Braco Dimitrijević

Braco Dimitrijević

Louvre is my studio, street is my museum

CHARTA

Contents / Sommaire

Lóránd Hegyi

Empathic Conceptualism

The Human Context of Casuality in Braco Dimitrijević's Work

". . . Someone once wrote to me that in my triptychs the artwork stood for the center piece of the classical triptych. But actually there is no center piece, all three elements are given equal weight, and if one is missing the work ceases to exist. Hierarchy has been canceled, all three elements have been placed on a pedestal together, the pedestal serving as an altar and calling things into question." This is what Braco Dimitrijević said in an interview with Jean-Hubert Martin about his *Triptychos Post Historicus*.[1] This anti-hierarchic position, which relativizes absolutized and mythicized historical necessity by resorting to the notion of coincidence and thus challenges hierarchical systems of values, alludes not just to fundamental historical and philosophical considerations but also to basic ethical principles such as tolerance, participation, empathy, and compassion. This humanist commitment characterizes the artist's aesthetic approach, it being understood that his (post)conceptual methodological practice has been embedded, right from the outset, in a context of cultural history and sociology. Coincidence and the effects of accidental events are no abstract, sterile moments that would occur in a clinical setting, interfering with a self-contained system. Rather, in the art of Braco Dimitrijević, such moments are invariably and inextricably connected to human destiny, as well as to concrete personal stories.

When exhibiting a sculpture by Andjelko Hundić in a portrait gallery next to a portrait-sculpture of Leonardo da Vinci placed on a marble pedestal, he shows the same anti-hierarchic attitude as the one found later, in the 1980s, in the program of *Triptychos Post Historicus*. When putting up a marble obelisk in the park of Charlottenburg Palace with an engraved text in golden letters that displays the date selected by an unknown casual passer-by, Peter Malwitz, he pays homage to an unfamiliar contemporary who just happened to be in a specific place at a specific time. By doing so, he puts a stranger's birth date exactly where you would normally expect to find highly important, well-known, distinguished, and venerated personalities.

Casual Passer-by I met at 1:43 PM, Venice, 1976
Collection: Tate Modern, London

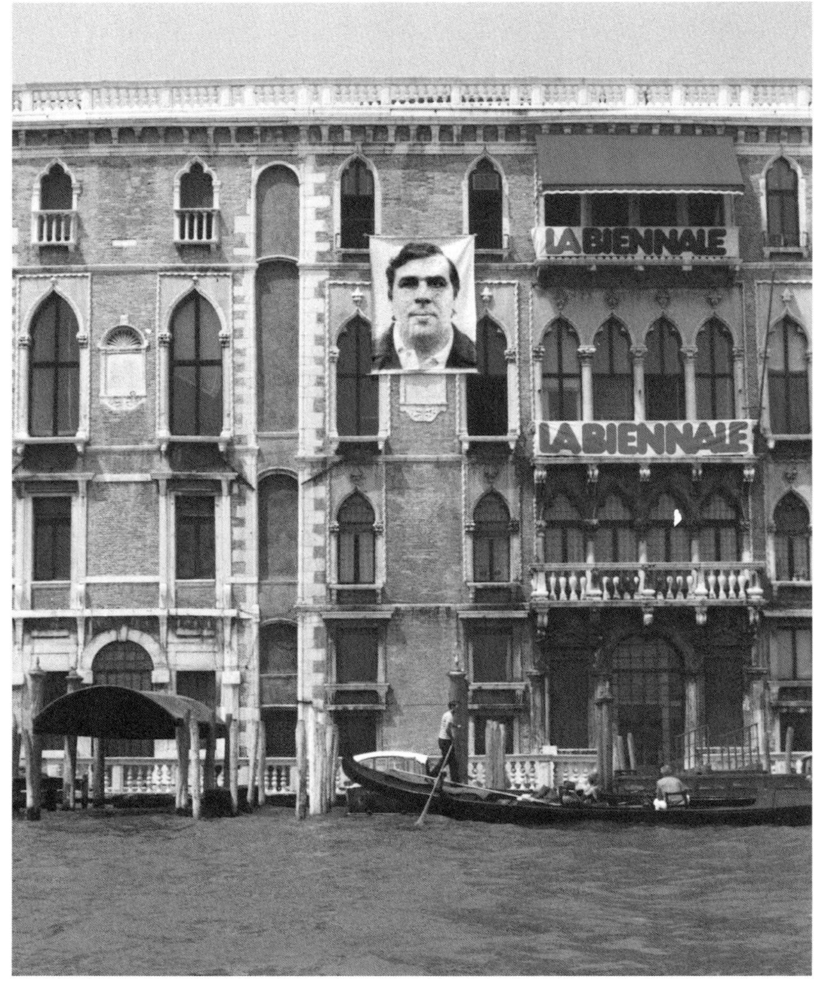

Braco Dimitrijević has always pursued a two-pronged strategy. It was only during the period of the *Triptychos Post Historicus*, i.e. following 1976, that another broader dimension of historical and cultural references was added to his oeuvre. In his early works he addressed evaluation mechanisms, hierarchies, and the impact of chance on human destiny placed in a socio-cultural context; he also empathically worshipped anonymous people who he felt were never perceived and assessed by others. Thanks to the artist's involvement and empathy, these works demonstrate that there is no hierarchy, no difference in value between famous people and those who are generally ignored. At the same time, he stresses how important the element of chance is—it turns one human being into a celebrity and the other one into the opposite. This implies that his art is not a neutral and sterile manifestation detached from personal destiny. Braco Dimitrijević wants to show no auto-referential models. On the contrary, his goal is to allude to the human dimension of coincidence, to the human notion of contradictory closed-off systems. Achille Bonito Oliva, in his essay on Braco Dimitrijević's "Casual Passer-by" series, comments on this aspect as follows: "Already then Braco Dimitrijević introduced a typically European ideological component into the analytic neutrality of conceptual art that generally tended towards self-contemplation and preferred the theoretical 'workshop.'"[2]

The work *Story about Two Artists* from 1969 displays almost all facets of Braco Dimitrijević's ethical and empathic attitude, as well as a distinctly European position within (post)conceptual art. On a black marble tablet we can read the laconically written, simple, but poignant and significant story of two painters who lived and worked in the same place at the same time. Accidentally, the king met one of the two painters in his garden to where his dog had eloped. This painter was invited to the royal court, he was admired and made quite a name for himself. The name of the other painter, in contrast, fell into oblivion a long time ago.

This work is key to Braco Dimitrijević's entire artistic practice. His slightly melancholy historical paraphrasing and his vaguely sentimental ethical commitment to a radical and anti-hierarchic recognition of every human being is a typical Central European trait. His subtle irony draws on real historical experiences, not just theoretical, exemplary, and auto-referential considerations. Braco Dimitrijević resorts to paraphrases that lend themselves to interpretations in a specific, historically determined socio-cultural context shaped by human activities. Consequently, his demonstrations are both paraphrases and realities of life, disclosing stark exposure as well as the cathartic, anarchic openness of every situation.

The monument for David Harper erected in London in 1972 and the monument for Alberto Vieri installed in Turin in 1973—both dedicated to persons the artist just happened to meet on the street—introduce the public to unknown, and thus allegedly insignificant, people placed on a pedestal, this act investing them with honor and a sense of acknowledgement. The documentary photographs taken at the time show pedestrians curiously gazing at the bronze statues in the park; clearly, they don't know these men immortalized by the monuments. The latter serve to legitimize the veneration by a community whose members perform the act of worship as a conventional process.

This series of works touches upon various aspects of communal values and their formation. Once again, coincidence is not seen as an indifferent or neutral tool for mind-games, but as a factor of ethical interference powerful enough to influence human destiny in a positive or negative way. Braco Dimitrijević had met David Harper accidentally on the street, at 1:30 pm, and that's how the man became well-known. In this context, the artist plays the role of king whose dog ran away and who, looking for it, meets the painter who then rises to fame on account of this chance encounter. This unintentional and unavoidable arbitrariness is part of a complex and multi-layered human reality. There is no need for moral justification: coincidence is just that—coincidental. But there is comprehension, reason, and modesty that teach us to put evaluations into perspective. Everybody may become famous, or remain anonymous, quite accidentally. This subversive and anti-hierarchic act of relativizing societal assessment mechanisms and conventional forms of veneration points to the wise and fatalistic modesty with which the artist makes us realize that we shouldn't accept conventions without any critical in-depth evaluation on our part.

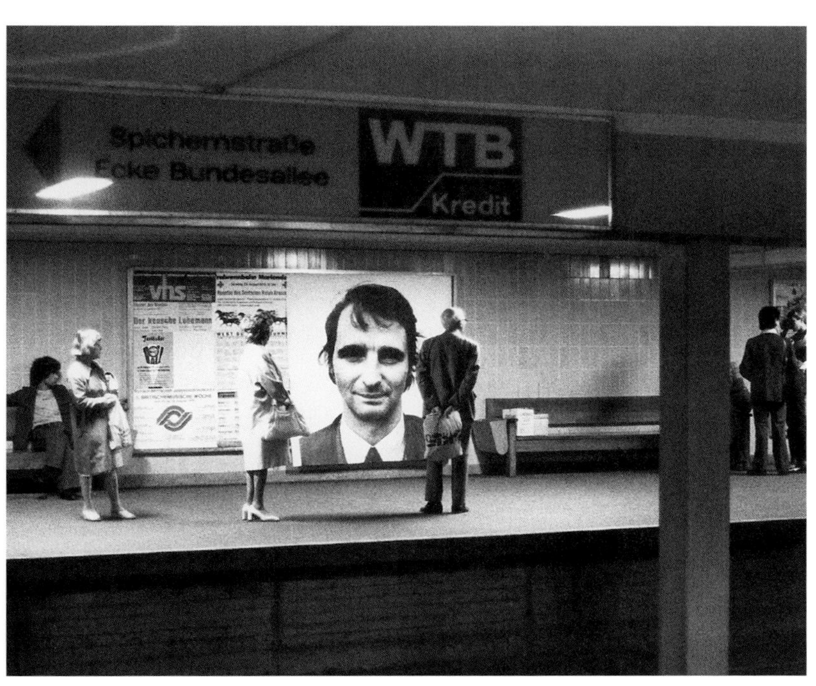

Casual Passer-by I met at 4:30 PM, 1976
Collection: Museum of Modern Art, New York

But there is also another level of meaning that implies the artist's emotionality and empathy—his genuine respect of fellow human beings who are perhaps never acknowledged by their immediate environment, but who may very well have the same important and valuable qualities (albeit somewhat hidden) as those found in universally adored contemporaries. Braco Dimitrijević's message is: every person is worth having a monument put up in his or her name. Every person is important, and should be recognized and acknowledged by others as such. Every person has the right to be perceived as significant. Braco Dimitrijević writes the name of a casual passer-by, Gerda Bollen, on a huge sign placed on the façade of the Palais des Beaux-Arts—a place usually reserved for announcements of exhibitions devoted to renowned artists. He also shows large-format portrait photographs of people who just happened to walk past him on the street on the façade of the Zagreb City Hall—a place usually reserved for portraits of Marx, Engels, Lenin, and Tito that adorned political parades. By doing so, the artist erects a monument for unknown people and proves his reverence for every human being. Thanks to this interpretation of the artistic act, his anti-hierarchic, radically humanist, and directly effective veneration of contemporaries moves center stage. Sheer coincidence turns selection into a relativizing moment, and social hierarchy is challenged as an arbitrary mechanism that should by no means be automatically accepted.

Just like persons who Braco Dimitrijević just happens to meet or see, accidental places or dates may also acquire a social dimension. A stone tablet placed in front of the Cologne Cathedral in 1980 read: "This could be a place of historical importance." And indeed, why shouldn't this place be significant for humanity, for human history, for our collective memory? Who decides what is important and what is unimportant? Who should have the power to determine hierarchies of significant and insignificant objects, places, dates, and persons?

Coincidence, errors, manipulation, wrong decisions, the process of forgetting—all of these factors make the evaluation of things ambiguous and unsatisfactory. Places, dates, persons, or events are incessantly appraised and reappraised; their importance is relative, arbitrary, mutable, fluctuating. This conviction shines through the entire *Triptychos Post Historicus* cycle, whose theoretical underpinnings were summarized by Braco Dimitrijević in his *Tractatus Post Historicus* in 1976. Even though, from the mid-1970s onwards, he paid more and more attention to metaphors gleaned from art history, as well as to art-historical objects, pictures, and sculptures, the conceptual basis of these more recent works is still formed by questions pertaining to hierarchy, evaluation systems, the function of coincidence, and ethics. Hence, it needs to be stressed that the interest the artist takes in the effects of chance is aroused mainly in a social, cultural, and political context.

With his provocative and yet simple, straightforward, evident, and transparent paraphrases, Braco Dimitrijević sheds light on the relativity of the selection process, the fragile credibility of hierarchy, and the dubious role played by evaluation mechanisms. He suggests anarchic freedom, but also generosity, tolerance, openness, modesty, and irony, and these qualities keep us from absolutizing our own conventions and from blindly accepting a seemingly natural hierarchy of persons and events. Evelyn Weiss comments on this as follows: "The works of Braco Dimitrijević are pictorial parables for the freedom of human beings and their creativity. It is only thanks to creativity that people could break free from the shackles of evolution; thanks to creativity, people are able to assume responsibility for their own decisions, and can thus lead their lives in dignity and hope."[3]

This subversive, anarchic, ironic, anti-hierarchic, as well as skeptical and relativizing attitude is highlighted impressively in the obelisk put up in 1979 in the park of Berlin's Charlottenburg Palace. The date engraved in the marble—March 11—is not explained, as if it were as clear as daylight to which event it refers, why it is so significant, and why it ought to leave an indelible imprint in our memory. Braco Dimitrijević's method is that of radical irony that helps him disclose assessment mechanisms. The fact that this date is engraved in a marble monument legitimizes its importance in the eyes of society. The only explanation given by the artist is: it wouldn't be there if it weren't significant. The mere existence of the obelisk with its engraved, and thus immortalized, date proves its importance without providing any additional information. The fact that the obelisk exists makes explanations superfluous. The monument expounds on its own content.

However, when viewed more closely, this tautology is no pure tautology because it was specified in a social, cultural, and political context. This tautology can only exist in a socially conditioned mentality that is legitimized by conventions and educational systems and marked by the imposed credibility of prevailing hierarchies and universally accepted representational systems. A mentality which explicitly states that whatever is venerated must, in fact, be venerated and that whatever is celebrated must, in fact, be celebrated. Hence, this tautology is neither objective nor neutral. It is conditioned by conventional representational systems, and therefore determined exclusively in socio-cultural terms.

Paradoxically, this work by Braco Dimitrijević also offers an interpretation of empathy, radical humanism, and solidarity, an interpretation that propagates human dignity and equality. Below the date we see a sentence that addresses the original relativity of its appraised significance in two ways: "This could be a day of historical importance." We already know the information conveyed by this sentence but here it is invested with another layer of meaning. March 11 is, in fact, the real birthday of a real human being who the artist accidentally met on the street and who was asked by the artist to name any date that would come to his mind. Peter Malwitz, a casual passer-by, encountered the artist by sheer coincidence. He chose a date that was then immortalized by Braco Dimitrijević in the form of a traditional monument. The conventional context in which this monument is embedded suggests something of extraordinary importance for society at large.

It is right here, in this act, that we are able to comprehend the dual aesthetic strategy pursued by Braco Dimitrijević. On the one hand, he demonstrates the lack of credibility of selection procedures as well as the relativity of evaluation mechanisms. The date chosen and the person encountered by pure chance supplant dates and persons that are collectively worshipped and legitimized by conventional representational systems. This artistic act elucidates the absurdity of conventional notions such as necessity, logic, rationality, justice, and hierarchy since it is coincidence that overrides everything. For this very reason, decisions must be relativized. A casual passer-by becomes the subject of a monument, and a randomly selected birthday is immortalized on a marble obelisk and thus respectfully acknowledged by society. And then the following questions arise: why shouldn't it be possible for immortalized and venerated persons for whom monuments have been put up to be the product of sheer coincidence? Is it not conceivable that these celebrated and

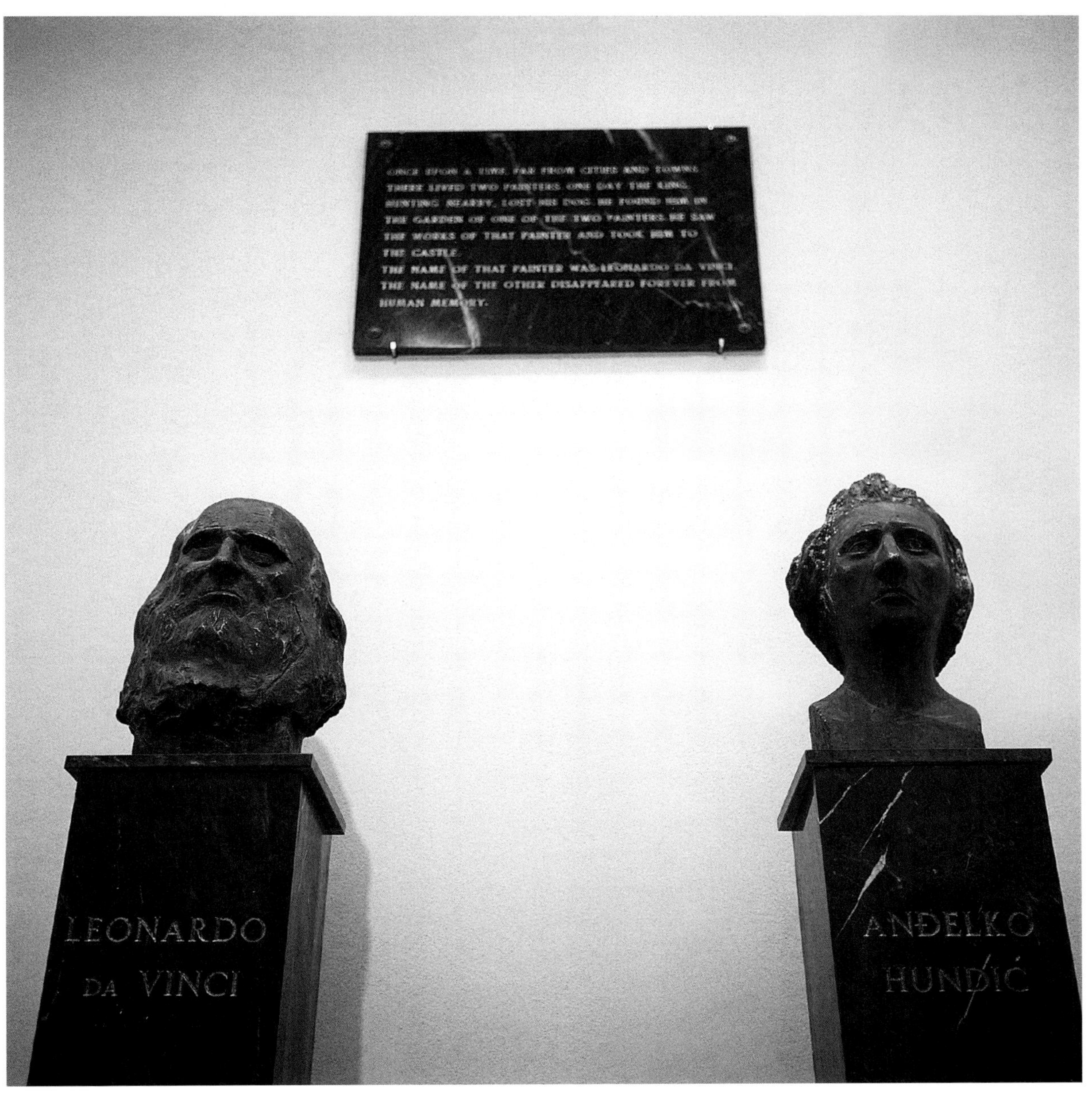

ONCE UPON A TIME, FAR FROM CITIES AND TOWNS, THERE LIVED TWO PAINTERS.
ONE DAY THE KING, HUNTING NEARBY, LOST HIS DOG.
HE FOUND HIM IN THE GARDEN OF ONE OF THE TWO PAINTERS.
HE SAW THE WORKS OF THAT PAINTER AND TOOK HIM TO THE CASTLE.
THE NAME OF THAT PAINTER WAS LEONARDO DA VINCI.
THE NAME OF THE OTHER DISAPPEARED FOREVER FROM HUMAN MEMORY.

B.D. 1969

Dialectical Chapel, Leonardo – Hundić, Venice Biennale, 1976
Collection: Stedelijk Museum voor Actuele Kunst, Ghent

Story About Two Artists, 1969

publicly displayed figures are part of our collective memory only by pure chance?

On the other hand, Braco Dimitrijević talks about something else, too. His monument is not just a paraphrase but a genuine alternative, a real possibility, and even an ethical challenge: every person is historically significant, the date of birth of every person is a historical date, and potentially every day is historically important since someone has been born. This solidarity, empathy, and admiration felt for fellow human beings imbues Braco Dimitrijević's conceptual considerations with true emotionality, passionate commitment, as well as radical and humanist romanticism.

"It is very likely that a single moment in post-history is much richer and more differentiated than all of history,"[4] posits Braco Dimitrijević, alluding to the boundless opportunities of artists living in the post-historical era. Linear historical developmental processes as well as logical, necessary, fatalistic, and mechanic structures no longer determine the direction and purpose of history. Rather, history is radically called into question and the juxtaposition of various connotation systems and referential levels becomes entirely legitimate. Dimitrijević's *ars poetica* heralds the acceptance of pluralism and the coexistence of contradictory concepts and aesthetic strategies. Additionally, it demands that artists themselves become active and engaged proponents of the post-historical age. In his art, radical interventions in history are not tantamount to an aesthetic adaptation to earlier stylistic patterns; there is no harmonization of the present with the past and no aesthetic role-play that would offer a certain poetic freedom to empathic strategies. On the contrary—history and its appraisal and the hierarchy of significance are radically challenged. The direct confrontation of artistic experiences is metaphorically projected onto the experiences gained by multi-cultural media societies of the 1980s and 1990s. Unambiguous, self-contained, and homogenous information structures cease to exist.

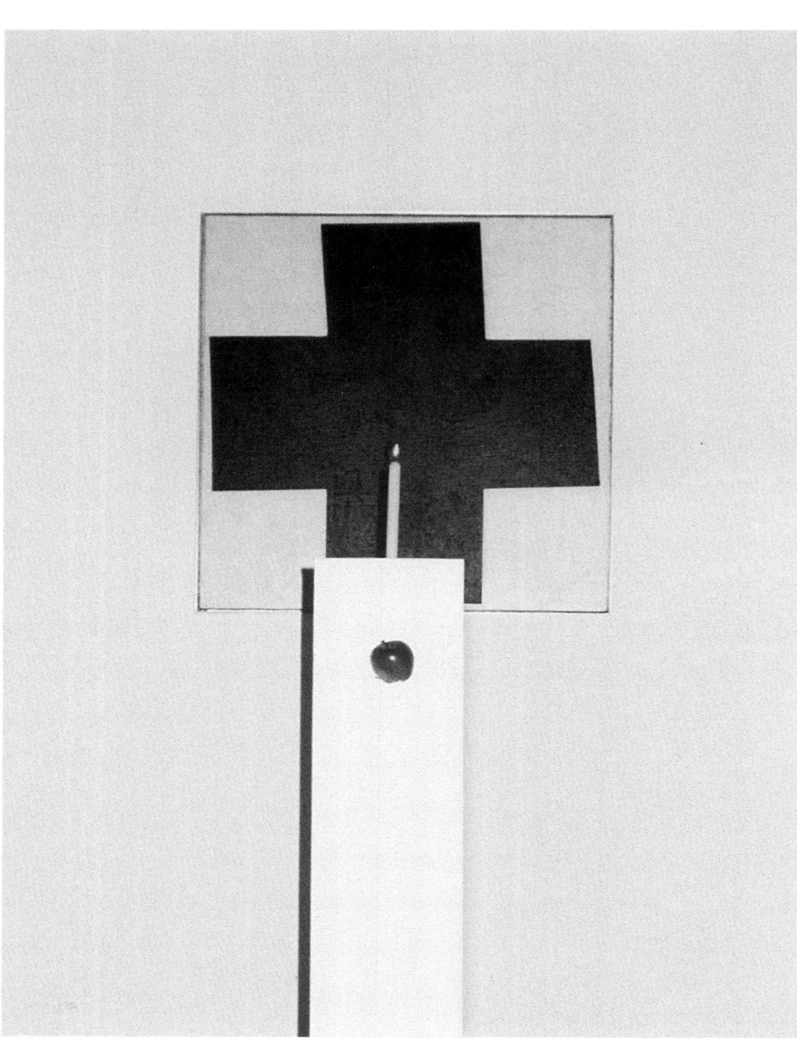

Triptychos Post Historicus
Musée National d'Art Moderne, Centre Georges Pompidou, Paris, 1981

I: *Black Cross*, Kasimir Malevich, 1915
II: Candle lit by Tchepo Kaleb on October 19, 1981; III: Apple

In the works belonging to the *Triptychos Post Historicus* cycle Braco Dimitrijević continues to address the notion of coincidence, but he also delves into the effects of chance in a socio-cultural context. Art-historical references and the real artworks included in his installations focus not so much on locations in public space and their cultural and political rituals; rather, they provide ample room for provocative connotations. A salient feature of Braco Dimitrijević's methodology is the transfer of certain elements from the realm of culture to areas outside its purview and, conversely, the aesthetic heroicizing and emphasis placed on various non-cultural moments so as to "elevate" them to the realm of culture. This deliberate mingling of different referential levels and his mixing of artistic signs with non-artistic ones yield a poetically powerful and provocative eclecticism which not only alludes to art, but above all to the experience of a crisis of history and historical awareness, evaluation mechanisms, and the credibility of representational systems.

"The triptychs, therefore, are a synthesis of the artist's ideas, the complete expression of the concept of post-history. In effect, the work of art he has borrowed undergoes a process of temporal alienation, since it has been removed from the 'sacred' context of the museum and subjected to an operation whose objective is simply to use it as a component of a new artistic creation. In the triptychs, real objects and vegetable matter combine to make the latent semantic messages in the artwork used emerge, thus establishing new levels of interpretation and adding new meanings to the work itself . . . Thus Dimitrijević adopts a conceptual strategy in his triptychs that is similar to that adopted in Venice in 1976, when the bronze busts of Leonardo da Vinci and Andjelko Hundiç, a man he had randomly stopped in the street one day, were exhibited together." This is what Stefano Marson has to say about the latent links existing between the apparently tautological photographs and the *Triptychos Post Historicus* series conjuring up provocative connotations.[5]

When, for instance, Braco Dimitrijević presents a suprematist picture by Kasimir Malevich together with a black bicycle and a yellow lemon, he mingles aesthetic perceptive processes at one level and creates an entirely new, radically eclectic structure of meaning at another. A poetic and arbitrary reconstitution of a historically possible situation cannot be precluded. The first level permits a formal and phenomenological reading. The black and red squares in Malevich's painting are homogenized with the circular shapes of bicycle wheels in a common geometric structure; the yellow reflector attached to the rear wheel and the yellow lemon appear as a formal vocabulary complementing each other. These formal similarities and parallels seem confusing, bewildering, alienating, and yet poetic, liberating, almost heroic, courageous, and provocative. The non-representational world of suprematism loses its transcendence, the painting is turned into a pictorial object, a component of the material world. Trivial everyday objects such as the bicycle and the lemon are torn from their material, functional, practical, and utilitarian context and reinterpreted to act as elements of a non-objective, universal formal structure.

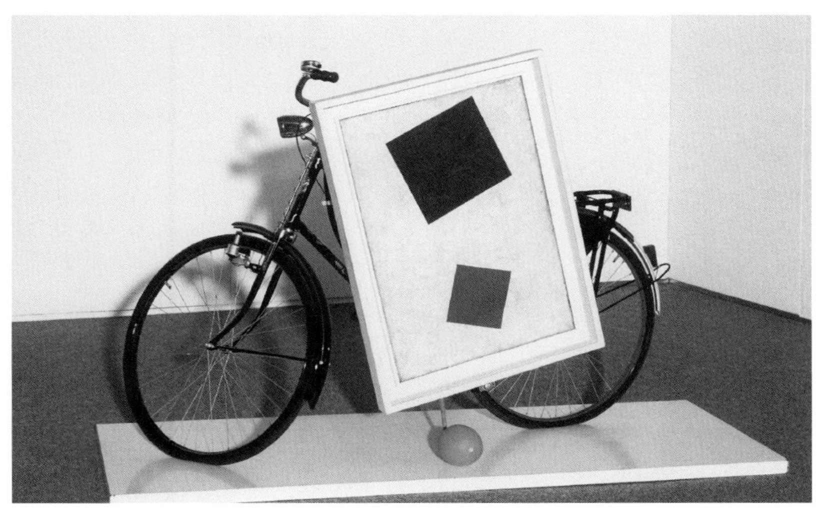

Triptychos Post Historicus
Wilhelm-Hack-Museum, Ludwigshafen, 1985

I: *Black and Red Square*, Kasimir Malevich, 1915
II: Bernhard Holeczek's bicycle;
III: Melon
Collection: Wilhelm-Hack-Museum, Ludwigshafen

The essential feature of aesthetic restructuring, however, becomes tangible at the second level only—the black bicycle carries Malevich's painting like a parcel, like the postman delivering the mail. Thus, Malevich's autonomous, aesthetic world of non-representational suprematism becomes a portable object, a specific, physical thing sending out a concealed message just like a letter tucked into an envelope. When we dredge up certain images from our cultural and historical memory, such as Agitprop elements from the October Revolution in Russia or the geometric abstract patterns for mass demonstrations painted on wooden walls, this very simple combination of objects becomes a tool for sensitizing history or for encouraging us to transgress history as an obsolete notion of how mankind developed. The artist of the post-historical age rides his black bicycle straight into history, confusing the temporal framework of historical existence and mingling different referential systems of visual and three-dimensional experiences; these can no longer act as exclusive, authentic structures because we can no longer believe in monolithic, causal, and logical systems.

The art-historical significance of Braco Dimitrijević's oeuvre—in the East as well as in the West—stems from this sensitization to the crisis affecting decision-making mechanisms. The latter challenge interpretations of historical processes as well as systems for assessing hierarchies in socio-cultural contexts. Therefore, his work can be seen from the vantage point of (post)conceptual and post-historical discourses. His empathic and romantic commitment to real human constellations determined by specific socio-cultural mechanisms and micro-political rituals places his attitude in a broader, more complex, and more diverse field of ethical participation. The situations presented in his installations and videos invariably convey dignified, critical, creative, anarchic, free, and independent notions. The oeuvre of Braco Dimitrijević is sovereign and poetic, provocative and subversive, engaged and empathic because he unswervingly believes in the inseparability of life, art, and anthropological realities. His interest, to put it in a nutshell, centers on the human context.

1. Jean-Hubert Martin, "Interview with Braco Dimitrijević," in *Braco Dimitrijević "Culturscapes" 1976–1984*, Museum Ludwig, Cologne and Kunsthalle, Bern, 1984, p. 64.
2. Achille Bonito Oliva, "The Justice of Art," in *Braco Dimitrijević*, Studio d'Arte Contemporanea Pino Casagrande, Rome, 2004, p. 9.
3. Evelyn Weiss, "Zufall: Geschichte – Evolution: Freiheit. Zu den Arbeiten von Braco Dimitrijević," in *Braco Dimitrijević "Culturscapes" 1976–1984*, Museum Ludwig, Cologne and Kunsthalle, Bern, 1984, p. 16.
4. Frank Perrin and Olivier Zahm, "Beyond Dualism" in *Braco Dimitrijević: Rooms and Thoughts*, Obalne Galerije Piran, 1991.
5. Stefano Marson, "Braco Dimitrijeviç and Italy," in *Braco Dimitrijević*, Studio d'Arte Contemporanea Pino Casagrande, Rome, 2004, p. 32.

Lóránd Hegyi

Conceptualisme empathique

Le contexte humain d'occasionnalité dans l'oeuvre de Braco Dimitrijević

… « Un jour, quelqu'un m'a écrit que dans mon *Triptychos*, l'œuvre d'art représentait le panneau central du triptyque classique. Or pour moi, il n'existe pas d'élément central. Les trois volets du triptyque ont tous autant d'importance, si l'un d'entre eux vient à manquer, l'œuvre n'existe plus. Toute hiérarchie des objets en est absente et les trois composantes sont présentées ensemble sur un socle qui sert d'autel et de point d'interrogation », dit Braco Dimitrijević dans un entretien avec Jean-Hubert Martin sur son *Triptychos Post Historicus*[1]. Cette attitude anti-hiérarchique relativise la mythique obligation historique par le hasard et remet en cause les systèmes de valeurs hiérarchisés. Elle intègre une réflexion philosophique de l'histoire et surtout des valeurs éthiques telles que la tolérance, la participation, l'empathie et la compassion. Cet engagement humaniste marque de son sceau toute la réflexion esthétique de Braco Dimitrijević, sa pratique méthodologique et (post)conceptuelle s'inscrit initialement dans un contexte culturel historique et sociologique. Le hasard et autres conséquences d'événements imprévus ne sont pas des moments de laboratoire abstraits et stériles destinés à troubler un système en vase clos. Pour Braco Dimitrijević, ces moments sont toujours et par principe indissociables du destin humain, de l'histoire concrète d'une personne.

Lorsque dans une galerie de portraits il place sur un socle de marbre une sculpture d'Andelko Hundic à côté de celle de Léonard de Vinci, il manifeste la même attitude anti-hiérarchique que quelques années plus tard, dans les années 1980, dans le programme des *Triptychos Post Historicus*. Lorsqu'il installe dans le parc du château de Charlottenburg un obélisque de marbre sur lequel est gravé en lettres dorées un texte avec la date de naissance d'un passant inconnu, un certain Peter Malwitz, il honore un homme qui se trouvait là incidemment et lui accorde un espace réservé usuellement à des personnalités de grand renom, l'élevant ainsi au même rang qu'eux.

Braco Dimitrijević développe une double stratégie dès ses premières œuvres, mais il faut attendre la période des *Triptychos Post Historicus*, après 1976, pour qu'elle prenne toute sa dimension et s'élargisse à des références historico-culturelles. Au départ, il travaille sur la problématique des mécanismes de valeur, de la hiérarchie, de l'effet du hasard sur la destinée humaine dans un contexte socioculturel précis. Ou alors il valorise avec empathie un concitoyen anonyme peut-être jamais reconnu dans son milieu social. Braco Dimitrijević démontre ainsi avec engagement et empathie que la hiérarchie n'existe pas, qu'il n'y a aucune différence de valeur entre les personnes célèbres et celles qui restent inconnues. Ce faisant, il révèle l'importance du hasard dans le jeu de la notoriété. Pas de démonstration neutre, stérile ou dissociée du destin personnel : les modèles autoréférentiels n'intéressent pas Braco Dimitrijević. Il a envie de présenter leur exact contraire, la dimension humaine du hasard face à la contradiction des systèmes fermés. Dans son essai sur la série « Casual Passer-by » de Braco Dimitrijević, Achille Bonito Oliva note en ce sens que cet artiste a introduit une composante idéologique typiquement européenne dans la neutralité analytique de l'art conceptuel, avec une approche moins tournée vers l'introspection que sur l'atelier théorique et pratique[2].

L'œuvre intitulée « Story About Two Artists » qui date de 1969 démontre presque tous les aspects de la prise de position éthique et de l'empathie de Braco Dimitrijević, qui est aussi une attitude européenne par excellence dans le milieu de l'art (post)conceptuel. Sur une plaque de marbre noire, un texte très laconique et pourtant significatif raconte l'histoire de deux peintres ayant vécu et travaillé à la même époque. Un roi avait rencontré l'un des deux peintres dans son jardin, où s'était égaré le chien du roi. Ce peintre fut invité à la cour et connut la célébrité. Le nom de l'autre peintre est tombé dans l'oubli depuis longtemps.

Cette œuvre est au centre de toute la pratique artistique de Braco Dimitrijević. Il est vrai que la paraphrase mélancolique et l'engagement éthique vaguement sentimental sont typiques pour une sensibilité d'Europe centrale, lorsqu'il s'agit du respect et de la valorisation radicalement anti-hiérarchique de toute personne. L'ironie subtile de Braco Dimitrijević se réfère à des expériences historiquement réelles, pas seulement théoriques, exemplaires et autoréférentielles. Il travaille avec des paraphrases interprétables dans un contexte socioculturel concret, déterminé historiquement par les activités humaines. Ses démonstrations sont donc à la fois paraphrases et réalités vécues, elles manifestent que toute situation contient une part de contrainte mais ouvre aussi une brèche subversivement libératrice.

Les monuments dédiés à David Harper en 1972 à Londres et à Alberto Vieri en 1973 à Turin célébraient des personnes rencontrées par hasard dans la rue. Inconnus du grand public et pour cela décrétés insignifiants, ces personnages sont élevés sur un piédestal, un acte qui leur confère honneur et gloire. Des prises de vue d'époque montrent des promeneurs de ce parc regardant avec intérêt ou étonnement ces bustes de bronze, car ils ne reconnaissent aucune des personnalités ainsi immortalisées. Le monument est une convention admise qui symbolise et légitime la reconnaissance sociale.

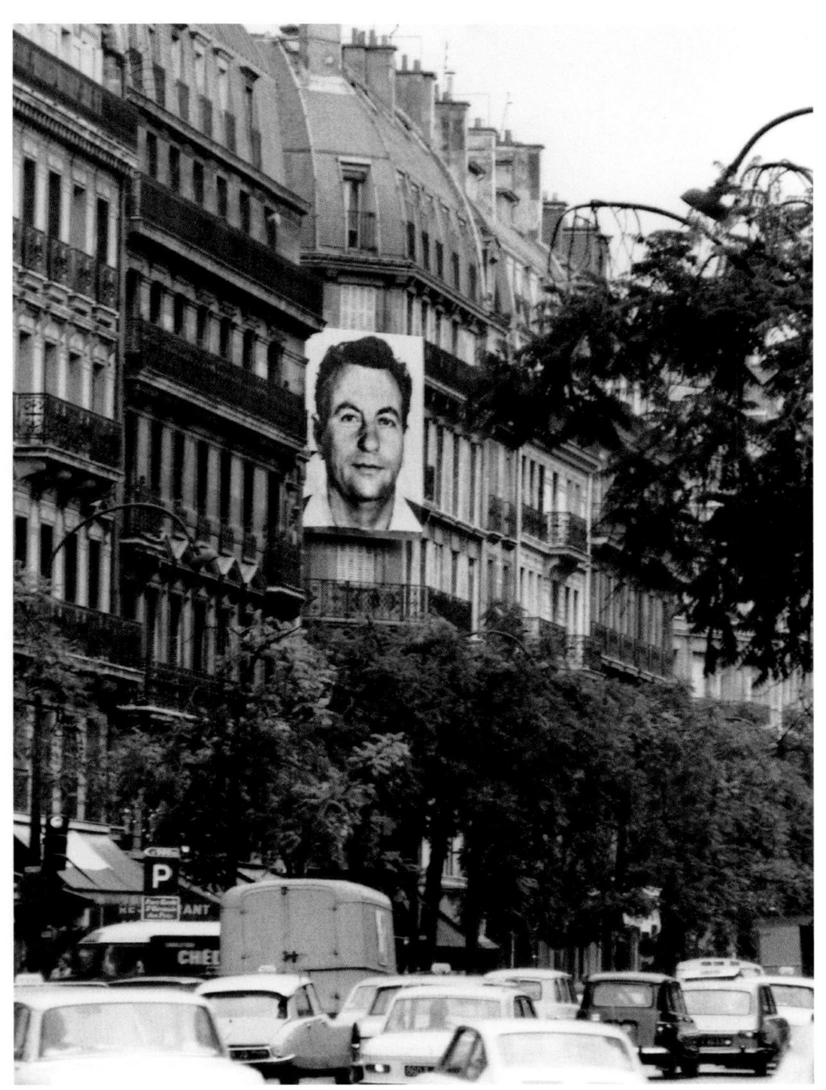

Casual Passer-by I met at 11:09 AM, Boulevard St. Germain, Paris, 1971
Collection: Musée National d'Art Moderne, Centre Georges Pompidou, Paris

Cette série de travaux interpelle différents aspects de l'échelle des valeurs sociales. Le hasard n'y est pas l'outil indifférent et neutre d'un jeu intellectuel, c'est un facteur de discorde éthique qui peut transformer toutes les destinées humaines, en bien ou en mal. David Harper est connu aujourd'hui parce que Braco Dimitrijević l'avait rencontré dans la rue à 13h30, c'est tout. L'artiste joue ici le rôle du roi dont le chien avait trouvé refuge dans le jardin du peintre, ce qui avait conduit à la notoriété de ce dernier.

La coïncidence non intentionnelle fait partie de la complexité irréductible de la réalité humaine ; pas besoin de justification morale, le hasard reste le hasard. Et pourtant, avec un peu de compréhension, de raison, de modestie nous pouvons apprendre à relativiser les jugements de valeur. Chacun d'entre nous peut, selon le jeu du hasard, connaître ou non la célébrité. Cette remise en question subversive et anti-hiérarchique des mécanismes de jugement social et des conventions honorifiques est le fruit du discernement intelligent et fataliste de l'artiste, lequel nous incite à n'accepter aucune convention sans l'avoir auparavant évaluée personnellement de façon critique.

Il existe aussi un autre niveau de signification pour l'émotionnalité et l'empathie précitées, c'est la véritable glorification de certains de nos contemporains peut-être jamais honorés dans leur milieu immédiat. Ils possèdent des qualités sans doute tout aussi profondes et dignes de reconnaissance que leurs contemporains célèbres, sauf qu'elles n'ont jamais été dévoilées et honorées. Chaque être humain vaut la peine qu'on lui érige un monument, dit l'artiste. Chaque personne a de l'importance et mérite l'attention et la reconnaissance des autres. Chacun a le droit d'être traité comme une personne importante. Lorsque Braco Dimitrijević écrit le nom de Gerda Bollen, cette passante rencontrée par hasard, sur la grande banderole recouvrant la façade du Palais des Beaux-Arts, il lui donne la place réservée habituellement aux noms des grands artistes et de leurs expositions. Lorsqu'il recouvre de portraits d'inconnus la façade de l'Hôtel de Ville de Zagreb, un emplacement réservé à cette époque, durant les grandes parades politiques, aux portraits de Marx, Engels, Lénine ou Tito, l'artiste élève un monument à la gloire du passant inconnu, démontrant ainsi que chaque personne a droit à la célébrité. Dans cette lecture de l'acte artistique, la célébration anti-hiérarchique, radicalement humaniste et immédiate de l'humain est au premier plan. D'un côté le choix est thématisé par le simple hasard comme moment à relativiser, de l'autre, la hiérarchie sociale est critiquée car tout aussi aléatoire, ses mécanismes ne devant en aucun cas être acceptés systématiquement.

Tout comme les personnes rencontrées par hasard, les lieux et dates peuvent eux aussi prendre une

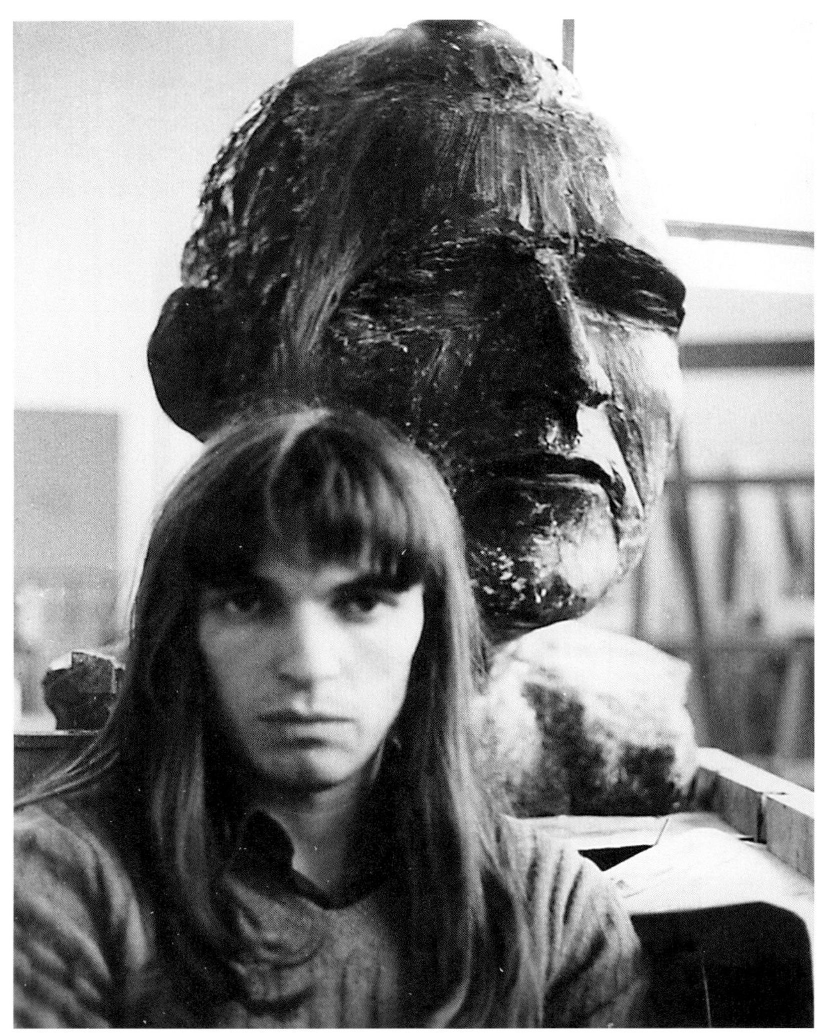

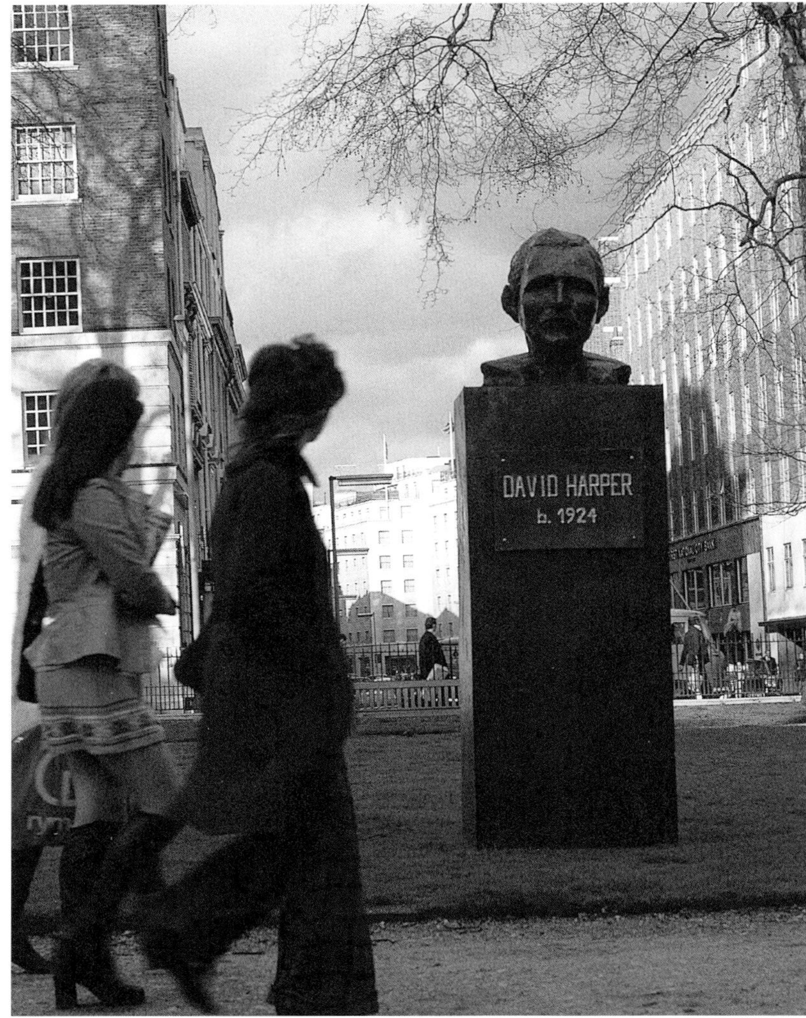

Braco Dimitrijević at St. Martin's School of Art, London, 1972

Monument to David Harper, the *Casual Passer-by I met at 11:28 AM*, London, 1972
Collection: Sylvain Perlstein, Paris

dimension sociétale, à un moment ou un autre. Une stèle de pierre installée en 1980 sur le parvis de la cathédrale de Cologne porte cette inscription : « This could be a place of historical importance » (Ce lieu pourrait avoir une importance historique). Une évidence, car pourquoi ce lieu précis ne pourrait-il pas devenir déterminant pour l'humanité et la mémoire collective ? Qui tranche sur l'importance ou l'insignifiance ? Qui est capable de décider de la hiérarchie à donner à des objets, des lieux, des dates, des personnes ?

Le hasard, l'erreur, une fausse décision, le processus de l'oubli, tout cela embrouille le jugement, ne le rend pas satisfaisant. L'importance des lieux, des dates, des personnes et des événements est sans cesse redéfinie, elle est relative, aléatoire, changeante. Cette certitude se retrouve dans tout le cycle des *Triptychos Post Historicus* et Braco Dimitrijević en a résumé la théorie en 1976 dans son *Tractatus Post Historicus*. Même si depuis le milieu des années 1970, il travaille plus intensément avec des métaphores, des objets, peintures et sculptures directement issus de l'histoire de l'art, ces travaux s'édifient toujours autour des questions de hiérarchie, de systèmes de classification, du rôle du hasard et de ses aspects éthiques. C'est toujours – et il faut le souligner - dans le contexte socioculturel et politique que la confrontation avec les conséquences du hasard se concrétise.

Lorsque Braco Dimitrijević démontre avec ses paraphrases provocantes, mais si évidentes et transparentes, la relativité du processus de choix, la fragile crédibilité de la hiérarchie, l'ambiguïté des mécanismes de valorisation, il suggère une libération via l'anarchie, mais nous incite parallèlement à faire preuve de générosité, de tolérance, d'esprit d'ouverture, de modestie et d'humour. Ceci afin d'éviter l'absolutisme de nos propres conventions et pour ne pas suivre aveuglément les hiérarchies apparemment évidentes concernant les personnes et les événements. Comme le formule Evelyn Weiss : « Ces travaux de Braco Dimitrijević sont des paraboles en images sur le libre-arbitre de l'homme et sa créativité, les seules valeurs lui permettant d'échapper à la chaîne évolutive, car les seules à lui donner la responsabilité de ses décisions, c'est-à-dire de la dignité et de l'espoir »[3].

Une telle attitude subversive et anarchiste, ironique, anti-hiérarchique et sceptique est exprimée très fortement dans l'obélisque érigé en 1979 dans le jardin du château de Charlottenburg à Berlin. La date gravée dans le marbre, le 11 mars, ne fait l'objet d'aucune explication, tant elle semble évidente, tant la référence doit être connue de tous, une date à graver pour toujours dans nos mémoires, rien de plus. La méthode de Braco Dimitrijević est celle de l'ironie radicale, c'est sa façon de mettre à nu les mécanismes de valorisation. Le simple fait que cette date soit écrite sur un monument légitime son importance aux yeux de la société. Si elle n'avait pas d'importance, elle ne serait pas inscrite ici - voilà pour l'explication. L'existence de l'obélisque et la pérennité de cette inscription dans le marbre légitime son importance, aucune explication supplémentaire n'est requise. La présence de l'obélisque supprime le besoin d'explication, le monument explique la raison d'être du monument.

En réalité, cette tautologie n'est pas vraiment une simple tautologie, car elle se concrétise dans un contexte socioculturel et politique précis. Elle exige une mentalité socialement conditionnée par des conventions et par son éducation, en confiance totale avec les hiérarchies existantes et les systèmes de représentations acceptés collectivement. D'après la formule « célébrons ce qui est déjà honoré et fêtons ce qui doit être fêté ». Cette tautologie n'est donc ni objective ni neutre, elle obéit à des systèmes de représentations conventionnelles et à des exigences socioculturelles.

Paradoxalement, cette œuvre de Braco Dimitrijević appelle aussi une lecture empathique, radicalement humaniste et solidaire, qui affirme la dignité et l'égalité humaine. Sous la date, une phrase thématise la relativité de la signification dans deux voies possibles : « This could be a day of historical importance » (Cette date pourrait avoir une importance historique). Nous connaissons déjà le pendant de cette phrase, mais ici, elle peut avoir une signification additionnelle. La date du 11 mars est celle d'un anniversaire réel, celui d'un passant rencontré par hasard et auquel l'artiste a demandé une date. Peter Malwitz a donné celle de son anniversaire et l'artiste l'a éternisée sous la forme d'un monument traditionnel, si monumental que dans un contexte conventionnel, il suggère un événement extraordinairement important pour la collectivité.

Marble plaque bearing the inscription *This could be a place of historical interest* may be at any location. The first such plaque was placed in Greek Street in Soho, London, 1971
Collection: Tate Gallery, London

C'est justement ici, dans cet acte, que nous pouvons mesurer la double stratégie esthétique de Braco Dimitrijević. Il opère certes en démontrant l'invraisemblance du système de sélection, c'est-à-dire en relativisant le mécanisme d'évaluation. Une date ou une personne trouvée fortuitement prend la place de la date ou de la personne qui aurait été légitimée par les systèmes conventionnels de représentation, reconnue collectivement, donc crédible. Cet acte artistique démontre l'absurdité des schémas traditionnels sur la nécessité, la logique, la rationalité, la justice et la hiérarchie. Comme c'est le hasard qui décide de tout, il nous faut relativiser les apparences. Tout comme un promeneur quelconque peut devenir le sujet d'un monument, tout comme sa date de naissance peut être gravée dans le marbre d'un obélisque et considérée avec respect par la société, ainsi peut-il également advenir que des personnalités immortalisées sur des monuments ne s'y trouvent que par hasard, que ces figures emblématiques n'aient pris place dans la mémoire collective que par chance.

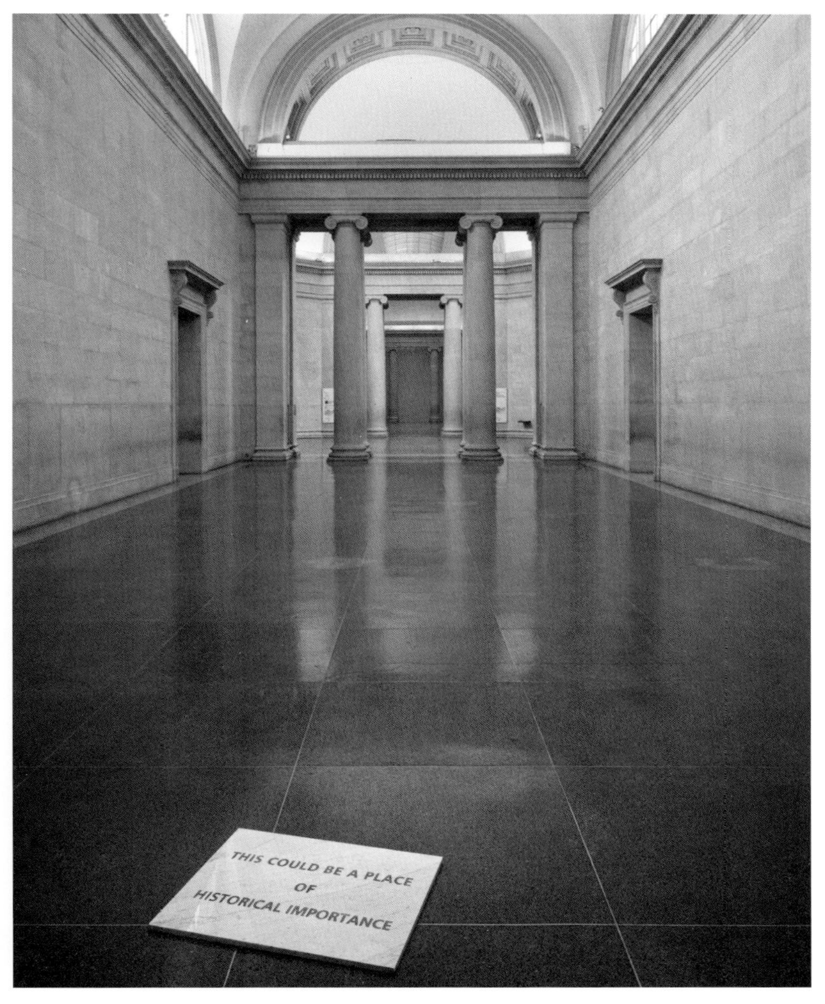

Mais Braco Dimitrijević a encore un autre objectif. Son monument n'est pas qu'une paraphrase, c'est une véritable alternative, une possibilité réelle, même un défi éthique : chaque être humain a sa place dans l'histoire ; la date de naissance de quelqu'un est une date historique ; chaque jour peut devenir une date historique importante, car il donne le jour à telle et telle personne. Cette empathie solidaire et la célébration de ses concitoyens confèrent aux réflexions conceptuelles de Braco Dimitrijević une émotionnalité incontestable, témoignent d'un engagement profond et d'un romantisme radicalement humaniste.

« Il est probable qu'un moment de la post-histoire soit beaucoup plus riche et différencié que l'histoire dans son ensemble » [4]. Ainsi

Braco Dimitrijević souligne-t-il les possibilités infinies de l'artiste de la période post-historique. L'orientation et les objectifs historiques ne sont plus régis par des processus de développement historique linéaires ou par des structures de développement inévitables et mécaniquement fatalistes, c'est l'histoire elle-même qui est entièrement remise en question. L'existence simultanée de différents systèmes de connotation et niveaux référentiels devient absolument légitime. L'*Ars poetica* de Dimitrijević préconise non seulement l'acceptance du pluralisme, la coexistence de concepts et de stratégies esthétiques contradictoires, il exige aussi de l'artiste qu'il participe lui-même activement à cette époque post-historique. Intervenir radicalement dans l'histoire ne signifie pas pour Dimitrijević une adaptation esthétique à des formules stylistiques passées, une harmonisation entre le présent et le passé ou un jeu de rôle esthétique – bien que celui-ci offrirait une certaine liberté poétique quant aux stratégies intuitives. Au contraire, une telle intervention jette le doute sur l'histoire et toutes ses règles, sur la hiérarchie des priorités en tant que telles. La confrontation directe des niveaux d'expériences artistiques est projetée par métaphore sur les expérimentations de la société médiatique multiculturelle des années 1980 et 1990, l'information n'y est plus ni clairement structurée ni homogène.

Dans les œuvres du cycle des *Triptychos Post Historicus*, Braco Dimitrijević poursuit sa réflexion sur le hasard ou plutôt sur les conséquences du hasard dans un contexte socioculturel donné, mais les références à l'histoire de l'art et les réelles œuvres d'art incluses dans les installations mettent moins l'accent sur les lieux de l'espace public et sur les rituels culturels et politiques, elles s'ouvrent davantage aux connotations provocantes. La méthodologie de Braco Dimitrijević se distingue en particulier par la transposition de certaines connotations du domaine culturel vers des pratiques artistiques hors-champs et à l'inverse, par l'apologie esthétique et la survalorisation de divers moments non culturels, afin de les catapulter dans le royaume de la Culture. Cette confusion voulue entre les divers niveaux de référence et le mélange du langage des signes artistiques et non-artistiques créent un éclectisme poétiquement efficace qui ne se réfère plus seulement à l'art, mais surtout à l'expérience historique de l'histoire en crise et de la conscience historique, ainsi qu'aux mécanismes de valorisation et à la crédibilité des systèmes de représentations.

Triptychos Post Historicus
Solomon R. Guggenheim Museum, New York, 1987
I: *Woman Ironing*, Pablo Picasso, 1904; II: Cornelia Lauf's coat; III: Apple
Color photograph, 160 x 120 cm
Private Collection, New York

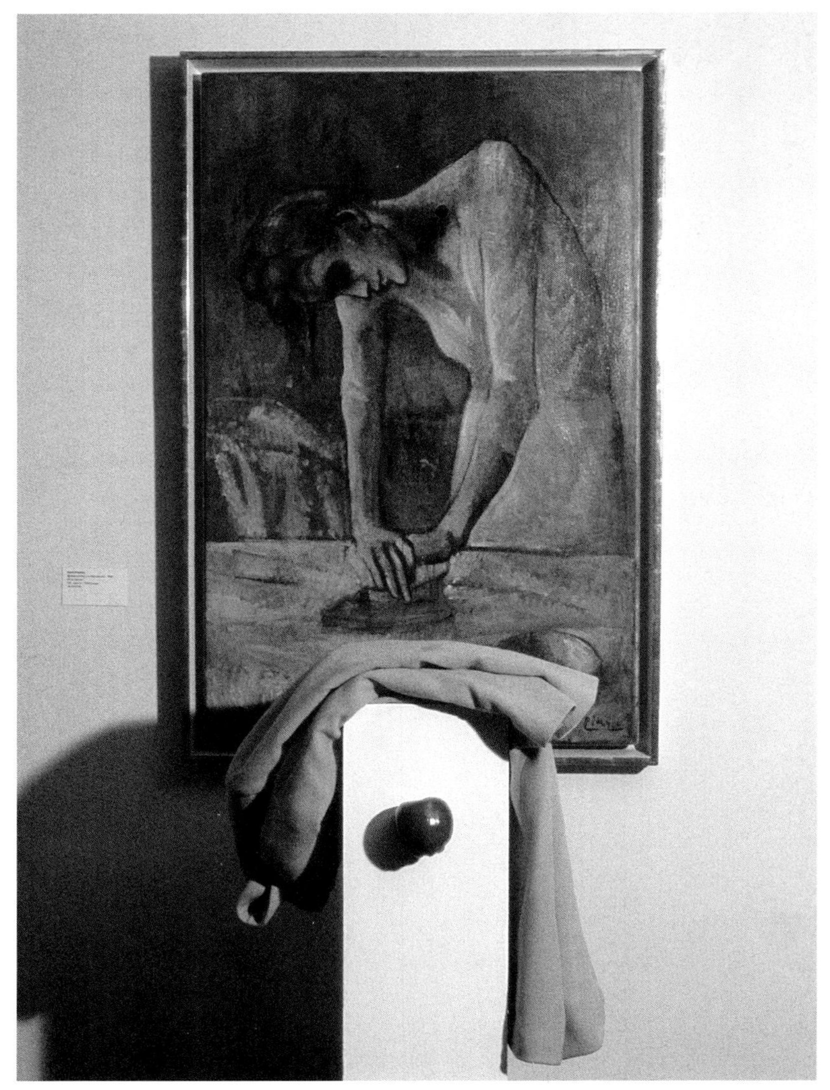

« Les triptyques représentent une synthèse entre les idées de l'artiste, ils sont l'expression absolue du concept post-historique. En effet, l'œuvre d'art que l'artiste a empruntée au musée subit un processus d'aliénation temporelle, car arrachée au contexte « sacré » du musée et soumise à une opération de création artistique où elle n'est plus qu'un simple élément. Dans les triptyques, des objets manufacturés et des matériaux végétaux sont combinés pour faire ressortir les messages sémantiques latents de l'œuvre d'art. Ceci tout en établissant de nouveaux niveaux d'interprétation et en ajoutant de nouvelles significations à l'œuvre elle-même. … Dimitrijević adopte dans ses triptyques une stratégie conceptuelle similaire à celle qu'il avait présentée à Venise en 1976, en juxtaposant les bustes de bronze de Léonard de Vinci et d'Andjelko Hundic, cet homme abordé un jour par hasard dans la rue ». Stefano Marson analyse ainsi le rapport latent entre des travaux photographiques d'une tautologie apparente et la série des *Triptychos Post Historicus* avec ses connotations provocantes[5].

Lorsque Braco Dimitrijević présente un tableau suprématiste de Kesimir Malevitch à côté d'un vélo noir et d'un citron jaune, il mêle les processus de perception esthétique à un niveau et crée une structure de sens éclectique, radicale et entièrement nouvelle à un autre niveau. Ce qui d'ailleurs n'exclut pas la reconstruction arbitrairement poétique d'une possible situation historique. Le premier niveau permet une lecture phénoménologique formelle : le carré noir et le carré rouge du tableau de Malevitch se fondent avec les cercles des roues de vélo en une structure géométrique commune, tandis que le réflec-

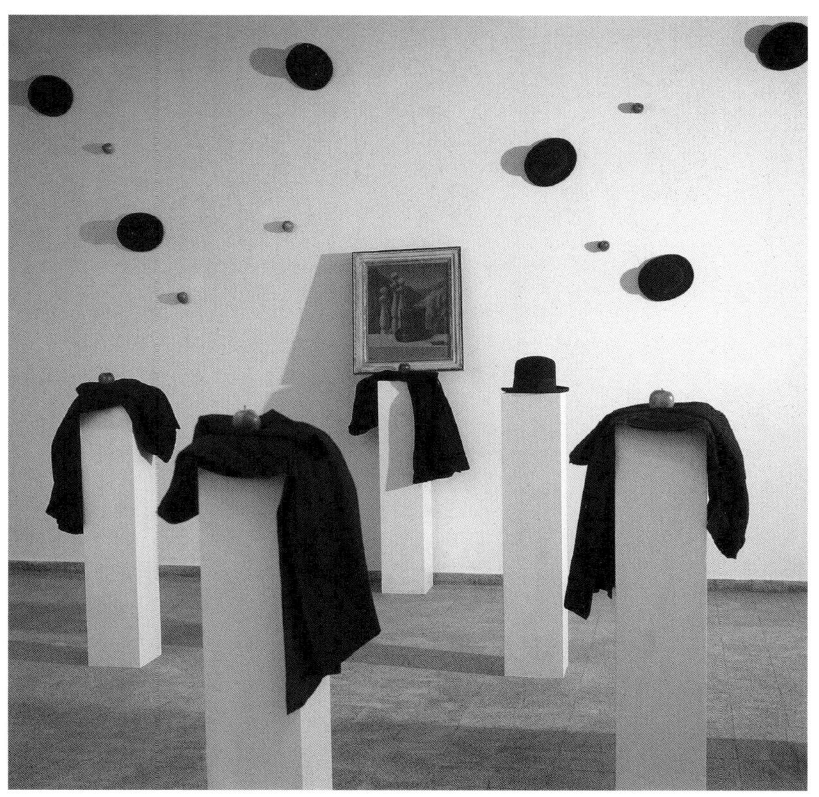

Triptychos Post Historicus or Hopes and Ways to Identity
Israel Museum, Jerusalem, 1990

I: *Le beaux ténébreux*, René Magritte, 1950
II: Coats from Mea She'arim, hats - gift of David Redberg; III: Apples
Collection: Israel Museum, Jerusalem

teur jaune de la roue arrière trouve son pendant dans le citron jaune, avec un vocabulaire formel commun. Ces ressemblances et ces parallèles dans la forme sont assez troublants mais il en découle aussi une certaine poésie, une sensation libératrice, un courage presque héroïque et provocateur. Le monde abstrait du suprématisme perd de sa transparence, le tableau n'est plus qu'une peinture-objet, un accessoire du monde matériel. Par ailleurs, un objet banal de la vie courante tel qu'un vélo ou un citron est extirpé de son contexte utilitaire et devient partie d'une structure abstraite universelle.

Ce n'est pourtant qu'au deuxième niveau qu'apparaît l'essentiel de la restructuration esthétique : la bicyclette noire porte le tableau de Malevitch comme un paquet, comme pourrait le faire un facteur. Ainsi, le monde esthétique bien autonome du suprématisme abstrait de Malevitch se transforme en un objet transportable, physiquement concrétisé, qui transmet un message caché, comme une lettre à l'intérieur d'une enveloppe fermée. Lorsque nous recherchons dans notre mémoire historico-culturelle certaines images comme les trains de propagande de la Révolution d'octobre en Russie ou les figures géométriques peintes sur les murs de bois pour les grandes manifestations, cette juxtaposition d'objets si simple éveille la sensibilité historique. Elle amène à dépasser l'histoire, qui n'est plus la forme apte à représenter l'essor de l'humanité. Sur son vélo noir, l'artiste de l'époque post-historique entre directement dans l'histoire, dérangeant le cadre temporel de l'existence historique, mêlant les différents systèmes de référence de l'expérience plastique visuelle, lesquels ne peuvent plus fonctionner comme les seules structures authentiques, tout simplement parce que les systèmes monolithiques soumis à une causalité logique ne sont plus crédibles.

L'œuvre de Braco Dimitrijević est importante dans l'histoire de l'art à l'Est comme à l'Ouest, car elle sensibilise à la crise des mécanismes de décisions ceux qui relativisent la lecture des processus historiques ou des systèmes d'évaluation de la hiérarchie dans les contextes socioculturels. Son œuvre semble donc localisée dans le contexte du discours (post)conceptuel et post-historique. Il fait preuve d'un engagement empathique et romantique pour les constellations humaines réelles et déterminées par des mécanismes socioculturels concrets et des rituels micro-politiques. Un engagement qui se présente pourtant dans le champ plus vaste, complexe et diversifié de la participation éthique. Les situations présentées dans ses installations et dans ses vidéos montrent toujours la perspective de nobles réflexions créatives et critiques, libres et anarchiques, indépendantes. L'œuvre de Braco Dimitrijević est souveraine, elle est poétique, à la fois provocante et subversive, engagée et empathique. Il croit encore et toujours que l'art est inséparable de la vie et des réalités anthropologiques. Le contexte humain est pour lui prioritaire.

1. Jean-Hubert Martin : Entretien avec Braco Dimitrijević
In: Catalogue : *Braco Dimitrijević « Culturscapes »* 1976 – 1984
Musée Ludwig, Cologne et Kunsthalle de Berne, 1984. p. : 64.
2. Achille Bonito Oliva : « The Justice of Art »
In : Catalogue : *Braco Dimitrijević*
Studio d'Arte Contemporanea Pino Casagrande, Rome 2004. p.9.
3. Evelyn Weiss : Zufall : « Geschichte – Evolution : Freiheit. Zu den Arbeiten von Braco Dimitrijević »
In : Catalogue: *Braco Dimitrijević « Culturscapes »* 1976 – 1984
Musée Ludwig, Cologne et Kunsthalle de Berne, 1984. p. : 16.
4. Frank Perrin et Olivier Zahn : Entretien avec Braco Dimitrijević in : *Beyond Dualism* 1991.
5. Stefano Marson : « Braco Dimitrijević and Italy » in : *Braco Dimitrijević* Studio d'Arte Contemporanea Pino Casagrande, 2004. p. : 32.

An Art Created for the World

I still remember the 1971 Paris Biennale, where I participated in the organization of the Italian Pavilion, and Braco Dimitrijević showed his *The Casual Passer-by I Met* in the section devoted to conceptual art. It is a photographic monument to an anonymous passer-by, a hymn to potential and unknown creativity, to the non-recognition of the artist-poet who is erased by history.

Braco Dimitrijević's first conceptual work, *Flag of the World*, was made as early as 1963, followed several years later by other outdoor works, *Accidental Sculpture* and *Painting by Kresimir Klika*. With these works, the artist establishes a direct relationship with the world, opposing the means of artistic language to the social conventions and codes of politics.

In the *Flag of the World*, Dimitrijević replaces an official sign, a national flag on his boat, with an alternative. His personal flag is that of a painter, the cloth for cleaning brushes. According to international conventions when entering foreign territorial waters, crossing from one country to another, the national flag is replaced with another country's flag, even if there is no land in sight. Dimitrijević's flag of art is universal, piercing through any frontier, surpassing any customary procedure, and confirming the free and nomadic nature of the artist.

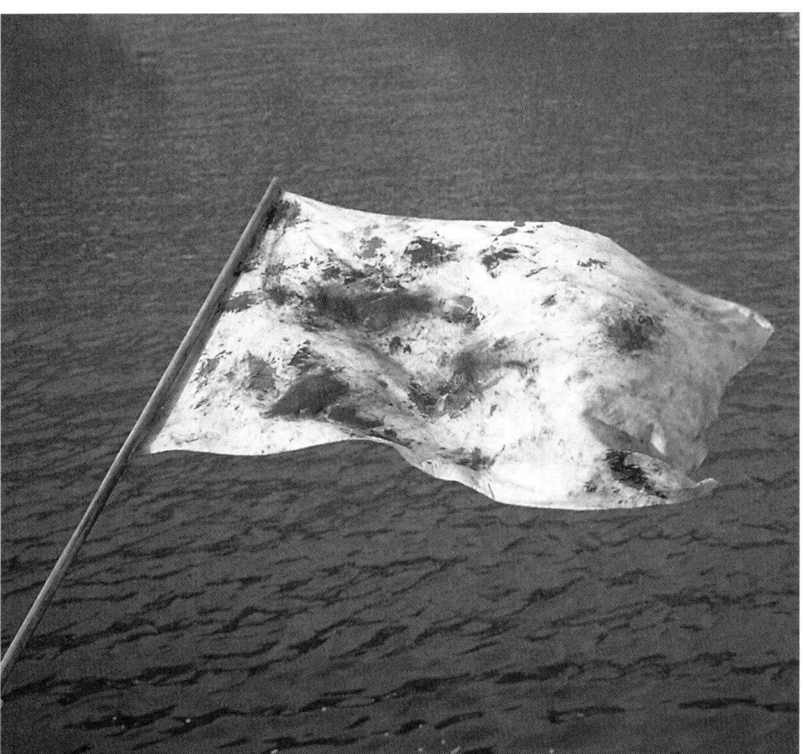

Flag of the World III, 1963

Accidental Sculpture (1968), a heap of plaster of Paris placed on the street by the artist, which becomes a sort of cloud when a car passes over, demonstrates both chance and freedom of the artist to occupy public space with innovative interventions.

Art material can also be a liquid, a milk splash on the street, as in *Painting by Kresimir Klika* (1969). We are in front of a monochrome painting which condenses all of the color spectrum to the whiteness of milk. At the same time an inversion of perspective takes place; the work of art is no longer placed vertically on the wall (of a house, a museum, or a gallery). Rather, it is placed horizontally on a street pavement. These works have their continuity in the *Casual Passer-by* series which Dimitrijević began at the end of the 1960s, in which the artist creates a substitution not of the national flag, but of icons of patriotism. Here the portraits of official personalities and media stars are replaced with those of unknown passers-by—a real and true democracy of the gaze.

Dimitrijević's conceptual art has always avoided the pragmatic neutrality of Anglo-Saxon art, by shifting creative emphasis towards indispensable and necessary elements of partiality. In so doing, he introduces a personal vision of the world.

Already then Braco Dimitrijević introduced a typically European ideological component into the analytic neutrality of conceptual art that generally tended towards self-contemplation and preferred the theoretical "workshop." In the following decades, he consistently conquered the conformist indifference of a bureaucracy which, as I still recall, ordered the police to remove the giant photograph of the unknown passer-by since it visually disturbed the public image of Paris.

Dimitrijević, with Cartesian rigor and Slavic irony, immediately pinpointed the problem of a mass culture that was increasingly subjected to the metastasis of an unstoppable kitsch that turns every historical complexity into schematic facts and every city into a picture postcard. Hence the conformist revolt of the authorities against the well-aimed incursion of the conceptual artist Dimitrijević.

Dimitrijević 's oeuvre from the 1960s to today can be inscribed under the sign of post-history. He introduced a concept of post-history that goes beyond a linear vision of progress, a purely evolutionistic and geometric conception of the past and present that denies any antinomies.

The planet Earth is a theater of conventions which have come to be called history. It is itself the fruit of a linear development that tries to give a meaning to everything under the name of progress. In his 1976 book *Tractatus Post Historicus*, Braco Dimitrijević elaborates an interpretation of that meaning in order to introduce a notion of post-history capable of defeating logocentrism—that completely Western, completely rational idea of historic progress, playing on the categories and distances between different realities that in fact surround each other.

From this vantage point, outside of the purely evolutional order subordinated to the ideology of Darwinism, Dimitrijević proposes prophetic works, accompanied by his theoretical text. His art has developed to a level of great maturity and at the end of the 1970s his artistic poetry escaped the ideological heaviness of the purely evolutionist linguistic Darwinism that had an almost superstitious power over most of the avant-garde art of those years.

Dimitrijević elaborates art that is concentrated on art itself, combining a situationist manner with Fluxus-like freedom as he puts together the high reality of art with the low reality of life, images derived from various moments in art history and elements belonging to nature. In the space of Dimitrijević 's post-history all distances become relative, temporal—between different periods of art (Renaissance, baroque, modernism)—as well as spatial, between fruits of earth united with a market cart and old paintings in museum frames.

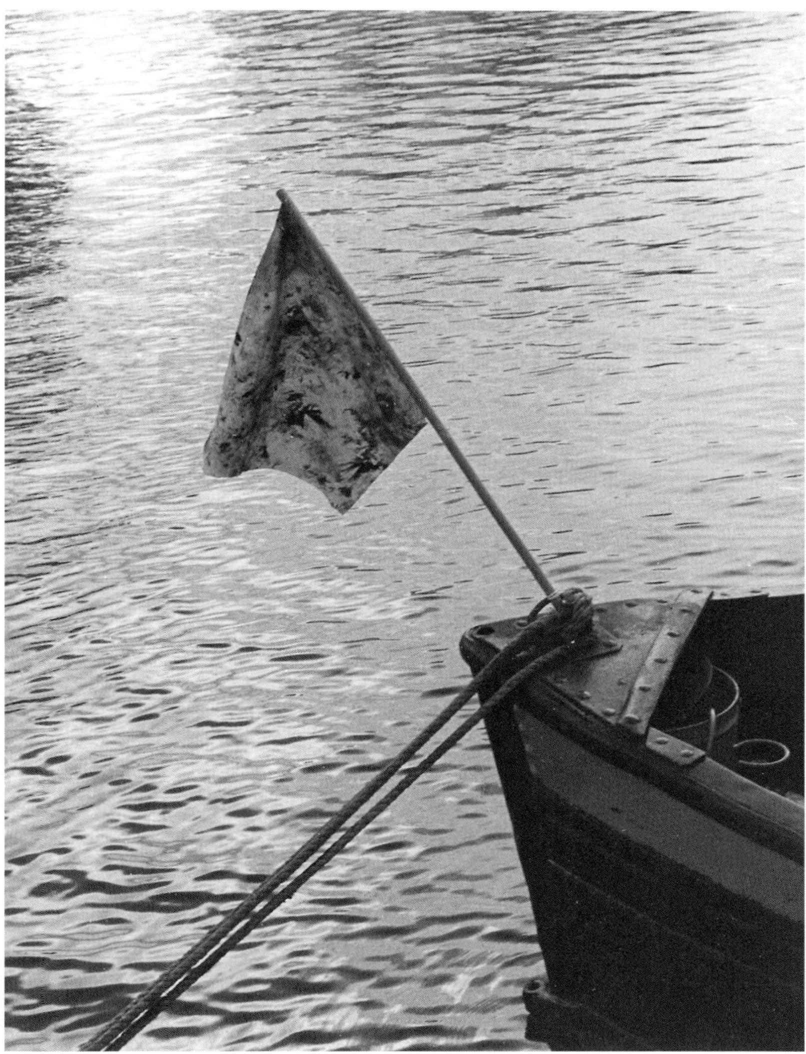

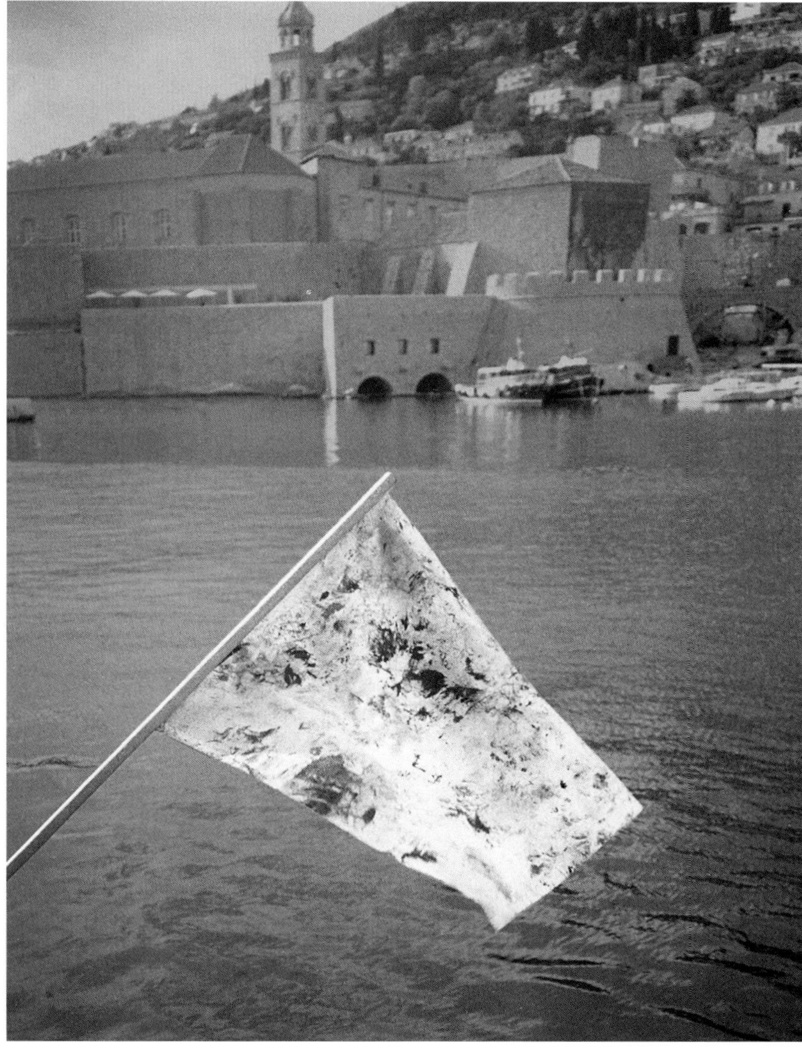

Flag of the World I, 1963
First outdoor work in which the official flag was replaced with a cloth for cleaning brushes

Flag of the World II, 1963

The installation *Van Gogh Goes to Paradise* made and exhibited in 2005, at the Musée d'Orsay, consisted of a market cart filled with oranges and lemons, in which was placed Van Gogh's self-portrait from 1889. Hanging on the wall next to this was another Van Gogh self-portrait from 1887. This was surrounded by oranges and lemons that were fixed to the wall, forming the shape of a comet.

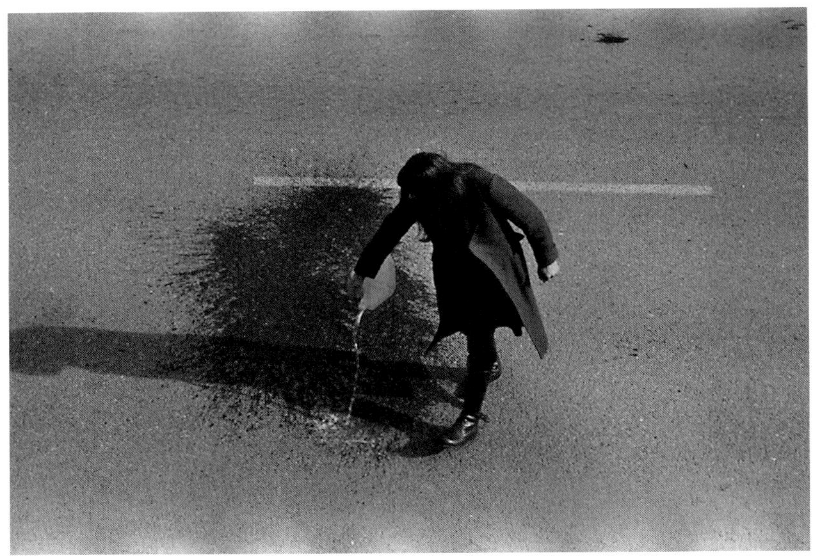

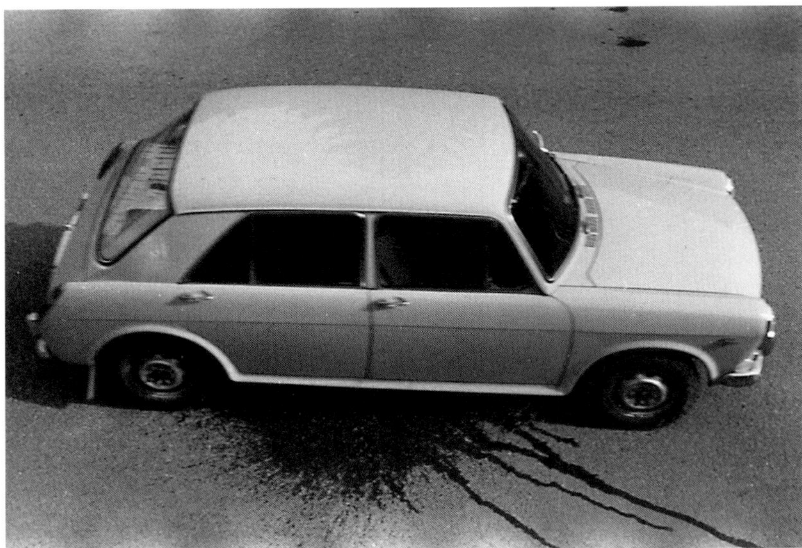

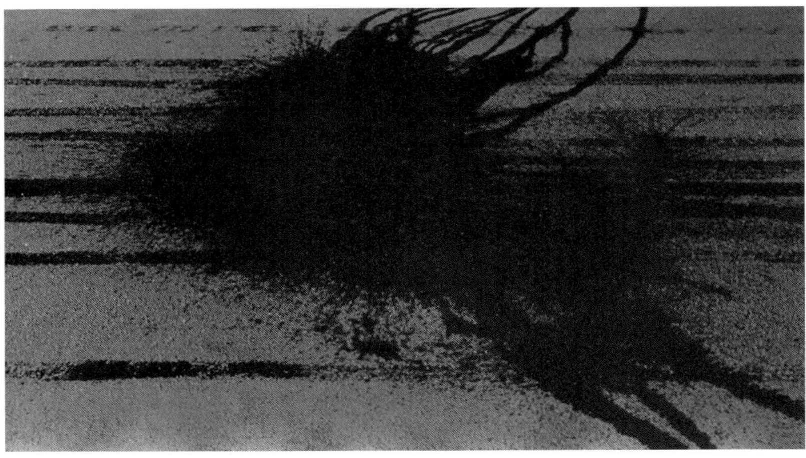

Accidental Painting IV, 1968
Oil on asphalt

Here Dimitrijević poetically assumes an astral perspective, a distant view that allows him not to make a distinction between the fruits of the earth and those of the imagination; oranges and lemons and the self-portrait of the great Dutch artist. In that way an interaction between art and life is established, rigorously resolved on the level of language. He jumps over the hierarchical order that substantially governs our everyday life and introduces the vitality of an encounter between the objects of different nature, united by their common belonging to the post-history of our planet.

Braco Dimitrijević uses the concept of the found object in order to construct a new typology of the readymade, able not only to strike metaphysically our way of seeing but to produce a shortcut between realities which are foreign to each other. Furthermore, he expands the limits of the conceptual art game, dislocating it from "dematerialization" and bringing it into contact with the matter of life, because, in the words of the artist, from a great distance there is no difference between the Louvre and the zoo. The mythical French museum becomes the artist's studio and a confined space within which is cultivated a love of art and a disciplined contemplation of the artwork, which at the same time pushes it towards the myth of untouchability. But since for Dimitrijević "the street is my museum," at the Musée d'Orsay the artist chose the paintings of Van Gogh and placed them in contact with the fruits of the earth. Van Gogh was given back his human dignity—that of a peasant—in tune with the natural landscapes of his pulsating painting.

From Kandinsky to Van Gogh, numerous artists have been taken as love hostages by Dimitrijević and linked to the natural reality of fruit, which in the closed space of a museum announces not the immobile time of immortality but the very minutes of our everyday life.

Dimitrijević has again confronted, both in his aesthetic and anthropological solutions, the totality of cosmic time (which contains present, past, and future) and the particularities of everyday life (which also contains death and desperation). In a site-specific work he has mixed the cultural heritage embodied by great masters, physical space, and pulsating life. Matter and concept, idea and form find their place in work which succeeds in affirming the relationship between art and life as a contradiction; the hell of life and the paradise of art. In fact, in the case of this work, we inhabit a condition in which time and space interlace in a relationship that is simultaneously concrete and symbolic.

In the Musée d'Orsay the air was filled not only with the emanations of the historic master paintings but also with the near loss of gravitational weight of fruits of the earth since they were now displayed on the museum wall. Dimitrijević seems to have introduced in this sacred space the freedom of a vacuum, which makes every thing levitate, and permits connections between things of different natures, organic and artificial, to be seen from the viewpoint of cosmic time which does not distinguish between centuries and months, between real oranges and lemons and the painted products of the earth. Braco Dimitrijević happily confirms the contradiction of art, the possibility of a vision capable of breaking the limits of historic reality of good common sense in favor of a positive vacuum, the ritual of an artwork that is able to affirm the hell of life and the paradise of art.

At the 1990 Venice Biennale, Dimitrijević presented another constellation work in the exhibition *Ubi Fluxus Ibi Motus*, this time a comet of apples on the floor serving as a pedestal to a bicycle to which was attached a work by Duchamp.

Once more the artist was playing a creative game which implies different linguistic options but only one compositional strategy: to make a universe out of fragments by creating a system of harmonious relationships between high and low, full and empty, history and nature, figurative and abstract, matter and form.

Braco Dimitrijević created a great work at the Jardin des Plantes zoo, Paris, in 1998, with the motto "If one looks from the moon, there is virtually no distance between the Louvre and the zoo," demonstrating the artist's ability to create an itinerary for the spectator, to absorb him in the place where in different cages cohabit the animal world and world of culture—lions with paintings belonging to art history. The zoo became a space of regeneration, an Indian reservation in the best sense of the world, in which energies gathered from different universes created an iconographic and formal miracle. The zoo was taken out of the ghetto of Nature and transformed into a place in which cages looked like minimalist structures, the paintings threw off their cultural rhetoric, and animals became gentle creatures able to host a *Gesamtkunstwerk*. In this way the artist transferred language from a purely metaphoric plane onto a completely metonymic one.

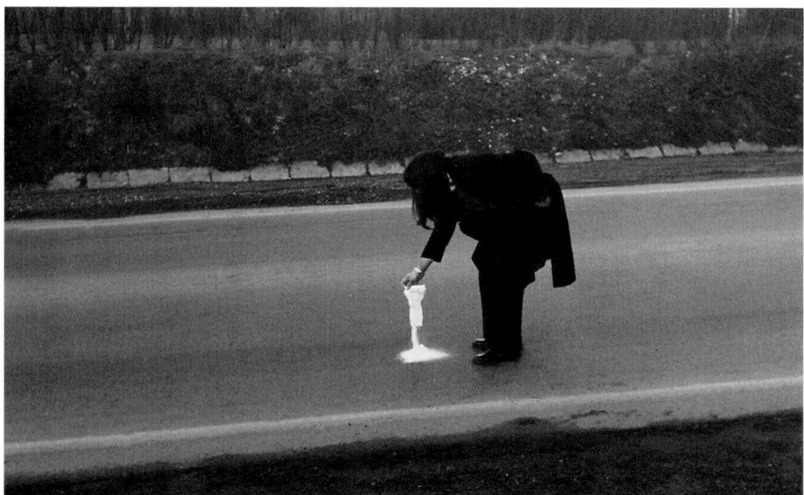

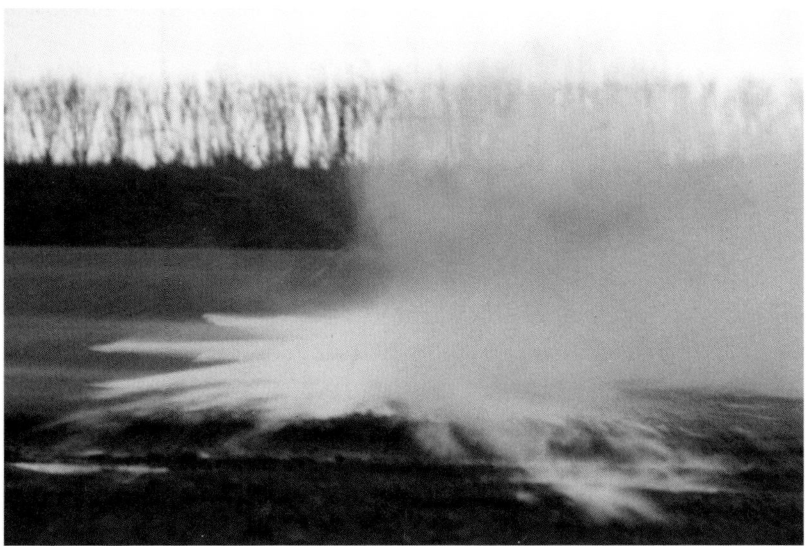

Accidental Sculpture, 1968
Plaster of Paris
Collection: FRAC Limousin

In recent works, Dimitrijević juxtaposes portraits of various personalities with everyday objects and tools, choice of which hints at the artist's judgement of these personalities or the social context in which they lived. Tatlin, Goncharova, Malevich, Matisse, Magritte, Marinetti, Picabia, Kafka, Ravel, Tesla, Gershwin, Rachmanivov, Dostioevski, and Wittgenstein—all these figures are accentuated by an assemblage procedure that associates the icons of art and culture with metal bars, cellos, bicycles, market carts, trombones, axes, boats, and shoes.

All this indicates, in rigorous linguistic terms, that Dimitrijević lives a creative process as a kind of universal judgement, a sort of compensation for the omissions of history and wrong social judgements. Accordingly, he alternates indoor and outdoor visual forms, mixing photographs and real objects. The choice of these objects does not have a purely aesthetic function, and instead reflects an ethical value linked to the artist's judgement regarding chosen personalities.

While kitsch is a virus malignantly attacking the collective imagination of mass society, on the other hand the icon, the image of the popular myth, is definitely the visible flipside of all this. Taking this as his premise, Braco Dimitrijević began to demolish the false myths of cultural history and international politics. Or, as in one of his more recent works, he stigmatizes and punishes the musical kitsch of operetta. Here we see Émile Blanchet, Oskar Strauss, Johann Strauss, Victor Herbert, and Victor Massé photographed and framed in a casual arrangement gazing at us from the wall. They each have a pickaxe outrageously breaking the icon's protective glass of authority, accompanied by rivulets of red blood, red chilli peppers reminiscent of coagulated blood. Here Dimitrijević brings the circle of the discourse begun in 1971 to a close and shows the other side of the coin. While the unknown passer-by is celebrated and rendered monumental on public buildings and at the entrance to the exhibition, and is thus turned into an involuntary icon, now by contrast Dimitrijević punishes and demolishes, by executing the historic icons of musical kitsch. Now he glaringly and poetically executes the creators of a light music that floated blissfully unaware over *finis Austriae,* stealing space and recognition from a culture that was instead investigating the crisis not only in the Austro-Hungarian Empire but the whole of Western society in general.

The explicit violence of the pickaxe that shatters and offends the respectability of the personalities is Dimitrijević 's attempt to remove conceptual art from the analytical limbo of pure ideological research and make it a political and emotional incursion into history. Through the weapon he uses he also refers

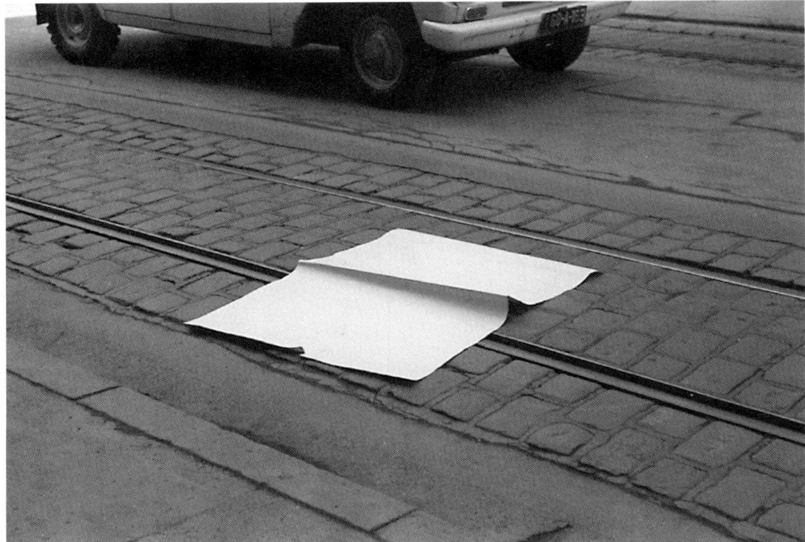

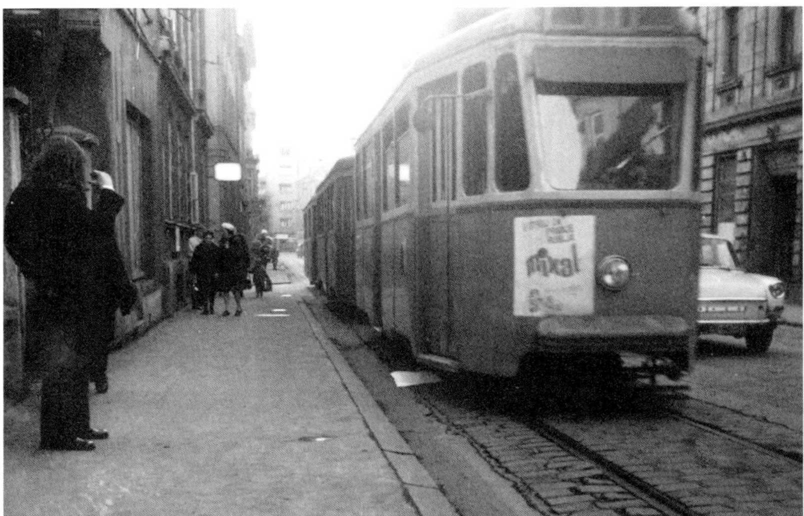

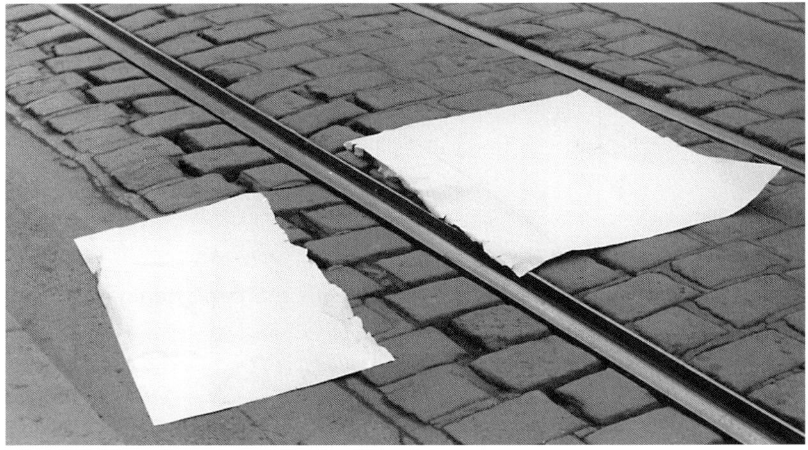

Accidental Drawing, 1968

to another assassination—that of Trotsky in Mexico City at the hand of a hired assassin employed by Stalin. Thus the weapon of a crime ceases to be an instrument of murderous destruction, but is paradoxically the tool of creative and constructive work conferring a different identity in art.

On other occasions the work unites other elements not always related to ideas of violence and death. At the Bienal de São Paulo in 1996, Dimitrijević presented the work *Against Historic Sense of Gravity*, a sequence of photo portraits including the painters Malevich and Modigliani, the inventor of psychoanalysis—Freud—the scientist Nikola Tesla, and the writer Kafka. Attached directly to the wall were various coconuts, which naturally evoked the tropical Brazilian context and whose display formed an astral image of the Great Bear. In this already stellar space in which these great representatives of culture are shown, five cellos were planted in the wall like spears. With the help of the musical instruments every kind of violence was transformed into spirituality, which arms all artistic creativity and engages the mind. If the law of gravity brings everything down, then art overcomes this force and spins the icons of artists and thinkers towards the constellation of the Great Bear, which in this case smelt erotically of the tropical fruit.

He has consistently been inspired by the material culture of the countries in which he has made his works. For example, when working in Latin America, coffee has been both a material and a color that he has adopted to create mainly installation images that are the fruit of a blend of nature and culture, photographs and elemental objects.

Dimitrijević develops his own poetic, conceptual investigation by contextualizing the work in the geographic, historic, and cultural space in which he makes the work. At the 1997 Havana biennial he made the work *Last Road to Paradise*, another shortcut between nature and culture, presenting three carts with three tons of sugar cane on which he placed big photographic portraits of Proust, Kafka, and Dostoevsky. The creators of individual utopias furthered the ferment of history, just as the sugar cane was fermenting in the carts. In any case utopias and sugarcane both end up in a *cul de sac*—the exhibition. The whole of European culture, from the Urals to the Mediterranean, precipitates itself into the Caribbean space, in the wagon of a collision, which represents relation and not domination, dialogue and not colonization. Braco Dimitrijević's work always pushes the notion of value to extremes, implying a coexistence of differences, sometimes celebrated through linguistic conflict between the objects from diverse origins, art and the everyday, related to each other as *objet trouvé*.

The short circuit between imagination and everyday materials leads the spectator towards a judgement, which is always accompanied by irony and passion, which liberates itself by taking a certain distance, as Goethe would say. This refers both to the artist who projects and to the spectator who contemplates.

An agnostic *œuvre*, this work of Braco Dimitrijević aims to provoke emotions and consciousness. It intends to redeem great personalities that have been unjustifiably forgotten, pulling them out of their iconographic anonymity. In the same way as the casual passer-by is immortalized, enlarged, and celebrated on the street under the interested or indifferent gaze of other passers-by.

European art theoreticians have been accustomed to the debate on the "death of art" as it has been absorbed in philosophical milieu. In any case, the common platform for Marxist and non-Marxist posi-

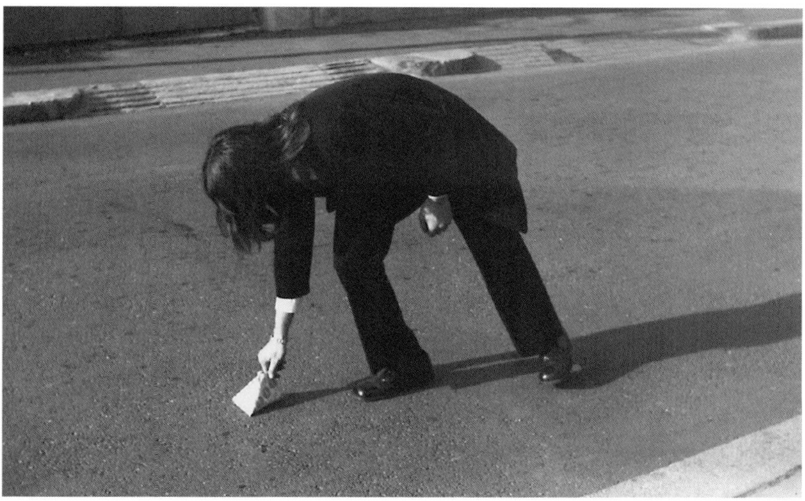

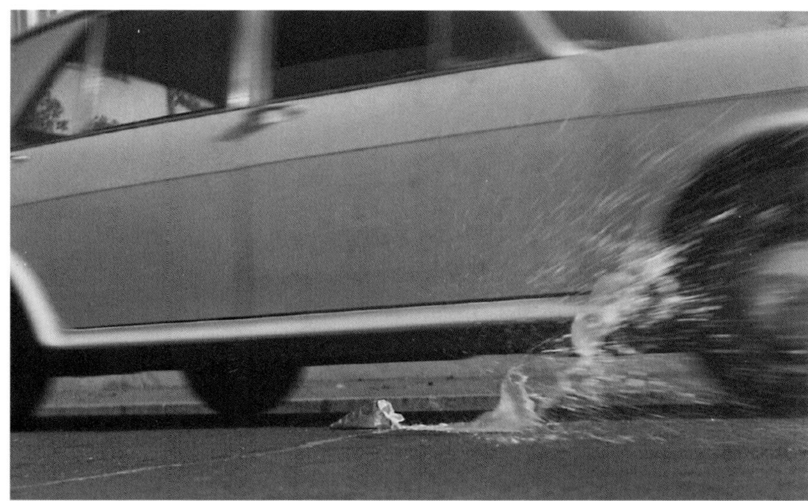

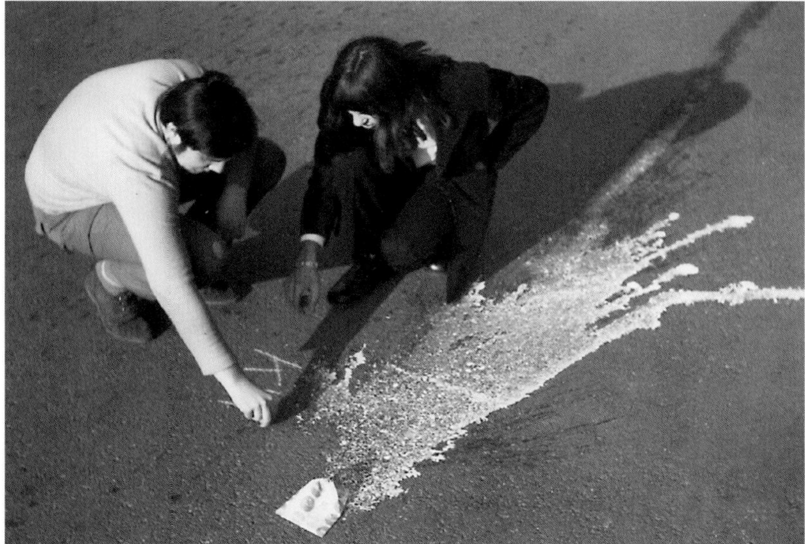

Painting by Krešimir Klika, Zagreb, 1969
Braco Dimitrijević installed a milk carton on the street waiting for a car to run it over. He stopped the driver and asked him to sign the milk splash
Collection: FRAC Limousin

tions alike is the concept that creation is progressively absorbed by all-devouring technical developments.

From then onwards, all contemporary art from impressionism to today, from the mid-nineteenth century to the end of the twentieth century seems to represent the artist's challenge to an era marked by technical reproducibility. In an evolutionary sense, contemporary art rested upon an ideology that in 1971 I termed "linguistic Darwinism," conveying the idea of research developed along linear lines, according to historicist ideas of progress.

The progress of history and the progress of art constituted a parallel convergence, and reflected a productive and experimental optimism regarding art and society of which it is expression.

The crisis of the 1970s brought with it a revision of art, and the theoretical passage from evolutionist linearity, from *the global*, and from neo-avant-gardes to productive discontinuity, to the *non-global*, to the Transavanguardia. The end of big narratives meant for some the much desired "death of art," absorbed by its unavoidable analytical character which undoubtedly marks technical culture.

Dimitrijević assumes in the theoretical field an anthropological view in which the creative process as a fertile metamorphosis includes in itself proofs of its own reality through its form. The form becomes style, and becomes visible proof of the transformation of life.

While socialist realism appears as an apology of existence, a servile activity to a metaphysical entity consisting of ideology, Dimitrijević confirms the ambivalent autonomy of art and its interaction with the world around it.

This is not to celebrate the hegemonic, superior value of the creative process, but rather to experience. At the same time it points out the permanency with which the everyday reality makes part of the artistic strategy in the complexity of a universe dominated by telematics.

Here pure information regarding world news is transformed into *formal and elaborate* meaning (Steinbach) capable of engraving itself into collective consciousness by a creative process of art, which is never a statistical evidence but constantly morphs itself into persistence. This work affirms a passage from space to time, from gesture to permanency.

The visibility of art is measured through the consistency of form, and is able to witness the joyful fatigue of life and the risk to live temporal verticality of the present in the horizontal posture of history. Post-history is positively cunning in preventing destructive dispersion into pure present.

Just as in the prophecy of Joseph Roth, between irony and lamentation, the model of the new man, the "man of tomorrow, but also this of after tomorrow, is a man of all forms that we have passed through and will be passing through." Art after 2000 represents the search to create iconographic counterpoint to the reality which surrounds man, by means of visual fiction but towards the cognitive and liberating ends. Without respecting any conventions, in tune with Gottfried Benn's prescription in *Getting Old: Problem for Artists*: "Formulate your propositions in a manner most deprived of any consideration."

This is a style that produces an ethics of how to make art, as well as respectable art movements. Even in the third millennium. Because, as Guy Debord says in *The Society of the Spectacle*, at this point in the world's journey all forms of expression start turning into void and becoming their own parody. In this parody-like imitation, in sterile mimicry through the special effects of art for the survival of a very artifi-

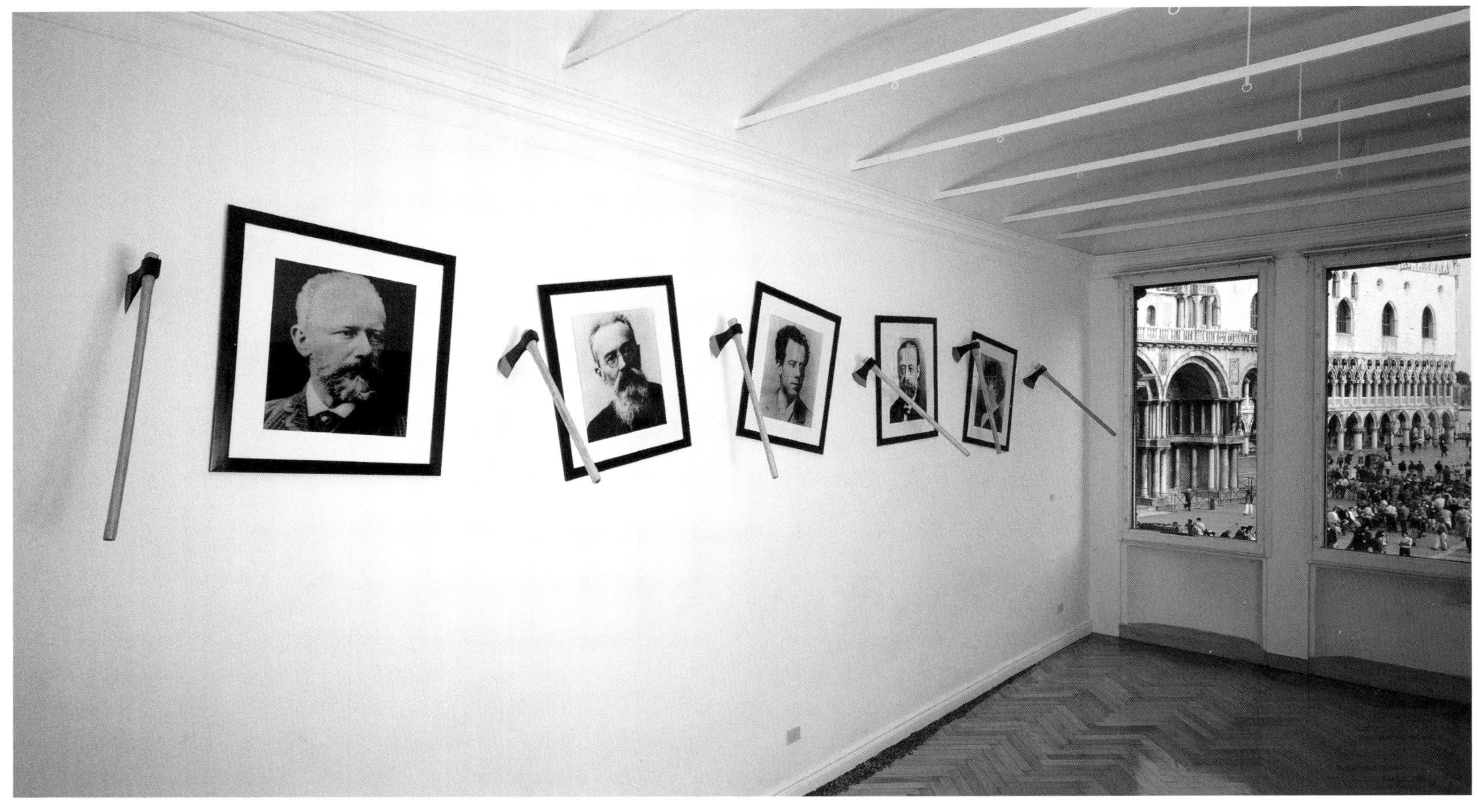

Citizens of Sarajevo
Venice Biennale, 1993
5 b/w photographs, 6 axes, beans, dimensions 860 x 300 cm
Collection: Museum Moderner Kunst, Vienna

cial nature, one affirms one's preference for the ultimate effect, the probable surprise of a better future. "Who says you have to follow the times, but for what reason if the times are wrong?" (Ingres). Indeed.

Out of conflict of art with conventions of the world is born the rehabilitation of history, of neo-history and the narrative of impossible future. An acrobatic act, vertically cut on the flat horizon of "unified thought." This art is a sign of difference. Even beyond 2000.

At the end of science, diagnosed by John Organ in 1996, the lack of great discoveries in the field of theoretical physics and molecular biology tend to overcome telematics with virtual omnipotence of *God Games*, and neo-design which projects new collective instruments for the development of minds. But always in the inevitably productive logic of the global. Instead, art seems to still promise unknown models of world particularities.

Art also confirms in its appearance the theorem, elaborated by Kurt Godel in 1931, of "indecisiveness" being an axiomatic truth and also an un-provable evidence which does not answer to mathematical norms of logics, objectively founded on demonstration, but rather on discontinuity of the subjective need to break the entropic equilibrium of the world.

Art uses the *pathos* of technological distance, of television re-run, in order to produce a testimony of future memory—of a quantity of death which seems to be cruelly proportional to the mass society which contemplates it now.

The rigorous artistic oeuvre of Braco Dimitrijević, which started in 1960s and continues today into a new century, contains a possibility of signalizing hope for a new way, the passage from post-history to neo-history. His iconography is a grand visual fresco of a vision of the world, never static, but also capable of using the principle of dialectics outside of any mechanical contraposition to affirm the idea of a total art and its anthropological value.

An art, as Pablo Picasso said, that focuses on the world.

But also, as Braco Dimitrijević is saying with his entire oeuvre, an art created for the world.

Achille Bonito Oliva

Un art crée pour le monde

Je me rappelle encore la Biennale de Paris en 1971, dont j'étais commissaire pour le Pavillon italien, où Braco Dimitrijević présentait dans la section consacrée à l'art conceptuel son *The Casual Passer-by I Met* (Le Passant anonyme que j'ai rencontré), monument photographique dédié à un passant inconnu, hymne à la créativité potentielle et ignorée, à la non-reconnaissance de l'artiste - poète effacé par l'histoire.

L'œuvre conceptuelle de Braco Dimitrijević le *Drapeau du Monde* fut réalisée déjà en 1963, suivie plusieurs années plus tard par une autre œuvre extérieure *Sculpture Accidentelle* et *Peinture par Kresimir Klika*. Avec ses œuvres, l'artiste établit une relation directe avec le monde opposant les moyens du langage artistique aux conventions sociales et aux codes de la politique. Dans le *Drapeau du Monde*, Dimitrijević remplace un signe officiel, un drapeau national sur son bateau par une alternative. Son drapeau personnel est celui d'un peintre, le chiffon utilisé pour nettoyer ses pinceaux. Selon les conventions internationales lorsque l'on pénètre dans les eaux territoriales étrangères, en naviguant d'un pays à l'autre, le pavillon national est remplacé par le pavillon de l'autre pays, même s'il n'y a aucune terre en vue à l'horizon. Le drapeau de l'art de Dimitrijević traverse toute frontière, surpasse toute procédure douanière et confirme la nature libre et nomade de l'artiste.

La sculpture accidentelle de 1968, un tas de plâtre de Paris placé sur la route par l'artiste, qui se transforme en nuage lorsqu'une voiture roule dessus, démontre à la fois la chance et la liberté qu'a l'artiste d'occuper l'espace public avec ses interventions innovantes.

Le matériel artistique peut aussi être un liquide, une éclaboussure de lait, comme dans *Peinture par Kresimir Kilka* . Nous sommes confrontés à une peinture monochrome qui condense toutes les couleurs du spectre dans la blancheur du lait. En même temps se produit une inversion de la perspective ; l'œuvre d'art n'est plus placée verticalement sur le mur (d'une maison, d'un musée ou d'une galerie), mais horizontalement sur la route. Ces œuvres trouvent leur continuité dans les séries du *Passant Occasionnel* (Casual Passer-by) que Dimitrijević commença à la fin des années soixante, dans lesquelles l'artiste crée une substitution, non du drapeau national, mais cette fois des icônes mêmes du patriotisme visuel. Là, les portraits des personnalités officielles et des stars des médias sont remplacés par ceux de passants inconnus. Une réelle et vraie démocratie pour le regard.

L'art conceptuel de Dimitrijević a toujours évité la neutralité pragmatique de l'art anglo-saxon, faisant prévaloir la partialité d'un regard jamais uniquement visuel, mais investigateur et juge à la fois.

Braco Dimitrijević a introduit, à partir de cette époque, une composante idéologique, typiquement européenne, dans la neutralité analytique de l'art conceptuel anglo-saxon, généralement porté à l'auto réflexion et à la primauté du laboratoire théorique.

Avec une extrême cohérence, dans les décennies suivantes, il a vaincu l'indifférence bien-pensante de la bureaucratie qui - et ce n'est pas un hasard, je m'en souviens encore - s'empressa, avec l'intervention de la police, de décrocher la gigantesque photographie du passant inconnu de l'endroit où elle avait été placée, parce qu'elle était une atteinte à l'image de Paris.

Braco Dimitrijević, avec une rigueur cartésienne et une ironie slave, a tout de suite identifié le problème de la culture de masse, de plus en plus soumise aux métastases d'un kitsch inexorable qui transforme toute complexité historique en fait schématique et toute ville en carte postale. D'où la révolte bien-pensante du pouvoir contre l'incursion ciblée de l'artiste conceptuel Dimitrijević.

Toute l'œuvre de Dimitrijević, depuis les années soixante jusqu'en 2009, peut être inscrite sous le signe de la Post-Histoire. Ce concept va au-delà de la vision linéaire du progrès purement évolutionniste et géométrique, du passé au présent, qui dénie toute antinomie.

La planète Terre est le théâtre d'une convention qu'on appelle histoire, résultat d'un développement linéaire qui cherche à donner un sens à toute chose sous le nom de progrès. Braco Dimitrijević, dans son livre *Tractatus Post Historicus* de 1976, développe une lecture dans ce sens, pour introduire la notion de posthistoire capable de l'emporter sur le sens logocentrique, tout à fait occidental, totalement rationnel, d'un progrès historique qui joue sur les catégories et la distance entre les diverses réalités qui nous entourent.

A partir de là, en dehors d'un ordre purement évolutif soumis à l'idéologie du darwinisme, Dimitrijević propose des œuvres prophétiques, sur la base de son texte théorique.

L'œuvre développe avec une grande maturité la poétique de Dimitrijević qui, depuis les années 70, évite le poids d'une idéologie du darwinisme linguistique, purement évolutionniste, qui imprégnait de façon presque superstitieuse la plupart des œuvres d'art d'avant-garde de ces années-là.

Il élabore un art concentré sur le monde de l'art dans lequel, à la manière des situationnistes et avec la liberté du groupe Fluxus, il met en contact la réalité haute de l'art et la réalité basse de la vie, une iconographie qui s'inspire de différentes périodes artistiques et d'éléments appartenant à la nature. Dans l'espace de la posthistoire de Dimitrijević, toutes les distances deviennent relatives : celles, temporelles, de l'art (Renaissance, baroque, modernité) et celles, spatiales, entre fruits de la terre en court-circuit avec des charrettes et œuvres d'art anciennes dans le cadre du musée.

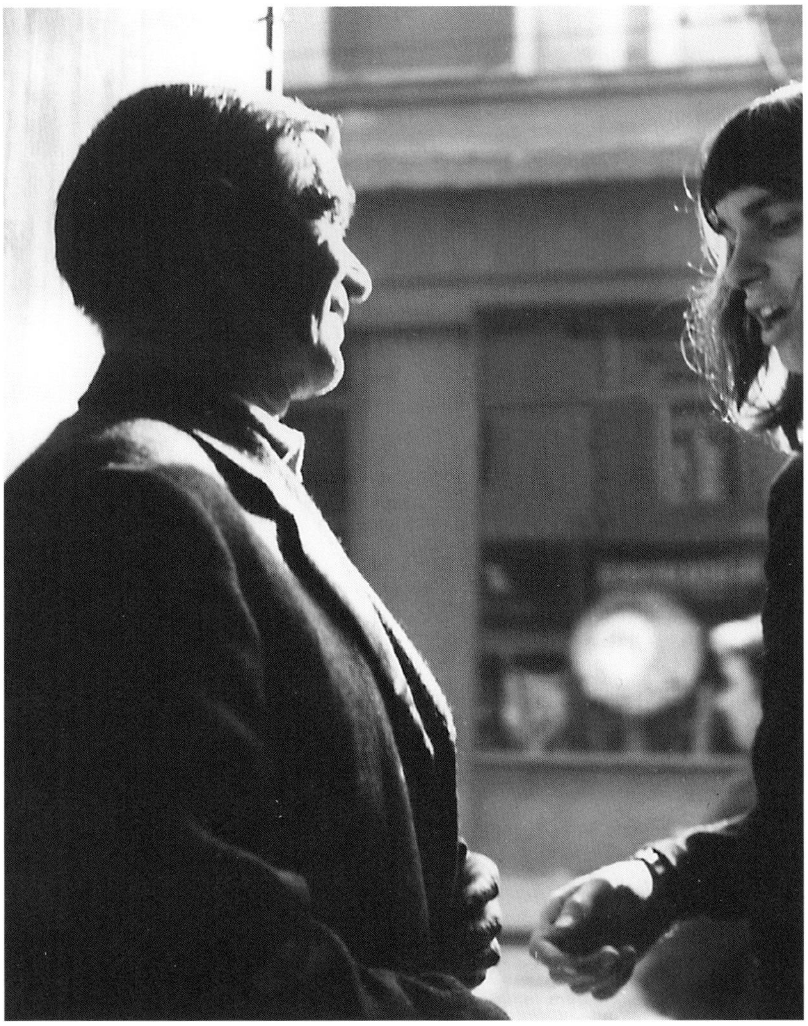

L'installation *Van Gogh enfin au paradis,* exposée au musée d'Orsay en 2005, est composée d'une charrette contenant des oranges et des citrons au-dessus desquels trône l'autoportrait de Van Gogh de 1889. A côté, sur le mur, un autre autoportrait du même artiste de 1887, est entouré d'oranges et de citrons fixés au mur de manière à former une comète.

Ici Dimitrijević assume poétiquement la distance sidérale d'un regard lointain qui permet de ne pas faire de différence entre les fruits de la terre et ceux de l'imagination, oranges ou citrons et autoportraits du grand artiste hollandais.

Ainsi se réalise une interaction entre l'art et la vie, rigoureusement résolue sur le plan du langage. Dimitrijević saute par-dessus l'ordre hiérarchique qui régit substantiellement le quotidien de notre vie et introduit la virtualité d'un contact entre objets de nature différente, unis entre eux par leur appartenance à la post-histoire de notre planète.

Braco Dimitrijević utilise le concept d'objet *trouvé* pour construire un nouveau type de ready-made, capable non seulement de frapper métaphysiquement notre regard, mais aussi de créer un court-circuit entre des réalités étrangères les unes aux autres. Plus encore, il repousse les limites du jeu de l'art conceptuel en sortant celui-ci de toute « dématérialisation » et en contact avec la matière de la vie parce que, au dire de l'artiste, vu de loin, il n'y a pas de distance entre le Louvre et le zoo.

Tihomir Simcić in conversation with Braco Dimitrijević, Zagreb, 1969

Le mythique musée français devient l'atelier et l'espace clos où se cultive l'amour de l'art et où se manifeste aussi une contemplation disciplinée de l'œuvre qui pousse celle-ci vers le mythe de l'intouchabilité. Mais puisque pour Dimitrijević « la rue est mon musée », l'artiste extrait du musée d'Orsay les œuvres de Van Gogh et les met à son gré en contact avec les fruits de la terre. Van Gogh retrouve la dignité d'une civilisation, la culture paysanne, à l'image des paysages naturels qu'il a su restituer dans sa peinture si vibrante.

De Kandinsky a Van Gogh, nombreux sont les artistes que Dimitrijević a pris amoureusement en otage et a rattachés à la réalité naturelle des fruits qui scandent, dans l'espace clos du musée, non pas le temps immobile de l'immortalité, mais le temps précis de notre quotidien.

Dimitrijević se confronte une fois de plus, sur le plan esthétique et anthropologique, à la totalité du temps cosmique (qui comprend présent, passé et futur) et au caractère partiel de la vie (qui comporte aussi la

p. 29
With a slab of clay Braco Dimitrijević waited behind the entrance door of an apartment house in Ilica Street, Zagreb. The first person that opened the door made an imprint with the door handle in the clay. The passer-by Tihomir Simcić agreed to sign the work

Sculpture by Tihomir Simcić, 1969

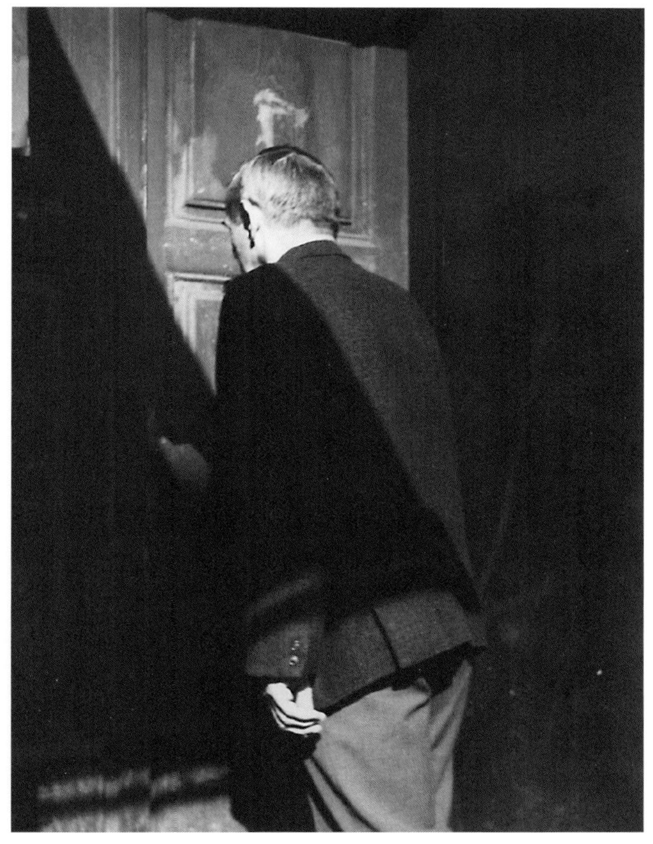

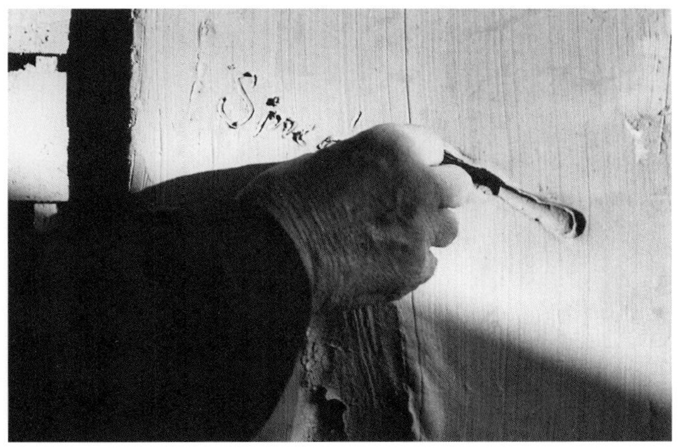

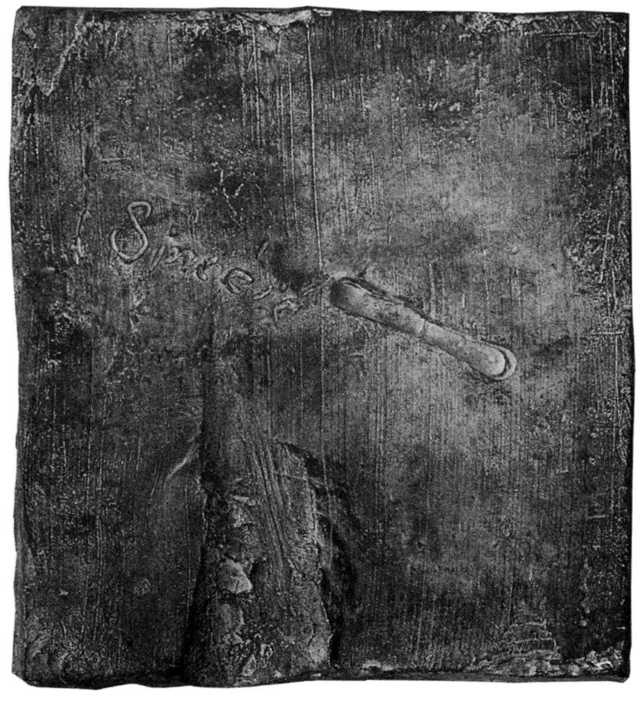

mort et le désespoir). Il résout sur le plan iconographique, grâce à une installation *in situ*, en mélangeant les éléments de l'héritage culturel reçu des grands maîtres exposés, espace physique et pulsion de la vie.

Matière et concept, idée et forme prennent place dans l'œuvre qui réussit à affirmer la relation entre art et vie à la manière d'un oxymore, l'enfer de la vie et le paradis de l'art. En effet, ici se vit une situation dans laquelle temps et espace nouent entre eux une relation à la fois concrète et symbolique.

Au musée d'Orsay, s'élèvent dans l'air non seulement les émanations des images des chefs-d'œuvres historiques, mais également la quasi-absence de pesanteur des fruits de la terre suspendus au mur du musée.
Dimitrijević semble avoir introduit dans cet espace sacré la liberté d'un vide qui fait flotter toutes choses et permet d'établir les liens entre éléments de nature différente, naturels et artificiels, vus dans l'optique d'un temps cosmique qui ne fait pas de différence entre les siècles et les mois, entre les oranges et les citrons naturels et les produits de la terre peints. Braco Dimitrijević confirme avec bonheur la contradiction de l'art, la possibilité d'une vision capable d'évacuer la réalité historique du bon sens quotidien en faveur d'un vide positif, le caractère rituel d'une œuvre en mesure d'affirmer l'enfer de la vie et le paradis de l'art.

Lors de la Biennale de Venise de 1990, Dimitrijević a présenté une nouvelle œuvre-constellation dans le cadre de l'exposition *Ubi Fluxus Ibi Motus* ; ici une comète de pommes sur le sol servait de piédestal à une bicyclette à laquelle était attachée une œuvre de Duchamp.

Une fois de plus, l'artiste jouait un jeu créatif comportant plusieurs options linguistiques mais une seule stratégie compositionnelle : fabriquer un univers à partir de fragments, en créant un système de rapports harmonieux entre haut et bas, plein et vide, histoire et nature, figuratif et abstrait, matière et forme.

Braco Dimitrijević a créé une grande œuvre au zoo du Jardin des Plantes à Paris en 1998, portant la devise “en regardant depuis la lune il n'y a pratiquement aucune distance entre le Louvre et le zoo,” montrant la capacité qu'a l'artiste de créer un parcours destiné au spectateur, d'absorber celui-ci dans un lieu où en diverses cages se côtoient le monde animal et le monde de la culture – lions et tableaux appartenant à l'histoire de l'art. Le zoo est devenu ainsi un espace de régénération, une réserve indienne au meilleur sens du mot, où des énergies recueillies à partir d'univers différents créaient un miracle iconographique et formel. Le zoo était sorti du ghetto de la Nature et transformé en un lieu où les cages prenaient des allures de structures minimalistes, où les peintures abandonnaient le discours culturel et les animaux devenaient de douces créatures capables d'accueillir un *Gesamtkunstwerk*. Ainsi, l'artiste faisait-il passer le langage d'un plan purement métaphorique à un plan entièrement métonymique.

Dans d'autre cas aussi Dimitrijević a rajouté aux photographies de certains personnages des objets quotidiens et des outils qui indiquent le jugement porté par l'artiste sur ces personnages : Tatlin, Goncharova, Malevitch, Matisse, Magritte, Marinetti, Picabia, Kafka, Ravel, Tesla, Gershwin, Rachmanivov, Dostoïevski, Wittgenstein, toutes ces figures sont mises en évidence à travers une procédure d'assemblage qui réunit les images de ces grands personnages avec des barres de métal, des violoncelles, des bicyclettes, des charrettes de campagne, des trompettes, des haches, des barques, des chaussures.

Tout cela indique dans des termes rigoureusement linguistiques la manière avec laquelle Dimitrijević vit le processus créatif comme une sorte de justice universelle et l'œuvre comme une réparation d'un oubli de l'histoire ou d'un jugement mauvais du corps social. Ainsi se succèdent à l'intérieur et à l'extérieur les formes visibles émergeantes de l'assemblage de photographies et d'objets réels. L'usage de ces objets n'a pas une fonction purement esthétique mais acquiert sûrement une valeur éthique liée au jugement de l'artiste en regard du personnage choisi.

Si le kitsch est le virus déferlant qui pénètre malignement dans l'imaginaire collectif de la société de masse, par ailleurs l'icône, l'image du mythe populaire, en est sans aucun doute le revers visible. Partant de telles prémisses, Braco Dimitrijević commence en toute logique à s'attaquer aux faux mythes de l'histoire culturelle et de la politique internationale. Ou bien, comme dans sa dernière œuvre, il stigmatise et condamne le kitsch musical de l'opérette.

Voilà donc Emile Blanchet, Oskar Strauss, Johann Strauss, Victor Herbert et Victor Masse, photographiés et encadrés, qui regardent en ordre dispersé depuis le mur et offrent chacun la présence outrageante d'une hache qui brise la vitre protectrice de l'autorité de l'icône, accompagnée de ruisselets de sang, extraits d'un piment rouge, qui évoquent des filets de sang coagulé.

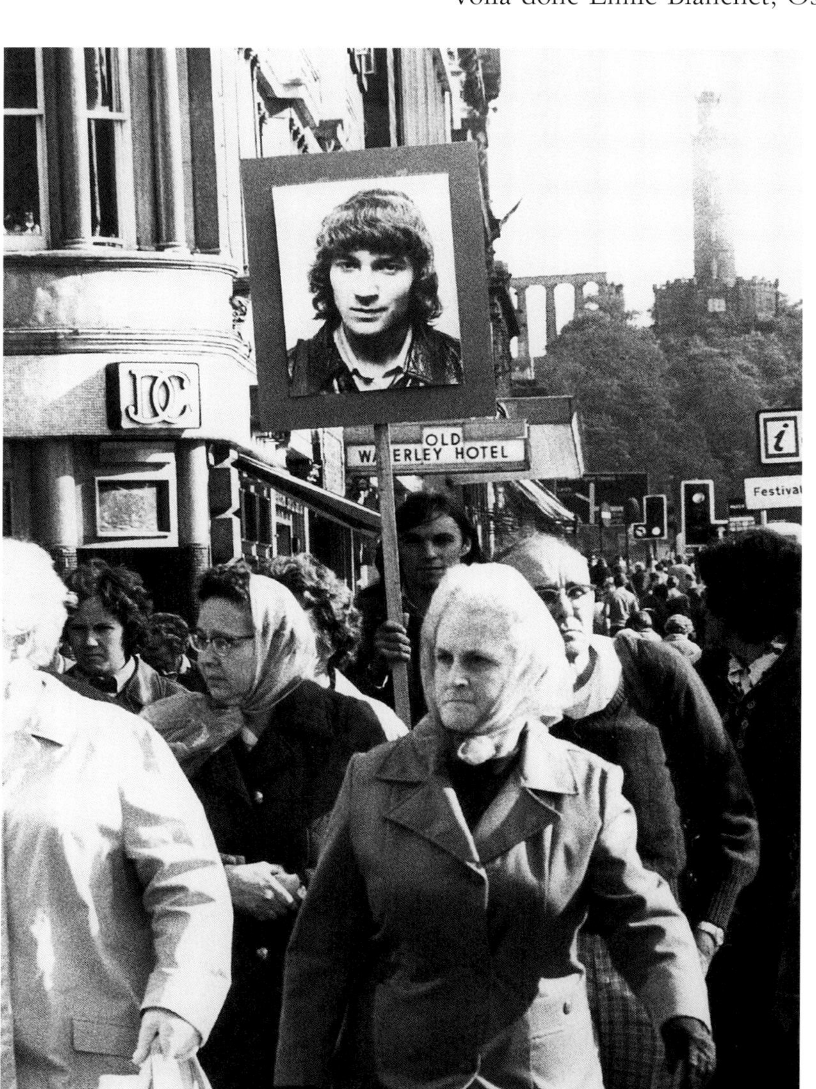

Casual Passer-by I met at 4:57 PM,
Edinburgh, 1975
Collection: Scottish National Gallery of Modern Art, Edinburgh

Dimitrijević referme ainsi le cercle du discours commencé en 1971 et montre le revers de la médaille. Si le passant inconnu était célèbre et figurait de façon monumentale sur les édifices publics et à l'entrée de l'exposition, transformé ainsi en une icône involontaire, maintenant au contraire Dimitrijević attaque et condamne en justicier les icônes historiques du kitsch musical. Ici sont fustigés de manière ostensible et poétique les auteurs d'une musique légère qui voguait béatement et avec inconscience sur la *finis Austriae,* empêchant la visibilité et la reconnaissance d'une culture qui, au contraire, enquêtait sur les crises non seulement de l'Empire austro – hongrois, mais aussi de la société occidentale en général.

La violence explicite de la hache qui transperce et offense la respectabilité des personnages est pour Dimitrijević le moyen de tenter de soustraire l'art conceptuel aux limbes analytiques, à la pure investigation idéologique, et d'en faire une incursion politique et sentimentale dans l'histoire.

Il rappelle aussi, avec l'arme utilisée, le souvenir d'un tout autre assassinat, celui de Trotski à Mexico, par un agent de Staline. Voici que l'arme du crime se rapproche de sa fonction d'instrument de violence homicide et devient paradoxalement l'outil d'un travail créatif et constructif d'une identité de l'art différente.

En d'autres occasions, l'œuvre unit d'autres éléments pas toujours liés à des idées de violence et de mort. A la Biennale de São Paulo en 1996, Dimitrijević a présenté l'œuvre *Against Historic Sense of Gravity*, une séquence de photo-portraits de personnages comme les peintres Malevitch et Modigliani, Freud l'inventeur de la psychanalyse, le scientifique Nikola Tesla ou l'écrivain Kafka. Accrochées directement au mur, quantité de noix de coco évoquaient naturellement le contexte tropical du Brésil, dans une disposition qui formait une image astrale de la Grande Ourse. Dans cet espace déjà stellaire où sont montrés ces grands représentants de la culture, cinq violoncelles étaient plantés dans le mur comme des lances.

Grâce aux instruments de musique, toute forme de violence était transformée en cette spiritualité qui arme toute créativité artistique et engage l'esprit.

Si la loi de la gravité fait chuter tout corps, alors l'art surmonte cette force et fait tournoyer ces icônes d'artistes et de penseurs vers la constellation de la Grande Ourse, qui à cette occasion dégageait le parfum érotique du fruit tropical.

L'artiste est régulièrement inspiré par la culture matérielle des pays où il réalise ses œuvres. Pour ses travaux en Amérique latine, par exemple, le café sert à la fois de matériau et de couleur qu'il adopte pour créer des images principalement d'installations qui sont le fruit d'un mélange de nature et de culture, de photographies et d'objets élémentaires.

De manière cohérente, il s'est toujours référé à la culture matérielle des pays d'Amérique latine dans lesquels il a réalisé ses œuvres. Le café, par exemple, a été un matériau et en même temps une couleur qu'il a adoptée pour créer des images qui étaient essentiellement des installations, fruit d'hybridation de nature et de culture, de photographies et d'objets élémentaires.

Dimitrijević développe sa propre enquête poétique et conceptuelle en situant l'œuvre dans le contexte de l'espace géographique, historique et culturel où il la réalise. Lors de la Biennale de La Havane de 1997, il produit l'œuvre *Last Road to Paradise*, autre raccourci entre nature et culture, en présentant trois charrettes contenant trois tonnes de canne à sucre et sur lesquelles il a placé de grands portraits photographiques de Proust, de Kafka et de Dostoïevski. Tout comme la canne à sucre fermentant dans les charrettes, ces créateurs d'utopies individuelles ont fait progresser le ferment de l'histoire. Quoiqu'il en soit, les utopies comme la canne à sucre mènent à cette impasse qu'est l'exposition. Toute la culture européenne, de l'Oural à la Méditerranée, se précipite dans l'espace caraïbe, dans le wagon d'une collision, représentant non la domination mais la relation, non la colonisation mais le dialogue. L'œuvre de Braco Dimitrijević porte toujours à l'extrême la notion de valeur, suggérant une cohabitation de différences, parfois exaltées à travers le conflit linguistique entre objets d'origines diverses, artistique ou quotidienne, mis en rapport comme autant d'objets trouvés.

Milan Simurdić, Casual Passer-by I met at 12:16 PM, Belgrade, 1974

Mr. and Mrs. Braco Dimitrijević request the pleasure of your company at a cocktail party to be held in honour of

Mr. Milan Simurdić

on April 18, 1974
at Gallery of Studentski kulturni centar
Maršala Tita 48 – Beograd
from 7.30 p. m. to 8.30 p. m.
R. S. V. P.

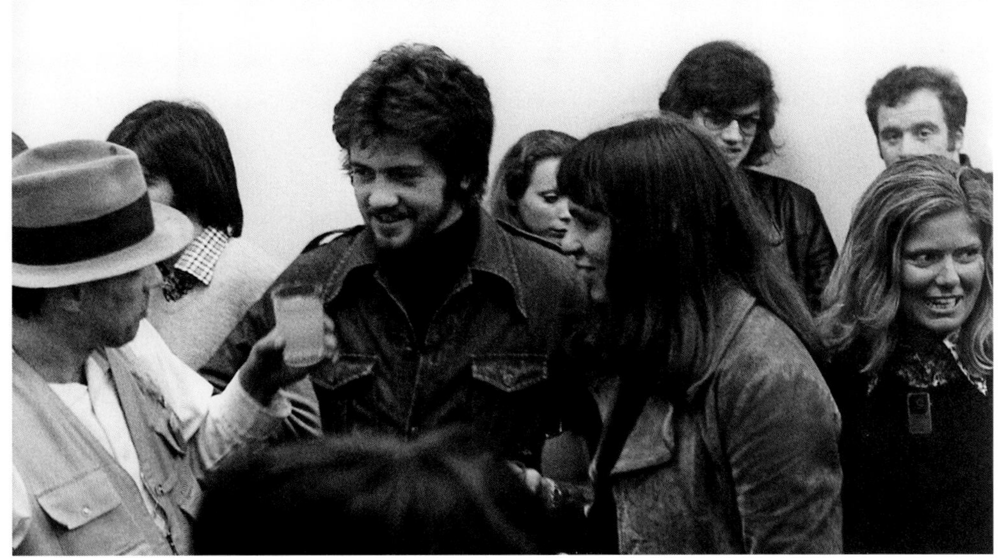

From left to right: Joseph Beuys, Milan Simurdić, Braco Dimitrijević, Ingrid Dacić

Dans tous les cas, le court-circuit entre les images et les matériaux quotidiens prédispose le spectateur à un jugement toujours accompagné d'ironie, la passion qui s'est libérée dans la distanciation, comme le dit Goethe. Cela vaut pour l'artiste qui projette et pour le spectateur qui contemple.

Une œuvre agnostique comme celle de Braco Dimitrijević veut produire des émotions et une prise de conscience. Il veut sauver les grands personnages, injustement oubliés, de leur iconographie anonyme et de même pour le passant occasionnel qui se retrouve immortalisé, agrandi et célèbré par la rue sous l'œil curieux, mais peut être aussi indifférent, des autres passants.

Les théoriciens de l'art européen nous avaient habitués à un débat considérant la « mort de l'art » comme son absorption dans le milieu philosophique. Dans tous les cas la plate-forme commune, pour les marxistes et les non-marxistes, était constituée par un concept de la création progressivement absorbé par le développement omnivore de la technique.

Depuis ce moment, tout l'art contemporain, de l'impressionnisme à aujourd'hui, de la moitié du XIXème siècle à la fin du XXème siècle, semblait un défi lancé par l'artiste à une époque marquée par la reproductibilité technique. Le sens évolutionniste du contemporain était donc supporté par une idéologie que j'ai définie en 1971 comme le « darwinisme linguistique », fruit du développement linéaire de la recherche et d'une empreinte de l'historicisme sur le progrès.

Le progrès de l'histoire et la progression des langues constituent une convergence parallèle en regard d'un optimisme productif et expérimental pour la société et l'art par elle exprimé.

La crise des modèles des années soixante-dix a comporté une révision dans le domaine de l'art, celui du passage théorique de la linéarité « évolutive », *global*, des néo-avant-gardistes à la discontinuité productive, pour cela *non-globale*, de la Transavangarde. La fin des grandes narrations, pour certains, a signifié la tant souhaitée « mort de l'art », absorbée par l'inéluctable caractère analytique qui indubitablement marque la culture de la technique.

Dimitrijević assume dans le domaine du théorique une vision anthropologique grâce à laquelle le processus créatif comme de fertiles métamorphoses inclut en soi les preuves de la vraie réalité à travers la forme. La forme dans le temps se transmute en style et donc devient la preuve visible de la transformation de la vie. Tandis que le réalisme socialiste apparaît comme l'apologie de l'existence, organique activité grégaire à l'entité métaphysique constituée par l'idéologie, la théorie de Dimitrijević affirme l'ambivalence de l'autonomie de l'art et son interaction avec le monde qui l'entoure.

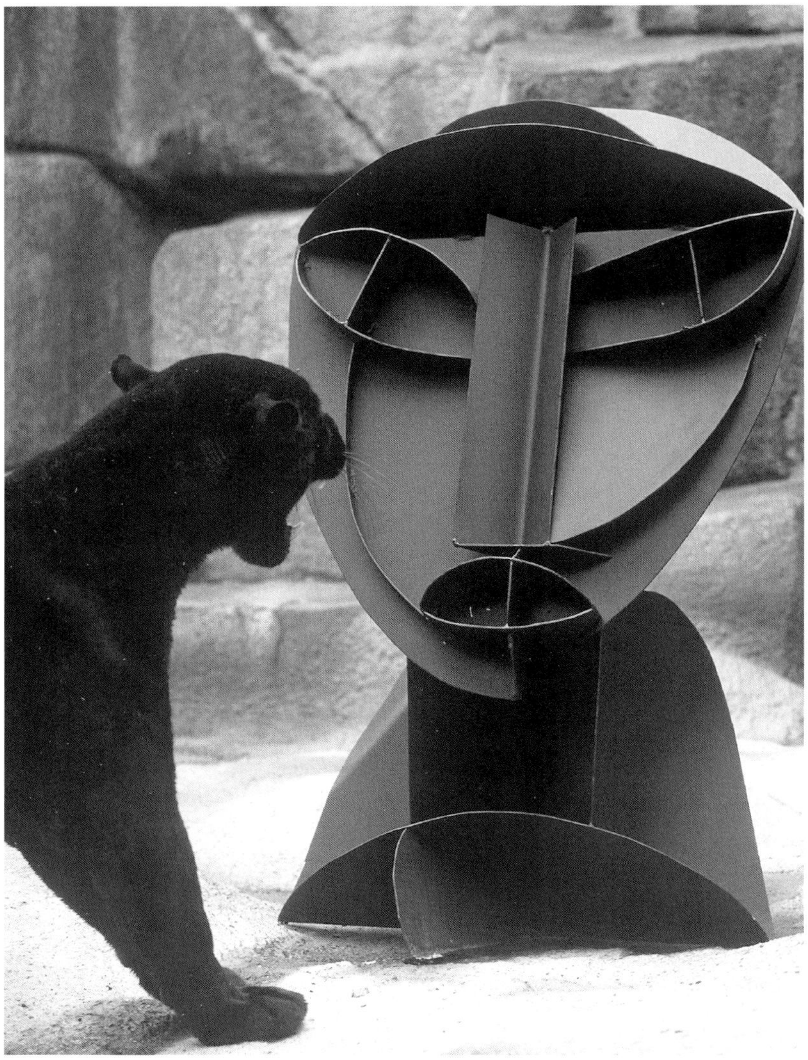

Ici ne se célèbre pas une superbe valeur hégémonique du processus créatif, mais plutôt s'affirme la capacité d'incision de l'expérience esthétique sur l'expérience quotidienne. En même temps se distingue la manière permanente de cette dernière d'accompagner la stratégie de l'artiste dans la complexité d'un univers dominé par la télématique.

Et voilà que la pure information concernant les notions du monde se transforme en *formel élaboré* (Steinbach) capable d'avoir une incidence sur la conscience collective à travers le processus créatif d'un art qui n'est jamais une évidence statistique mais toujours la métamorphose vers le persistant.

En définitive, la visibilité de l'art se mesure à travers la consistance de la forme, capable de témoigner de la joyeuse fatigue de vivre et de la délivrance de la verticalité temporelle du présent, en maintien horizontal, pourtant complexe de l'histoire. La post-histoire est l'astuce positive qui permet de figer dans la durée le destructif désespoir du pur présent.

Se confirme ainsi la prophétie de Joseph Roth, entre ironie et lamentation, sur le profil de l'homme nouveau, « l'homme de demain mais aussi celui de l'après-demain, l'homme de toutes les formes à travers lesquelles nous devrons passer ». L'art au-delà de l'an 2000 cherche donc à créer un contrechamps iconographique à la réalité qui entoure l'homme à travers un champs de finition visuel mais avec une finalité consciente et libératoire. Sans tenir compte de conventions, selon la prescription de Gottfried Benn dans *Vieillir : préoccupation d'artistes* : « Formulez vos thèses sans égard aucun ».

Cas d'evolution, 1998
Ménagerie du Jardin des Plantes, Paris
Collection: Fonds National d'Art Contemporain

C'est le style qui produit l'éthique du faire, le mouvement par excellence de l'art. Dans le troisième millénaire aussi. Parce que, comme le dit Guy Debord dans la *Société du spectacle*, à ce point du cheminement du monde toutes les formes de l'expression commencent à tourner en rond et constituent leur propre parodie.

A l'imitation parodique, à la stérilité mimétique de l'effet spécial, l'art, pour la survie de sa propre nature artificielle, affirme la préférence pour un effet ultérieur, celui de la vraisemblable surprise d'un futur meilleur. « On dit qu'il faut aller avec le temps, mais pour quelle raison, si le temps a tort ?» (Ingres). En effet.

Du conflit de l'art avec les conventions du monde naît la réhabilitation de l'histoire, la néo-histoire, la narration du futur impossible.

Un saut acrobatique à la verticale sur l'horizon plat de la « pensée unique ». L'art c'est cela : signe de la différence.

Au moment où la science, comme l'a diagnostiqué John Organ en 1996, est en manque de grandes découvertes dans le domaine de la physique théorique et de la biologie moléculaire, l'homme cherche à substituer la télématique à l'omnipotence virtuelle des *God Games* (Jeux de Dieu) et au néo-design

Those who sensed earthquakes, 2007
B/W photograph, snake
Courtesy Slought Foundation, Philadelphia

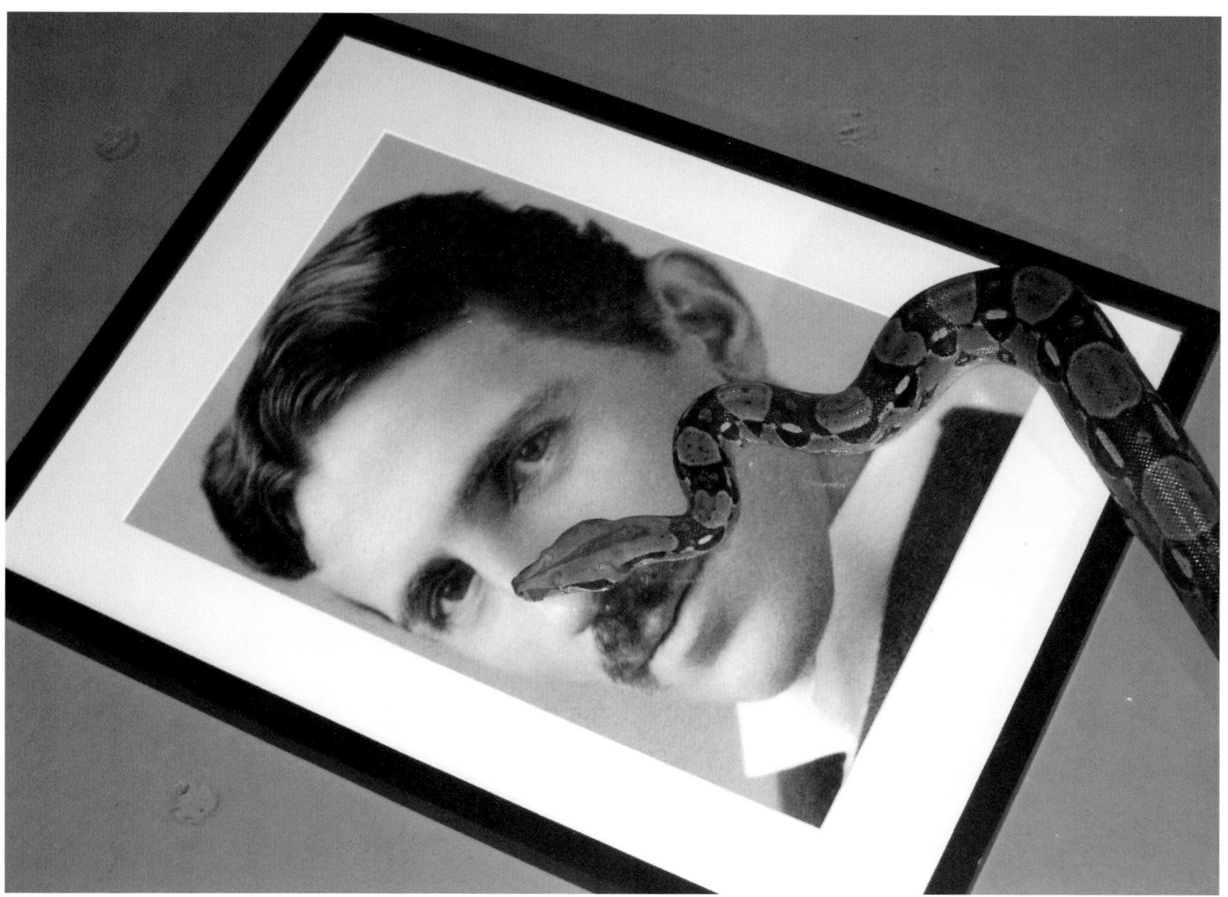

qui propose de nouveaux instruments collectifs pour le développement du mental. Mais toujours dans l'inévitable logique productive du global. Cependant l'art semble encore promettre des modèles mondiaux et inédits de singularité.

L'art en outre confirme en apparence le théorème élaboré en 1931 par Kurt Gödel « de l'indicibilité » étant une vérité axiomatique et aussi une évidence indémontrable qui ne répond pas aux normes mathématiques de la logique, objectivement fondées sur la démonstration, mais à la discontinuité du besoin subjectif de rompre l'équilibre entropique du monde.

L'art utilise le pathos de la distance technologique, la reprise télévisuelle, afin de produire un témoignage à la future mémoire d'une quantité de mort qui semble cruellement proportionnelle à la société de masse qui la contemple en ce moment même.

En conclusion, la production artistique rigoureuse de Braco Dimitrijević, qui a débuté dans les années soixante et se prolonge dans la première décade du nouveau siècle contient en elle la possibilité de pouvoir indiquer l'espérance d'un chemin, le passage de la Post-Histoire à la Néo-histoire. Son iconographie est une grande fresque d'une vision du monde jamais statique, capable au contraire d'utiliser le principe de dialectique, hors de toute opposition systématique, pour affirmer une idée d'art total et sa valeur anthropologique. Un art, comme disait Pablo Picasso, qui se focalise sur le monde.

Mais aussi un art, comme disait et dit avec toute son œuvre Braco Dimitrijević, en faveur du monde.

Letter to Braco Dimitrijević about Post-History

Dear Braco Dimitrijević,

In many African communities, the role of the *griot* (traveling black African poet and musician) consists of telling the history of the tribe that gathers together traditionally under the branches of the "tree of endless discussions." Endless discussions because that story is always a subject to be treated with caution and always a controversial one: never does the *griot* tell the same version of that immensely flexible history. In the Jewish tradition of the Talmud, these discussions are referred to as *pilpul*, which are all the more delightful since the truth is never discovered, which is, by the way, far from being their aim: the commentary itself needs to be commented, since objective truth is a result of negotiations. That is quite far from Hegel and his vision of History as "the realization of an idea," far from the Christian and Marxist-Leninist teleologies, and far from the progressive dogma influencing Western modernism.

In the Middle Ages, theology was considered an integral science: it is history, the "fake science," as you call it, that took its place at the level of illusions coagulated into Truths. In both cases, the belief in the absolute sense of the collective narrative crushes the multitude of versions and hypotheses. The world has a meaning, and this meaning is the only one. Conspiracy theories, so fashionable nowadays, reinforce this idea while they claim to oppose it. When you wrote for the first time, in 1969, that "there are no mistakes in History," but that "the whole of History is a mistake," a thesis appearing in your book entitled "Tractatus Post Historicus" published in 1976, you take a step beyond the dogma of the avant-gardes of the time who perpetuated a banal Messianism based on a strict historization of artistic "gestures."

In your work, since at least the beginning of the 1970s, you have sought to replace this monolithic narrative with the idea of coexisting truths and to confuse the tracks that lead to that single line by which the West has imposed its colonial power upon the entire world. Thus, for a long time, humanity lived as if watching only one television channel: you were either within History or totally without it in that ahistorical zone generally allocated to "the savages," in other words, without any particular importance. Your idea of the "post-history" compares to the invention of channel-hopping: we are talking about switching between different sources of broadcasting, each of which portrays a version of History.

In 1912 an international conference confirmed the notion of "universal time" divided into time zones. A century later, the idea of global economy running twenty-four hours a day validates a notion of the universal that does not dare to identify itself any more, promoting, on the contrary, "differences" and multiculturalism (the vernacular or national culture having become fictional) in order to better mask the genuine uniformization implemented by it. What is linked to these two dates is the fiction of a linear history of mankind, a modernist history whose postmodern hypocrisy today consists in arranging the scenery. For the ideology of the "end of history," inseparable from postmodernism, represents most of all the will to freeze the image in order to neutralize all vague political attempts to transform the world and fix its course along a "new economic order" that would be the final one. In your words: "What we call History is nothing more than one subjectivity imposed on the whole world as objective opinion."[1]

But when you talk about a "post" state of History it has nothing to do with its end. Quite the contrary, your works and your writings prompt an outburst of creativity, a multitude of histories, their versions and their hybridization. Regarding History, Louis Althusser talked about a "process without a subject" in the 1960s: an audacious idea going against the ideologies of the era that could think of no other subject of History than the people or the fighting proletariat. However, post-history has no subject, either. And especially not the Earth itself, Gaia, the maternal idol transformed into a monotheistic ersatz by radical ecologists and New Age groups. The fact that there is no subject for post-history liberates a multitude of subjects, that is, us: as Serge Daney put it: "Have we failed to such an extent in replacing God, the father of mankind, the brother that the terrible matriarchy of our mother, the Earth, should return?"[2]

The "casual passer-by," the central theme of your work, this individual that becomes a subject only when encountering the device of inscription implemented by you is the true inhabitant of post-history. In a way, he appears as the tenant of glory, in this respect, he is a contemporary of Warhol's "becoming famous for fifteen minutes."

An animal or some fruit, an ordinary object, a piece of art. In your "post-historical triptychs" you show that Cézanne or Picasso, whose works we comprehend and evaluate in their relation to a narrative event, in other words, as signals emitted by history, can also be perceived as natural phenomena or tools. A picture by Kazimir Malevich, hatchets placed at an angle, associated with apples put on stands: this arrangement, created in St. Petersburg in 2005, imitates the array of colors of the painter whose composition (*Vanka*, 1928–1929) presents a human figure seen from behind in the first place in post-suprematist style, but heading to a much more realistic farm situated in the background of the picture. You have placed your stands in such a way so as to recall the wake of that walking man, and having hung the painting in one of the corners of the room, you have evoked the first suprematist exhibition in Petrograd in 1915 in which the "black square on white" by the same Malevich was displayed in a similar position: at the top of the wall and in the corner. And in the most well-known photo of that "historic" exhibition, a chair can be found among the works.

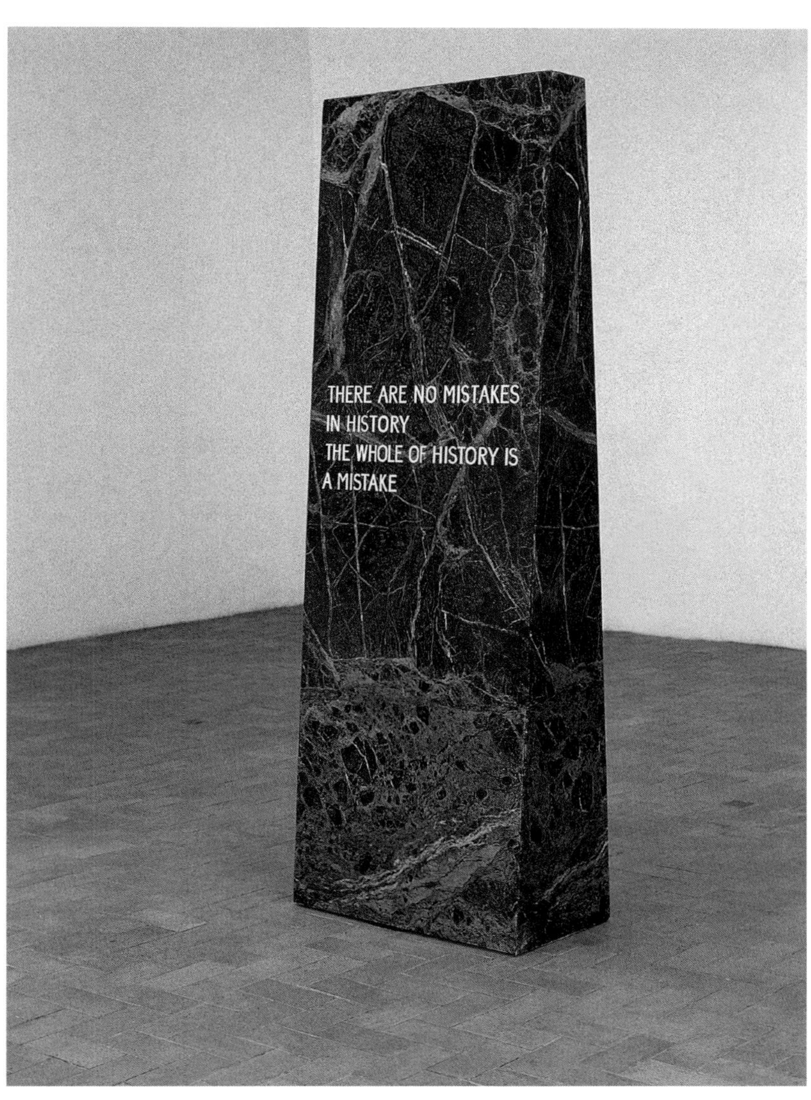

Post-Historic Landmark, 1969–1979
Private Collection, Paris

Your "post-historical" arrangements evoke the status of the icon, a generic image which assembles three elements that you summon: in *Between Eternity and Geniuscide* (1994), it is made explicit since you place candles in front of photographic portraits of Kafka and Modigliani, perched on a sea of red beans. This votive dimension constituting the icon assembles in a stable unit that of the arrangement, the organic, artistic, and functional elements that compose the *Triptychs*. Post-history as you see it reveals itself spontaneously in the form of an absolute timelessness of which the icon constitutes the privileged visual framework. Nevertheless, in your work, the timeless is only a precondition to post-history and not its last say. The *zeitlos*, the Eternal, the atemporal, the long historical duration are but some motives, among others, of a vision of time stripped of all imposed figures. In other words, the icon is only a moment of the image: more precisely, the moment of its crossing from historical time to the ambiguity of the timeless.

So which age does that "casual passer-by" belong to that you met in London at 11:28 on an October morning in 1972? In any case, not to the ordinary one: the day is the only element missing. He belongs to the history of art to the extent that this encounter resulted in a piece of art that eternalizes him; to your personal history, for it is your wandering and the fact that you were in London that day that allow him to exist for us. But he also belongs to that chaotic time without chronology in which Malevich encounters an apple and a hatchet to the liking of the chromatic harmonies. André Malraux wrote in *L'Intemporel* that "the Events of a life converge rather than follow each other." Art is a nave around which this convergence may be organized and which may create coherence that the chronological ideology just cannot perceive. Our memory is achronological itself: it wanders in recent times, then in the faraway irrespective of dates. Chronology is nothing more than an idealist version of time that materialism, that of signs and colors, has destroyed in your "post-historical" compositions.

You claim that "there are no schisms in creation, but breakdowns of perception." Along the same lines, Paul Valéry thought that one could write a literary history without using the authors' names, narrating only the modifications that took place in the ways of reading. But time will not necessarily flow from the past towards the future: when writing about Franz Kafka, Jorge Luis Borges considers his work as a historic shock that transforms the past thoroughly; an entire branch of literature emerges as the "forerunner of Kafka." Similarly, in the 1960s, Georges Perec and OULIPO invented the notion of "plagiarist by anticipating," which points out the reversible and multidirectional time of culture. With the progress of globalization (that in harmony with the Hegelian tradition, some perceive only as the "end of history"), we are heading towards a civilization exploded into countless fragments. According to that conception of history, the opposite of the idea of universal progress, history is no one-way street; instead, there are local crises, micro-narratives, briefly, a whole of temporal distortions that one needs to learn to read together. To this future archipelago of the world, brought about by globalization, corresponds a new notion of time comprising all the historical narratives, all of the chronologies, the sum of accelerations and slowdowns: in a word, heterochrony. It is a temporality in which time flows from the future towards the past, and from global present towards all the particular times.

In 1967 Robert Smithson elaborated the notion of "ruins in reverse" in relation to his piece entitled *The Monuments of Passaic.* Exploring the uncultivated countryside of the state of New Jersey, Smithson qualifies all recent and future constructions as "ruins in reverse." Earlier, romantic ruins (the ones that Hubert Robert presented in his paintings) symbolized the flight of time and incited to a nostalgic meditation over the past; the vaguely modernist constructions designed by Smithson, however, are programmed to become ruins even before their existence, the ruins of a modernist ideology in which future and linear scenarios are much more real than the present or the past. Naturally, entropy, that generic notion around which Smithson articulates his work, is a slowdown. However, paradoxically, this loss of speed results in the acceleration of the future obsoleteness of these "ruins in reverse." As Claudio Magris puts it: "There is no one flow of time going at a constant speed into one specific direction; sometimes we pass another train coming from the opposite direction, from the past, and for a moment, we have this past near us, next to us, in our present." Your post-historical arrangements work like these Smithsonian "ruins in reverse": they

Tractatus Post Historicus, 1976
Edition Dacic Tubingen

Tractatus Post Historicus, 1976
Table of Contents

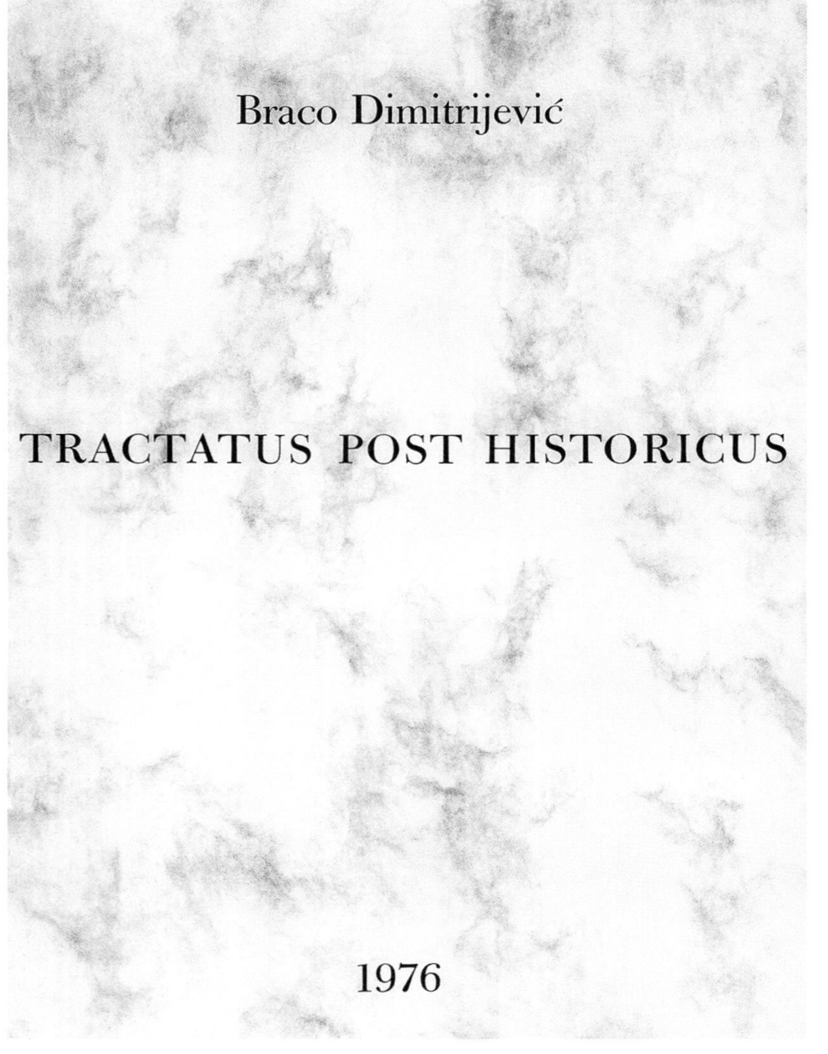

Table of contents

Introduction

Chapter One

THE ETHICS OF FORM OR ESTHETICS OF LOGIC
Art History as the History of Formal Evolution
Style as a Form of Racism in Art
Myth is the Best Investiment;
Formal Innovation. Macro and Micro Style.
Two Logical Spaces;
ERC System. $E_1R_1C_1$ System
Method
Chance
Formal Non-originality; Principle of Ready Esthetics
Artificial Myth or Esthetic of Logic

Chapter Two

STATUS HISTORICUS
Story about Two Artists

Chapter Three

STATUS POST HISTORICUS
About Two Artists. Dialectic Chapel.

Chapter Four

THREE MUSEUM EXHIBITONS
Decentralization of Art

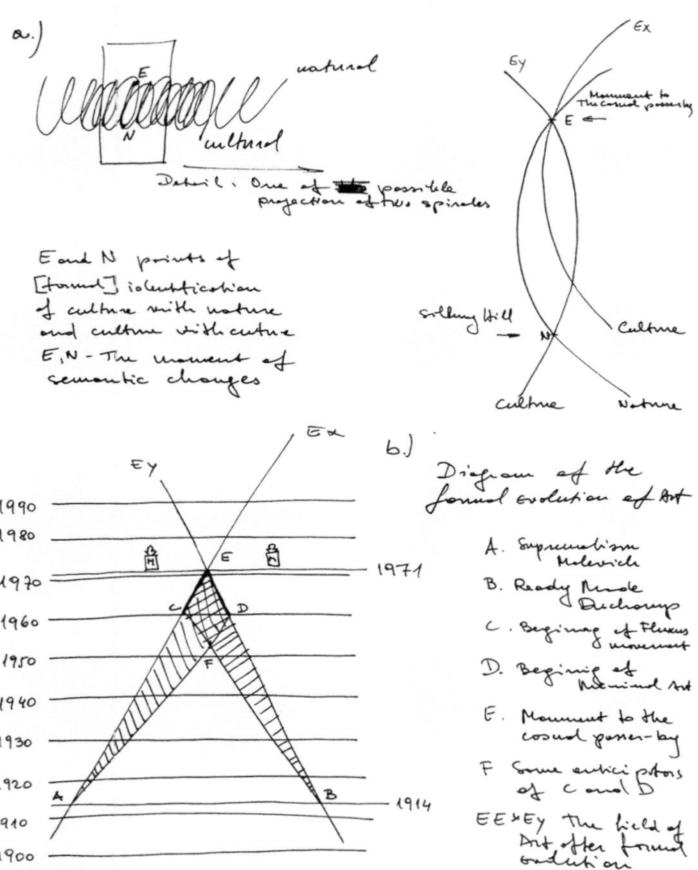

STÄDTISCHES MUSEUM MÖNCHENGLADBACH

TELEFON (02161) 270394 TELEX 852510 SKMG D 4050 MÖNCHENGLADBACH BISMARCKSTRASSE 97

Z e r t i f i k a t

über den Ankauf der Idee, die Bronzebüste des Malers Max Roeder, die sich bereits unter der Inventarnummer 6534 in den Sammlungsbeständen des Städtischen Museums befindet, die darin verbleiben wird, aber die von jetzt an ebenso als ein Werk von Braco Dimitrijević im Sinne "Dies könnte ein Meisterwerk sein" verstanden werden darf.

Der Kaufbetrag wird auf das Konto von Braco Dimitrijević bei der Kreditna Banka Zagreb überwiesen.

Mönchengladbach, den 11. Juni 1975

Dr. Cladders
Museumsdirektor

Braco Dimitrijević

Diagram of Formal Evolution of Art, 1975
A Suprematism: Malevich
B Ready-made: Duchamp
C The beginning of the Fluxus movement
D The beginning of minimal art
E Monument to the *Casual Passer-by*
F Some precursors of C and D
CEDF Overlapping BCE (the spirit of conceptualism) with ADE (cold minimalist presentation) we get the field of so-called conceptual art
CE Development of minimal art
ABF Movements of relative importance for conceptual art. Left from AEEy and right from BEEx: activity which imitates art
EExEy The field of art after formal evolution

Monchengladbach Document, 1975
Certificate of purchase of an idea. "The bronze bust of a painter Max Roeder is stored under stock number 6134 in the collection of the Stadtisches Museum, where it will stay. From now on it can also be regarded as a work of Braco Dimitrijević, *This Could Be a Masterpiece*. (The purchase amount will be transferred to the account of Braco Dimitrijević at Kreditna Banka Zagreb.)"

go from the future towards the past, their point of departure being modern art and their destination, the Lascaux caves.

The portrait of the "casual passers-by" that you hang up like official posters on the front walls of buildings designate the possibility of a junction in History: when one is in front of them, one is always under the impression of entering a parallel reality or having overslept and inexplicably missed a moment of official History, for this institutional narrative is made up of forgotten things, more or less voluntary omissions, subtle hierarchies and implicit codes. The "casual passers-by" remind us that History is created by all of us and that the essence of mankind, as stated by Karl Marx, is no other than the result of what we do together. As a means and as a territory, your work is a zone of junctions: a space in which history turns back, goes off the rails, makes a false step.

In a way, history ceases to be "universal" when it spatializes, when it demands its own territory: contemporary reality is an open book in which, by turning its pages, artists may simultaneously explore the strata of the past and the traces of the times to come. For modernism, the past represented tradition that the new supplanted. For postmodernism, it was a kind of catalogue or repertoire. Nowadays, it simply constitutes a new area of which artists are the privileged archaeologists and geographers, since they glance through it by going from form to form far from the strictness that the discursive linearity imposes upon thinkers and ideologists. In your work, I admire that obstinacy that is shaped around a strong and premonitory vision. Were you not an artist, you would be a kind of preacher or a traveling monk, the one that hammers in, further and further, a painful but salutary nail.

1. In the catalogue *Braco Dimitrijeviç*, Edizione Charta, Milan, 2006 (like all subsequent quotations).

2. Serge Daney, *L'exercice a été profitable, monsieur*, Éditions POL, Paris, p. 341.

Lettre a Braco Dimitrijević sur la Post-Histoire

Cher Braco Dimitrijević,
La fonction du griot, dans nombre de communautés africaines, consiste à raconter l'histoire de la tribu, qui se réunit traditionnellement sous les ramures de "l'arbre à palabres". Palabres, parce que cette histoire est toujours sujette à caution et à controverses ; le griot ne raconte jamais la même version de l'histoire, infiniment élastique. Dans la tradition juive du talmud, on parle de "pilpoul" pour qualifier ces discussions d'autant plus savoureuses que la vérité n'en sort jamais, et qu'il ne saurait d'ailleurs en être question : le commentaire lui-même doit se voir commenté, car la vérité objective est un produit de négociations. Nous nous trouvons là fort loin de Hegel et de sa vision de l'Histoire comme "réalisation d'une idée", loin des téléologies chrétiennes ou marxistes-léninistes, loin du dogme progressiste qui a marqué le modernisme occidental.

Au Moyen-âge, la théologie était considérée comme une science à part entière ; c'est l'histoire, "fausse science", écris-tu, qui a pris sa place au rang des illusions coagulées en Vérités. Dans les deux cas, la croyance au sens absolu du récit collectif écrase la multitude des versions et des hypothèses. Le monde a un sens, et ce sens est unique. Les théories du complot, très à la mode aujourd'hui, ne font que conforter cette idée tout en prétendant s'y opposer. Lorsque tu écris pour la première fois, en 1969, qu' "Il n'y a pas d'erreur dans l'Histoire", mais que "c'est toute l'Histoire qui est une erreur", proposition reprise dans ton livre *Tractacus Post Historicus* paru en 1976, tu fais un pas en-dehors du dogme des avant-gardes de l'époque, qui perpétuaient un messianisme banal s'appuyant sur une historisation stricte des "gestes" artistiques.

Dans ton travail, depuis au moins le début des années 1970, tu cherches à substituer à ce récit monolithique l'idée d'une coexistence des vérités, à brouiller les pistes qui mènent à cette voie unique, par laquelle l'occident a assis son pouvoir colonial sur le monde entier. L'humanité a ainsi longtemps vécu en regardant une seule chaîne de télévision : on était soit dans l'Histoire, soit totalement en dehors, dans cette zone anhistorique habituellement circonscrite aux peuples "sauvages", autrement dit sans importance particulière. Ton idée de la "post-histoire" équivaut à l'invention du zapping ; il s'agit de passer entre différentes sources émettrices qui, chacune, porteraient une version de l'Histoire.

Gianfranco Martina, Casual Passer-by I met at 3:28 PM, San Sicario, 1976

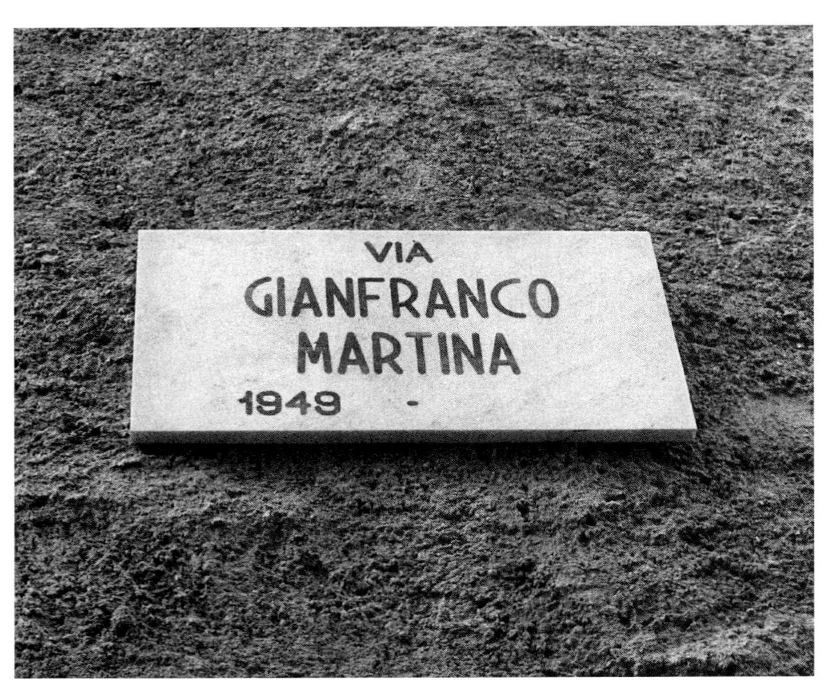

En 1912, une conférence internationale a entériné la notion de "temps universel" divisé en fuseaux horaires ; un siècle plus tard, l'idée d'une économie globale, fonctionnant vingt-quatre heures sur vingt-quatre, valide une conception de l'universel qui n'ose plus dire son nom, mettant au contraire en avant les "différences" et le multiculturalisme (la culture vernaculaire devenant le fait national lui-même, fictionnalisé) afin de mieux masquer l'uniformisation réelle qu'elle met en place. Ce qui s'organise autour de ces deux dates, c'est la fiction d'une histoire de l'humanité linéaire, une histoire moderniste, dont l'hypocrisie postmoderne consiste aujourd'hui à aménager les décors. Car l'idéologie de la "fin de l'histoire", inséparable du postmodernisme, représente avant tout la volonté de faire un arrêt sur image, afin de neutraliser toute vélléité politique de transformation du monde et de fixer son cours sur un "nouvel ordre" économique, qui serait définitif. "Ce que nous appellons l'Histoire, dis-tu, n'est rien de plus qu'une subjectivité qui est imposée au monde entier comme une opinion objective."[1]

Mais quand tu parles d'un "après" (post) de l'Histoire, cela n'a rien à voir avec sa fin. A l'opposé, tes œuvres et tes écrits incitent à un déchaînement créatif, au pullulement des histoires, de leurs variantes et de leur hybridation. Au sujet de l'Histoire, Louis Althusser parlait, dans les années 1960, d'un "procés sans sujet": une idée forte, à contre-courant des idéologies de l'époque, qui n'imaginaient pas d'autre sujet de l'Histoire que le peuple ou le prolétariat en lutte. Or il n'y a pas non plus de sujet de la post-histoire. Et surtout pas la Terre elle-même, Gaïa, idole maternelle transformée en ersatz monothéiste par les écologistes radicaux ou les groupes new age. Qu'il n'y ait pas de sujet de la post-histoire, cela libère la multitude des sujets, c'est-à-dire nous : comme l'écrivait Serge Daney, "avons-nous à ce point échoué dans notre remplacement de Dieu le père par l'homme le Frère pour que revienne le terrible matriarcat de notre mère la Terre ?"[2] Le "Casual passer-by" qui est le sujet central de ton travail, cet individu qui ne devient sujet que par sa rencontre avec le dispositif d'inscription que tu mets en place, est le véritable habitant de la post-histoire. En quelque sorte, il se présente comme le locataire de la gloire, contemporain en cela de l'injonction warholienne à "devenir célèbre pendant quinze minutes".

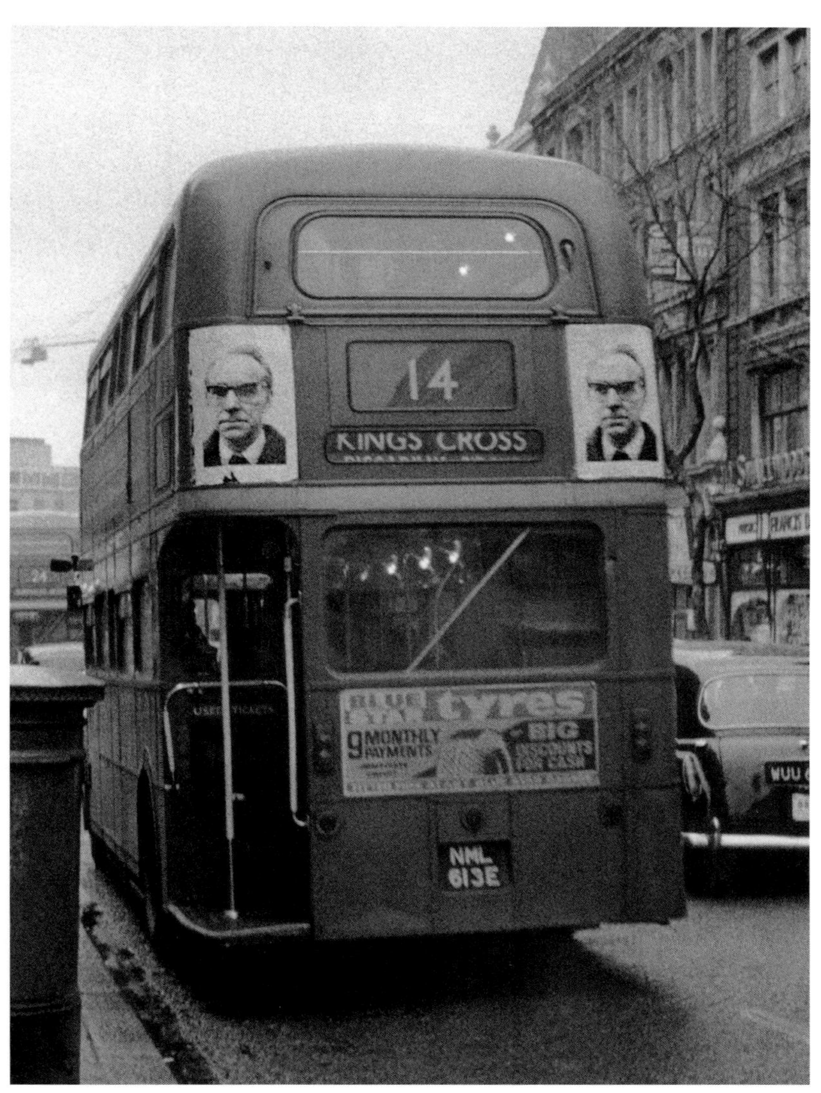

Casual Passer-by I met at 11:28 AM, London, 1972
Collection: Tate Gallery, London

Un animal ou un fruit, un objet usuel, une œuvre d'art. Dans tes "triptyques post-Historiques", tu montres que Cézanne ou Picasso, dont on comprend et évalue l'œuvre dans son rapport avec un déroulement narratif, c'est-à-dire comme autant de signaux émis par l'histoire, peuvent également être perçus comme des phénomènes naturels ou des outils. Un tableau de Kezimir Malevitch, des haches planteés obliquement, associées à des pommes disposées sur des socles : cette installation, réalisée à Saint Pétersbourg en 2005, reprend la gamme de couleur du peintre, dont la composition ("Vanka", 1928-1929) représente une figure humaine vue de dos, au premier plan, dans un style post-suprématiste, mais se dirigeant vers une ferme bien plus réaliste située à l'arrière-plan du tableau. Tu as disposé les socles de telle manière qu'ils évoquent le sillage de cet homme qui marche, et accroché l'oeuvre dans un coin de la pièce, rappellant ainsi la première exposition suprématiste à Pétrograd en 1915, dans laquelle le "Carré noir sur fond blanc" du même Malevitch se trouvait dans une disposition similaire, tout en haut du mur et dans un coin. Et dans la photographie la plus connue de cette exposition « historique », une chaise se trouve au milieu des œuvres.

Tes installations « post-historiques » renvoient au statut de l'icône, image générique par laquelle s'assemblent les trois éléments que tu convoques ensemble : dans « Between eternity and geniuscide » (1994), c'est d'ailleurs d'une manière explicite, puisque tu apposes des bougies devant les portraits photographiques de Kafka ou Modigliani, juchés sur une mer de haricots rouges. Cette dimension votive, constitutive de l'icône, rassemble en une unité stable, celle de l'installation, les éléments organiques, artistiques et fonctionnels qui composent les « Triptyques ». La post-histoire, telle que tu la conçois, se donne à voir spontanément sous la forme d'une intemporalité absolue, dont l'icône constitue le régime visuel privilégié. L'intemporel n'est toutefois, dans ton œuvre, que le préalable de la post-histoire, et non pas son dernier mot. Le « zeitlos », l'Éternel, l'atemporel, la longue durée historique, ne sont que des motifs parmi d'autres d'une vision du temps dénuée de toute figure imposée. En d'autres termes, l'icône n'est qu'un moment de l'image ; plus exactement, le moment de son passage du temps historique à l'ambigüité de l'intemporel.

A quelle époque appartient donc ce « casual passer-by » que tu as rencontré à Londres, à onze heures vingt-huit du matin, en octobre 1972 ? Pas au quotidien, en tous cas : le jour (la date) est le seul élément manquant. Il appartient à l'histoire de l'art, dans la mesure où cette rencontre a donné lieu à une œuvre qui l'éternise ; à ton histoire personnelle, puisque ce sont tes déambulations, et le fait que tu te trouvais ce jour-là à Londres, qui le font exister pour nous. Mais il appartient aussi à ce temps chaotique et sans chronologie dans lequel Malevitch rencontre une pomme et une hache, au gré des accords chromatiques. André Malraux écrivait dans « L'Intemporel » que « les Événements [d'une] vie convergent plus qu'ils ne se succèdent. » L'art est un moyeu autour duquel peut s'ordonner cette convergence, et se déployer une cohérence que l'idéologie chronologique ne peut pas percevoir. Notre mémoire, elle, est a-chronologique : elle erre dans le proche, puis dans le lointain, sans se soucier de datations. La chronologie n'est rien de plus qu'une version idéaliste du temps, que le matérialisme, celui des signes et des couleurs, vient détruire dans tes compositions « post-historiques ».

« Il n'y a pas de ruptures dans la création, mais des ruptures de perception », dis-tu. Paul Valéry pensait, d'une manière analogue, que l'on pourrait écrire une histoire de la littérature sans employer de noms propres d'auteurs, mais uniquement par le récit des modifications qui se sont opérées dans les modes de lecture. Mais le temps ne va pas forcément du passé vers l'avenir : Jorge Luis Borges, lorsqu'il écrit sur Franz Kafka, considère son œuvre comme un ébranlement historique qui transforme en profondeur le passé ; toute une branche de la littérature se révèle ainsi comme celle des « précurseurs de Kafka ». Dans le même sens, Georges Perec et l'OULIPO inventent dans les années 1960 la notion de « plagiaire par anticipation », qui caractérise le temps réversible et multidirectionnel de la culture. Avec l'avancée de la globalisation (que certains ne perçoivent, selon la tradition hégelienne, que comme la « fin de l'histoire »), nous nous dirigeons vers une civilisation éclatée en multiples fragments. Selon cette conception de l'histoire, opposée à l'idée du progrès universel, il ne peut pas exister de sens unique de l'histoire, mais des crises locales, des micro-récits, bref un ensemble de distorsions temporelles qui doivent apprendre à se lire ensemble. Au devenir-archipel du monde, provoqué par la globalisation, correspond une nouvelle conception du temps qui englobe la totalité des récits historiques, l'ensemble des chronologies, la somme des vitesses et des lenteurs : en un mot, une hétérochronie. Une temporalité dans laquelle le temps irait du futur vers le passé, et du présent global jusqu'à tous les temps singuliers.

En 1967, Robert Smithson élabore la notion de « ruine à l'envers » (ruins in reverse), à propos de sa pièce « The Monuments of Passaic ». Explorant les paysages en friches de l'état du New Jersey, Smith-

Between Eternity and Geniuscide II,
1994
4 B/W photographs, candles, beans
Dimensions: 9 x 1.2 x 1 m
Collection: Israel Museum, Jerusalem

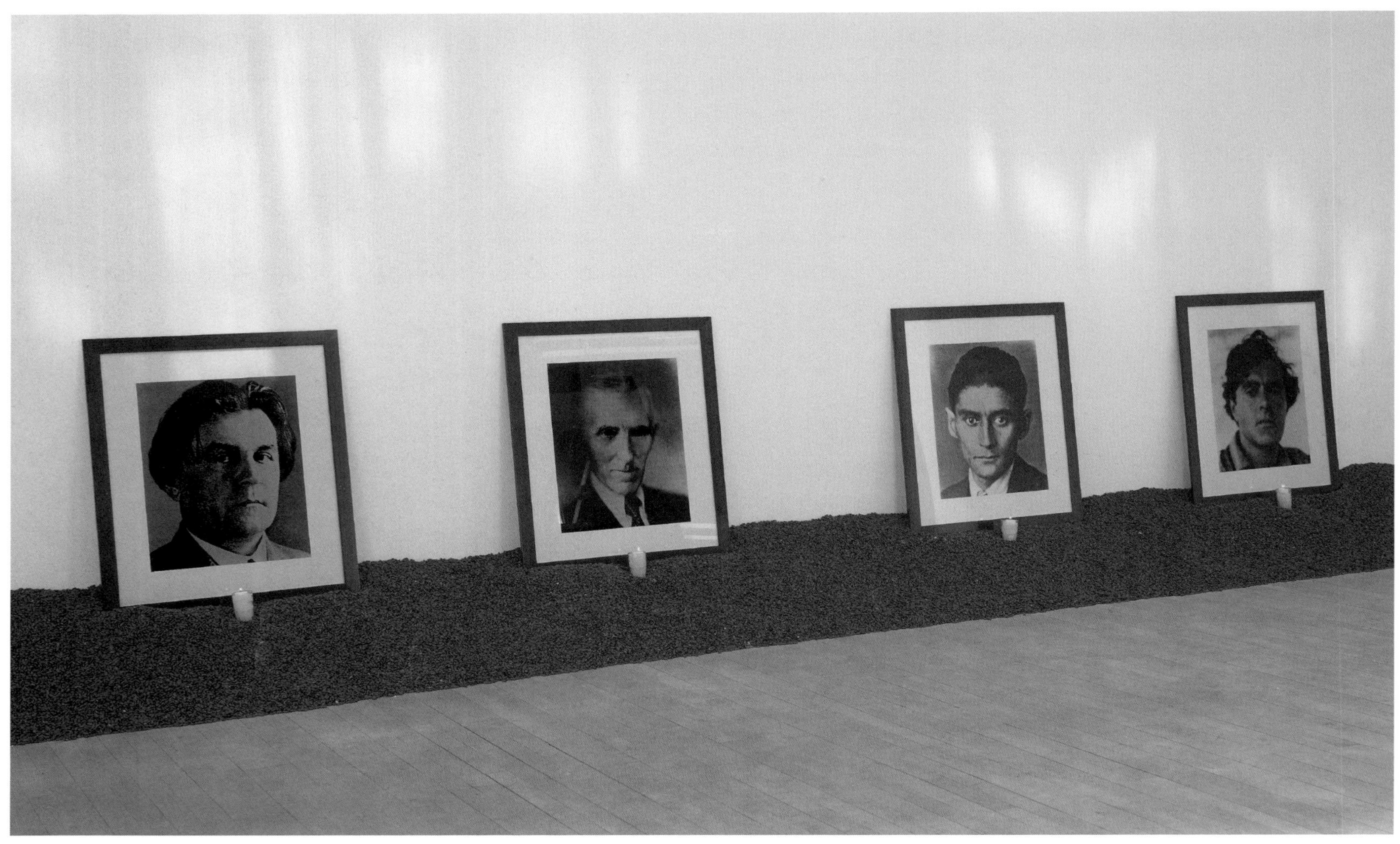

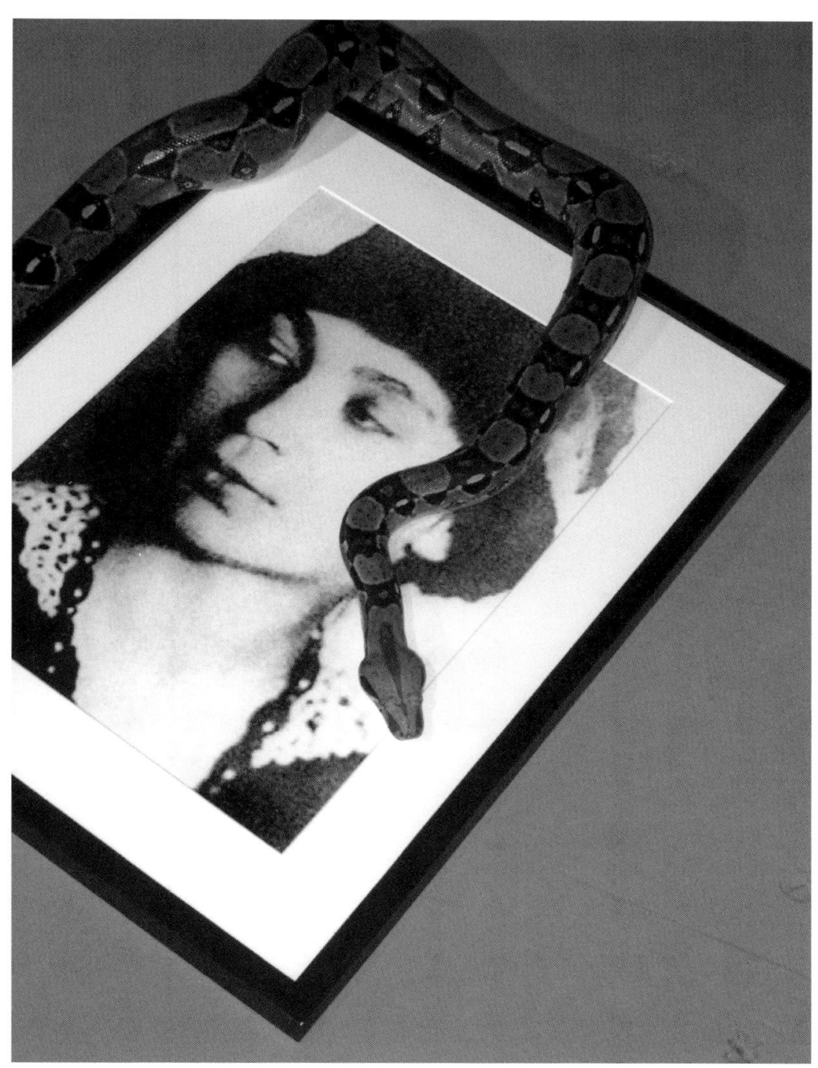

Those who sensed earthquakes (Gontcharova), 2007
B/W photograph, snake
Courtesy Slought Foundation, Philadelphia

son qualifie de « ruines à l'envers » toutes les constructions récentes et à venir. Jadis, la ruine romantique (celle que Hubert Robert figurait dans ses toiles) représentait la fuite du temps, en incitant à une méditation nostalgique sur le passé ; les constructions vaguement modernistes désignées par Smithson, elles, sont programmées pour devenir des ruines avant même d'exister, les ruines d'une idéologie moderniste dans laquelle les scénarios du futur, linéaires, étaient bien plus réels que le présent ou le passé. Certes, l'entropie, cette notion générique autour de laquelle Smithson articule son travail, est une décélération. Mais paradoxalement, cette perte de vitesse aboutit à l'accélération du devenir-obsolète de ces « ruines à l'envers ». Comme l'écrit Claudio Magris, « Il n'y a pas un train unique du temps, roulant à vitesse constante dans une direction unique ; parfois on croise un autre train qui vient d'en face, du passé, et pendant un moment nous avons ce passé près de nous, à côté de nous, dans notre présent. Tes installations « post-historiques » fonctionnent comme ces « ruines à l'envers » smithsoniennes : elles vont du futur vers le passé, partant de l'art moderne pour aller jusqu'à la grotte de Lascaux.

Le portrait des « casual passers-by », que tu accroches comme des affiches officielles au fronton des bâtiments, désignent la possibilité d'une bifurcation dans l'Histoire : lorsque l'on se retrouve en face d'eux, on a toujours l'impression d'entrer dans une réalité parallèle, ou d'avoir inexplicablement raté un moment de l'Histoire officielle pour avoir trop dormi, car ce récit institutionnel est fait d'oublis, d'omissions plus ou moins volontaires, de hiérarchies subtiles, de codes implicites. Les « casual passers-by » nous remettent en mémoire que l'Histoire est faite par tous, et que l'essence de l'humanité, comme Karl Marx l'écrivait, n'est autre que le résultat de ce que nous faisons ensemble. Dispositif, territoire, ton travail est une zone de bifurcations : un espace à l'intérieur duquel l'histoire rebrousse chemin, déraille, fait un pas de côté.

D'une certaine manière, l'histoire cesse d'être « universelle » lorsqu'elle se spatialise, lorsqu'elle se fait territoire : la réalité contemporaine est un livre ouvert, dans lequel les artistes, en en tournant les pages, peuvent explorer à la fois les strates du passé et les traces de l'à-venir. Pour le modernisme, le passé représentait la tradition, que le nouveau venait supplanter. Pour le postmoderne, il faisait figure de catalogue ou de répertoire. Aujourd'hui, il forme tout simplement un nouveau territoire, dont les artistes sont les archéologues et les géographes privilégiés, car ils le parcourent en allant de forme en forme, loin des rigueurs que la linéarité discursive impose aux penseurs ou aux idéologues. J'admire, dans ton oeuvre, cette obstination qui s'articule autour d'une vision forte, prémonitoire. Si tu n'étais pas artiste, tu serais une sorte de prédicateur, ou un moine vagant, celui qui enfonce toujours plus loin un clou douloureux mais salutaire.

1. In catalogue *Braco Dimitrijević*, Edizioni Charta, tout comme les citations qui suivent. « What we call History is nothing more than one subjectivity which is imposed on the whole world as objective opinion. »
2. Serge Daney, *L'exercice a été profitable, monsieur*, Éditions POL, page 341.

Probing History and Its Displays: Conceptual Interventions

A monumental image of Mao Zedong lives from the fact that the depicted person is a national and international icon, politically influential and recognized by everyone. Artists such as Gerhard Richter and Andy Warhol, who were deeply engaged with mass media imagery, both addressed the iconicity of the Mao portrait in different ways. Richter represented him in a small, out-of-focus print in 1968, both heightening and dissolving its aura; Andy Warhol depicted Mao as a monumental pop icon in 1973, and one year later he irreverently turned the icon into wallpaper. Dimitrijević's monumental portraits of ordinary citizens, which he began in 1970, mimicked existing pictorial conventions such as the propaganda portrait and intervened in an already coded cultural and political landscape of representation.

With several bodies of work from the early 1970s, such as his casual passers-by, his public monuments, commemorative plaques, and "history photographs," Braco Dimitrijević recognized the cultural and political significance of institutionalized markers of history, and how they quietly reinforce accepted historical narratives. Monumental portraits of party leaders were popular in the Eastern Block throughout the 1960s and 1970s, although they clearly grew out of the propaganda traditions of the communist and fascist regimes earlier in the century. The oversized portrait banner, often used during parades and party events, were constant reminders of state power. Politically, Dimitrijević's native Yugoslavia walked a fine line during the Cold War because it neither conformed to the narrow doctrines of Russian-style communism nor did it align itself wholeheartedly with the capitalist model.[1] Traveling through Yugoslavia during this period, Tito's portrait and name was ever present. In public squares and government buildings, and most startling of all, even in remote countrysides where his name was spelled out in capital letters over entire hillsides with piles of stones. In contrast to the personality cult of socialist or communist propaganda machineries, Braco Dimitrijević turned the tables when he bestowed the grandiose forms of monumental portraiture upon everyday people. The selection process was left to chance: casual encounters with people in the street (he approached the first person he ran into) determined who would be represented. With the person's permission, the artist displayed the portrait in public spaces, on billboards, buses, or strikingly, on monumental building banners without identification or comment.

Monument to Alberto Vieri, the *Casual Passer-by I met at 4:16 PM*, Turin, 1973
Collection: Gian Enzo Sperone, Rome – New York

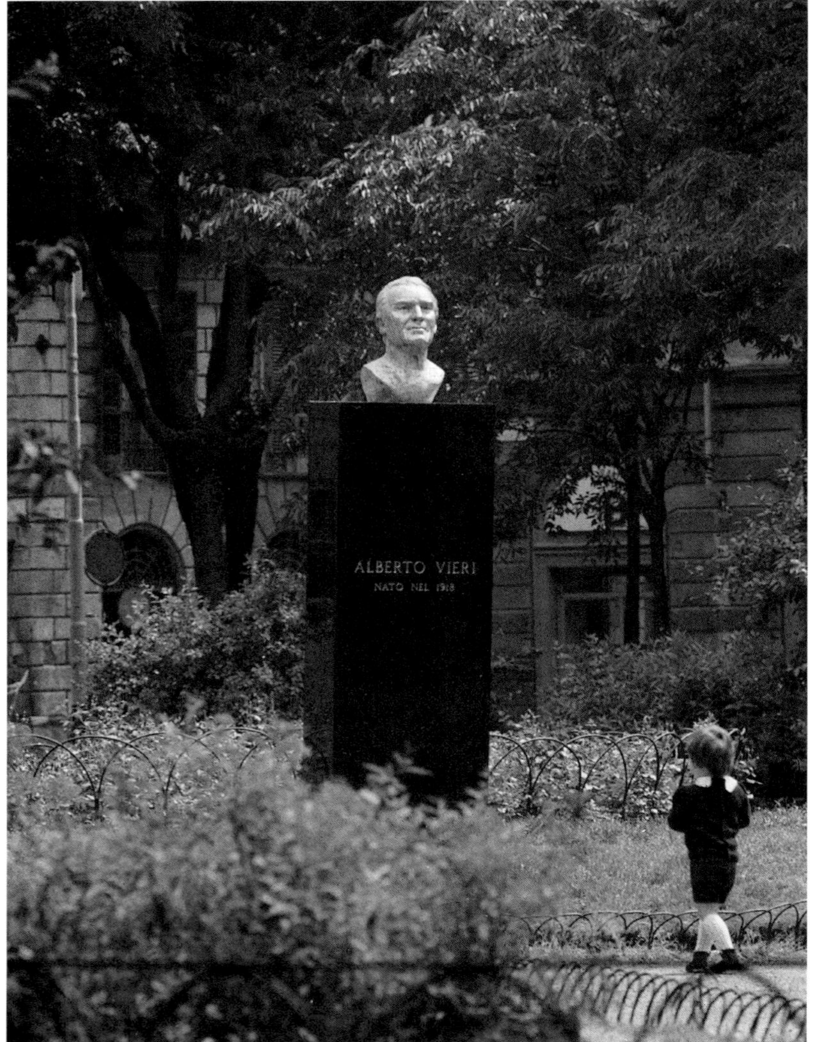

From the beginning, Dimitrijević used conceptual strategies to intervene in public spaces but he went beyond the parameters established in the 1960s. Many early conceptualists, especially in North America and Britain, turned to propositions, text, and photography, which gave rise to the notion of "dematerialization." The term, coined by Lucy Lippard and John Chandler in 1968 in reaction to the artistic developments in North America, was a provisional one (and somewhat misleading) but it tried to capture the new artistic emphasis on process and experience rather than a final and finite material object.[2] Lippard's subsequent anthology of exhibitions, events, and publications in the 1960s and early 1970s was still taking stock rather than offering set interpretations, although she was already adding a cautionary note about the term in her preface.[3] As Lippard was well

Casual Passer-by I met at 2:42 PM, London, 1971
"Sarah Knipe stayed here in 1971"
In his student days at St. Martin's School of Art in London, Braco Dimitrijević started installing memorial plaques inscribed with the names of casual passers-by

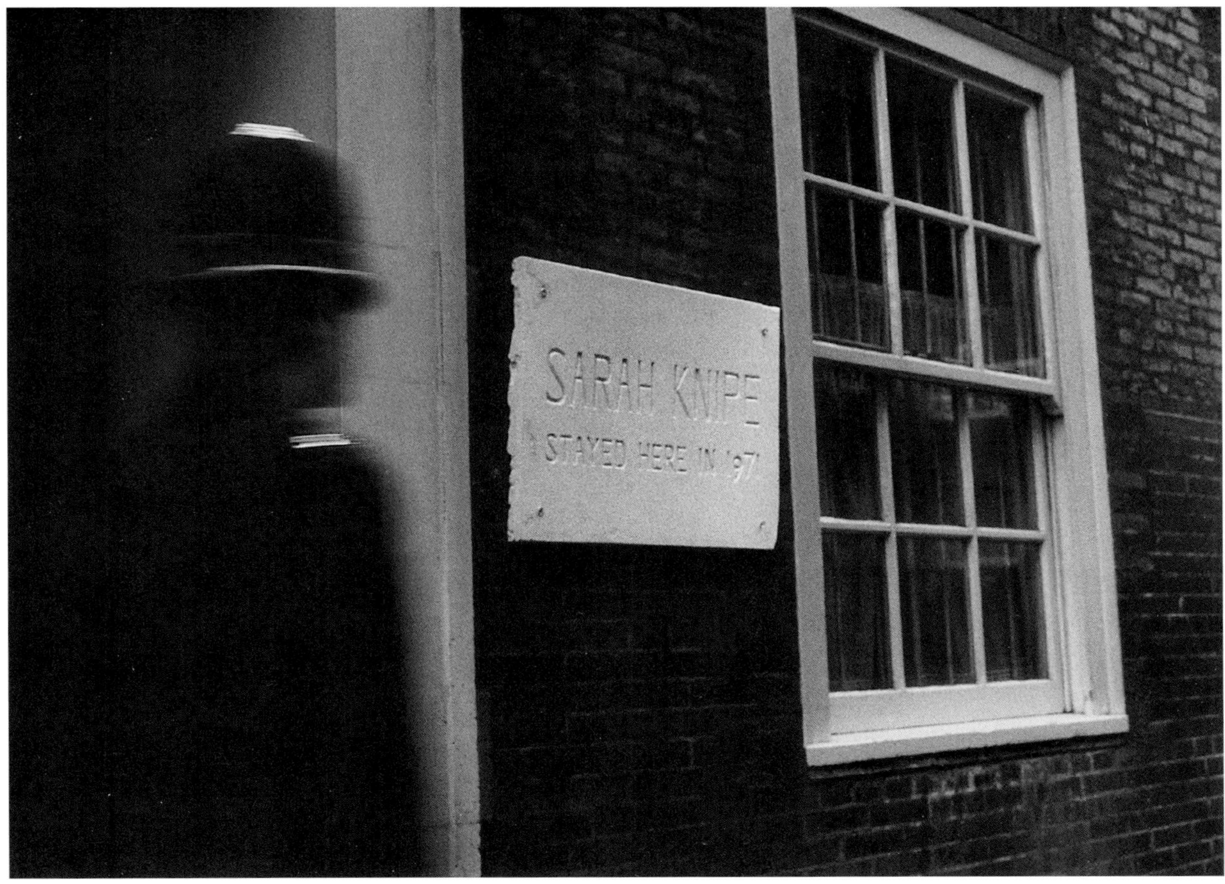

aware, an entire strain of conceptual artists developed their ideas directly from a dialogue with sculptural concepts, but other writers settled on a narrow interpretation of the evocative term "dematerialization" and made it the shorthand for conceptual art in the early 1970s: "The abolition of the art-object," wrote Ursula Meyer, "typical for conceptual art, eliminates the concern with 'style,' 'quality,' and 'permanence,' the indispensable modalities of traditional and contemporary art." Moreover, she argued that this shift from object to concept signaled a disdain for commodities and commodity culture.[4]

Meanwhile in continental Europe, the conceptual sensibilities of the Yves Klein and Zero variety were already familiar to audiences by the late 1950s. A decade later, several leading exhibitions introduced the newly emerging conceptual trends from North America, notably *Op Losse Schroeven* (Amsterdam, 1969), *When Attitudes Become Form* (Bern, 1969), and the Paris Biennale of 1971. Dimitrijević was represented at the Paris Biennale and again at the 1972 Documenta. The latter brings into focus Braco Dimitrijević's unusual adaptation of conceptual strategies. In Harald Szeemann's sprawling Documenta exhibition, several parallel developments in the arts appeared under one roof. The show's motto was *Probing Reality: Image Worlds Today* and the exhibition included an ambitious survey of everyday imagery (everything from advertisement, political posters, and religious imagery to currencies and garden decorations). The show reacted to a number of developments in the 1960s, notably to new artistic strategies that were not necessarily focused on a finite, material object. Questions of representation were framed through a critical inquiry of commodity culture, a topic near and dear to left critics and theoreticians, particularly in Germany. Throughout the politically volatile period of the 1960s, pop art was a catalyst for these debates. In one of the more fascinating misinterpretations in recent history pop in Germany was first embraced as an art that entailed a social critique of consumer culture, but by the end of the decade it came to be regarded as affirmative.[5] At a time when emerging artistic trends in North America were viewed under the catchphrase "dematerialization," insistent critiques of commodity culture, influenced by the writings of the Frankfurt School, dominated art criticism in Germany.

Throughout the Documenta exhibition but especially in the "Idea Art" section one could find a rigorous artistic engagement with photography and questions of representation. And yet, these critiques of representation, of spectacular society, or the perception of images and spaces, spelled out by conceptual artists at that exhibition went largely unrecognized by critics and theoreticians.[6] The curators of the "Idea Art" section ignored the role of photography in favor of non-visual concepts, and the aesthetic theory developed in the main catalogue text by the philosopher Hans-Heinz Holz, lamented what he saw as "the un-reflected adoption of everyday culture into the image, which marks US-American pop art." Unlike German critics in the mid-1960s, he viewed the representational forms of pop art as "the result of a loss of differentiated seeing," minimalism and earth works (and a few conceptual works he grouped with these) were to him a mere retreat to *l'art pour l'art* positions. Following Herbert Marcuse's much earlier text on the affirmative character of art, the big mantra amongst left theorists and art critics in Germany throughout the 1960s was a renewed social relevance of art and demands to reconnect art and life. Holz was no exception, in his view contemporary art was in crisis (caused by the loss of its ritual function therefore the rise of commodification). The solution to this crisis, he thought, would be in the political rather than the artistic arena.[7]

Dimitrijević's works, which were a late addition to show and thus not mentioned in the catalogue, connected a critical political perspective with conceptual methods.[8] He had a clear understanding of the institutional appropriation and coding of social life and public places. At the same time, he drew from, and indeed expanded, the existing repertoire of conceptual strategies.

Interesting in itself is the placement of his work at Documenta 5: between Rebecca Horn, Franz Erhard Walther, and Yoko Ono in the section "Personal Mythologies" rather than the conceptualists, where his work would have read rather differently. The fact that he was not only using "dematerialized" materials such as photography and text but also engaged very material public monuments, which set him somewhat apart.

Dimitrijević's commemorative plaques and public monuments were a logical extension of the *Casual Passer-By* works. Just as before, he engaged institutionalized markers in the public realm. It is helpful to remember that Barnett Newman and Claes Oldenburg had already begun to deconstruct the formal language of the war memorial in direct connection to the Vietnam War in the 1960s. Both works remained

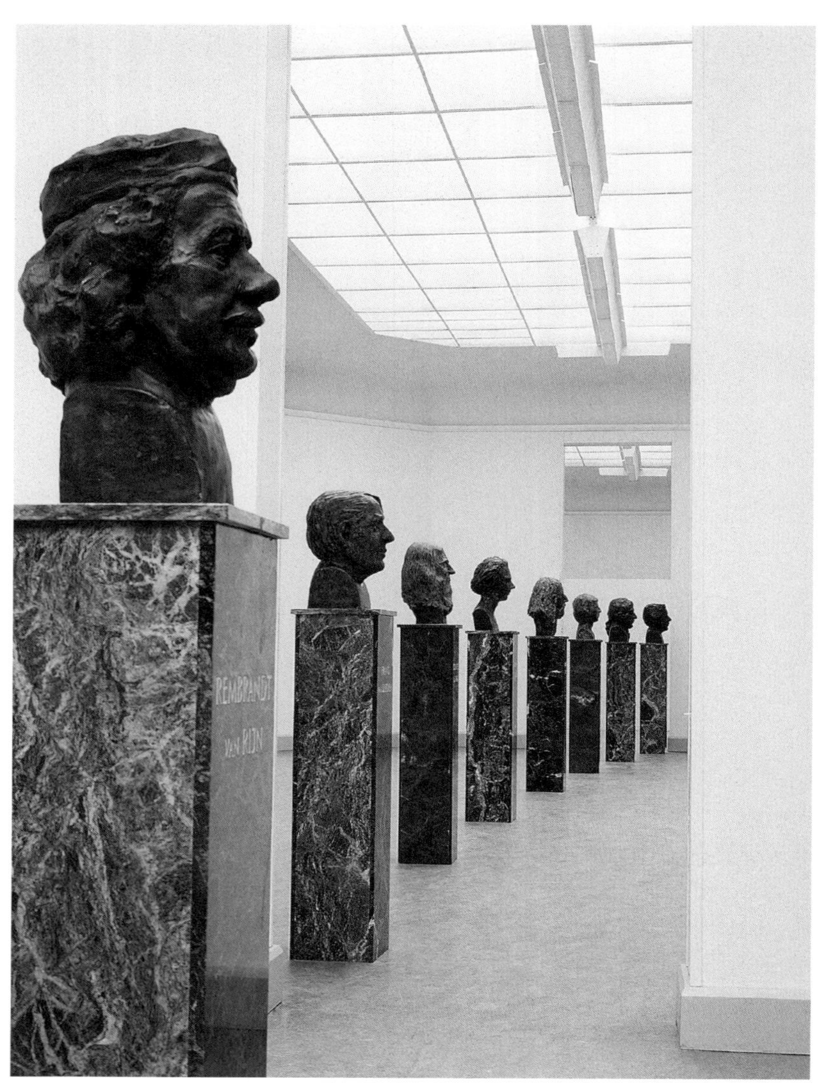

Louvre Colonnade, 1976–1979. One-man show at the Van Abbemuseum, Eindhoven
Rembrandt – Van Dooren. Collection: Van Abbemuseum, Eindhoven
Dürer – Someren. Collection: Neuesmuseum, Nuremberg
Turner – Rampton. Collection: Tate Gallery, London

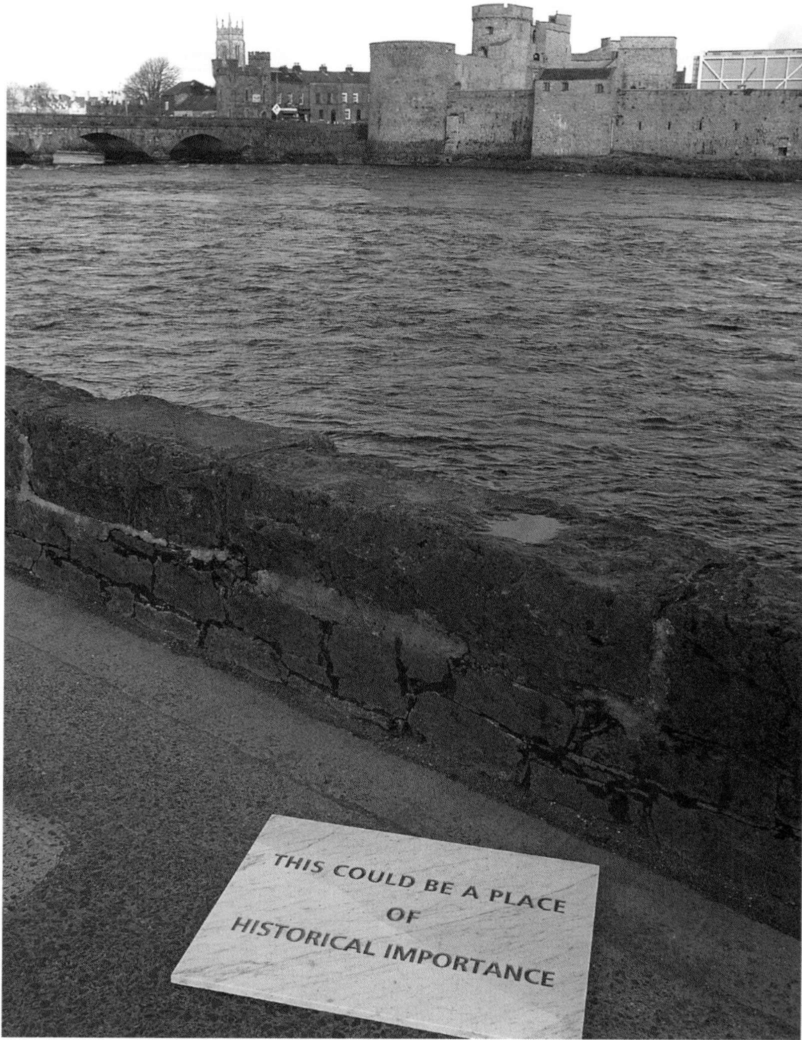

Limerick, Ireland, 1995

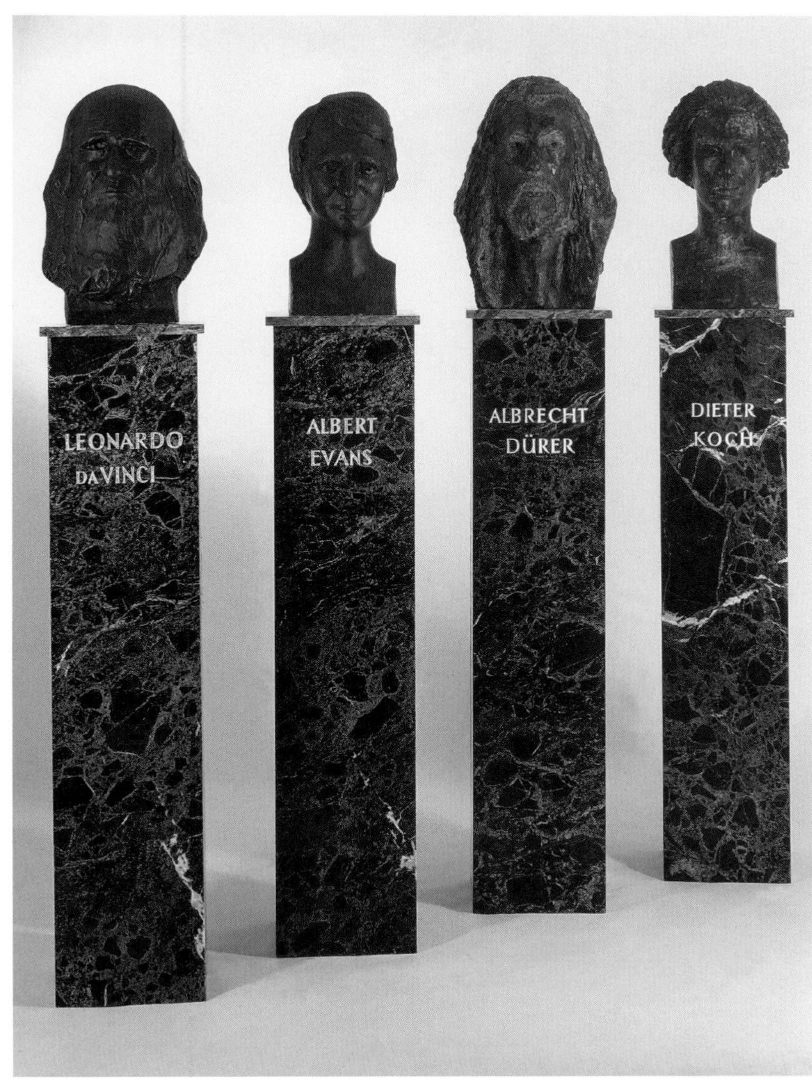

About Two Artists: Leonardo da Vinci – Albert Evans, 1979
Collection: Tate Gallery, London
About Two Artists: Albrecht Dürer – Dieter Koch, 1979
Collection: Dacic Tubingen

within contemporary aesthetic sensibilities and both functioned emphatically as political protests and anti-monuments: Newman's *Broken Odalisk* (1963–1969) used the formal vocabulary of minimalism, while Oldenburg's inflatable *Lipstick (Ascending)* (1969) underscored the phallic appearance of the tank gun as much as the erect obelisk and rendered it limp and impotent. By contrast, Dimitrijević undertook surreptitious public interventions, and his formal vocabulary followed much older traditions. He capitalized on the fact that Europe's public sites are to a sometimes absurd degree covered by monuments and historic markers. The names of philosophers, writers, artists, musicians, scientists, aristocratic rulers, and modern politicians are appended to streets, plazas, buildings, parks and gardens, tunnels and bridges whenever possible. With this form of inscription, the general public is constantly surrounded by and reminded of famous individuals and historic events. Freestanding monuments are common sights in parks and plazas. The portrait-bust, the full-length figure, and the equestrian statue elevated on plinths or massive bases are common forms of the genre. The most celebrated figures in prominent places become integral parts of the urban and social fabric in the form of landmarks as much as convenient meeting spots. Less prominent figures can become decorative structures that are part of the visual landscape yet paradoxically invisible. While every other town in Germany may have a statue named after Goethe or Schiller regardless whether the men had any direct connection to the place, commemorative plaques tend to be site-specific markers noting where a famous person lived or worked. At times they border on the trivial with inscriptions such as "At this establishment, Camus, Voltaire, Matisse, Shakespeare, Wagner, or Caruso, stayed a night or had a meal in (fill in date)." Due to the high concentration of names that populate public spaces there are invariably instances where the names are unfamiliar even to the locals. Marble plaques such as Dimitrijević's "Sarah Knipe stayed here in 1971" (London, 1971) or "John Forster lived here Oct. 1961–Feb. 1968" (London 1972) fit seamlessly into this cultural landscape and only the most discerning individuals will stop and ponder the name or the recentness of the dates. Going one step further, his *Monument to David Harper, the Casual Passer-by I met at 11:28 AM* (London, 1972) consisted of an over live-size bust of the man and was set on a massive stone plinth with a commemorative inscription: "David Harper b. 1924." Facilitated by the Situation Gallery, the sculpture was placed in Berkeley Square in London without further comment or context. Clearly, this was a "material object" in a traditional (pre-modern) art historical sense and while he worked on the sculpture he reportedly got into an argument with his teacher Anthony Caro at the St. Martins School, where he studied at the time.[9] The sculpture's realist style was in itself a politically charged topic. In the post-war period, the ideological divide between East and West concerned not only economic and political models but artistic styles as well. Abstraction, especially the gestural variety, was theorized in terms of artistic and intellectual freedom and became the lingua franca of the West. It connected contemporary artistic trends with the pre-war avant-garde and marked a stark departure from fascist preferences for idealized realist forms. The East, however, adhered to socialist realism as the preferred, government sanctioned style.[10] With his public monuments and commemorative plaques, Dimitrijević pioneered an entirely new form of appropriation. He de facto occupied existing artistic and cultural traditions and their formal manifestations and, with a work such as the David Harper bust, presented a "fake" monument.

Monuments are institutionalized markers of past achievements and glories, suggesting with the durability of their materials a view of history that is as definite and immutable as metal or stone. This appearance of durability and inevitability is of course an illusion. Political fortunes can change rapidly and the monuments of the old regimes can be quickly dismantled and replaced with new ones. If public monuments celebrating historical figures or events are inaugurated with much fanfare and ceremony, photography (or rather, documentary photography) is the quiet accomplice in the writing of history. Not surprisingly, many debates on photography since the 1960s have centered on the documentary image. Reinhard Matz aptly described it as the assumption that the documentary photographer can let the objects speak for themselves: "Once photographed, the object alone seems to be the sole cause and determining reason of a photograph as if natural and legitimate it draws all our attention onto itself."[11] Conceptual artists in the 1960s were at the forefront of articulating a critique of the seemingly factual image. A recurring feature was the undermining of beliefs in the mimetic depiction of "reality" and the rejection of photography as an object for aesthetic contemplation. Technical craftsmanship in a modernist sense was mostly opposed and instead images banal in subject matter and execution were created that pointed to the conditions of photographic representation and the construction of meaning. Through the deliberately staged slippage of signifier and signified—often achieved through a gap between image and title or through serialized images, the supposedly transparent medium and depicted "reality" emerged as oblique and culturally predetermined.

Roland Barthes (like Walter Benjamin and Bertolt Brecht before him) understood well that photographs in and of themselves did not carry a single meaning but relied on their context. In his well-known 1964 essay on the "Rhetoric of the Image" he distinguished between three messages: "a linguistic message, a coded iconic message, and a non-coded iconic message."[12] The first referred to the title or caption, the latter two described two different aspects of the visual image—one factual, the other cultural. While intricate cultural messages can be communicated through subtle clues inscribed in the literal, perceptual message, the most overt determinant of meaning comes from the caption; the linguistic message, which anchors the image and presents the viewer with a ready interpretation. With the technical revolution of digital technologies since the 1990s, and an increasingly sophisticated body of literature on photography and New Media, Barthes's theories are now often regarded as somewhat antiquated since they were formulated in the analogue era. But apart from the fact that our viewing habits have not advanced at the same speed as technology, it is important to remember that the conceptualists in the 1960s and early 1970s were precisely concerned with the questions outlined by Barthes. The relationship between image and title, caption, or accompanying text was thus a crucial point where pioneering photoconceptualists could intervene.[13]

In 1971, Braco Dimitrijević began a photographic series that grew out of his work with public monuments. It continued his interest in the commemoration of historic events and applied the same technique of a staged gap between image and text used by other conceptual artists but with a radical twist. He exploded the temporal frame of traditional documentary photography, where the image is called upon as a witness to testify to that "which has been," as Barthes famously argued in *Camera Lucida*. Photography's role in the writing of history is contingent on its evidentiary powers, which is anchored by a title, caption, or text. Dimitrijević does the opposite, and indeed the unthinkable by combining straight, non-descript photographs of quaint-looking wooded landscapes, the exterior of a small house, or a stone portal framed

This Could Be a Place of Historical Interest, installation view, Museum Fridericianum, Documenta VI, Kassel, 1977
Collection: Tate Modern, London

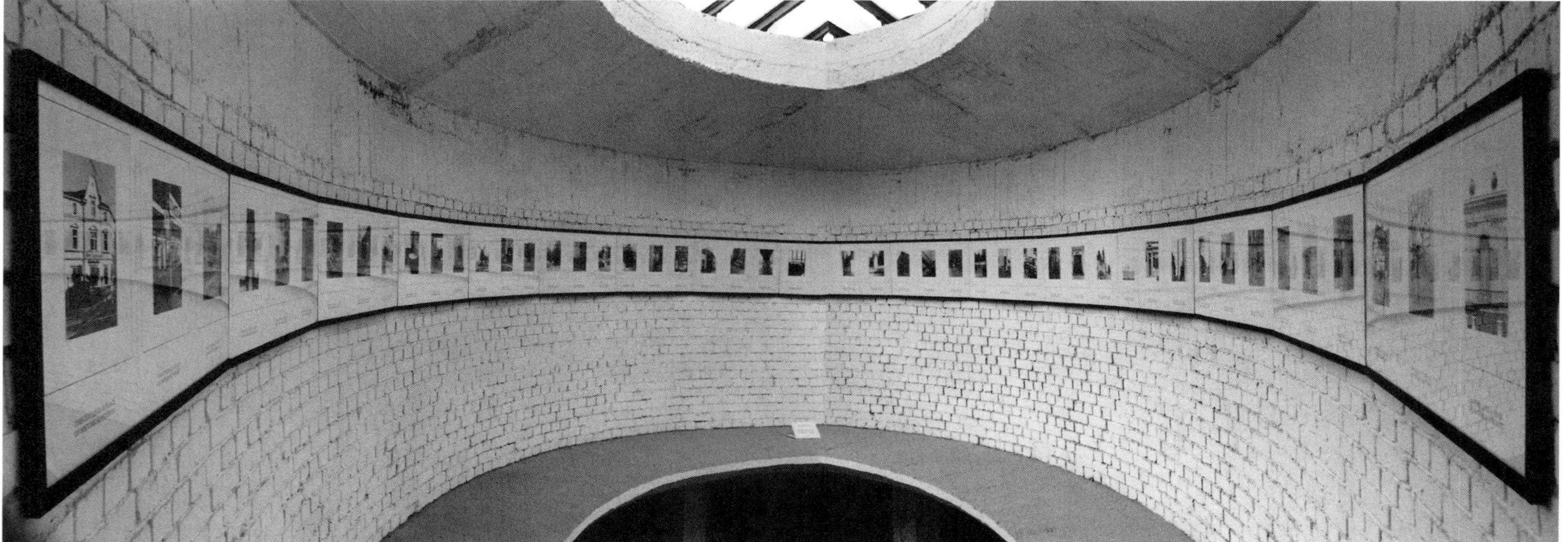

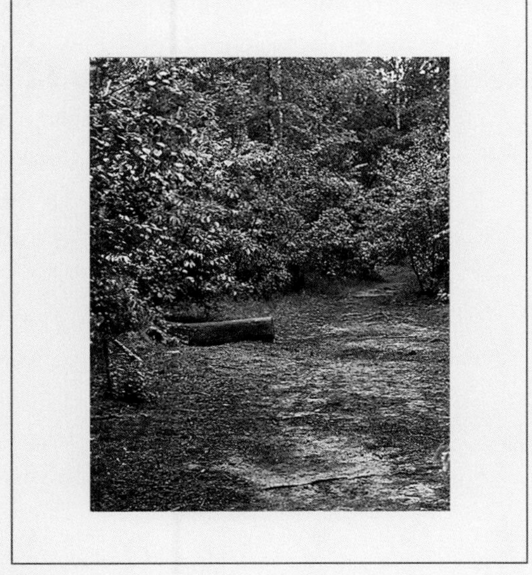

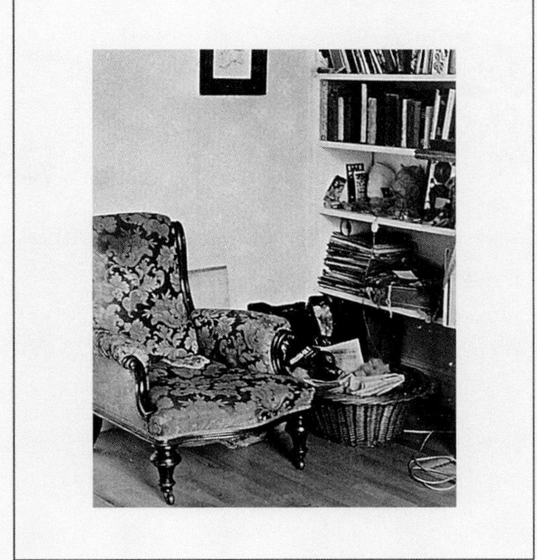

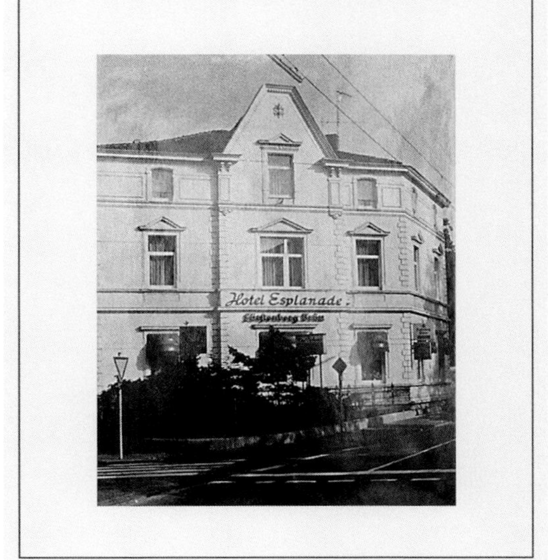

This Could Be a Place of Historical Interest, (detail), 1977
Collection: Tate Modern, London

by lush trees. None of the sites are identified or dated and all of them are void of people. The caption, "This could be a place of historic interest," does not identify a place, nor does it offer facts or narratives of any kind. Instead, this hypothetical directive mobilizes the viewer's powers of association and turns the everyday scene into something potentially significant or ominous. Any number of potential events could be projected onto the image, this could be the site of war crimes or a heroic battle, the place where a historic treaty is signed, a famous speech is held, or a seminal work of art or scientific discovery is made. Dimitrijević's strategy demonstrates in reverse how an ordinary photograph functions within a historical narrative when a definitive, factual context is provided and how that ephemeral photograph becomes a monument in its own right. But more importantly, he reminds us of the arbitrariness of historic events that make one site important and the next banal. In the artist's hometown of Sarajevo, one of the most famous, and accidental historical sites of the twentieth century can be found: the street where Archduke Franz Ferdinand, crown prince of the Austro-Hungarian Empire, and his wife were assassinated in June 1914, an event that precipitated World War I. Looking at Dimitrijević's prophetic photographic series from today's vantage point with the former Yugoslavia's recent history of ethnic war in mind, the work has gained an even greater and unintended and chilling resonance.

For his 10 meter-high obelisk in the gardens of Schloss Charlottenburg, Berlin in 1976–1979, Dimitrijević combined the hypothetical clause of his photographic series with his experiments in public space. The work resulted from the encounter with Peter Malwitz, another casual passer-by. Asked about a date for the inscription on the obelisk the man selected his birthday (March 11). In form and content the work followed well-worn traditions of historic monuments but the secondary inscription along the base, "This Could be a Day of Historical Importance," upends both form and cultural convention.

Dimitrijević's Berlin obelisk is inscribed with the birthday of a casual passer-by, in short a date of personal significance that is given the trappings of universal importance and public significance. Yet without a year, the date can refer to the past or to the future, and the associative power we bring to this date is only part of the equation. Equally important is the appropriation of a culturally and historically coded public space using pre-existing forms and formulas of public monuments and commemoration. As a result, Dimitrijević sets into motion a more complex process of reflection. He prompts us to consider not only the element of chance that determines historical events and subsequently dictates the way historical narratives are henceforth written but the formal language of monuments and commemorative plaques and their role in public space.

Dimitrijević's insistent focus on public monuments and the importance of visual markers (both sculpture and photography) in the writing and depiction of history (and art history) at this early stage remains striking. While the theoretical and artistic focus of many contemporaries in the late 1960s and 1970s was directed at commodity culture and the spectacular society, he conversely engaged the aesthetic objects of historic (and political) commemoration in their most potent public forms. The adequate means with which to address these was with the already existing materials and forms. His seemingly reactionary turn towards conventional sculptural materials such as marble and bronze were at odds with the narrow definition of "dematerialization" that came into circulation in the late 1960s and early 1970s.

As a conceptual artist, he was far ahead of his times and pioneered an area of investigation that would become increasingly significant in the 1980s and 1990s.[14]

1. On this topic see Nena Dimitrijević 's thoughtful analysis, "The Post Historical Dimension," in *Braco Dimitrijević*, Edizioni Charta, Milan, 2006, p. 23ff.
2. Lucy Lippard and John Chandler, "The Dematerialization of Art," *Art International XII*, no. 2, February 20, 1968, pp. 31–36.
3. "Since I first wrote on the subject in 1967, it has often been pointed out to me that dematerialization is an inaccurate term, that a piece of paper or a photograph is as much an object, or as 'material,' as a ton of lead. Granted. But for lack of a better term I have continued to refer to a process of dematerialization, or the deemphasis on material aspects (uniqueness, permanence, decorative attractiveness)." See Lucy Lippard, "Preface," in *Six Years: The Dematerialization of the Art Object, from 1966 to 1972*, first published in 1973, University of California Press, Berkeley, 1997, p. 5.
4. Ursula Meyer, *Conceptual Art*, E.P. Dutton and Co., New York, 1972, p. xv. A similar argument was made by Gregory Battcock in *Idea Art: A Critical Anthology*, Dutton, New York, 1973. This view was largely shared by Gregory Battcock who wrote the following year, "What they all seemed to have in common was a rejection of the 'bourgeois' aspects of traditional art. Works of Idea Art frequently did not exist as objects. Rather, they remained ideas; frequently what did exist was only some kind of documentation referring to the concept." See Gregory Battcock, "Introduction," in *Idea Art: A Critical Anthology*, Dutton, New York, 1973, p. 1.
5. A detailed description of these debates can be found in my dissertation, Catharina Manchanda, "Reconsidering the Object of Photography: German Artists, Curators and Critics in Light of 'documenta 5,'" Ph.D. thesis, City University of New York, Ph.D. Program of Art History, 2005.
6. The conceptual art section at Documenta V ("Idea Art") was co-curated by the art dealer Konrad Fischer and the art historian Klaus Honnef. The catalogue text was written by Honnef and Giesela Kaminsiki and their interpretations were guided by Lippard's texts as much as the more tightly framed definitions outlined by Ursula Meyer. Accordingly, dematerialization was interpreted as a move away from the object and a turn towards the concept. This led the authors to focus especially on text-based work while to equally potent conceptual photographic strategies went unrecognized. Instead, photographs (along with maps or drawings) were merely viewed as supporting documentation. A detailed analysis of this topic can be found in the last chapter of my dissertation. See citation in footnote 5.
7. See Hans-Heinz Holz, "Kritische Theorie des ästhetischen Zeichens," in *documenta 5: Befragung der Realität—Bildwelten heute*, exhibition catalogue, documenta GmbH, Kassel, 1972, pp. 1.1–1.86. Holz's knowledge of contemporary art and newly emerging artistic strategies appears cursory. His main points of reference were in the modernist arena, which clearly put him at a disadvantage. He was not alone in his appreciation of the strategies of the avant-garde in the modernist period, writing in the mid-1970s, Peter Bürger and Andreas Huyssen still looked in that direction and Huyssen was especially unappreciative of conceptual art. See Peter Bürger, *Theory of the Avant-Garde* (Theorie der Avant-Garde, 1974), translated by Michael Shaw, foreword by Jochen Schulte-Sasse (University of Minnesota Press, Minneapolis, 1984); and Andreas Huyssen, "The Cultural Politics of Pop: Reception and Critique of US Pop Art in the Federal Republic of Germany," *New German Critique*, 1-2, no. 5–6, 1975, pp. 77–97.
8. The following works by Braco Dimitrijević were shown at Documenta V: conceptual photo-text versions of his *Monument to David Harper*, 1972, *Casual Passer-by I met at 6:24 PM*, Düsseldorf, 1972 (this work was shown as a monumental banner hung from the Friedericianum and as photo-text version in the galleries). Further conceptual photo-text pieces of the *Casual Passer-by I met at 5 PM*, Naples, 1971 (as well as a group photograph), and the *Casual Passer-by I met at 10:05 PM*, London, 1972.
9. See Nena Dimitrijević, "The Post Historical Dimension," *Op. cit.*, p. 31.
10. That stylistic split between East and West was meant to be a topic at Documenta V as well. Entire sections were meant to be dedicated to socialist and communist styles but the respective governments ultimately declined their participation. The Documenta proposals and a few pages in the catalogue still testify to the original ambition.
11. Reinhard Matz, "Gegen einen naiven Begriff der Dokumentarfotografie (1981)," reprinted in Hubertus von Amelunxen, *Theorie der Fotografie IV 1980-1995*, Schirmer/Mosel, Munich, 2000, p. 96.
12. Roland Barthes, "Rhetoric of the Image" (1964), in *Image, Music, Text*.
13. One such example is Robert Barry's *Inert Gas Series* of 1969. It is a series of photographs that were staged in Los Angeles that pushed photography's abilities to the limit. The caption for one of the pieces *Inert Gas Series, Helium* described a sculptural process, "Sometime during the morning of March 5, 1969, 2 cubic feet of Helium will be released into the atmosphere"—a process that remained invisible to the human eye as well as the camera. Whether the artist actually released the gas or merely proposed to do so was of no consequence. What mattered was the description and photographic "documentation" of a process that could be imagined but remained imperceptible. Barry's work pointed to the limitations of photography's evidentiary abilities and questioned its supposed "objectivity." In staging an invisible process, he simultaneously critiqued the medium and outlined a notion of "sculpture" that lay beyond the realm of perception and in choosing a non-reactive, inert gas, he pointed to a material far more durable than any bronze or stone sculpture.
14. For a detailed discussion of this subject see Kai-Uwe Hemken, *Gedächtnisbilder: Vergessen und Erinnern in der Gegenwartskunst*, Reclam, Leipzig, 1996.

Explorer l'Histoire et ses représentations : interventions conceptuelles

L'image monumentale de Mao Tsé-Toung perdure grâce au fait que la personne dépeinte est une icône nationale et internationale, politiquement influente et reconnue de tous. Des artistes comme Gerhard Richter et Andy Warhol qui s'exposaient à l'imagerie des media ont chacun à leur manière traité l'iconicité du portrait de Mao. Richter le représenta en 1968 sur une petite impression floue, soulignant et dissolvant son aura ; Andy Warhol en 1973 le dépeint comme une icône Pop monumentale, un an plus tard il transforme sans scrupule l'icône en papier peint. Les monumentaux portraits de citoyens ordinaires commencés par Dimitrijević en 1970 miment les conventions picturales des portraits de propagande intervenant dans un paysage culturel et politique déjà codé.

Dans diverses séries de travaux datant du début des années 70, comme ses passants anonymes, ses monuments publics, ses plaques commémoratives, et ses « photographies d'histoire », Braco Dimitrijević reconnaît l'importance culturelle et politique des repères historiques institutionnels et la façon dont ils renforcent discrètement les narrations historiques établies. Les portraits monumentaux de dirigeants politiques étaient très populaires dans le bloc soviétique dans les années 60 et 70, même s'ils sont d'évidence issus de la propagande du régime communiste et fasciste des années précédentes. Les énormes portraits figurant souvent en bannières lors de fêtes et de défilés étaient un rappel constant du pouvoir de l'Etat. Politiquement, la Yougoslavie natale de Dimitrijević était dans une position ambiguë pendant la guerre froide parce qu'elle ne se conformait pas aux doctrines communistes étriquées à la soviétique, et ne s'alignait pas non plus sans réserve sur le modèle capitaliste[1]. Voyageant en Yougoslavie pendant cette période, les portraits et le nom de Tito n'avaient jamais été si présents. Sur les places publiques et sur les monuments du gouvernement, et le plus surprenant, même en pleine campagne où son nom s'étalait en lettres majuscules érigées en entassant des pavés sur les collines. Contrastant avec le culte de la personnalité et la machination de la propagande socialiste et communiste, Braco Dimitrijević renverse la situation en présentant des portraits aux formes monumentales de gens de tous les jours. Le processus de sélection était laissé au hasard : des rencontres informelles avec des gens dans la rue (il approchait la première personne qu'il apercevait) déterminaient qui allait être représenté. Avec la permission de la personne, l'artiste exposait le portrait sur les lieux publics, sur des panneaux, des bus ou, plus étonnant, sur des panneaux de bâtiments énormes sans identification ni commentaire.

Casual Passer-by I met at 1:15 PM, 4:23 PM, 6:11 PM, Zagreb, 1971
Collection: Museum Moderner Kunst, Vienna

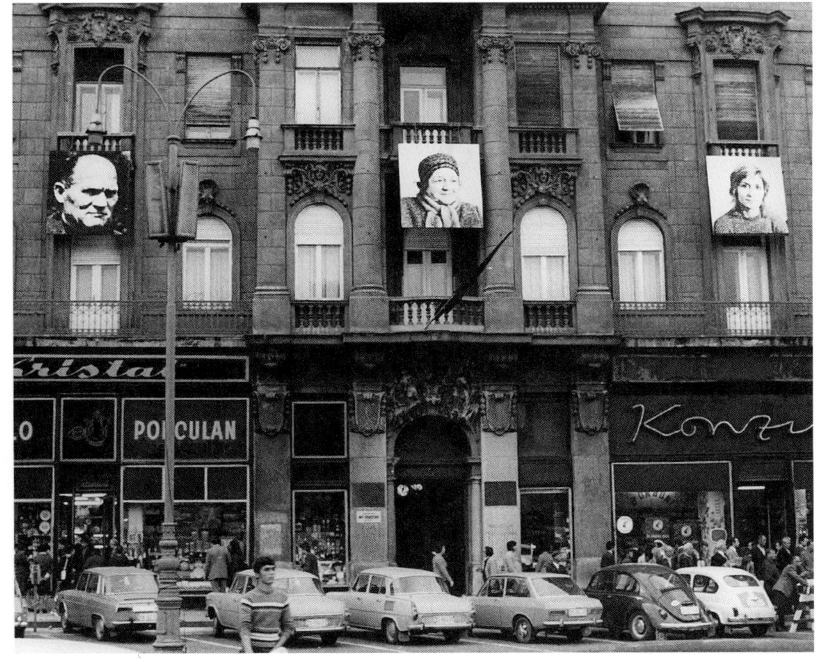

Dés le début, Dimitrijević utilisa des stratégies conceptuelles pour intervenir dans des endroits publics, mais il dépassa les paramètres préétablis des années 60. Plusieurs conceptuels des débuts, notamment en Amérique du nord et en Angleterre, se tournaient vers des positions, des textes et des photos, en précurseurs du concept de « dématérialisation ». Ce terme avancé par Lucy Lippard et John Chandler en 1968, en réaction à l'évolution artistique de l'Amérique du nord, se voulait provisoire (et d'une certaine manière trompeur) mais il tentait de capturer le nouvel accent artistique mis sur le processus et l'expérience plutôt que sur l'objet final et définitif[2]. L'anthologie des expositions, événements et publications ultérieurs de Lippard dans les années 60 et au début des années 70 faisait encore le point sur la situation plutôt qu'elle ne la fixait pas des représentations, même si, dans sa préface elle ajoutait une note de prudence sur le terme même de dématérialisation.[3] Comme Lippard le savait, toute une

Casual Passer-by I met at 10:05 PM, London, 1972
"John Foster lived here Oct. 1961 – Feb. 1968"

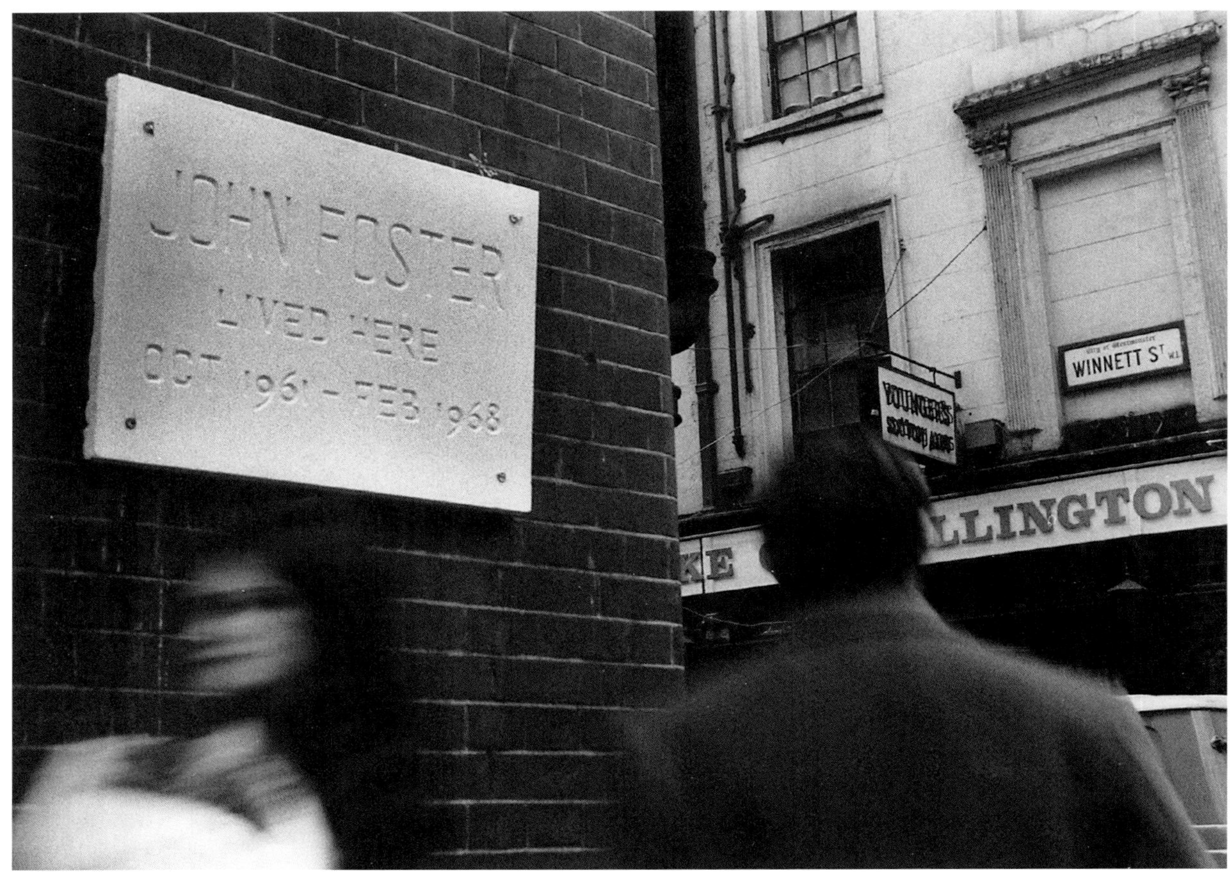

tendance d'artistes conceptuels puisait ses idées dans le dialogue avec les concepts sculpturaux, d'autres écrivains se contentaient de se mettre d'accord sur une interprétation du terme évocateur de la « dématérialisation ». Celle-ci était devenue la formule consacrée de l'art conceptuel du début des années 70 : « L'abolition de l'art objet, écrivit Ursula Meyer, typique de l'Art Conceptuel, élimine l'intérêt pour le style, la qualité et la permanence, les caractéristiques indispensables de l'art traditionnel et contemporain. » De plus, elle prétendait que le passage de l'objet au concept signifiait une forme de mépris pour la culture de la consommation[4].

Pendant ce temps en Europe continentale, la sensibilité conceptuelle d'Yves Klein et de Zero était déjà connue du public dès les années 50. Une décennie plus tard, plusieurs expositions majeures introduisirent les nouvelles tendances émergentes venues d'Amérique du nord, notamment « Op. Losse Schroeven » (Amsterdam, 1969), « Quand les attitudes deviennent formes » (Berne, 1969), et la Biennale de Paris en 1971. Dimitrijević fut représenté à la Biennale de Paris ainsi qu'à la Documenta de 1972. Cette dernière mit en lumière l'adaptation peu courante des stratégies conceptuelles de Braco Dimitrijević. Dans l'exposition tentaculaire d'Harald Szeeman à la Documenta, divers mouvements parallèles dans les arts ont été exposés sous le même toit. Le slogan de l'exposition était *Probing Reality : Image Worlds Today*, l'exposition proposait une enquête ambitieuse sur l'imagerie de la vie quotidienne (tout, de la pub, poster politique et imagerie religieuse aux monnaies et décorations de jardins). L'exposition se posait en réaction aux nombreux développements des année 60, notamment aux nouvelles stratégies artistiques qui n'étaient pas nécessairement orientées vers un objet matériel défini. Les questions de représentation se situaient dans le cadre d'une enquête critique de la culture matérialiste, sujet cher aux théoriciens et critiques de gauche, plus particulièrement en Allemagne.

Durant la période politique versatile des année 60, le Pop Art a catalysé tous les débats. Dans une des plus fascinantes incompréhensions de l'histoire récente, le Pop en Allemagne a été reçu comme un art qui portait une critique sociale de la culture de consommation, mais vers la fin de la décennie, il fut perçu comme positif [5]. A un moment où les tendances artistiques en Amérique du nord s'inscrivaient dans la formule de la « dématérialisation », les critiques insistantes de la culture matérialiste, influencées par les écrits de l'Ecole de Francfort, ont dominé la critique de l'art en Allemagne. Dans l'exposition de la Documenta, et plus particulièrement dans la section « Idea Art », on pouvait trouver un engagement artistique rigoureux dans la photographie et les problèmes de représentation. Malgré tout, ces critiques de la représentation de la société du spectacle ou de la perception des images dans l'espace, faites par les artistes conceptuels de cette exposition, ne furent pas reconnues par les critiques et les théoriciens.[6] Les commissaires d'exposition de la section « Idea Art » ont ignoré le rôle de la photographie en faveur de concepts non visuels ; la théorie esthétique développée dans le texte du catalogue principal par le philosophe Hans-Heinz Holz déplorait ce qu'il avait considéré comme «l'adoption irréfléchie de la culture quotidienne dans l'image, qui marque le Pop Art américain. »

A l'opposé des critiques allemands au milieu des années 60, il percevait les formes de représentation du Pop Art comme « le résultat d'une perte de vision diversifiée», le Minimalisme et le Land Art (ainsi que quelques travaux conceptuels) étaient pour lui un simple retour aux orientations de *l'art pour l'art.* À la suite du texte d'Herbert Marcus écrit précédemment sur le caractère affirmatif de l'art, le grand mantra parmi les théoriciens et les critiques d'art de gauche des années 60 était un renouvellement de la validité sociale de l'art et des demandes pour relier l'art et la vie. Holz n'était pas une exception, dans sa vision l'art contemporain était en crise (à cause de la perte de sa fonction de rituel et donc de la montée du matérialisme). La solution de cette crise, pensait-il, dépendait de la sphère politique plutôt qu'artistique.[7]

Les travaux de Dimitrijević, ajoutés plus tardivement à l'exposition et ne figurant donc pas au catalogue, combinaient une perspective politique critique avec des méthodes conceptuelles.[8] Il avait compris de quelle façon l'institution s'était appropriée et avait codifié la vie sociale et les espaces publics. En même temps, il s'est inspiré et nourri du répertoire des stratégies conceptuelles de l'époque. Le placement de son travail dans la Documenta 5 : entre Rebecca Horn, Franz Erhard Walther et Yoko Ono dans la section « Mythologies personnelles » plutôt qu'avec les conceptualistes, où son travail aurait été perçu différemment, le fait qu'il n'utilisait pas seulement des matériaux « dématérialisés » comme la photographie et le texte mais incorporait des monuments publics concrets, lui firent une place à part.

Les plaques commémoratives et les monuments publics de Dimitrijević étaient une extension logique de la série des « Casual Passer-By ». Comme il l'avait déjà fait auparavant, il engageait des marques institutionnelles dans la sphère publique. Il est utile de se rappeler que Barnett Newman et Claes Oldenburg avaient déjà commencé à déstructurer le langage formel des mémoriaux de guerre directement liés à la guerre du Vietnam dans les années 60. Leurs œuvres à tous deux correspondaient à la sensibilité esthétique contemporaine et fonctionnaient nettement comme des protestations politiques et des anti-monuments : le « Broken Odalisk (1963-1969) » de Newman utilisait le vocabulaire formel du Minimalisme, alors que le « Lipstick Ascending » (gonflable), 1969, d'Oldenburg soulignait l'apparition phallique du canon, ainsi que celle de l'obélisque en érection, et le rendait boiteux et impuissant. Au contraire, Dimitrijević participa discrètement à plusieurs interventions publiques, et son vocabulaire formel appartenait à des traditions plus anciennes. Il a tiré profit du fait que les places publiques en Europe sont couvertes, parfois dans des proportions absurdes, de monuments et de rappels historiques. Les noms de philosophes, écrivains, artistes, musiciens, scientifiques, éminents législateurs et politiciens modernes sont donnés à des rues, places, bâtiments, parcs et jardins, tunnels et ponts dans toutes les occasions... Ces formes d'inscriptions rappellent constamment au grand public l'existence de personnes connues et de faits historiques. On voit couramment des monuments érigés librement dans les parcs et sur les places publiques. Les bustes, statues en pied et statues équestres élevées sur des estrades ou des socles massifs sont des formes courantes du genre. Des personnages très célèbres de lieux importants deviennent partie intégrante du paysage urbain et social comme points de repère ou lieux de rencontre. Des personnages moins importants peuvent devenir des éléments de décoration et s'intégrer au paysage visuel tout en devenant paradoxalement invisibles. Si chaque ville allemande se doit d'avoir une statue du nom de Goethe ou de Schiller même si ces deux hommes n'ont aucun lien avec l'endroit, les plaques commémoratives sont en général des repères spécifiques à un lieu et évoquent une personne connue qui y a vécu ou travaillé. Elles frôlent parfois le ridicule avec des inscriptions comme « Dans cet établissement, Camus, Voltaire, Matisse, Shakespeare, Wagner, ou Caruso, a passé la nuit ou déjeuné le (avec la date) ». L'abondance des noms attribués aux lieux publics fait que dans bien des cas ces noms sont inconnus même des habitants. Des plaques de marbre comme celles de Dimitrijević « Ici a séjourné Sarah Knipe en 1971» (Londres 1971) ou « Ici a vécu John Foster d'octobre 1961 à février 1968 » (Londres 1972) s'inscrivent parfaitement dans le paysage culturel et seulement les passants les plus avertis se demanderont de qui il s'agit et pourquoi la date est si récente. Allant un peu plus loin, son « Monument to David Harper, The Casual Passer-by I met at 11:28 AM, London, 1972 » représentait le buste d'un homme plus grand que nature sur un socle en pierre avec une inscription commémorative : « David Harper né en 1924. » Avec l'aide de la Situation Gallery, la sculpture fut placée à Berkeley Square à Londres sans plus de commentaire ni d'explication. Clairement, ceci était un « objet matériel » dans le sens traditionnel (pré-moderne) de l'histoire de l'art et on raconte que, pendant qu'il travaillait sur une sculpture, il s'est disputé avec Antony Caro, son professeur à la St Martin School où il était alors étudiant.[9] Le style réaliste de la sculpture était lui-même un sujet chargé de politique. À l'époque de l'après-guerre, la division idéologique entre l'Est et l'Ouest touchait non seulement les modèles politiques et économiques mais même les styles artistiques. L'abstraction, notamment les différences gestuelles, devenait théorie en termes de liberté artistique et intellectuelle et devint le sabir de l'Ouest. Elle associait les tendances artistiques contemporaines à l'avant-garde de l'après-guerre. Elle se distingua des préférences fascistes pour les formes réalistes idéalisées. L'Est adhérait cependant au réalisme socialiste, le style préféré sanctionné par le gouvernement.[10] Avec ses monuments publics et ses plaques commémoratives, Dimitrijević fut à l'avant-garde d'une forme d'appropriation complètement nouvelle. Il a effectivement pris la place des traditions artistiques et culturelles de son époque ainsi que de leurs manifestations et avec une oeuvre comme le buste de David Harper, il a présenté un « faux » monument.

Les monuments sont des marques institutionnelles des réalisations et des victoires passées, évoquant grâce à leur matière durable une perception de l'histoire qui est aussi fixe et immuable que le métal ou la pierre. Cette apparence de durabilité et d'inévitabilité est bien entendu illusoire. Les fortunes politiques peuvent changer très rapidement et les monuments des anciens régimes peuvent être très rapidement abattus et remplacés par de nouveaux. Si des monuments publics à la gloire de personnages historiques sont inaugurés avec beaucoup de pompe et d'apparat, la photographie elle (ou plutôt la photographie documentaire) est le complice silencieux de l'écriture de l'histoire. Bien entendu l'image documentaire fait l'ob-

11 of March, This Could Be a day of Historical Importance
The date of March 11 was chosen by Peter Malwitz, a casual passer-by, because it was his birthday
Collection: Museum and Garden, Schloss Charlottenburg

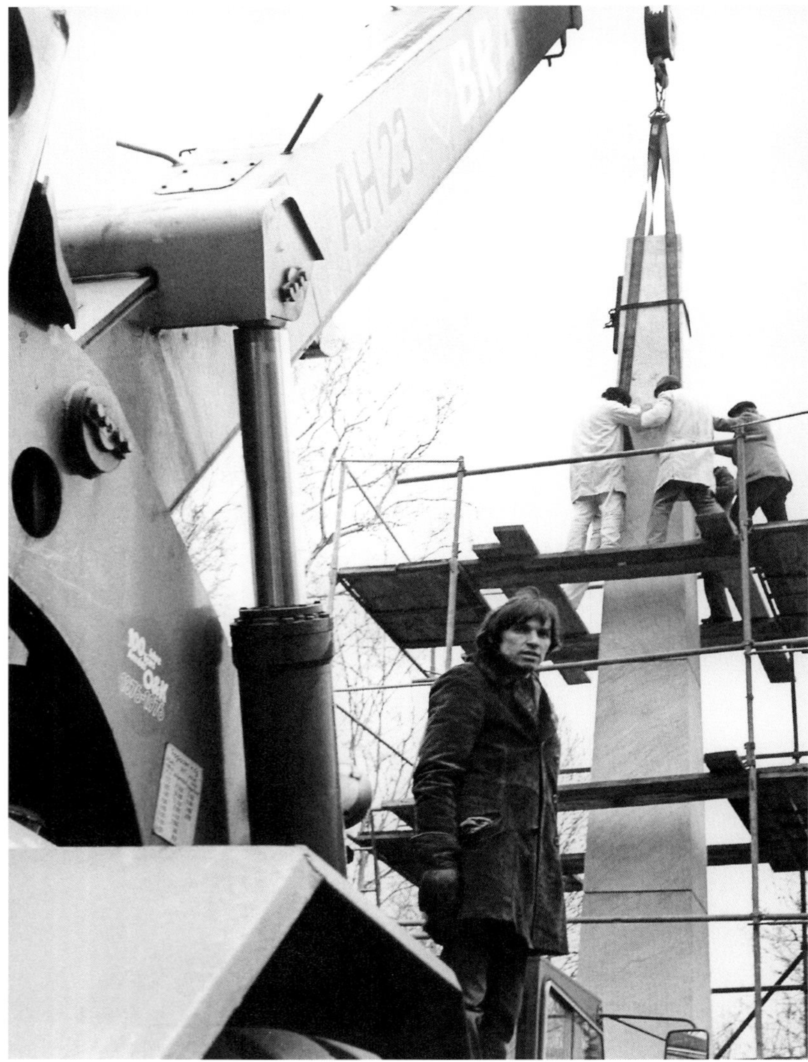

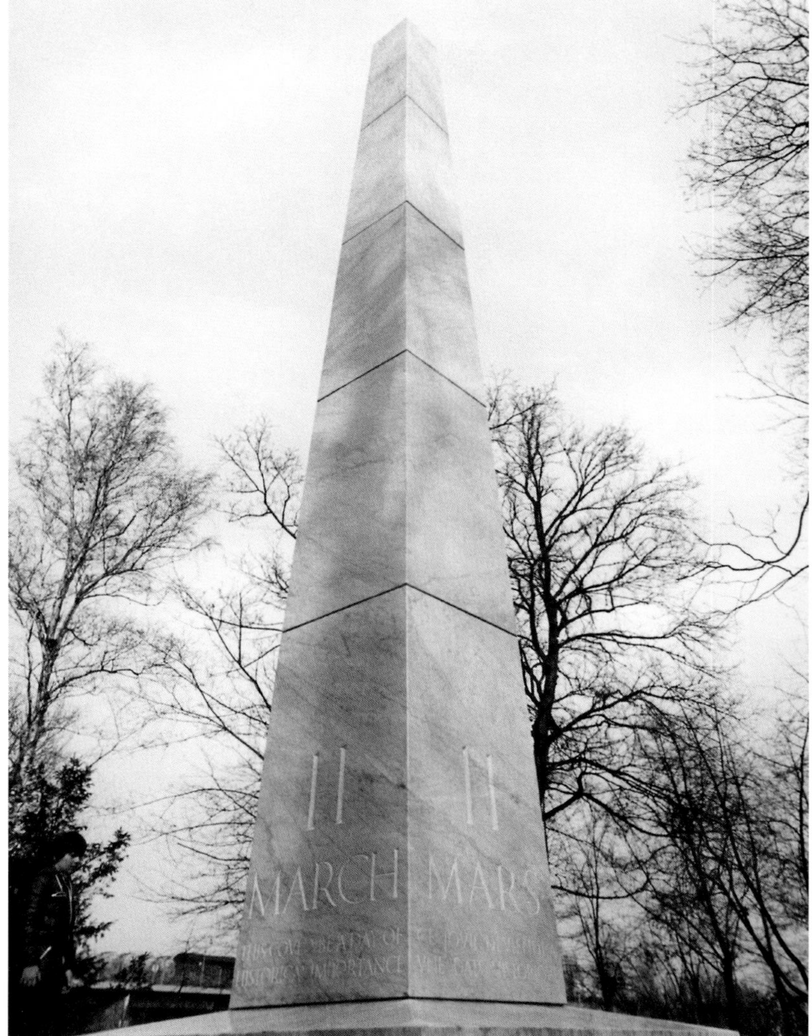

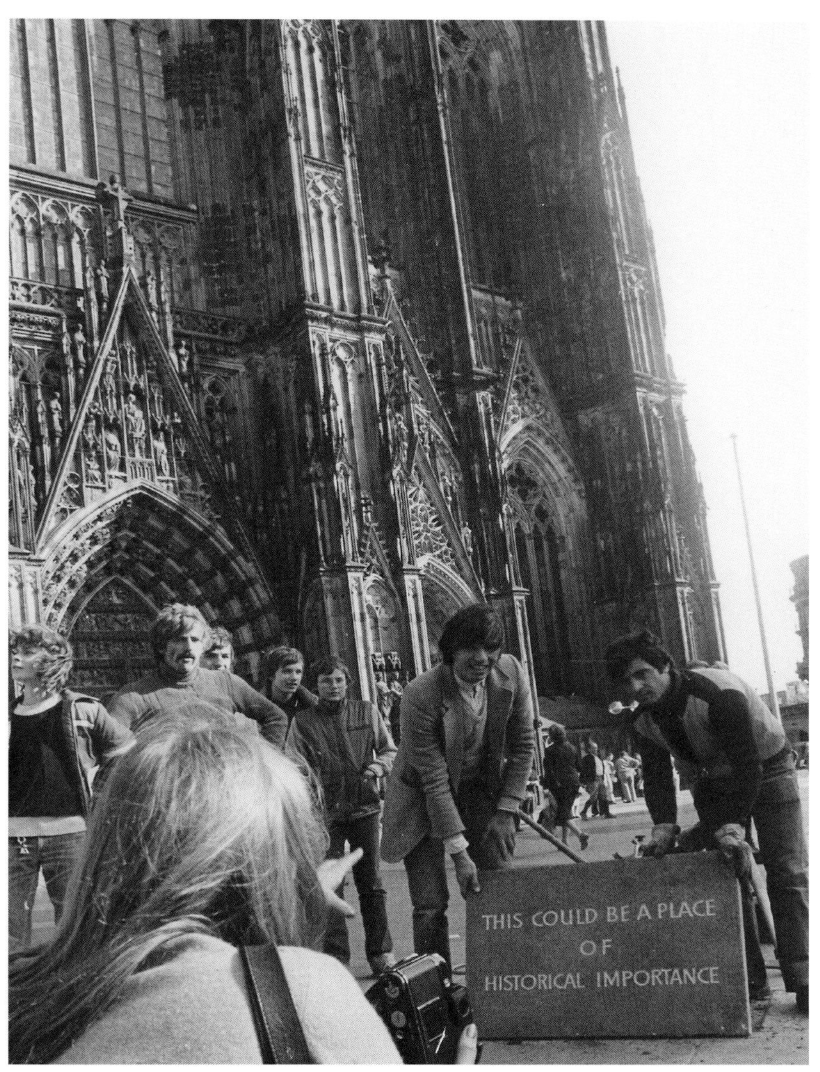

Granite slab built into the pavement in front of Cologne cathedral, 1980
Public comission, City of Cologne

jet de nombreuses discussions depuis les années 60. Reinhard Matz l'a habilement décrite en affirmant que les photographes documentaires peuvent laisser les objets parler par eux-mêmes : « Une fois photographié, l'objet seul semble devenir l'unique raison d'être de la photographie puisque, étant naturel et légitime, il porte toute l'attention sur lui. » .[11] Les artistes conceptuels des années 60 sont montés en première ligne pour critiquer l'image en apparence factuelle. Un prétexte souvent évoqué était l'ébranlement de la croyance en la description mimétique de la « réalité » et le rejet de la photographie en tant qu'objet esthétique de contemplation. On s'opposait à l'artisanat technique dans un sens moderniste et à sa place on créait des images d'un sujet et d'une technique banale, qui soulignaient les conditions de la représentation photographique et la construction du sens. À travers le dérapage délibéré du signifiant et du signifié souvent obtenu grâce à un décalage entre l'image et le titre, à travers des images en série, le médium en apparence transparent et la « réalité » dépeinte s'avèrent biaisés et culturellement prédéterminés.

Roland Barthes (comme Walter Benjamin et Bertolt Brecht avant lui) avait bien compris que les photographies en elles-mêmes n'avaient pas une seule signification mais étaient déterminées par le contexte. Dans son texte très connu de 1964 sur la « Rhétorique des images », il faisait la distinction entre trois messages : « un message linguistique, un message iconique codé et un message iconique non codé». [12] Le premier se référait au titre ou à la légende, les deux autres décrivaient deux aspects différents de l'image visuelle, un factuel et l'autre culturel. Alors que des messages culturels complexes peuvent être transmis grâce à des indices subtils inscrits littéralement dans le message de perception, le signifiant le plus évidemment déterminant est celui de la légende, le message linguistique qui ancre l'image et donne au spectateur une interprétation irréversible. Après une révolution des technologies digitales pendant les années 90, une littérature grandissante sur la photographie et les nouveaux médias, les théories de Barthes semblent aujour d'hui dépassées dès lors qu'elles appartiennent à cette époque. Mais, mis à part le fait que notre façon de voir n'avance pas à la même vitesse que la technologie, il est important de se souvenir que les conceptualistes des années 60 et 70 se préoccupaient précisément des problèmes décrits par Barthes. La relation entre l'image et le titre, la légende ou le texte d'accompagnement était donc un point crucial où pouvaient intervenir les pionniers de la photographie conceptualiste.[13]

En 1971, Braco Dimitrijević commença une série de photographies qui sortaient de son œuvre de monuments publics. Elle poursuivait l'intérêt qu'il portait à la commémoration d'événements historiques et appliquait la même technique d'un espace mis en scène, entre image et texte, utilisé par d'autres artistes conceptuels mais avec un tour plus radical. Il explosait le cadre temporel de la photographie documentaire traditionnelle, où l'image n'est qu'un témoin servant seulement à montrer « ce qui a été», selon l'argumentation célèbre de Barthes dans *Camera Lucida*. Le rôle de la photographie dans l'écriture de l'histoire dépend de sa capacité à fournir des preuves étayées par un titre, une légende, ou un texte. Dimitrijević fait le contraire et vraiment l'impensable en combinant simultanément des photographies non descriptives de paysages boisés pittoresques, l'extérieur d'une petite maison ou un portail de pierre encadré d'arbres luxuriants. Aucun des sites n'est identifié ou daté et aucune photographie ne contient de personnages. La légende « Ceci pourrait être un lieu historique » ne correspond pas à un lieu précis et ne présente ni faits ni narration. Au contraire cette directive hypothétique mobilise les facultés d'association du spectateur et donne à une scène de tous les jours le potentiel d'avoir du sens et d'être inquiétante. Autant d'événements potentiels peuvent être projetés dans l'image, ce pourrait être une scène de crimes de guerre ou d'une bataille héroïque, le lieu où fut signé un traité, prononcé un discours historique, réalisée une oeuvre d'art connue ou une découverte scientifique. La stratégie de Dimitrijević démontre au contraire

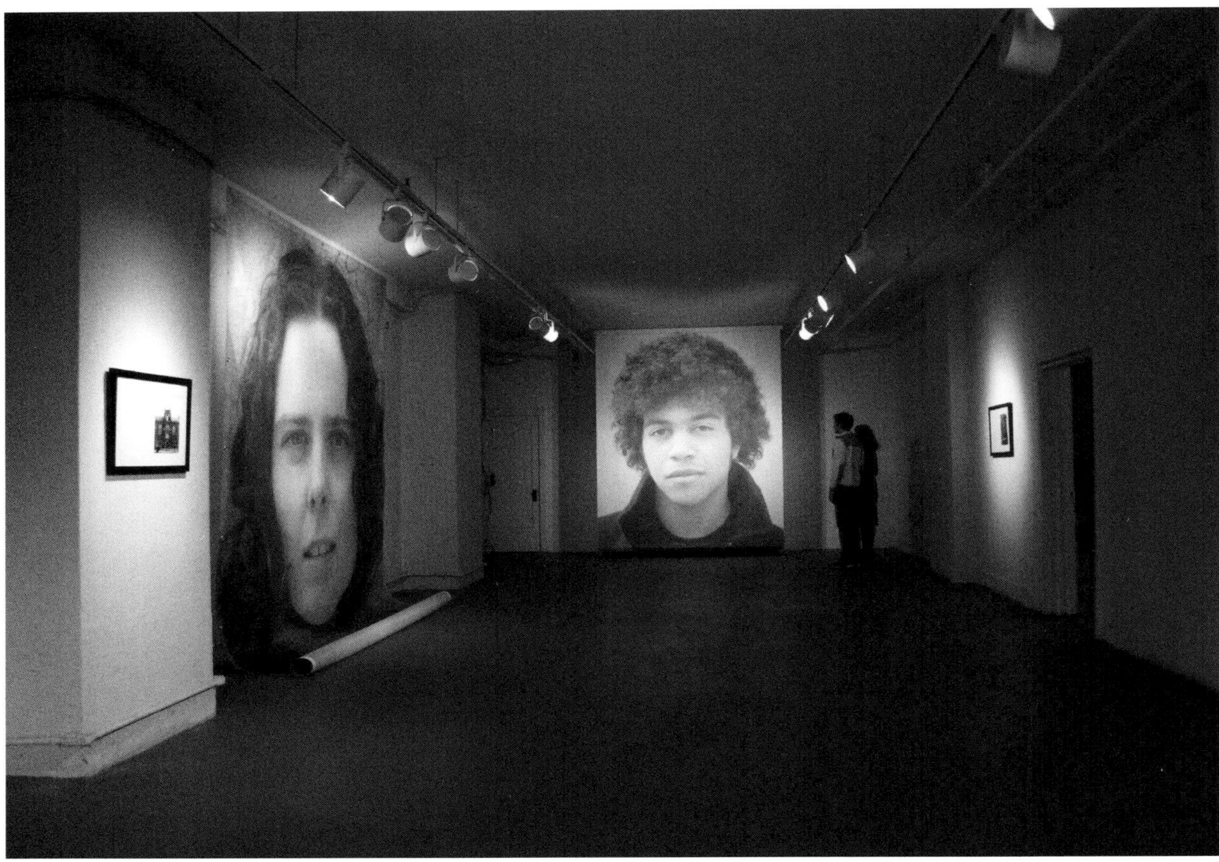

Installation view of exhibition Slought Foundation Philadelphia, 2007

qu'une photographie ordinaire fonctionne dans le cadre d'une narration historique lorsqu'un contexte définitif est effectivement donné et que cette photographie éphémère devient en elle-même un monument. Mais il nous rappelle essentiellement l'aspect arbitraire des événements historiques qui confèrent de l'importance à un site, de la banalité à un autre. A Sarajevo, la ville natale de l'artiste, on trouve l'un des lieux accidentels les plus connus du 20ème siècle : la rue où furent assassinés en juin 1914 l'Archiduc François Ferdinand, prince couronné de l'Empire austro-hongrois, et son épouse, événement qui précipita la Première Guerre mondiale. Si on observe la série des photographies de Dimitrijević devenues aujourd'hui prophétiques à la lumière des événements historiques récents de la guerre ethnique en Yougoslavie, son travail prend involontairement une résonance effrayante.

Pour son obélisque d'une hauteur de 10 mètres dans les jardins du Château de Charlottenburg, réalisé à Berlin en 1979, Dimitrijević a combiné la clause hypothétique de sa série de photographies avec ses expérimentations dans les lieux publics. Ce travail était le résultat d'une rencontre avec Peter Malwitz, un autre passant anonyme. Après qu'on lui a demandé de choisir une date pour l'inscrire sur l'obélisque, il choisit son anniversaire (le 11 mars). Dans sa forme et son contenu, ce travail suivait des traditions déjà en usage pour les monuments historiques mais l'inscription secondaire sur le socle « Ceci pourrait être un jour d'importance historique » déconstruit la forme ainsi que les conventions historiques.

Sur l'obélisque berlinois de Dimitrijević est inscrite la date d'anniversaire d'un passant anonyme, autrement dit on donne à une date ayant une signification personnelle une importance universelle et d'intérêt publique. Cependant sans l'inscription de l'année, la date peut se référer au passé ou à l'avenir et le pouvoir associatif que l'on donne à cette date fait seulement partie d'une équation. L'appropriation d'un espace public codé culturellement et historiquement est tout aussi importante dans ce travail où il utilise des formes existantes de monuments publics et de formules de commémoration. Par conséquent, Dimitrijević met en mouvement un processus de réflexion complexe. Il nous conduit à considérer non seulement la part de hasard qui détermine les événements historiques et par la suite dicte l'écriture des narrations historiques mais aussi le langage des monuments et plaques commémoratives et leurs rôles dans l'espace public.

L'attention insistante que porte Dimitrijević aux monuments publics et l'importance des marques visuelles (la sculpture et la photographie) dans les écrits et images de l'histoire (et de l'histoire de l'art) est remarquable dès ses débuts. Alors que l'intérêt théorique et artistique de ses contemporains se portait vers la culture matérialiste et la société du spectacle, lui à l'inverse se concentrait sur l'aspect esthétique des objets de commémoration historique (et politique) dans leurs formes publiques. La meilleure façon de traiter ce sujet était d'utiliser des formes et matières déjà existantes. Son tournant en apparence réactionnaire vers des matières de sculpture traditionnelles comme le marbre ou le bronze était en discordance avec la définition étroite de la « dématérialisation » qui était vogue dans les années 60 et au début des années 70. En tant qu'artiste conceptuel, il était en avance sur son temps et fut pionnier dans le département de la recherche qui fut à son apogée dans les années 80 et 90.[14]

1. Sur ce sujet référez-vous à l'analyse pointue de Nena Dimitrijević , "The Post Historical Dimension," dans *Braco Dimitrijević* (Milan-New York: Charta, 2006), p. 23
2. Lucy Lippard et John Chandler, "The Dematerialization of Art," *Art International XII*, no. 2 (February 20, 1968): 31-36.
3. « Depuis que j'ai écrit sur ce sujet en 1967, il m'a souvent été remarqué que la dématieralisation n'est pas un terme correct, qu'un bout de papier ou une photographie est tout autant un objet, ou tout aussi « matériel » qu'une tonne de plomb. Accordé. Mais comme je n'ai pas touvé de meilleur terme, j'ai continué de me référer au processus de dématerialisation ou à la diminution de l'intérêt de l'aspect matériel (le caractère, la permanence, l'attrait de la décoration.) » Se référer à Lucy Lippard, "Preface," *Six Years: The Dematerialization of the Art Object, from 1966 to 1972*, première publicatoin en 1973 (Berkeley, Los Angles, London: University of California Press, 1997), 5.
4. Ursula Meyer, *Conceptual Art* (New York: E.P. Dutton and Co., 1972), XV. Vous trouverez un argument similaire de Gregory Battcock dans *Idea Art: A Critical Anthology* (New York: Dutton, 1973). Cette vision était partagée par Gregory Battcock qui l'année suivante écrit, "What they all seemed to have in common was a rejection of the "bourgeois" aspects of traditional art. Works of Idea Art frequently did not exist as objects. Rather, they remained ideas; frequently what did exist was only some kind of documentation referring to the concept." See Gregory Battcock, "Introduction," *Idea Art: A Critical Anthology* (New York: Dutton, 1973), 1.
5. Une description détaillée de ces débats peut être trouvée dans ma thèse, Catharina Manchanda, "Reconsidering the Object of Photography: German Artists, Curators and Critics in Light of 'documenta 5,'" Ph.D. thesis, (City University of New York: Ph.D. Program of Art History, 2005).
6. La partie sur l'art conceptuel de la Documenta 5 ("Idea Art") était orchestrée par le marchard d'art Konrad Fischer et l'historien d'art Klaus Honnef. Le catalogue était écrit par Honnef et Giesela Kaminsiki et leurs interprétations étaient guidées par les textes de Lippard autant que par les définitions plus precises de Ursula Meyer. La dématérialisation été interprétée comme un éloignement de l'objet vers le concept. Ceci a amené les auteurs à se concentrer spécifiquement sur des travaux avec des textes alors que les stratégies photographiques ne furent pas reconnues. Au contraire, les photographies (ainsi que les plans et les dessins) furent perçues comme des documents d'accompagnement. Une analyse détaillée de ce sujet se trouve dans le dernier chapitre de ma thèse. Voire citation note 5.
7. Voir Hans-Heinz Holz, "Kritische Theorie des ästhetischen Zeichens," in *Documenta 5: Befragung der Realität—Bildwelten heute.* Catalogue d'exposition (Kassel: documenta GmbH, 1972, 1.1-1.86). La connaissance de l'art contemporain et d'autres stratégies artistiques émergeantes par Holz sont approximatives. Ses points de références majeurs était modernistes, ce qui ne l'avantageait pas. Il n'était pas le seul à l'époque moderniste à avoir cette opinion sur les avant-gardes. Peter Bürger et Andreas Huyssen écrivant dans les années 70, regardaient encore dans la même direction et Huyssen était particulièrement peu élogieux sur l'art conceptuel. Voir Peter Bürger, *Theory of the Avant-Garde* (Theorie der Avant-Garde, 1974), traduit pas Michael Shaw, préface de Jochen Schulte-Sasse (Minneapolis: University of Minnesota Press, 1984); et Andreas Huyssen, "The Cultural Politics of Pop: Reception and Critique of US Pop Art in the Federal Republic of Germany." New German Critique 1-2, no. 5-6 (1975), 77-97.
8. Les travaux suivants de Braco Dimitrijević étaient montrés à la Documenta 5: des versions conceptuelles de ses photo- textes conceptuels *Monument to David Harper, 1972, Casual Passer-by I met at 6:24 PM, Düsseldorf, 1972* (ce travail était exposé comme une bannière monumentale accrochée au Friedericianum et dans leur version photo-texte). Ainsi que d'autres photo-textes conceptuels du *Casual Passer-by I met at 5pm, Naples, 1971* (ainsi que des photographies de groupe) et le *Casual Passer-by I met at 10:05 PM, London, 1972*.
9. Se référer à Nena Dimitrijević , "The Post Historical Dimension,"31.
10. Cette différence de style entre Est et Ouest devait aussi être un sujet de la Documenta 5. Des sections entières devaient être dédiées au style socialiste et communiste, mais les gouvernements en question ne voulurent pas participer. La proposition de la Documenta et quelques pages dans le catalogue témoignent de l'ambition d'origine.
11. Reinhard Matz, "Gegen einen naiven Begriff der Dokumentarfotografie (1981)," ré imprimé à Hubertus von Amelunxen, *Theorie der Fotografie IV 1980-1995* (München: Schirmer/Mosel, 2000), 96
12. Roland Barthes, "Rhetoric of the Image" (1964), dans *Image, Music, Text*.
13. Tel l'exemple de Robert Barry *Inert Gas Series* de 1969. C'est une série de photographies prises à Los Angeles qui poussait la photographie dans ses limites. Une des pièces de *Inert Gas Series*, *Helium* décrit un processus sculptural, "Sometime during the morning of March 5, 1969, 2 cubic feet of Helium will be released into the atmosphere"—un processus qui demeurait invisible à l'oeil humain et à la caméra. Si l'artiste a effectivement émis des gaz ou bien a seulement proposé de le faire ne porte pas à conséquence. La description et la documentation photographique du processus de documentation qui pouvaytent être imaginés mais demeuraient imperceptibles comptaient le plus. Le travail de Barry soulignait les limites des soi-disant évidences et de l'objectivité de ce médium. En mettant en scène un processus invisible il critiquait simultanément le médium et énonçait un élément de la « sculpture » au-delà de la perception. De plus en choisissant un gaz non réactif il choisissait une matière plus durable que toute sculpture de bronze ou de pierre.
14. Pour une discussion détaillée de ce sujet se référer à Kai- Uwe Hemken, *Gedächtnisbilder: Vergessen und Erinnern in der Gegenwartskunst* (Leipzig: Reclam, 1996).

STATEMENTS AND THOUGHTS (1966–2009)

THERE ARE NO MISTAKES IN HISTORY. THE WHOLE OF HISTORY IS A MISTAKE.

POST-HISTORY IS TIME OF COEXISTENCE OF DIFFERENT VALUES, A TIME OF MULTI-ANGULAR VIEWING, SPACE WITH NO FINAL TRUTH.

I AM THE PHILOSOPHER WHO CHOOSES TO EXPRESS HIMSELF THROUGH VISUAL ARTS IN ORDER TO COMMUNICATE WITH THE SPEED OF LIGHT.

THE WHOLE OF HISTORY IS NOT AS RICH AS 1 SECOND OF POST-HISTORICAL TIME.

OUR ENVIRONMENT IS NOT PHYSICAL SPACE BUT CULTURAL HERITAGE.

LOUVRE IS MY STUDIO, STREET IS MY MUSEUM.

I AM JUST LIKE AN ORDINARY PAINTER EXCEPT THAT ON MY PALLET THERE ARE BICYCLES, SHOVELS, APPLES, MATISSES, REMBRANDTS, LIONS, AND CROCODILES.

IF ONE LOOKS FROM THE MOON, THERE IS VIRTUALLY NO DISTANCE BETWEEN THE LOUVRE AND THE ZOO.

CHANCE IS LOGIC BEYOND REASON.

IN COSMOS THERE IS NO ABOVE AND BELOW.

DARWINISM WOULD BE ACCEPTABLE IF IT WOULD IMPLY REVERSE ORDER.

I AM NOT A MAKER OF OBJECTS, BUT A CREATOR OF VISION.

I MADE WORKS WITH ANIMALS IN ORDER TO LEARN ABOUT MAN.

LASCAUX WAS AT THE SAME TIME THE LOUVRE AND THE ZOO.

FAME HAS TO DO WITH POLITICS, TALENT WITH NATURE.

WITH VISUAL MISERY IT'S DIFFICULT TO HELP THE MISERY OF THE WORLD.

REAL REVOLUTION DOES NOT HAPPEN WHEN PEOPLE EXPRESS THEIR ANGER BY THROWING TOMATOES AT PAINTINGS BUT WHEN A FRUIT IS GENTLY PLACED NEXT TO A PAINTING.

TRUTH HAS NO CHANCE IN FIGHTING THE MYTH; ONLY WHEN IT BECOMES THE LEGEND.

EVERY CASUAL PASSER-BY IS MY ALTER EGO, A SUPPLEMENT TO MY IGNORANCE.

WHERE WOULD I BE IF I WERE FOLLOWING THE TRENDS? DEFINITELY NOT IN THE POSITION TO MAKE THEM.

FASHION IS WHAT REMAINS UNDER THE NAIL WHEN YOU SCRATCH THE STYLE.

I AM NOT INTERESTED IN SMALL FORMAL SHIFTS, INVENTING USELESS OBJECTS, IN ADDING MORE WORDS TO THE VOCABULARY OF NONSENSE.

AT THE EDGE OF THE VOLCANO YOU REMEMBER THAT EARTH WAS ONCE A STAR.

NO THEORY IS ETERNAL.

EVERY ENERGY TURNS INTO A PICTURE.

MY ART RESUMES EVERY OTHER FORM OF ART, EVERY HANDWRITING THAT EXISTS IN THE UNIVERSE.

HISTORY IS ALWAYS REPRESENTED BY KITSCH, POST-HISTORY BY ART.

IN POST-HISTORY 1 SECOND EQUALS ETERNITY.

DÉCLARATIONS – PENSÉES 1966-2009

IL N'Y A PAS D'ERREURS DANS L'HISTOIRE. TOUTE L'HISTOIRE EST UNE ERREUR.

LA POST-HISTOIRE EST UNE ÉPOQUE OÙ COEXISTENT DES VALEURS DIFFÉRENTES, UNE ÉPOQUE DE VISION SOUS DES ANGLES MULTIPLES, L'ESPACE SANS VÉRITÉ ULTIME

JE SUIS LE PHILOSOPHE QUI CHOISIT DE S'EXPRIMER À TRAVERS LES IMAGES
AFIN DE COMMUNIQUER À LA VITESSE DE LA LUMIÈRE.

L'HISTOIRE TOUTE ENTIÈRE EST MOINS RICHE QU'UNE SECONDE DE TEMPS POST-HISTORIQUE.

NOTRE ENVIRONNEMENT N'EST PAS L'ESPACE PHYSIQUE MAIS L'HERITAGE CULTUREL.

LE LOUVRE EST MON ATELIER, LA RUE EST MON MUSÉE.

JE SUIS COMME UN PEINTRE ORDINAIRE SAUF QUE SUR MA PALETTE IL Y A DES VÉLOS, DES PELLES, DES POMMES, DES MATISSE, DES REMBRANDT, DES LIONS ET DES CROCODILES.

SI ON REGARDE LA TERRE DEPUIS LA LUNE IL N'Y A PRATIQUEMENT PAS DE DISTANCE ENTRE LE LOUVRE ET LE ZOO.

LE HASARD EST LA LOGIQUE AU-DELÀ DE LA RAISON.

DANS L'UNIVERS IL N'Y A NI HAUT NI BAS.

LE DARWINISME SERAIT ACCEPTABLE S'IL SUPPOSAIT UN ORDRE INVERSE.

JE NE SUIS PAS FAISEUR D'OBJETS, MAIS CRÉATEUR DE VISION.

J'AI FAIT DES ŒUVRES AVEC DES ANIMAUX AFIN D'EN APPRENDRE SUR L'HOMME.

LASCAUX ÉTAIT EN MÊME TEMPS LE LOUVRE ET LE ZOO.

LA CÉLÉBRITÉ EST UNE AFFAIRE DE POLITIQUE, LE TALENT UNE QUESTION DE NATURE.

AVEC UNE MISÈRE VISUELLE IL EST DIFFICILE DE PORTER SECOURS À LA MISÈRE DU MONDE.

LA VRAIE RÉVOLUTION ARRIVE, NON PAS LORSQUE LES GENS EXPRIMENT LEUR COLÈRE EN LANÇANT DES TOMATES SUR LES TABLEAUX, MAIS LORSQU'UN FRUIT EST PLACÉ GENTIMENT À CÔTÉ D'UN TABLEAU.

LA VÉRITÉ N'A AUCUNE CHANCE EN LUTTANT CONTRE LE MYTHE ; SAUF QUAND CELUI-CI DEVIENT LÉGENDE.

CHAQUE PASSANT OCCASIONEL EST MON ALTER EGO, UN SUPPLÉMENT À MON IGNORANCE.

OÙ SERAIS-JE SI JE SUIVAIS LES TENDANCES ? SÛREMENT PAS EN MESURE DE LES CRÉER.

LA MODE EST CE QUI RESTE SOUS L'ONGLE QUAND ON GRATTE LE STYLE.

JE NE M'INTÉRESSE PAS AUX PETITS CHANGEMENTS FORMELS, A L'INVENTION D'OBJETS INUTILES, A L'AJOUT DE NOUVEAUX MOTS AU VOCABULAIRE DU NON-SENS.

CE N'EST QU'AU BORD DU VOLCAN QU'ON SE SOUVIENT QUE LA TERRE A ÉTÉ UNE ÉTOILE.

AUCUNE THÉORIE N'EST ÉTERNELLE.

TOUTE ÉNERGIE SE TRANSFORME EN IMAGE.

MON ART REPREND TOUTE AUTRE FORME D'ART, TOUTE ÉCRITURE QUI EXISTE DANS L'UNIVERS.

L'HISTOIRE EST TOUJOURS REPRÉSENTÉE PAR LE KITSCH, LA POST-HISTOIRE PAR L'ART.

DANS LA POST-HISTOIRE 1 SECONDE ÉGALE L'ÉTERNITÉ.

Casual Passer-by

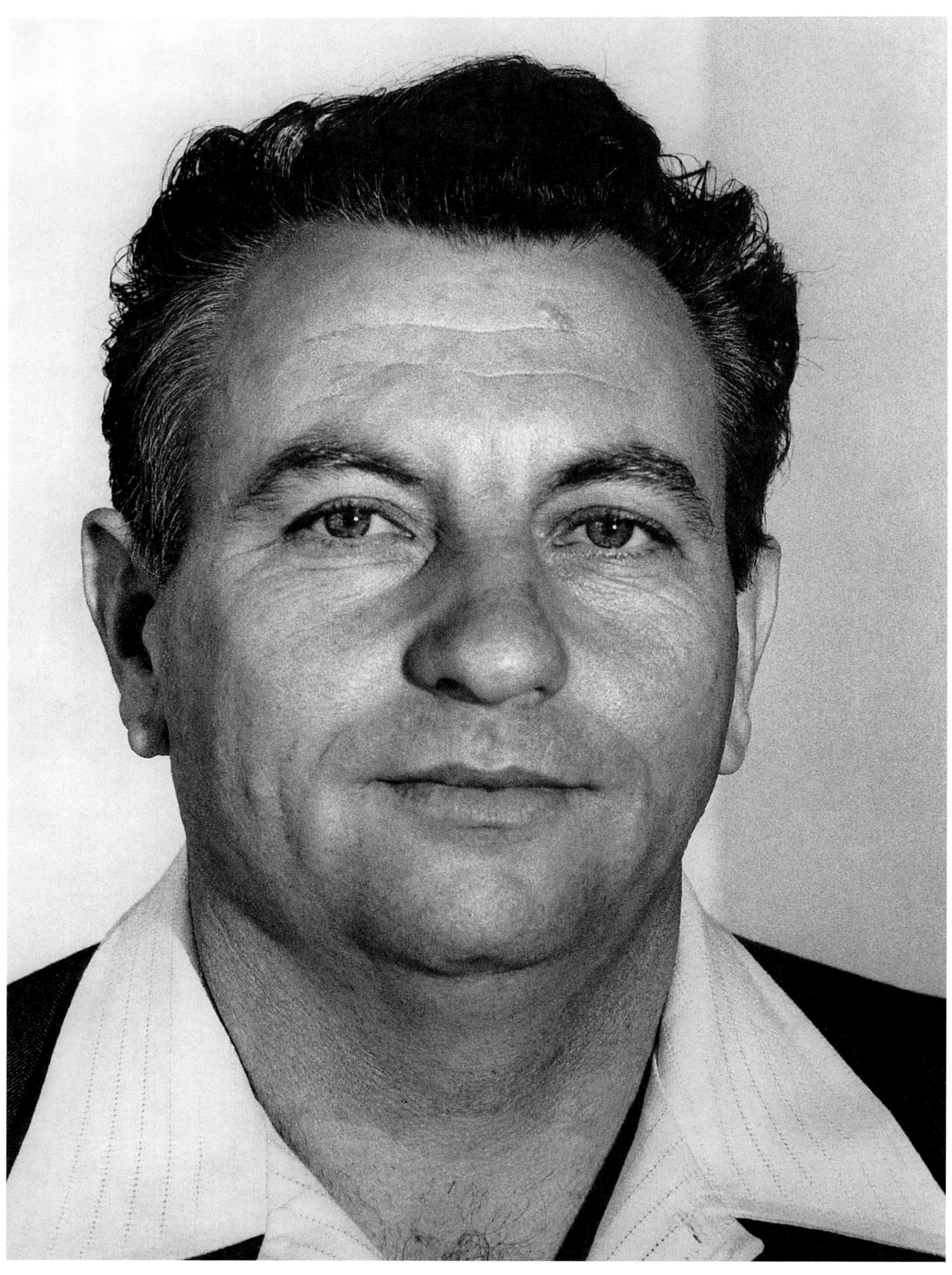

Casual Passer-by I met at 11:09 AM, Paris, 1971
Collection: Musée National d'Art Moderne,
Centre Georges Pompidou, Paris

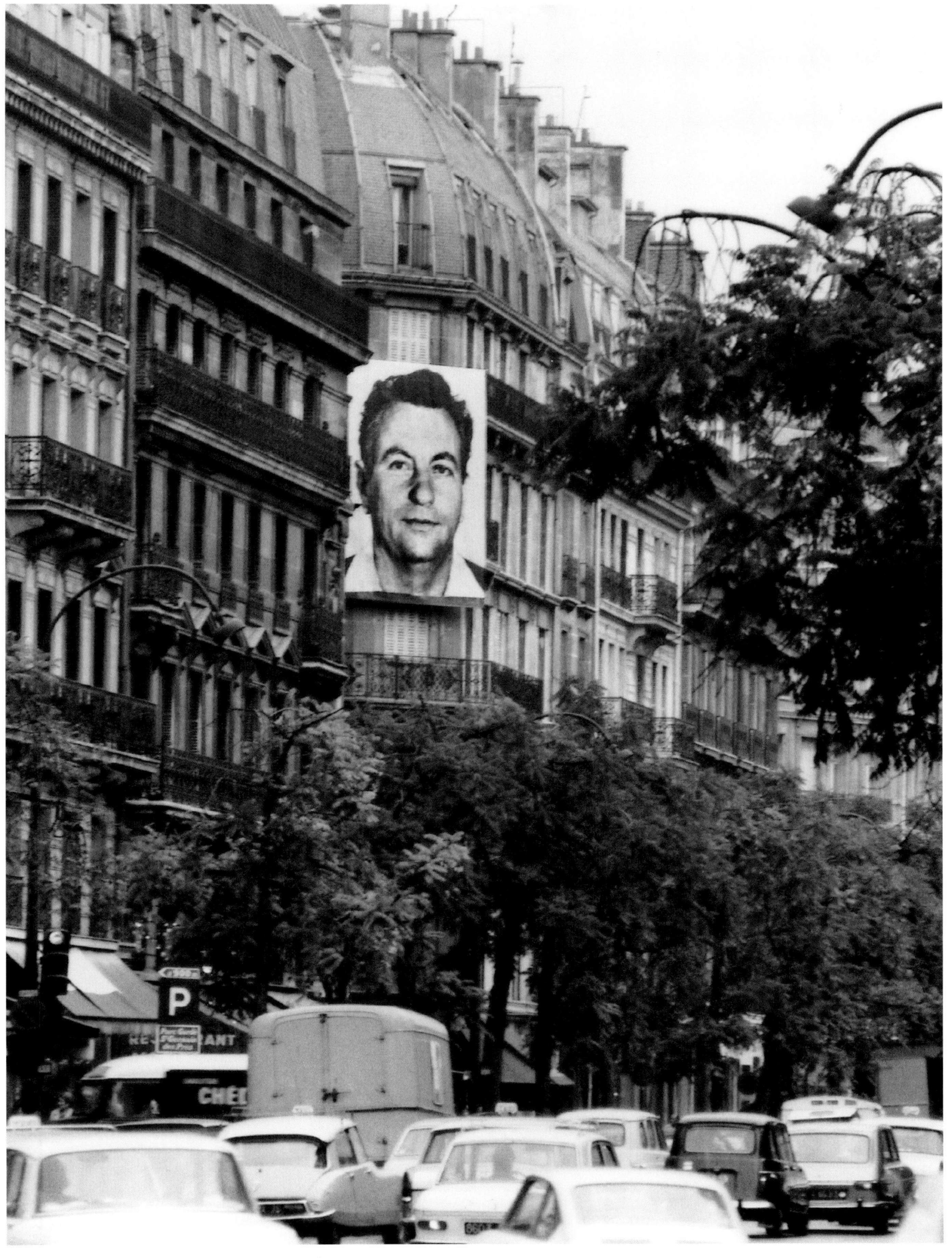

Boulevard St. Germain, Paris

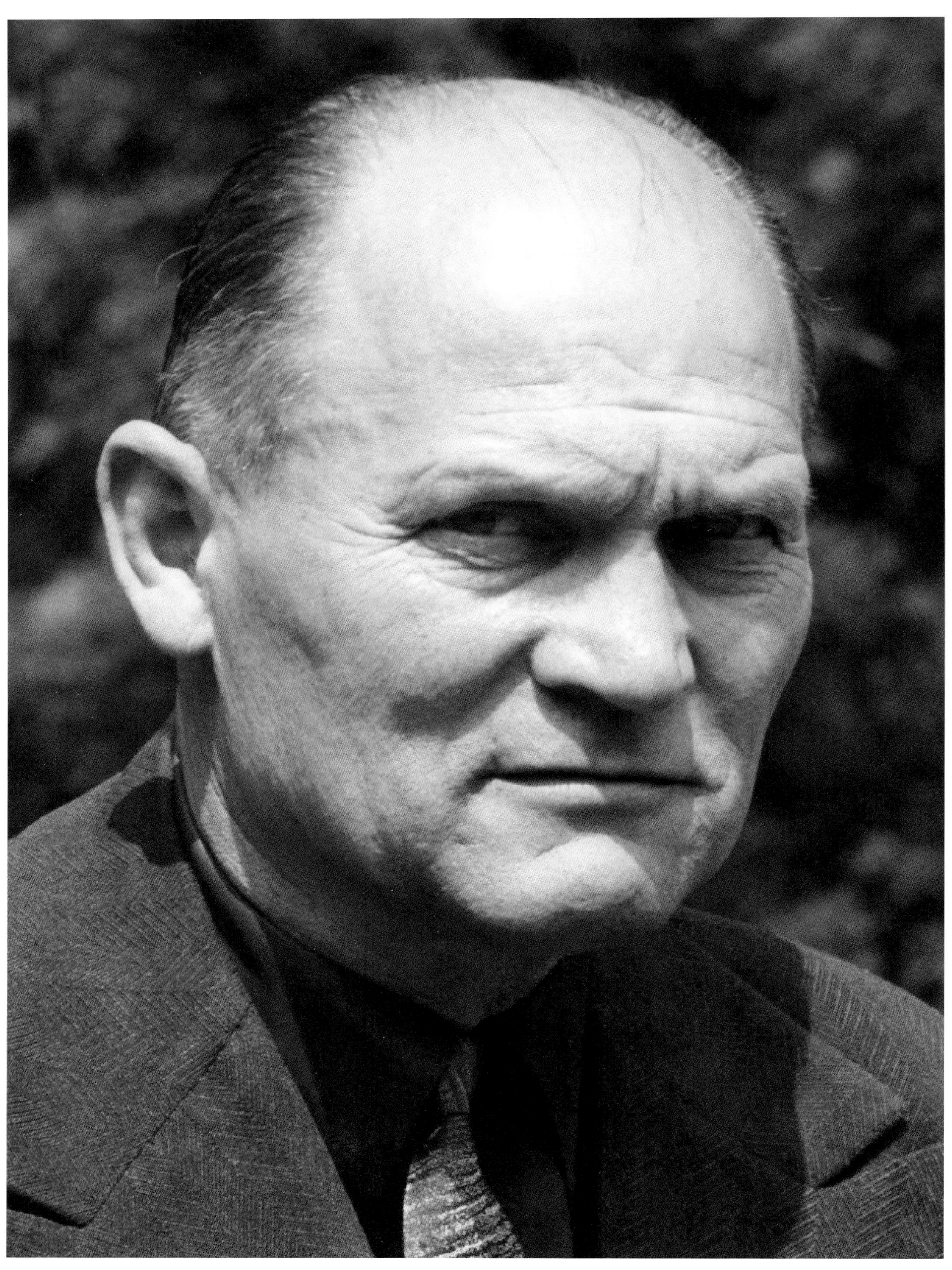

Casual Passer-by I met at 1:15 PM, Zagreb, 1971
Collection: Museum Moderner Kunst, Vienna

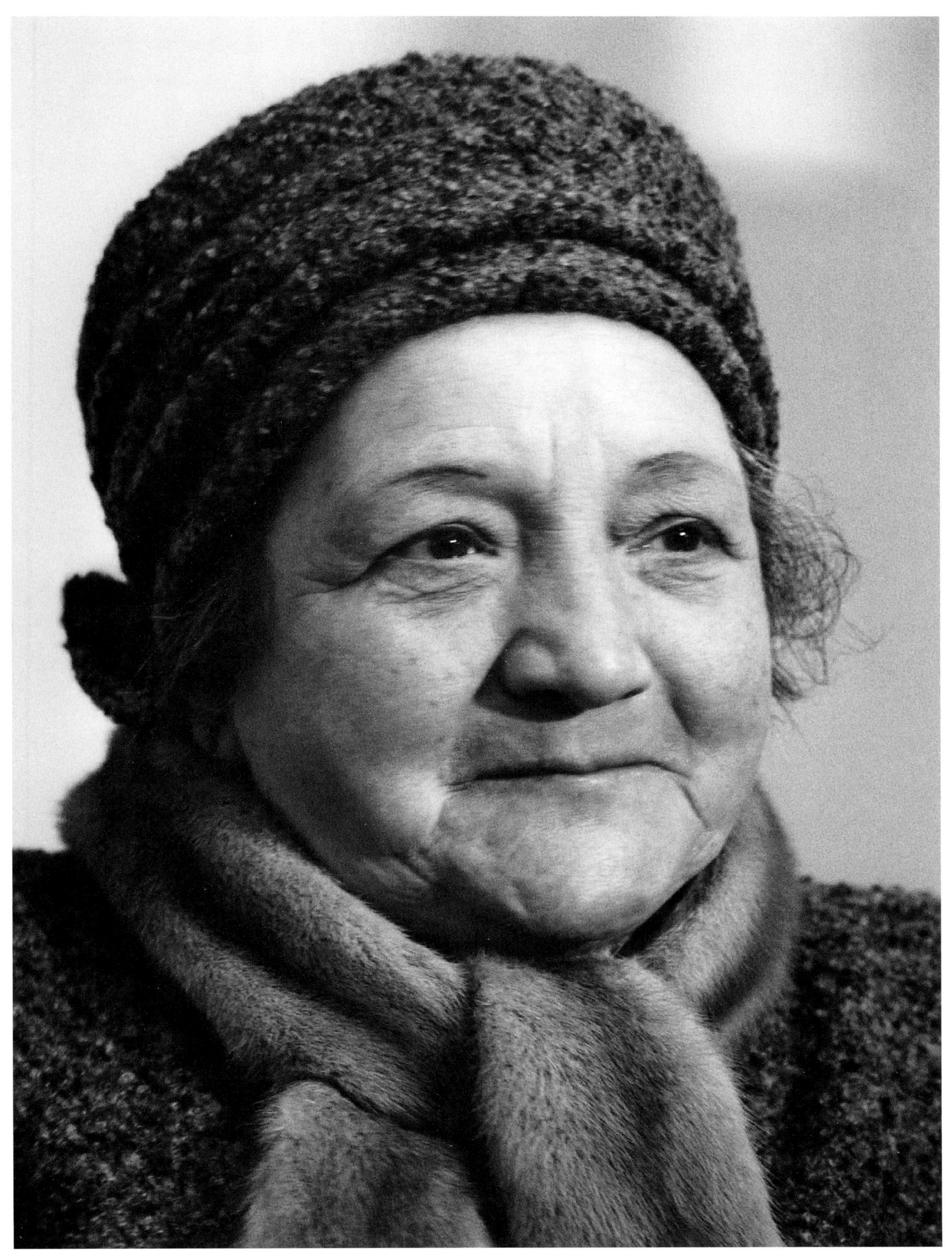

Casual Passer-by I met at 4:23 PM, Zagreb, 1971
Collection: Museum Moderner Kunst, Vienna

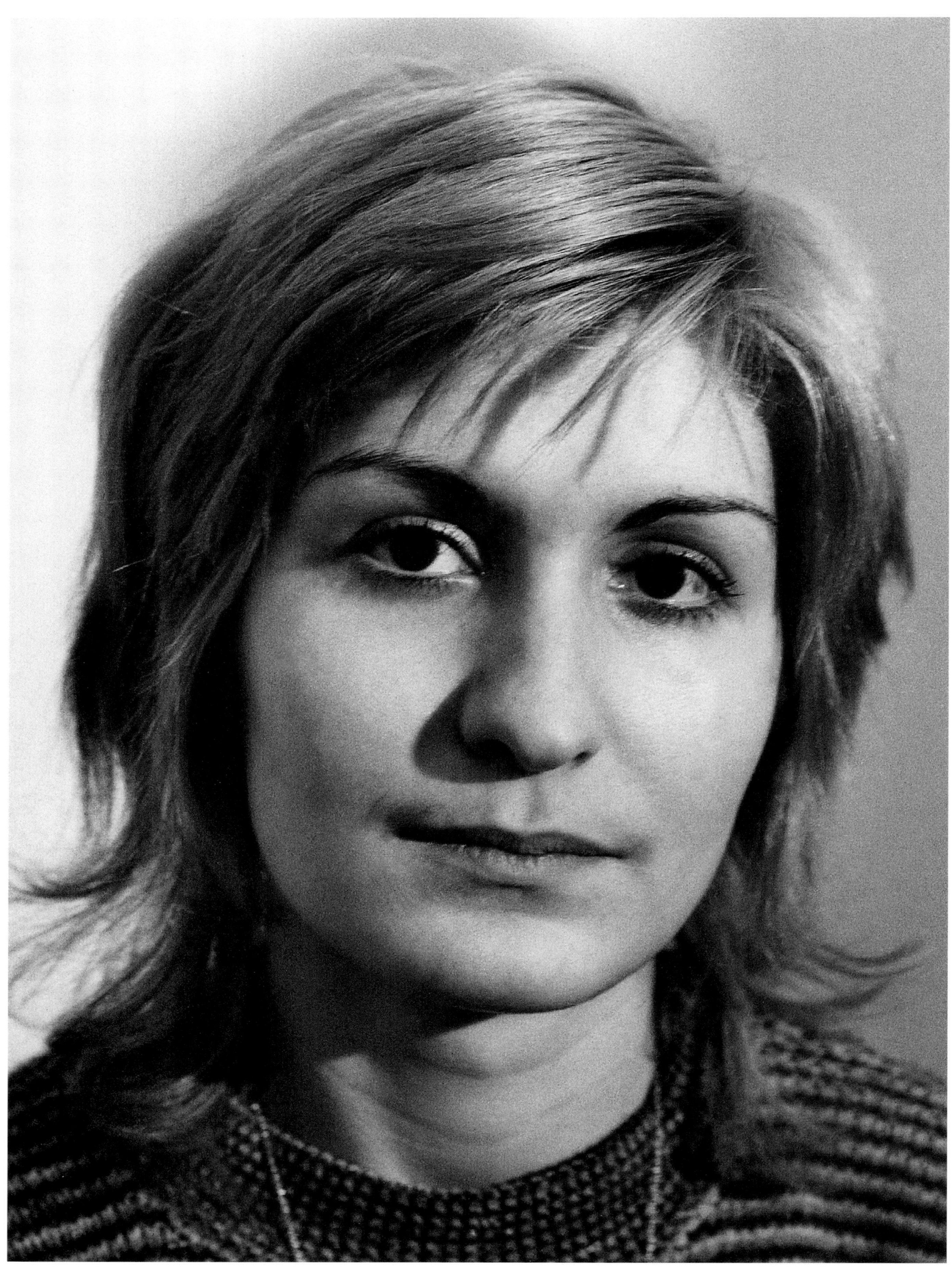

Casual Passer-by I met at 6:11 PM, Zagreb, 1971
Collection: Museum Moderner Kunst, Vienna

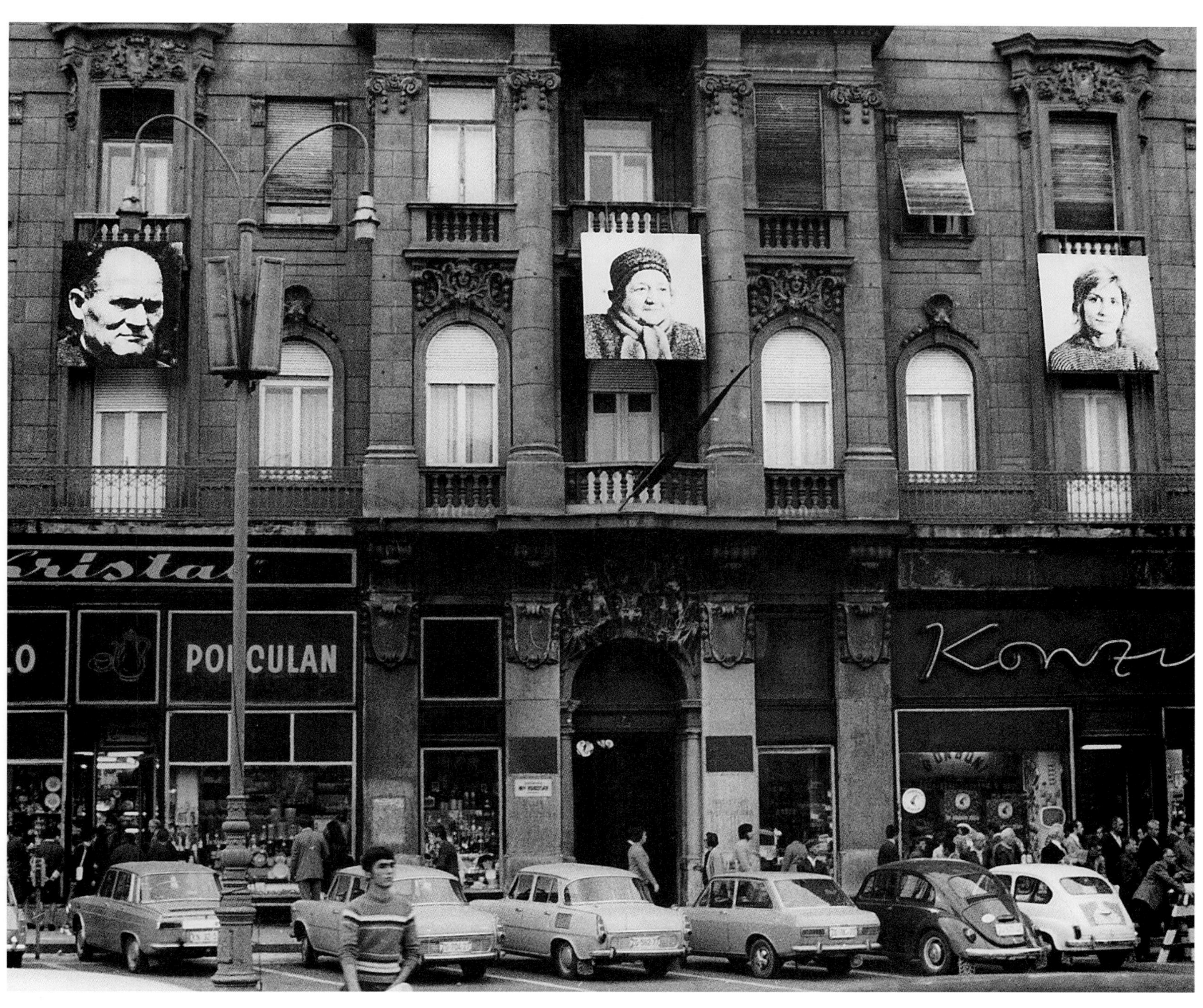

Trg Bana Jelacica, former Republic Square, Zagreb, 1971

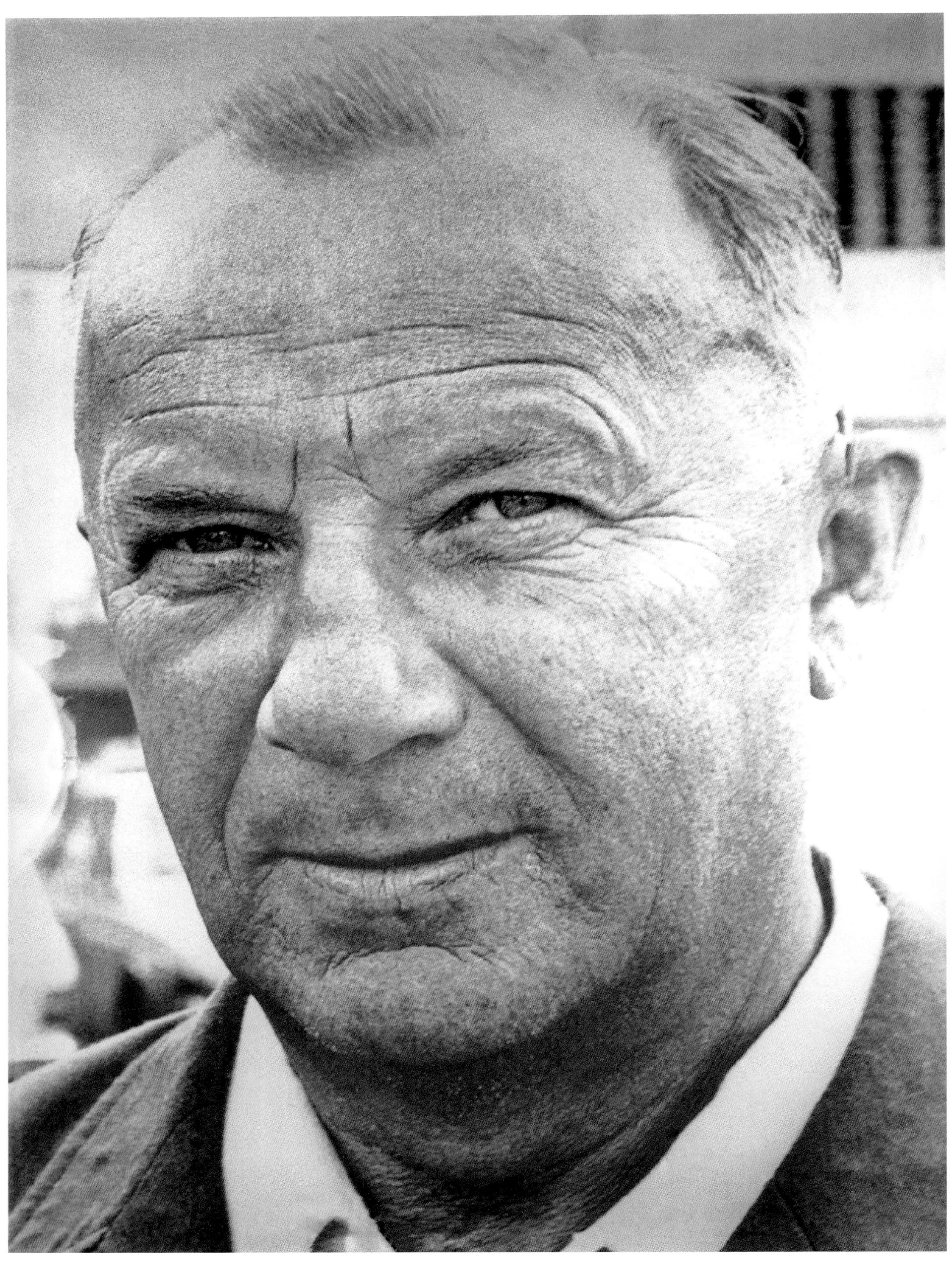

Casual Passer-by I met at 2:04 PM, Munich, 1970
Collection: Gerhard Richter, Cologne

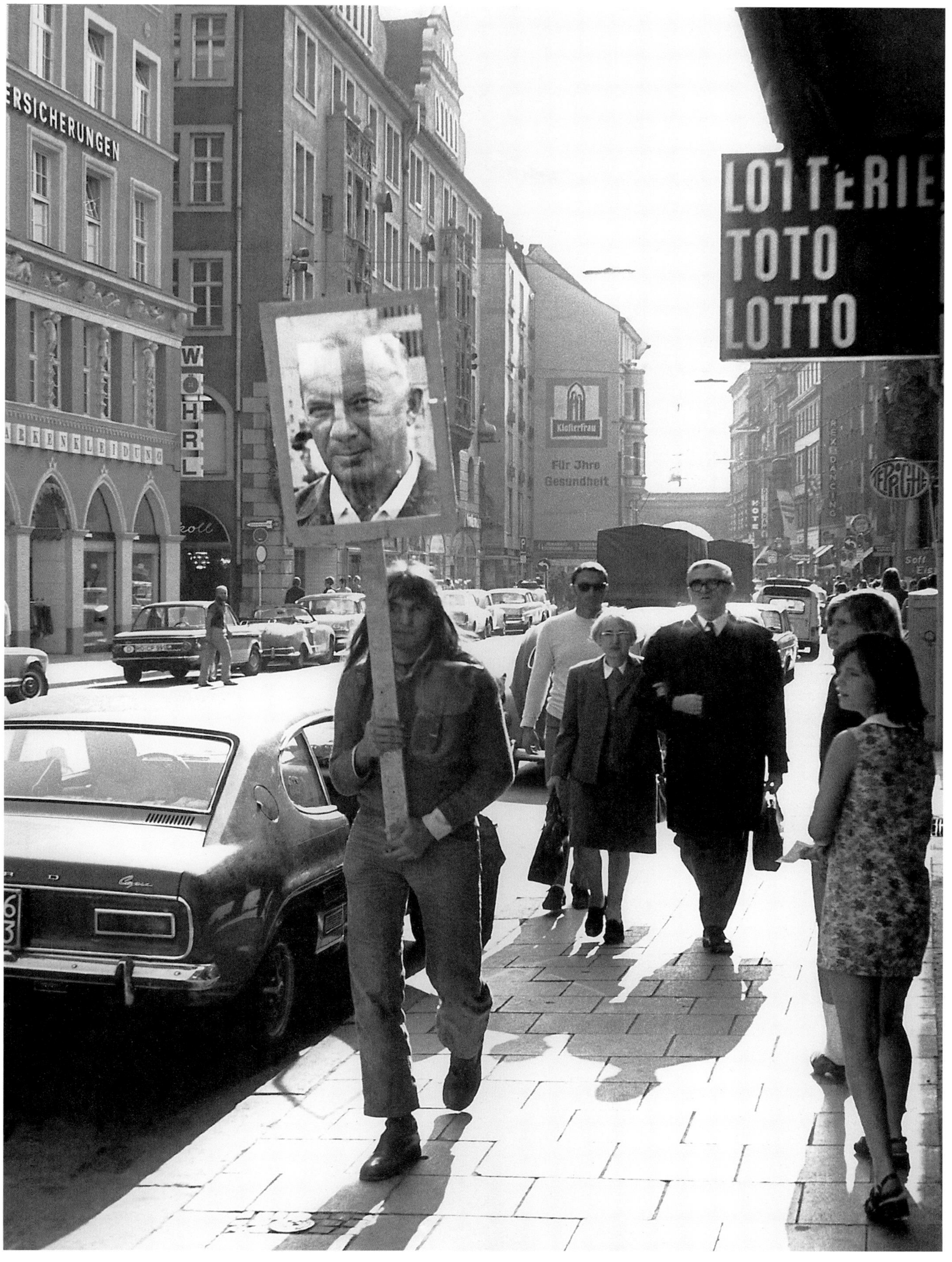
ERSICHERUNGEN
LOTTERIE
TOTO
LOTTO
Klosterfrau
Für Ihre
Gesundheit

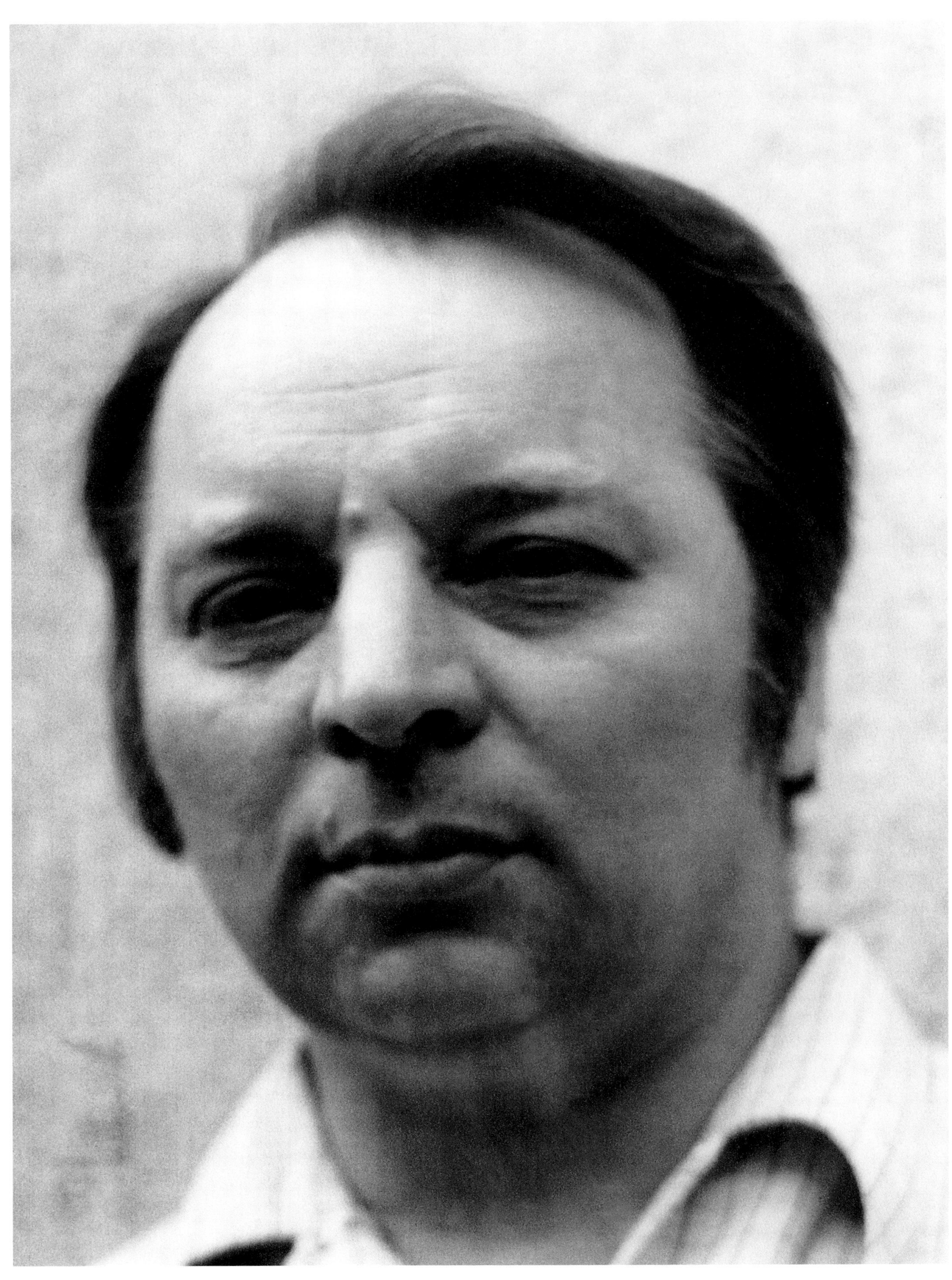

Casual Passer-by I met at 6:24 PM, Düsseldorf, 1972
Collection: Städtisches Museum Abteiberg, Mönchengladbach

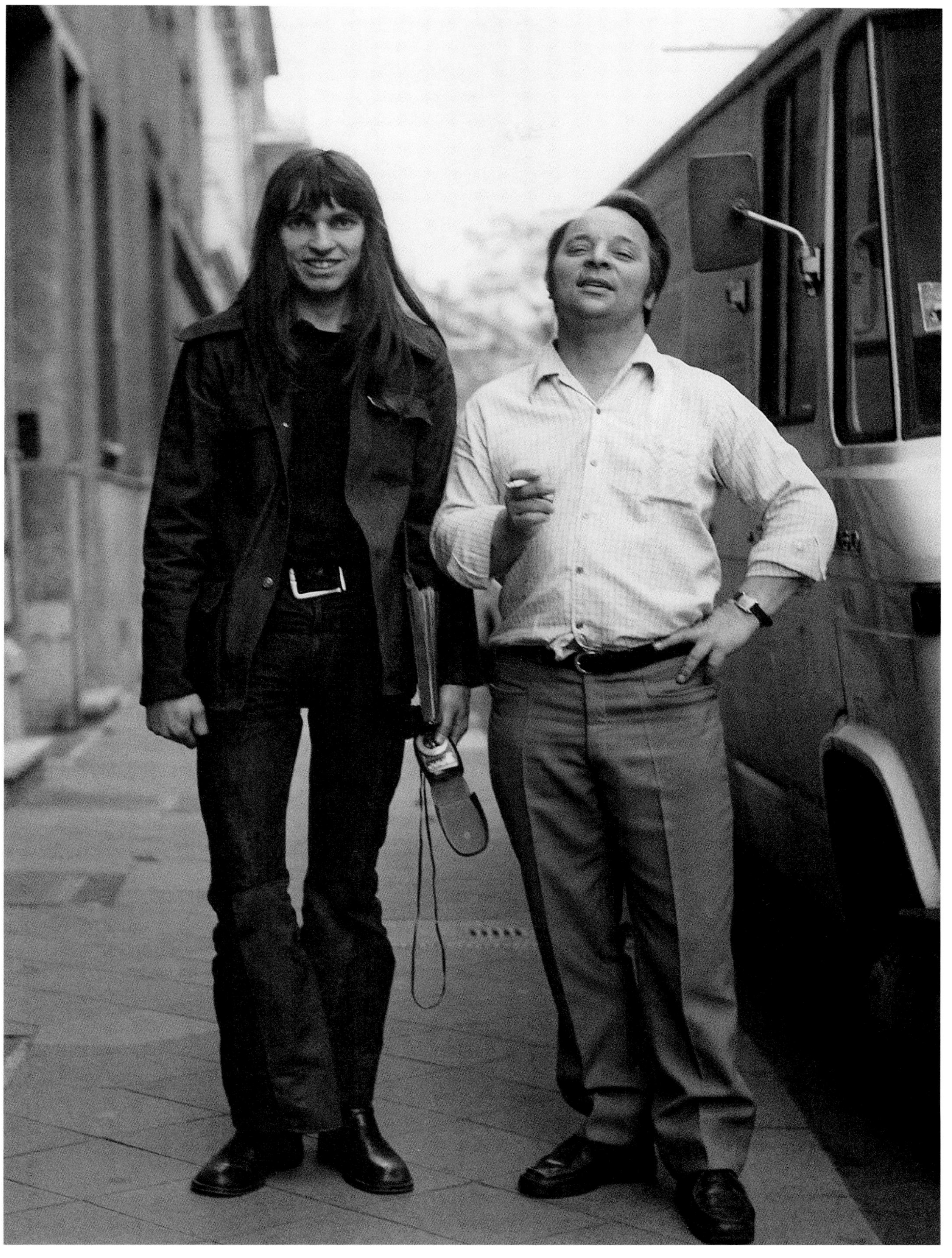

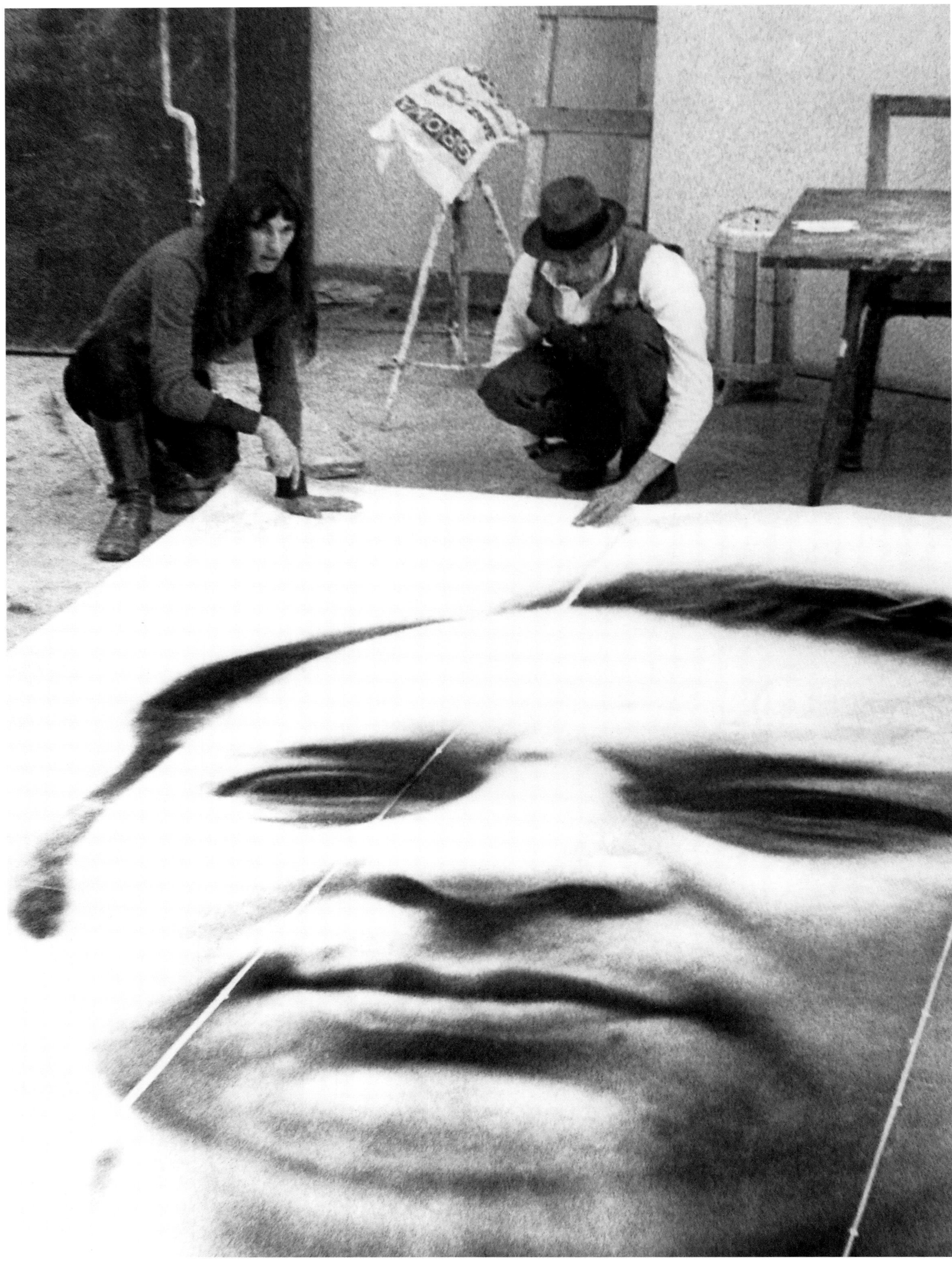

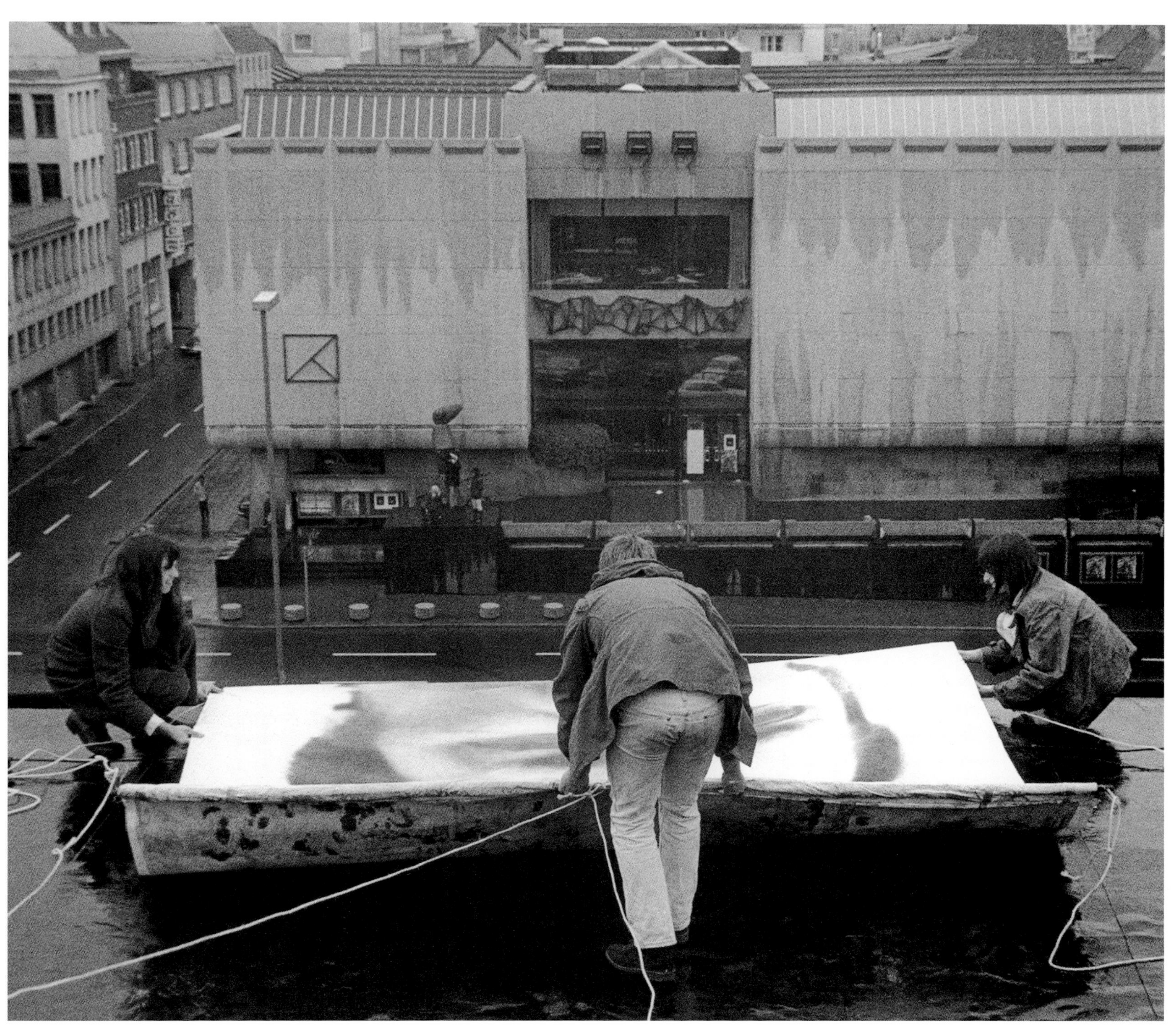

Preparing the work for the exhibition
at the Galerie Konrad Fischer in Beuys' studio in Düsseldorf

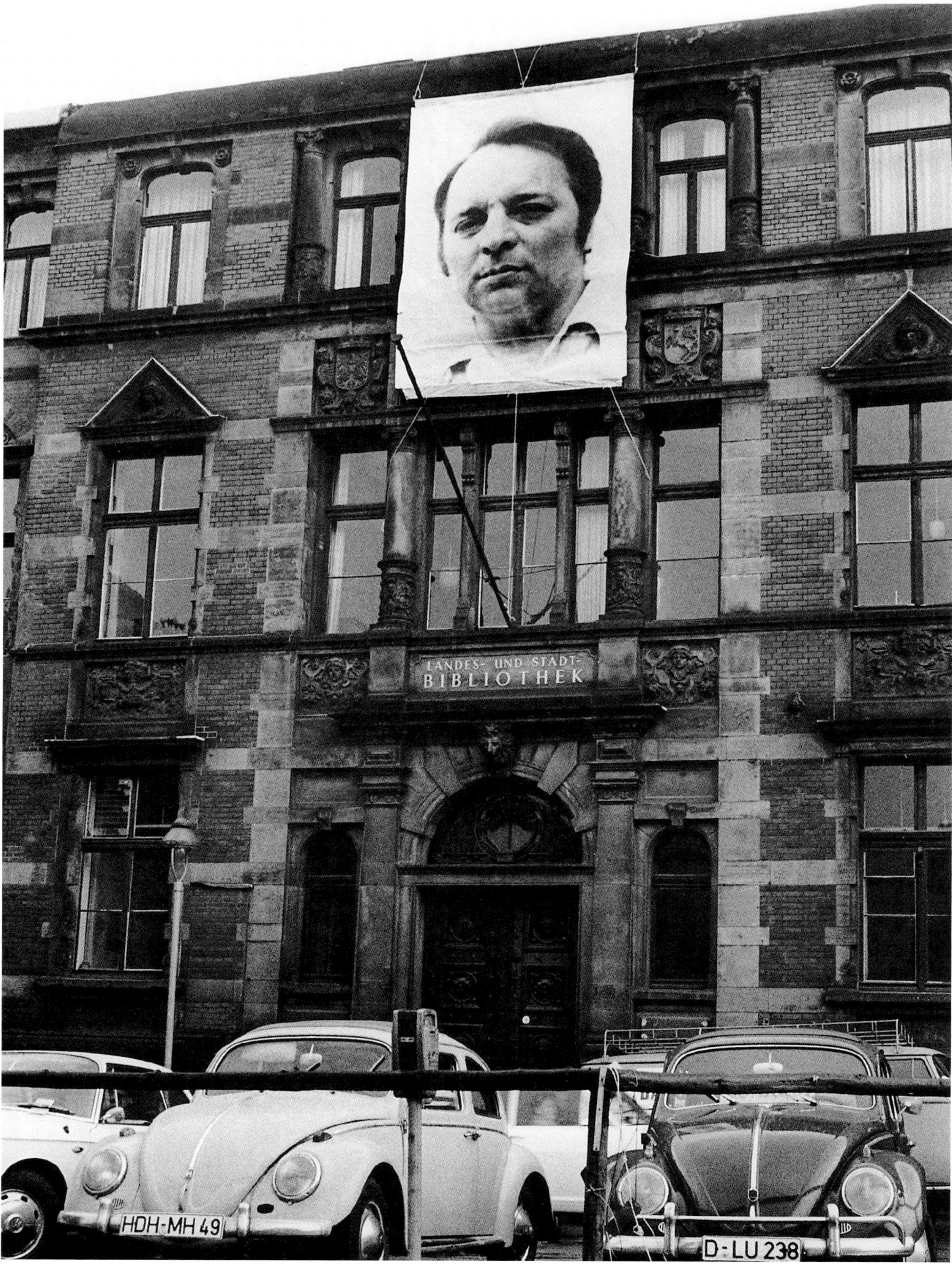

Grebbeplatz, Düsseldorf, 1972

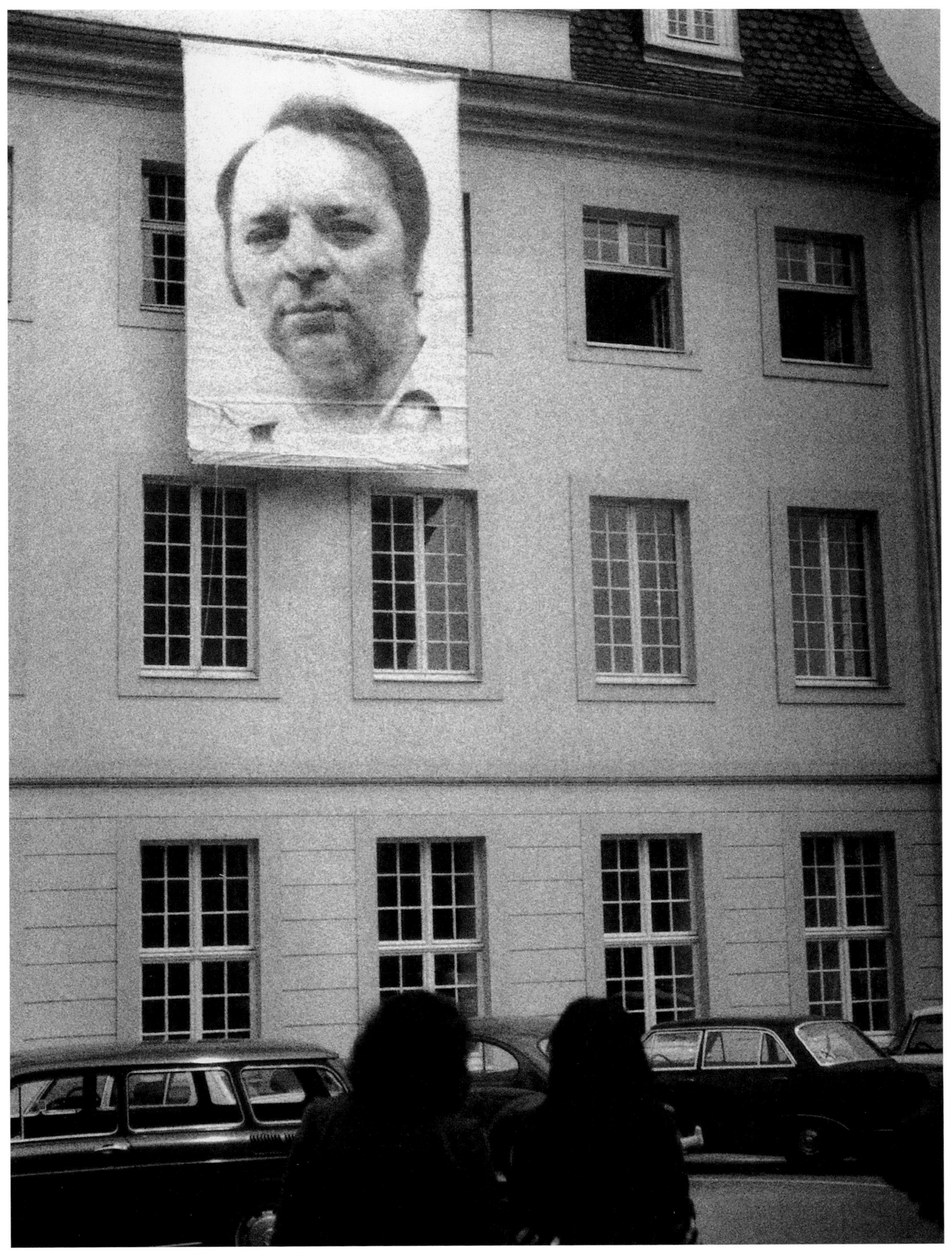

Documenta V, Kassel, 1972

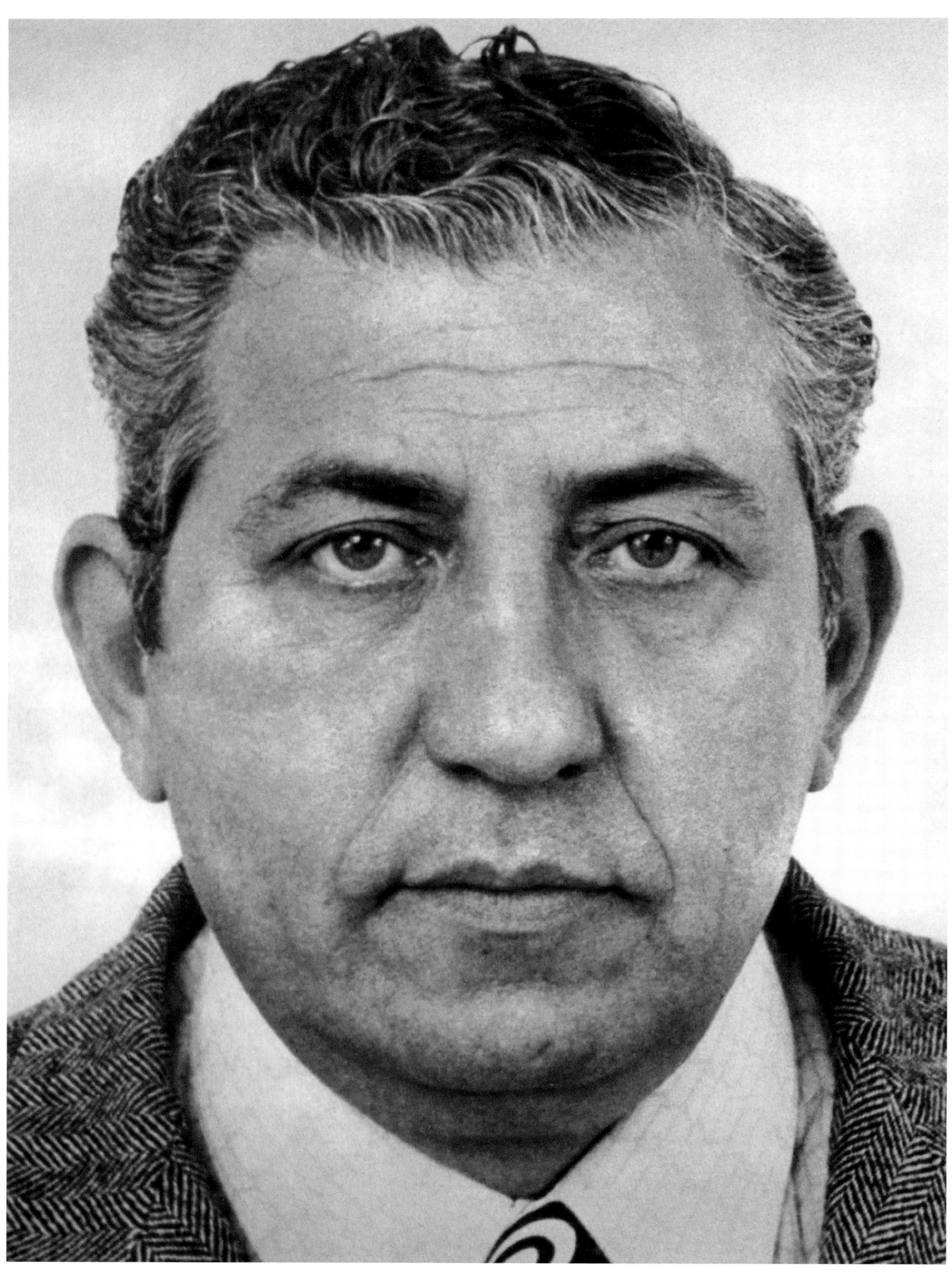

Casual Passer-by I met at 5 PM, Naples, 1971
Collection: Lucio Amelio, Naples

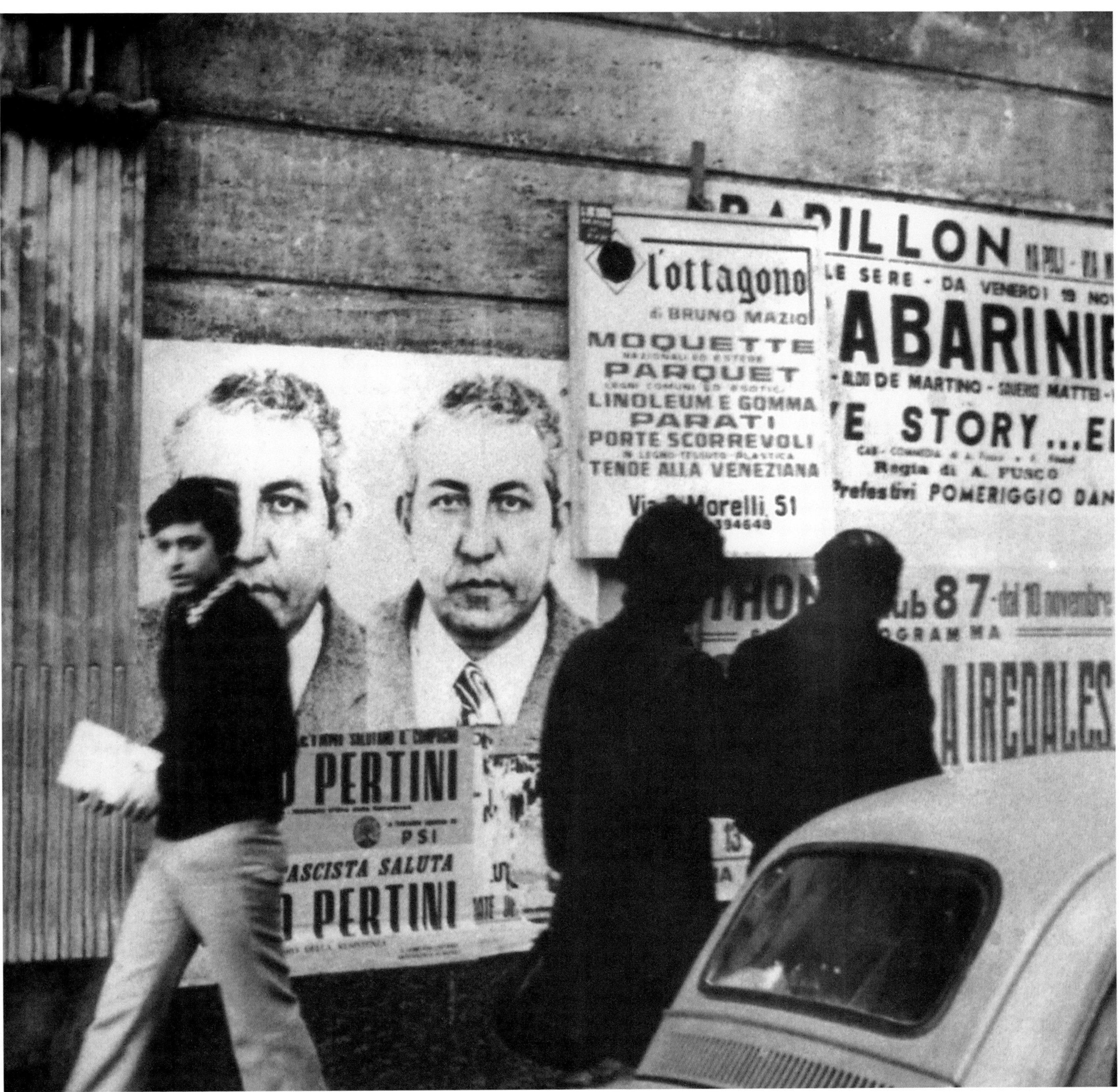
l'ottagono
di BRUNO MAZIO
MOQUETTE
PARQUET
LINOLEUM E GOMMA
PARATI
PORTE SCORREVOLI
TENDE ALLA VENEZIANA
Morelli, 51
ILLON
DA VENERDI 19
ABARINIE
DE MARTINO
STORY
Regia di A. FUSCO
Prefestivi POMERIGGIO
87 - dal 10 novembre
IREDALES
PERTINI
PSI
ASCISTA SALUTA
PERTINI

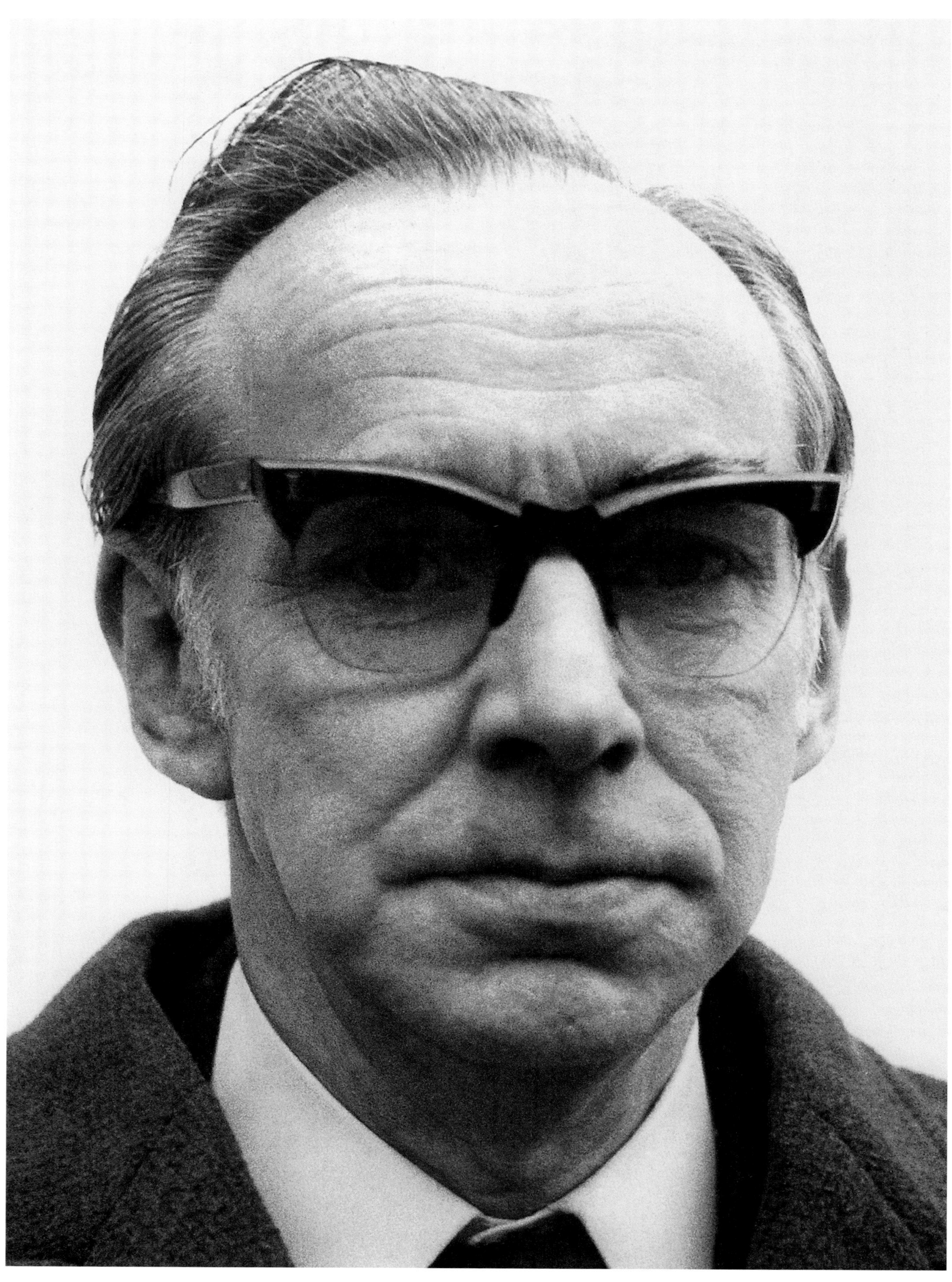

Casual Passer-by I met at 11:28 AM, London, 1972
Collection: Tate Gallery, London

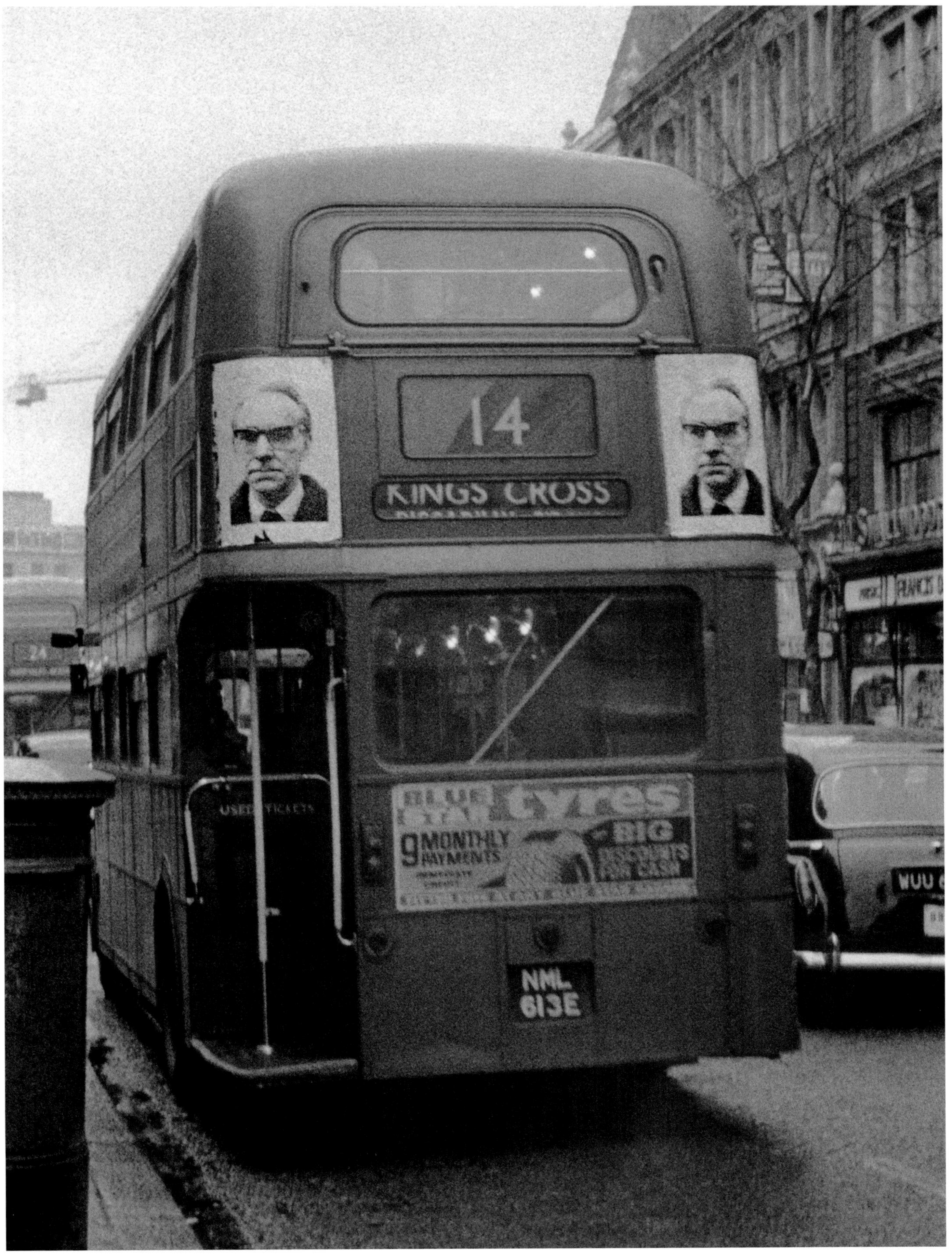
14
KINGS CROSS
USED TICKETS
tyres
9 MONTHLY PAYMENTS
BIG DISCOUNTS FOR CASH
NML 613E

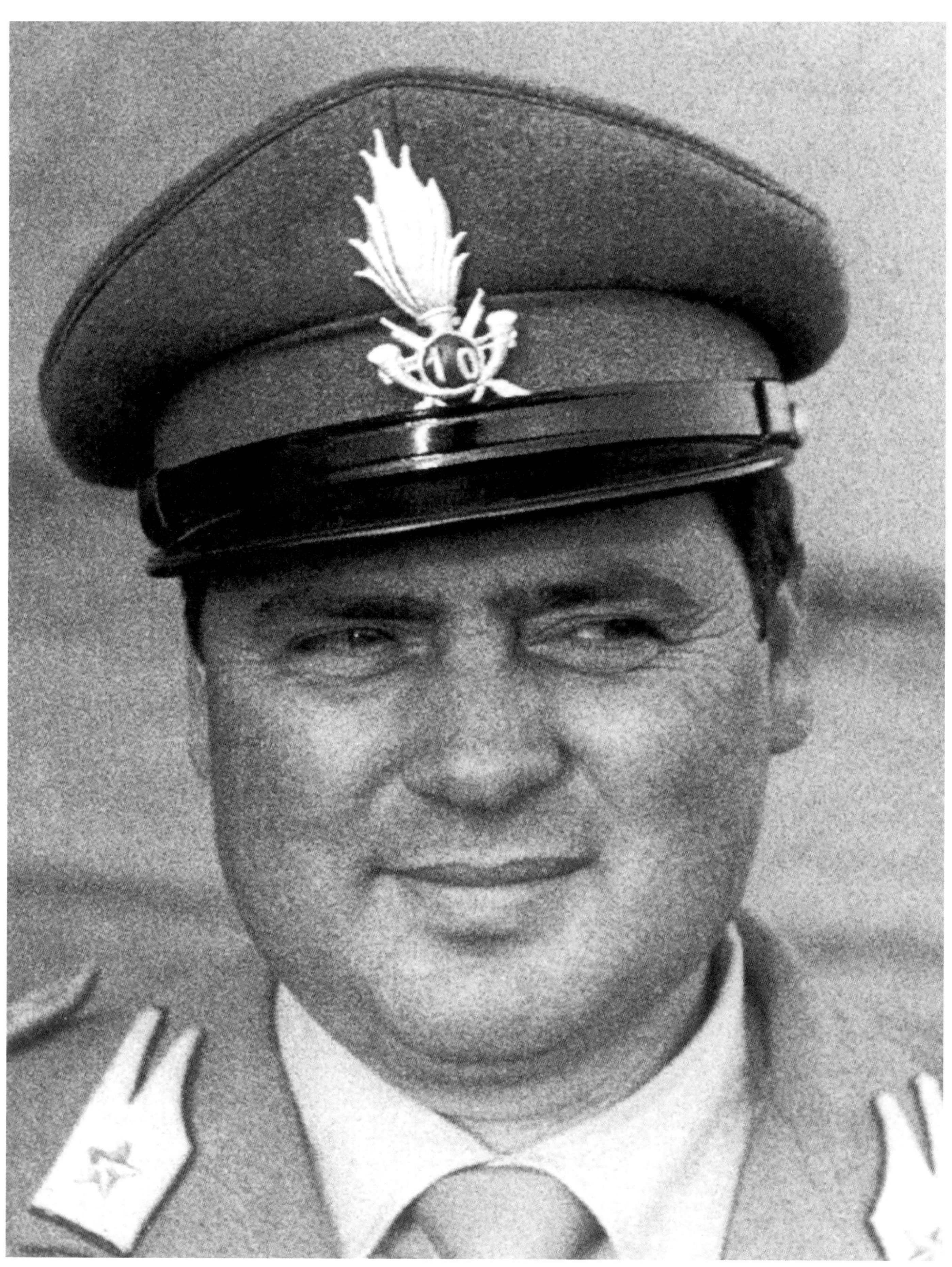

Casual Passer-by I met at 2 PM, Naples, 1971

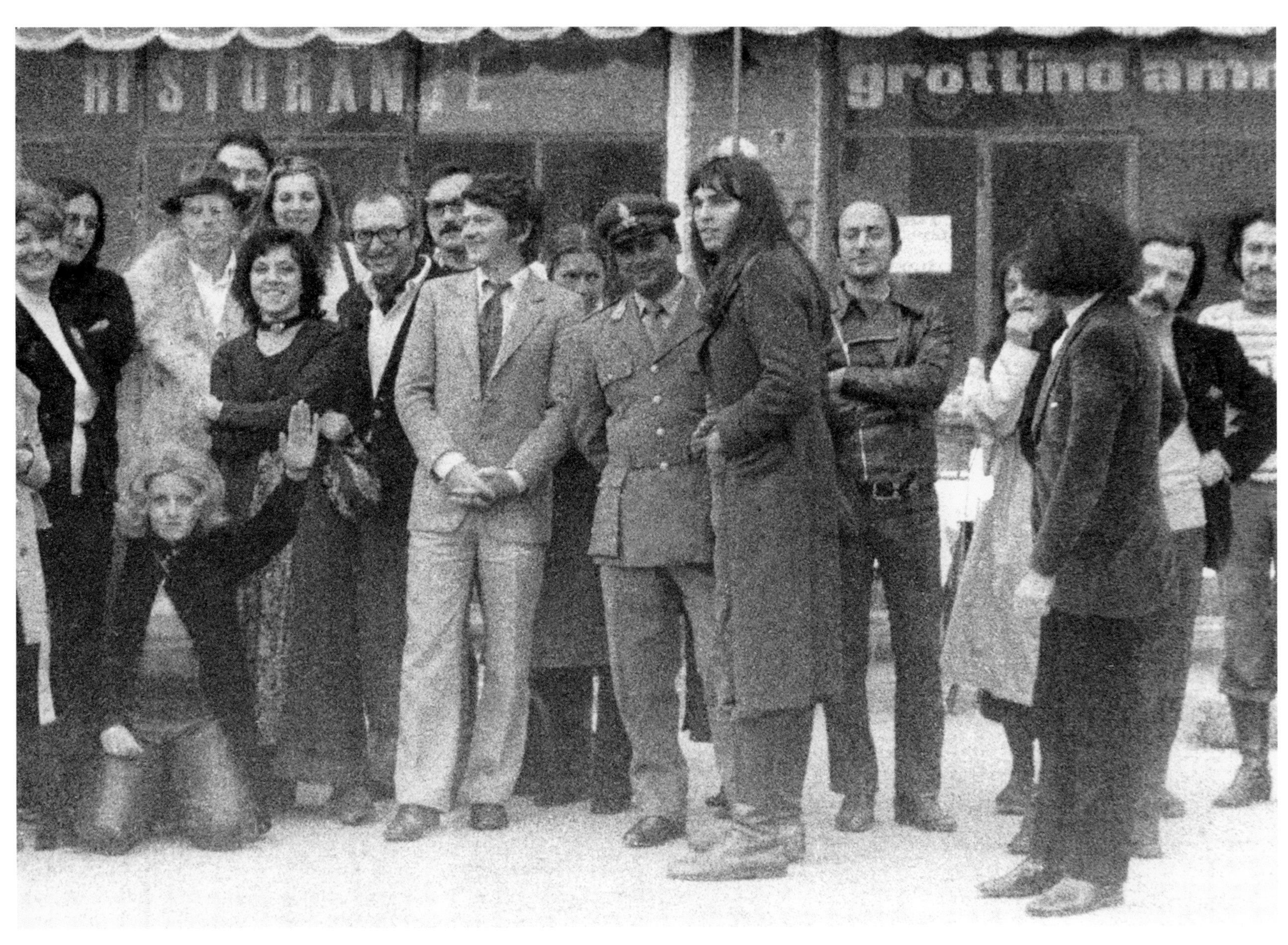

From left to right: Marinella Pirelli, Germano Celant, Mimma Pisani, Joseph Beuys, Lucio Amelio, Diana Alfano, Natalia Fesser, Pasquale Trisorio, Lutz Shirmer, Folker Skulima, Louisa Schubert, Francesco Abatiello, Braco Dimitrijević, Carlo Alfano, Marisa Merz, Vettor Pisani, Achille Bonito Oliva, Jannis Kounellis

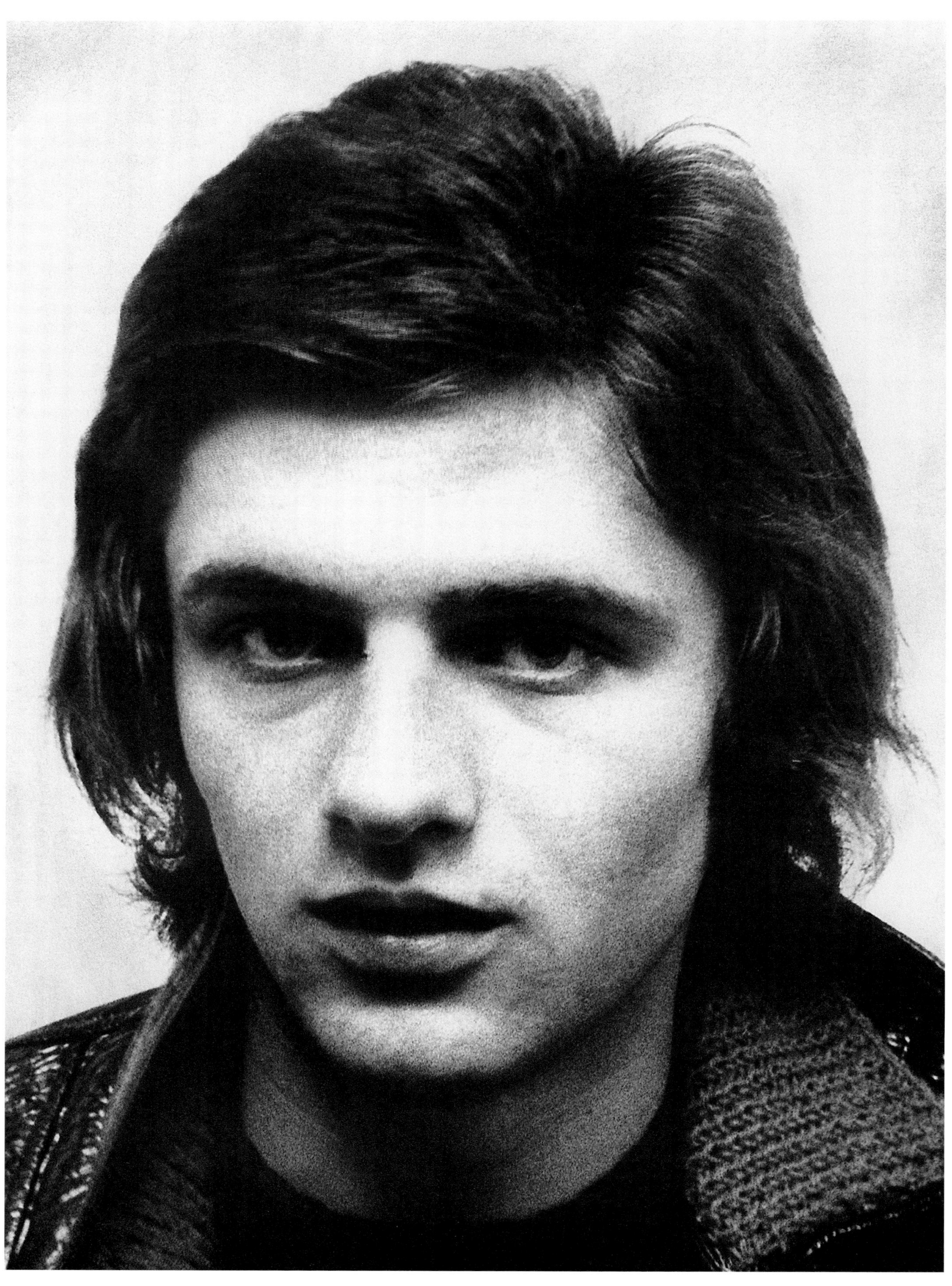

Casual Passer-by I met at 2:55 PM, Milan, 1974
Collection: Museo d'Arte Contemporanea, Trevi

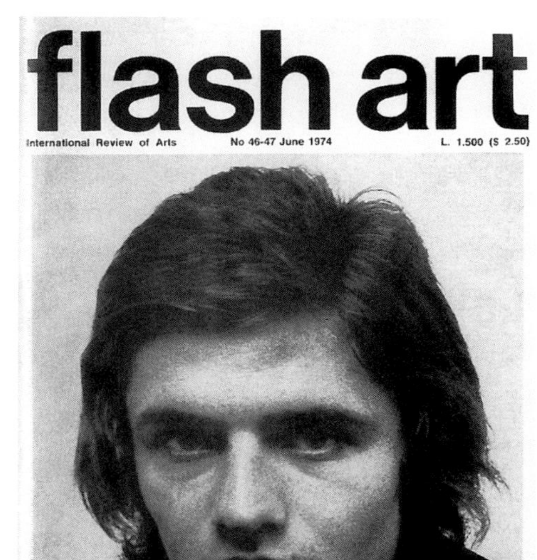

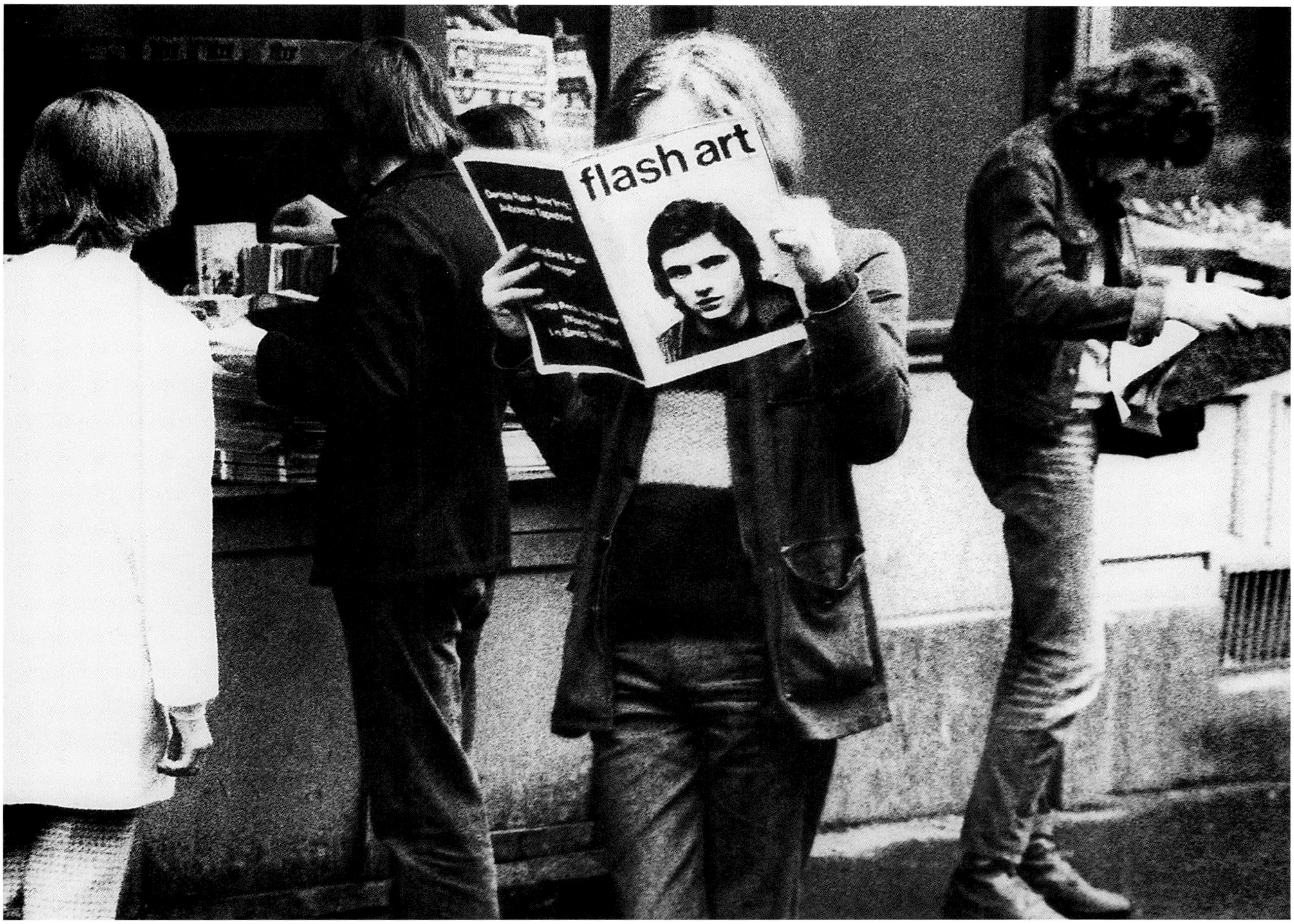

Cover of *Flash Art* magazine with the face of a *Casual Passer-by*, June 1974

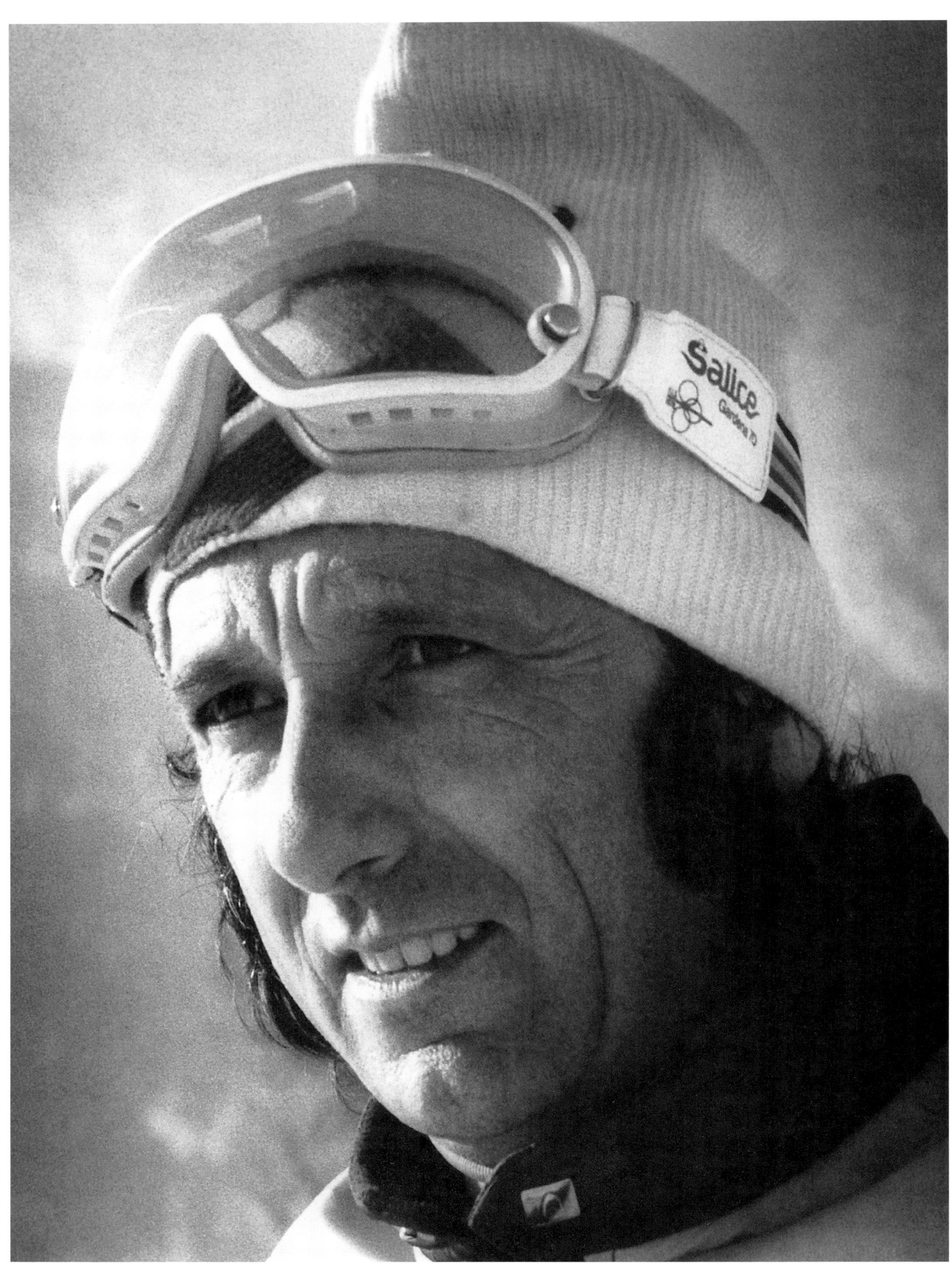

Casual Passer-by I met at 2:39 PM, San Sicario, 1974

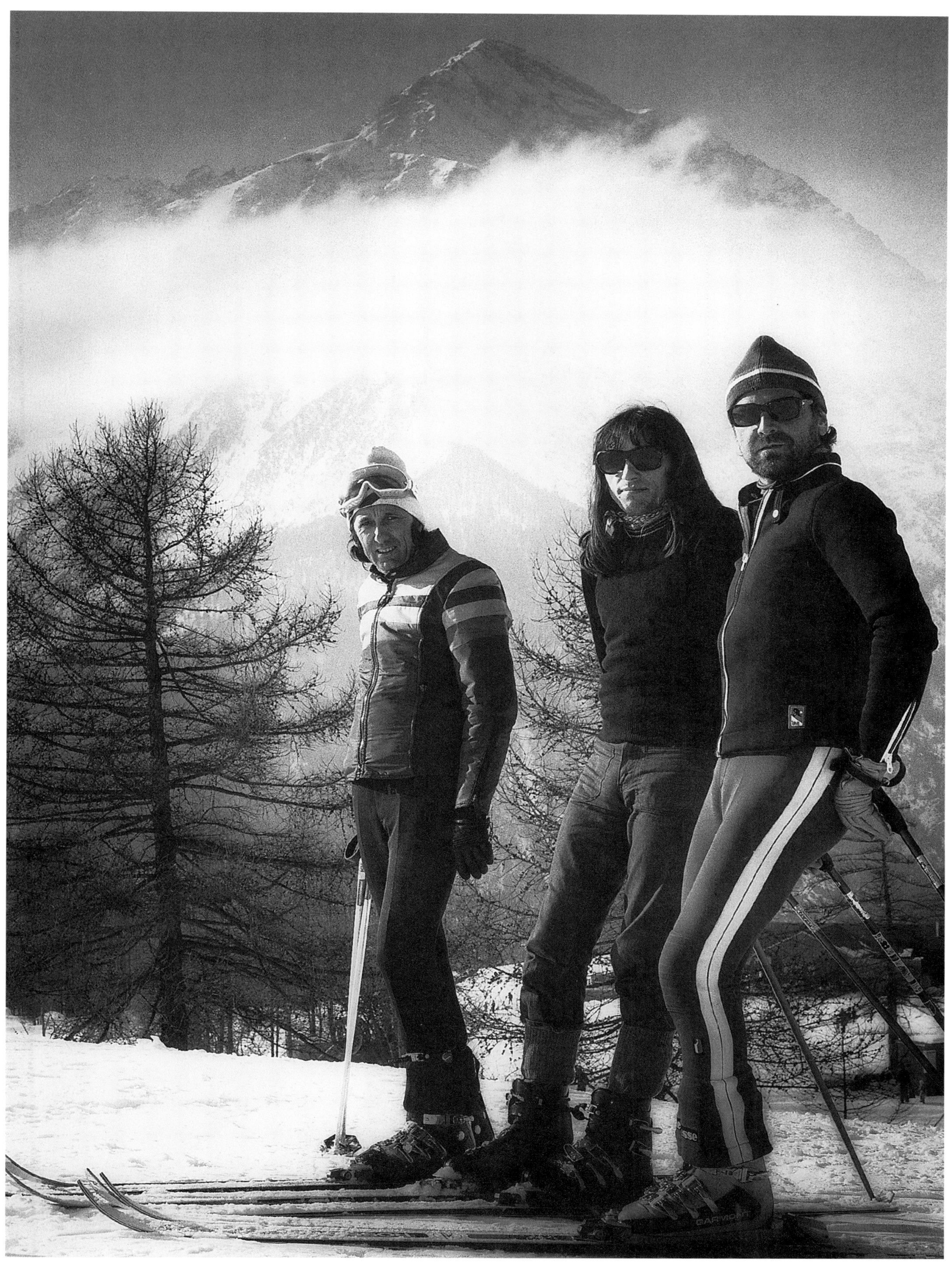

From left to right: Emilio Chiosso, Braco Dimitrijević, Michelangelo Pistoletto

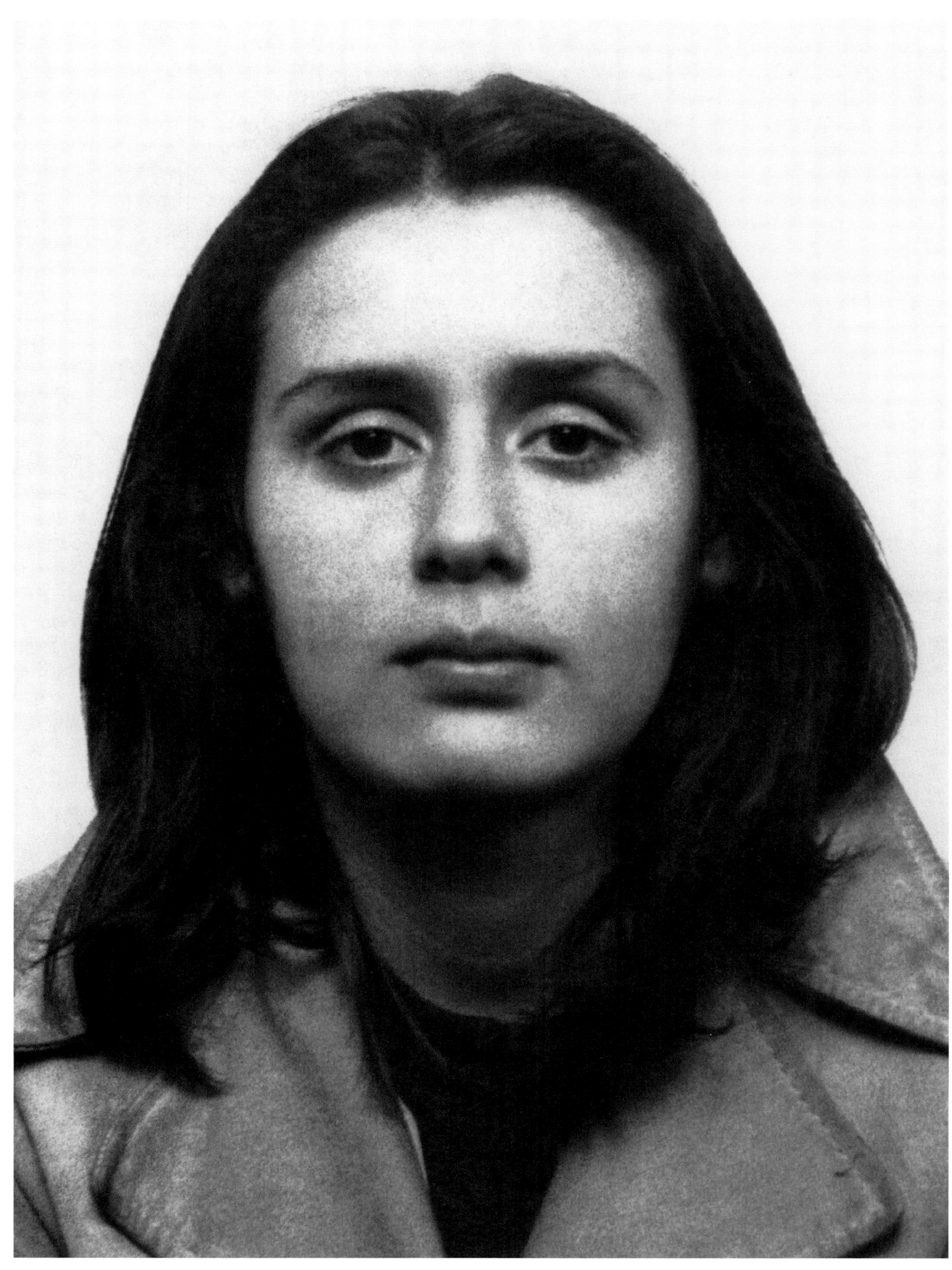

Casual Passer-by I met at 11:20 AM, Turin, 1974
Collection: Dacic, Tubingen

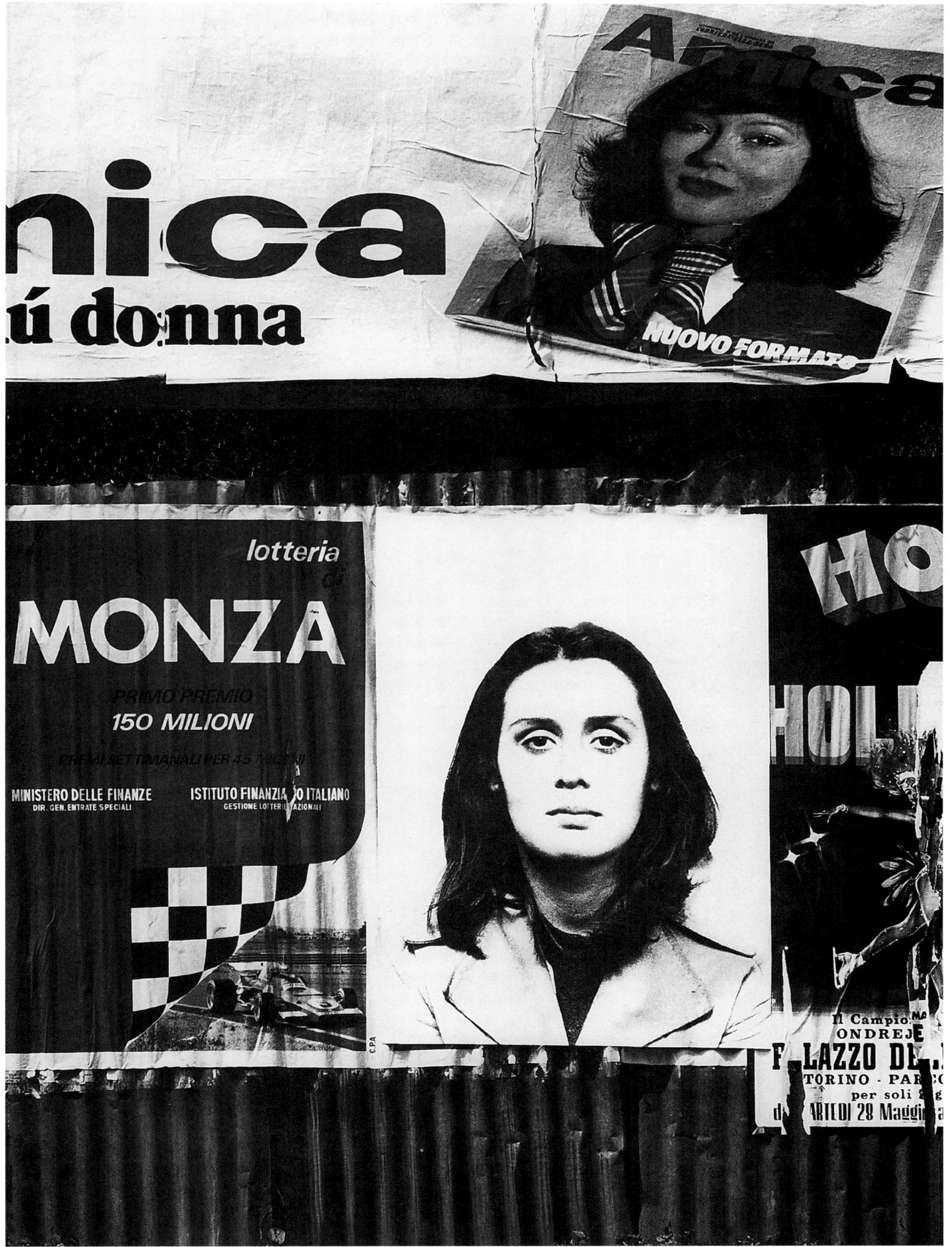
nica
ú donna
NUOVO FORMATO
lotteria
MONZA
PRIMO PREMIO
150 MILIONI
MINISTERO DELLE FINANZE
DIR. GEN. ENTRATE SPECIALI
GESTIONE LOTTERIE
C.P.A.
Il Campio
ONDREJ
LAZZO DE
TORINO - PARC
per soli
28 Maggi

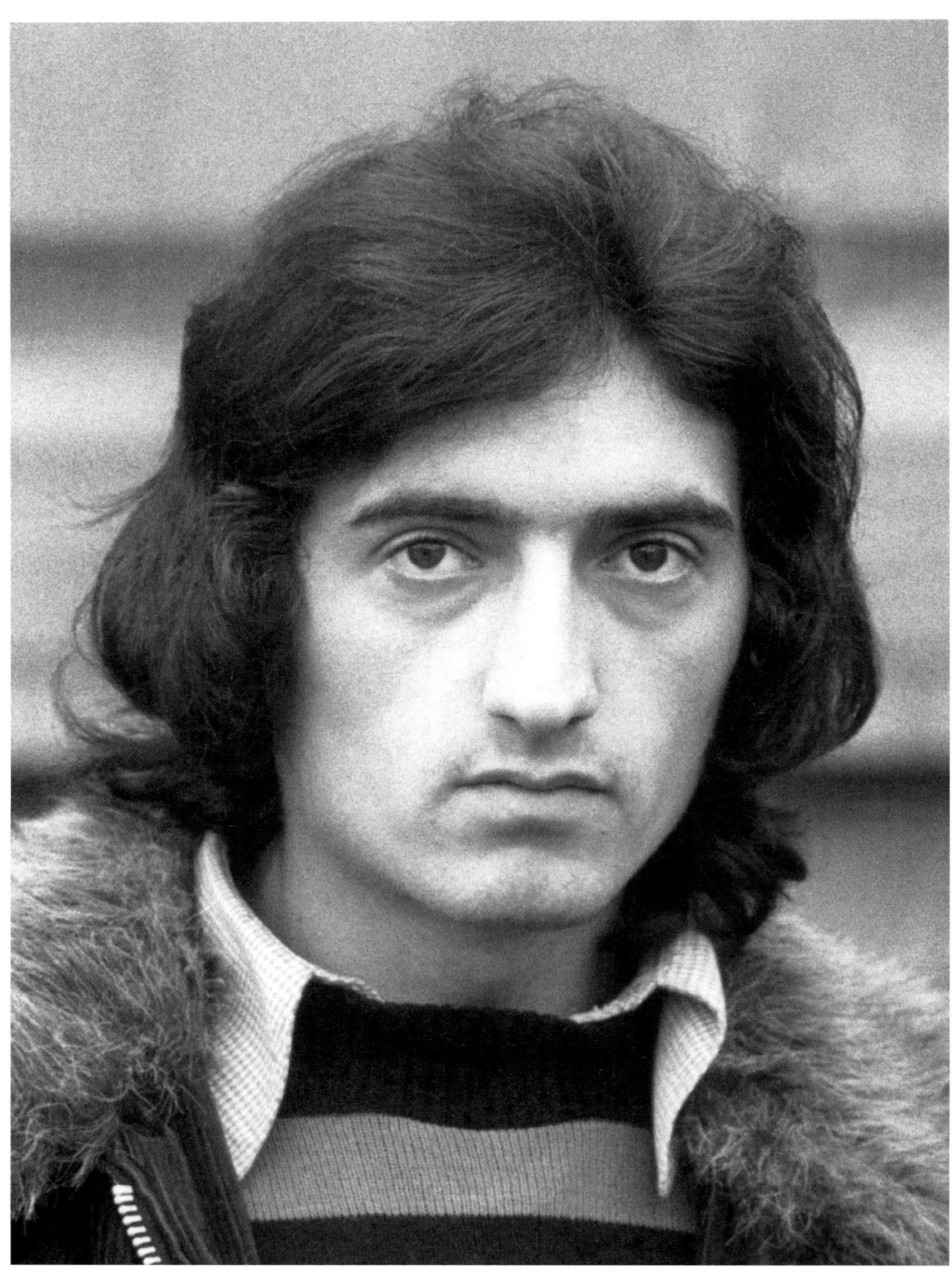

Casual Passer-by I met at 4:43 PM, Milan, 1974
Courtesy Galerie Françoise Lambert, Milan

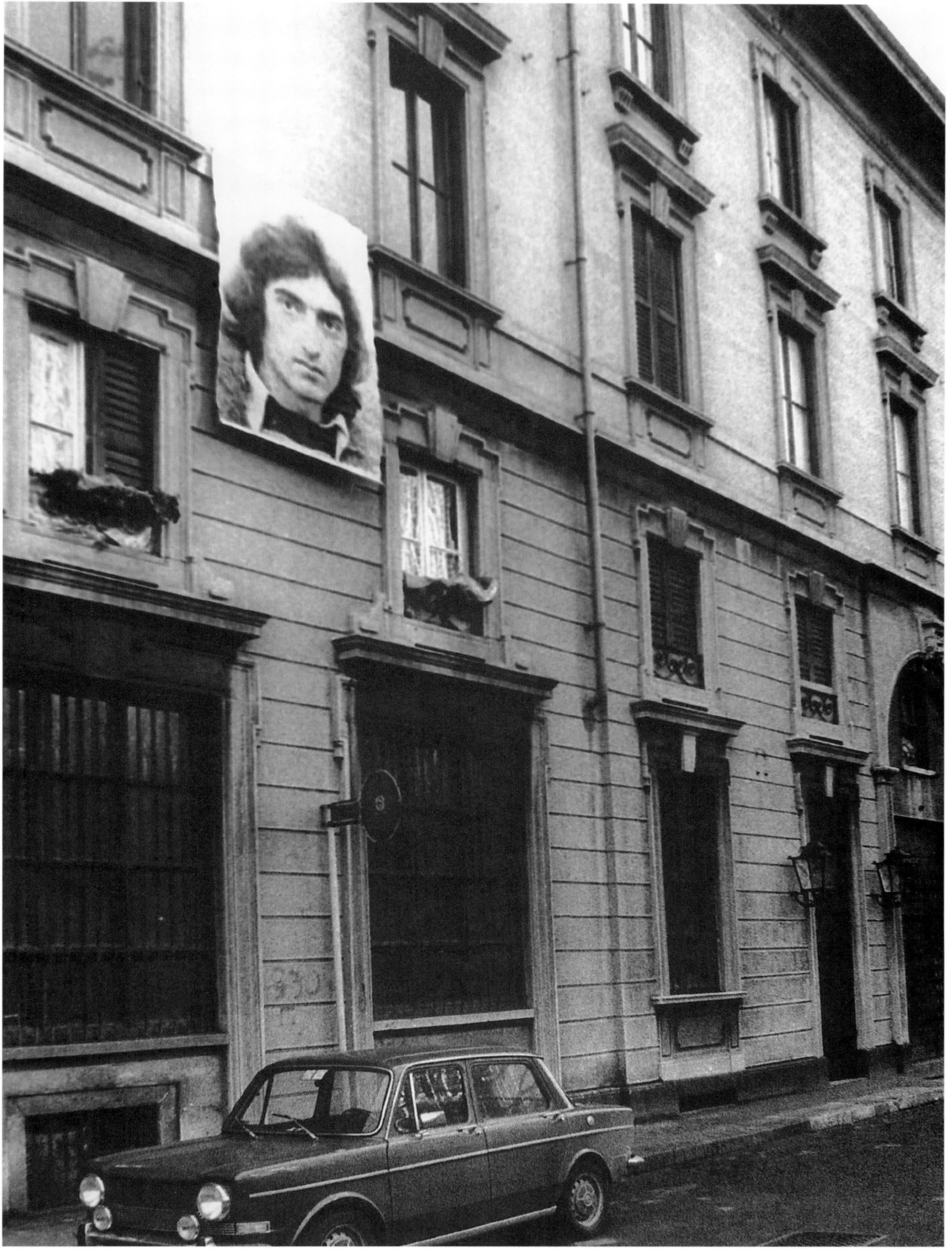

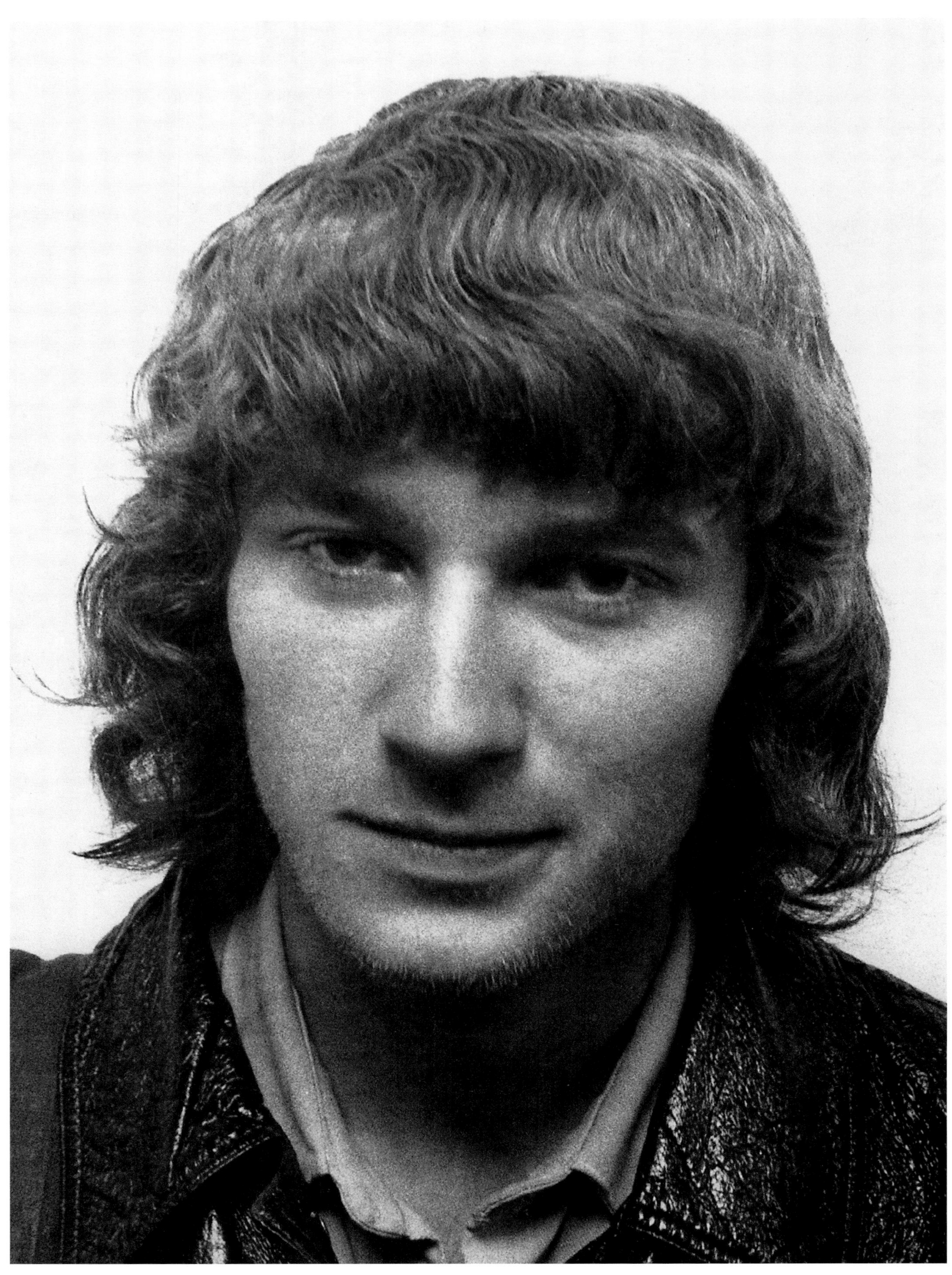

Casual Passer-by I met at 4:57 PM, Edinburgh, 1975
Collection: Scottish National Gallery of Modern Art, Edinburgh

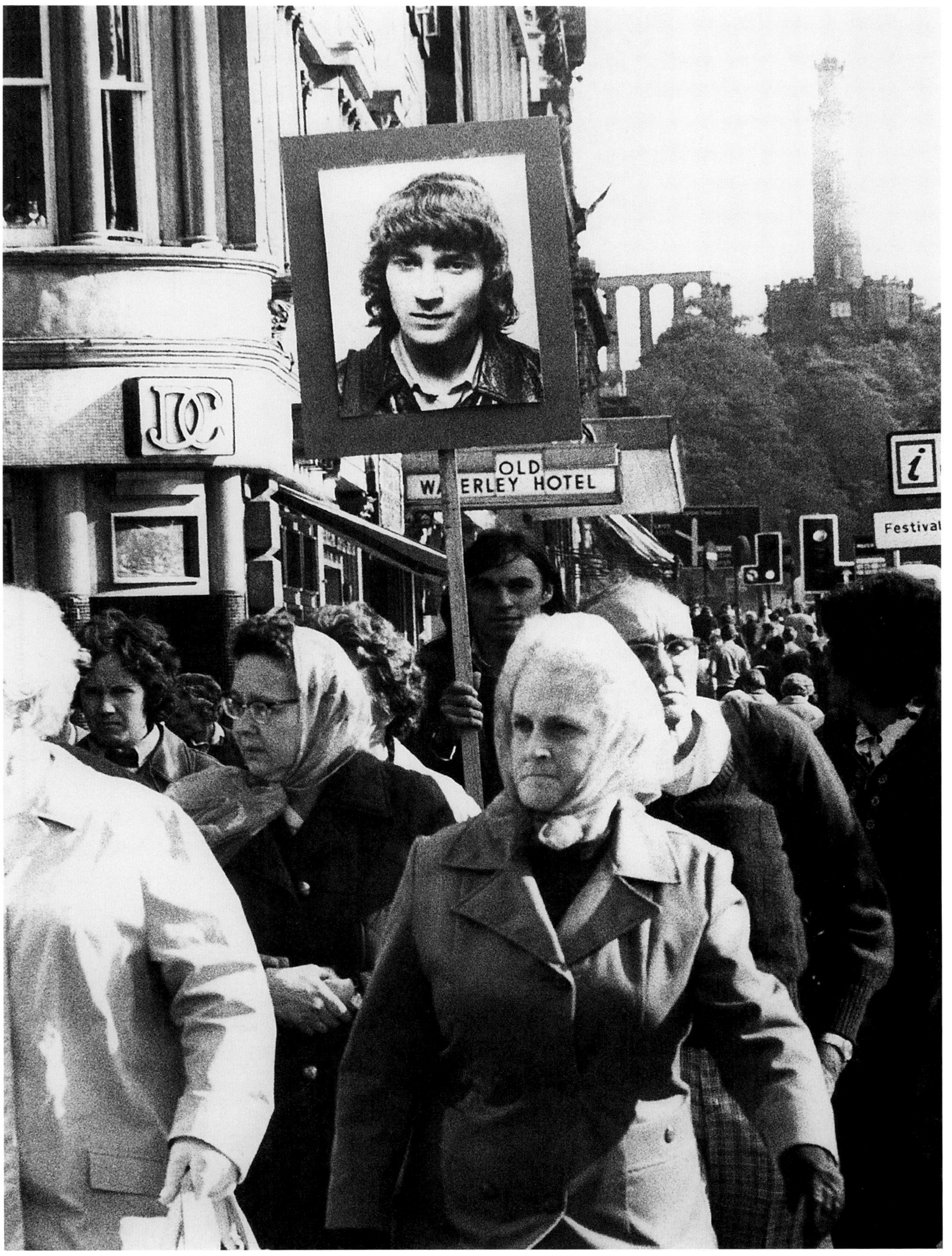
OLD
WA ERLEY HOTEL
Festival

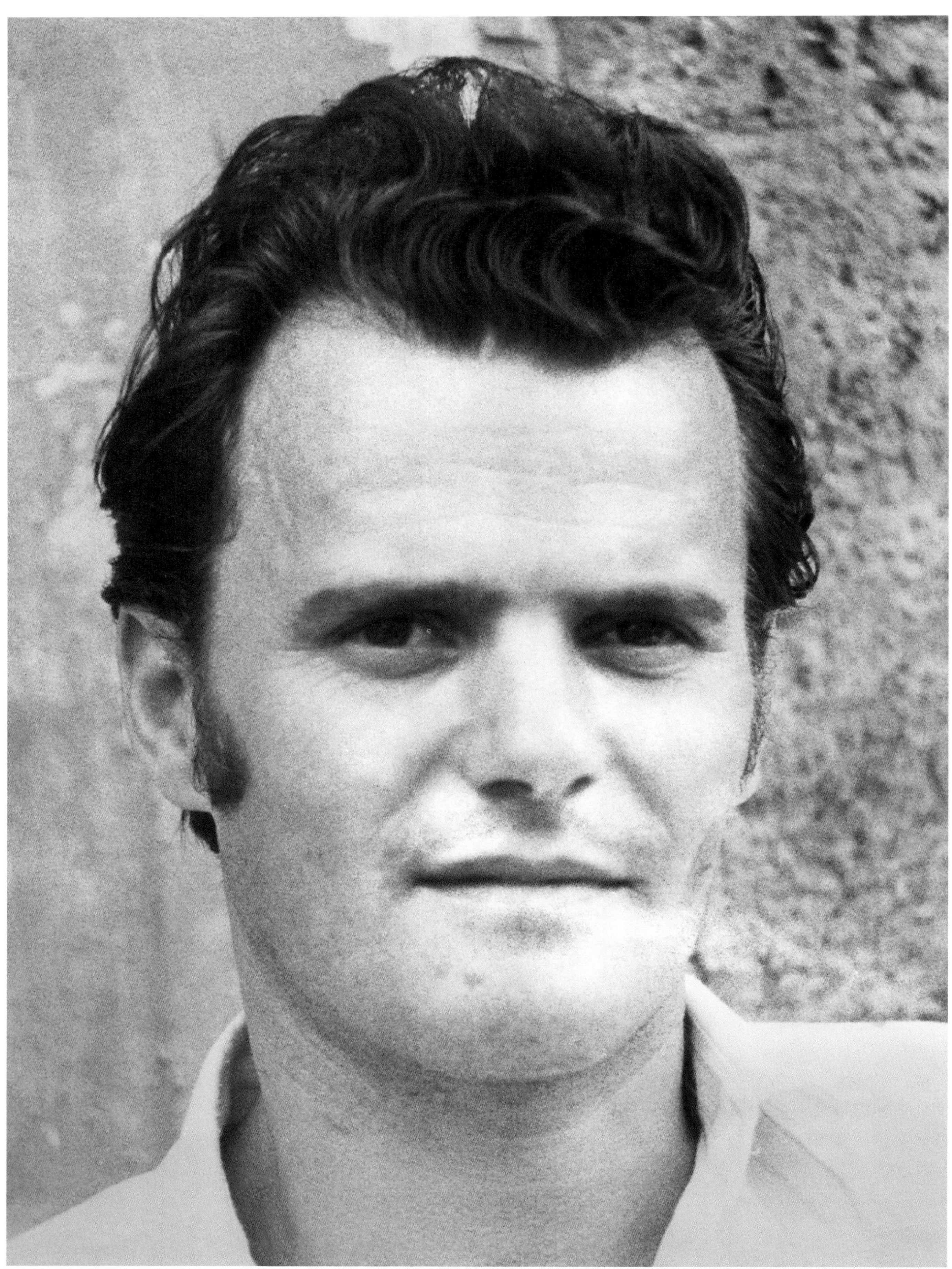

Casual Passer-by I met at 3:04 PM, Rome, 1972

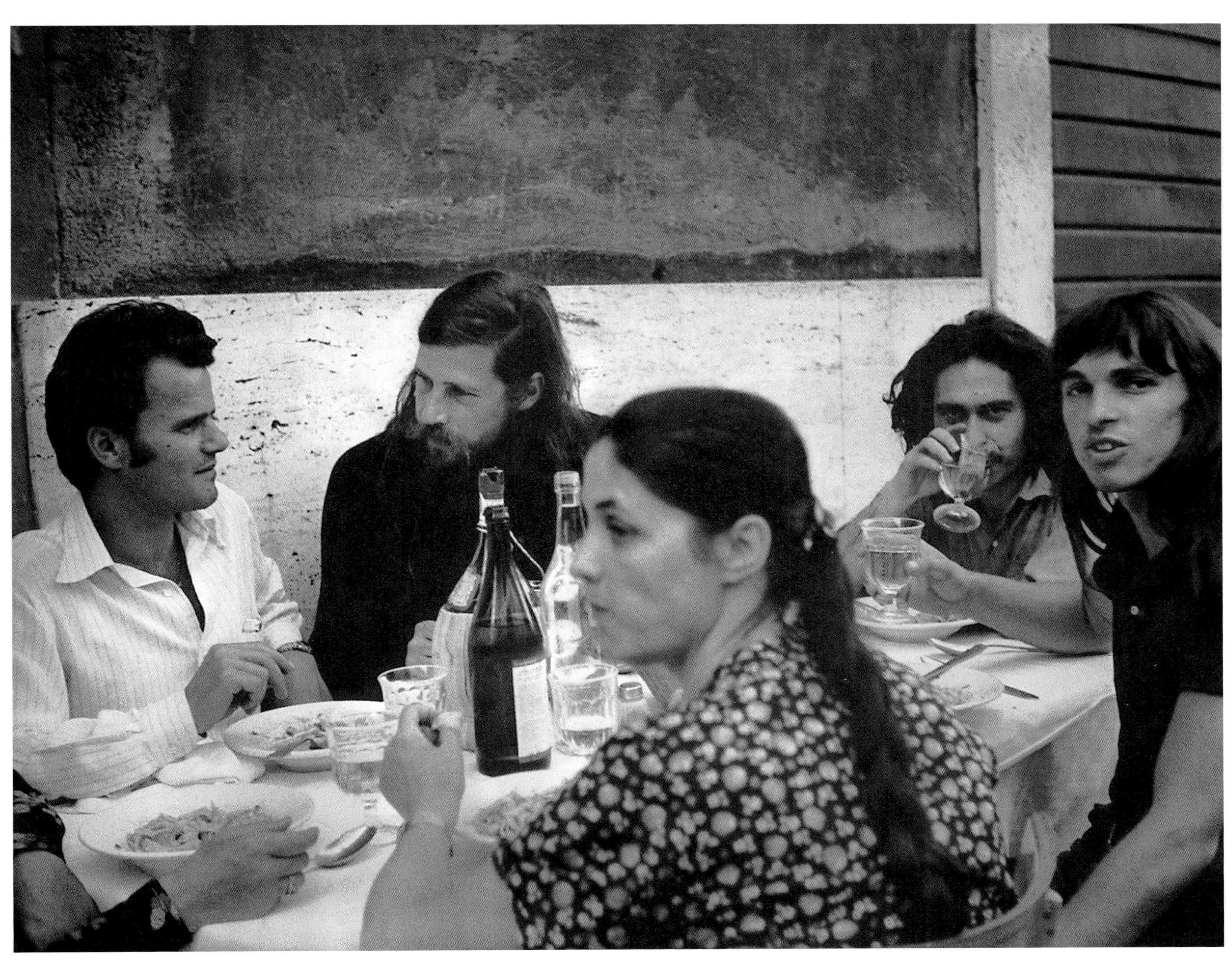

From left to right: Giuseppe Pietrolongo, Willoughby Sharp,
Efi, Jannis Kounellis, Braco Dimitrijević

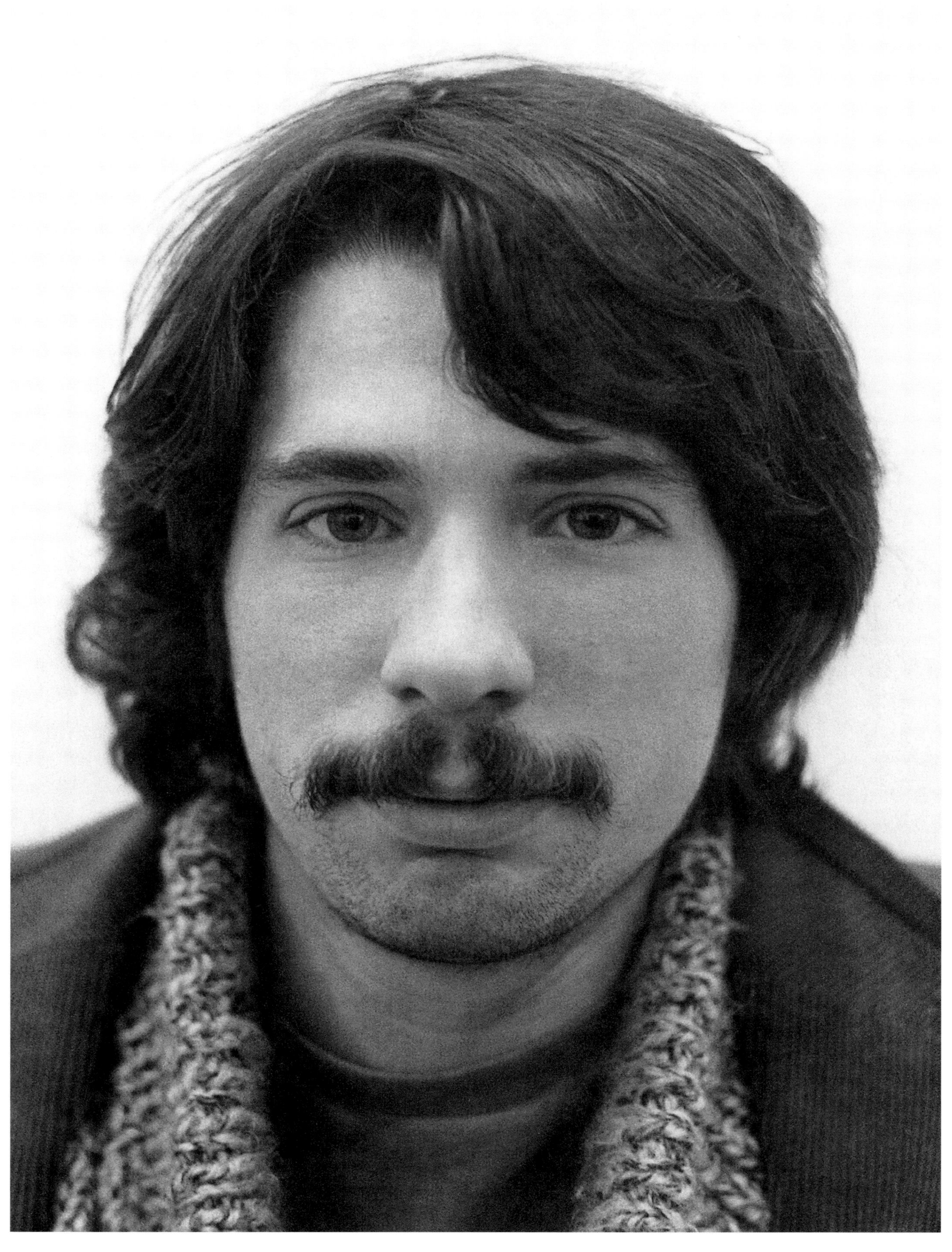

Casual Passer-by I met at 10:11 PM, Berlin, 1976
Collection: Hoffmann, Berlin

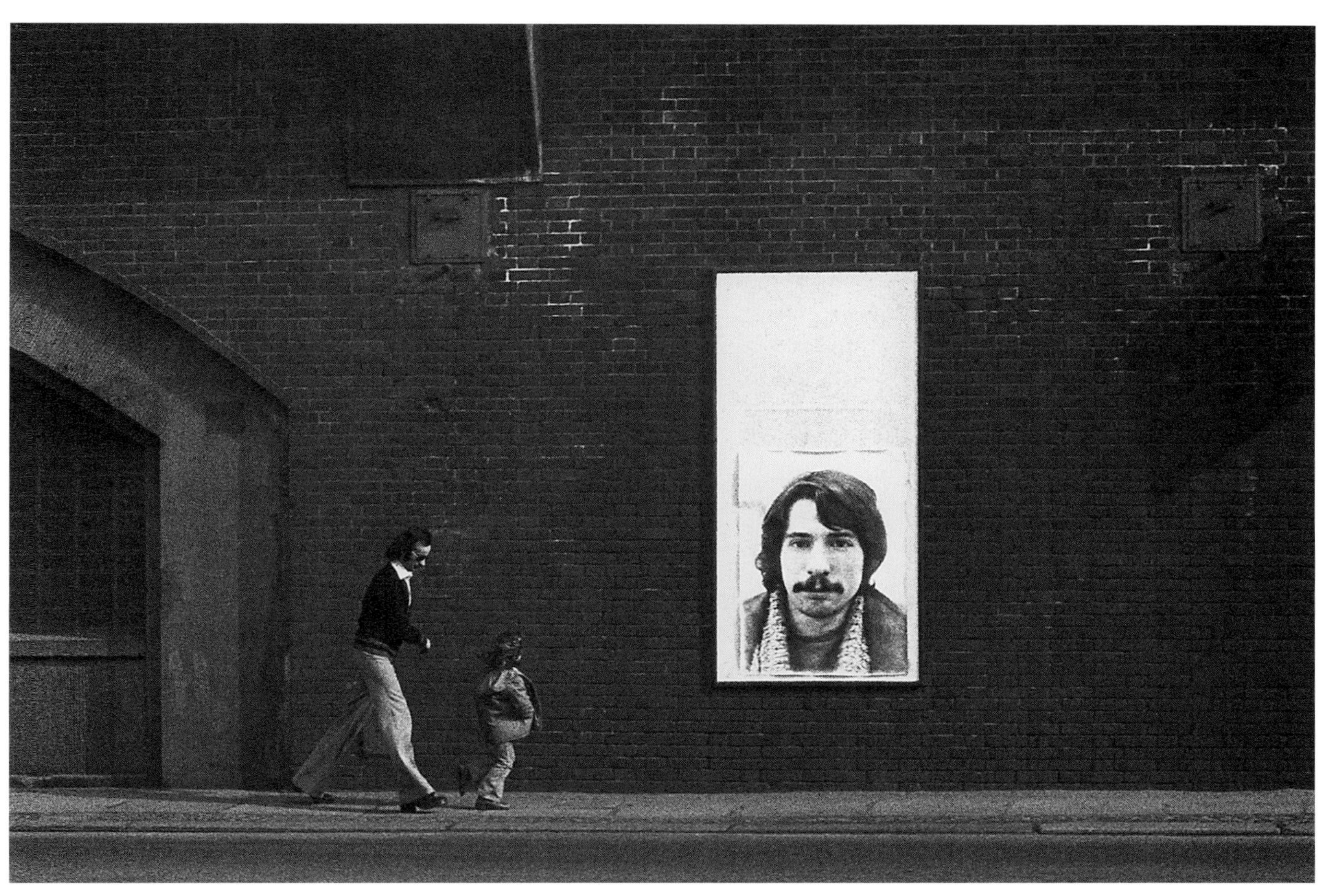

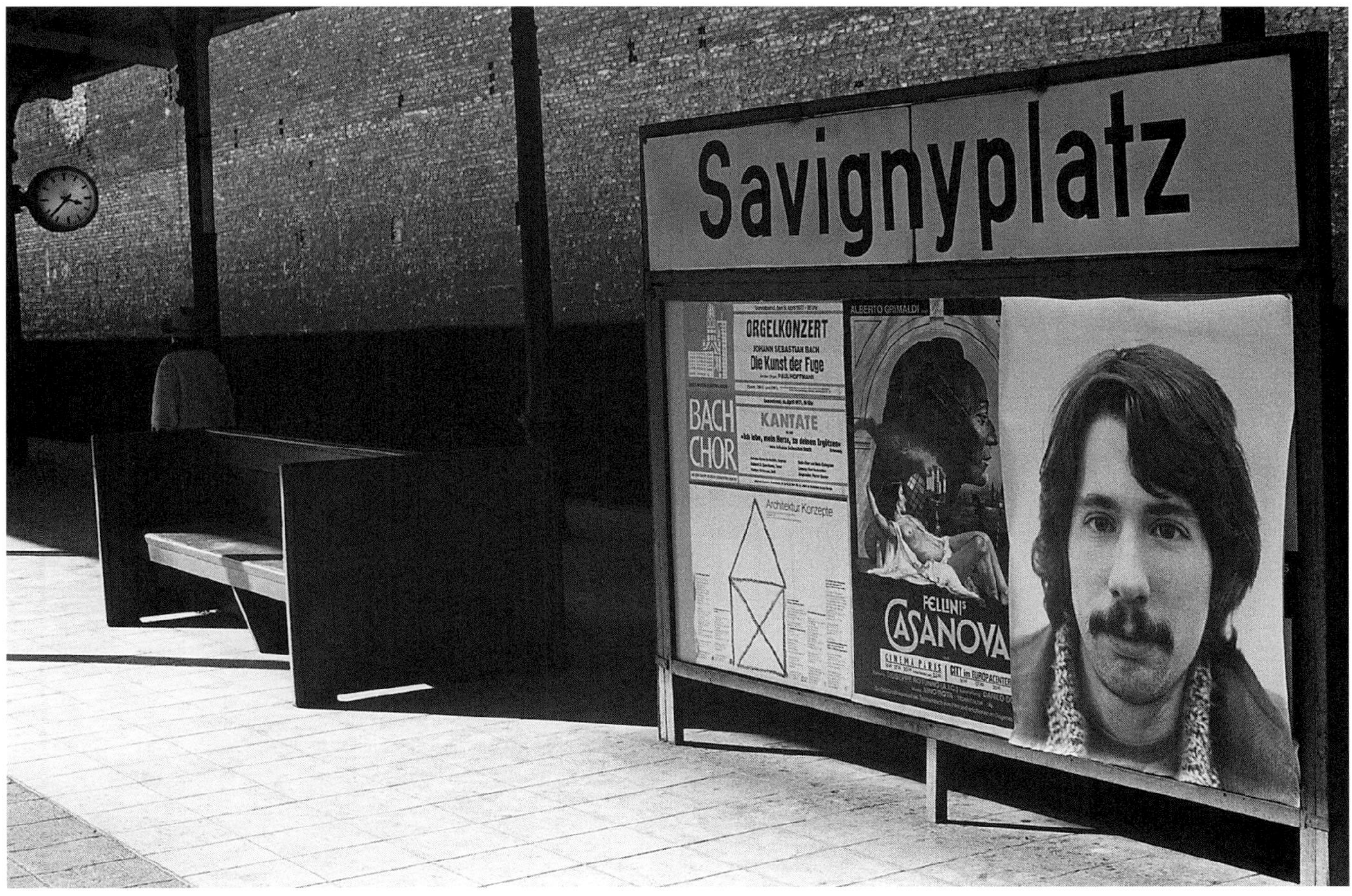
Savignyplatz
ORGELKONZERT
JOHANN SEBASTIAN BACH
Die Kunst der Fuge
BACH
CHOR
KANTATE
Architektur Konzepte
ALBERTO GRIMALDI
FELLINI's
CASANOVA
CINEMA PARIS

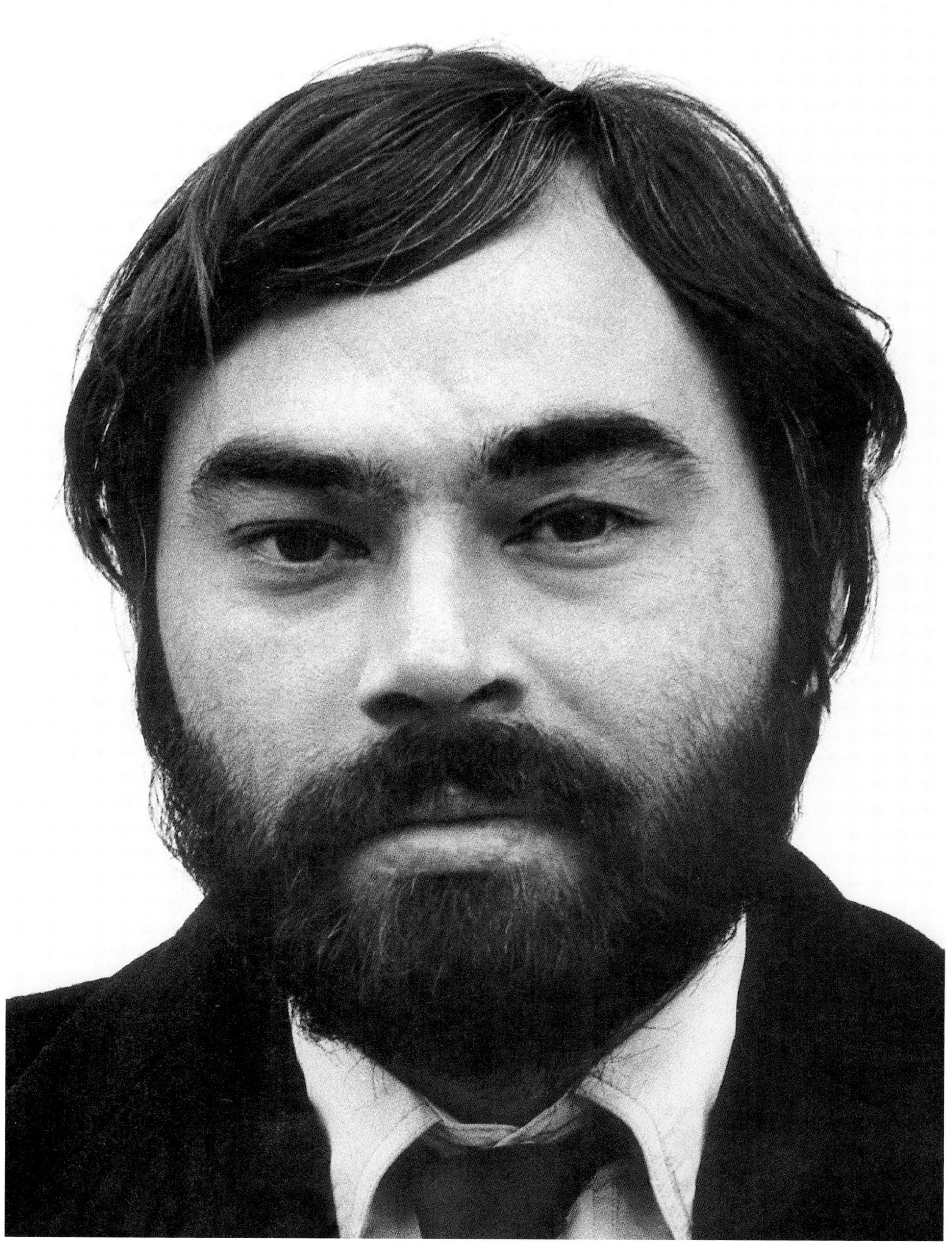

Casual Passer-by I met at 1:14 PM, London, 1978
Private Collection, Oxford

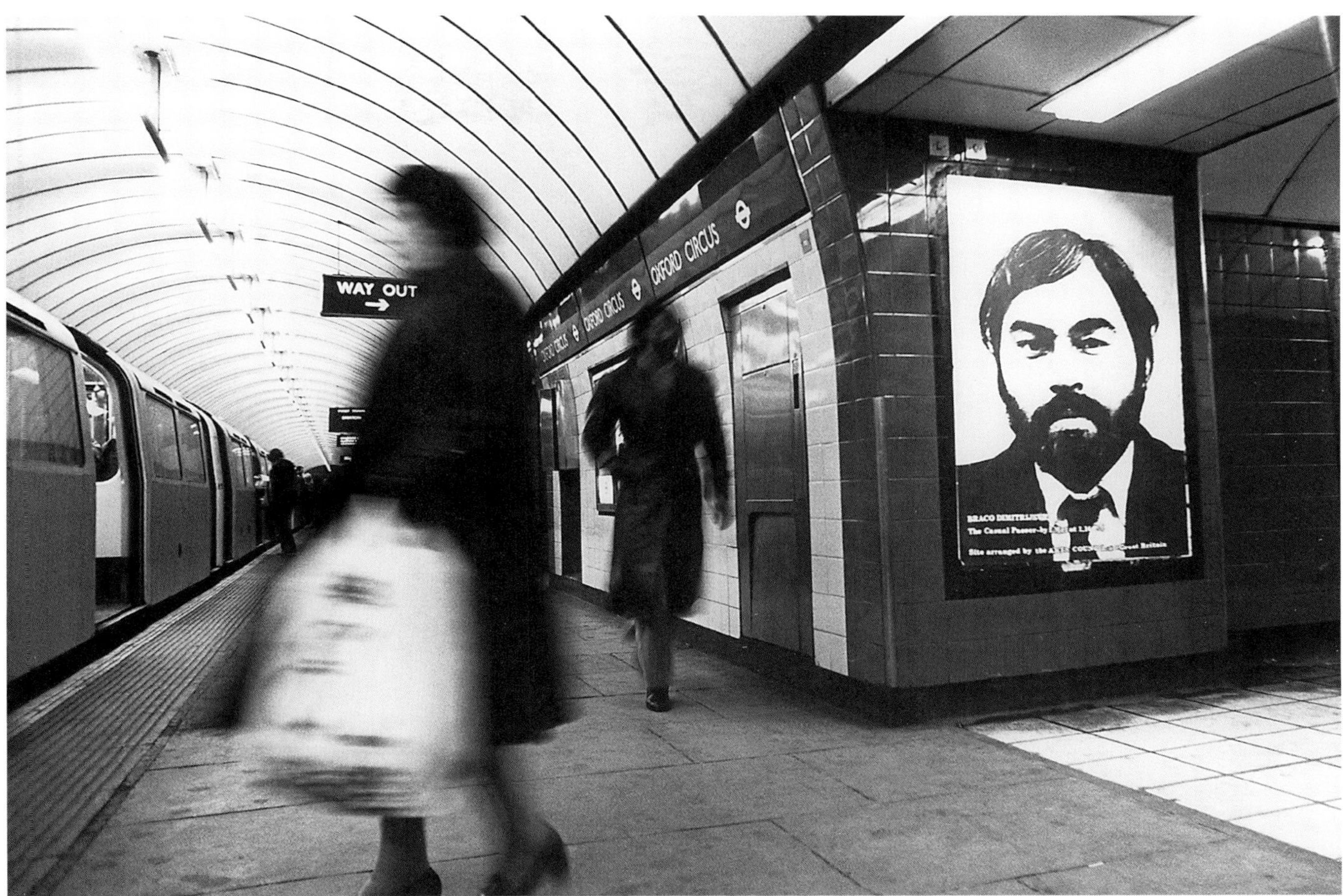

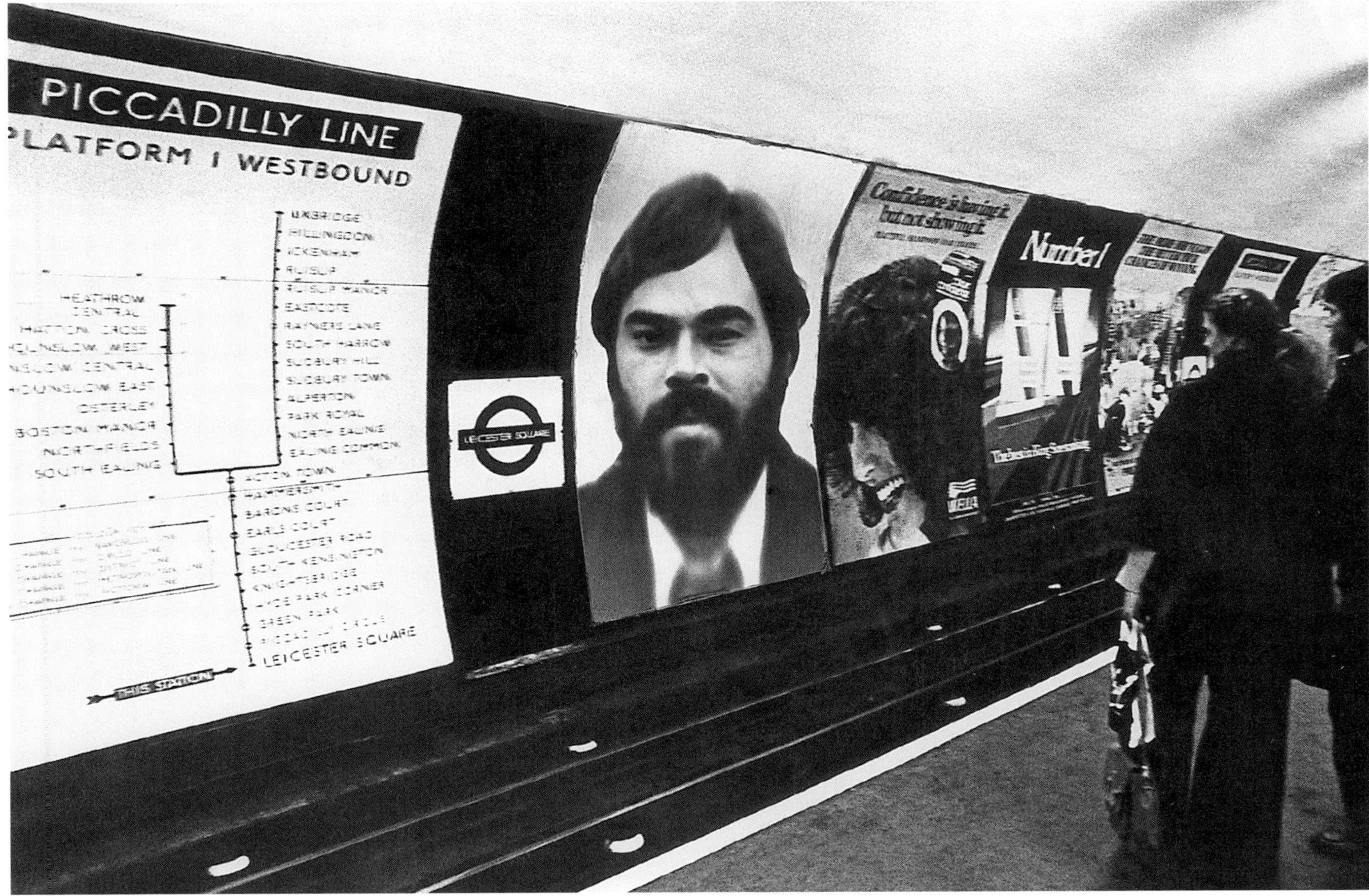

London Underground Stations

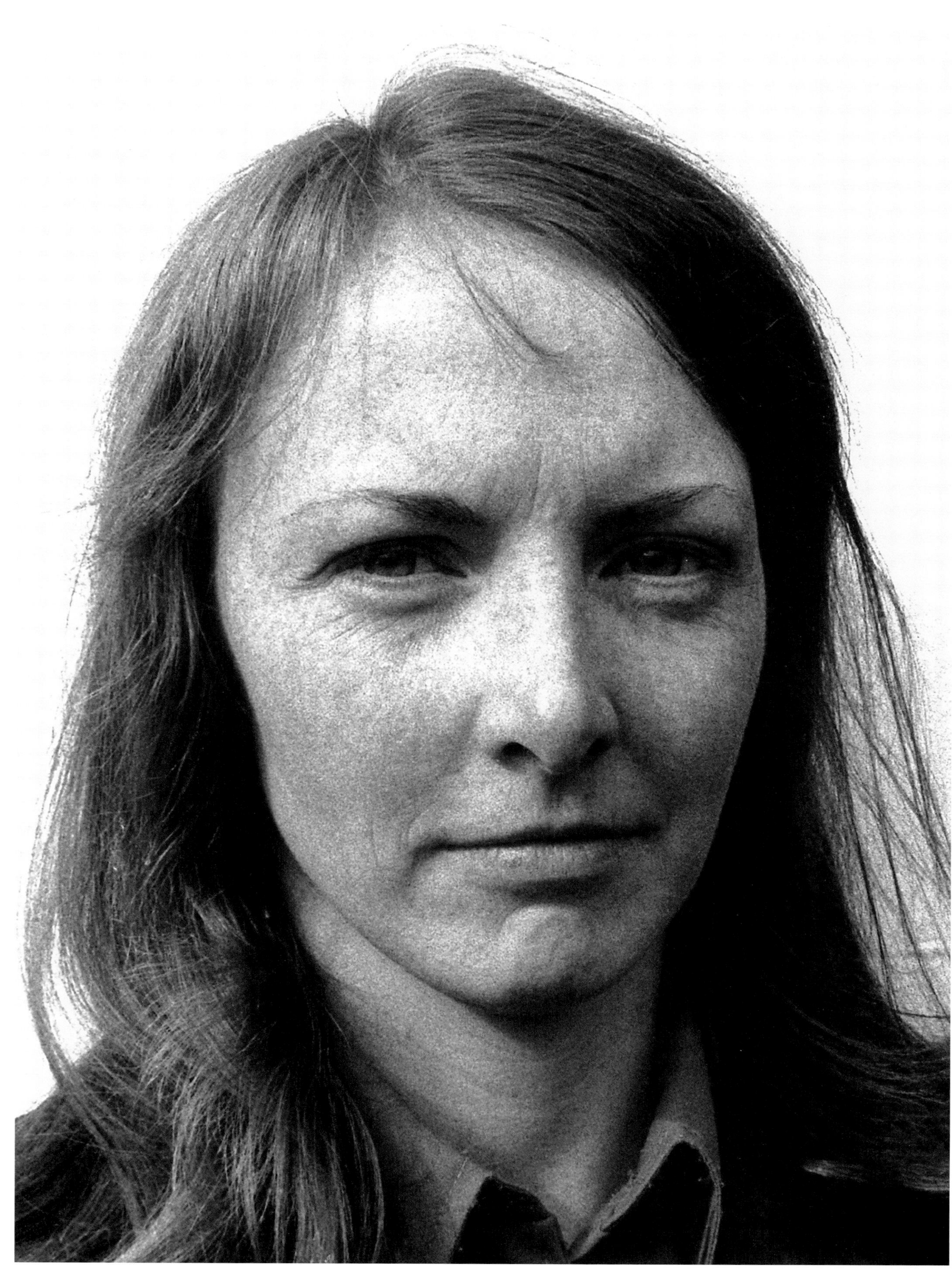

Casual Passer-by I met at 2:25 PM, Berlin, 1976

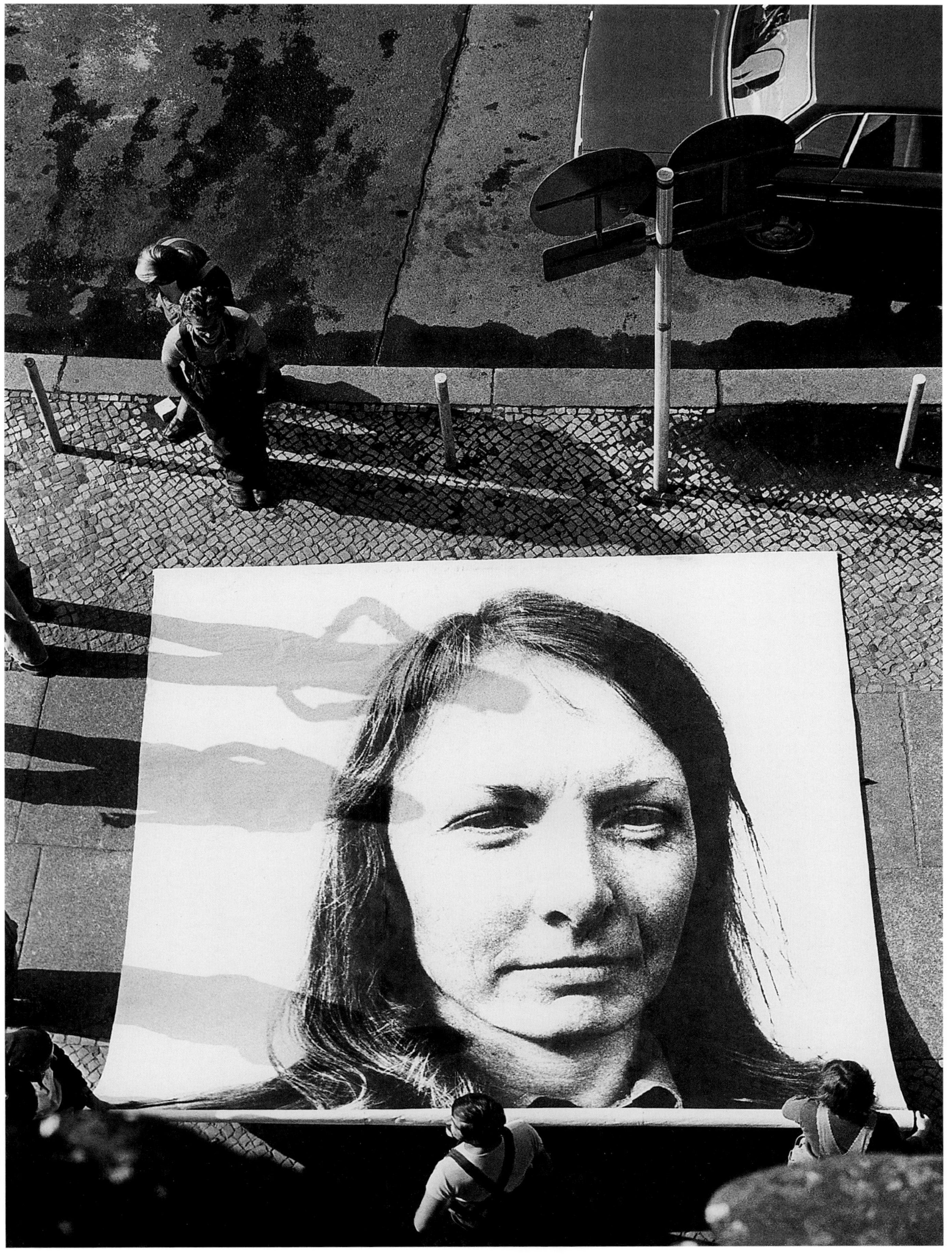

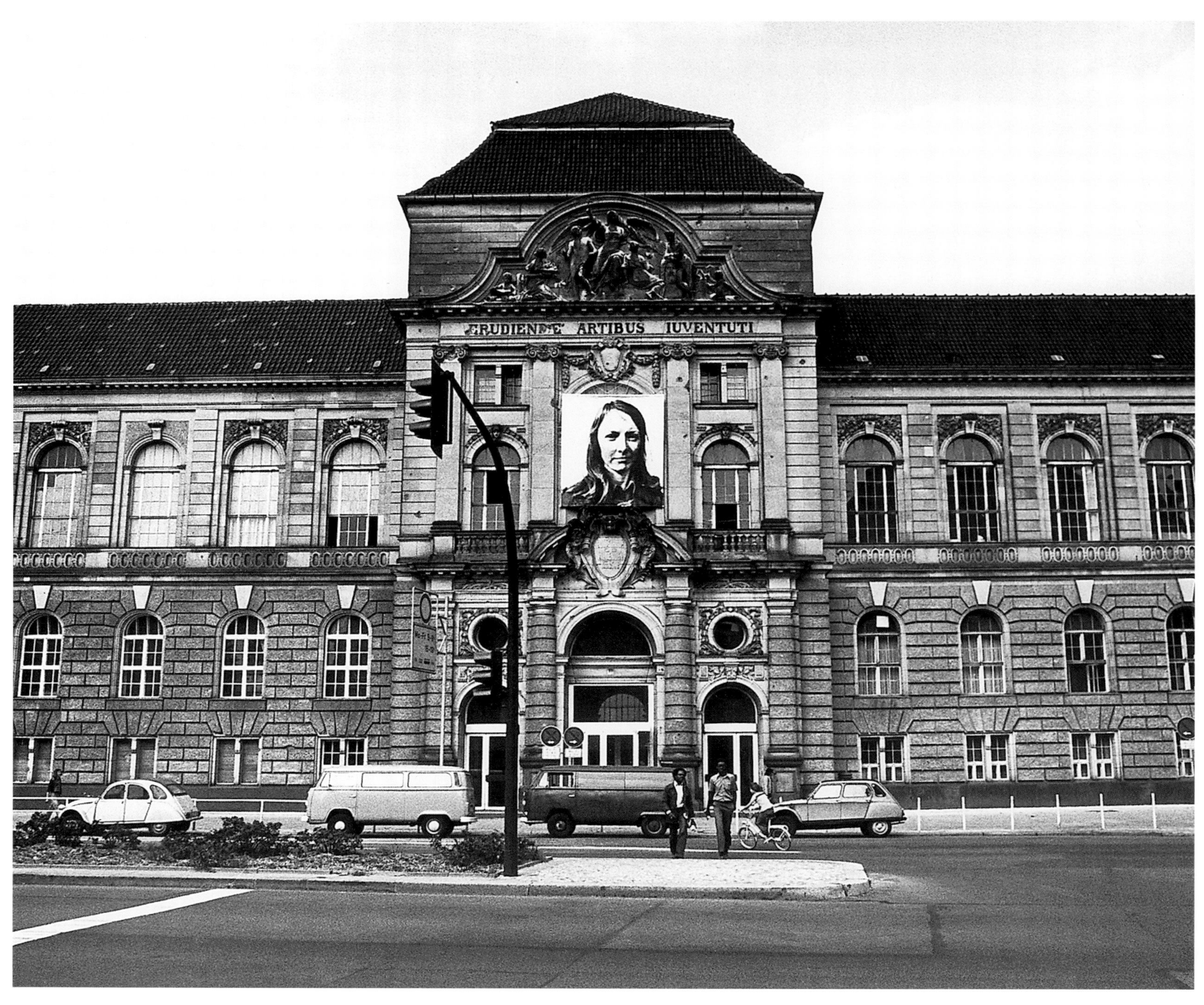

Steinplatz, Berlin, 1976

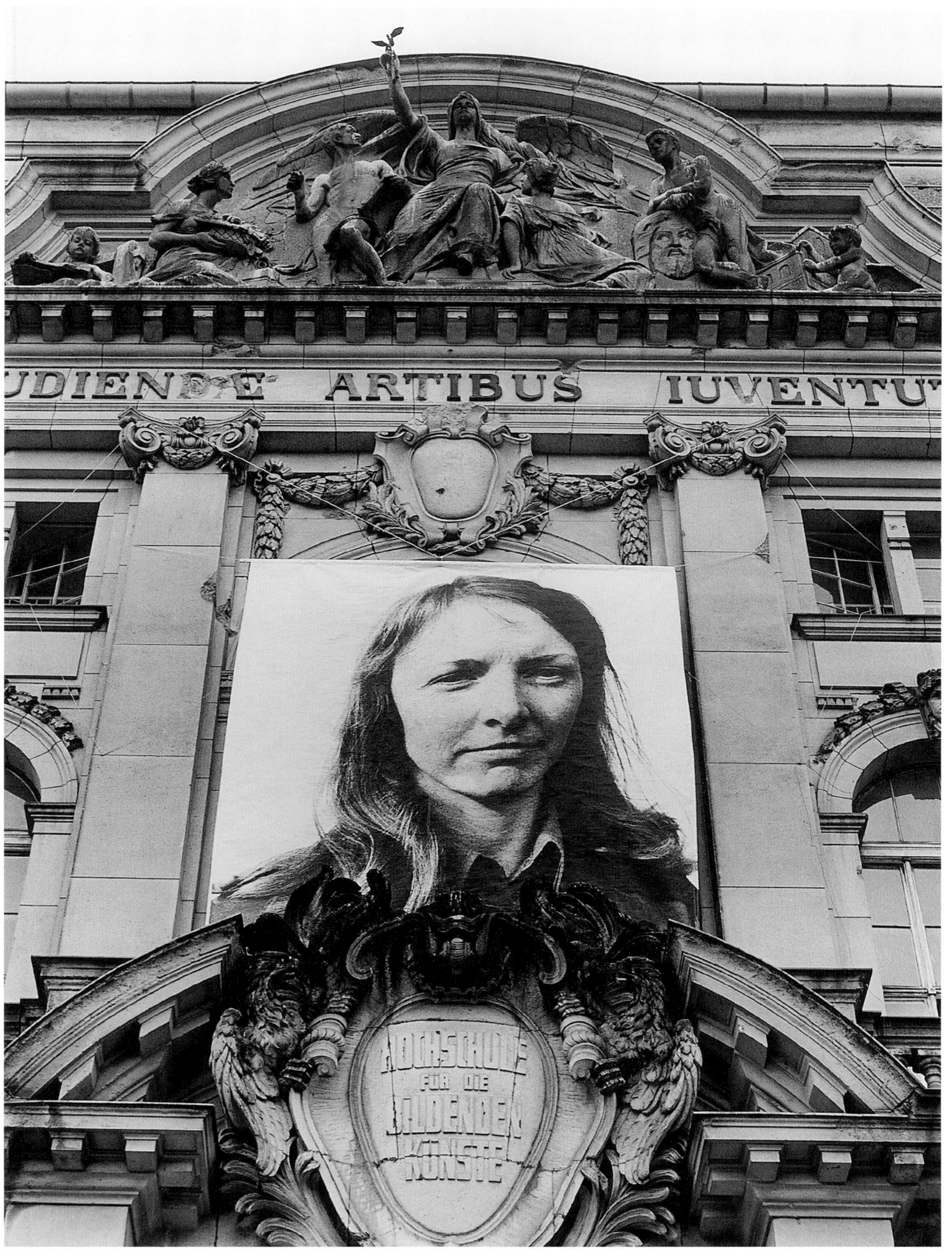
ARTIBUS
HOCHSCHULE
FÜR DIE
BILDENDEN
KÜNSTE

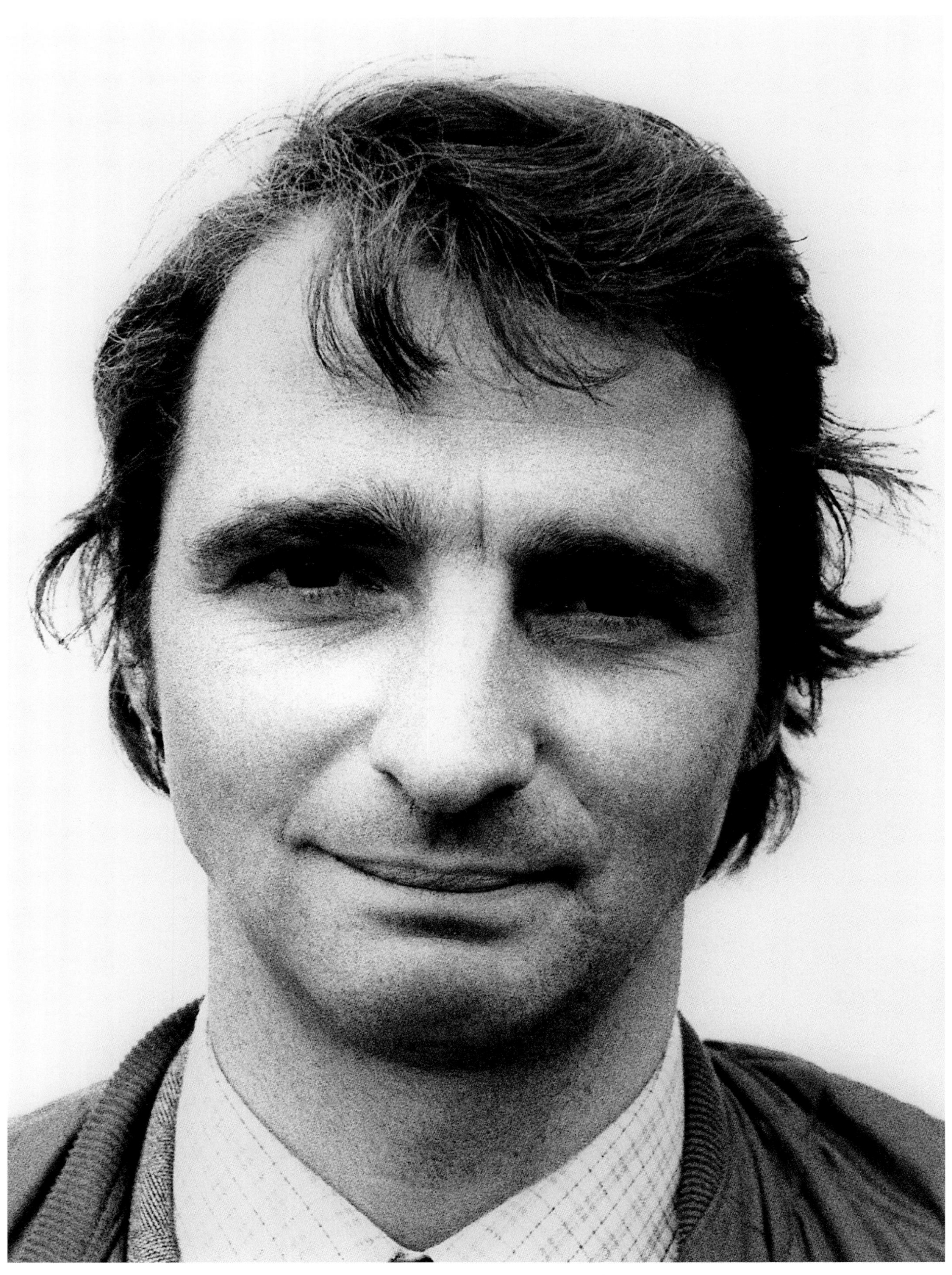

Casual Passer-by I met at 4:30 PM, Berlin, 1976
Collection: Museum of Modern Art, New York

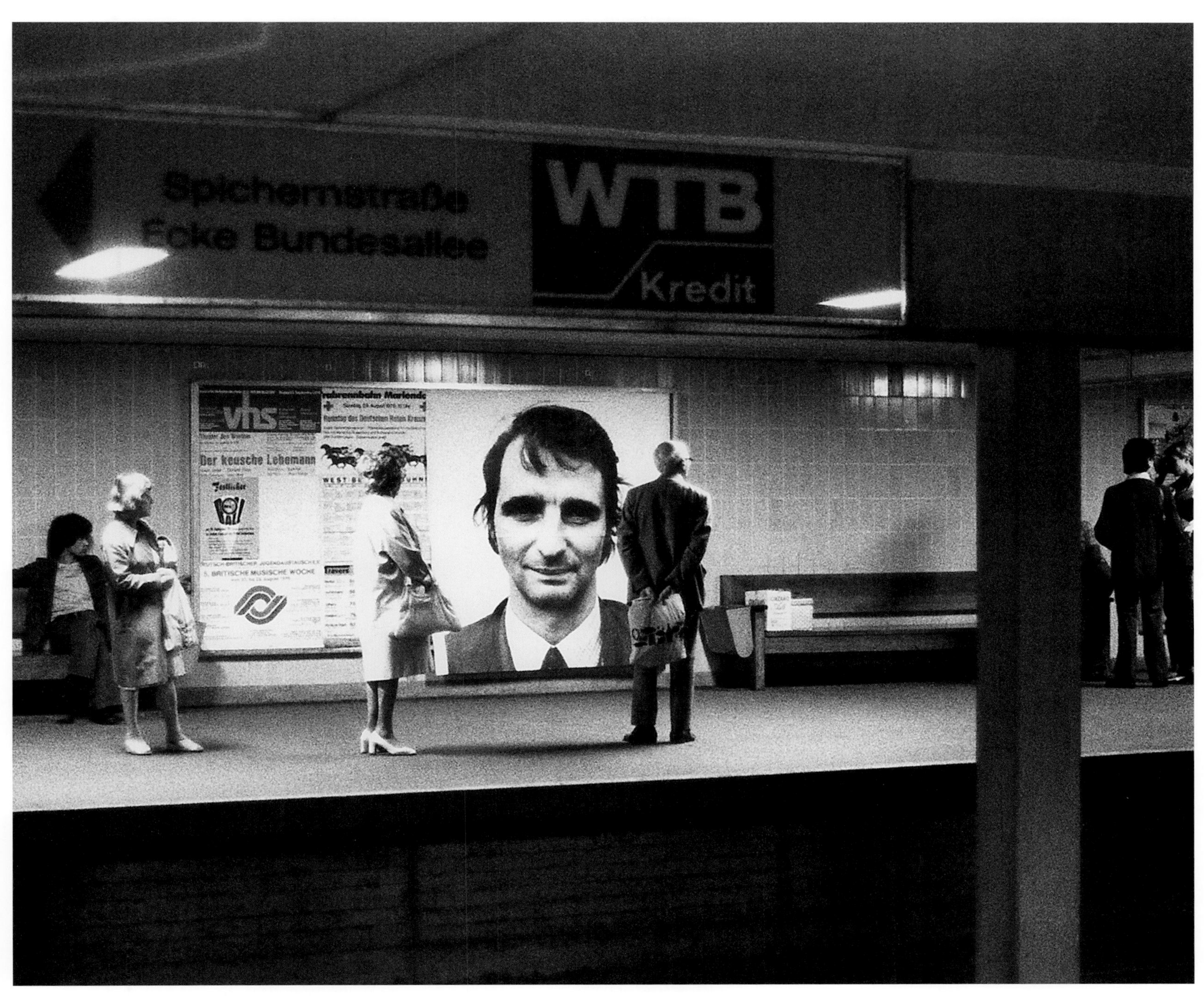

U-Bahn, Berlin, 1976

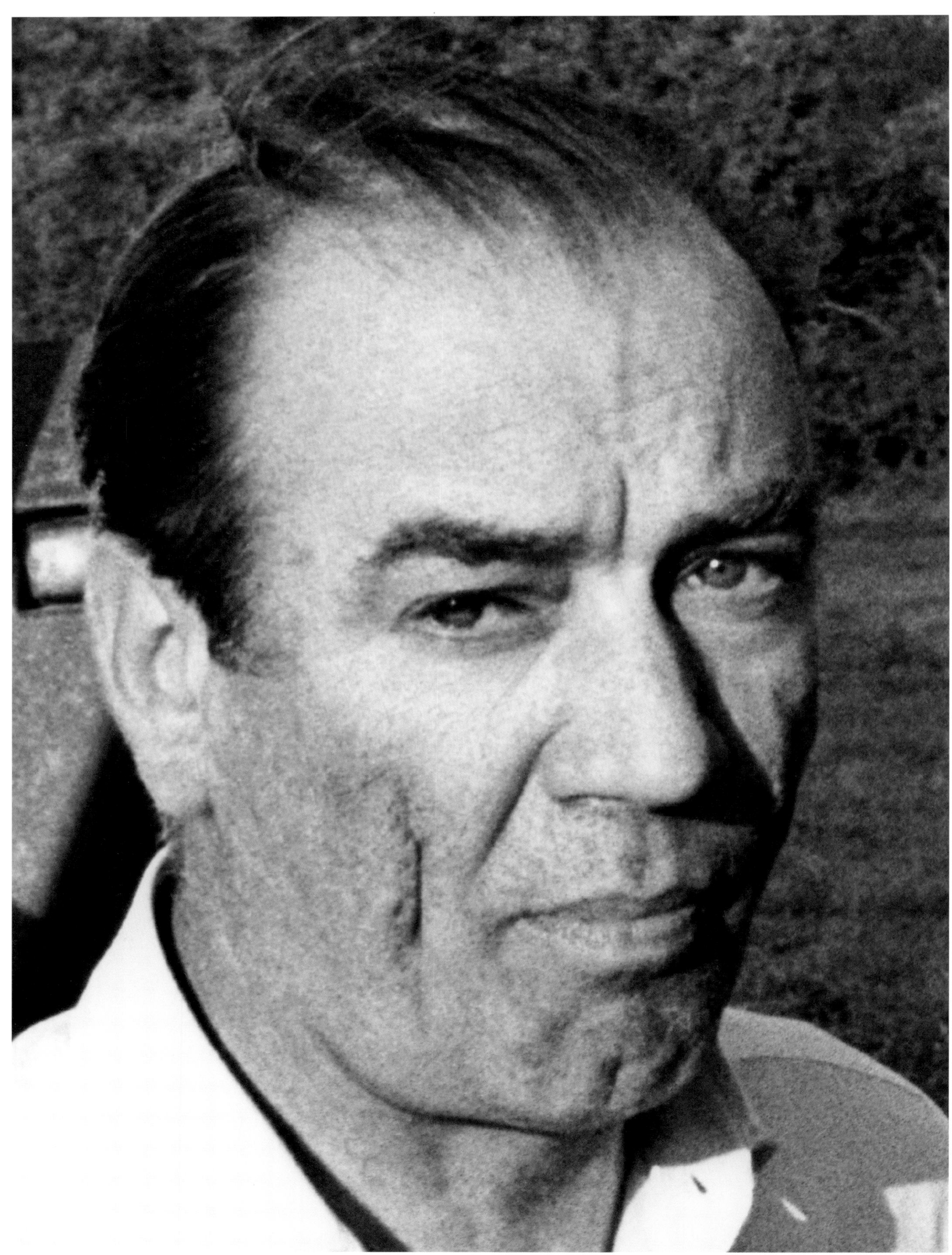

Casual Passer-by I met at 6:14 PM, Northend, Henley on Thames, 1978

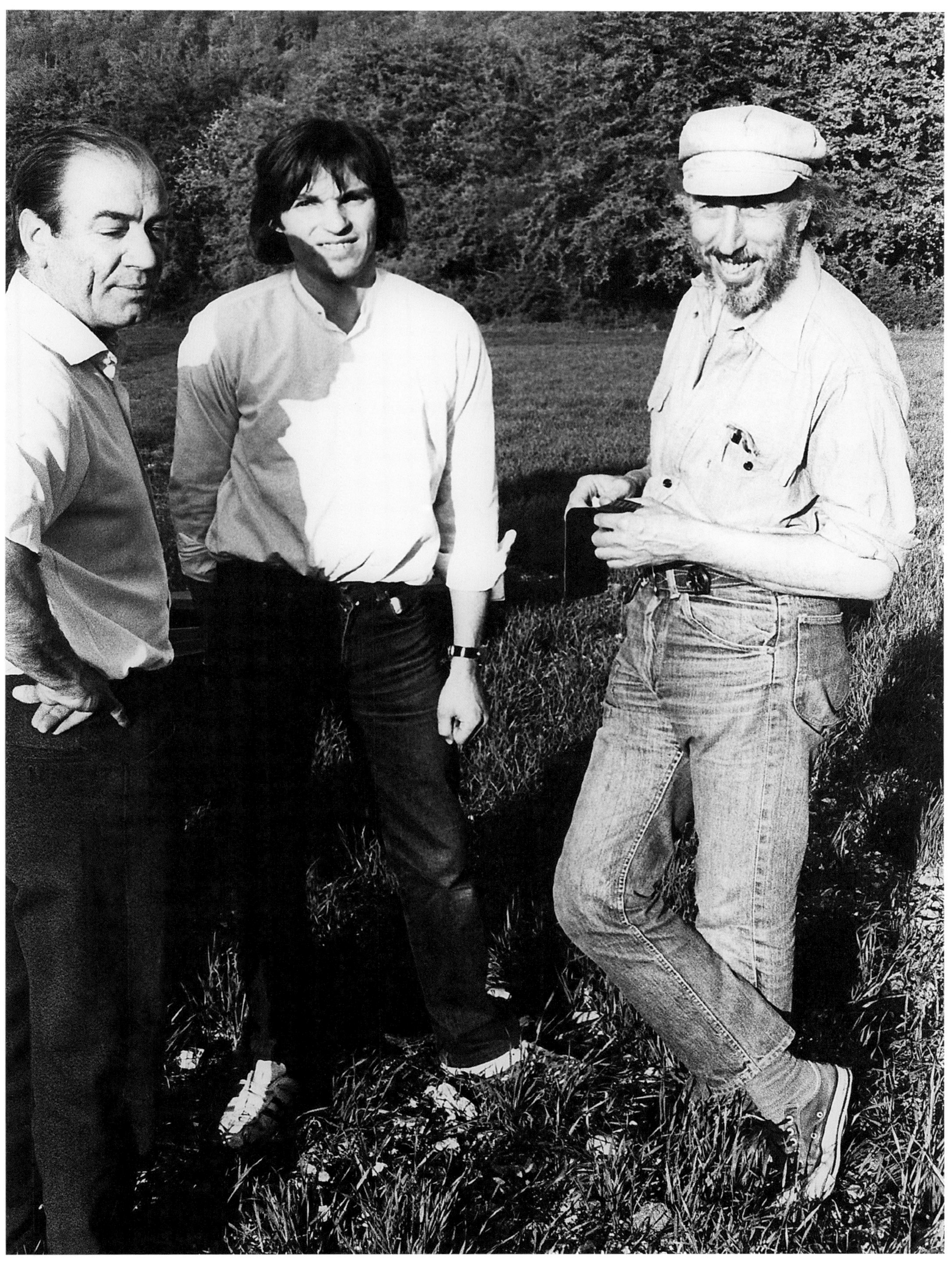

From left to right: John Fane, Braco Dimitrijević, Richard Hamilton

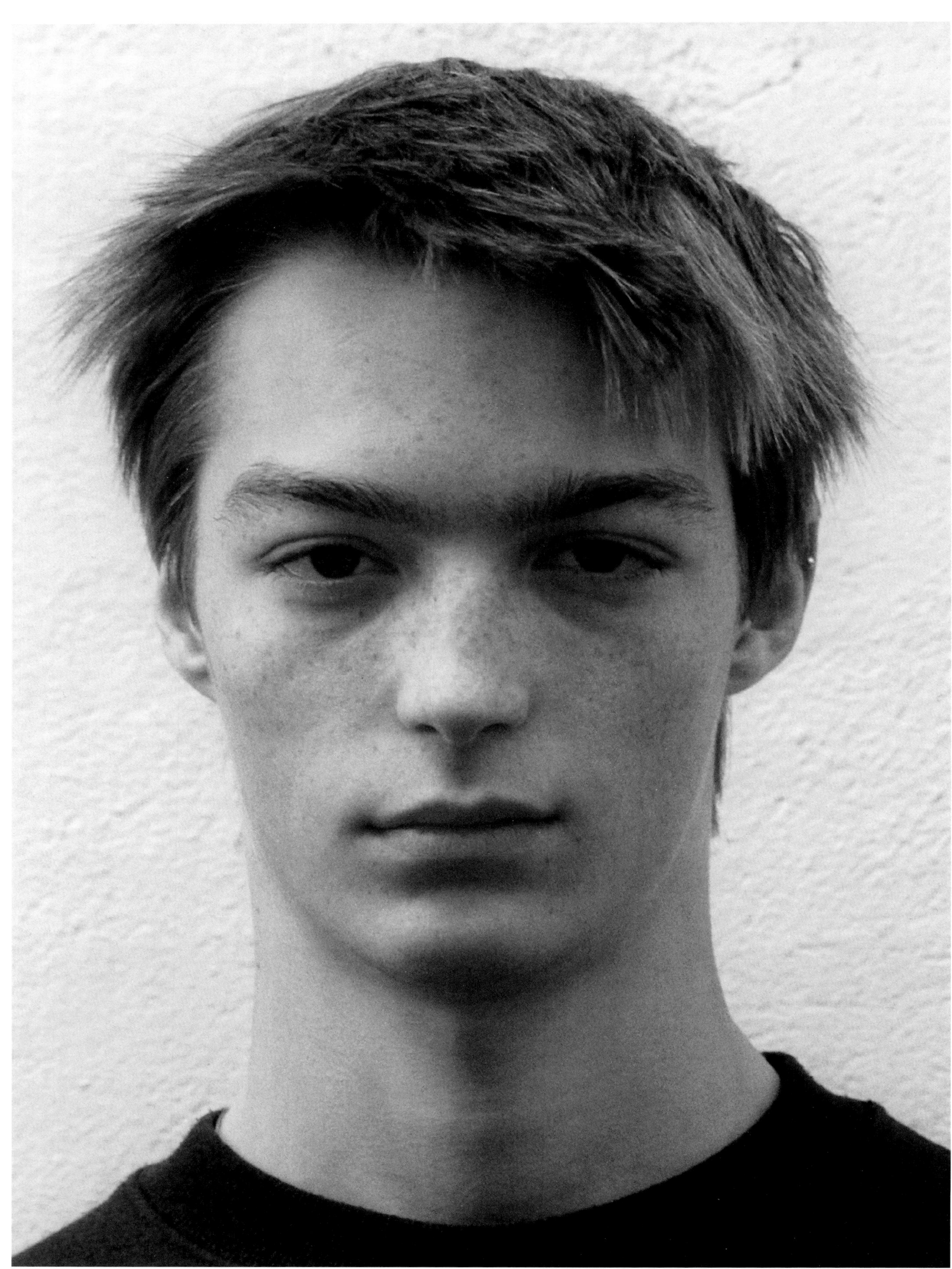

Casual Passer-by I met at 3:59 PM, Paris, 1982

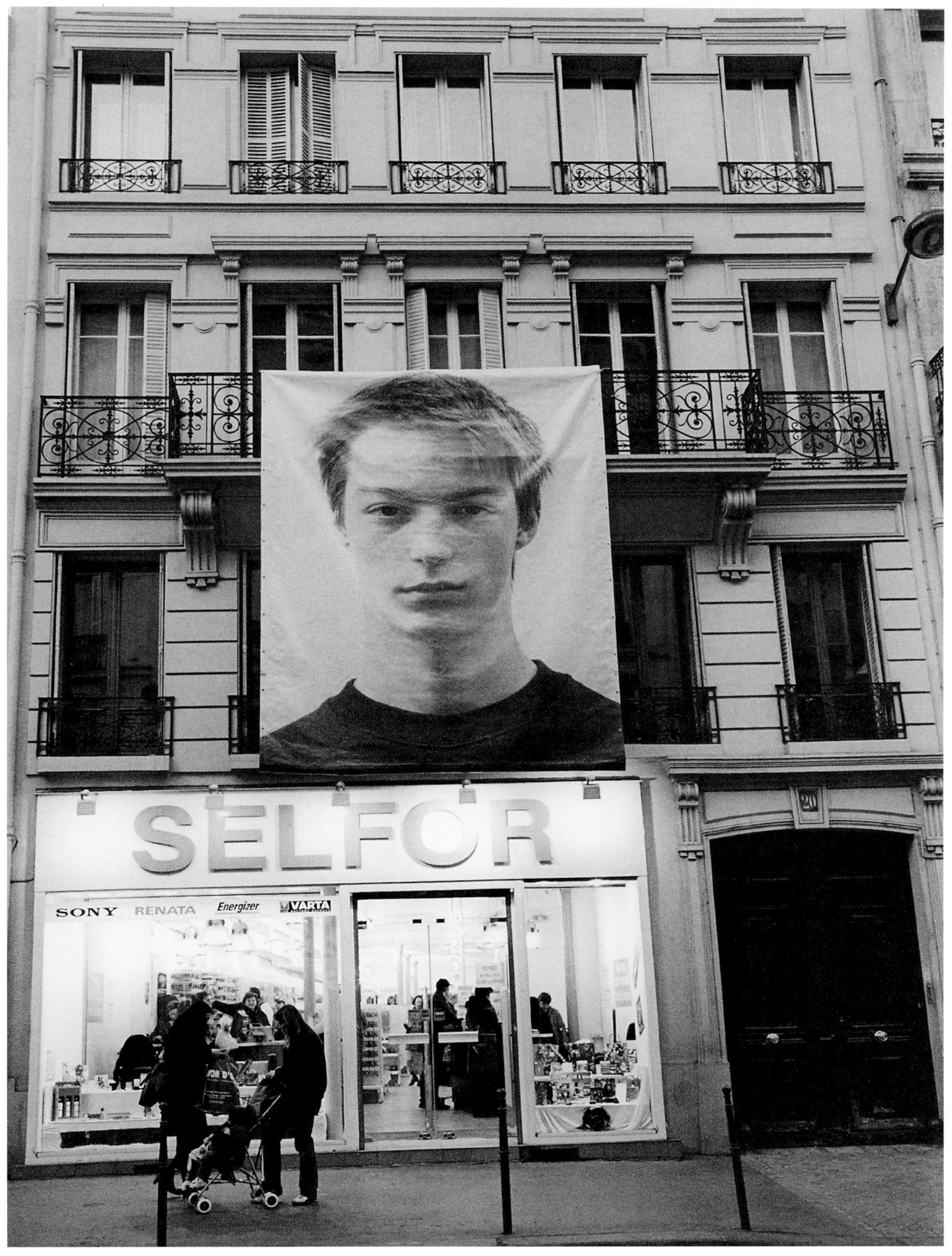
SELFOR
SONY
RENATA
Energizer
VARTA
20

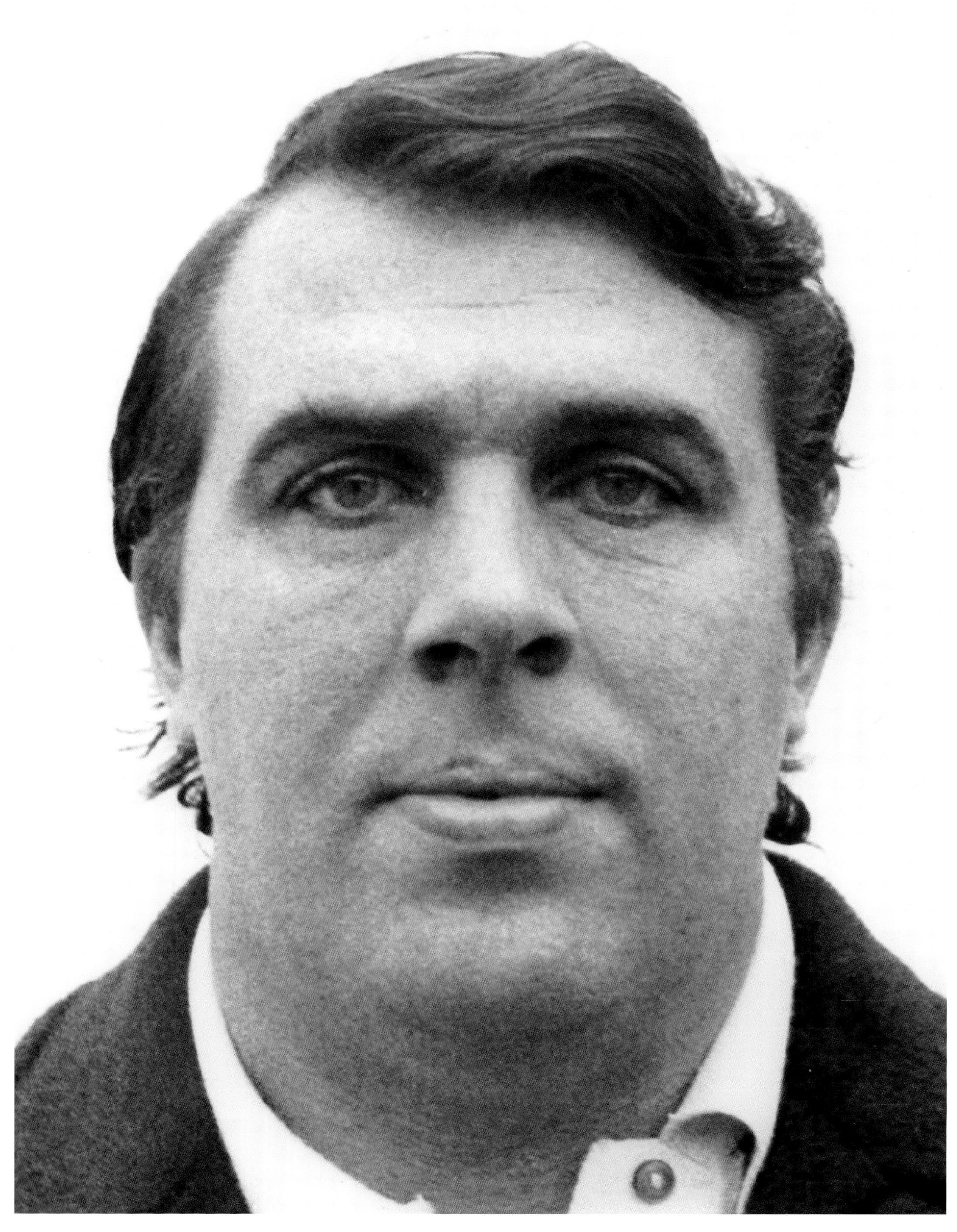

Casual Passer-by I met at 1:43 PM, Venice, 1976
Collection: Tate Modern, London

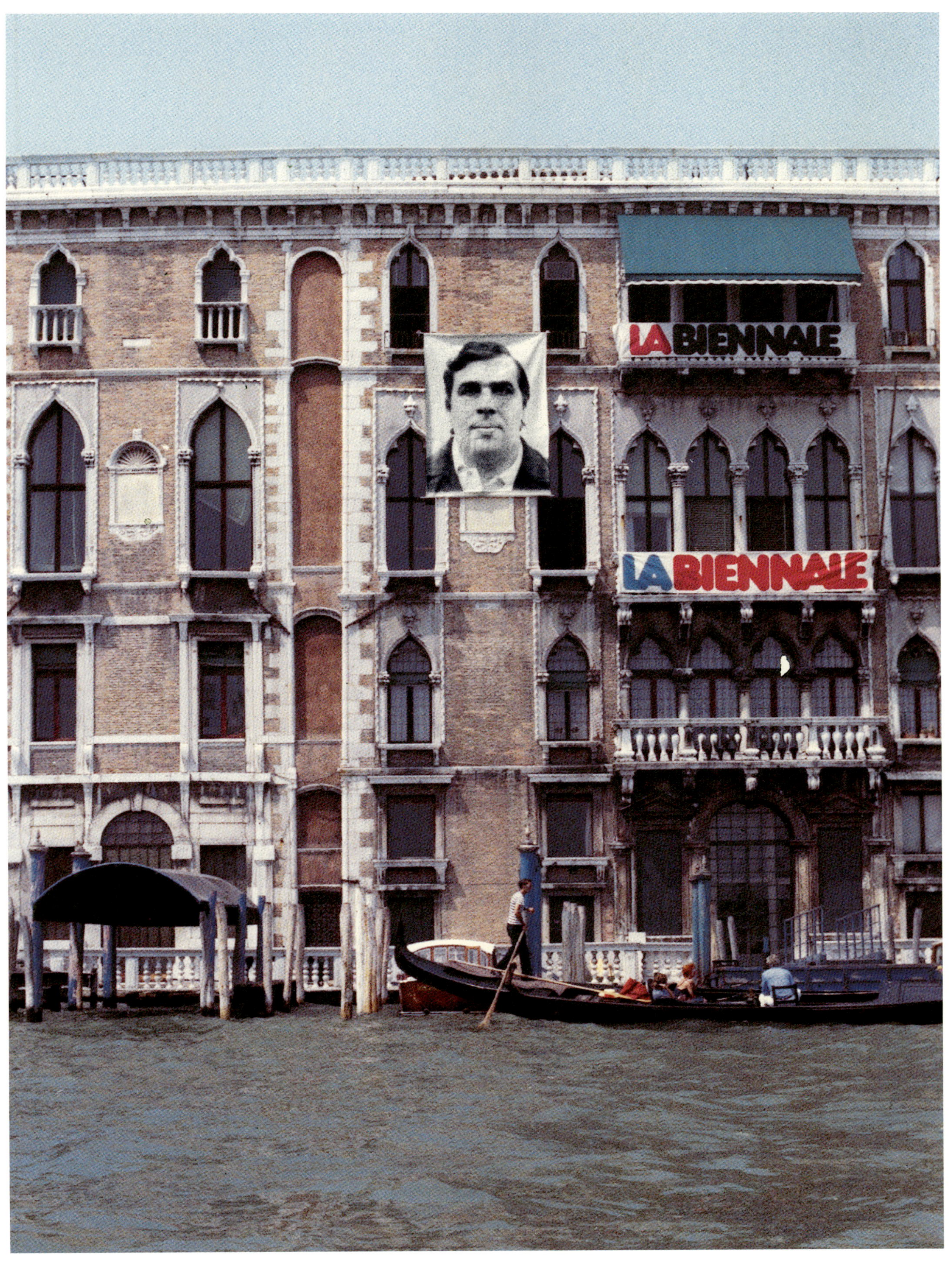

Venice Biennale, Grand Canal, 1976

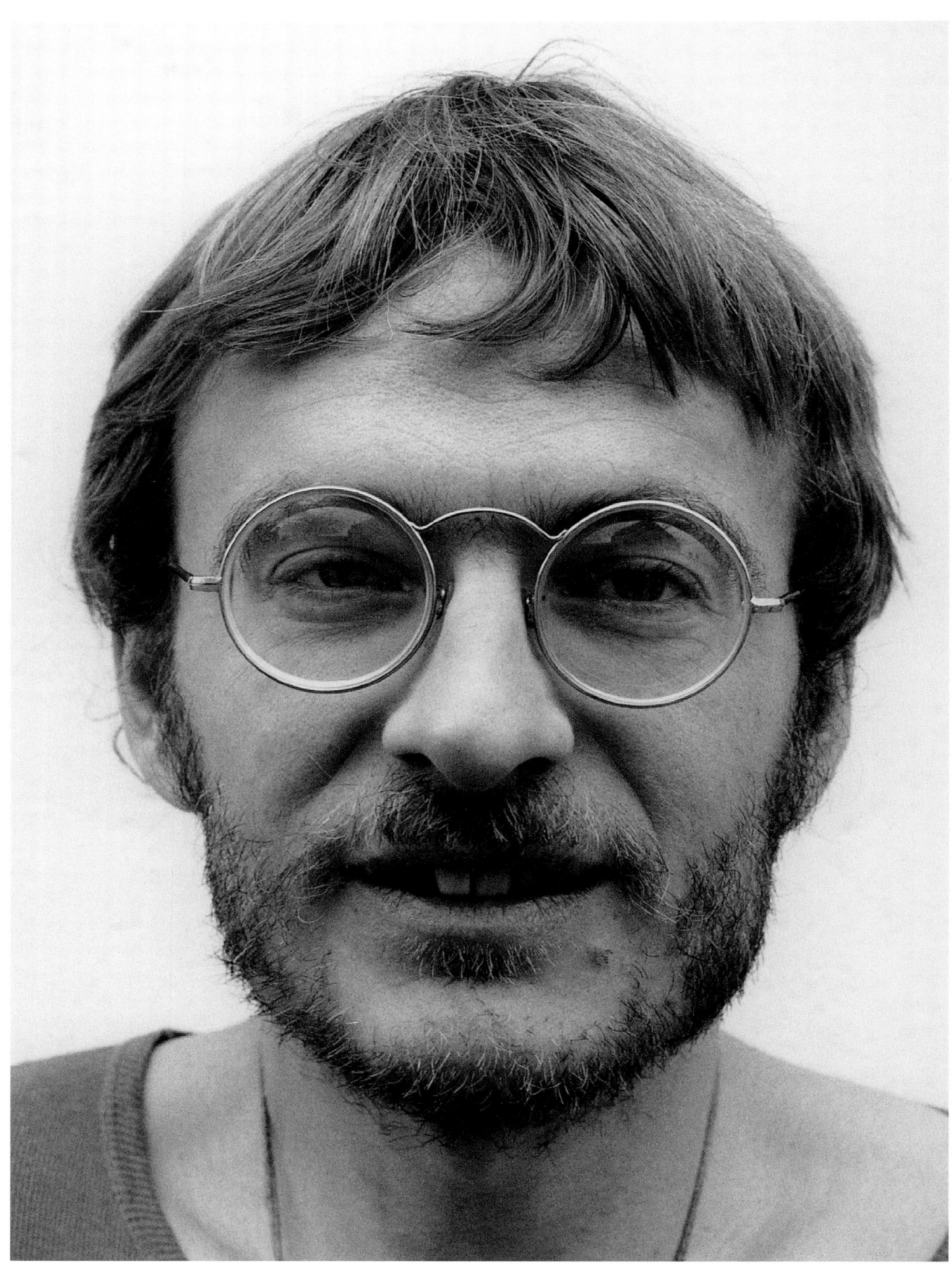

Casual Passer-by I met at 6:23 PM, Eindhoven, 1979

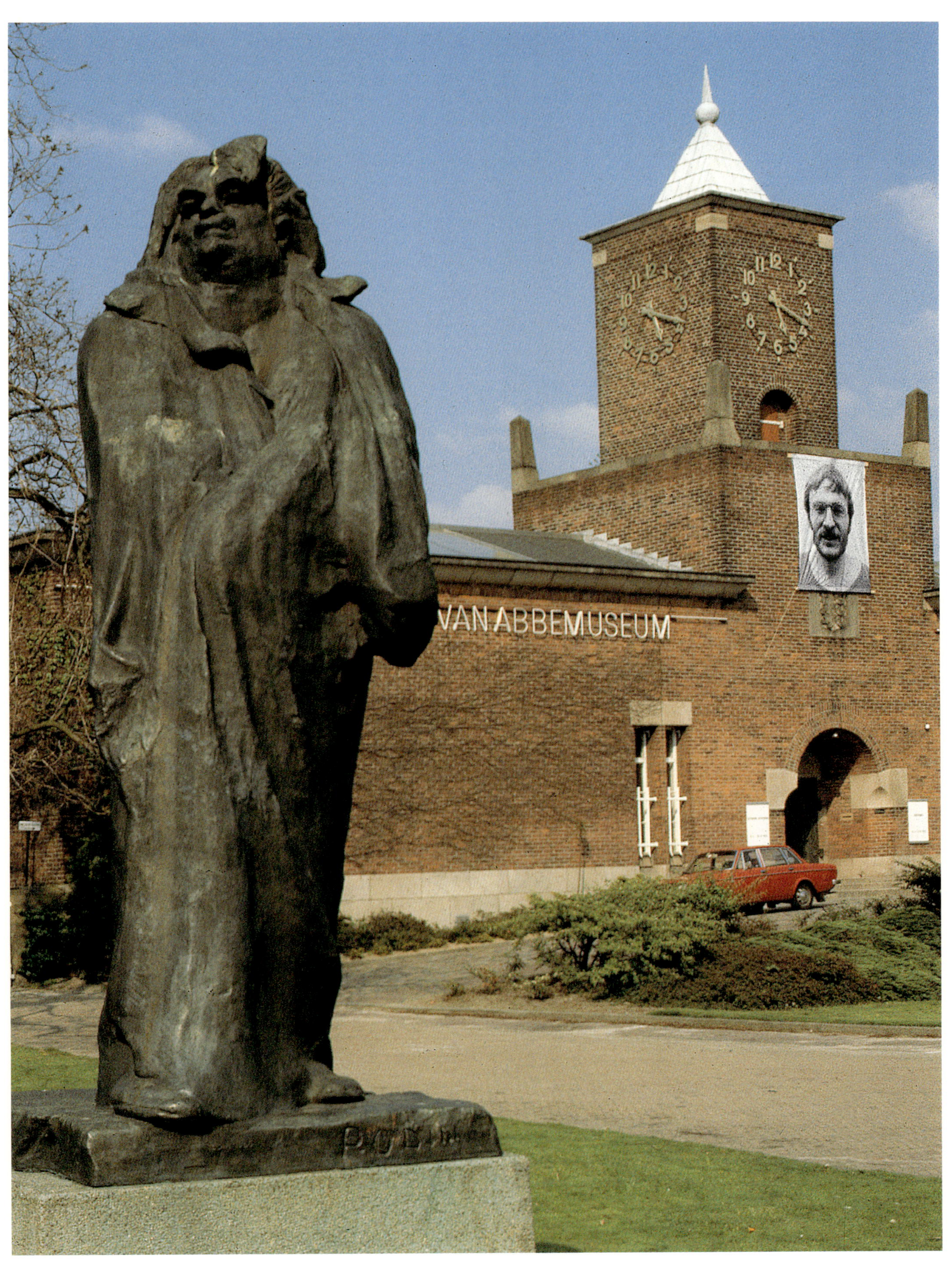

Stedelijk van Abbemuseum, Eindhoven, 1979
(*Balzac* by Rodin, *Casual Passer-by* by Braco Dimitrijević)

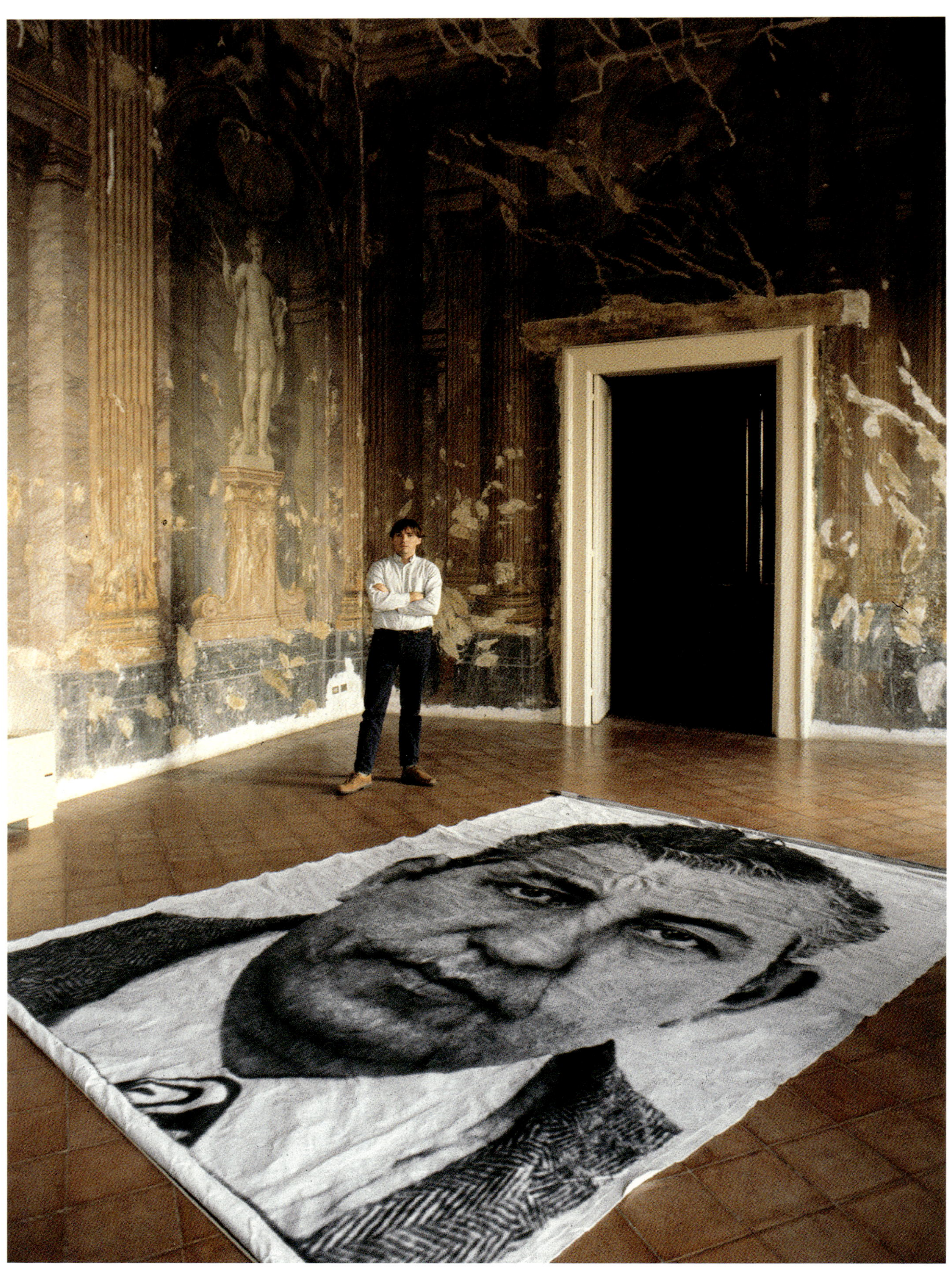

Preparing the work for the *Terrae Motus* exhibition,
Villa Campolieto, Herculaneum, 1986

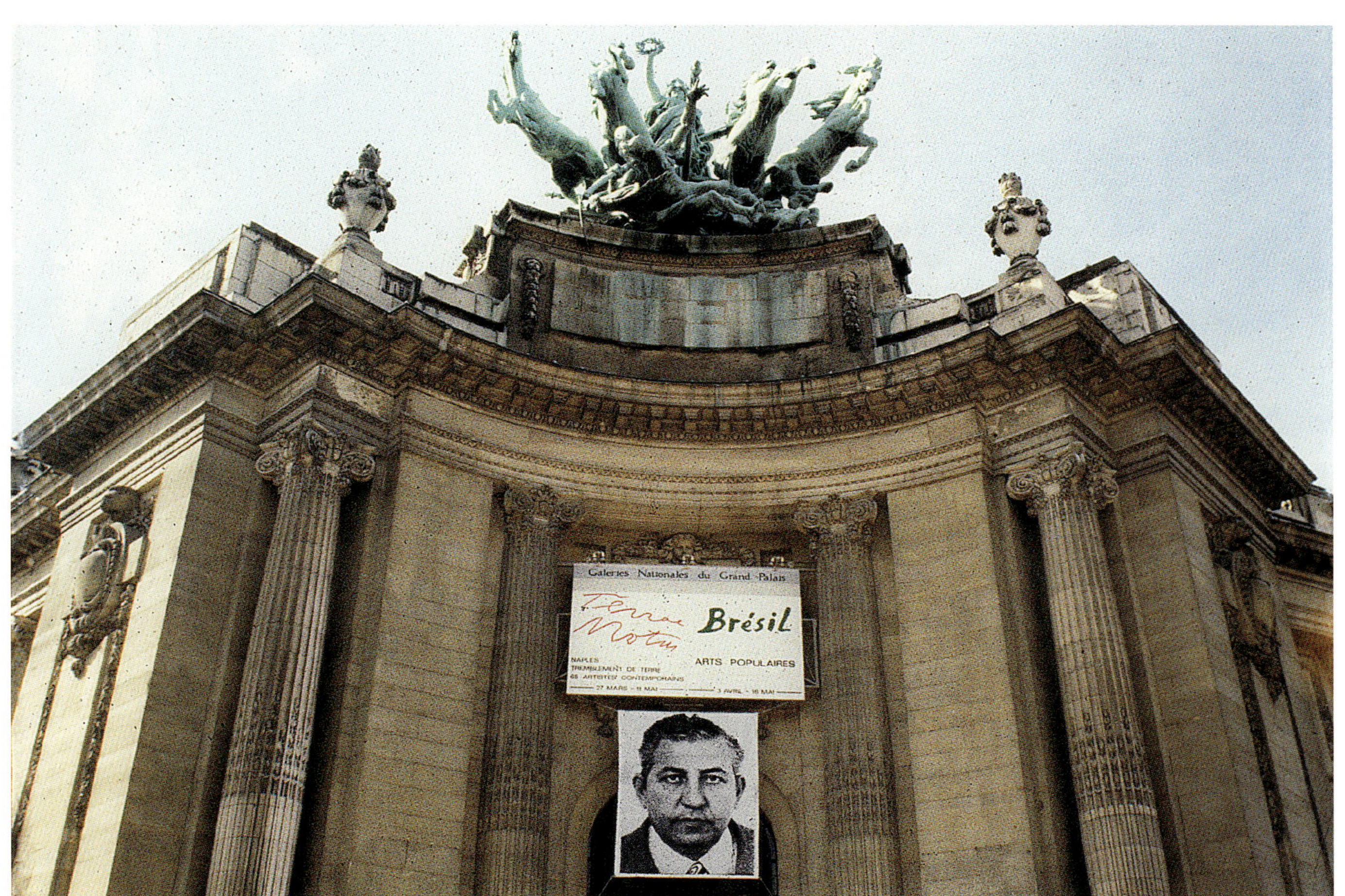

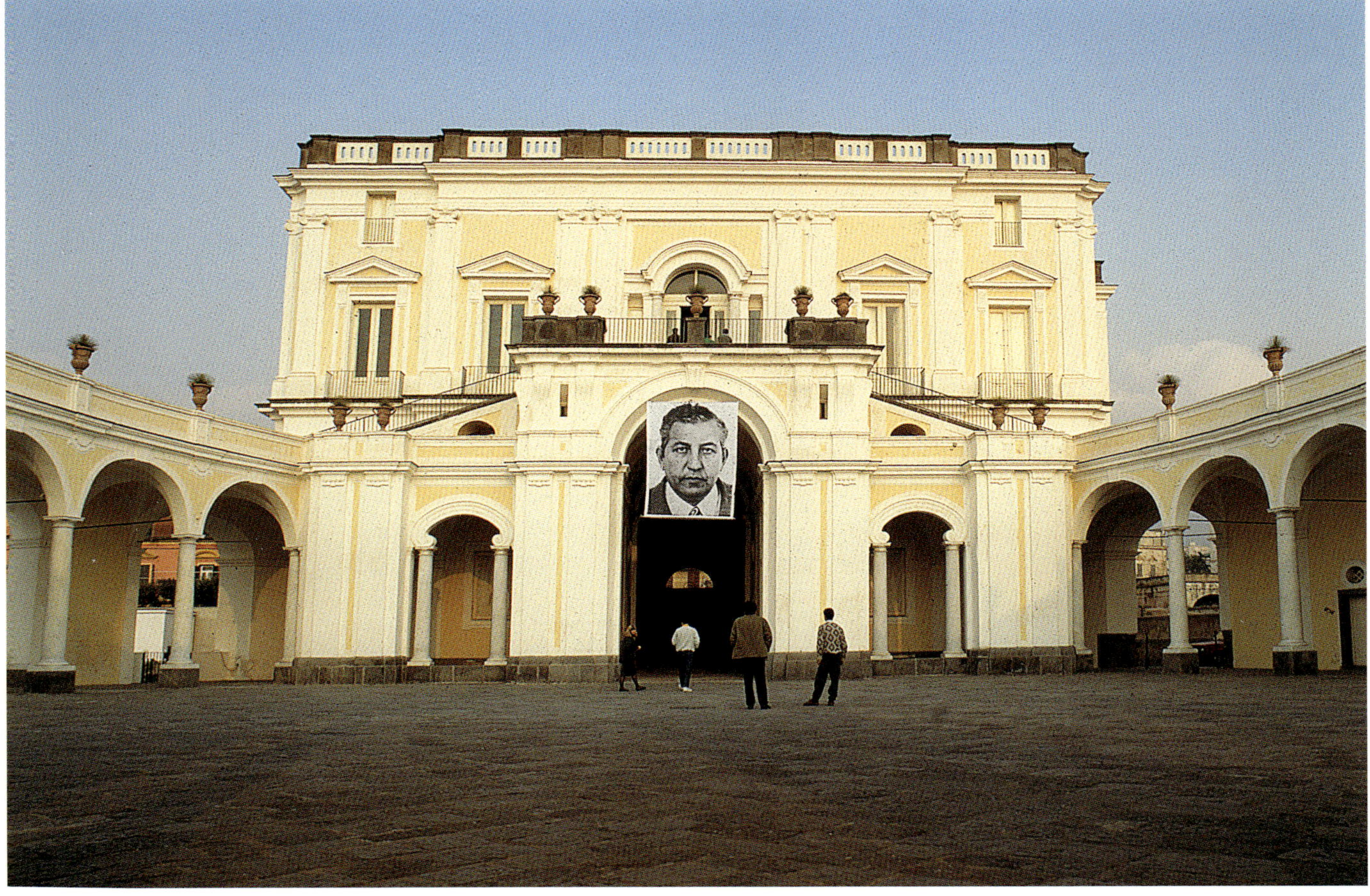

Grand Palais, Paris, 1986

Villa Campolieto, Herculaneum, 1986

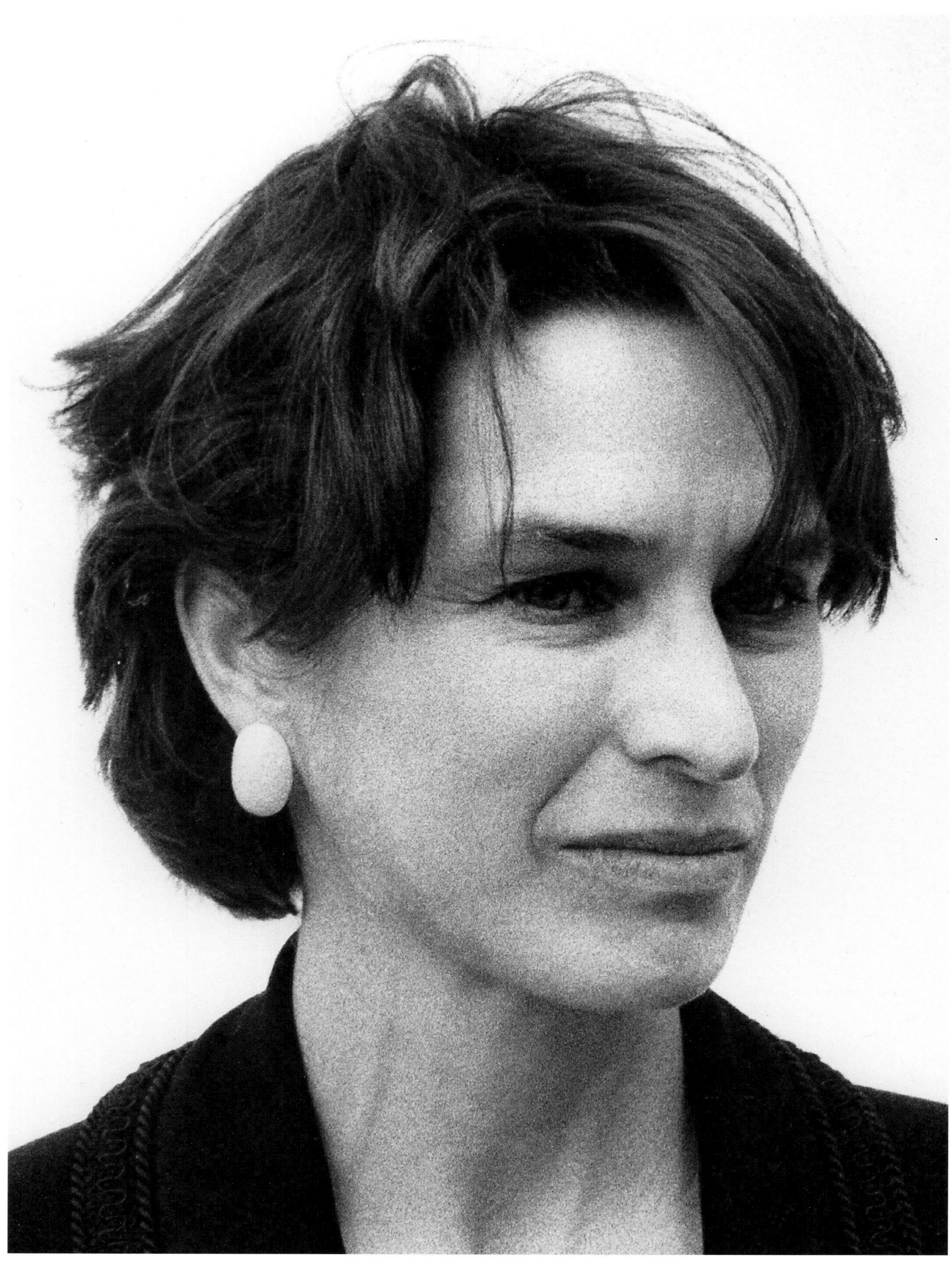

Casual Passer-by I met at 10:15 AM, New York, 1988

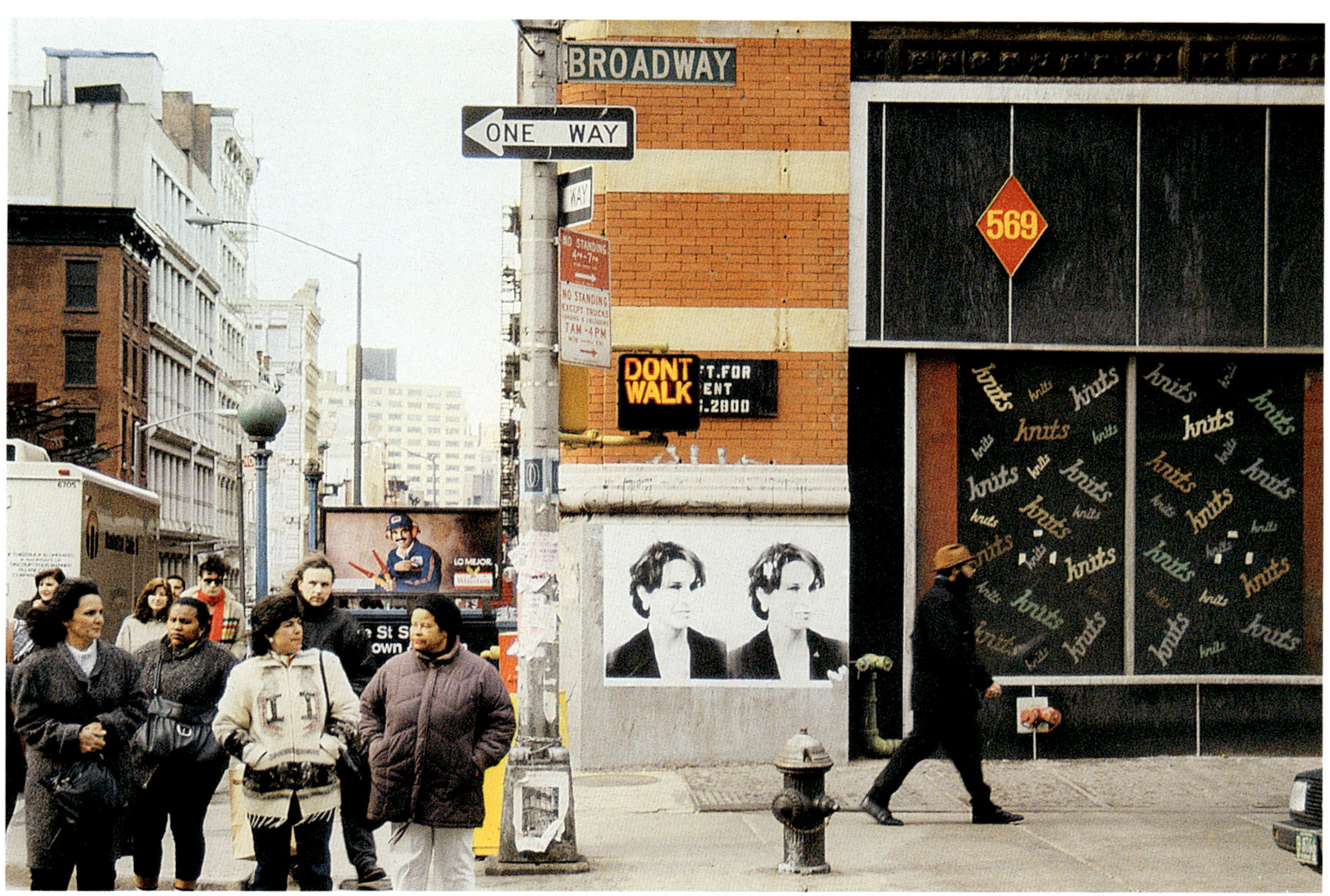

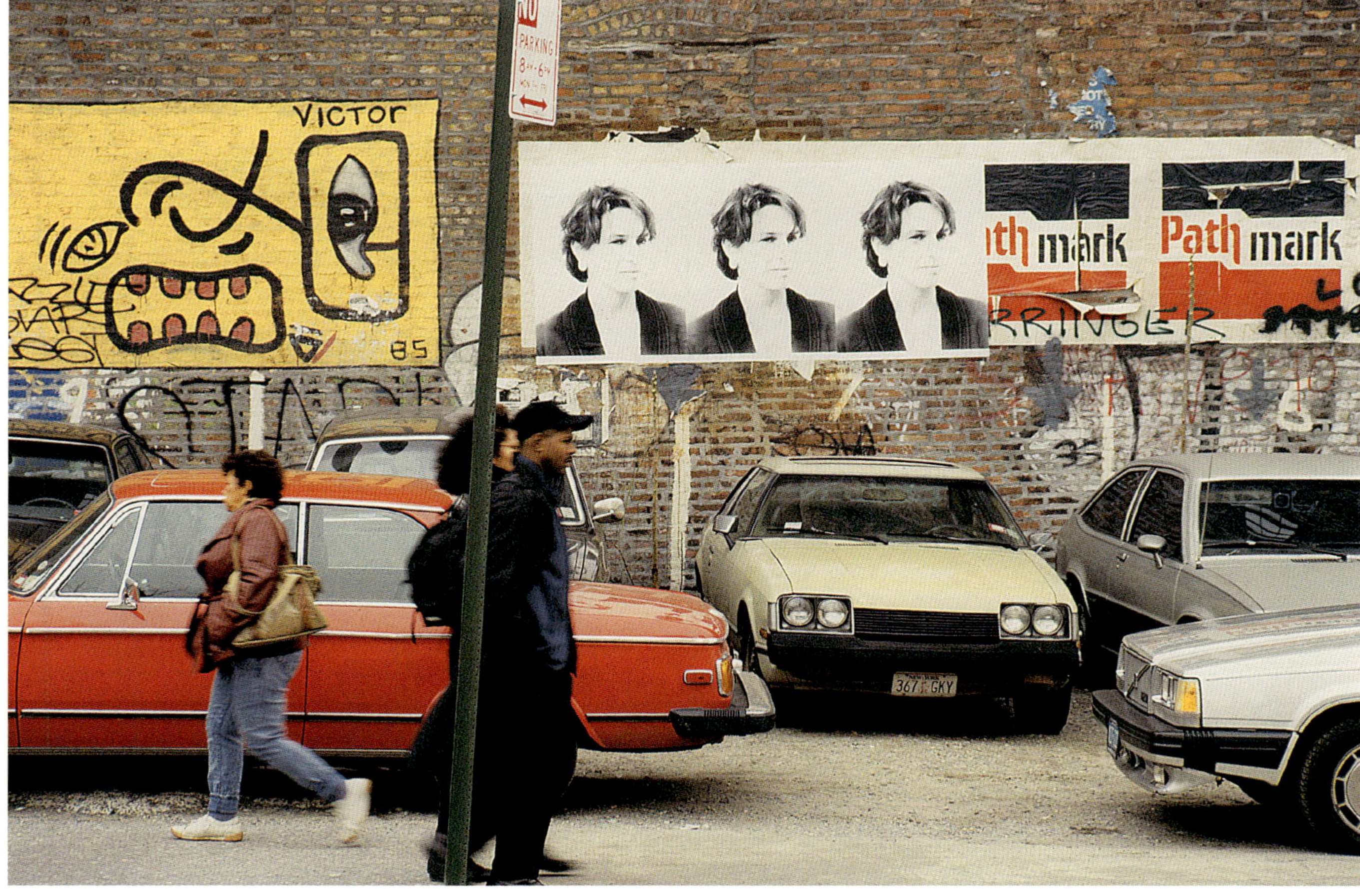

Downtown Manhattan, New York, 1988

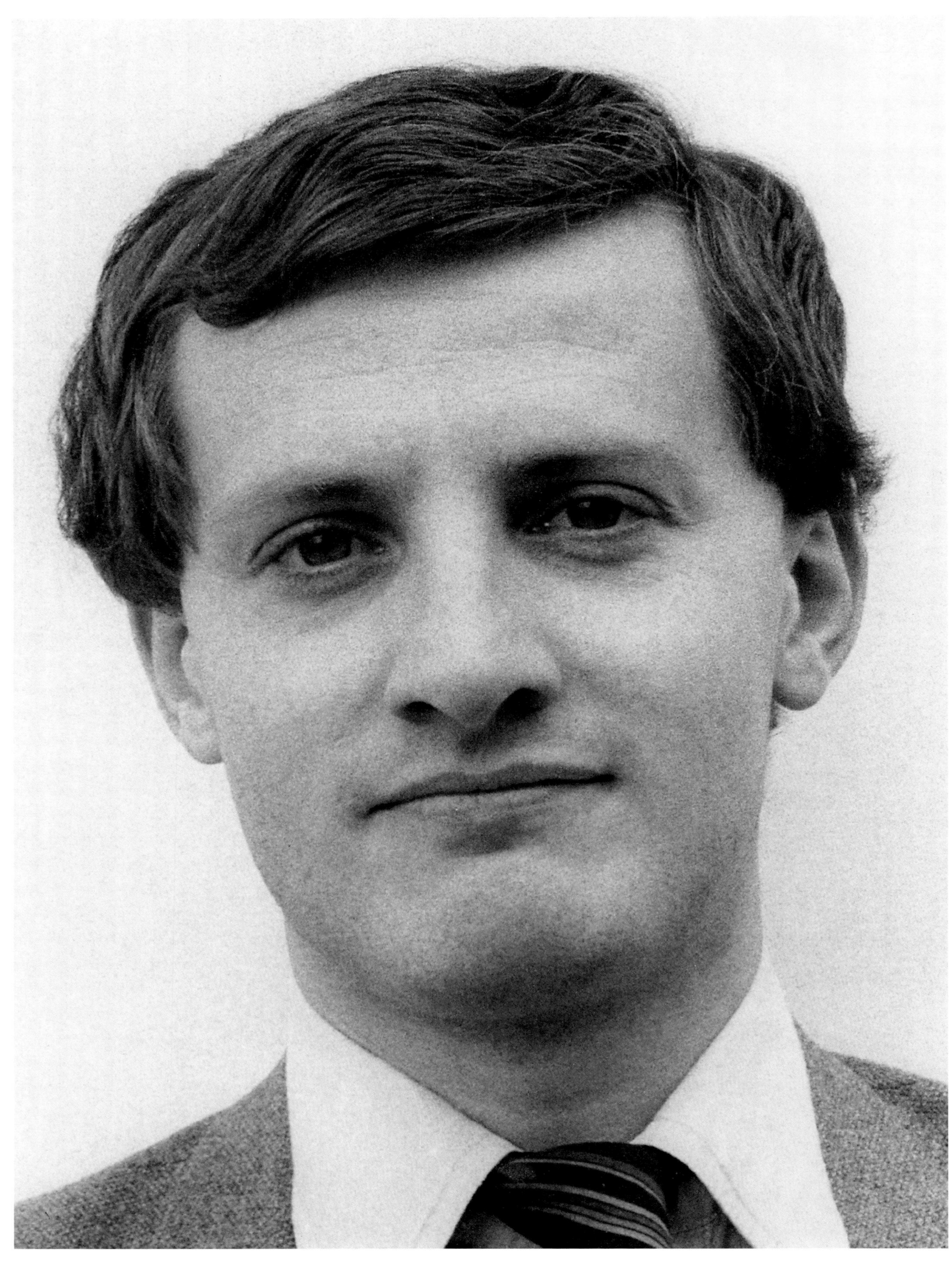

Casual Passer-by I met at 3:41 PM, New York, 1988
Private Collection, New York

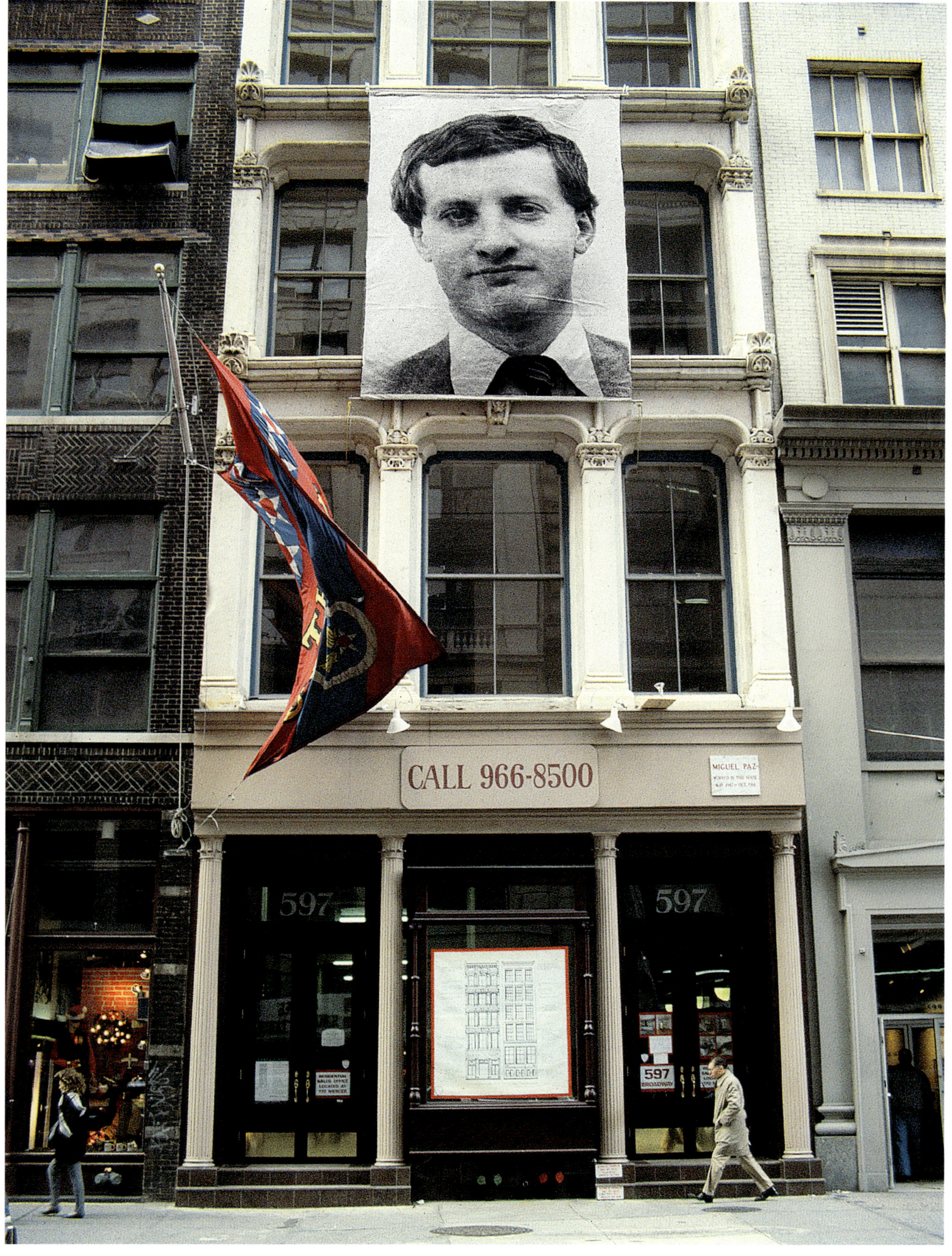

Broadway, New York, 1988

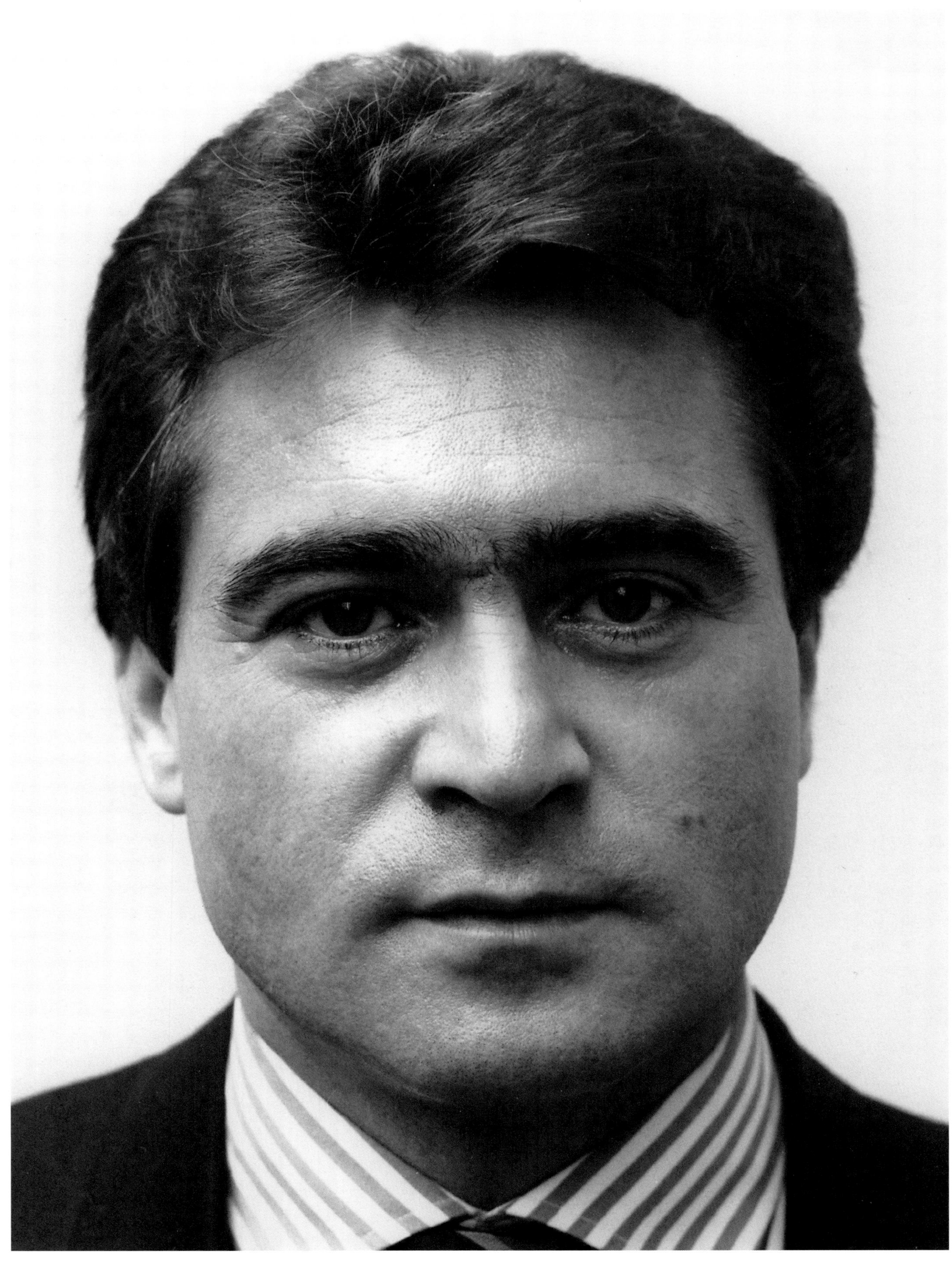

Casual Passer-by I met at 3:59 PM, Paris, 1989
Collection: Eric Fabre, Paris

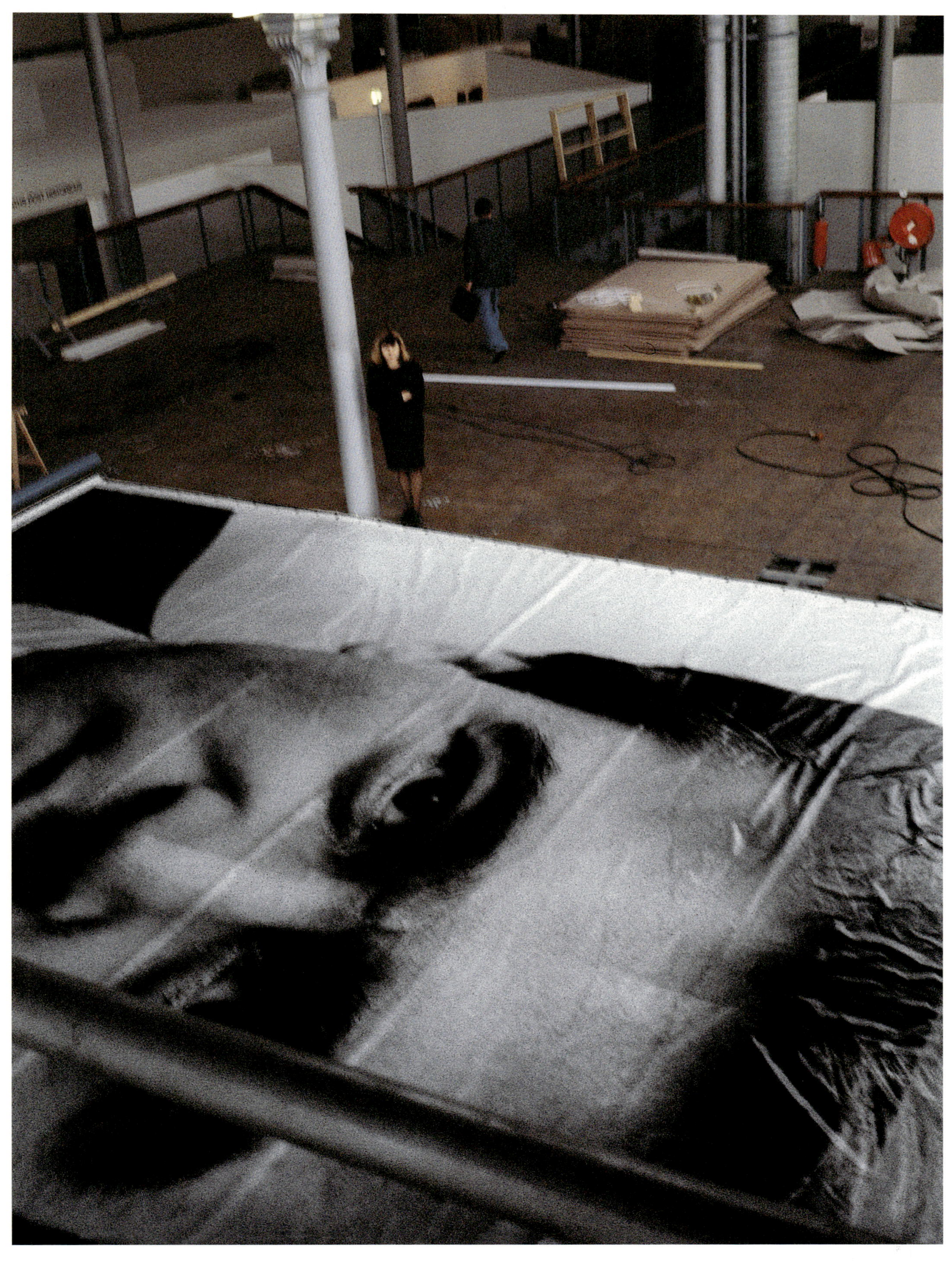

Preparation for the *Magiciens de la Terre* exhibition, 1989
Grande Halle de la Villette, Paris

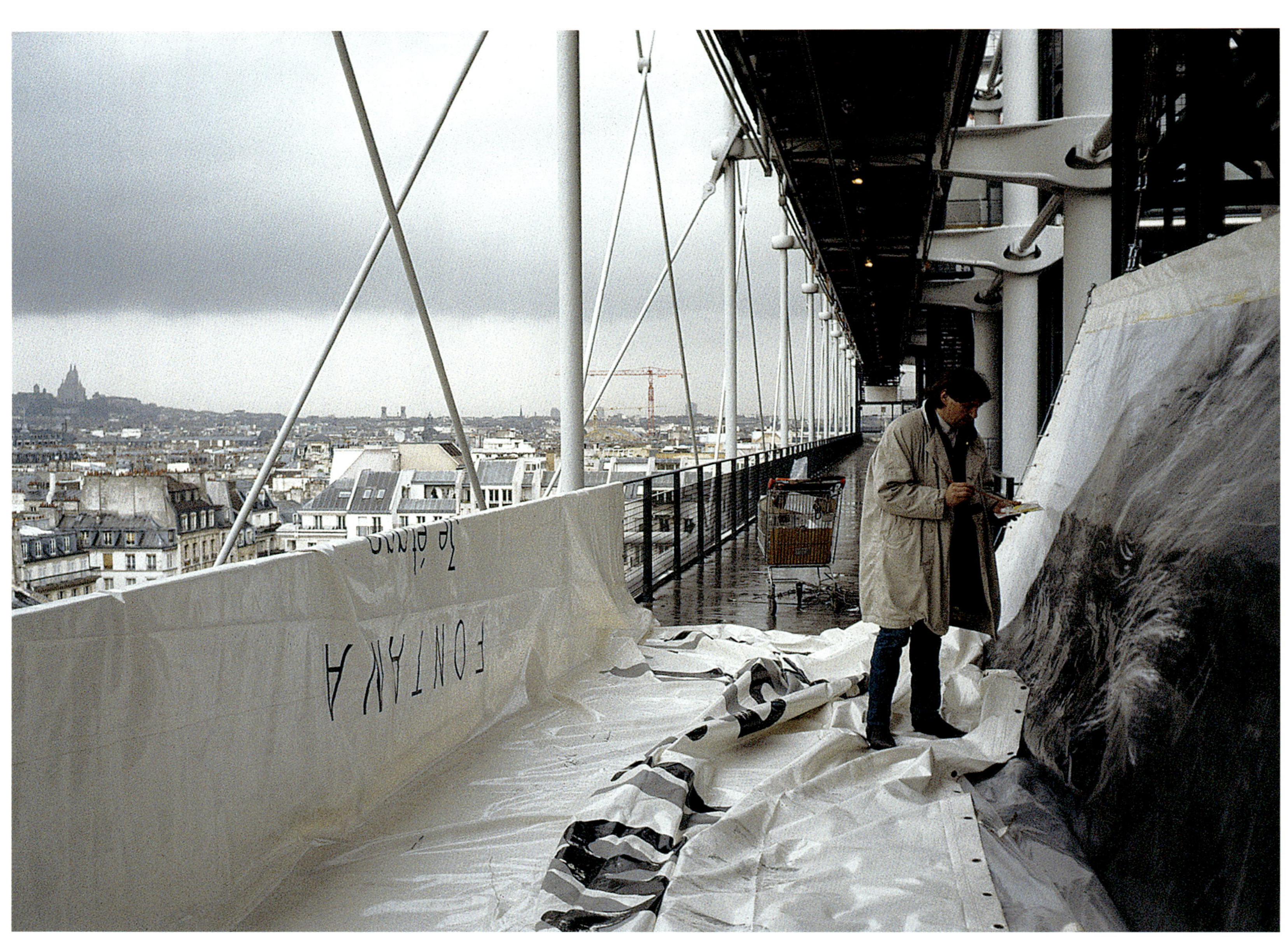

Magiciens de la Terre exhibition, 1989
Musée National d'Art Moderne, Centre Georges Pompidou, Paris

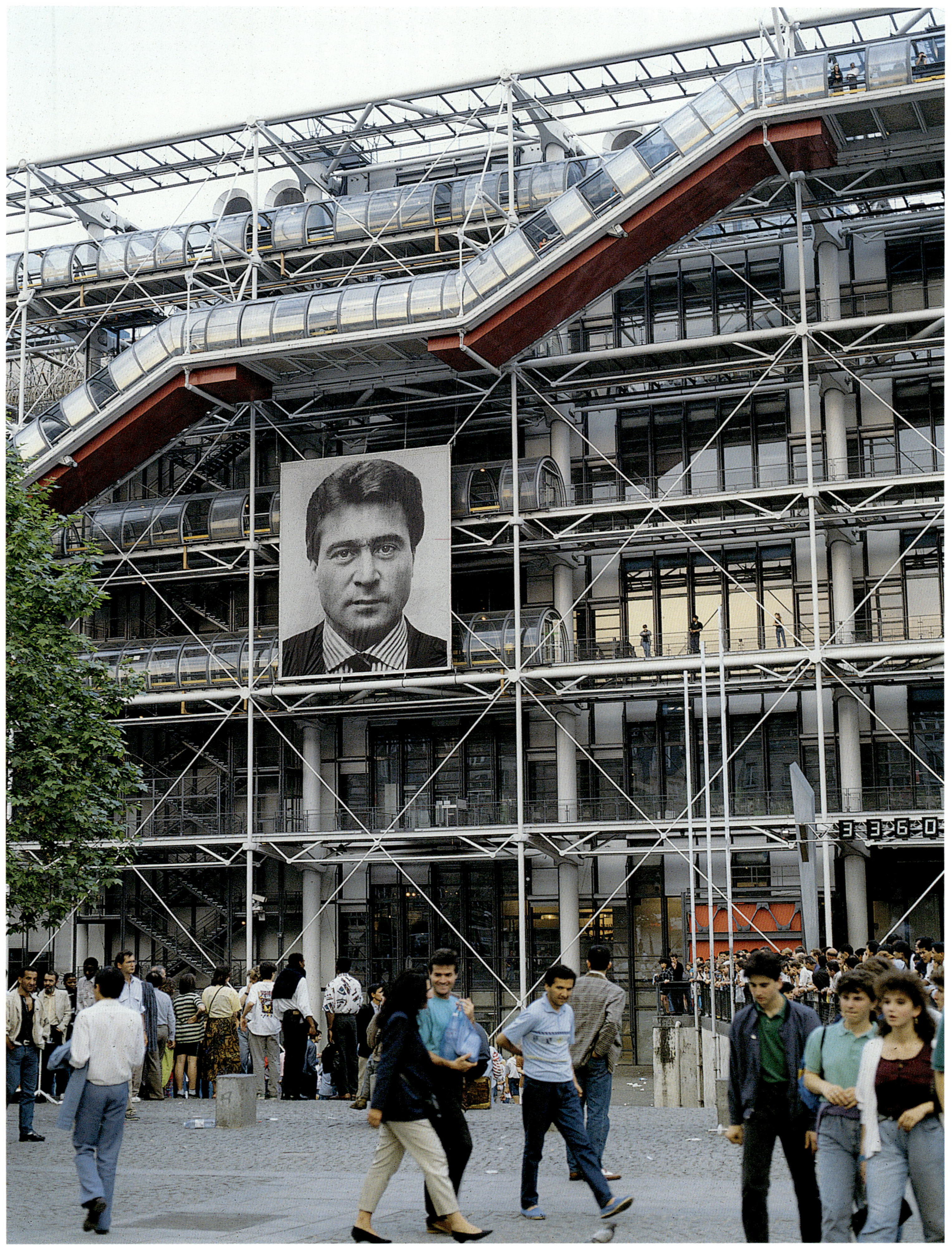

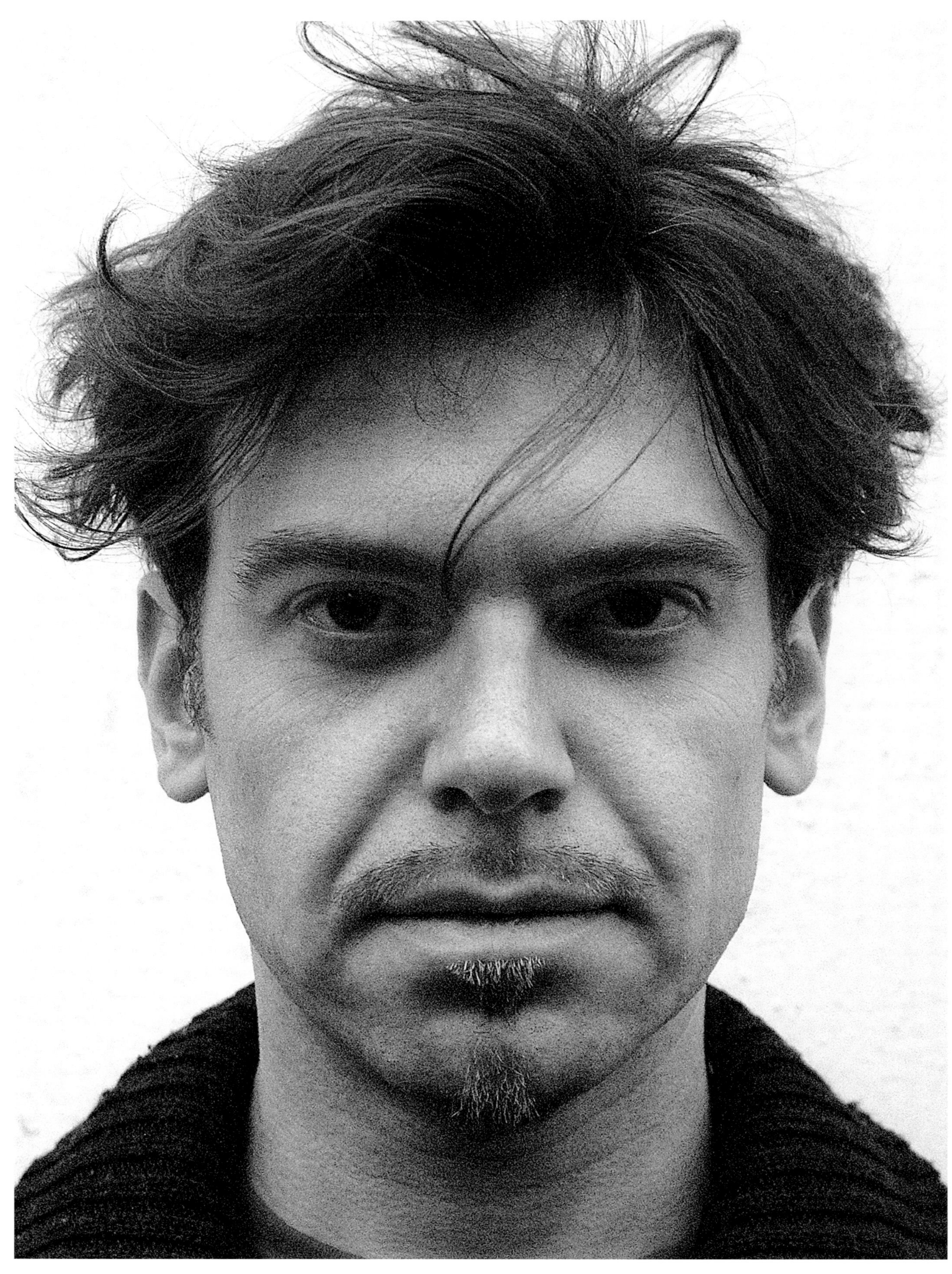

Casual Passer-by I met at 2:20 PM, Rome, 2004
Courtesy Galleria Pino Casagrande, Rome

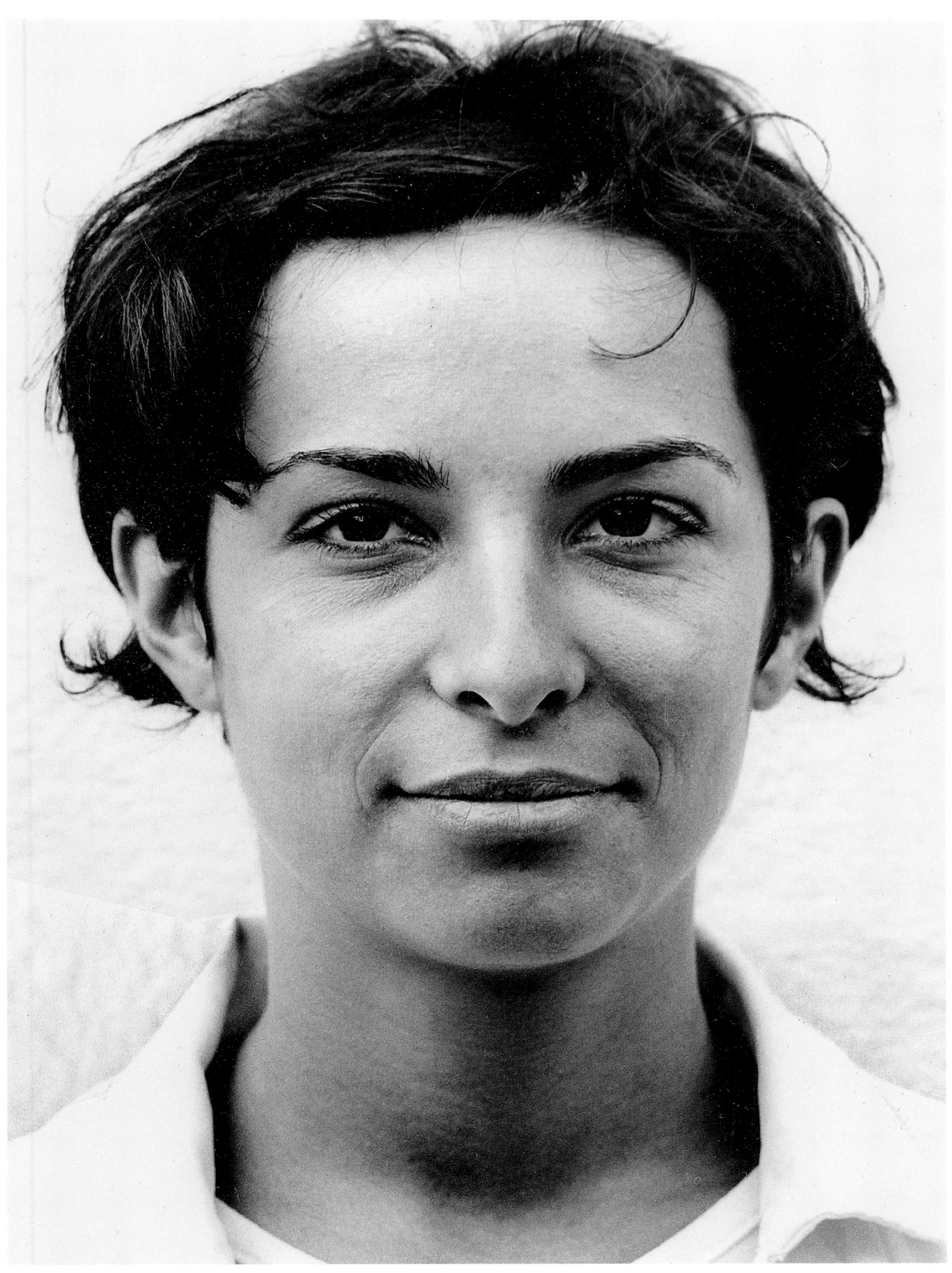

Casual Passer-by I met at 2:09 PM, Rome, 2004
Courtesy Galleria Pino Casagrande, Rome

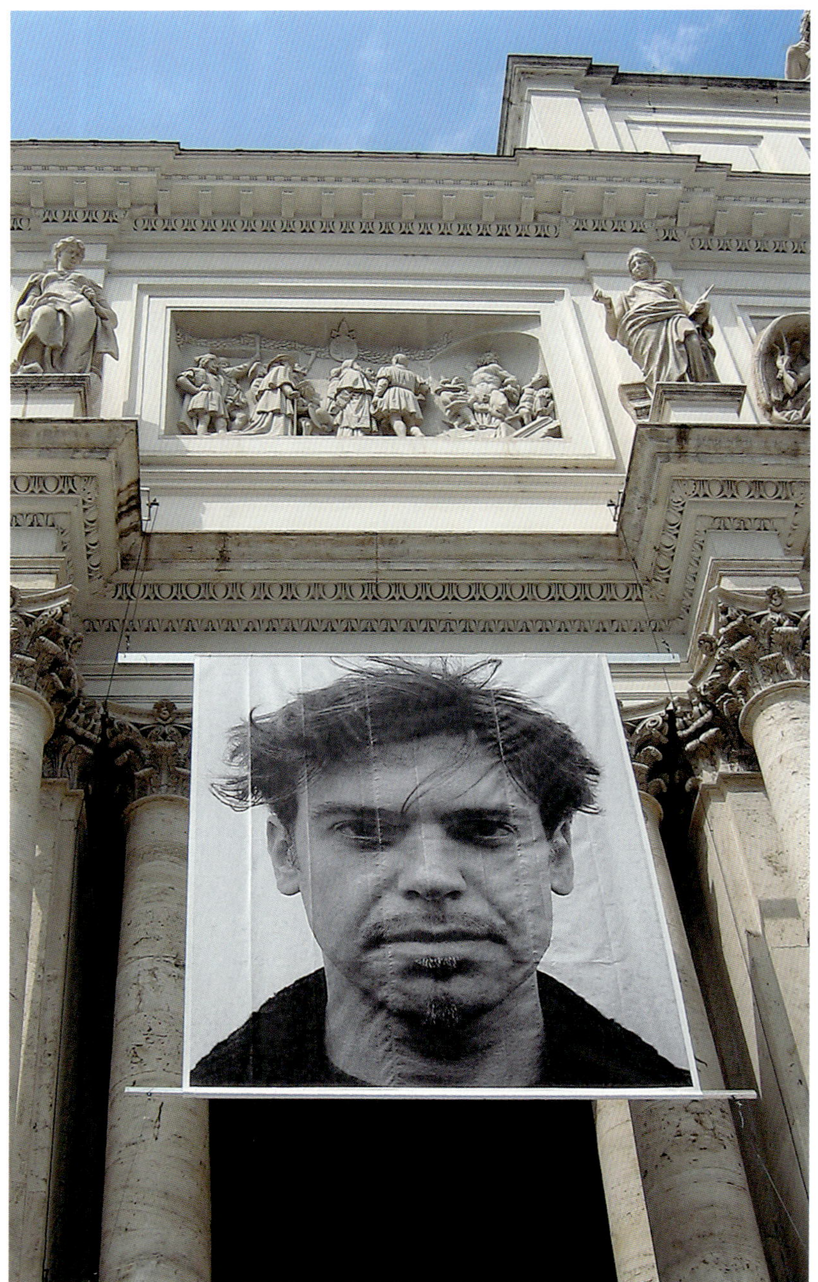

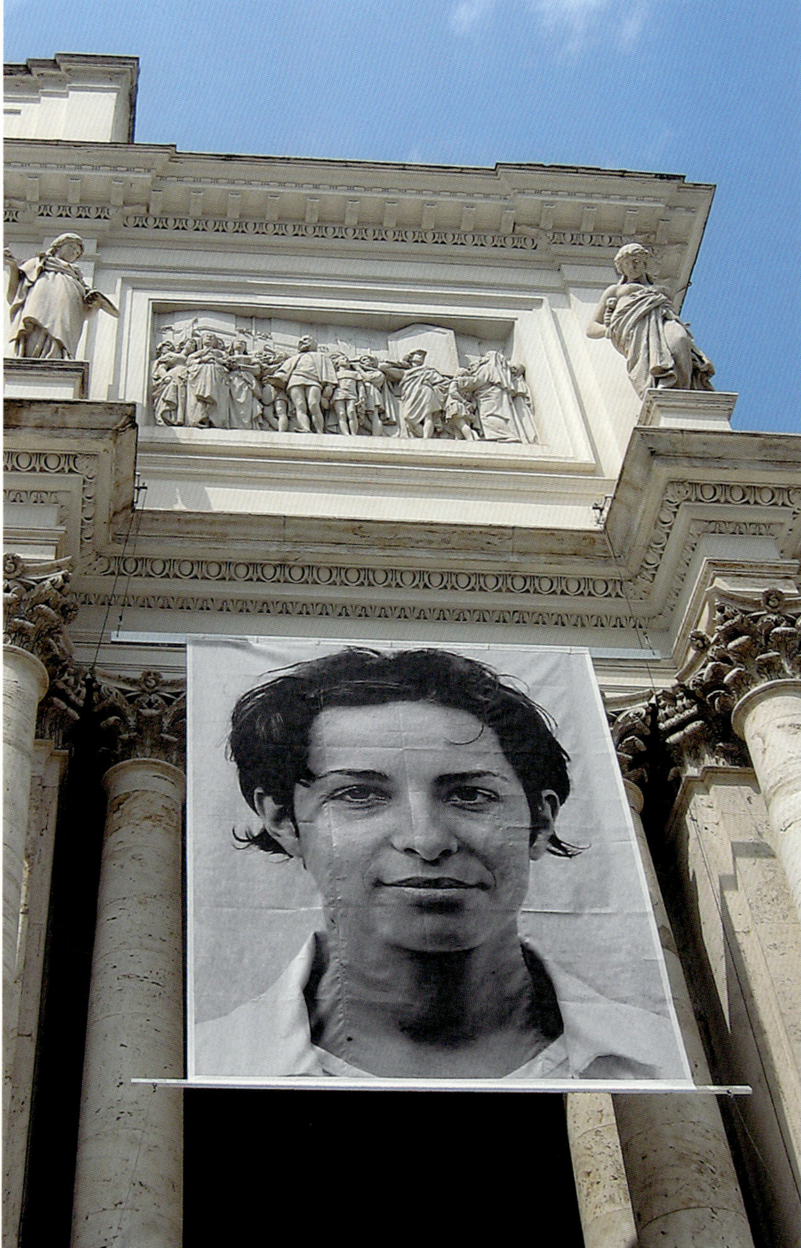

Palazzo delle Esposizioni, Rome, 2004

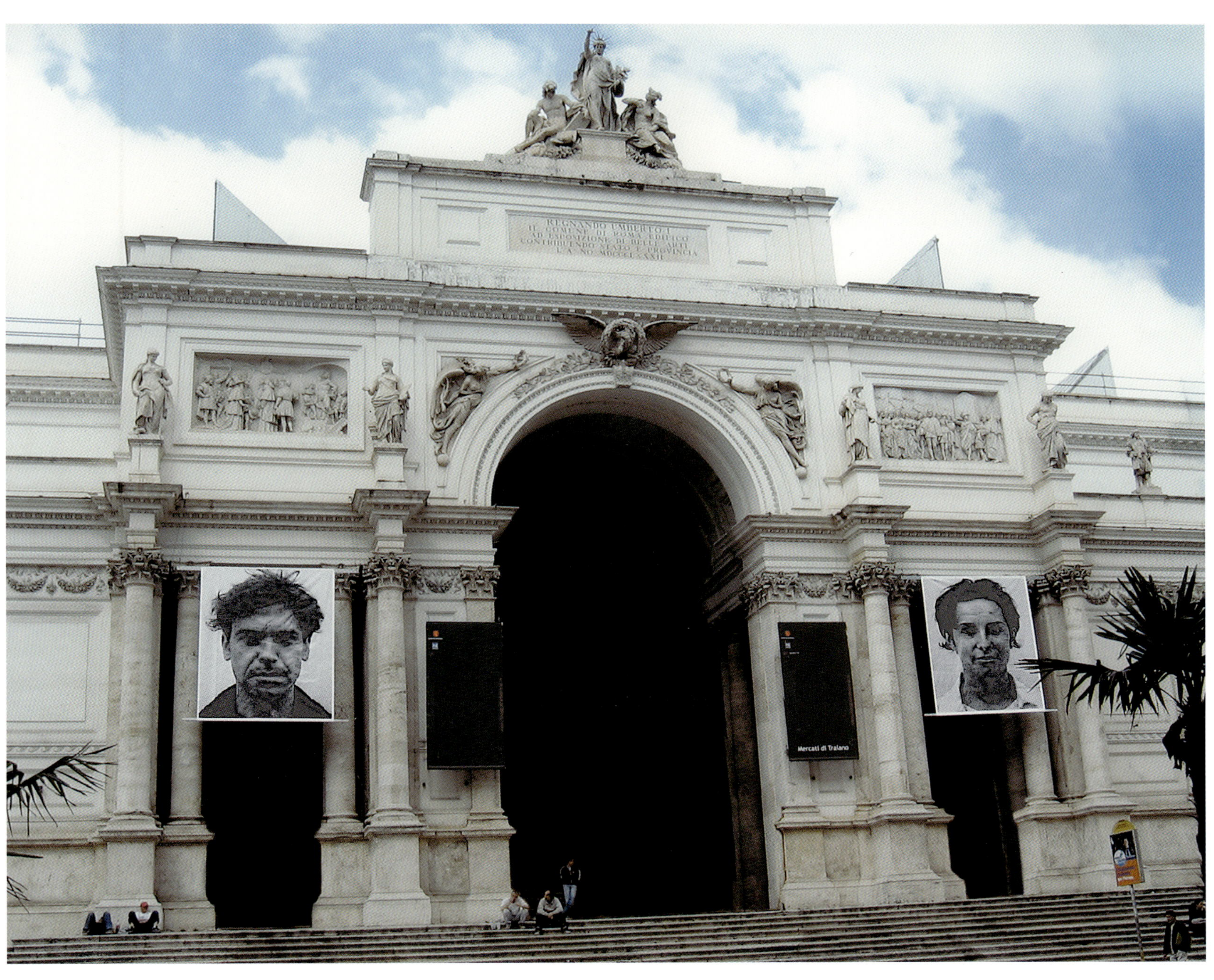
REGNANDO UMBERTO I
Mercati di Traiano

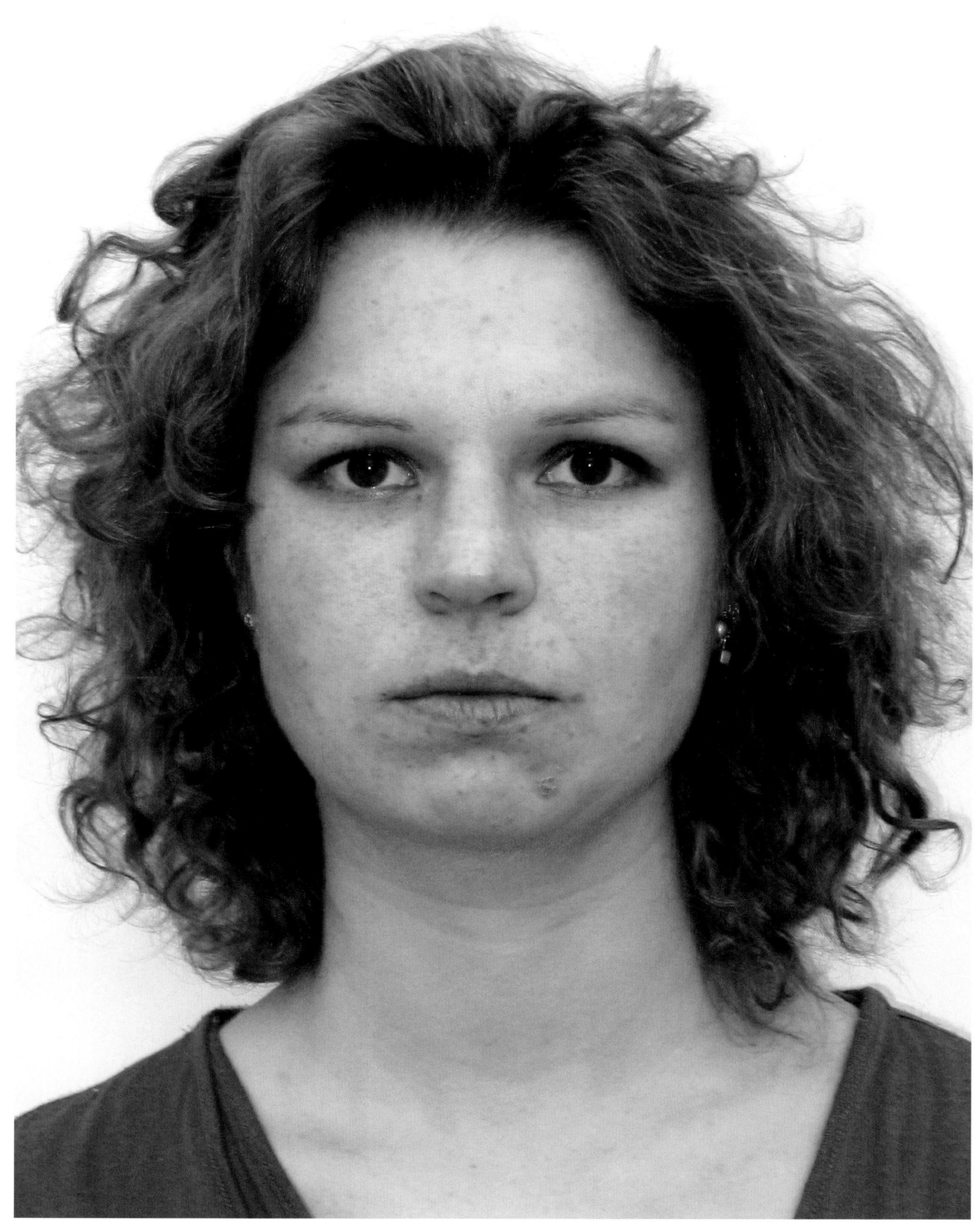

Casual Passer-by I met at 4:01 PM, Herford, 2005

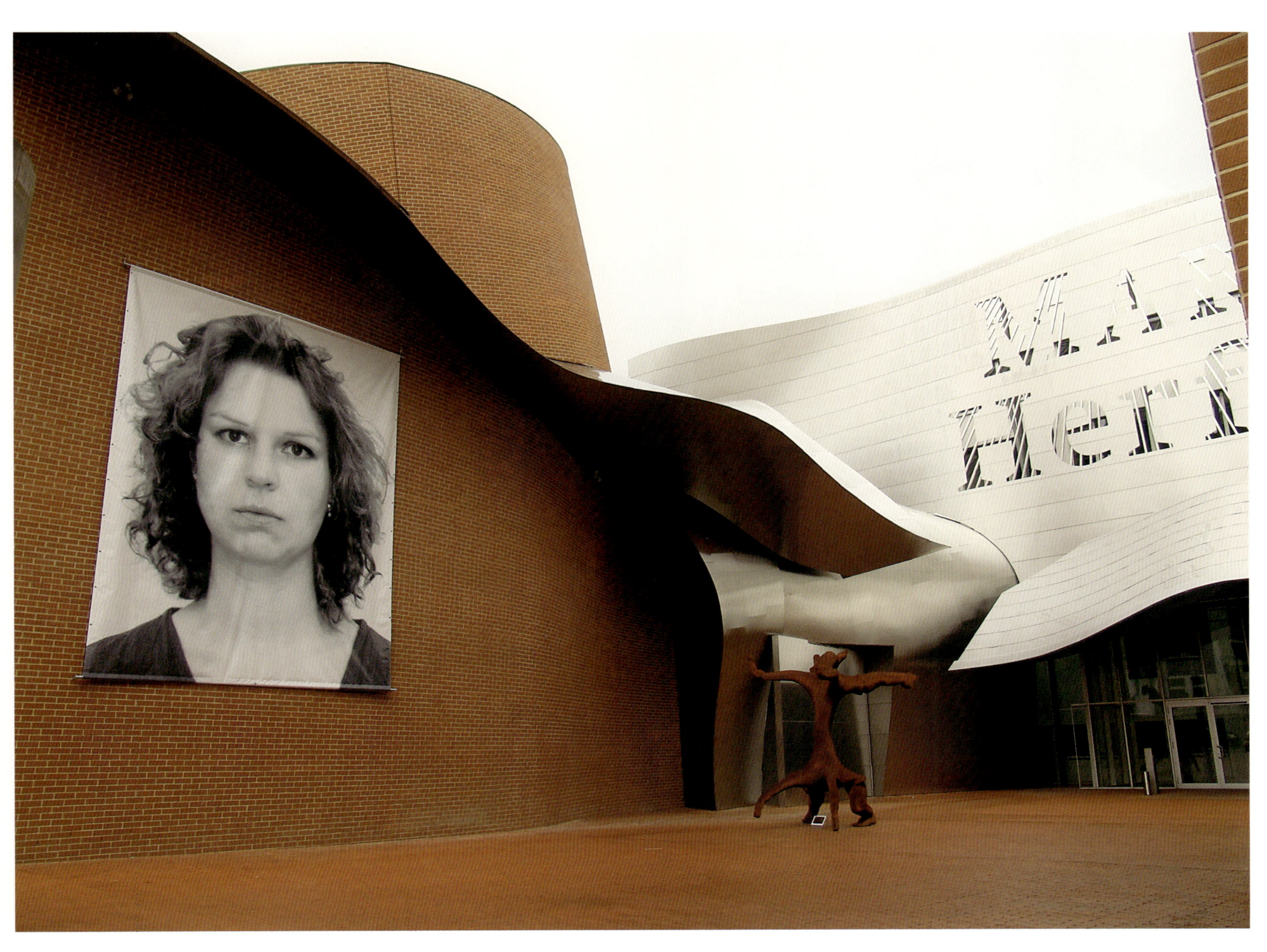

Marta, Herford, 2005

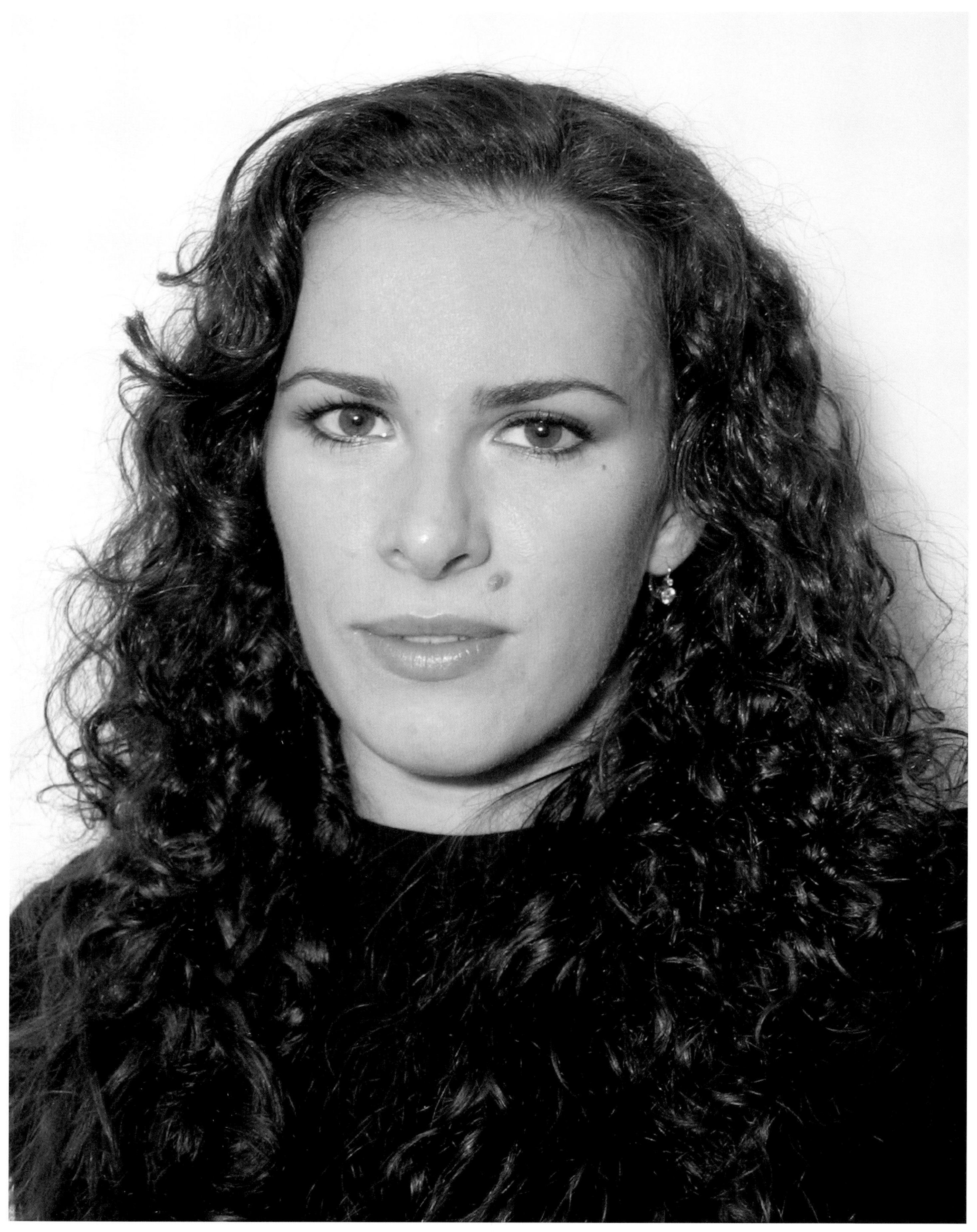

Casual Passer-by I met at 11:23 PM, London, 2005

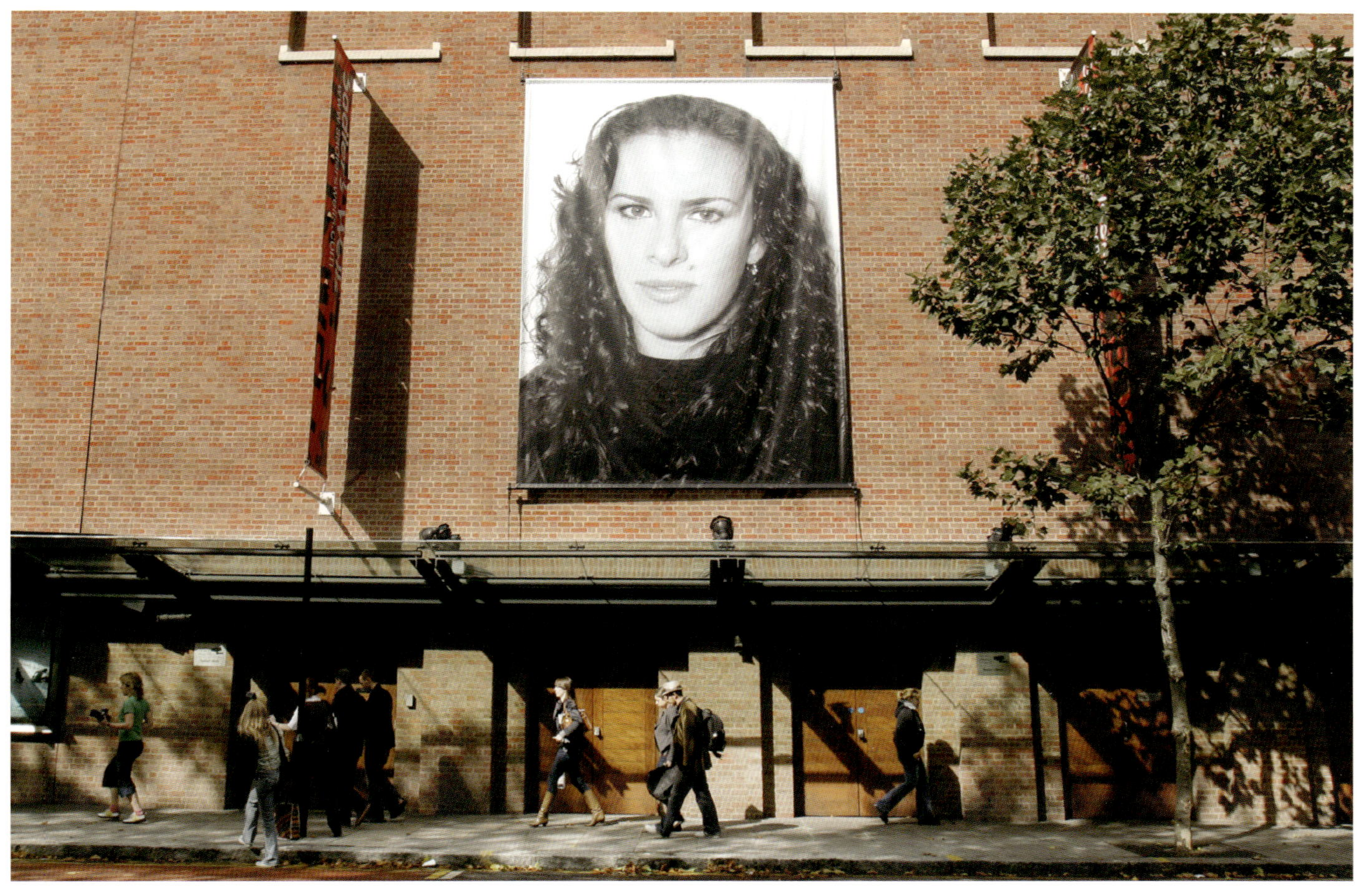

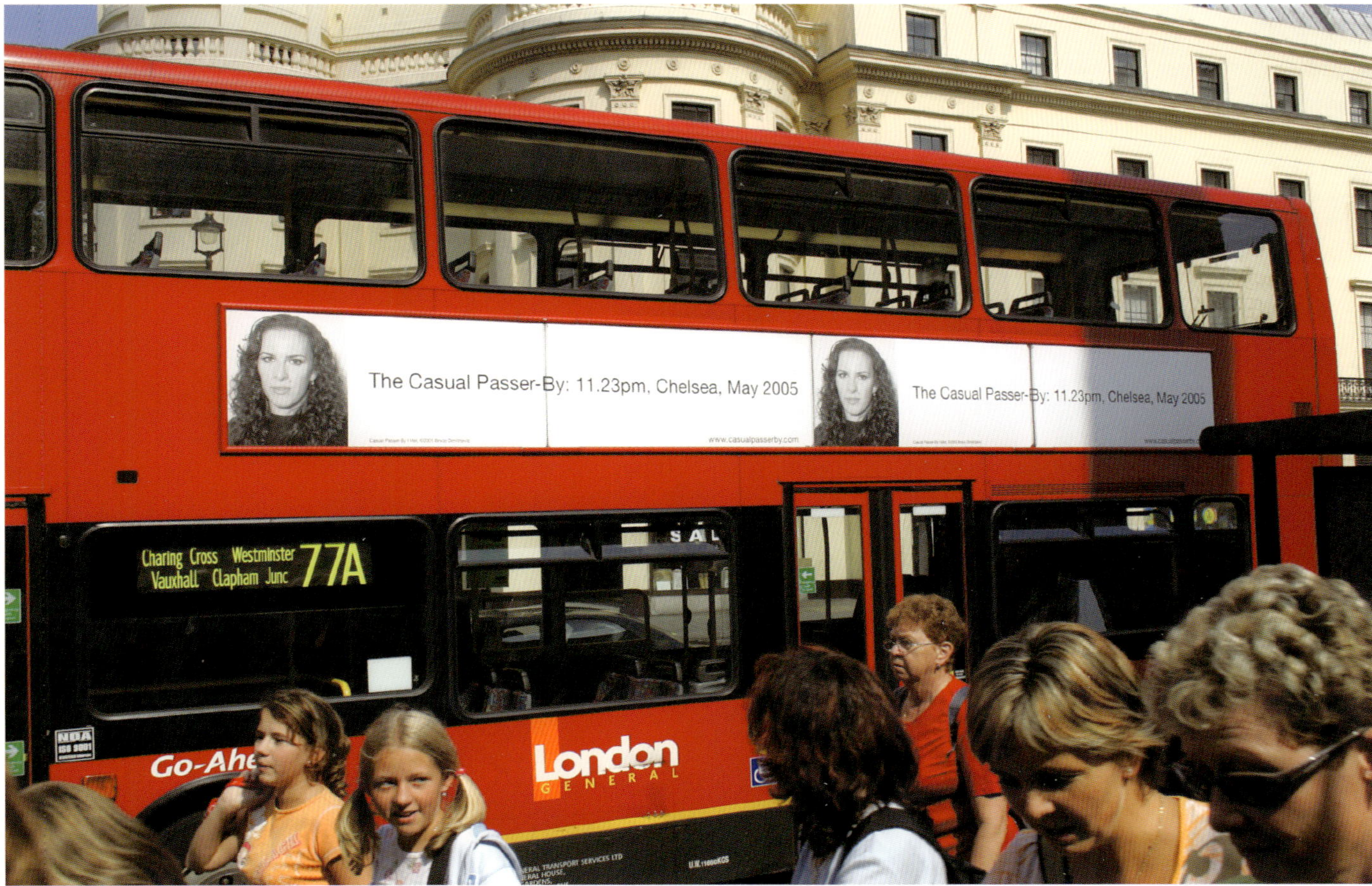

Casual Passer-by, project realized with Tate Modern, London Transport, Viacom Outdoor, and Sadler's Wells, London

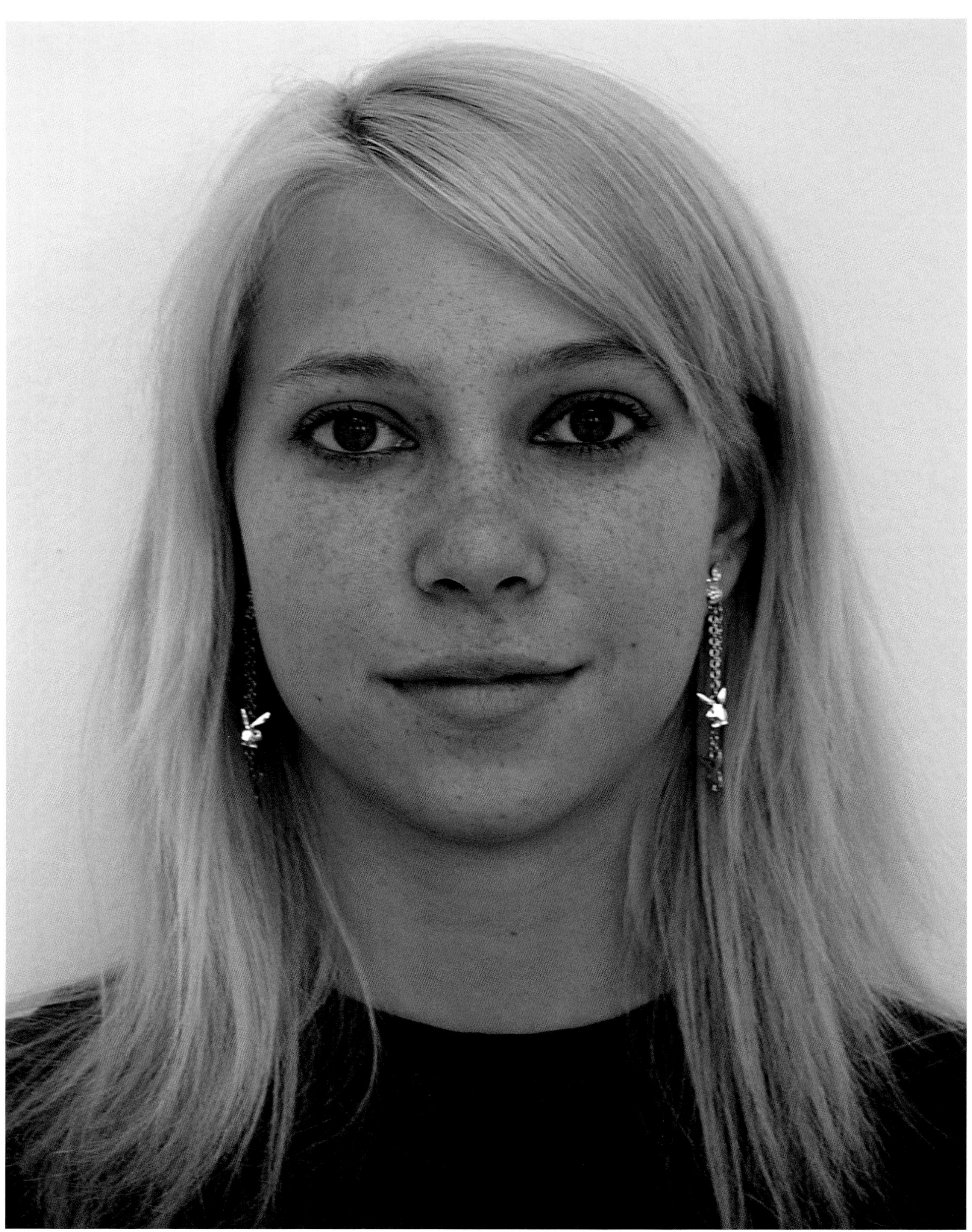

Casual Passer-by I met at 2:07 PM, Budapest, 2008

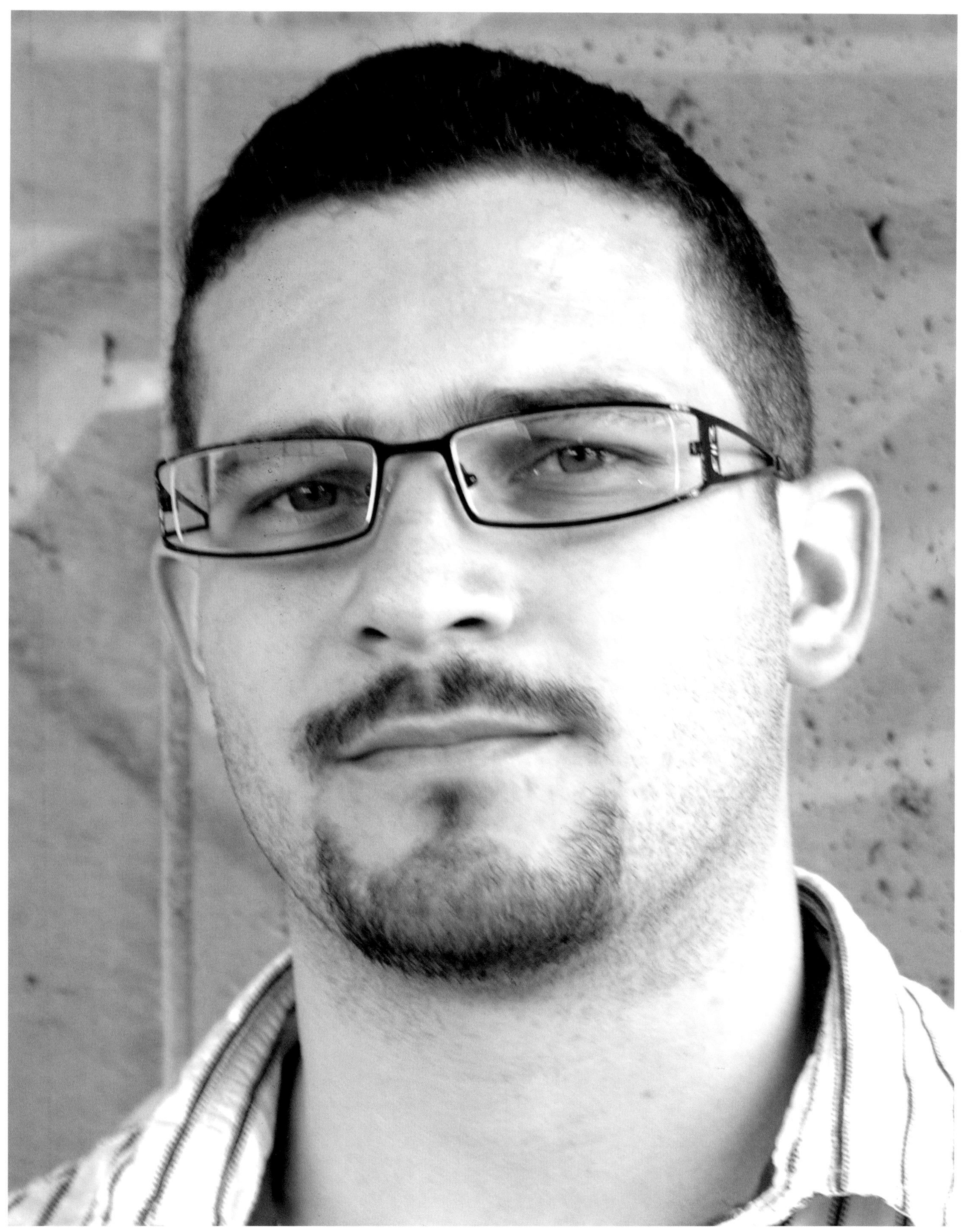

Casual Passer-by I met at 2:07 PM, Budapest, 2008

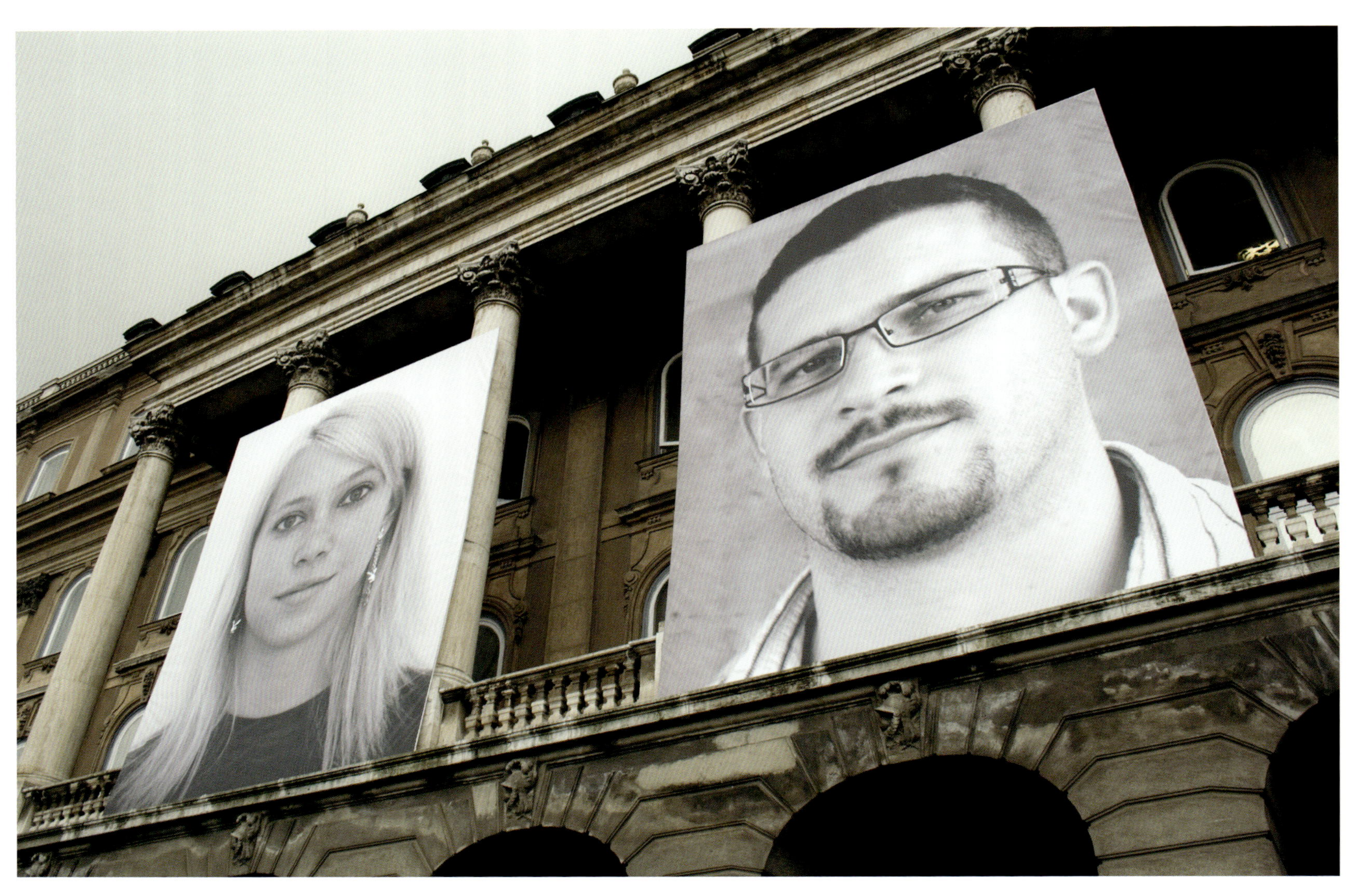

Buda Castle, Budapest, 2008

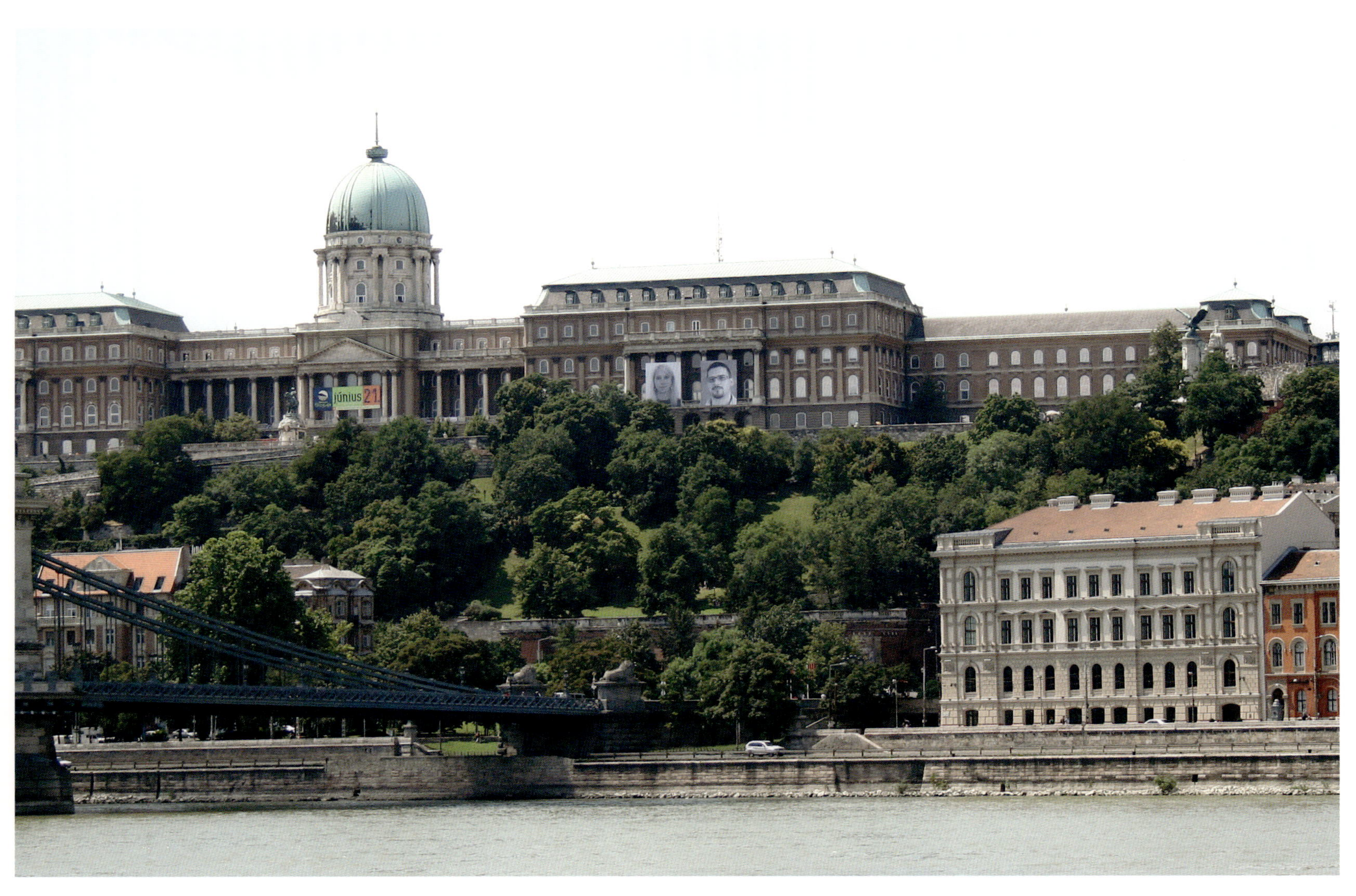

Buda Castle, view from Pest Side, 2008

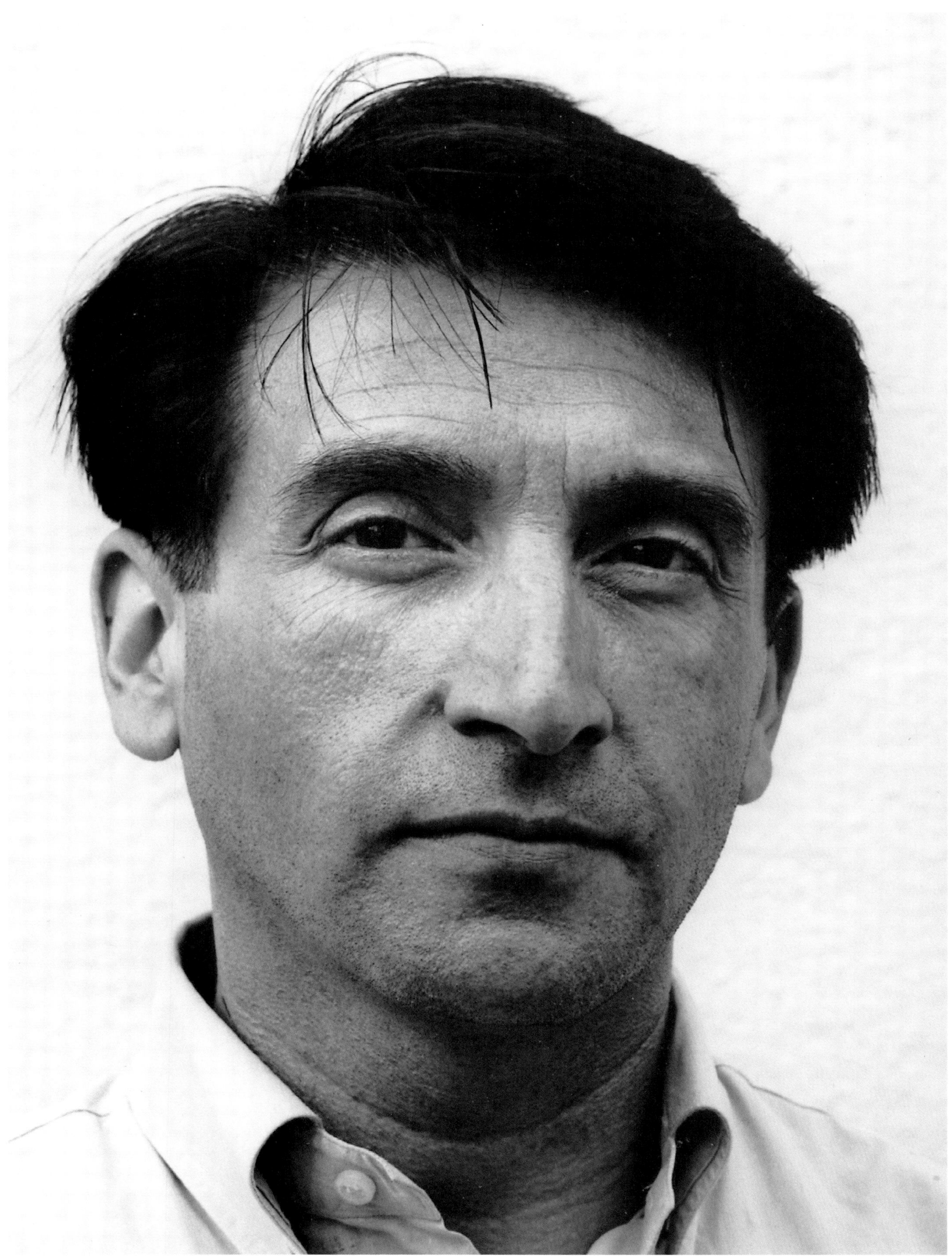

Casual Passer-by I met at 3:41 PM, Paris, 1999

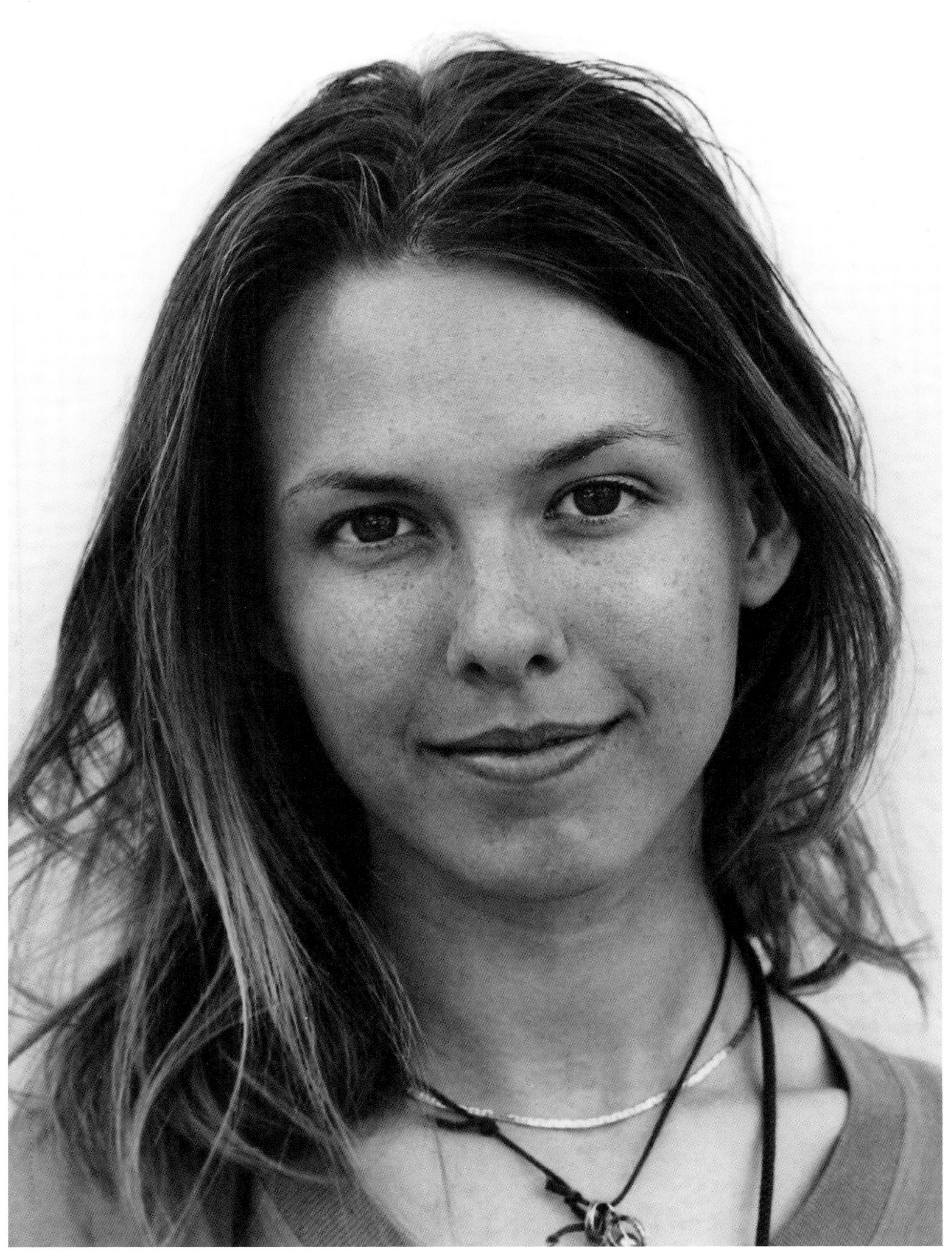

Casual Passer-by I met at 3:47 PM, Paris, 1999

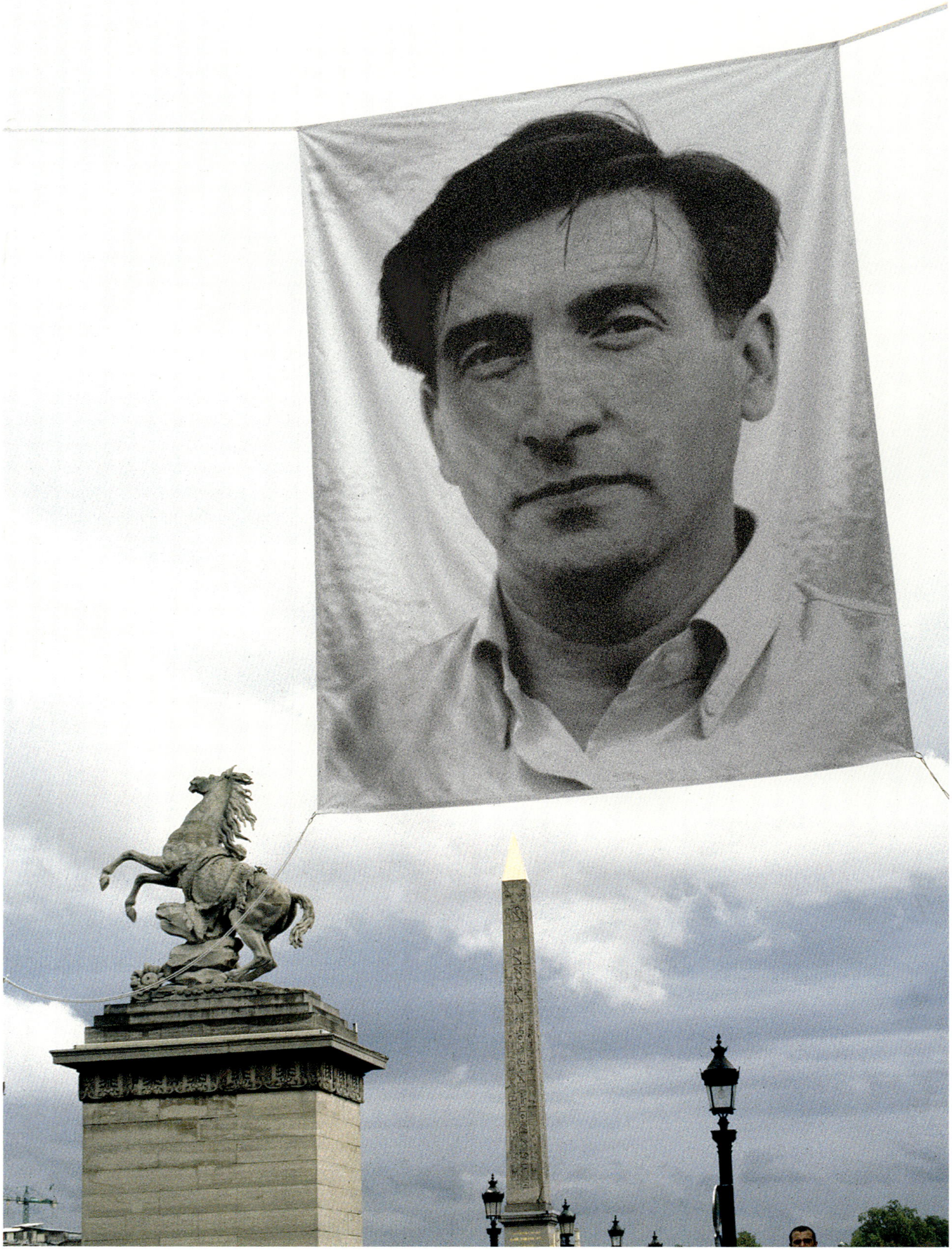

Place de la Concorde, Paris, 1999

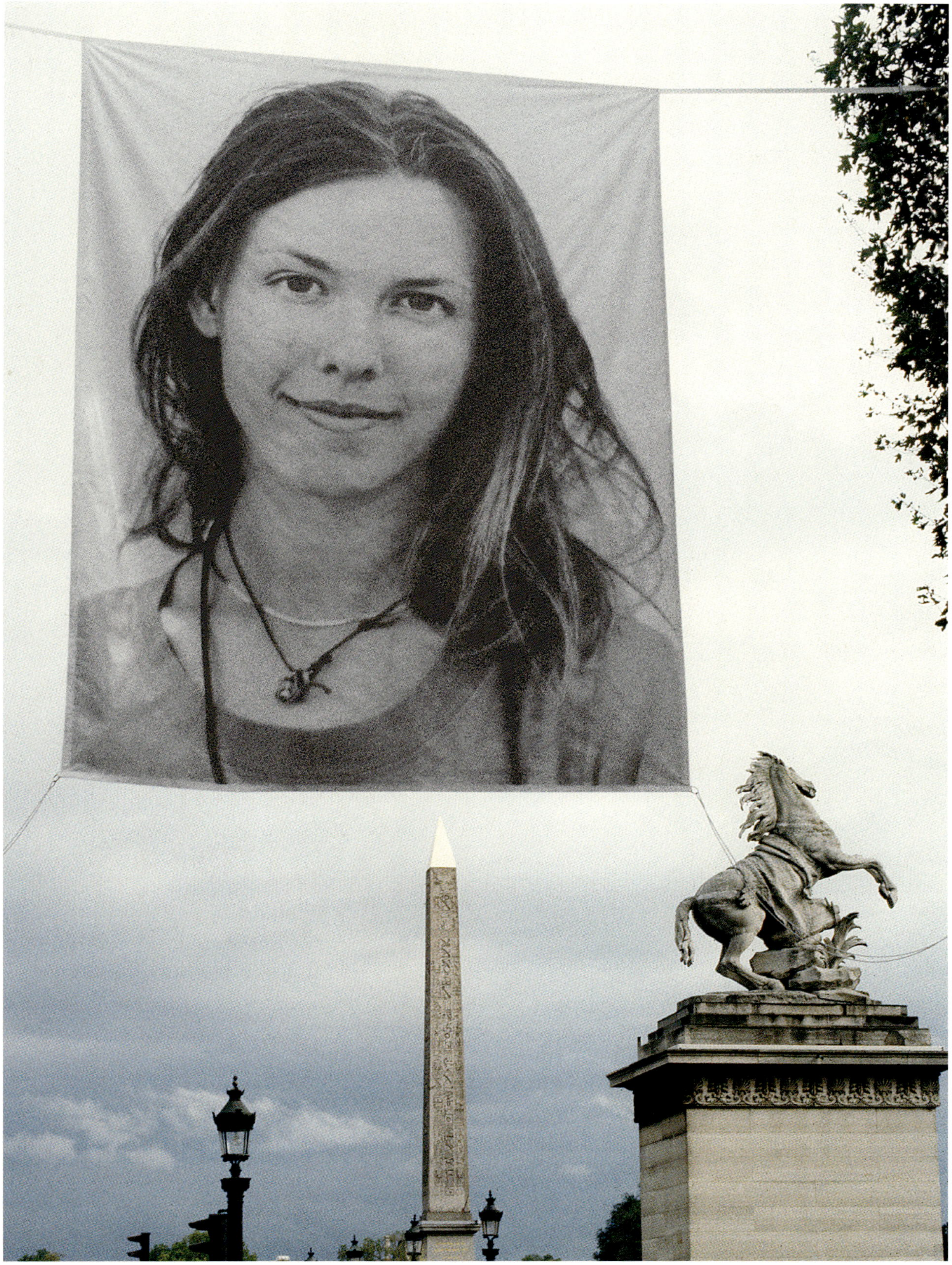

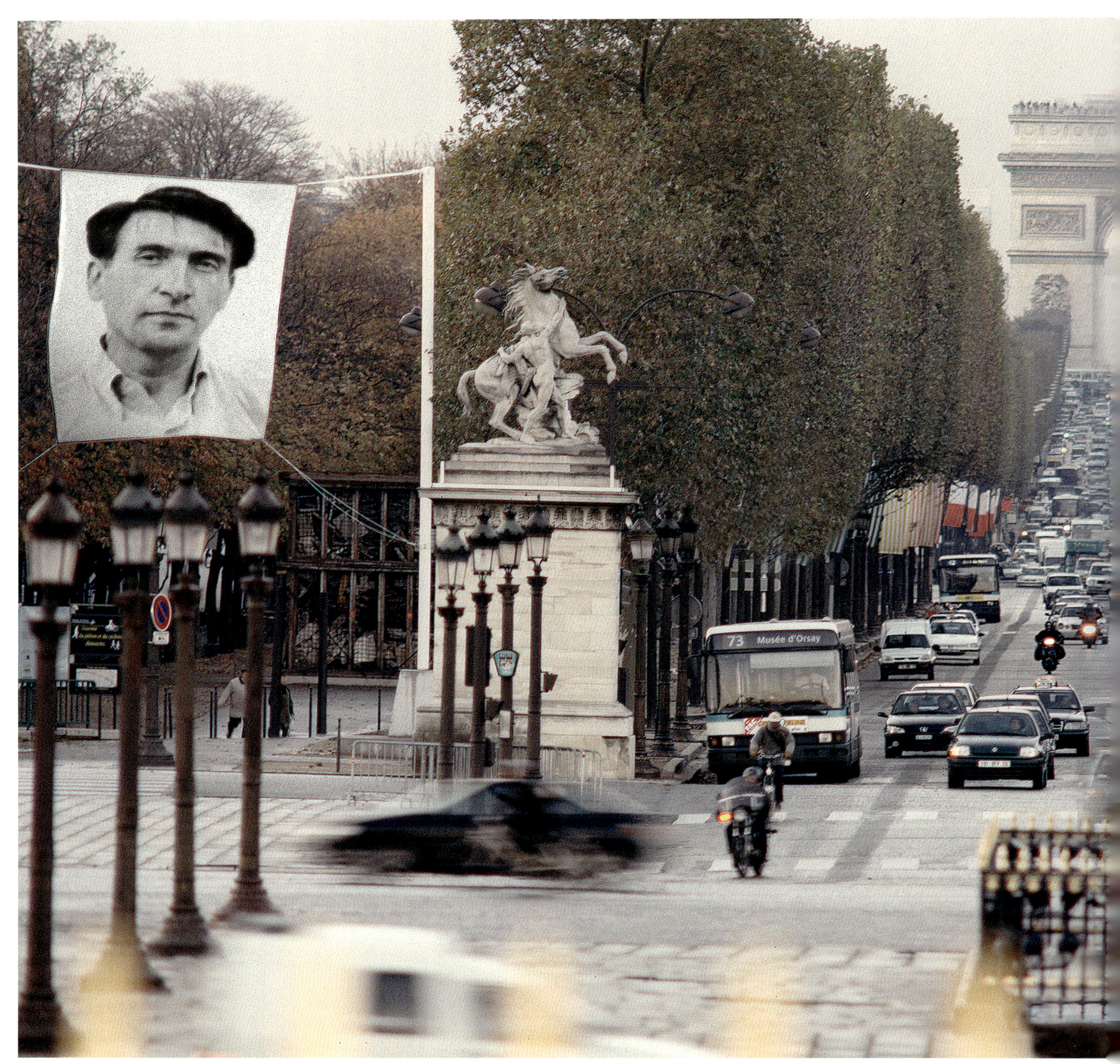

Les Champs-Élysées, Paris, 1999–2000

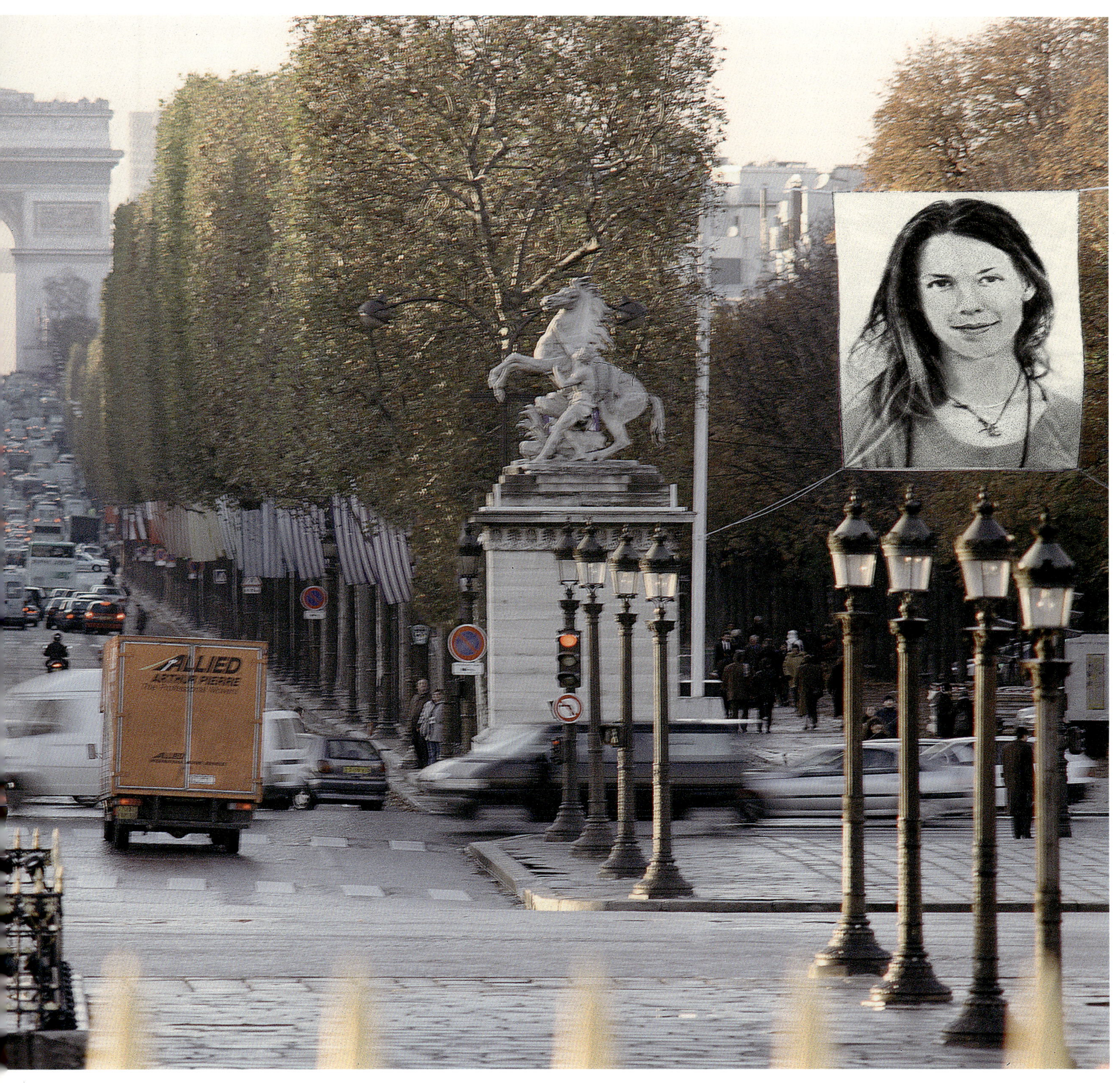
ALLIED
ARTHUR PIERRE

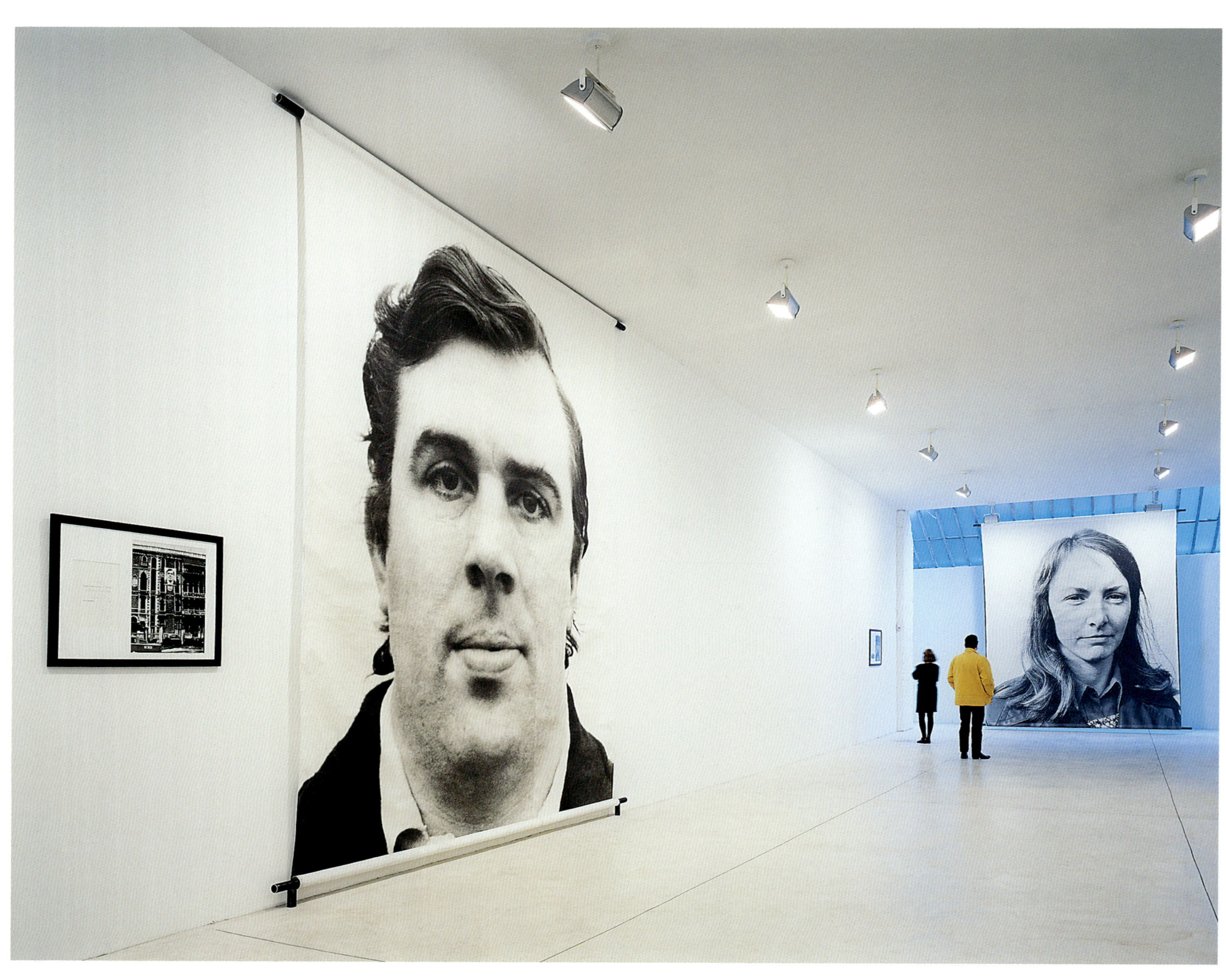

Early Works, 1968–1976
Pat Hearn Gallery, New York, 1990

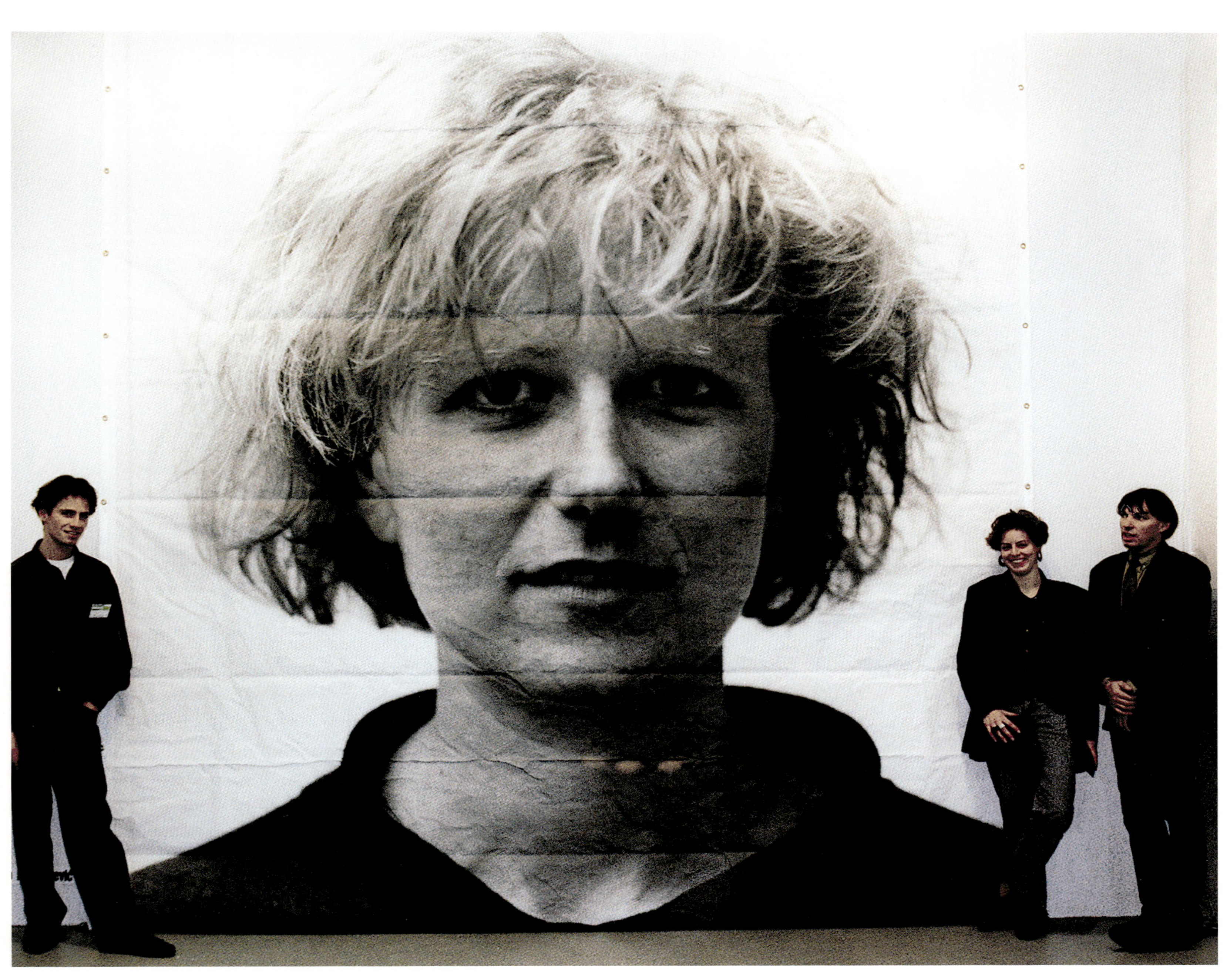

Casual Passer-by I met, London, 1982
Collection: Bernhard Starkmann, London

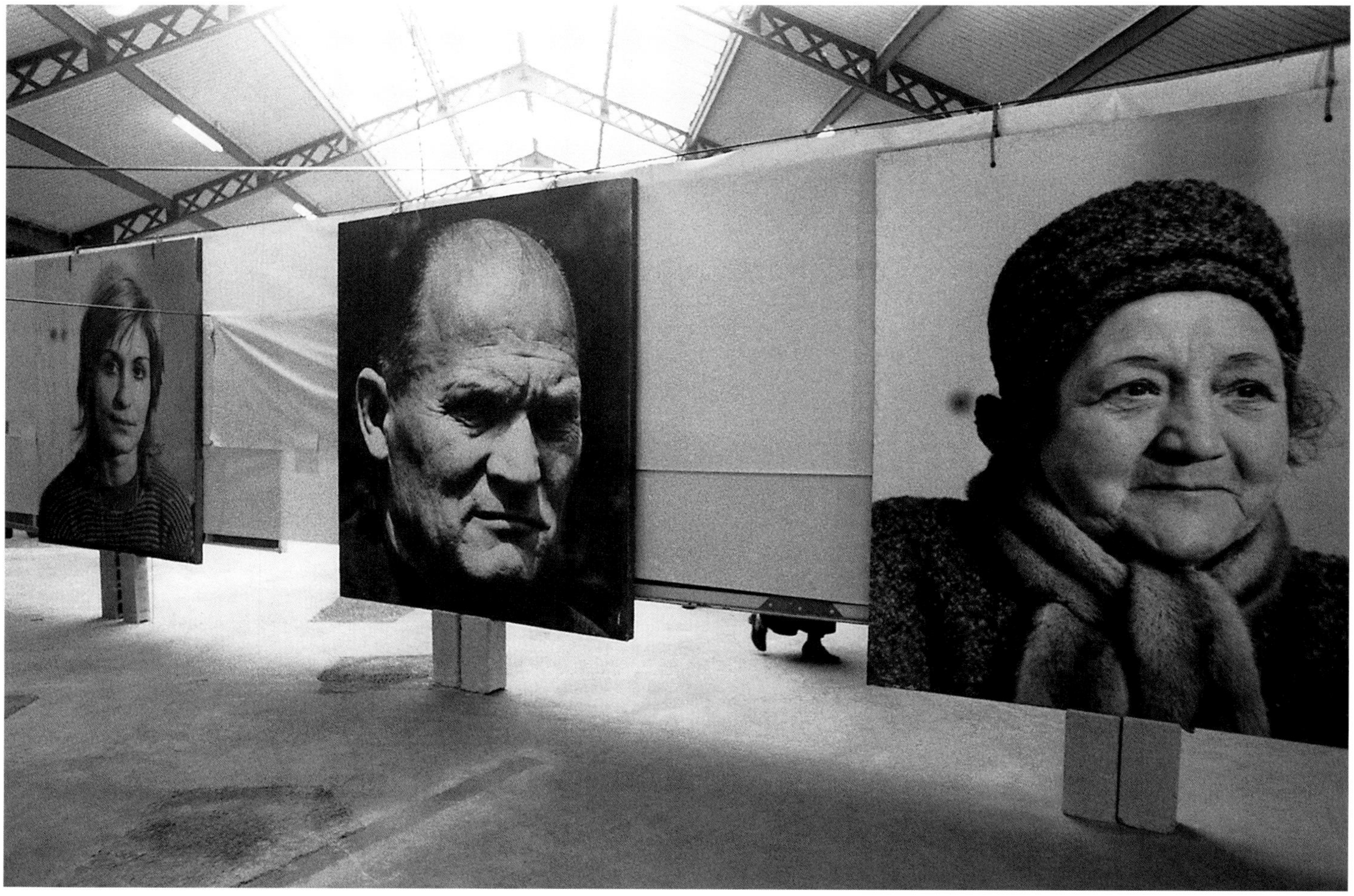

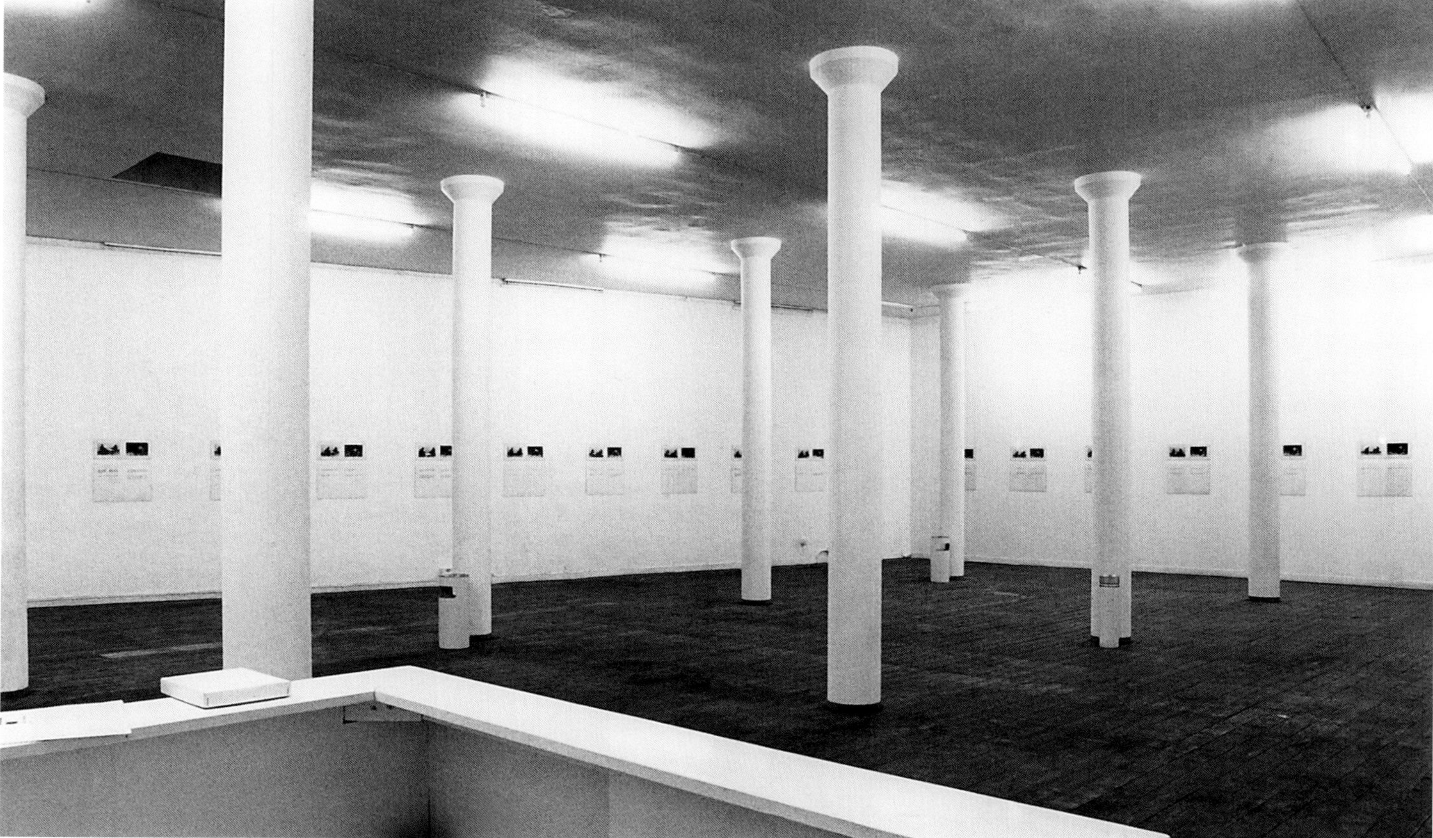

7th Paris Biennale, 1971

One-man exhibition at the Robert Self Gallery, London, 1975

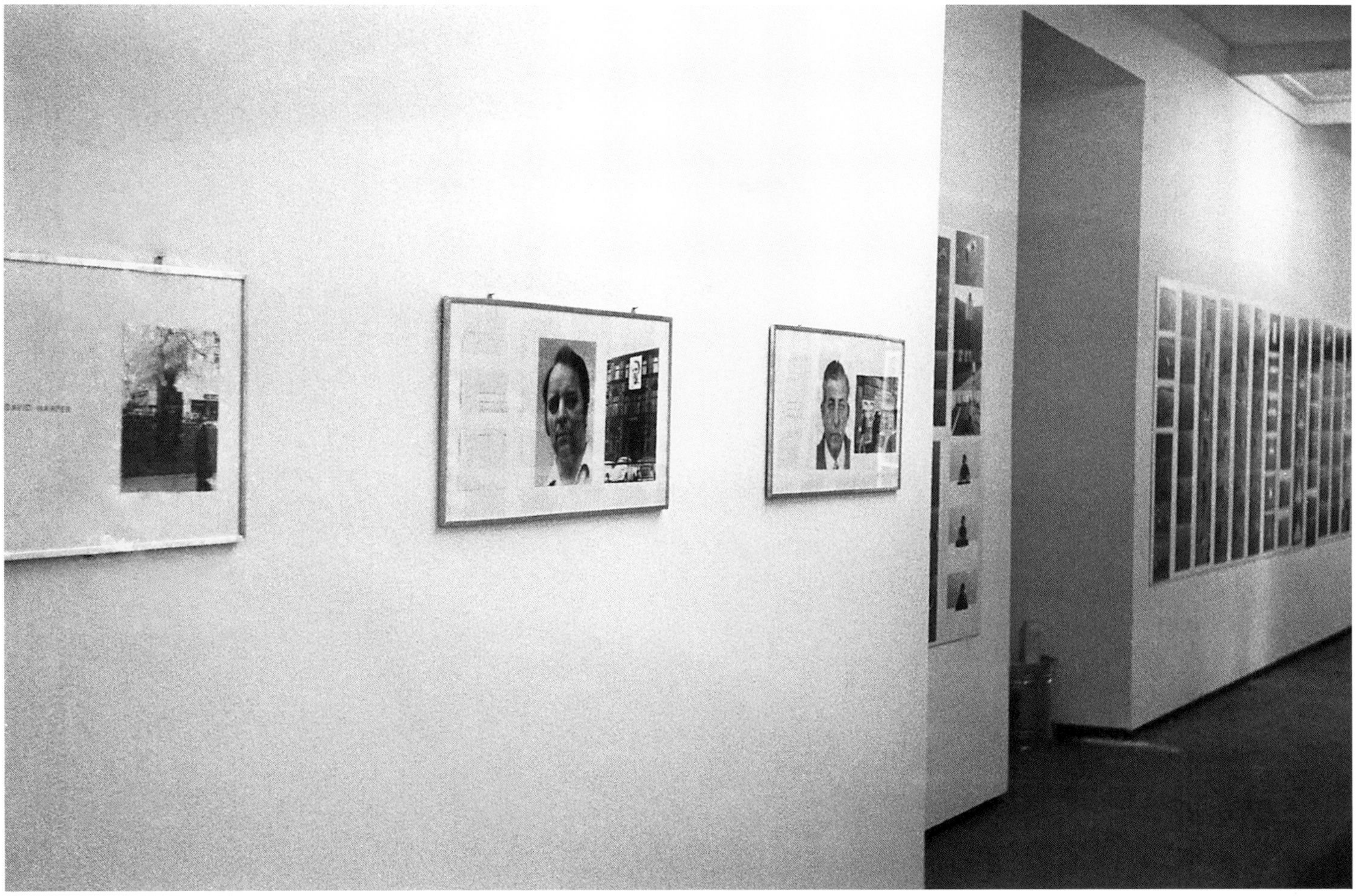

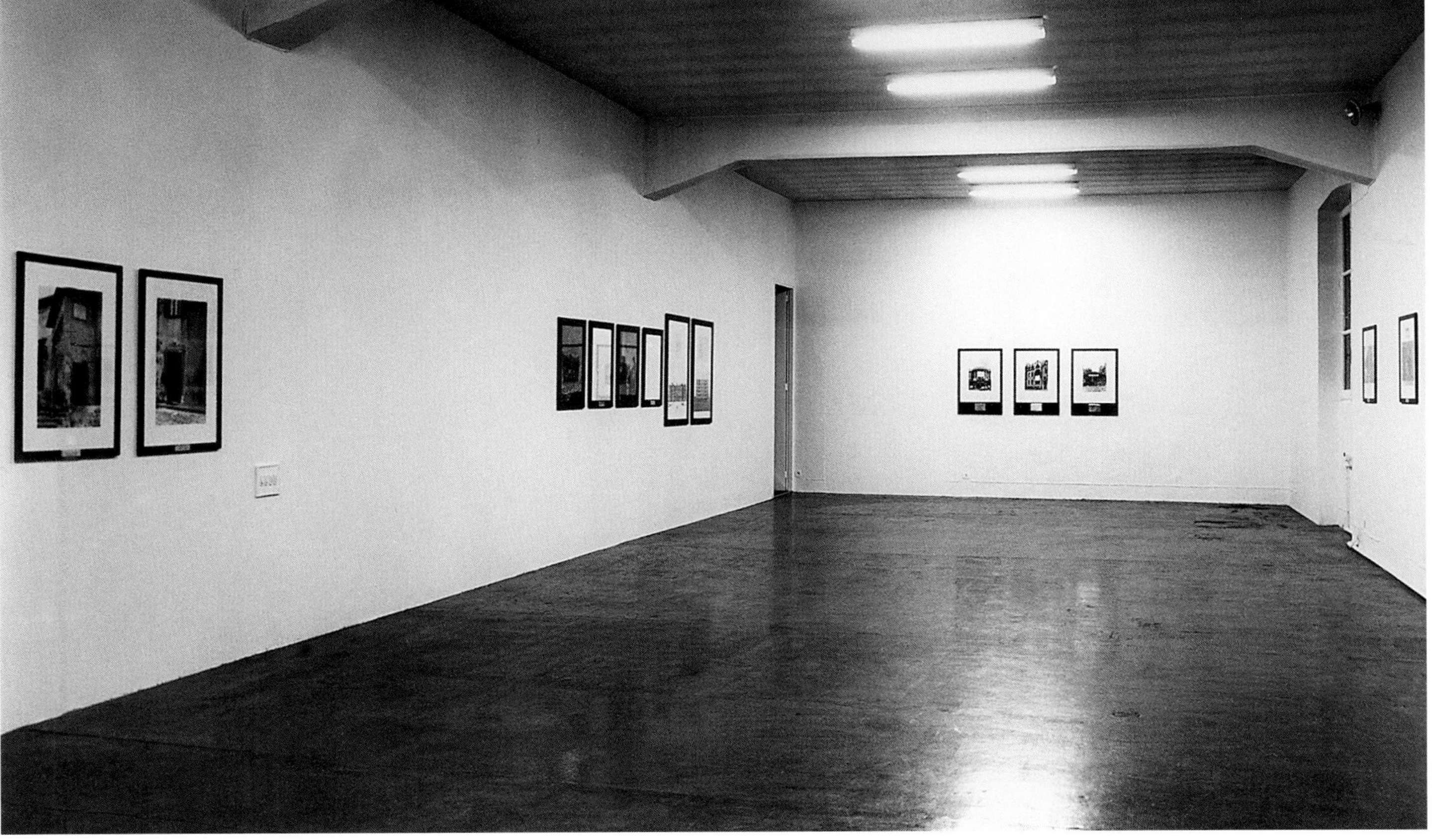

Documenta V, Fridericianum, Kassel, 1972

One-man exhibition at the Galleria Gian Enzo Sperone, Turin, 1974

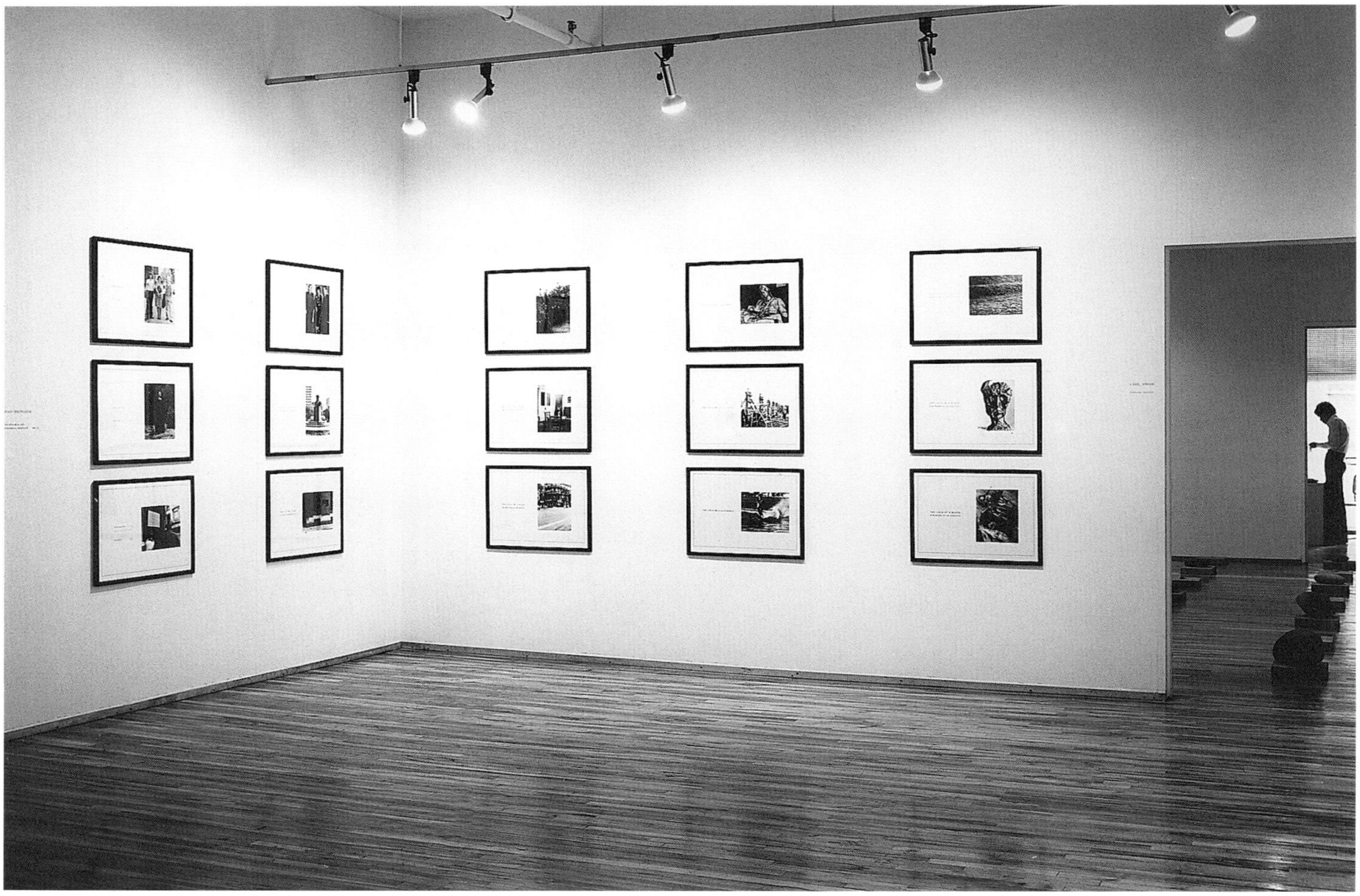

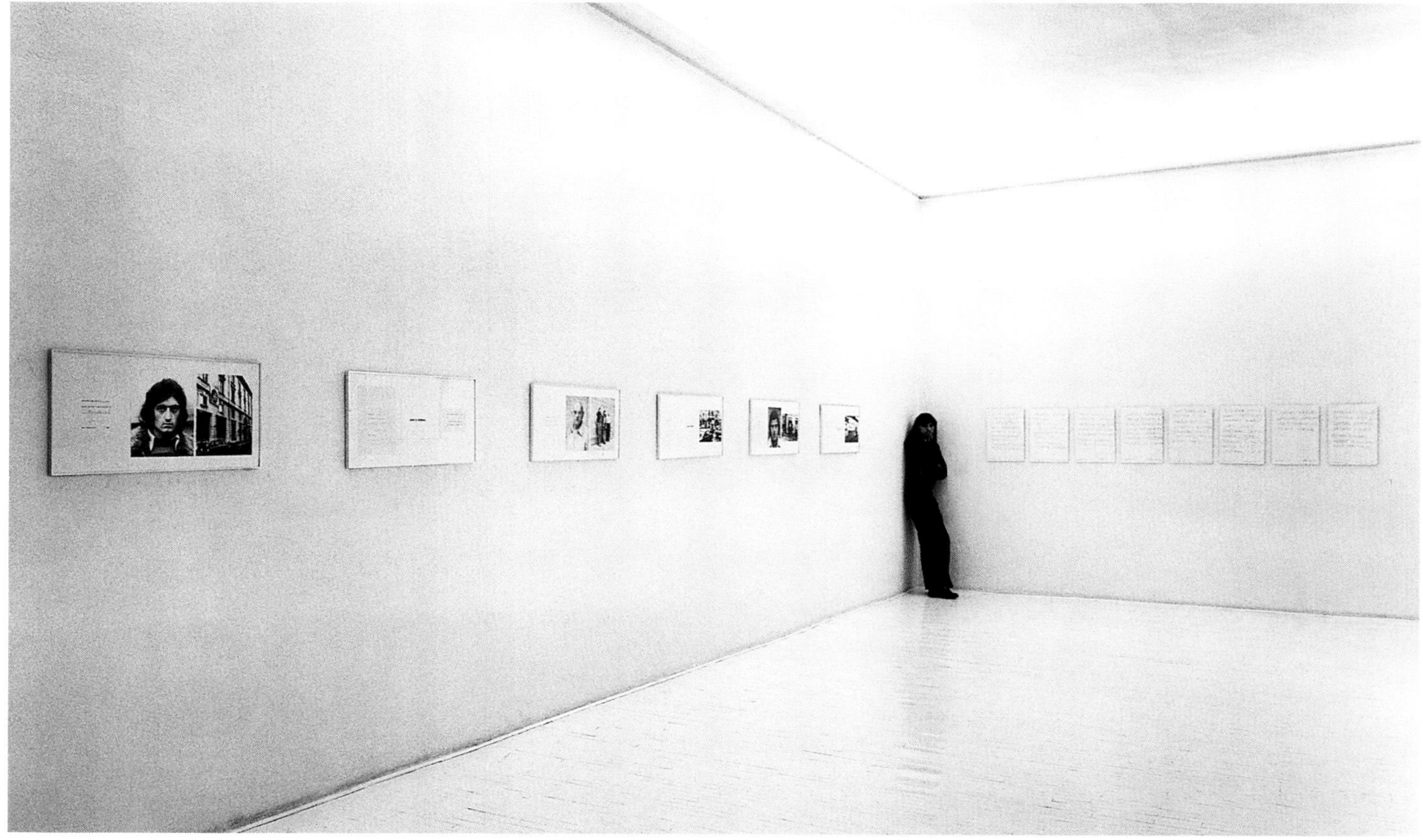

One-man exhibition at the Sperone Gallery, New York, 1975

One-man exhibition at the Galleria Francoise Lambert, Milan, 1974

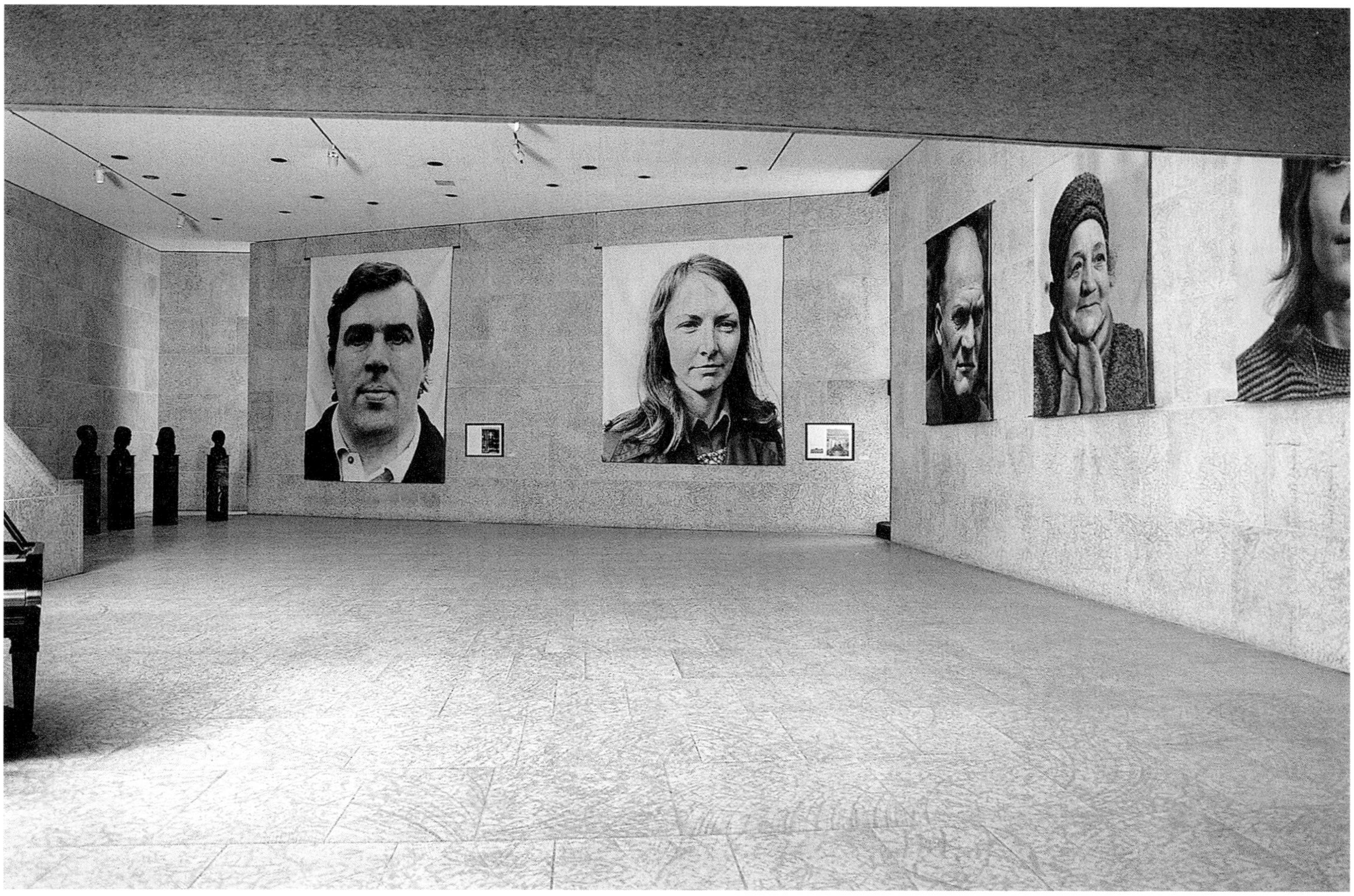

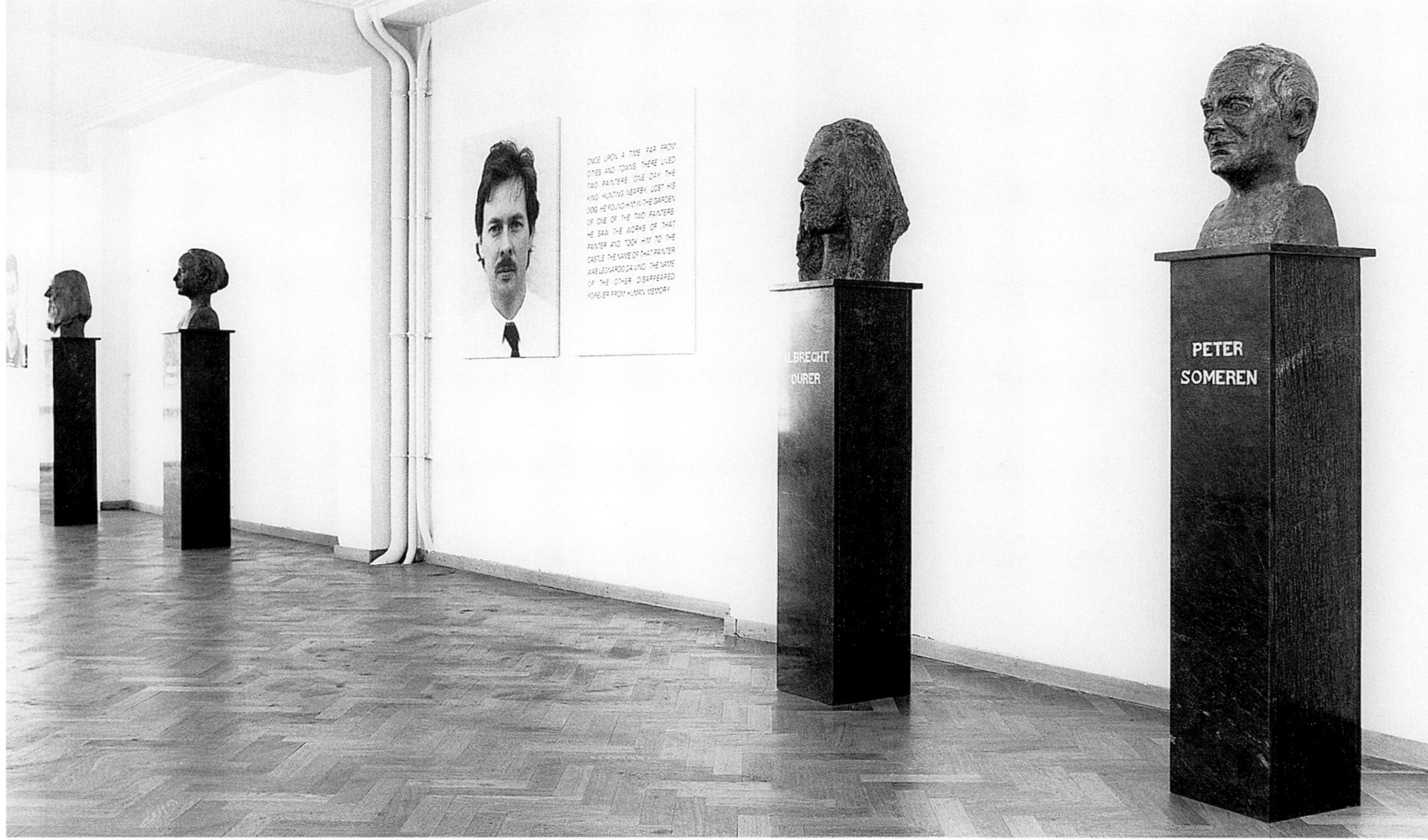

One-man exhibition at the Winnipeg Art Gallery, Canada, 1990

One-man exhibition at the Galerie Albert Baronian, Brussels, 1989

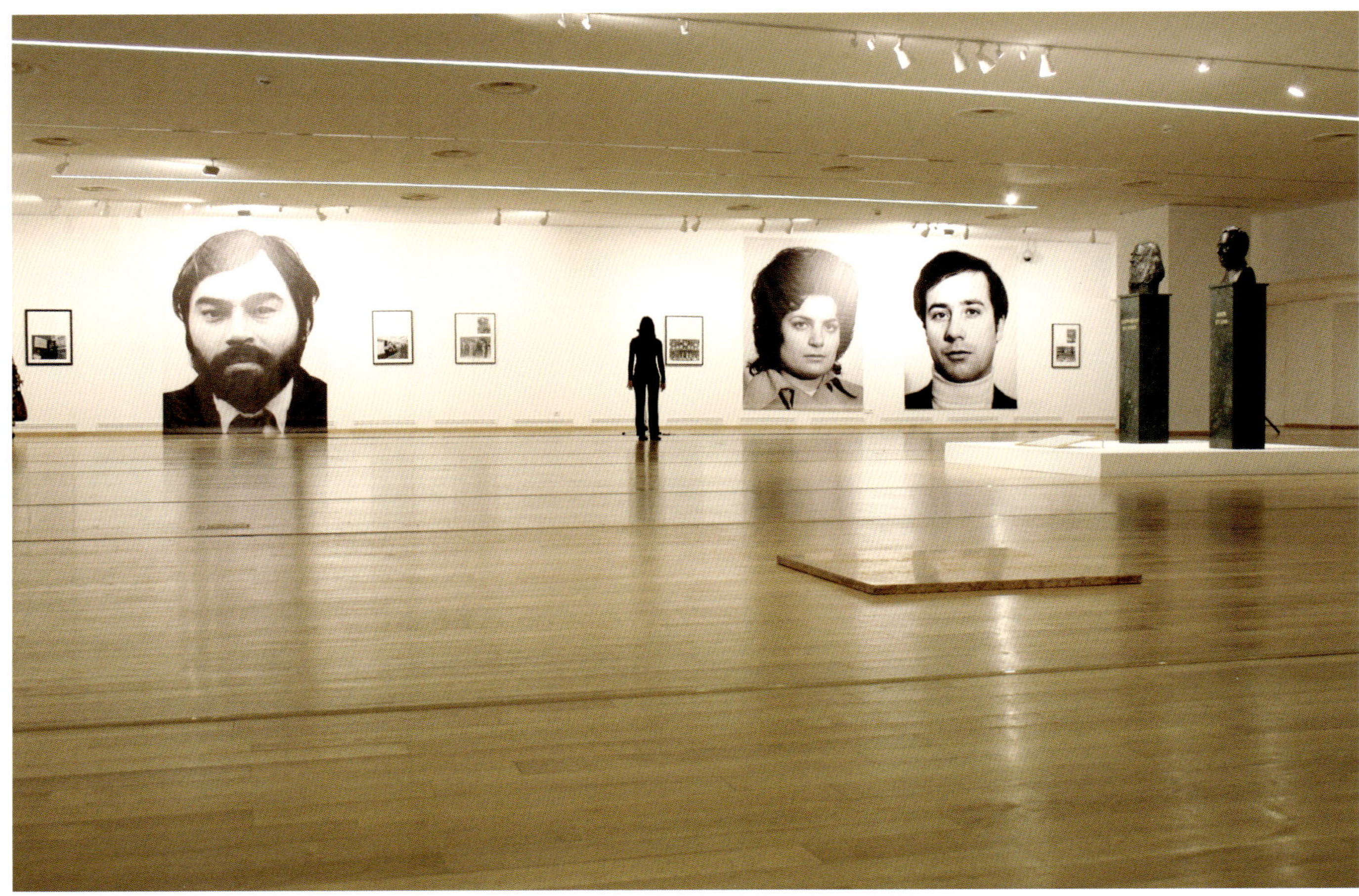

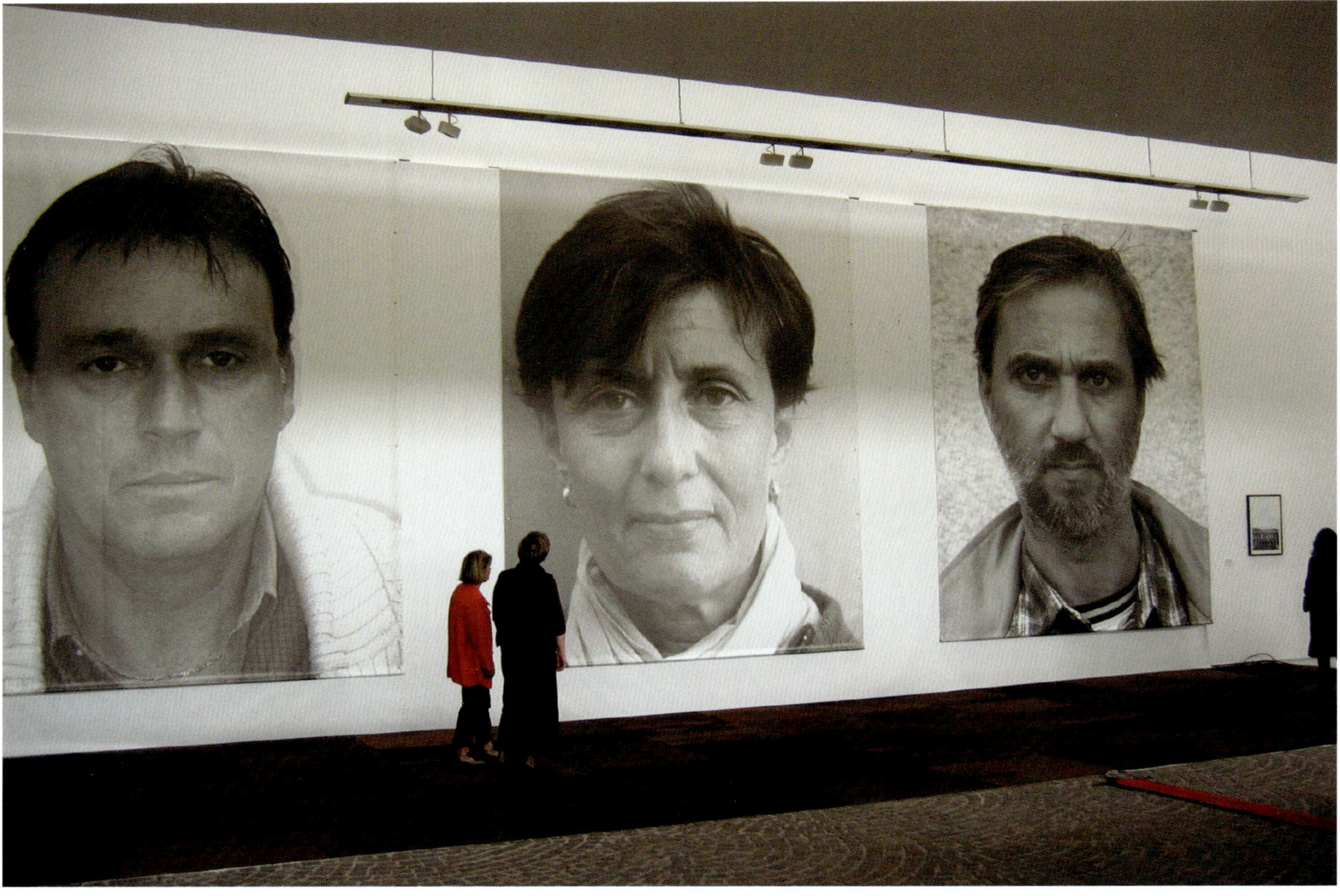

Retrospective at National Museum of Contemporary Art, Bucharest, 2008 *Casual Passers-by I met*, Musée d'Art Moderne, St. Etienne, 2004

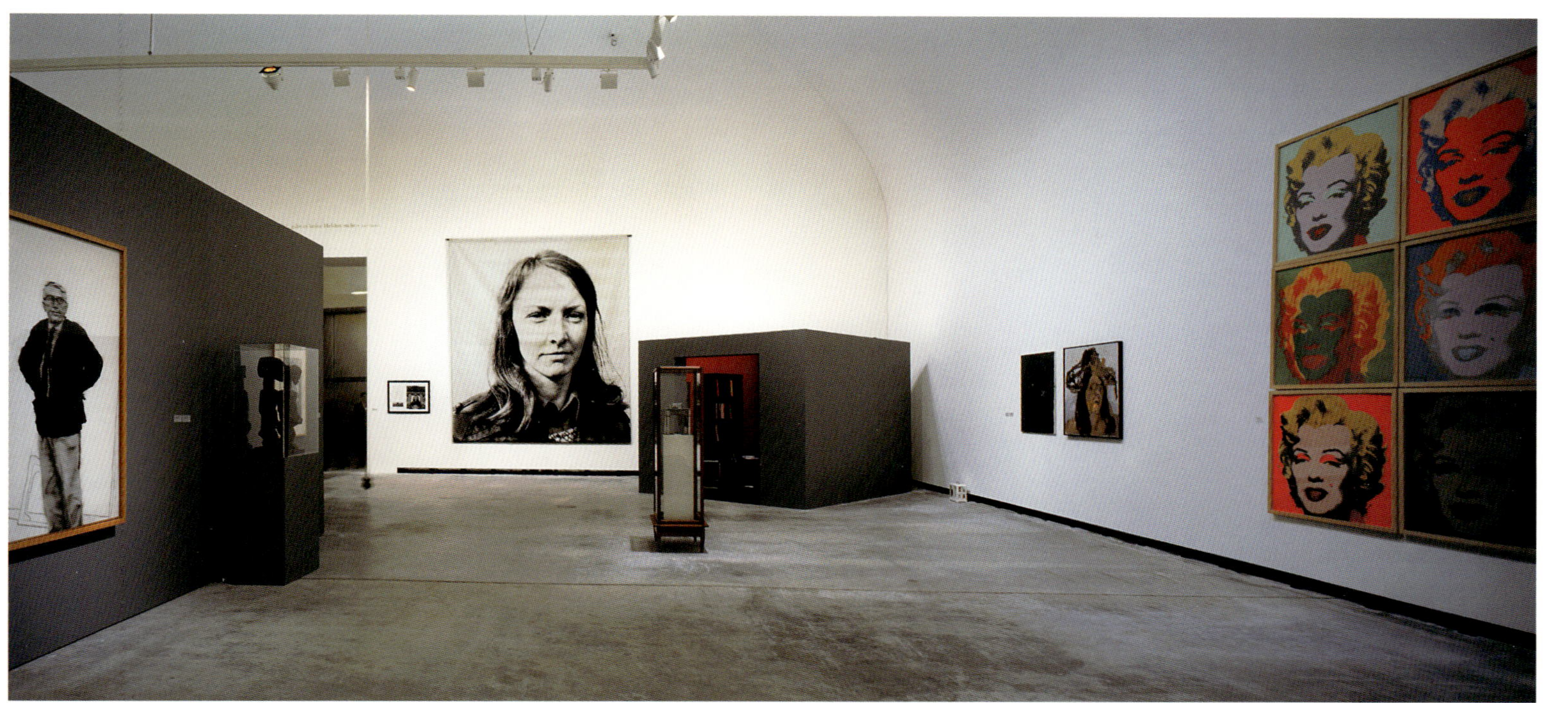

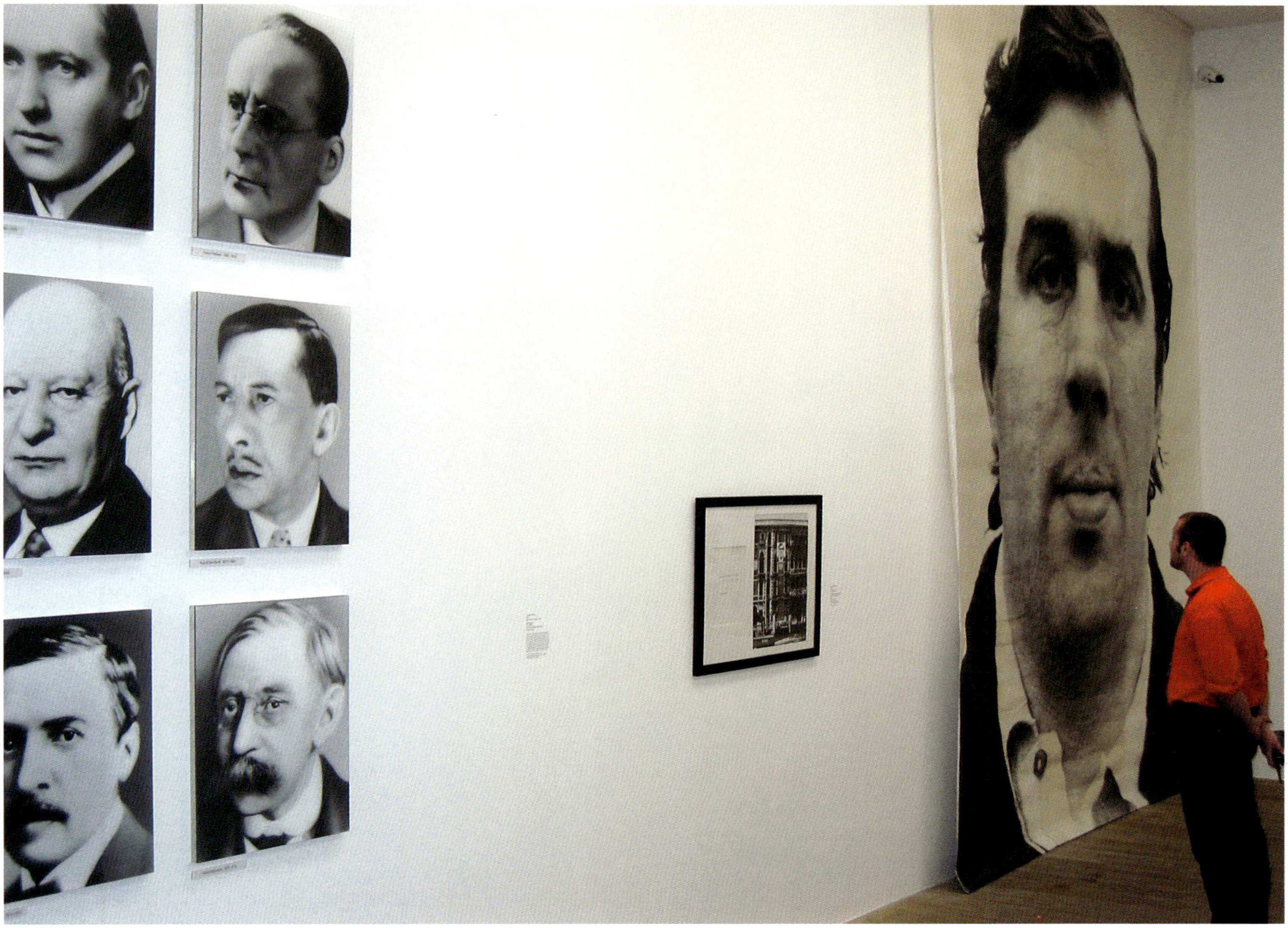

Installation view of *My Private Heroes* exhibition at MARTA, Herford, 2005

Installation view of *Open Systems* exhibition at Tate Modern, London, 2005

New Installations

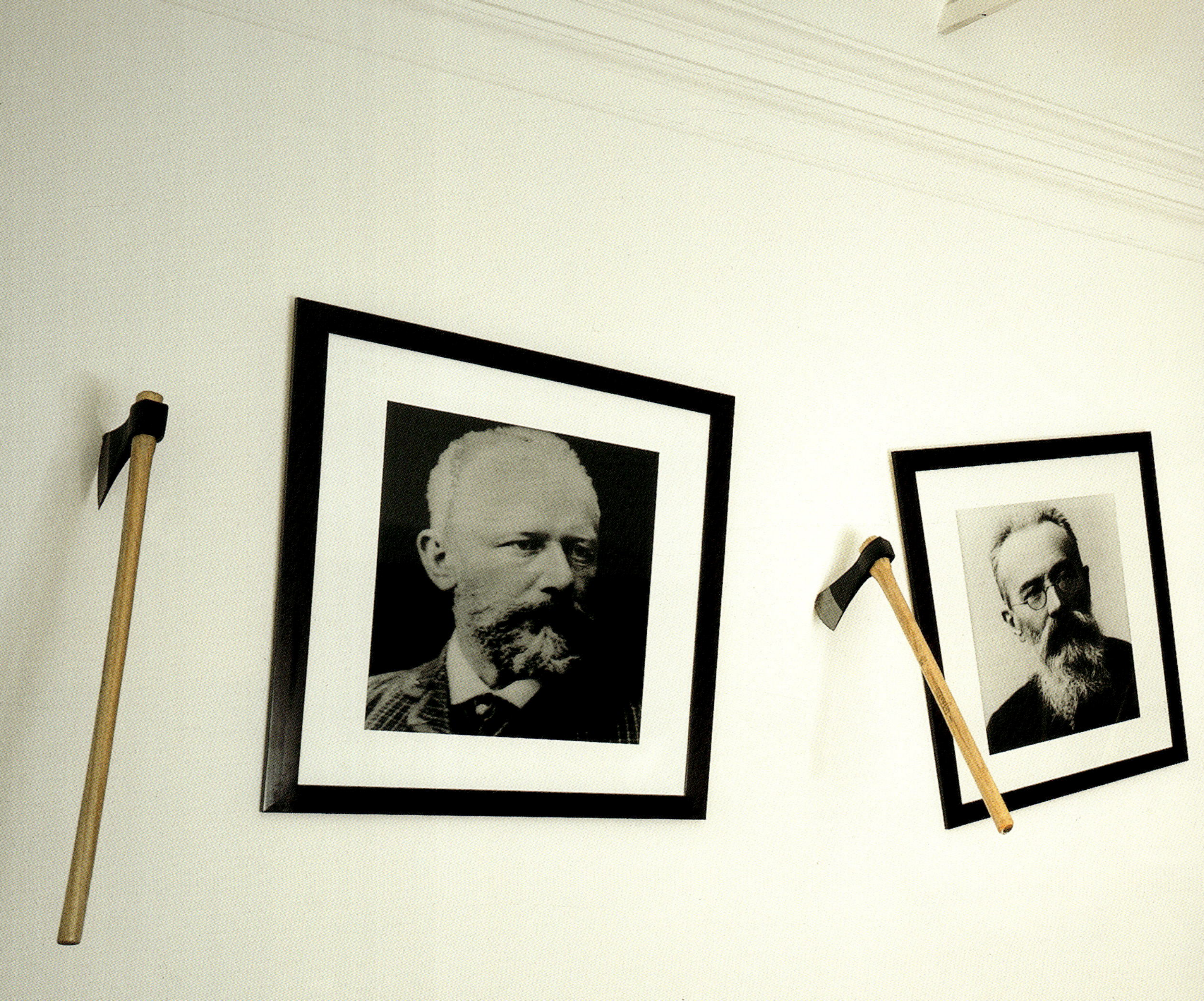

Citizens of Sarajevo
Venice Biennale, 1993

5 B/W photographs, 6 axes, beans, dimensions 860 x 300 cm
Collection: Museum Moderner Kunst Stiftung Ludwig, Vienna

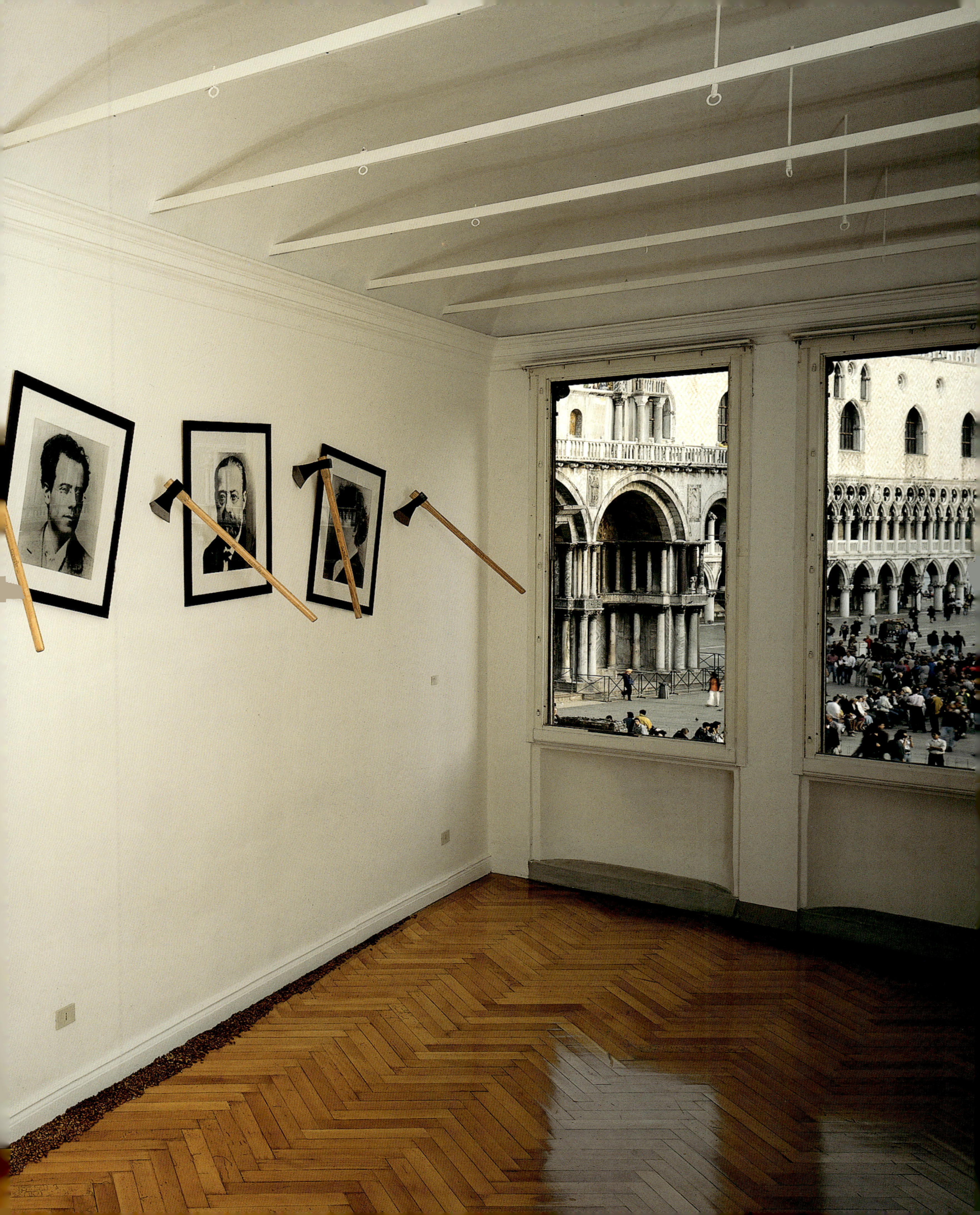

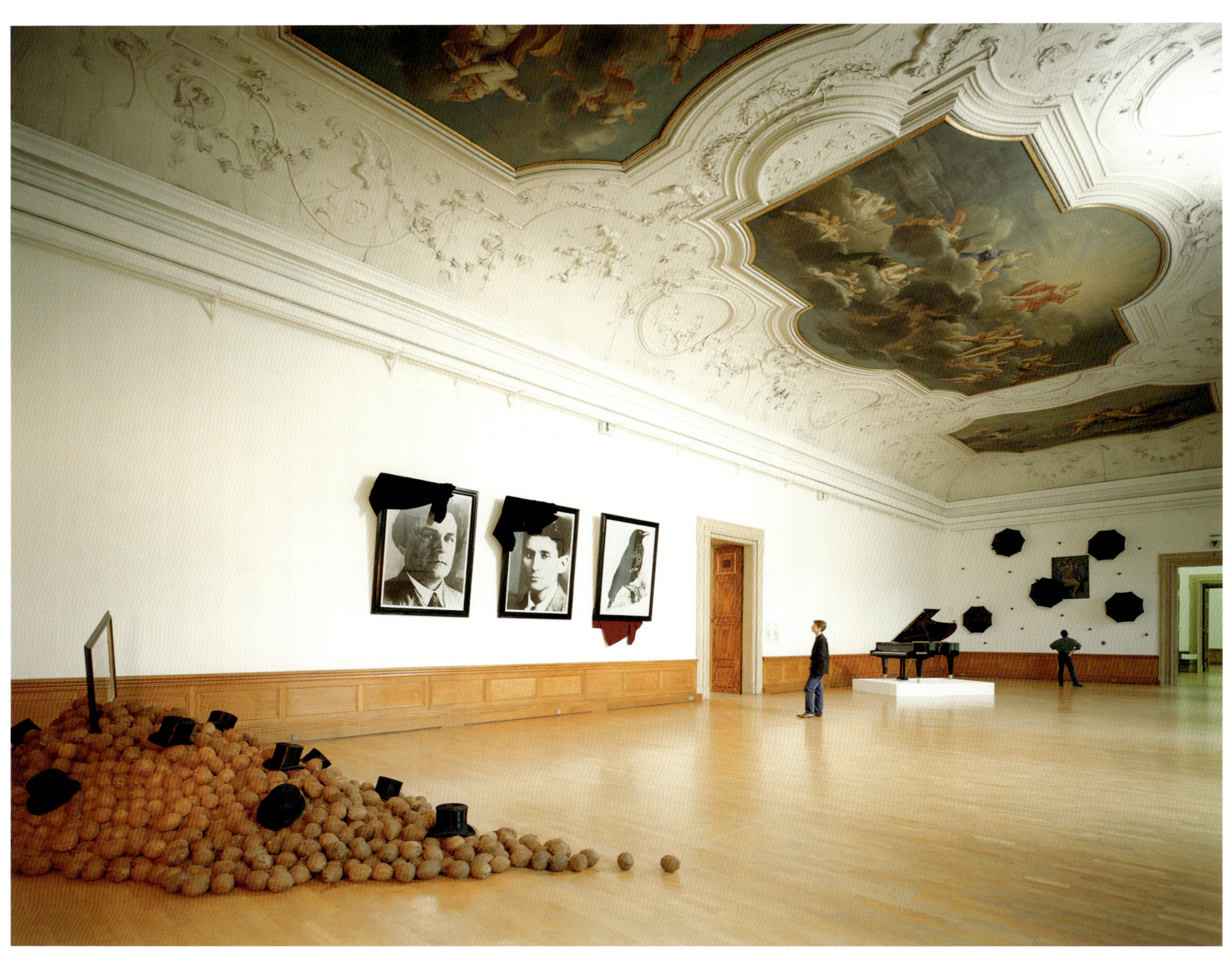

Installation view of retrospective exhibition
Slow as Light, Fast as Thought
Liechtenstein Palace, Museum Moderner
Kunst Stiftung Ludwig, Vienna, 1994

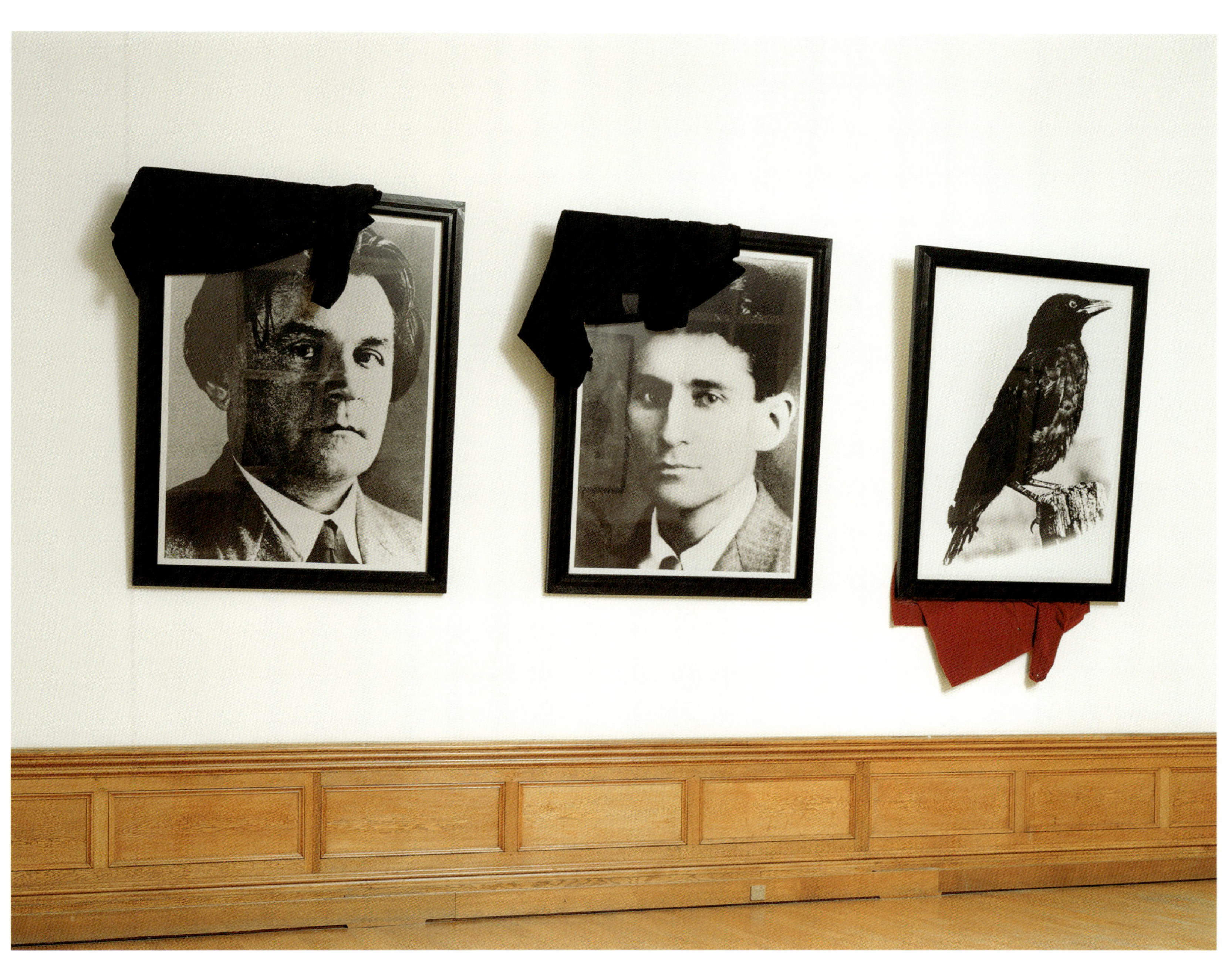

Between Eternity and Geniuscide,
for Malevich, Kafka, and Blackbird, 1994

Coats, B/W photographs, 200 x 150 cm each

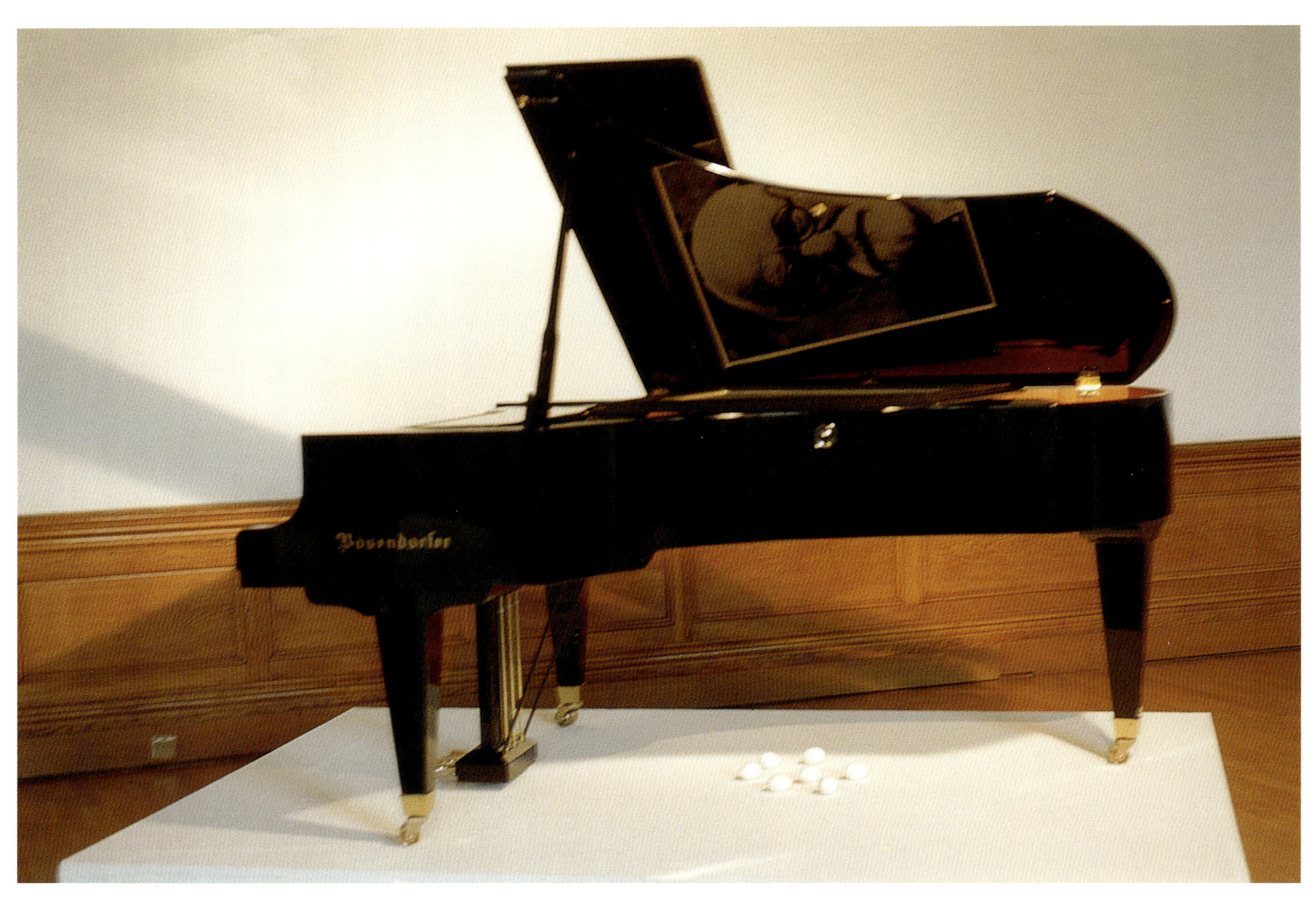

Portrait of Freud, 1994

B/W photograph, piano, eggs
Overall dimensions: 150 x 230 x 200 cm

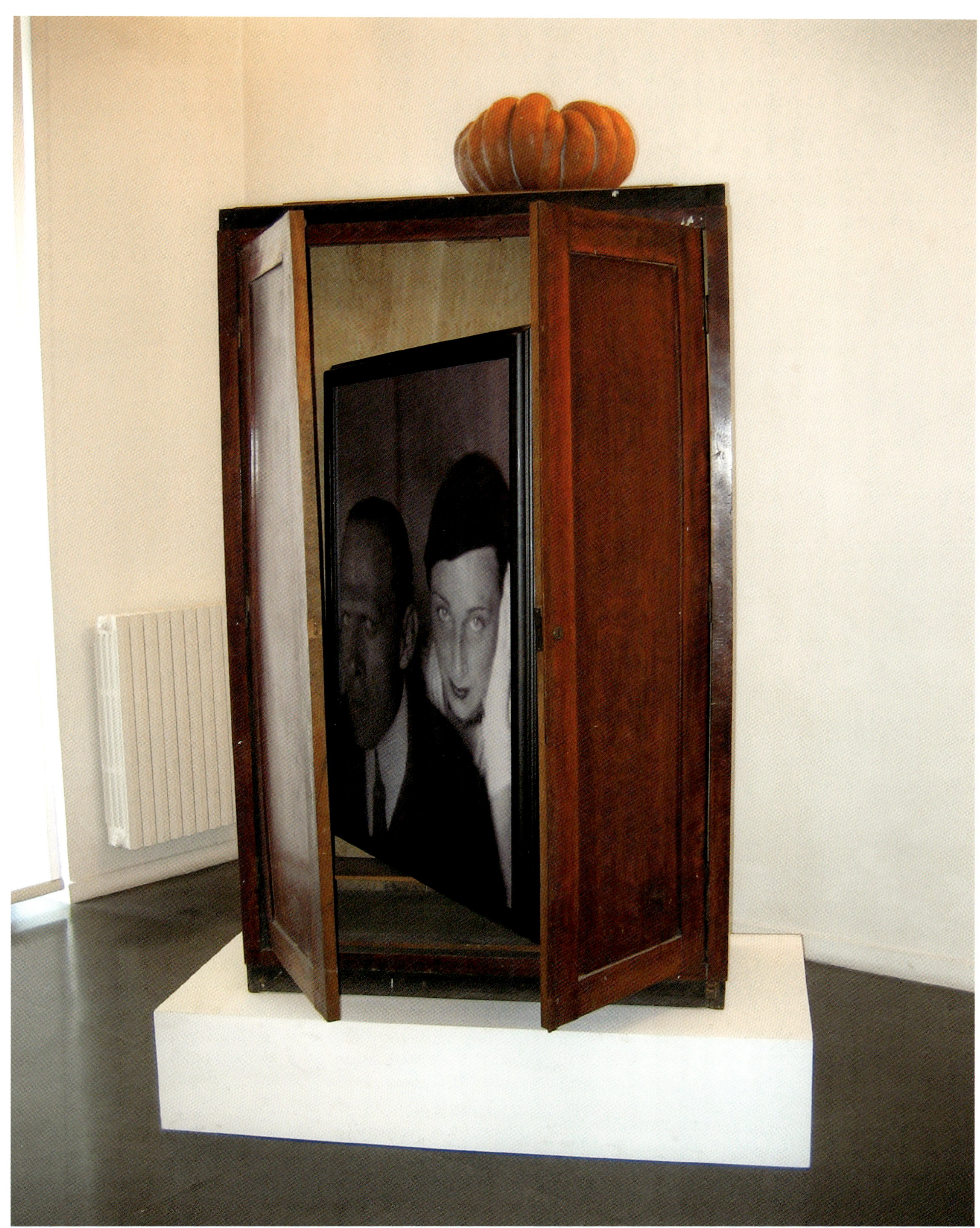

Case Harms, 2005

B/W photograph, wardrobe, pumpkin
Overall dimensions: 210 x 110 x 100 cm
Fondazione Mudima, Milan

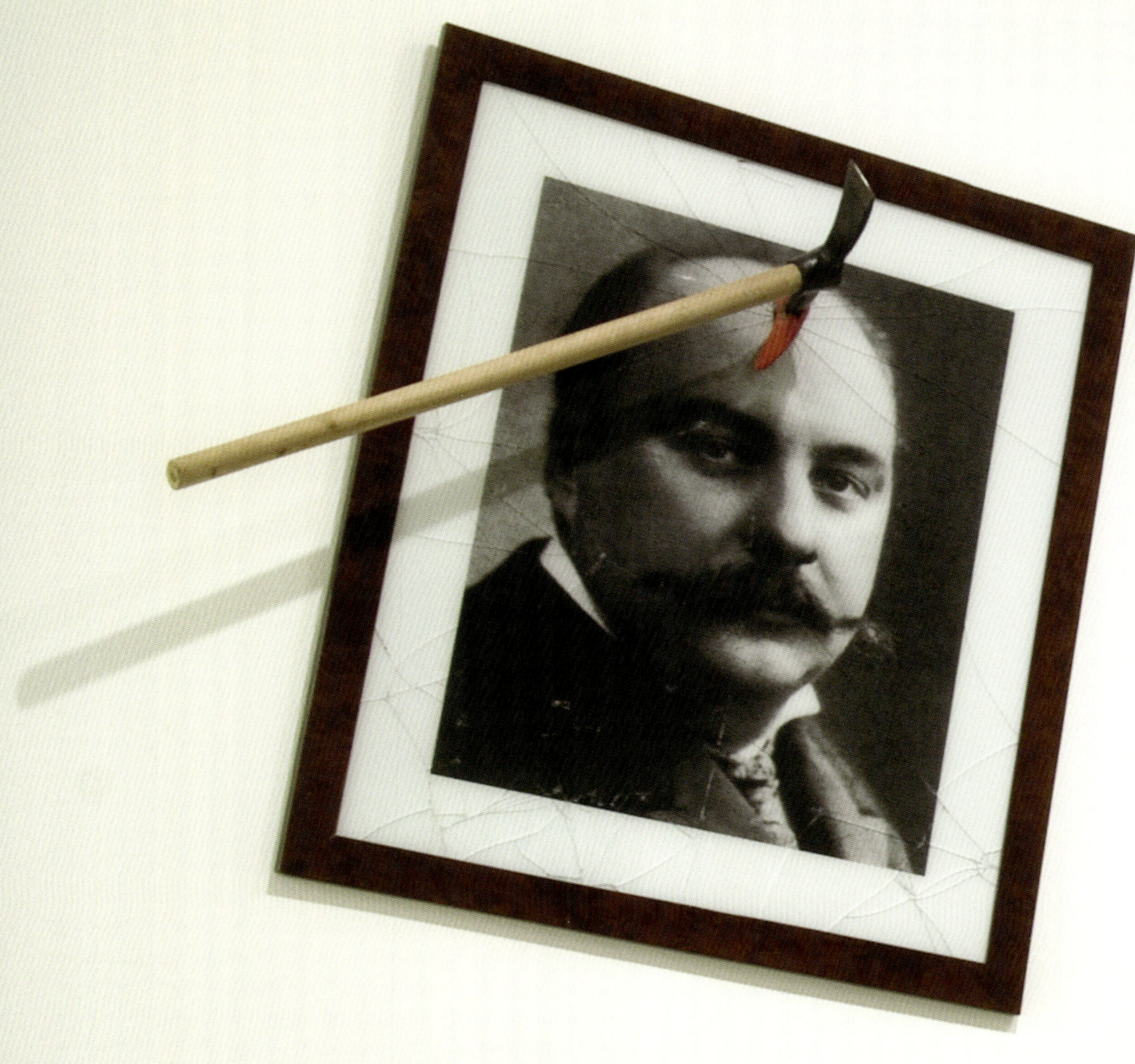

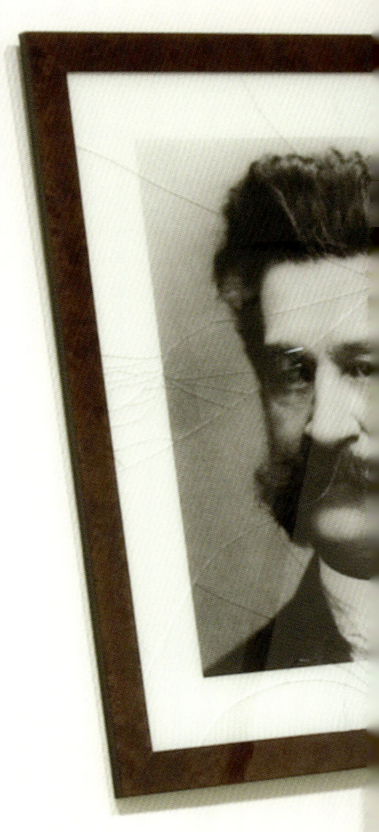

Balkan Walzer, 2004

7 B/W photographs, 7 pickaxes, red chili peppers
Dimensions: 12 x 3 m
Galleria Pino Casagrande, Rome

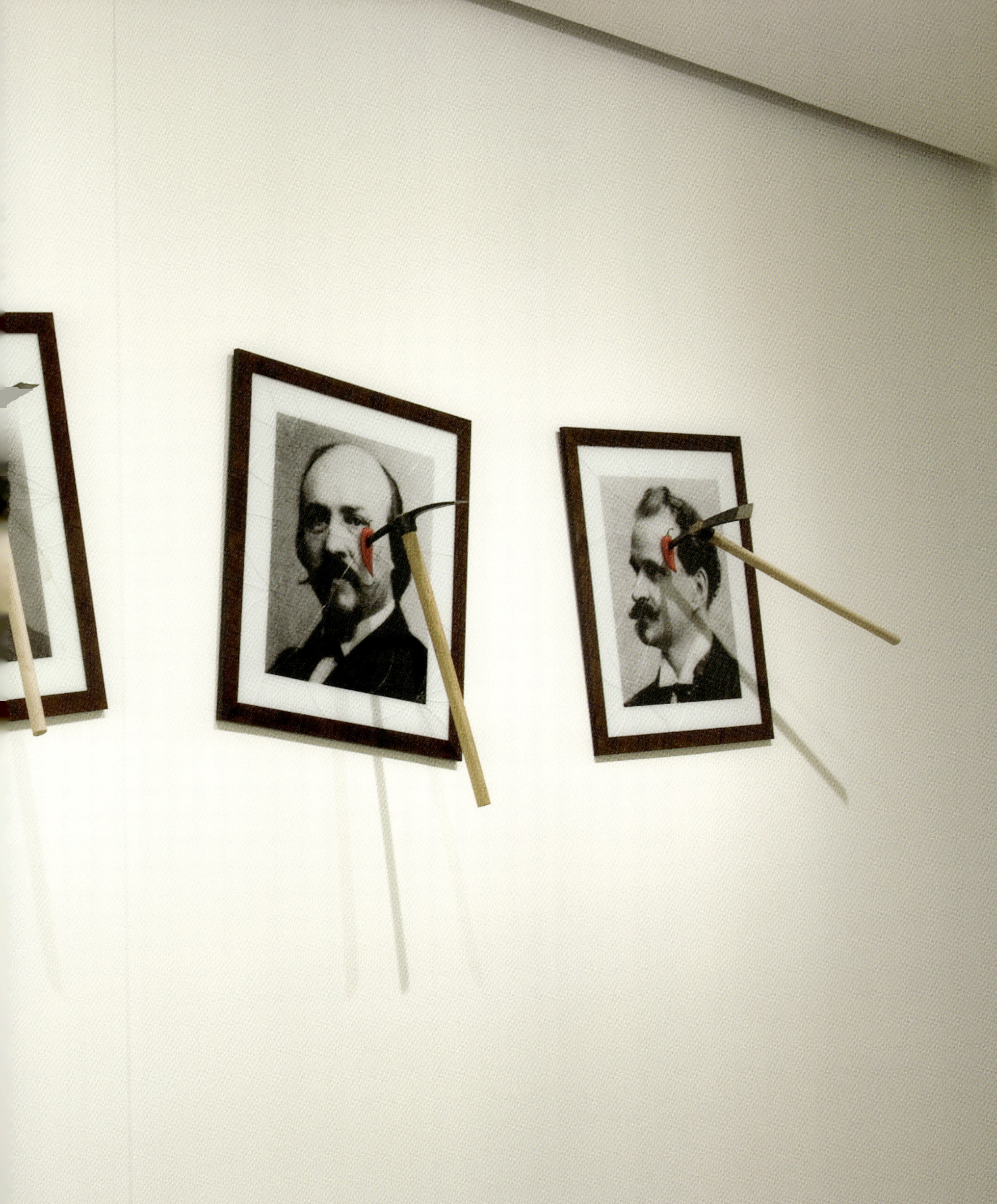

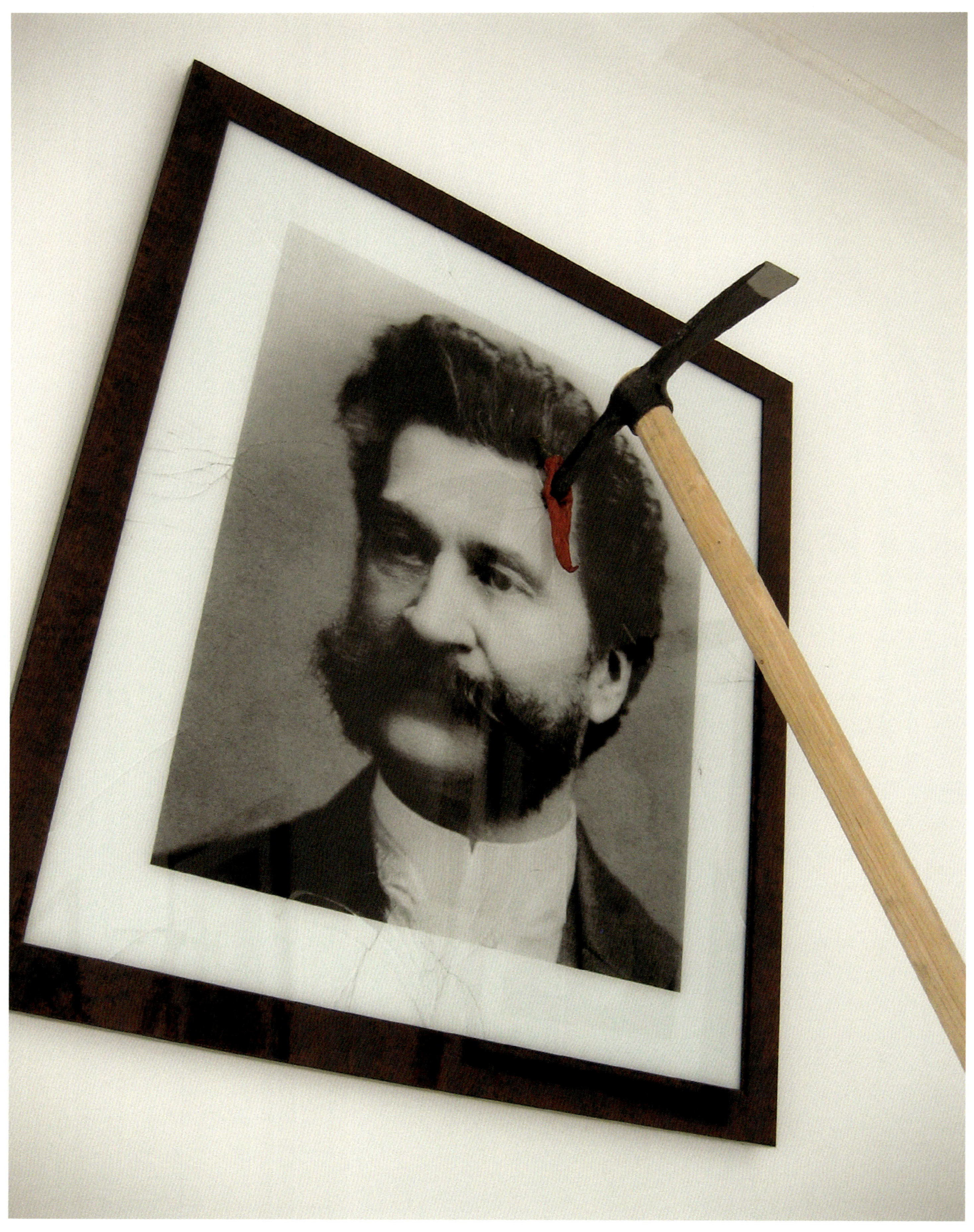

Balkan Walzer, 2004 (Johann Strauss)

B/W photograph, pickaxe, red chili pepper
Dimensions: 85 x 75 x 75 cm

Balkan Walzer, 2004 (Joseph Strauss)

B/W photograph, pickaxe, red chili pepper
Dimensions: 85 x 75 x 75 cm
Collection: Fondazione Raffaella and Stefano Sciaretta, Rome

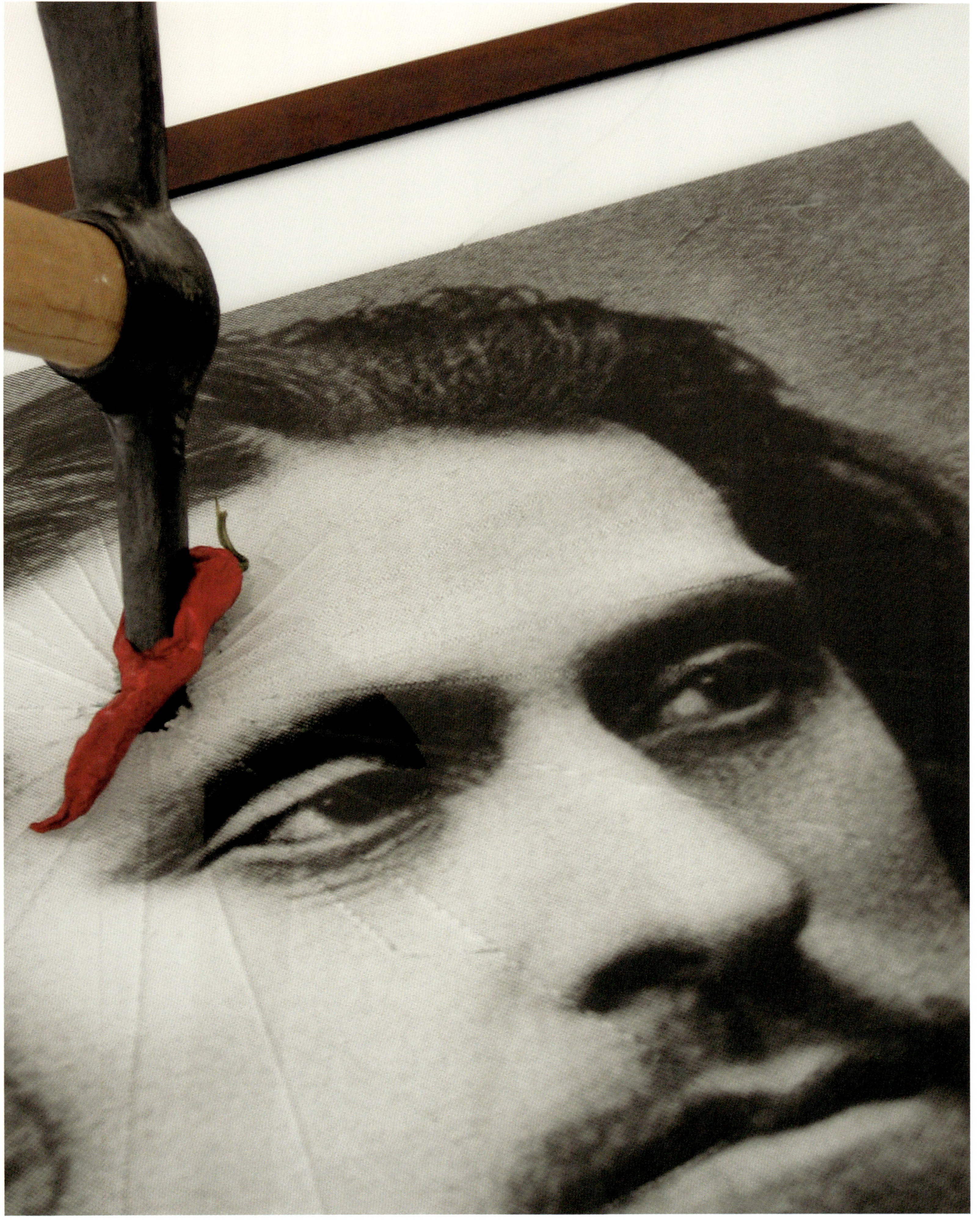

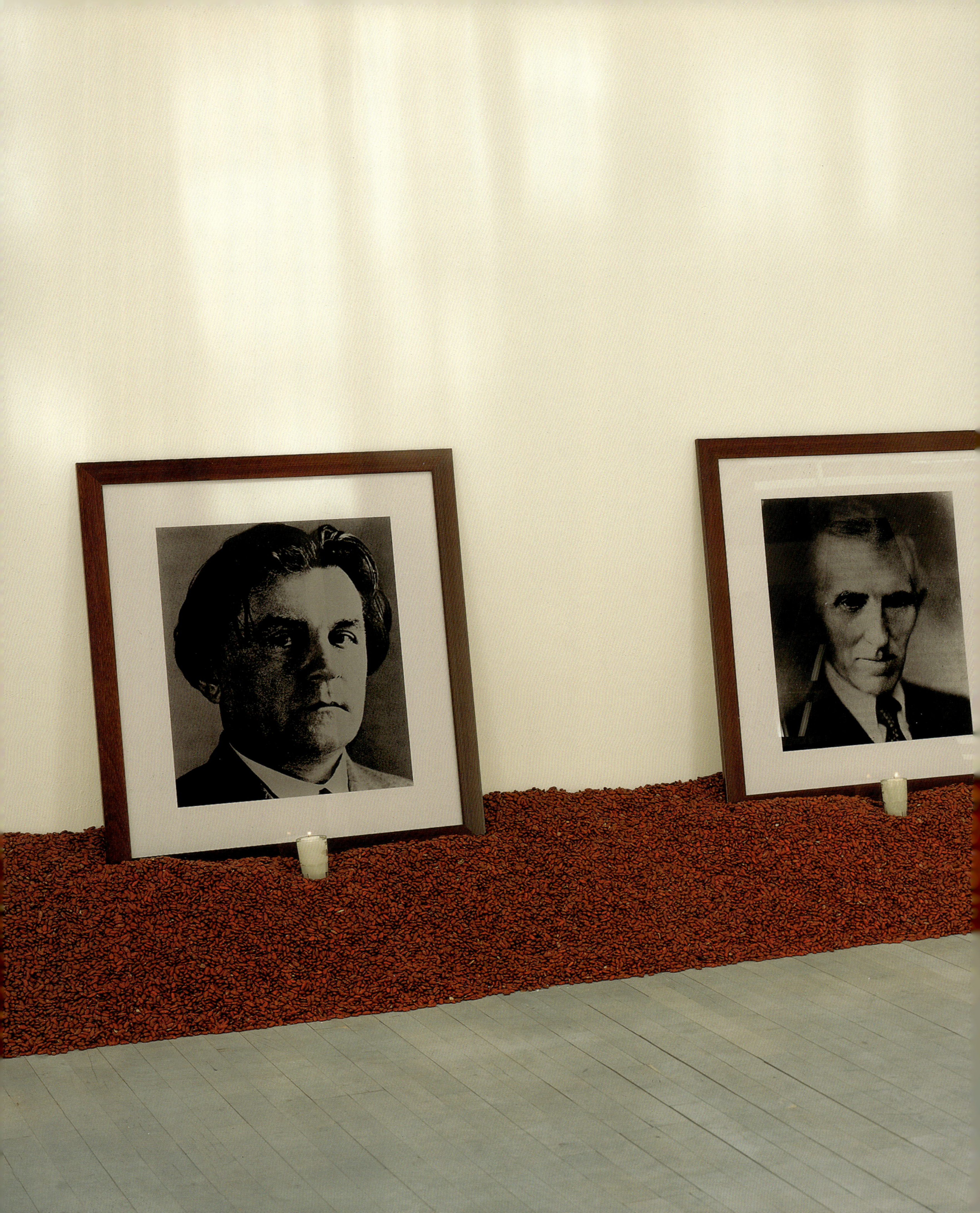

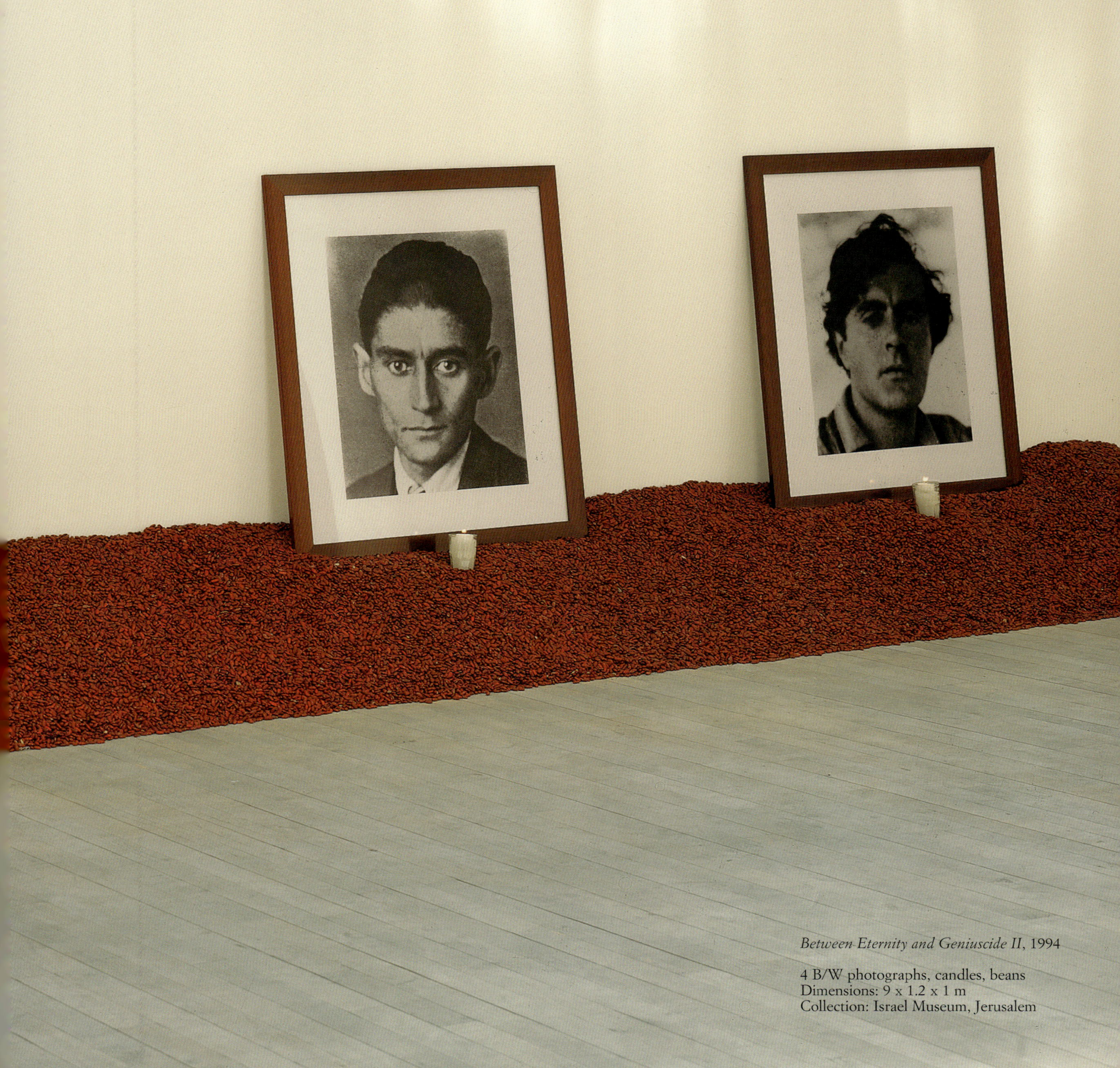

Between Eternity and Geniuscide II, 1994

4 B/W photographs, candles, beans
Dimensions: 9 x 1.2 x 1 m
Collection: Israel Museum, Jerusalem

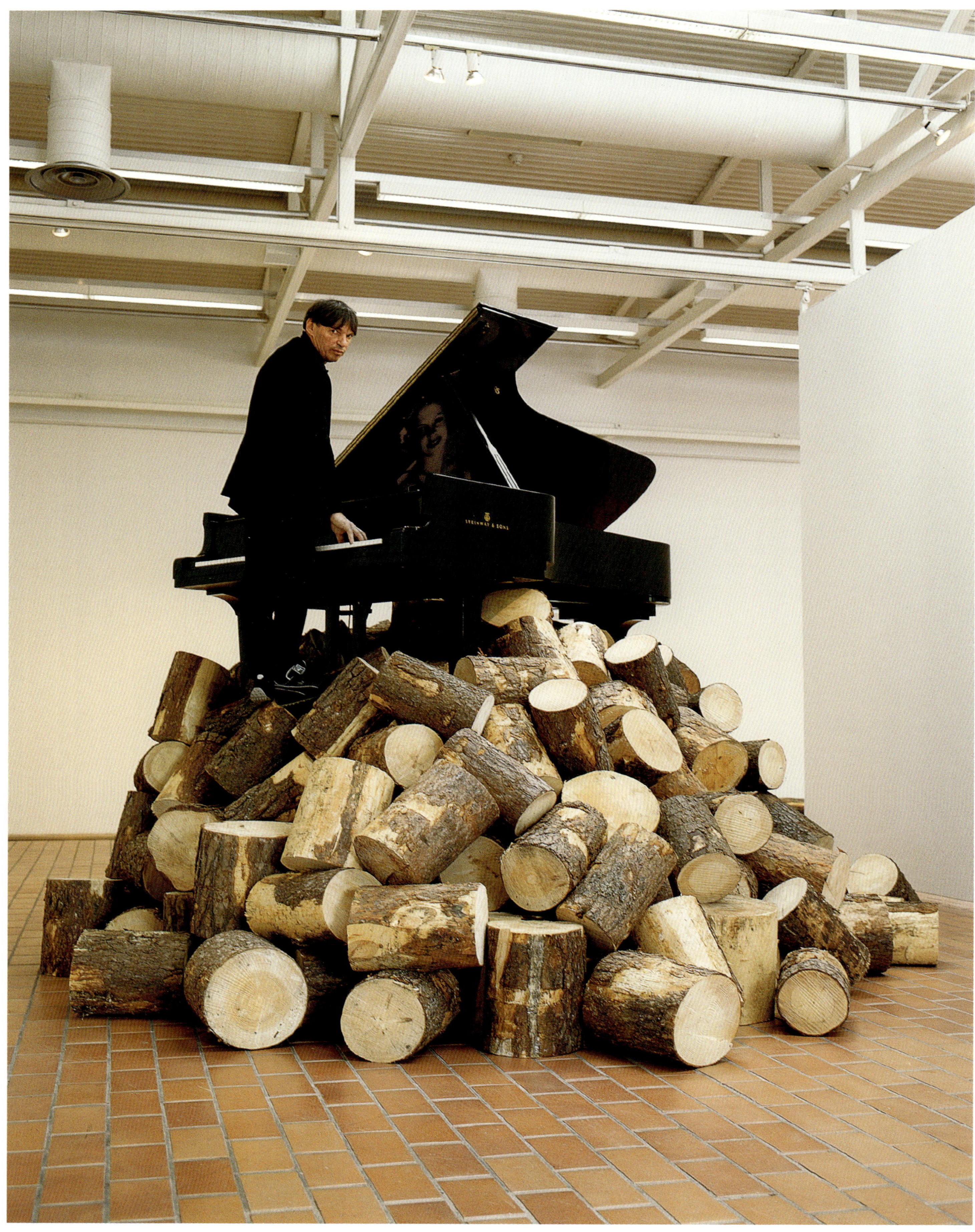

Finnish Rhapsody with Touch of Suprematism, 2000

B/W photograph, concert piano, logs
Overall dimensions: 380 x 550 cm
Porin Taidemuseo, Finland

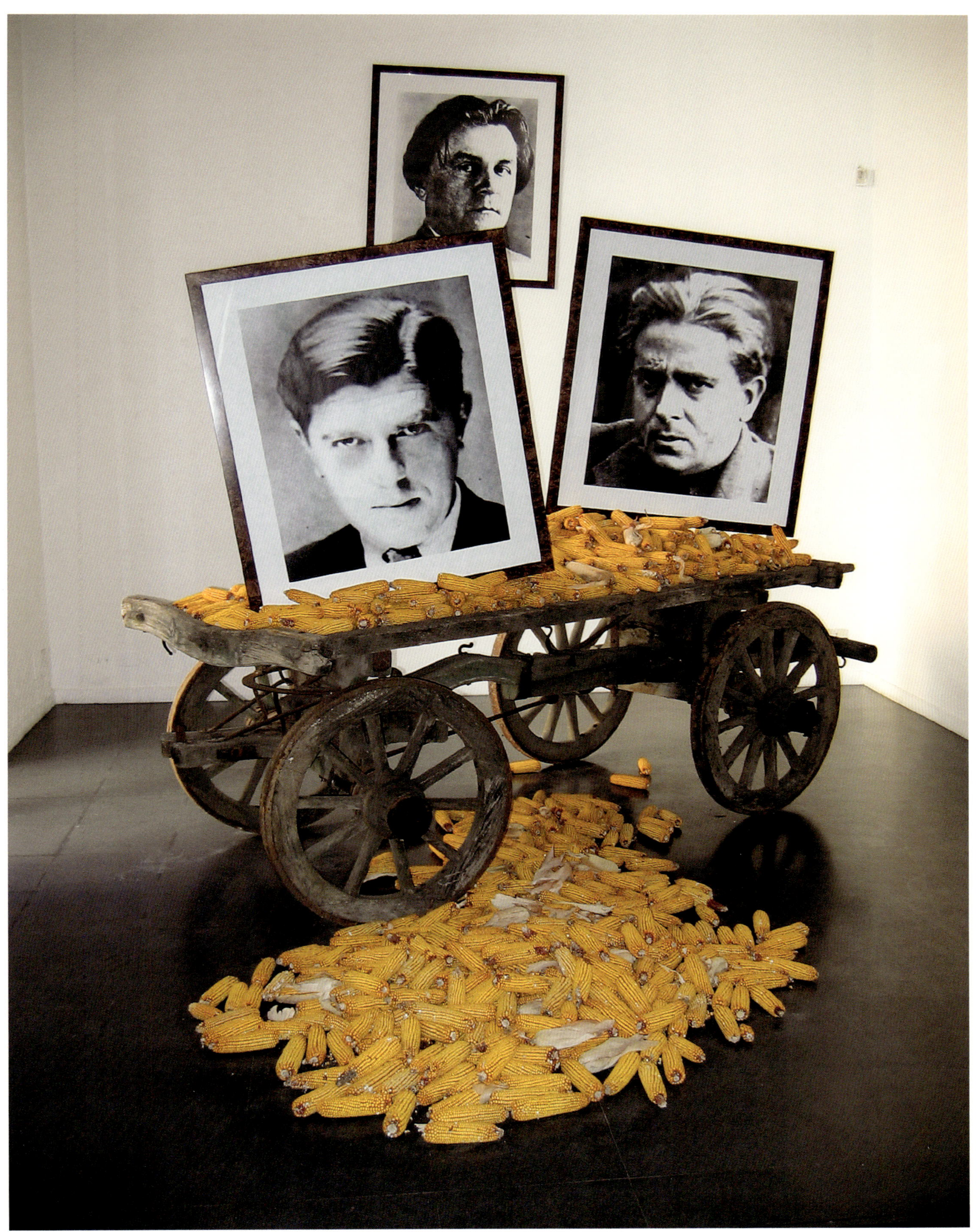

From here to Great Bear, 2005

3 B/W photographs, wagon, corn on the cob
Overall dimensions: 370 x 300 x 450 cm
Fondazione Mudima, Milan

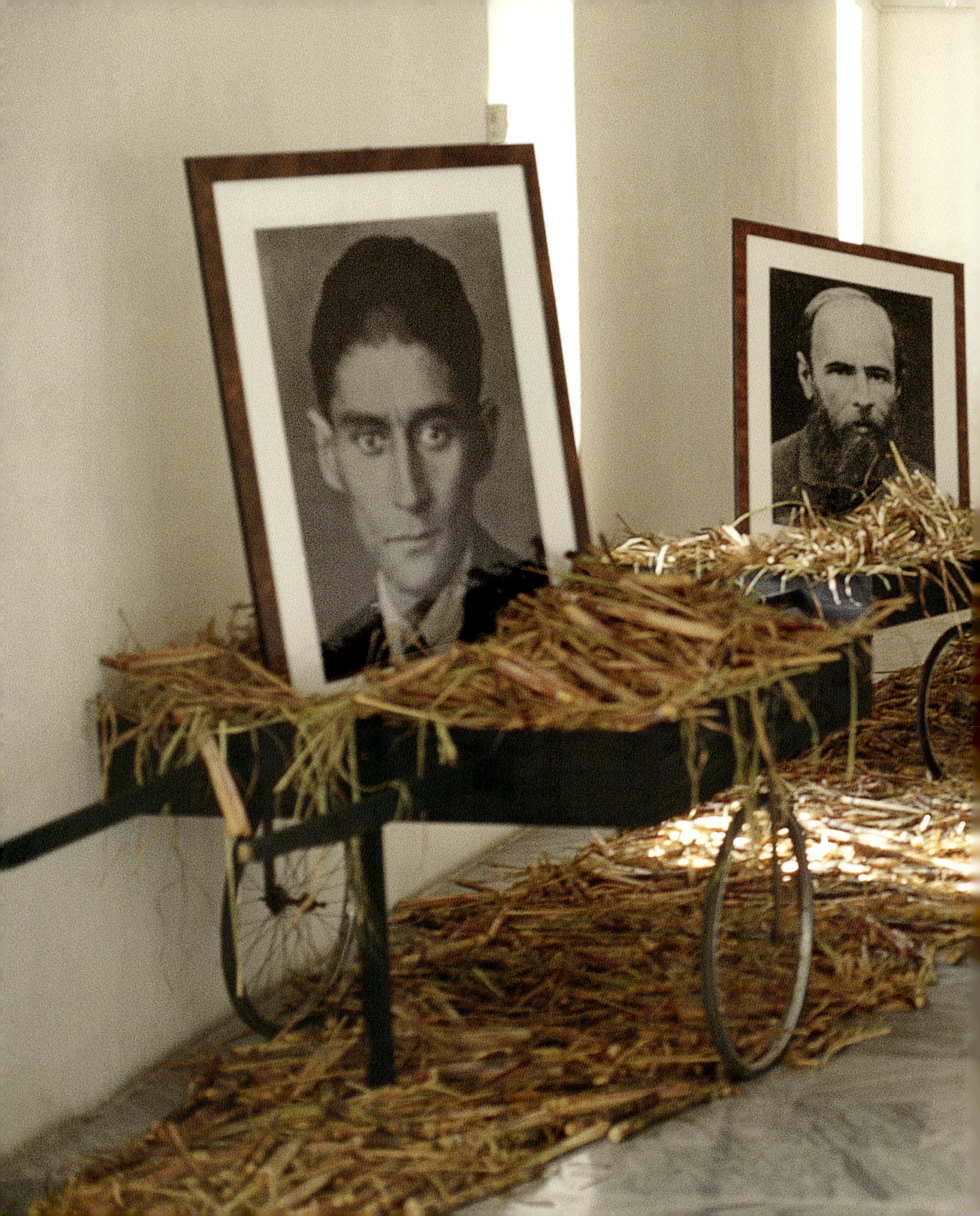

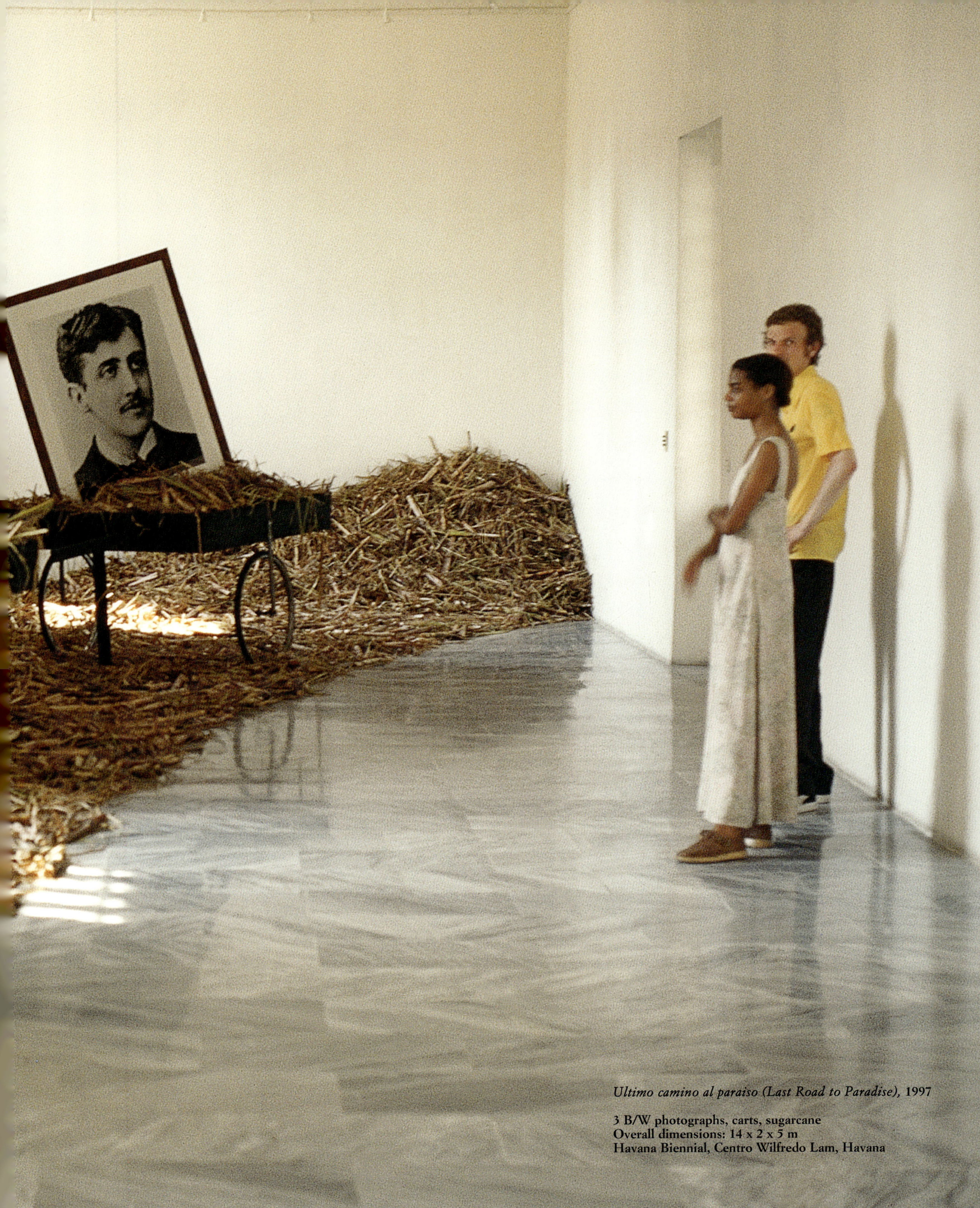

Ultimo camino al paraiso (Last Road to Paradise), 1997

3 B/W photographs, carts, sugarcane
Overall dimensions: 14 x 2 x 5 m
Havana Biennial, Centro Wilfredo Lam, Havana

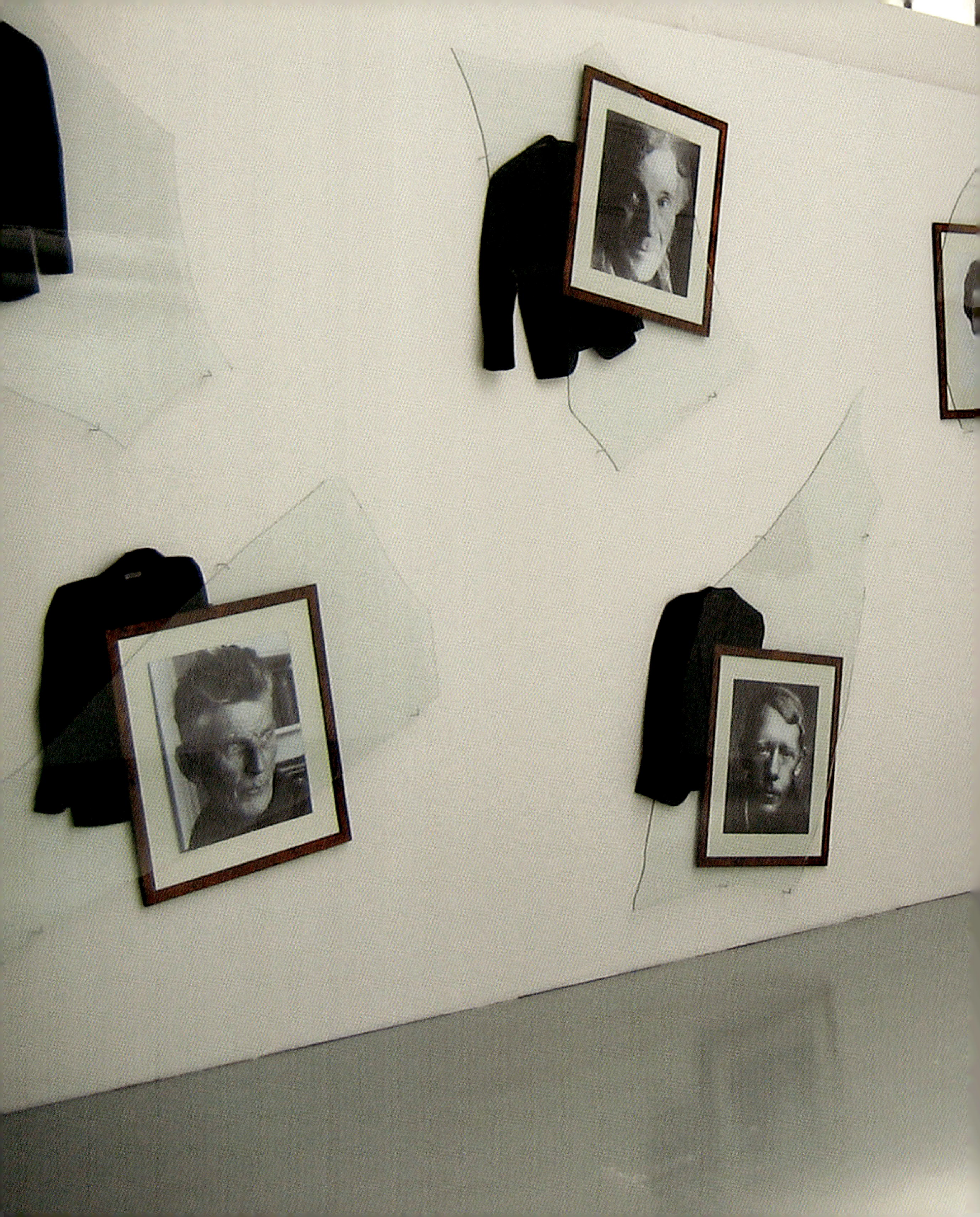

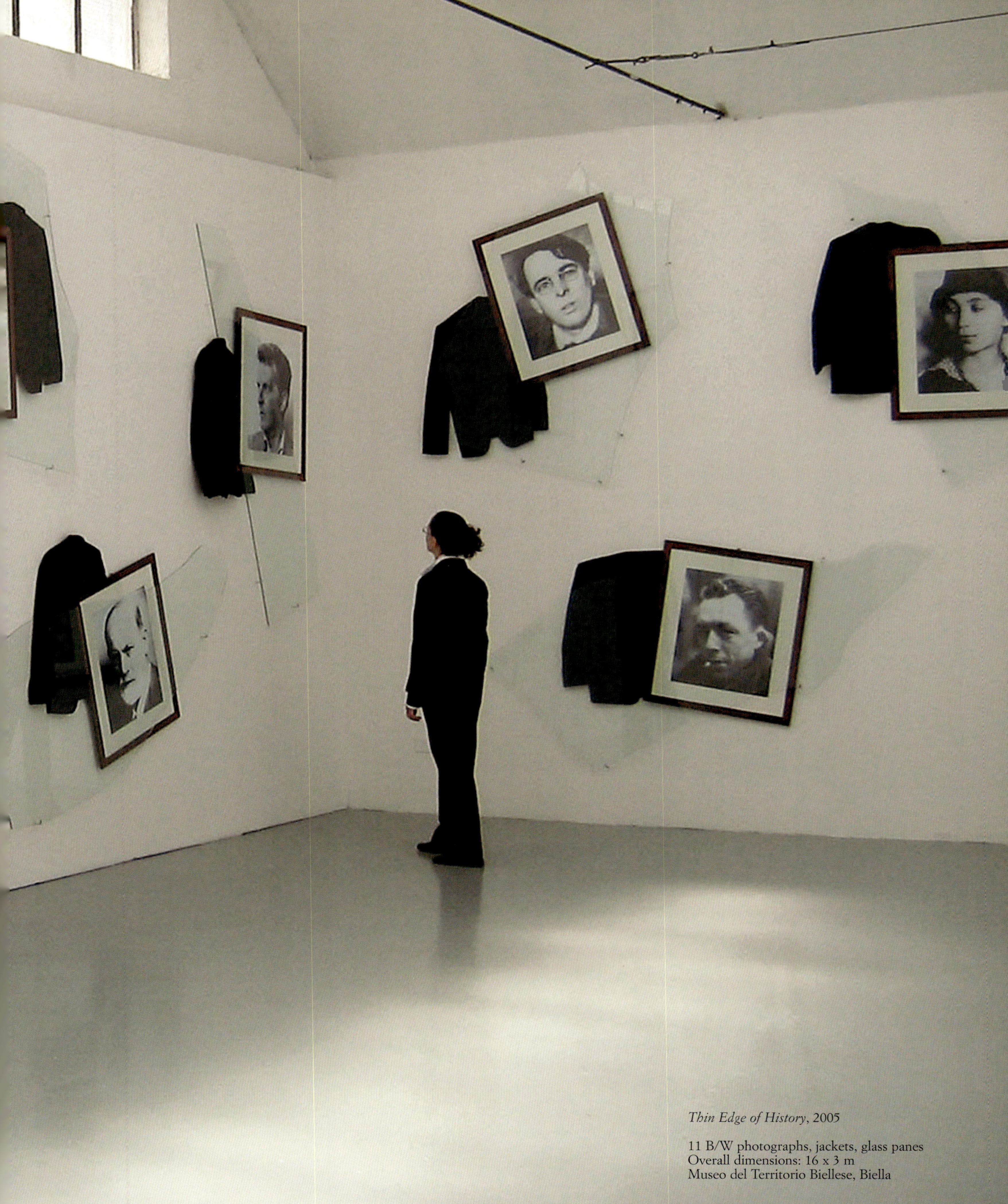

Thin Edge of History, 2005

11 B/W photographs, jackets, glass panes
Overall dimensions: 16 x 3 m
Museo del Territorio Biellese, Biella

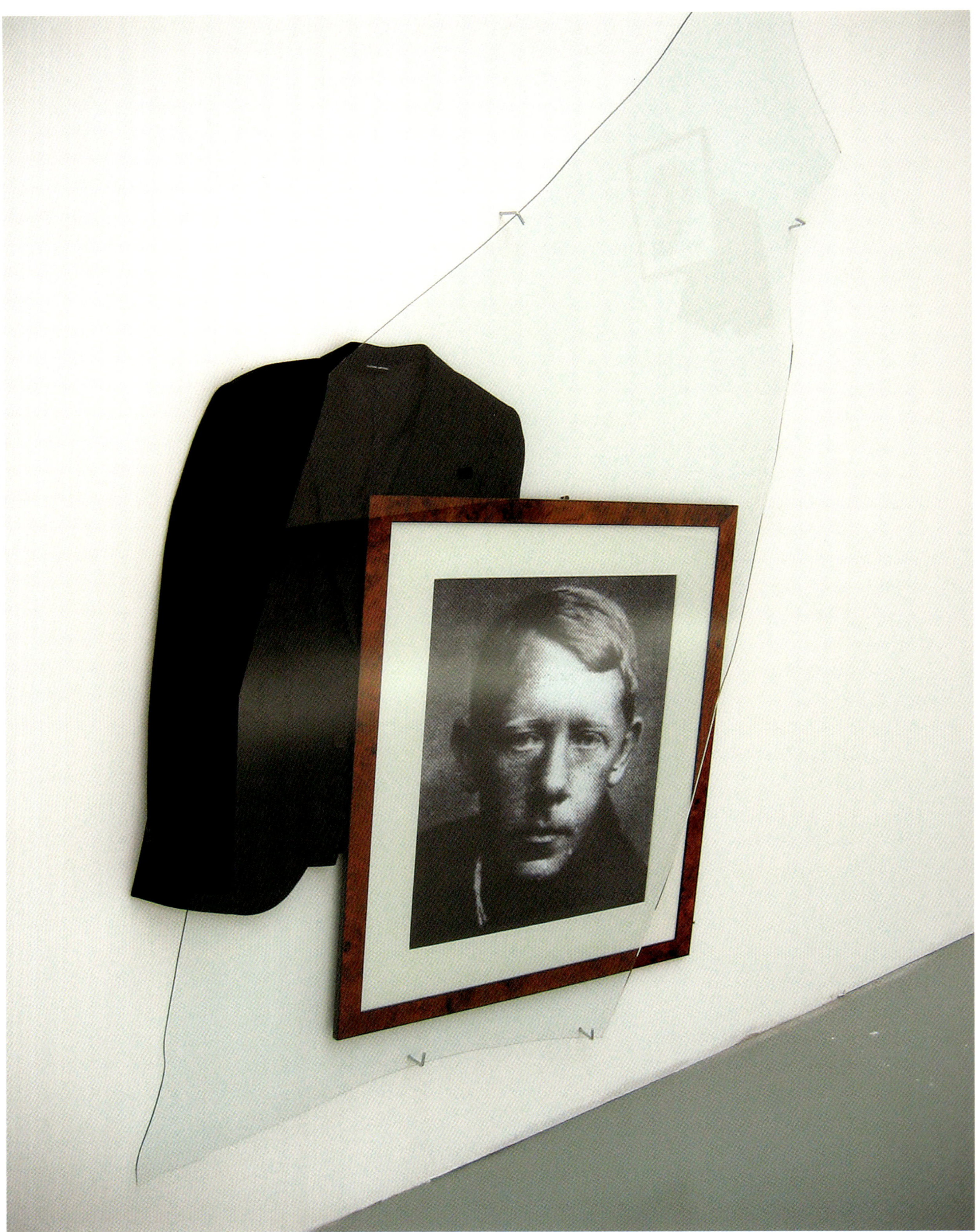

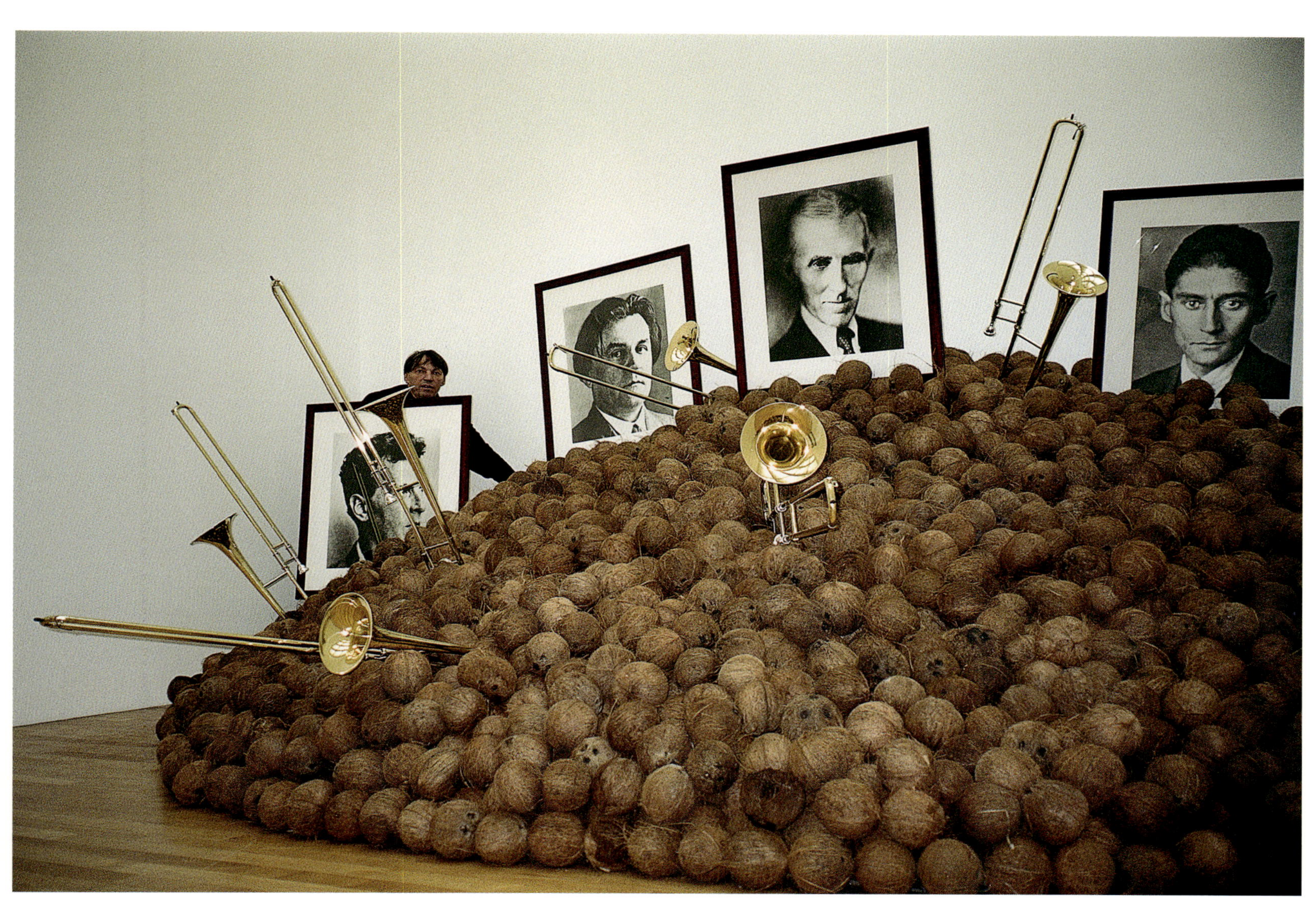

Thin Edge of History, 2005
(detail: Tatlin)

Heralds of Post History II, 1999 (detail)
Zeitwenden exhibition, Kunstmuseum, Bonn

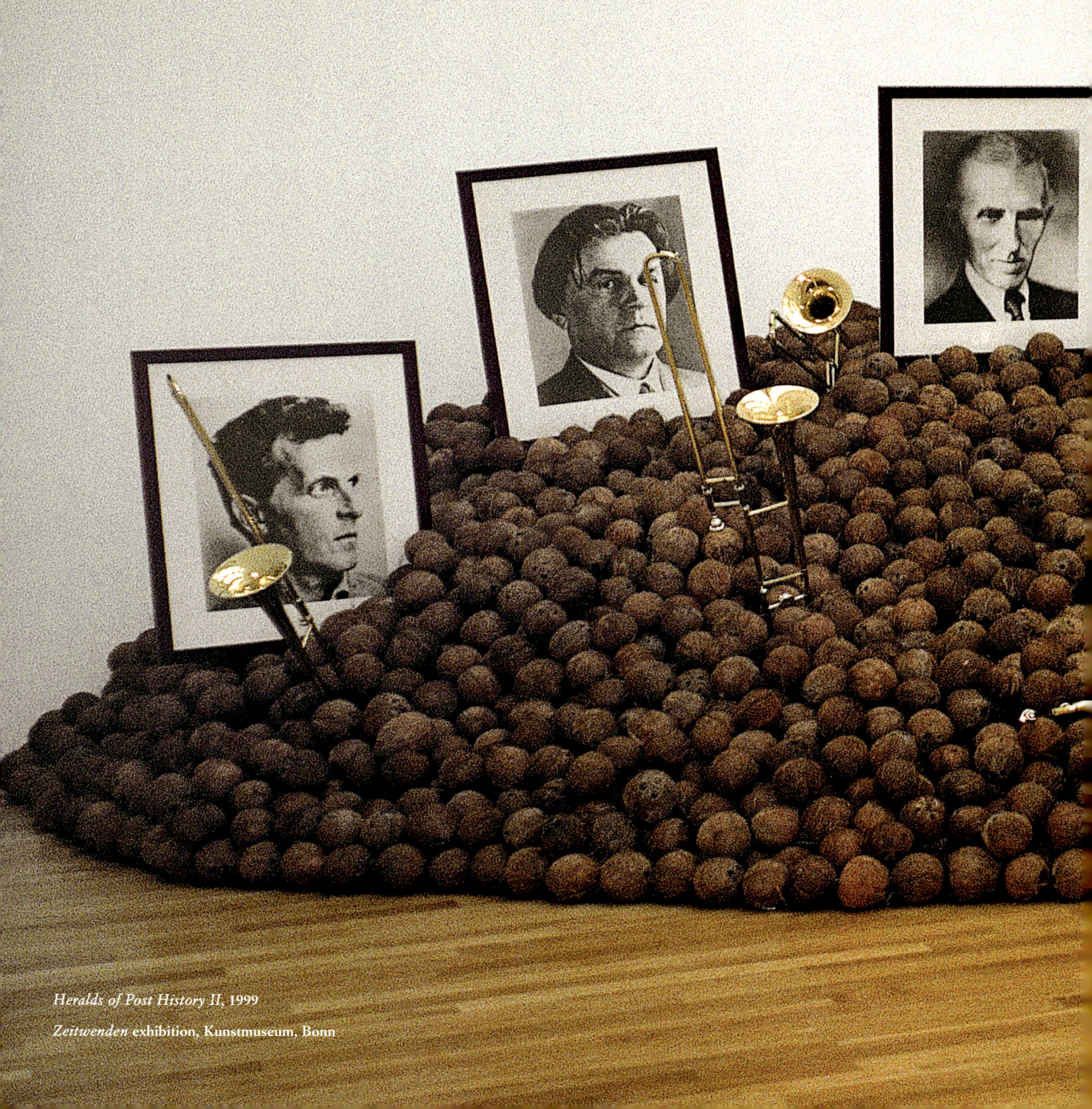

Heralds of Post History II, 1999

Zeitwenden exhibition, Kunstmuseum, Bonn

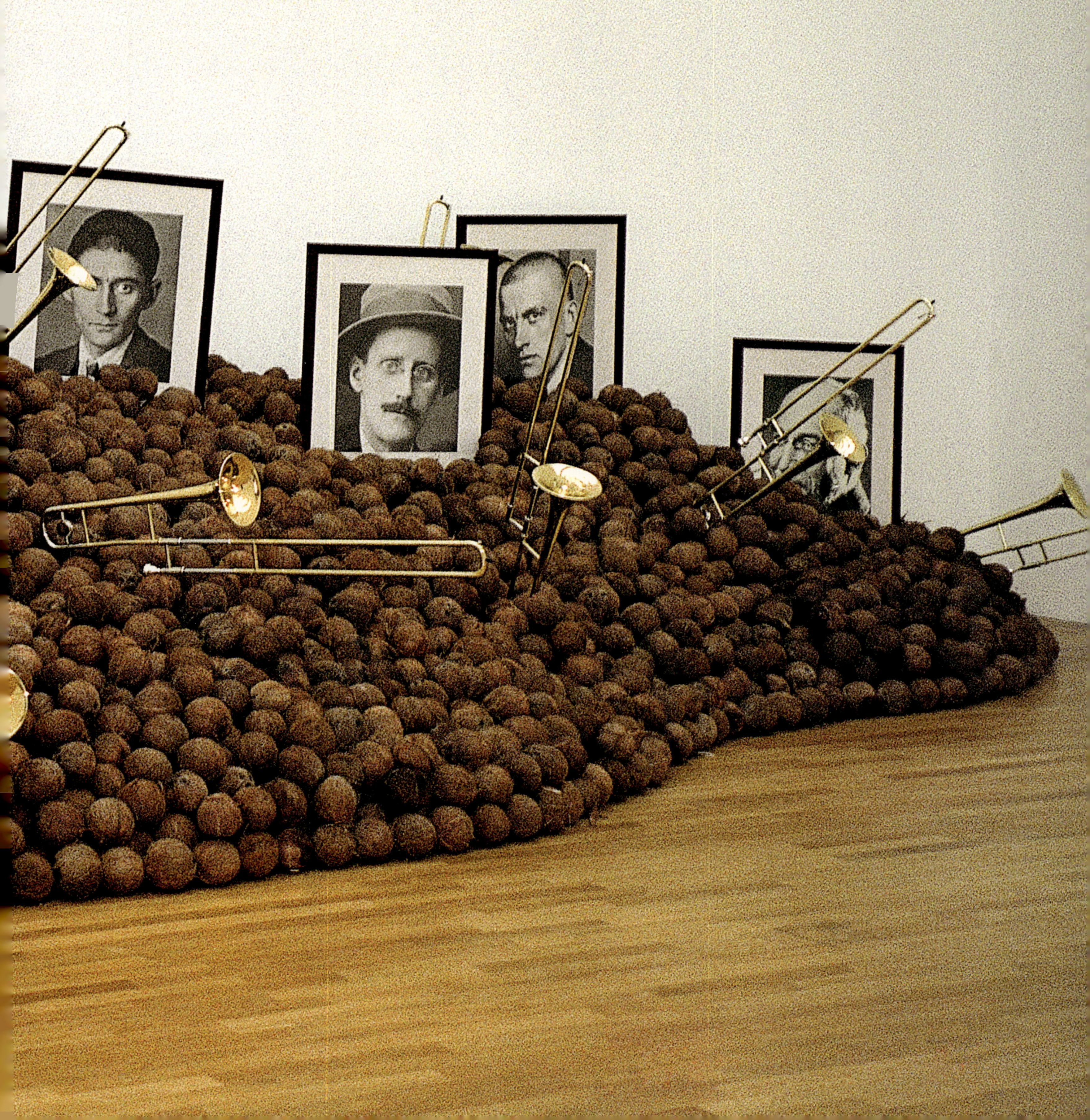

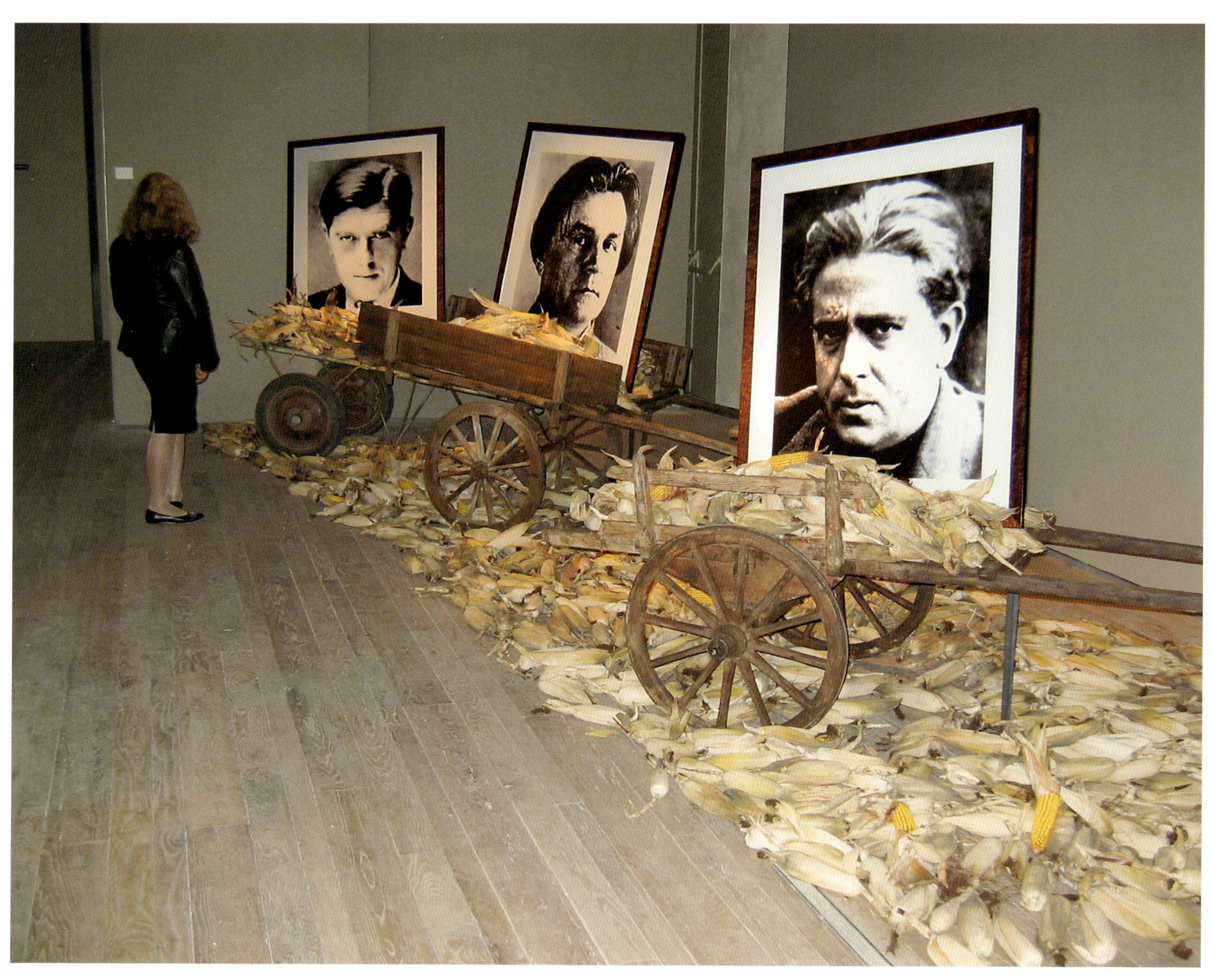

All about the Grain, 2004

B/W photograph, coat, roses
Dimensions: 15 x 6 m
Museo Santa Maria della Scala, Siena

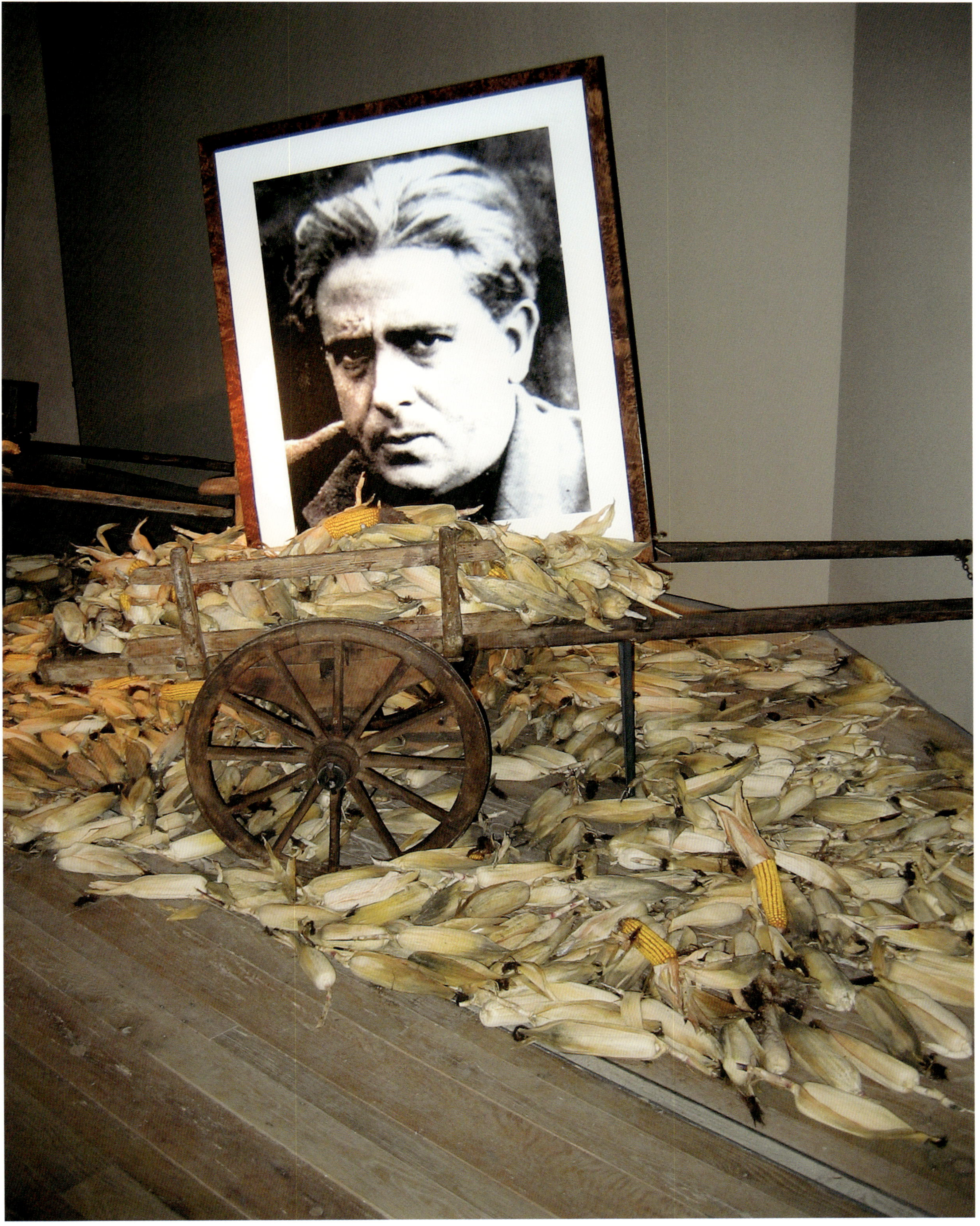

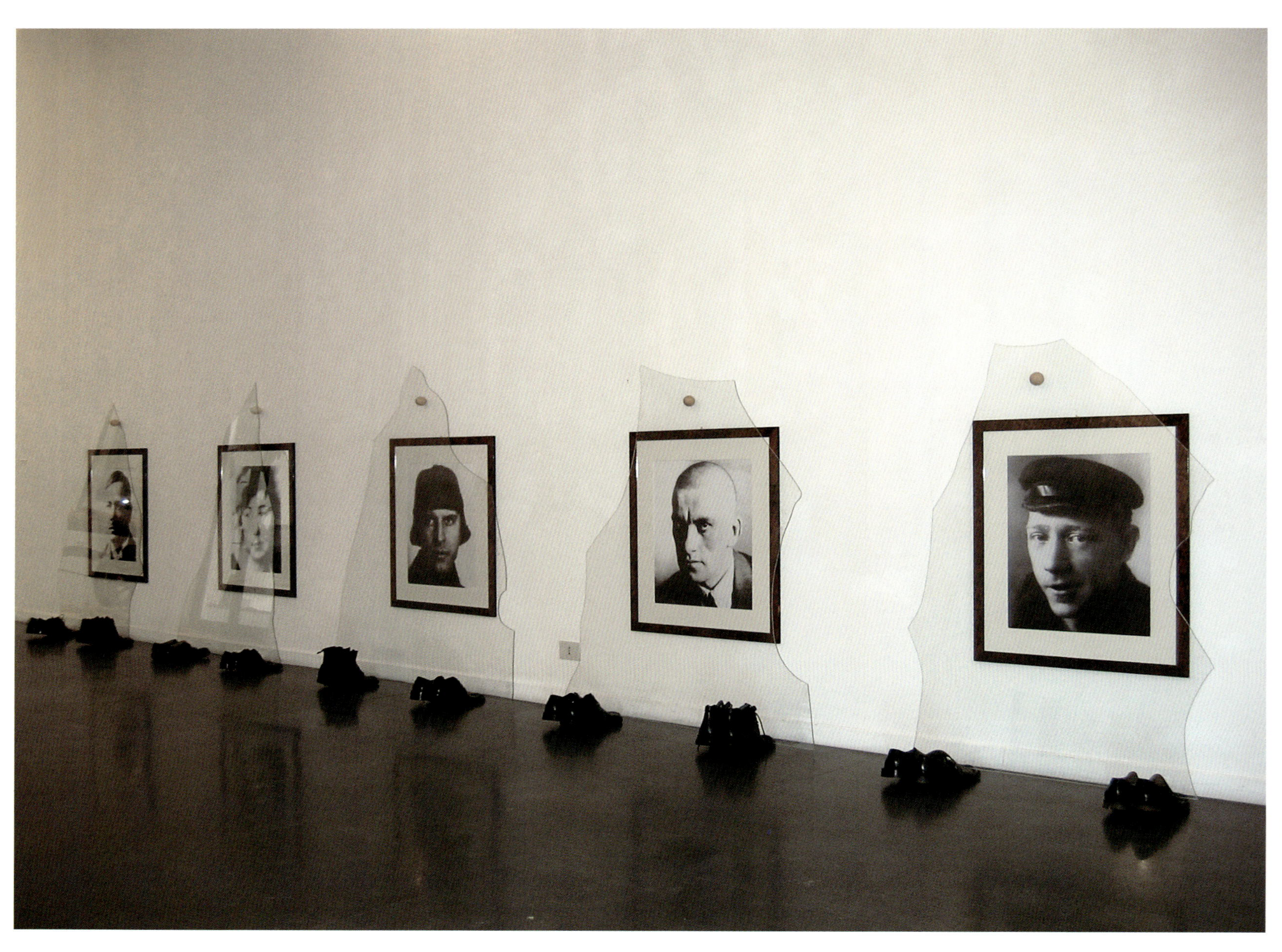

Thin Edge of Convention II, 1997–2005

5 B/W photographs, glass, eggs
Overall dimensions: 8 x 1.4 m
Grand Palais Paris, *La Force de l'Art*, 2006
Collection: Fonds National d'Art Contemporain

Thin Edge of Convention II, 1997–2005 (detail)

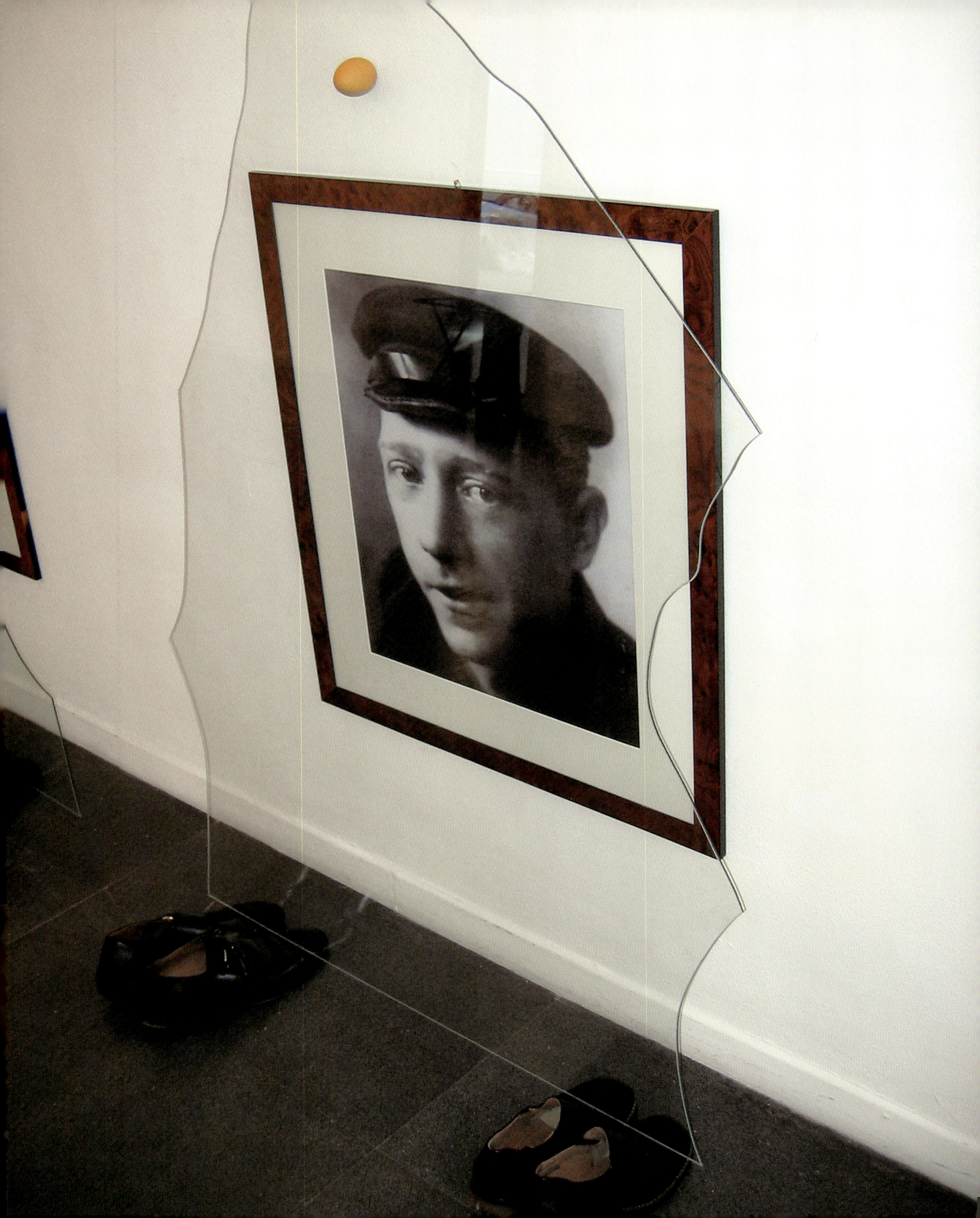

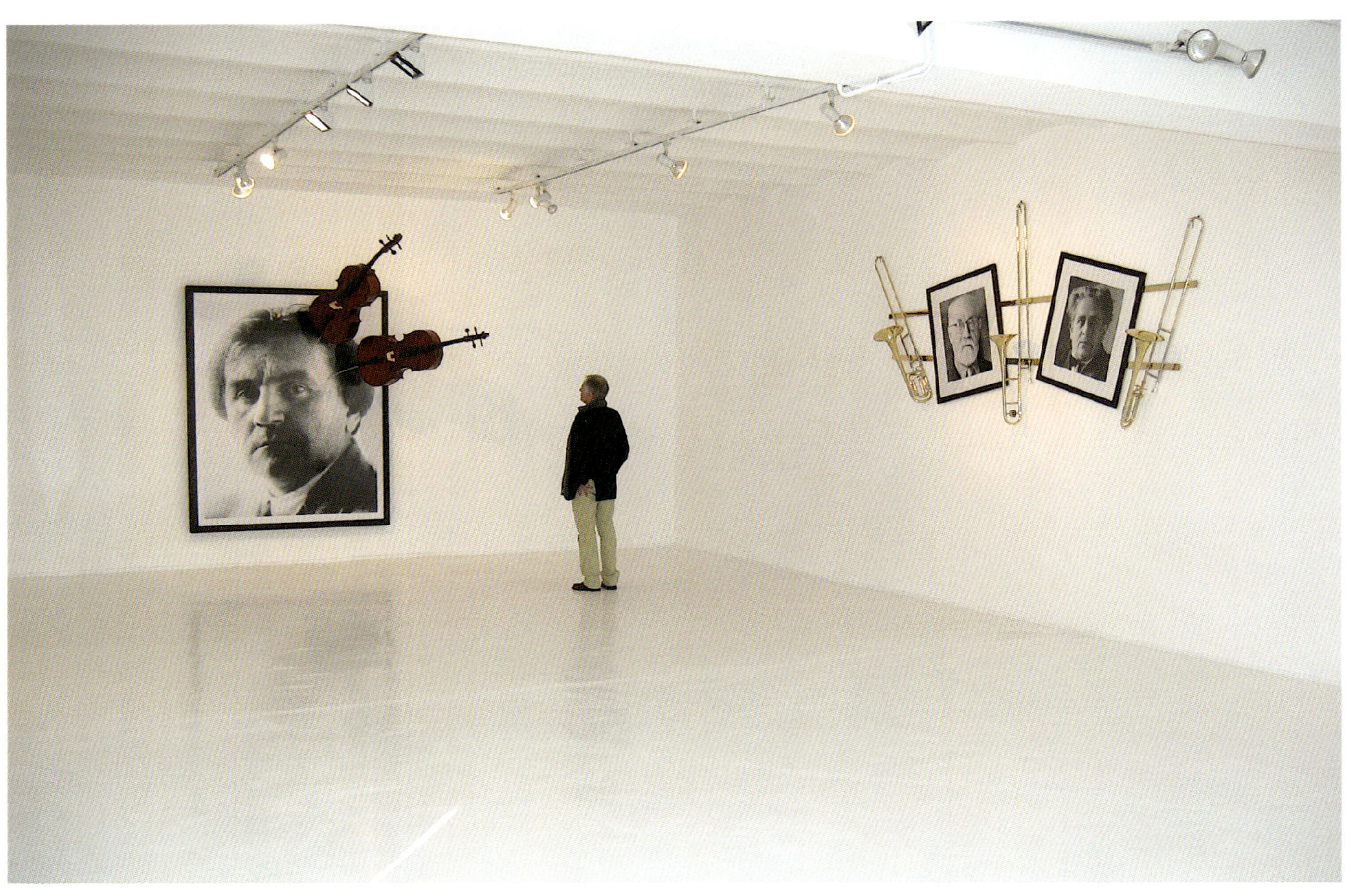

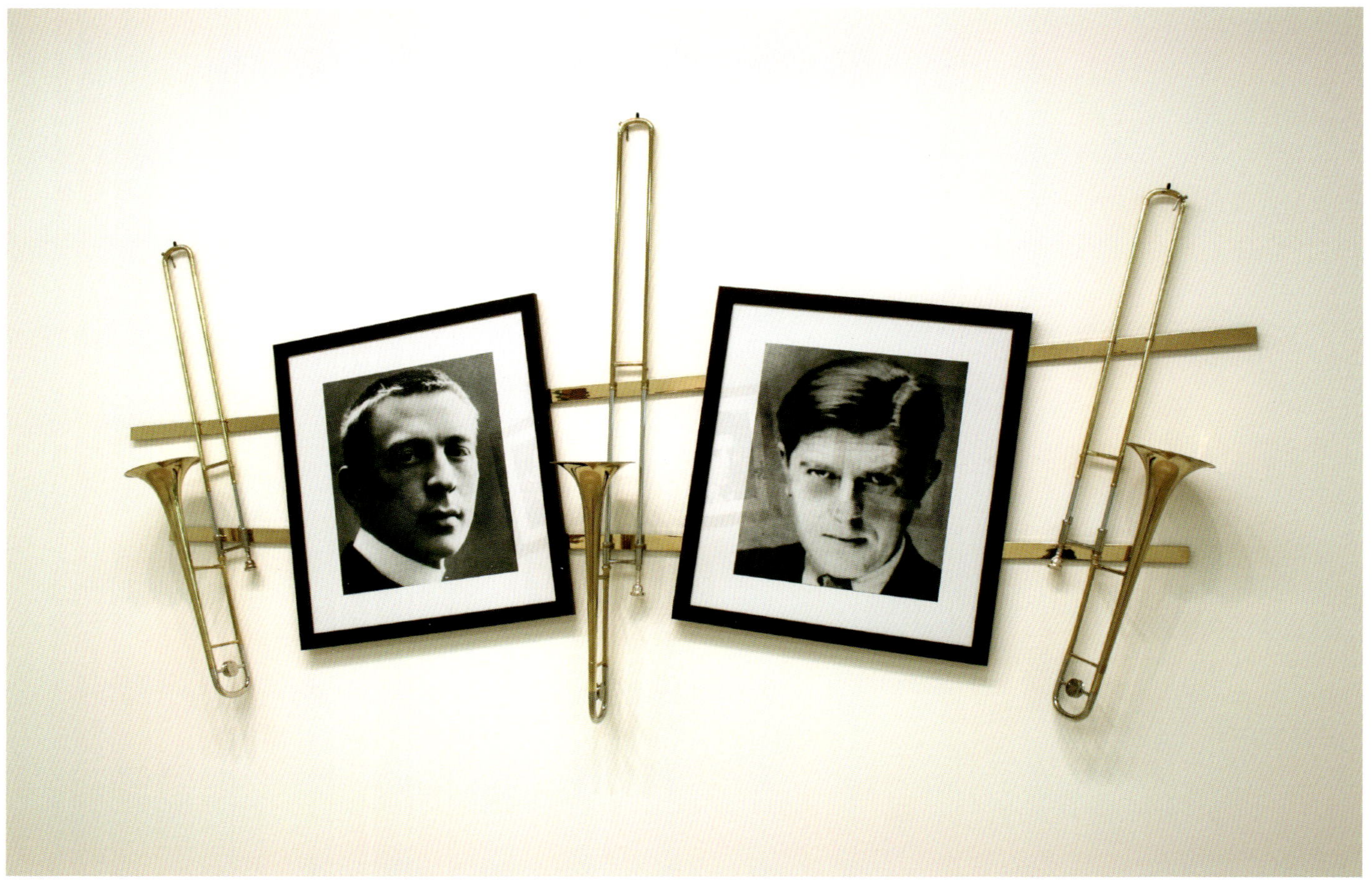

Installation view of solo exhibition
at Galleria Pino Casagrande, Rome 2006

Heralds of Post History V, 2006

B/W photographs, trombons, brass plates
Courtesy Galleria Pino Casagrande, Rome

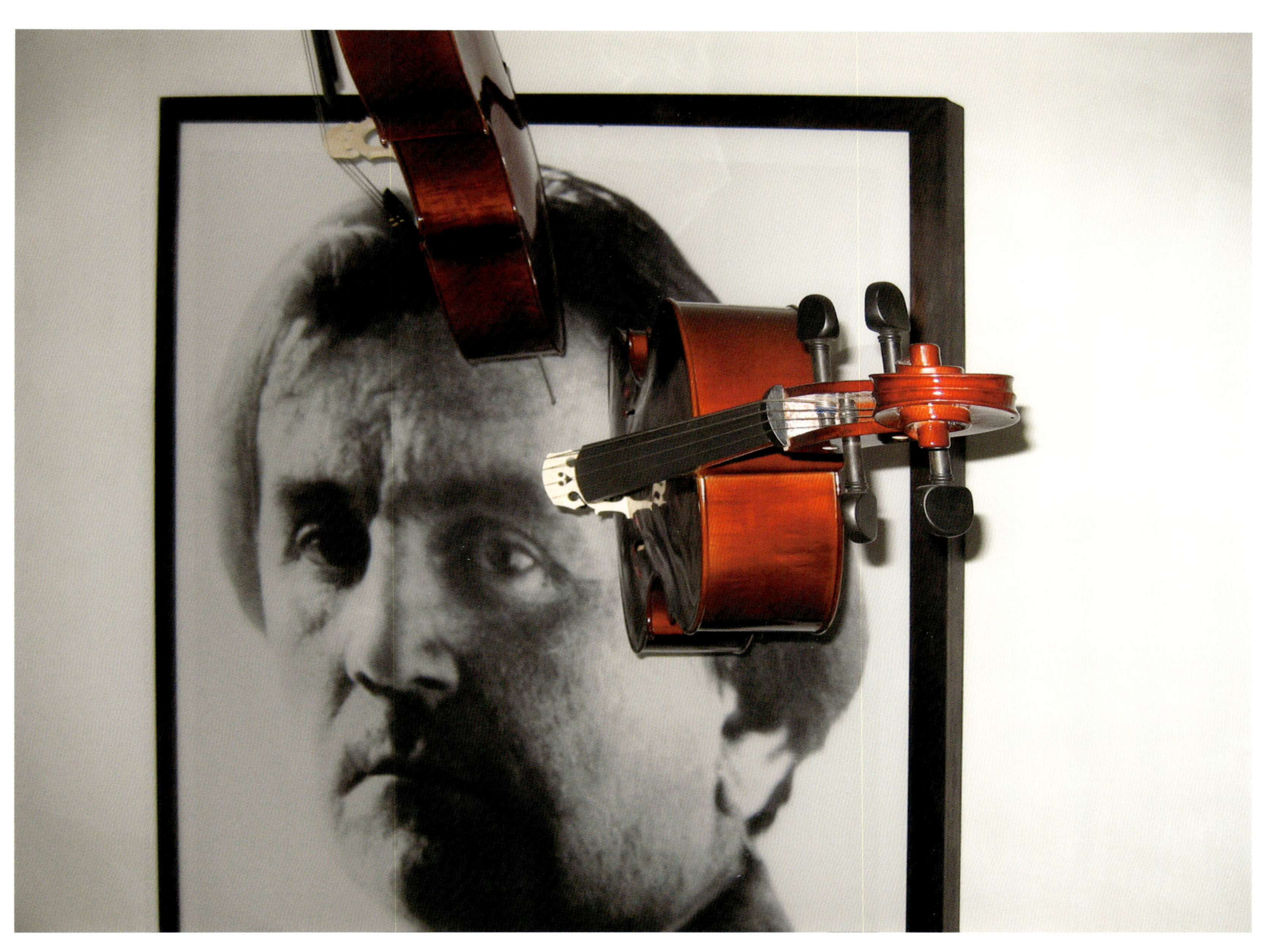

Dynamic Suprematism, 2006 (detail)

B/W photograph, violoncellos, 220 x 160 cm
Courtesy Galleria Pino Casagrande, Rome

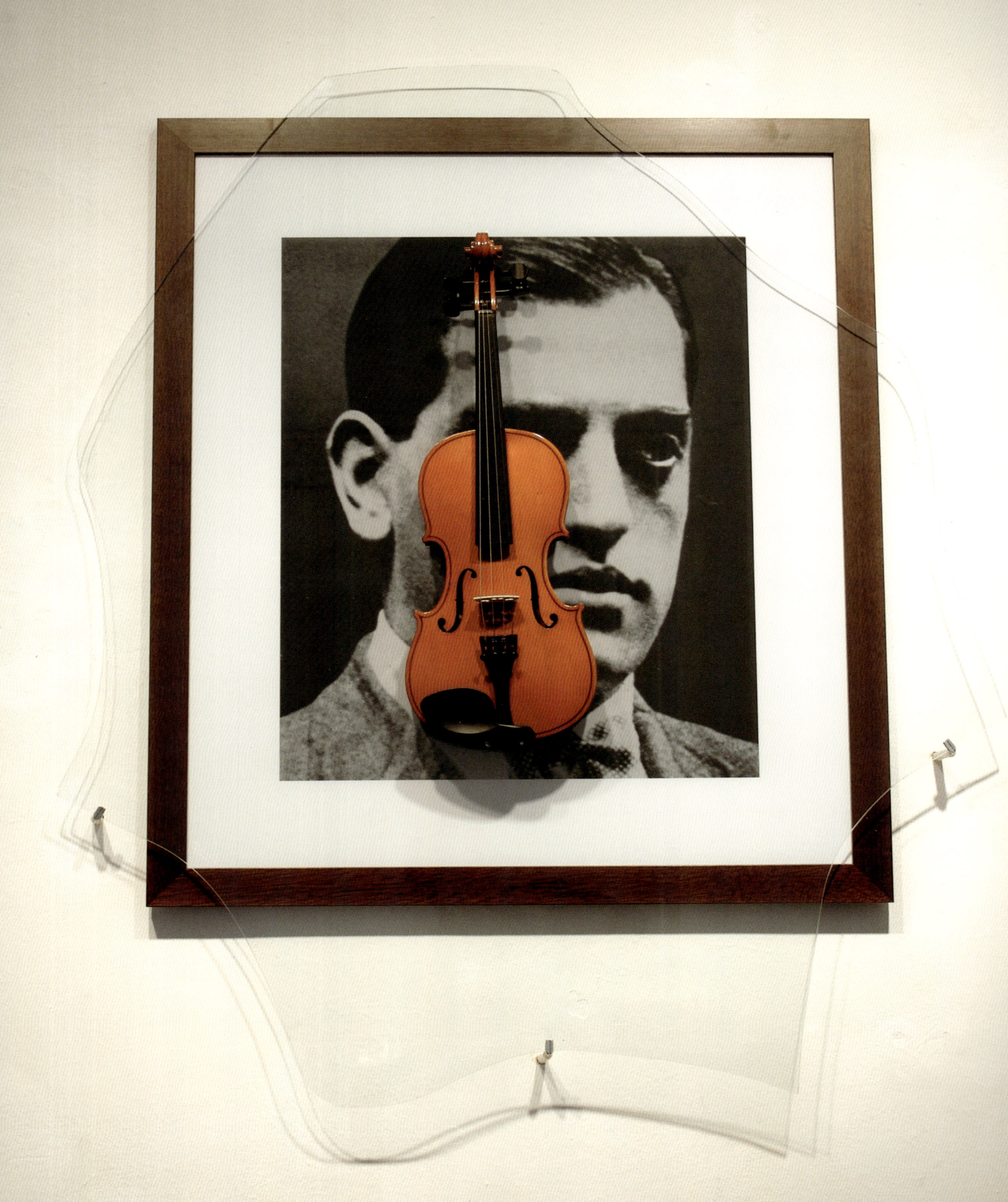

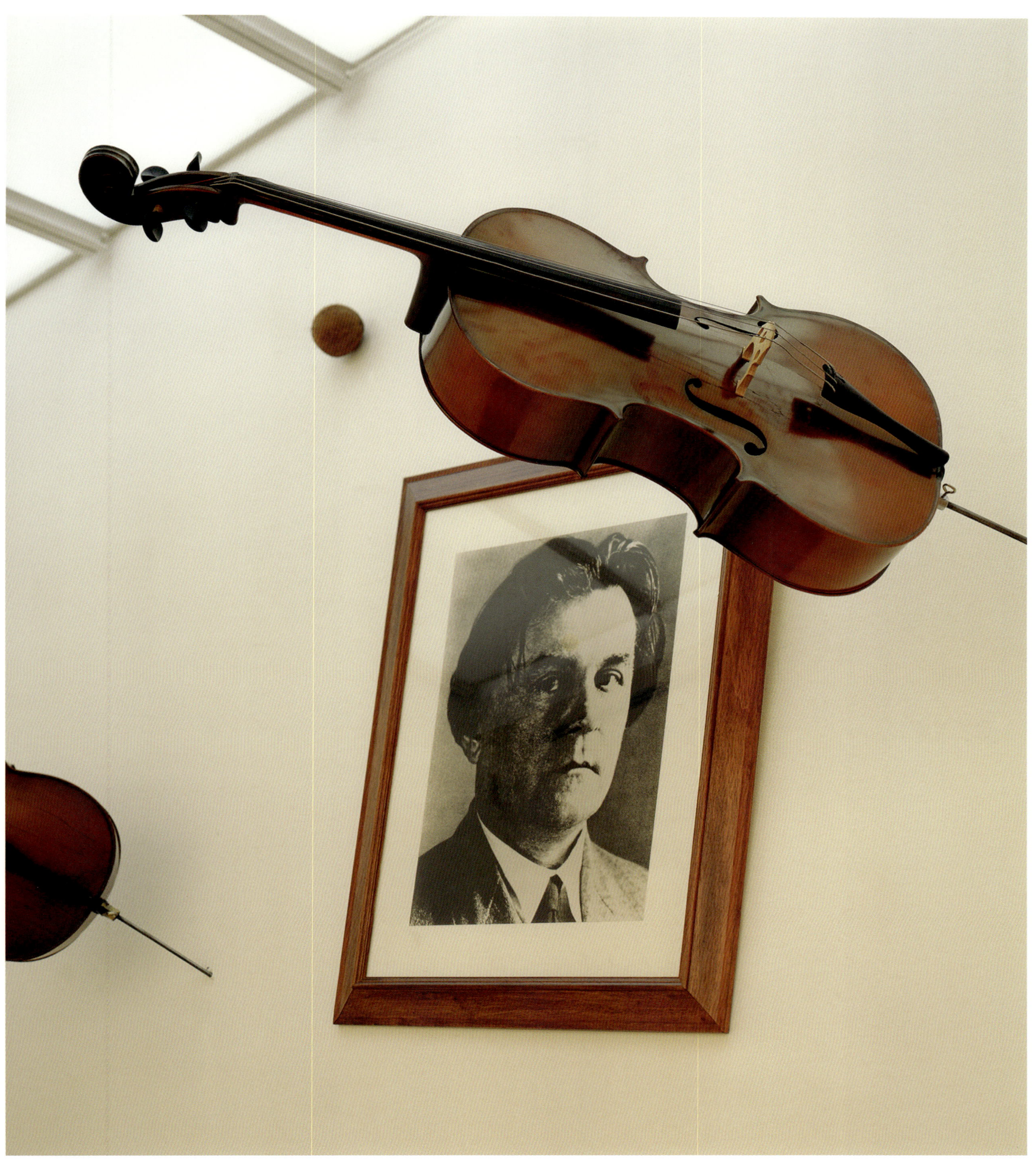

Stroke on Fifth Avenue, 2007

B/W photograph, violin, glass, 100 x 90 x 20 cm
Courtesy Galerie Heike Curtze, Berlin-Vienna

Against Historic Sense of Gravity II, 1996
(detail: Malevich)

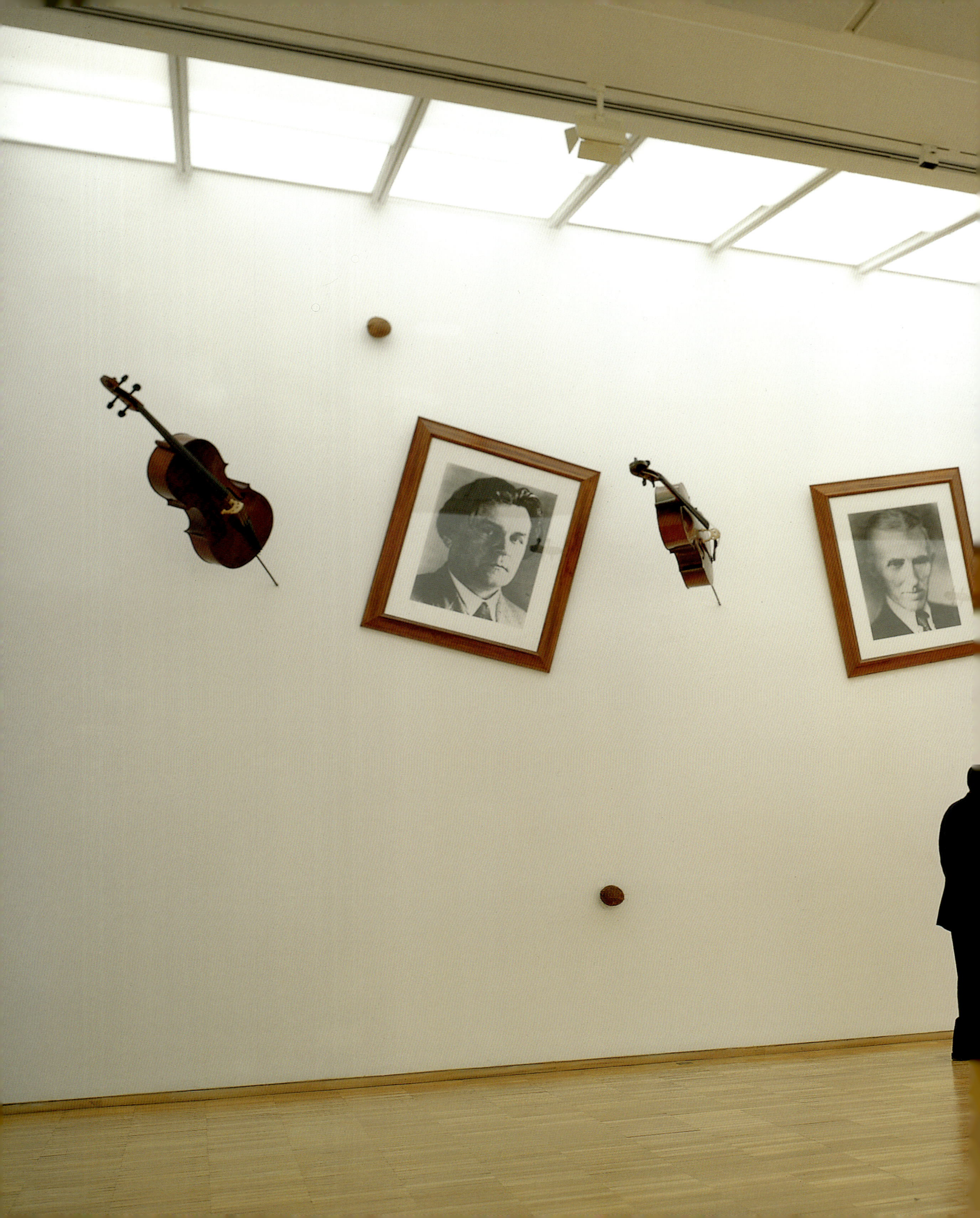

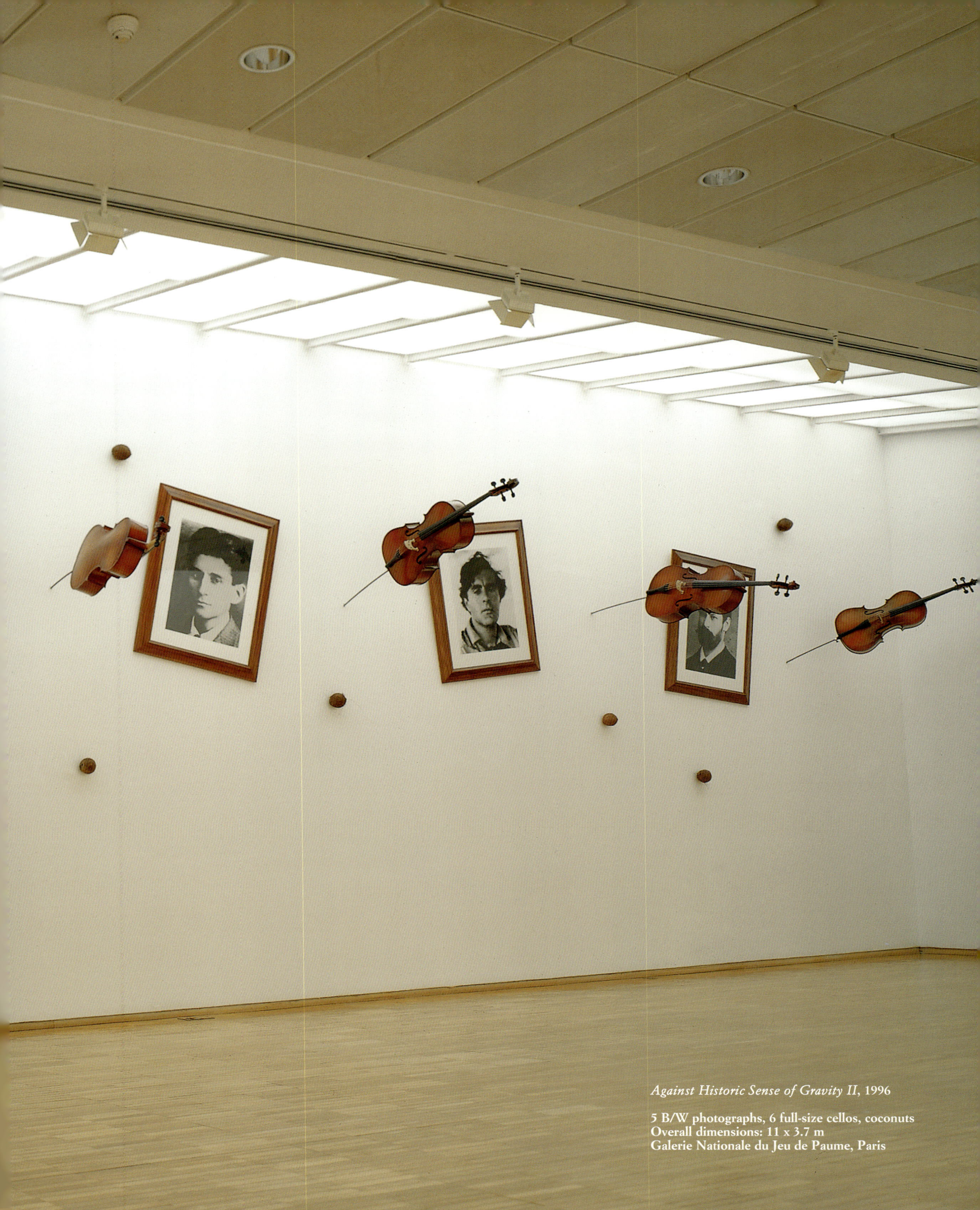

Against Historic Sense of Gravity II, 1996

5 B/W photographs, 6 full-size cellos, coconuts
Overall dimensions: 11 x 3.7 m
Galerie Nationale du Jeu de Paume, Paris

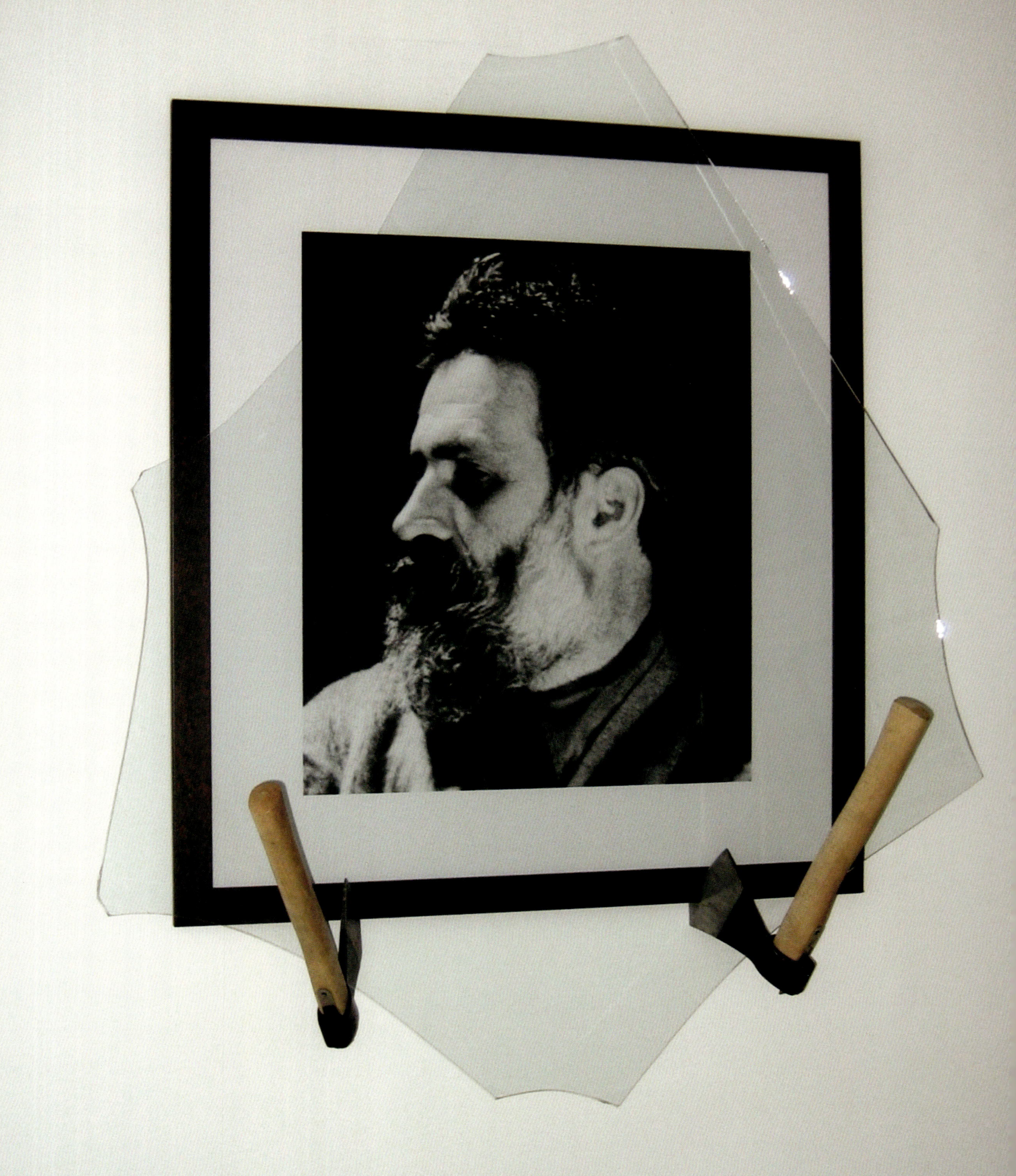

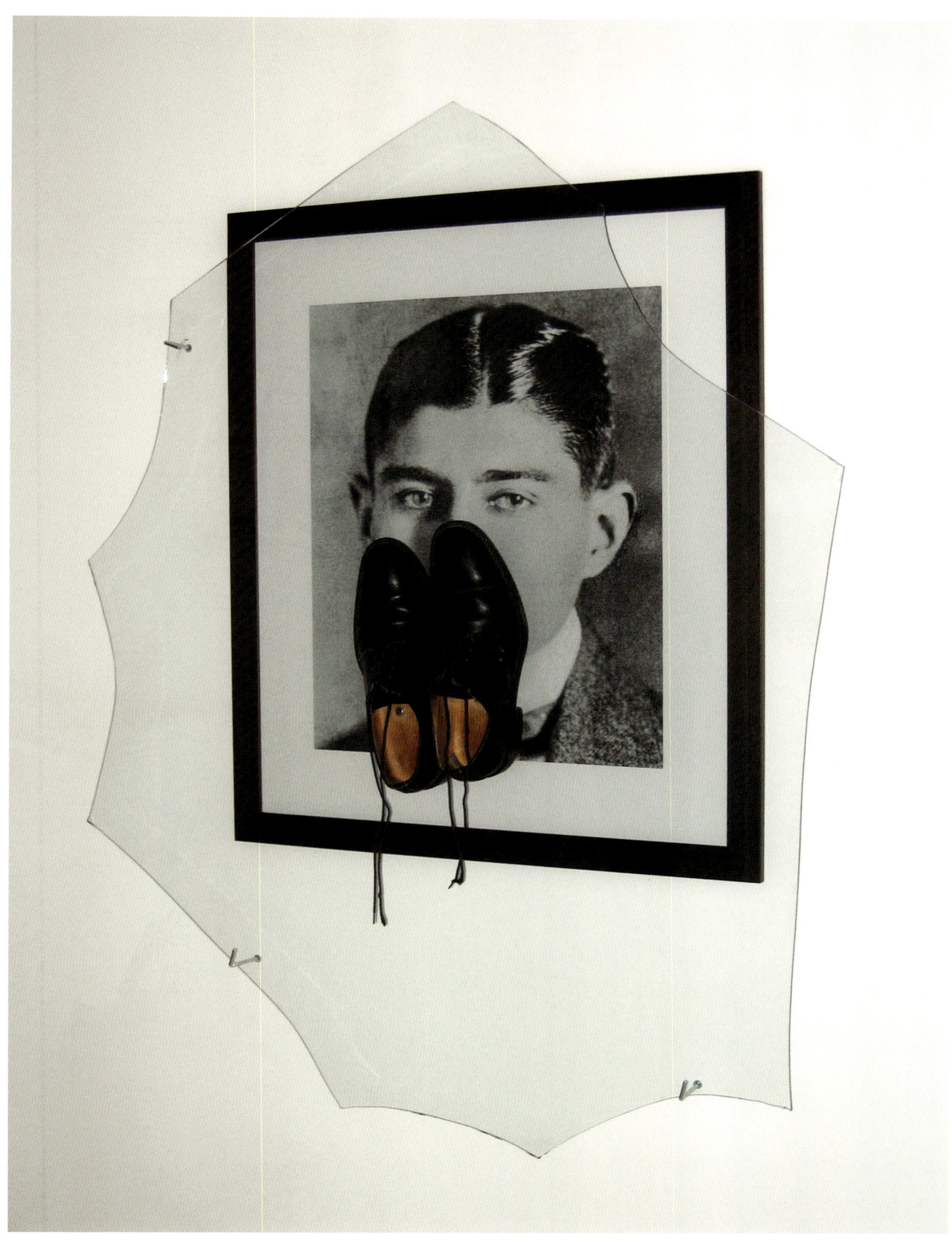

Endless Coloumn, 2006

B/W photograph, axes, glass, 110 x 90 x 30 cm
Courtesy Galerie Heike Curtze, Berlin-Vienna

Unwanted, 2007

B/W photograph, shoes, glass
Courtesy Galerie Heike Curtze, Berlin-Vienna

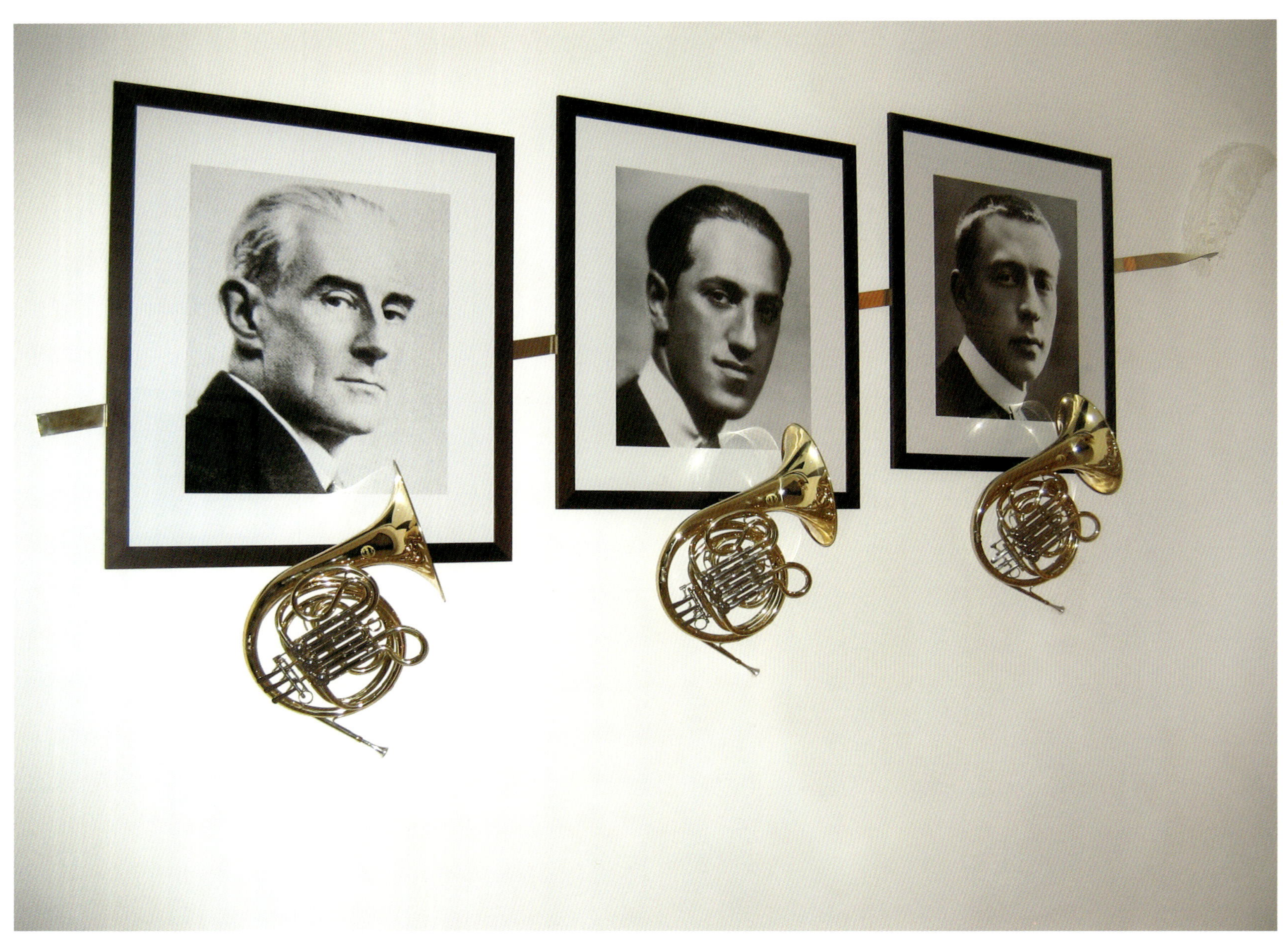

Heralds of Post History IV, 2006

B/W photographs, French horns, brass
Courtesy Galleria Pino Casagrande, Rome

Heralds of Post History - China, 2006 (detail)

B/W photographs, French horns, brass, ostrich feather
170 x 140 x 10 cm
Courtesy Xin-Dong Cheng Contemporary Art, Beijing

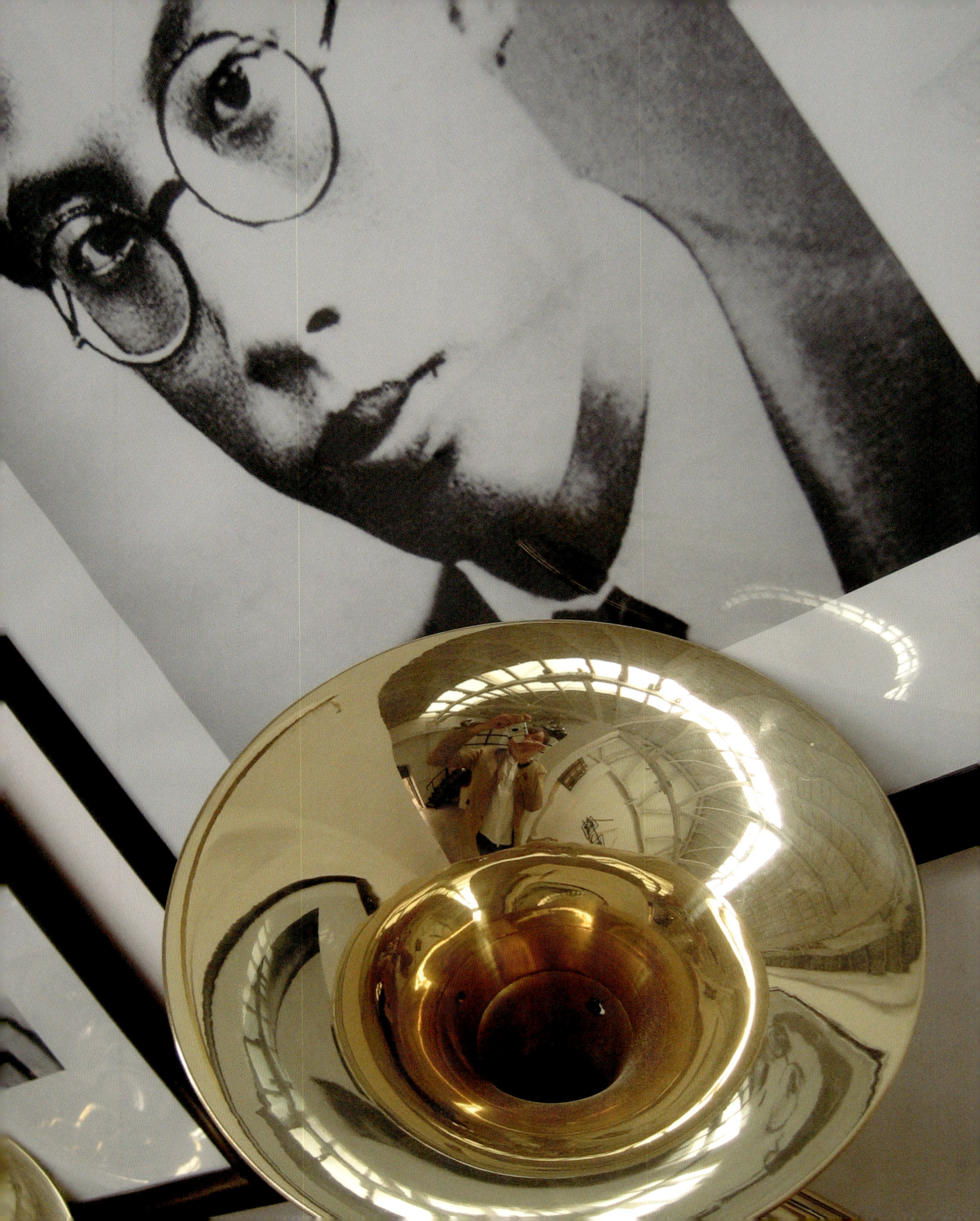

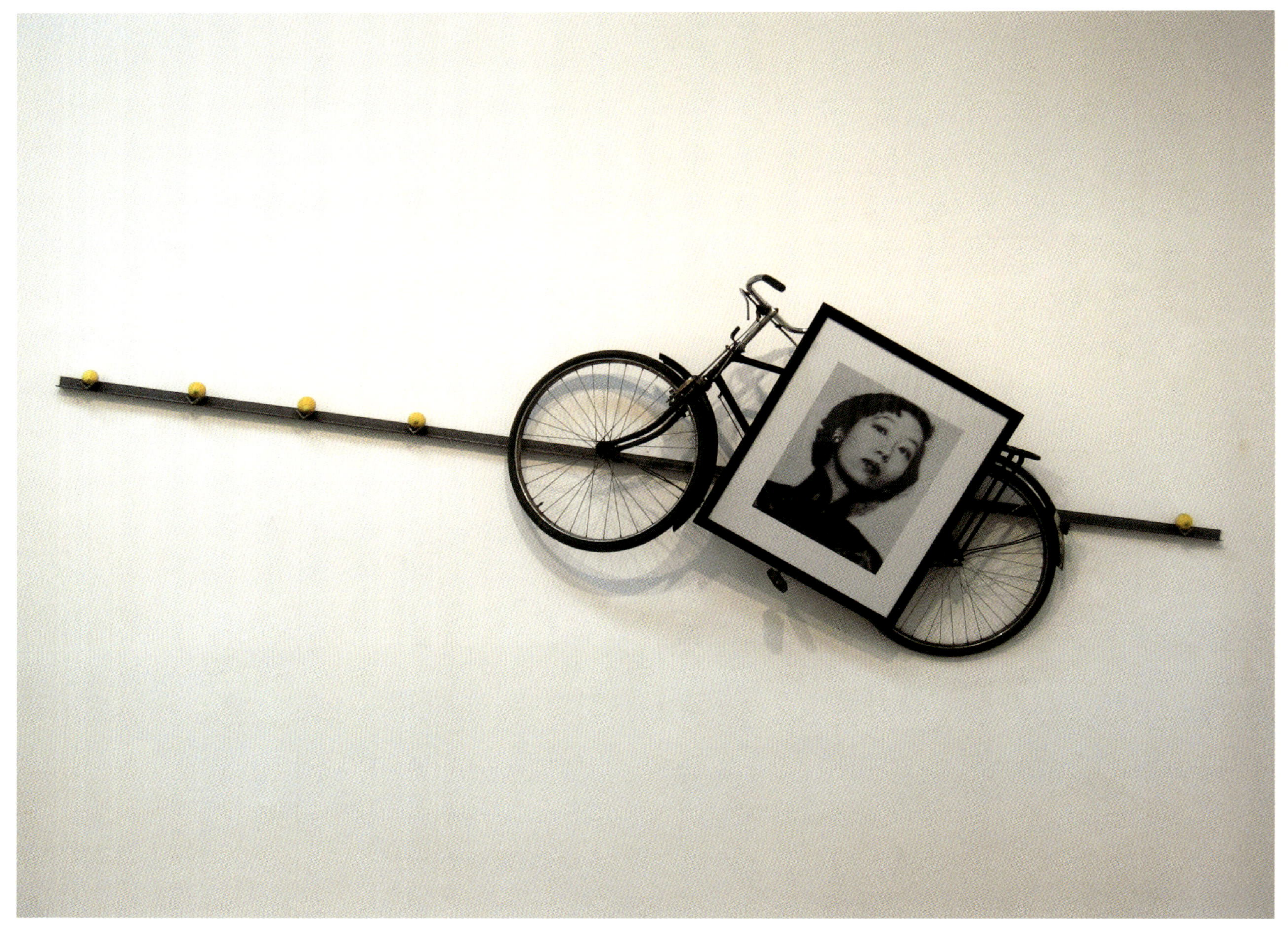

Untitled, 2006

B/W photograph, bicycle, metal bar
Private Collection, Beijing

Between Collective and Individual, 2006

Imperial College of China, Confucius Temple, Beijing
B/W photographs, bicycles, metal
Courtesy Xin-Dong Cheng Contemporary Art, Beijing

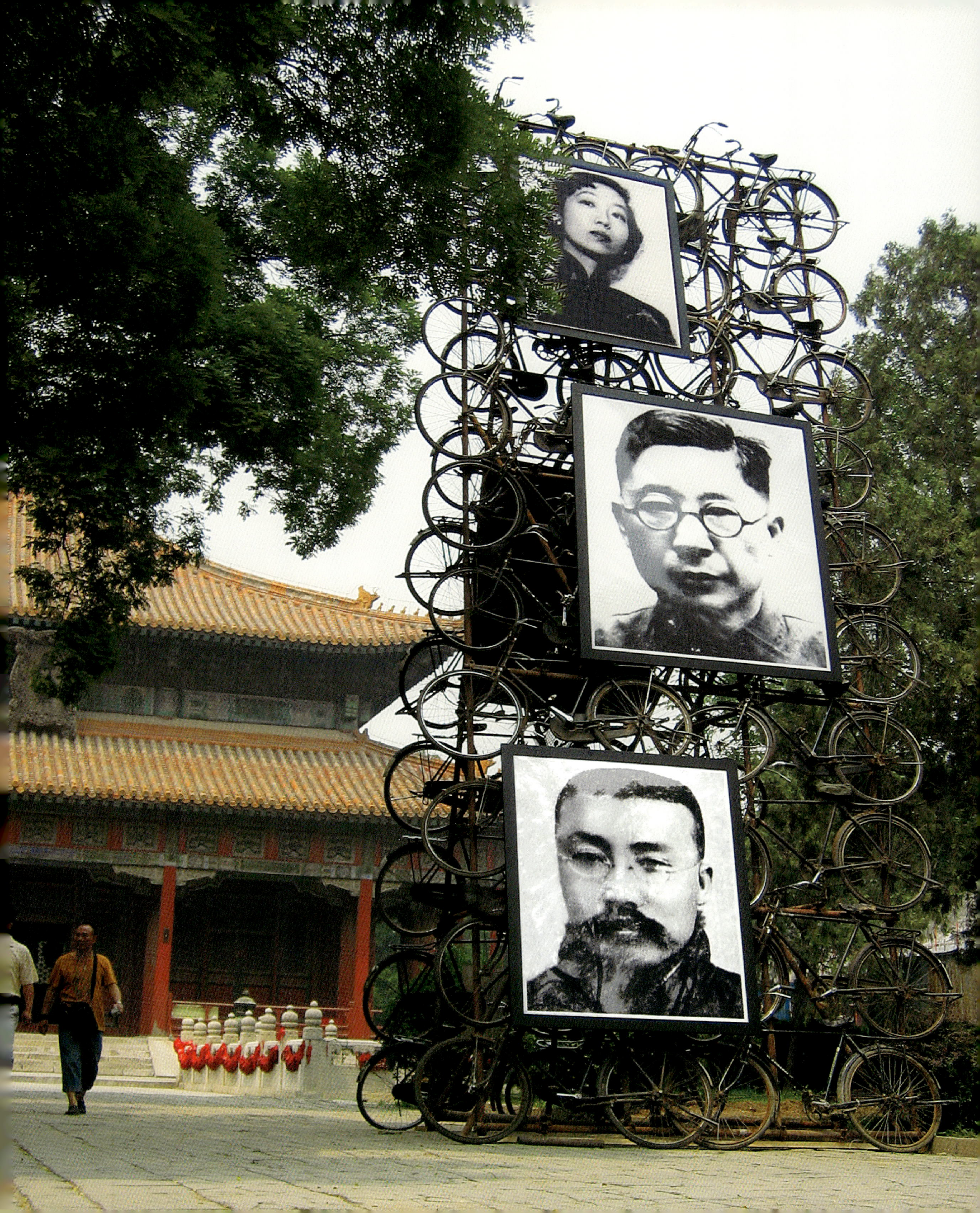

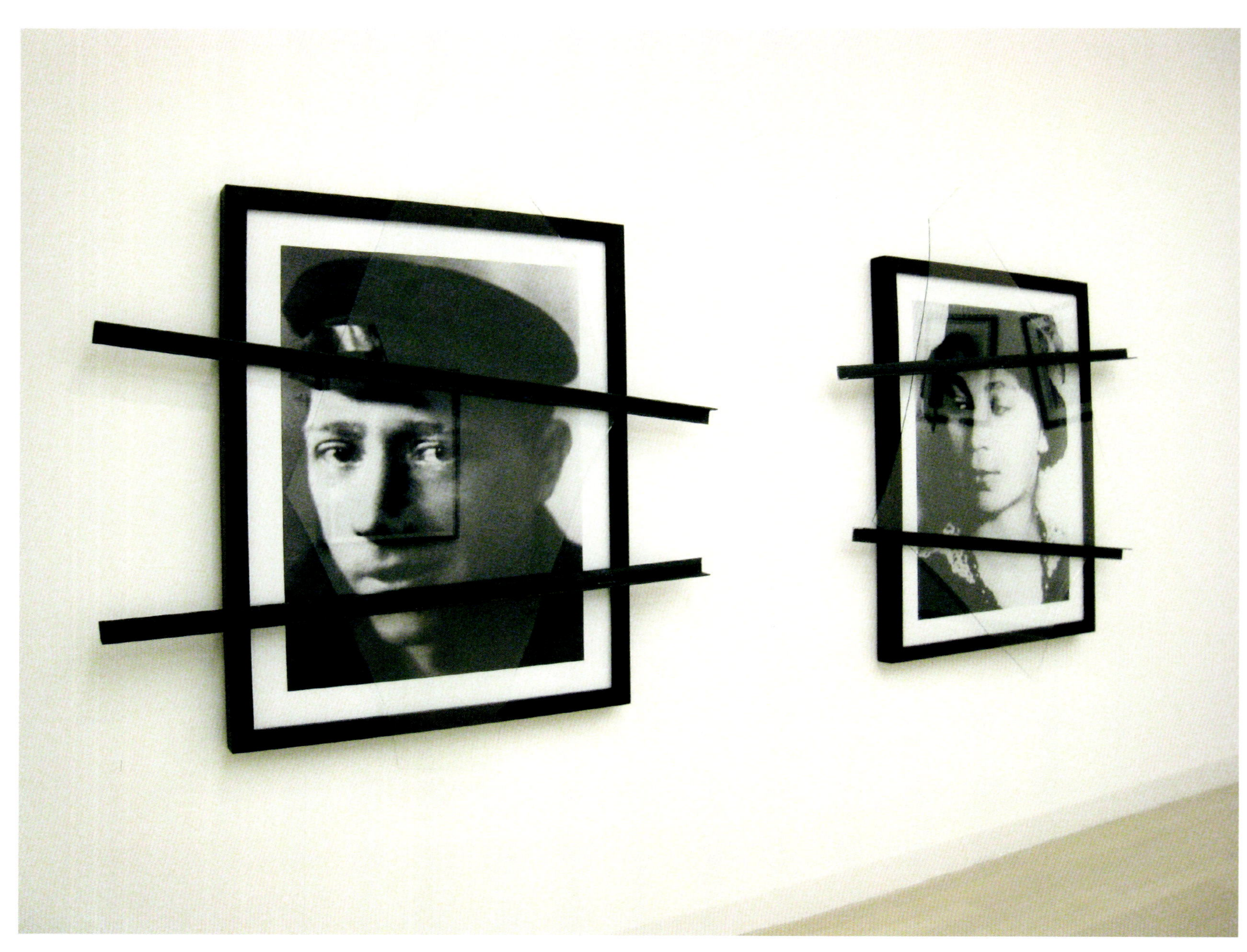

Crossed (Tatlin - Goncharova), 2007

B/W photograph, metal, glass, 170 x 140 x 10 cm
Courtesy Galerie Heike Curtze, Berlin-Vienna

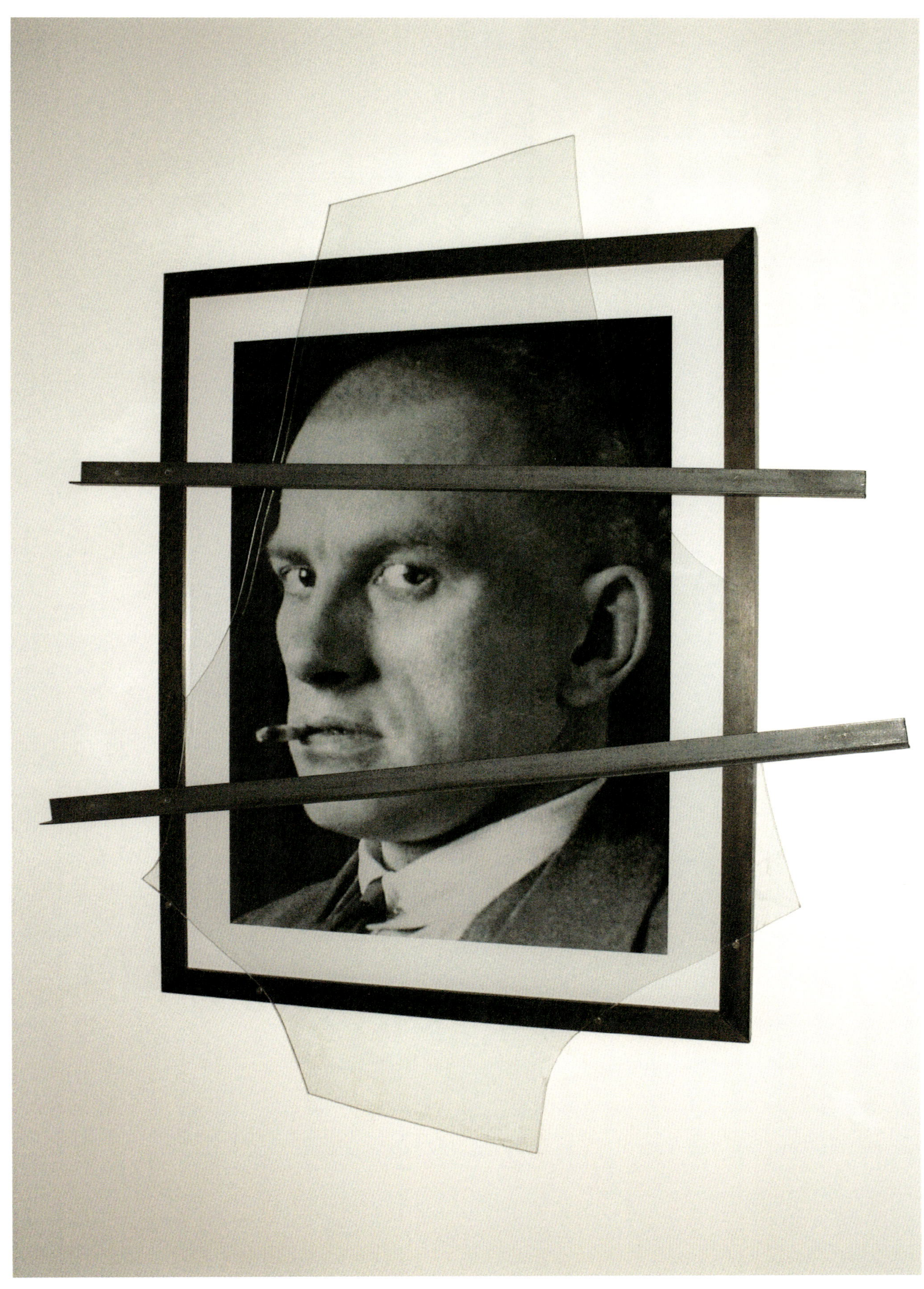

Crossed (Majakovski), 2007

B/W photograph, metal, glass, 170 x 140 x 10 cm
Courtesy Galerie Heike Curtze, Berlin-Vienna

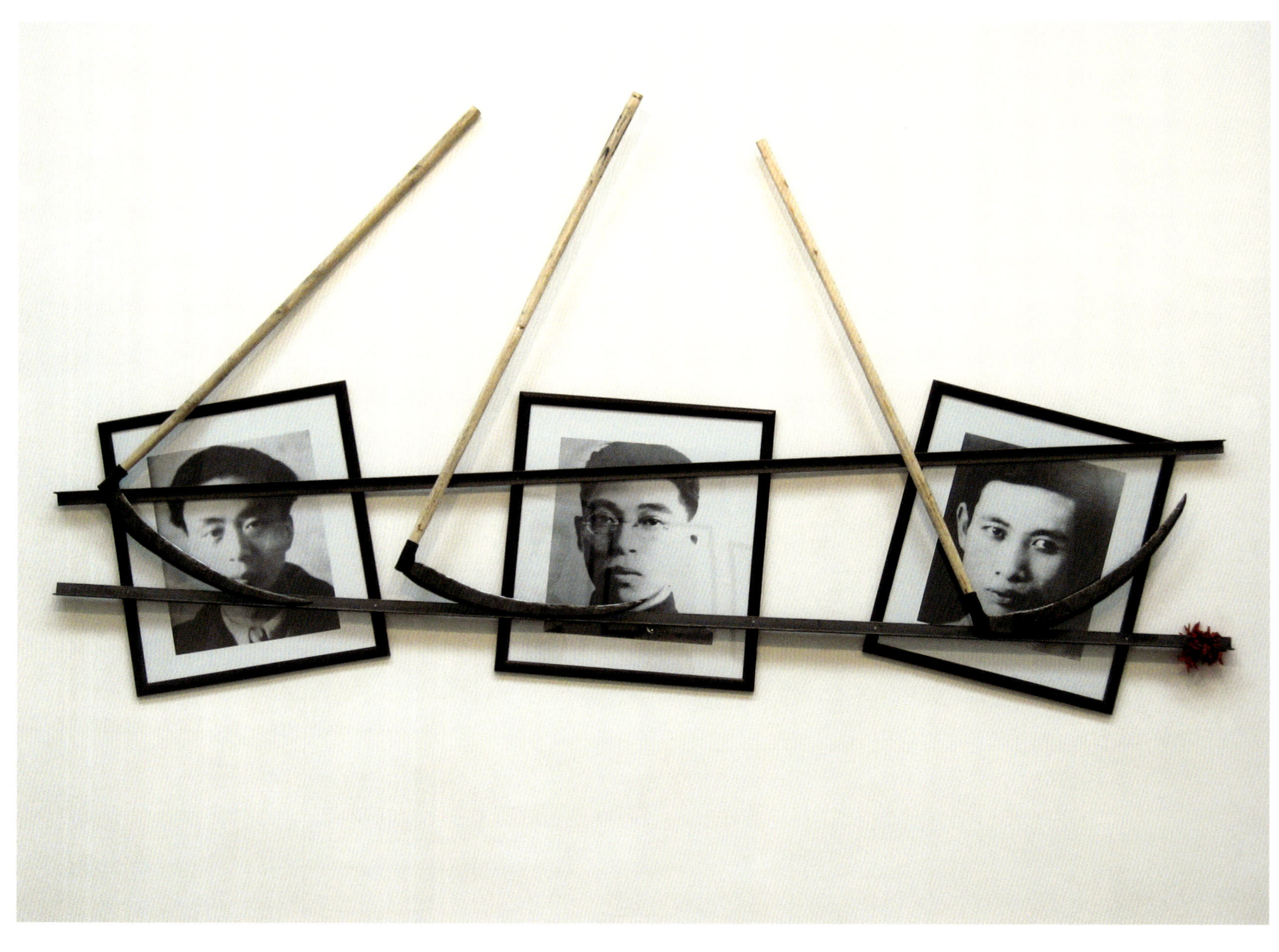

Poets in the Field, 2006

B/W photographs, metal, scythes
Private collection.

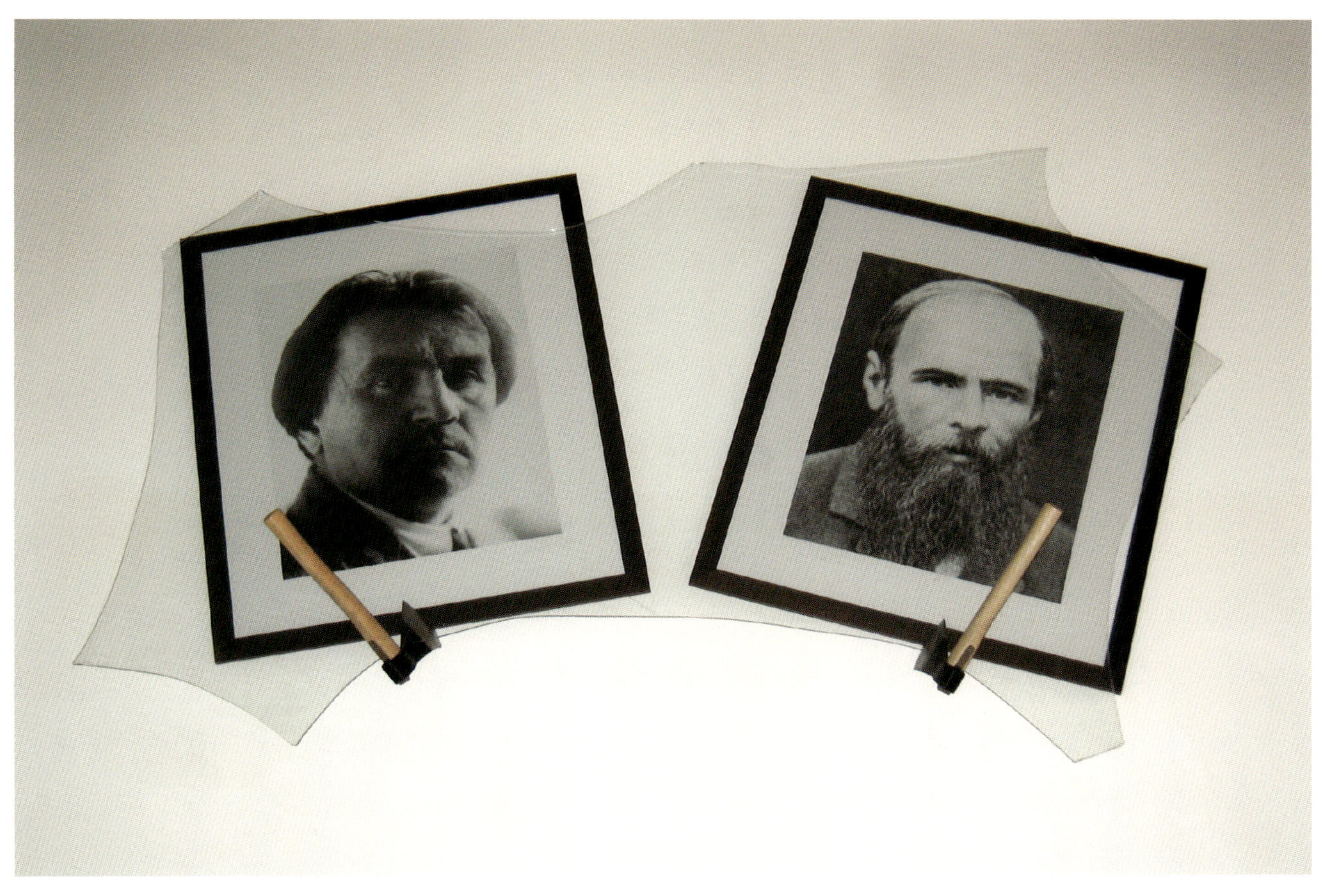

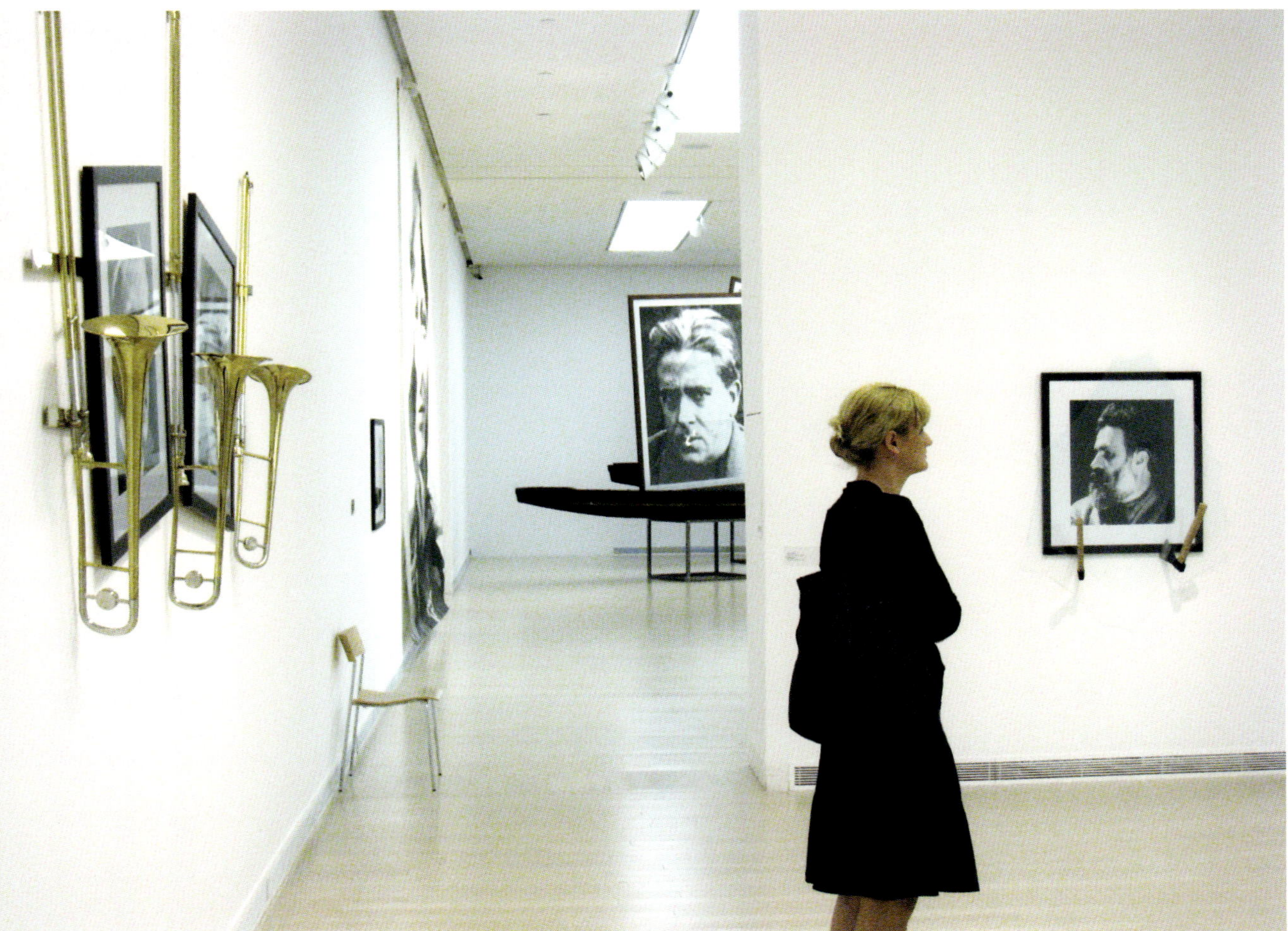

Russian Rapsody, 2006

B/W photographs, axes, glass
Courtesy Galleria Pino Casagrande, Rome

Installation view of retrospective exhibition
Ludwig Museum of Contemporary Art, Budapest, 2008

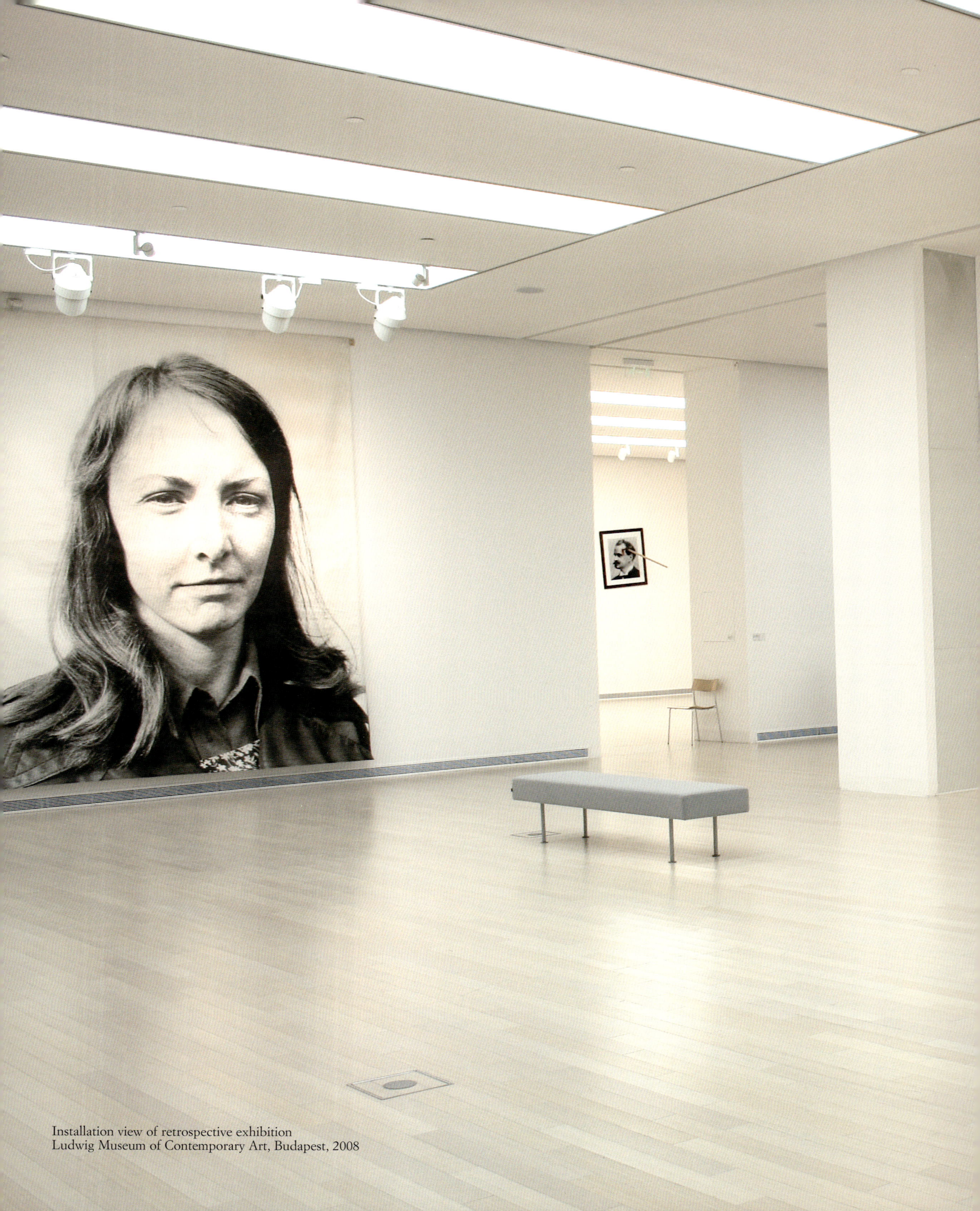

Installation view of retrospective exhibition
Ludwig Museum of Contemporary Art, Budapest, 2008

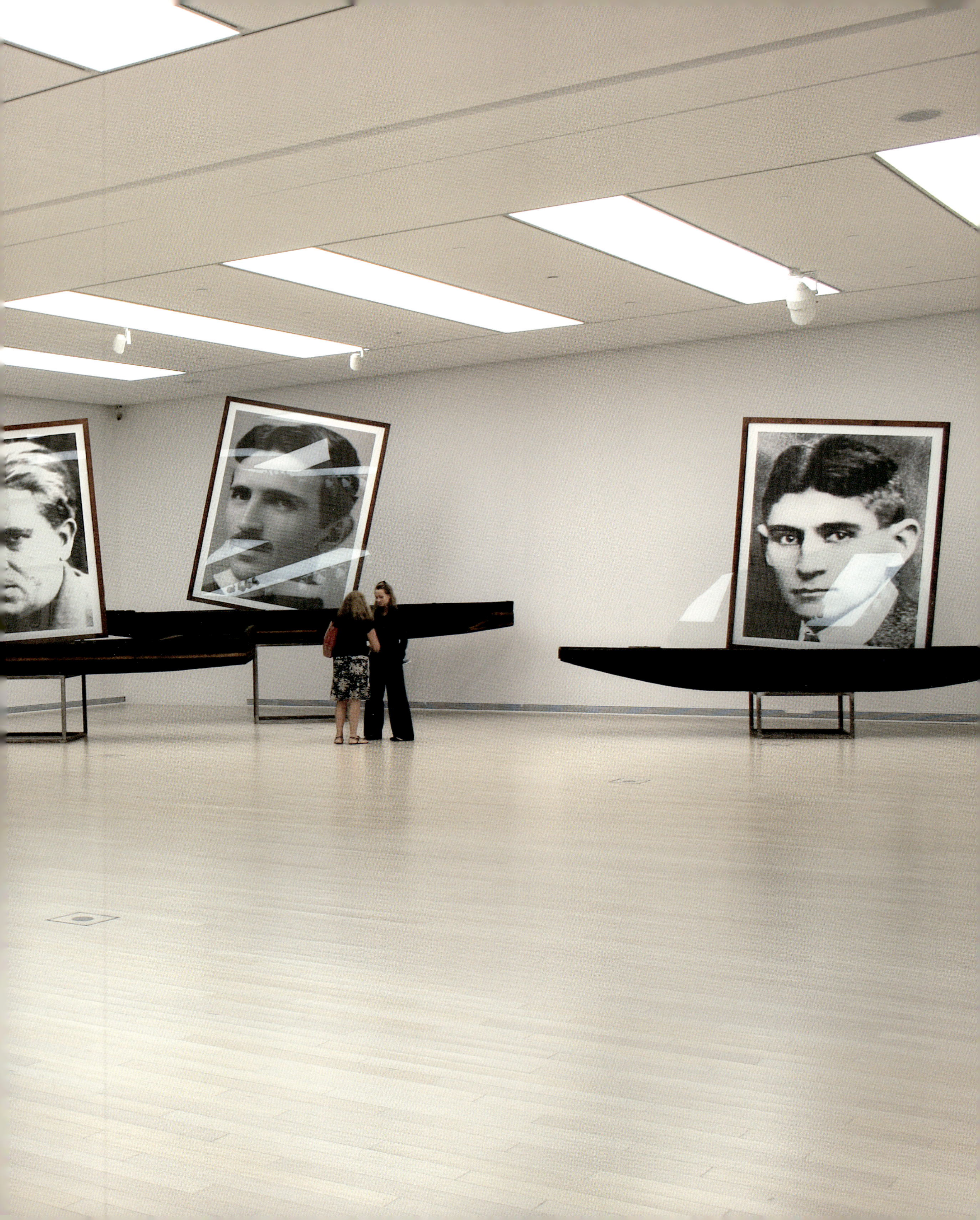

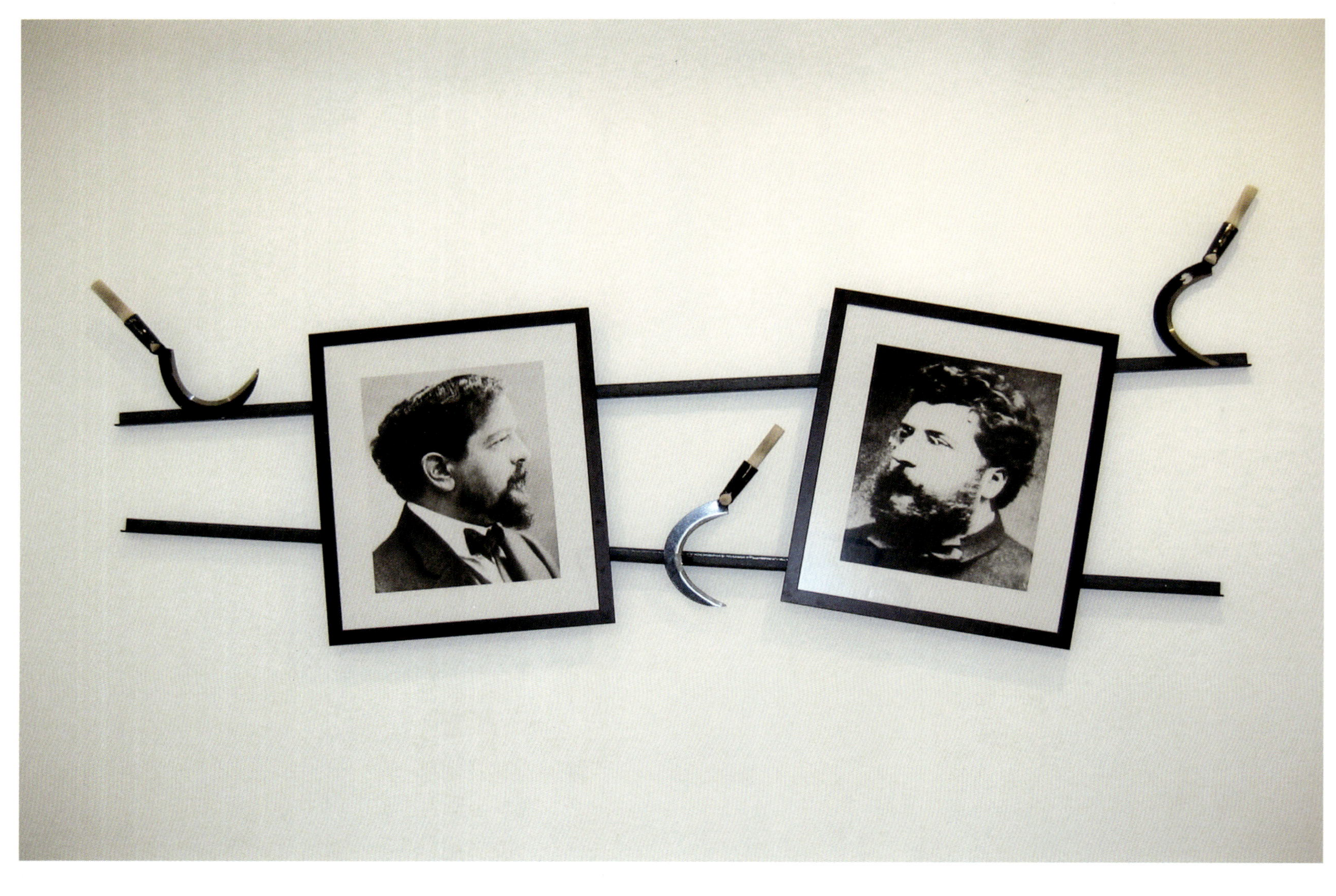

Constellation VII (Debussy, Bizet), 2007

B/W photographs, scythes, metal
Private Collection

Far from Harbour near the Stars, 2006

B/W photographs, boats, metal
Courtesy Galleria Pino Casagrande, Rome

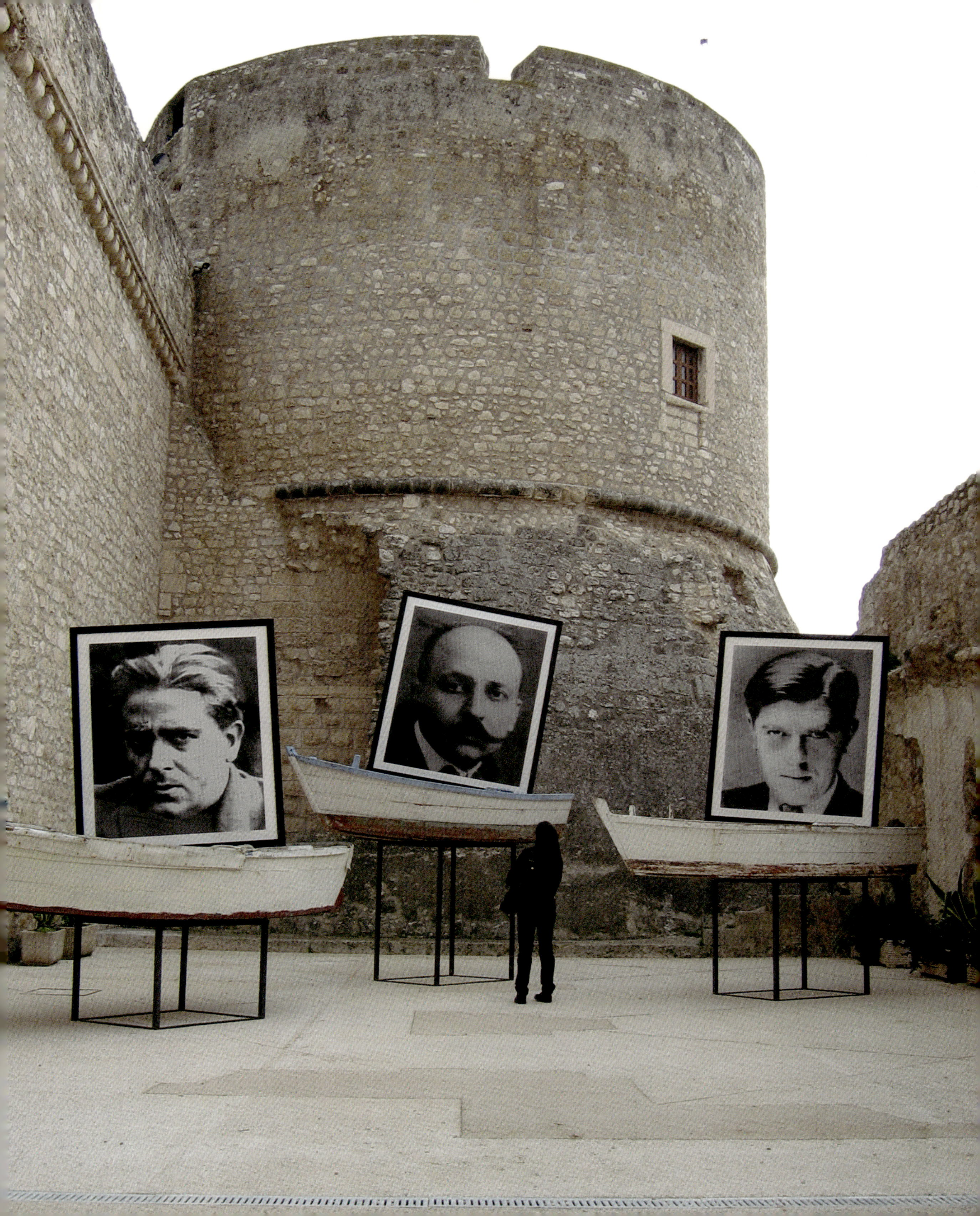

Culturescapes

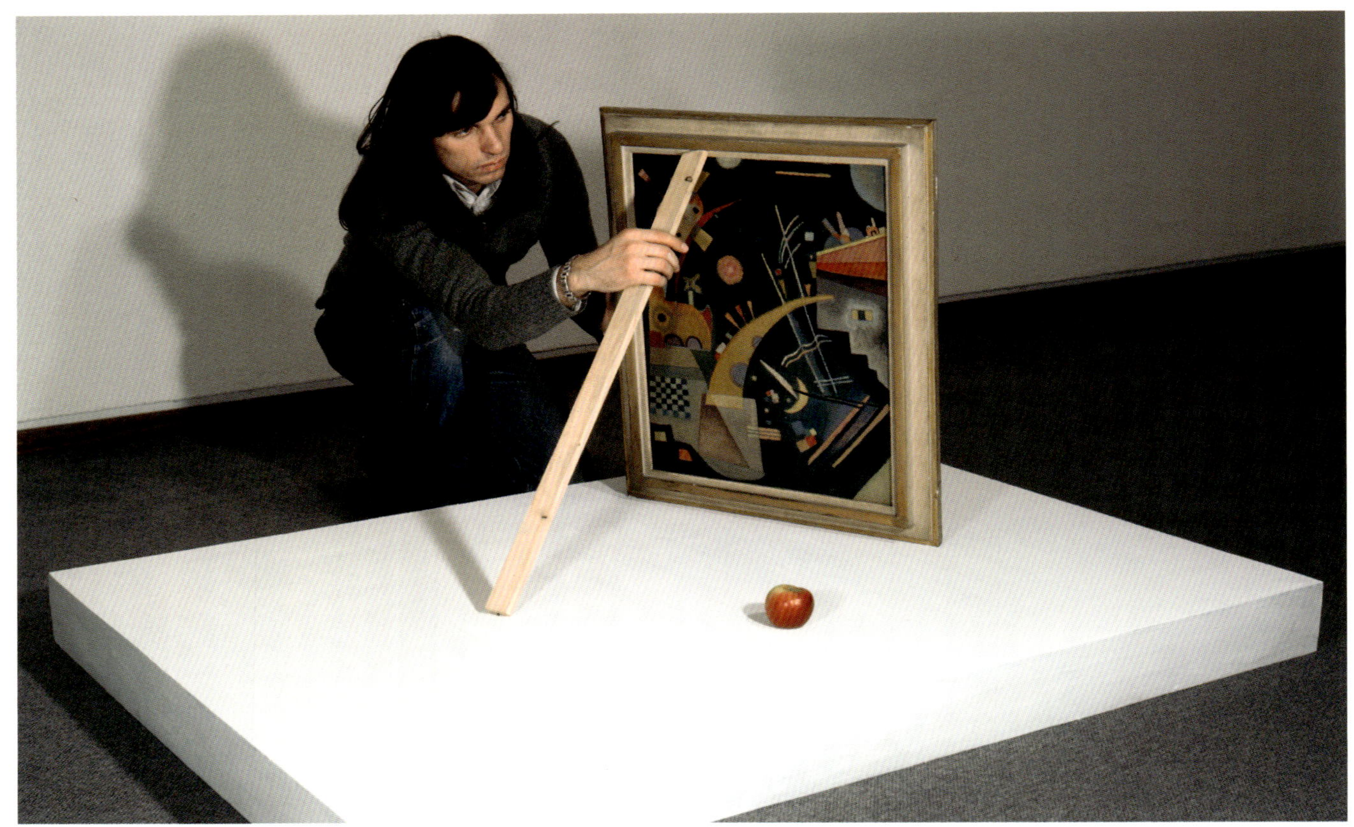

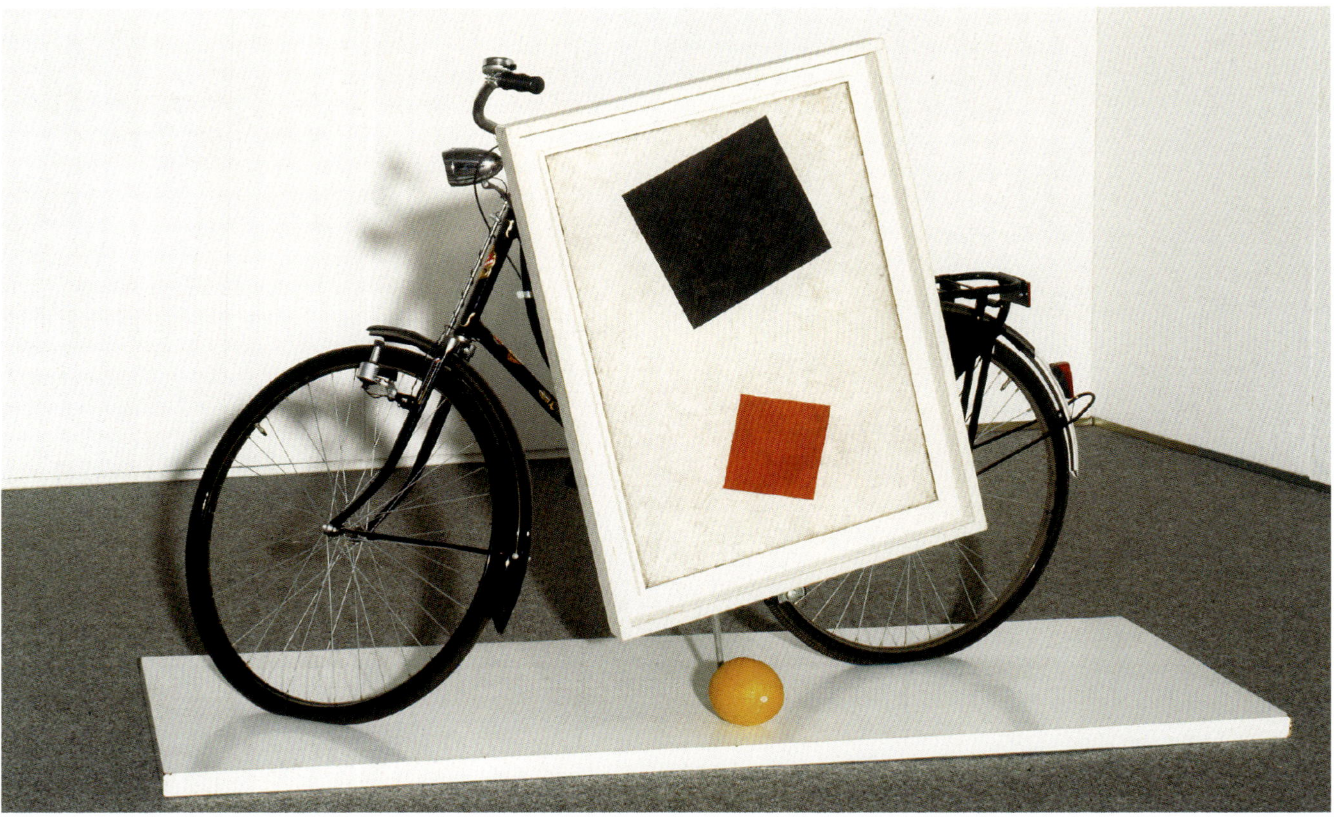

Installing *Triptychos Post Historicus with Kandinsky* at the Nationalgalerie, Berlin, 1976

Triptychos Post Historicus
Wilhelm-Hack-Museum, Ludwigshafen, 1985

I: *Black and Red Square*, Kasimir Malevich, 1915
II: Bernhard Holeczek's bicycle; III: Melon
Collection: Wilhelm-Hack-Museum, Ludwigshafen

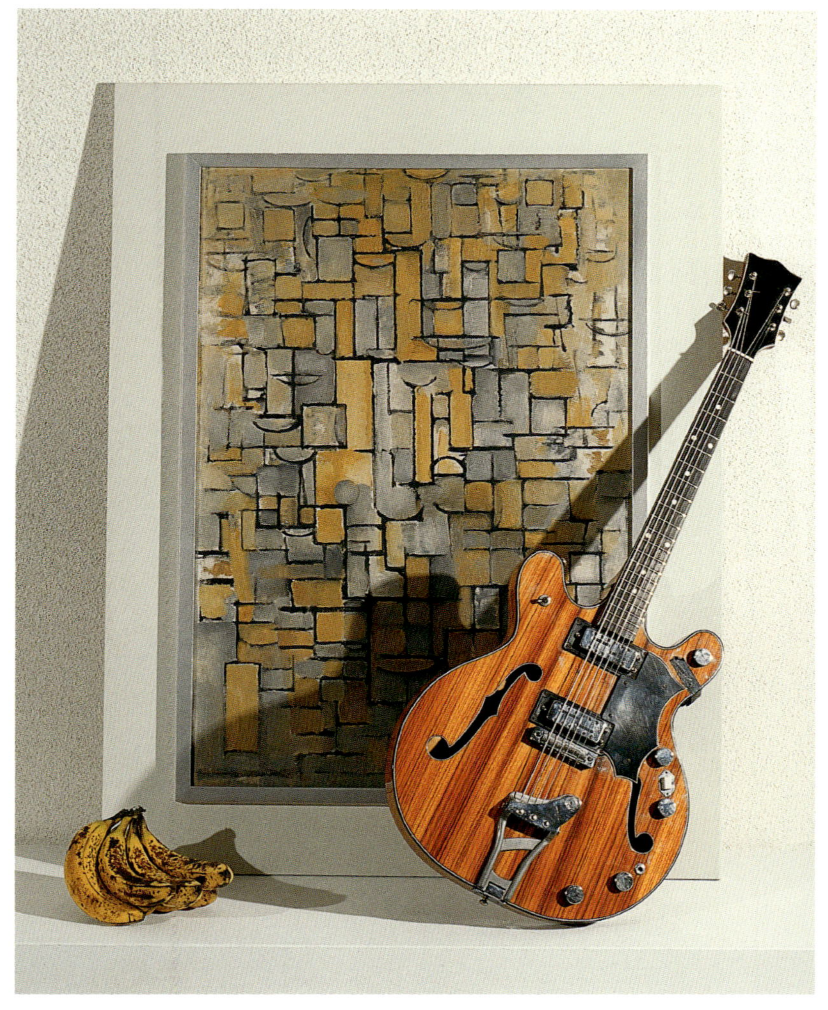

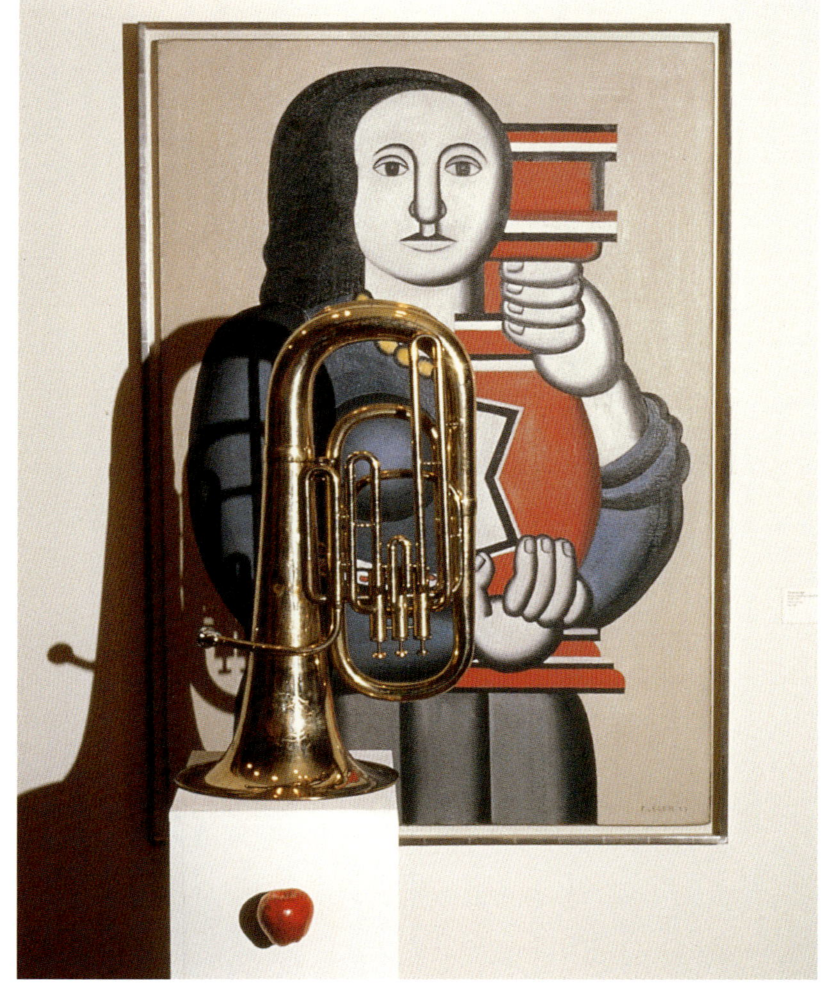

Triptychos Post Historicus
Stedelijk Van Abbemuseum, Eindhoven, 1978

I: *Composition XIV*, Piet Mondrian, 1913
II: Hans Biezen's guitar; III: Bananas

Triptychos Post Historicus
Solomon R. Guggenheim Museum, New York, 1988

I: *Woman with Vase*, Fernand Léger, 1937
II: Baritone trombone played by Tchepo Kaleb; III: Apple

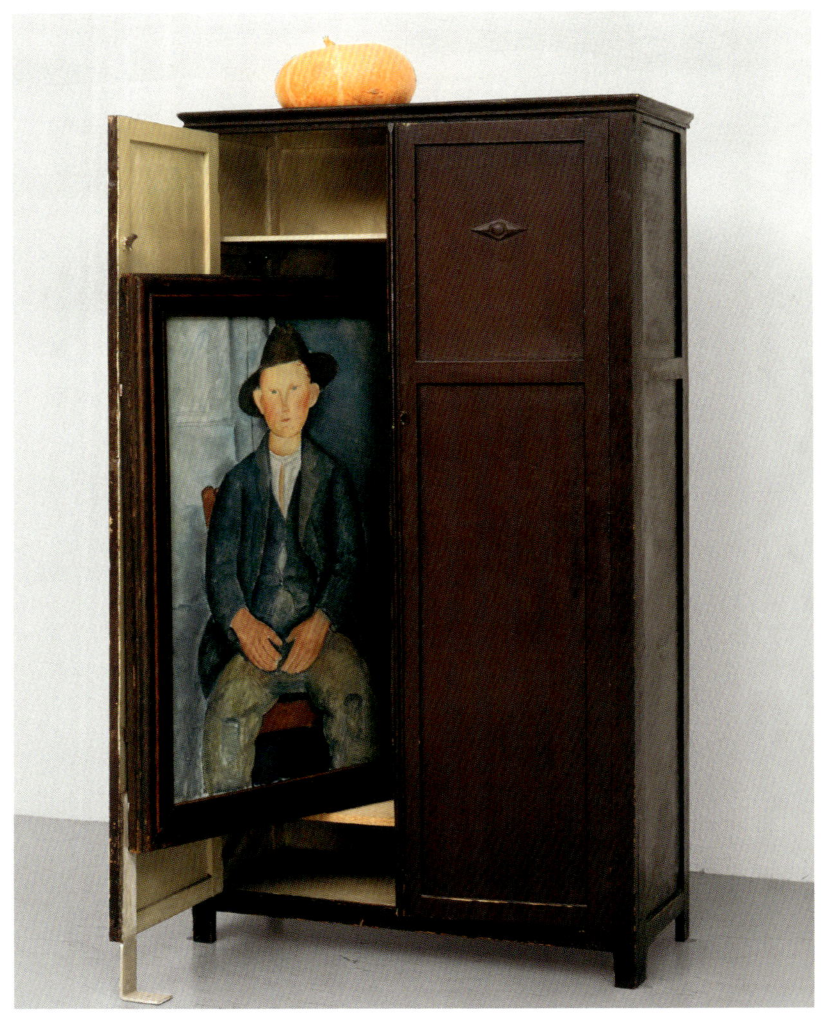

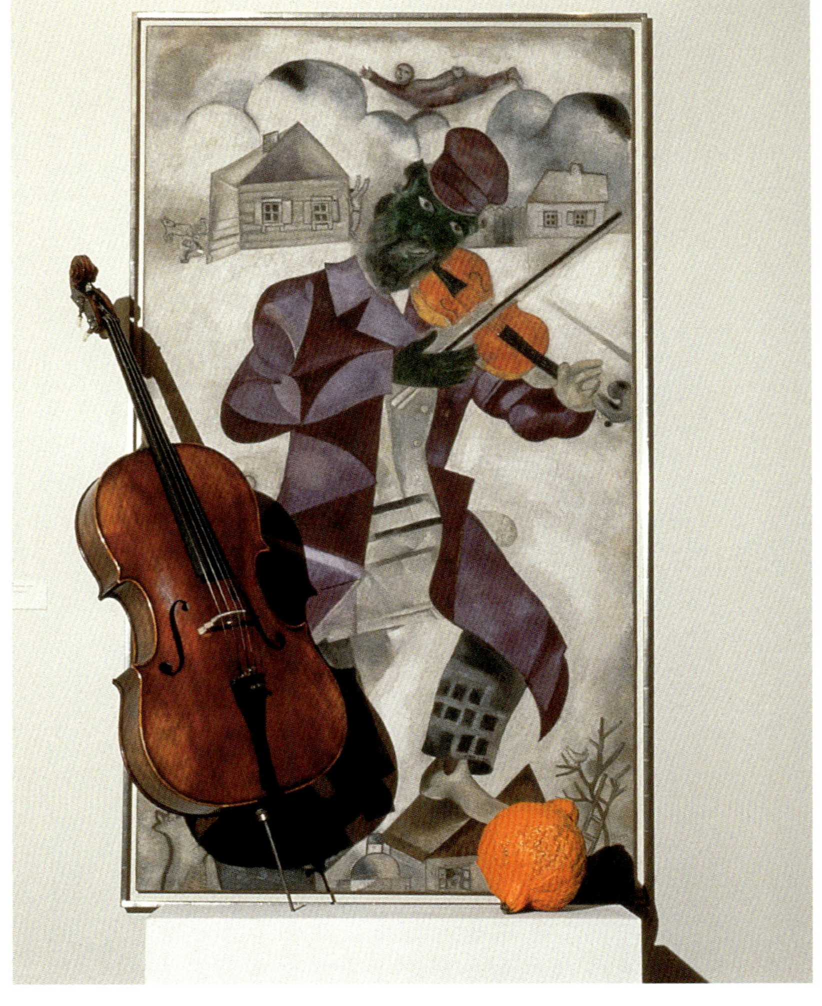

Triptychos Post Historicus or Repeated Secret
Tate Gallery, London, 1978–1985

I: *The Little Peasant*, Amedeo Modigliani, 1919
II: Wardrobe painted by Sarah Moore; III: Pumpkin
Collection: Tate Gallery, London

Triptychos Post Historicus
Solomon R. Guggenheim Museum, New York, 1988

I: *Green Violinist*, Marc Chagall, 1923–1924
II: Cello played by Anne Skolnick; III: Squash

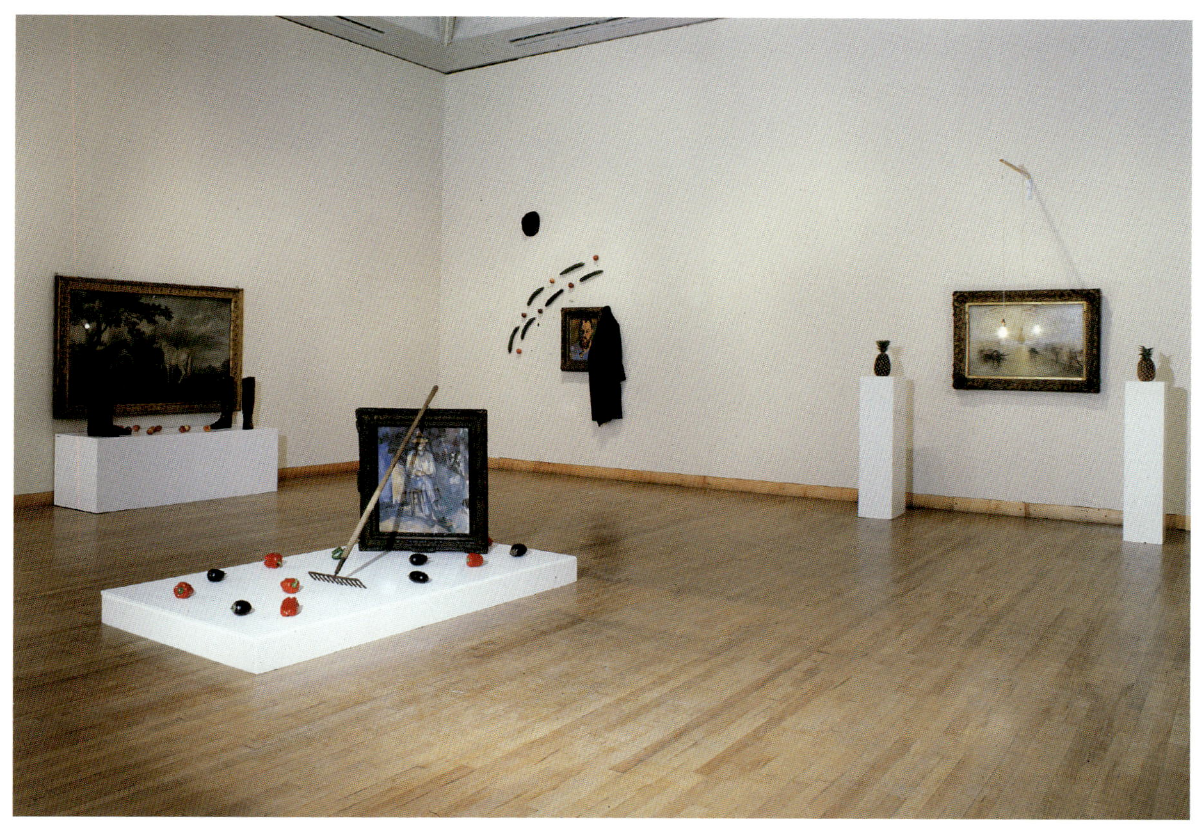

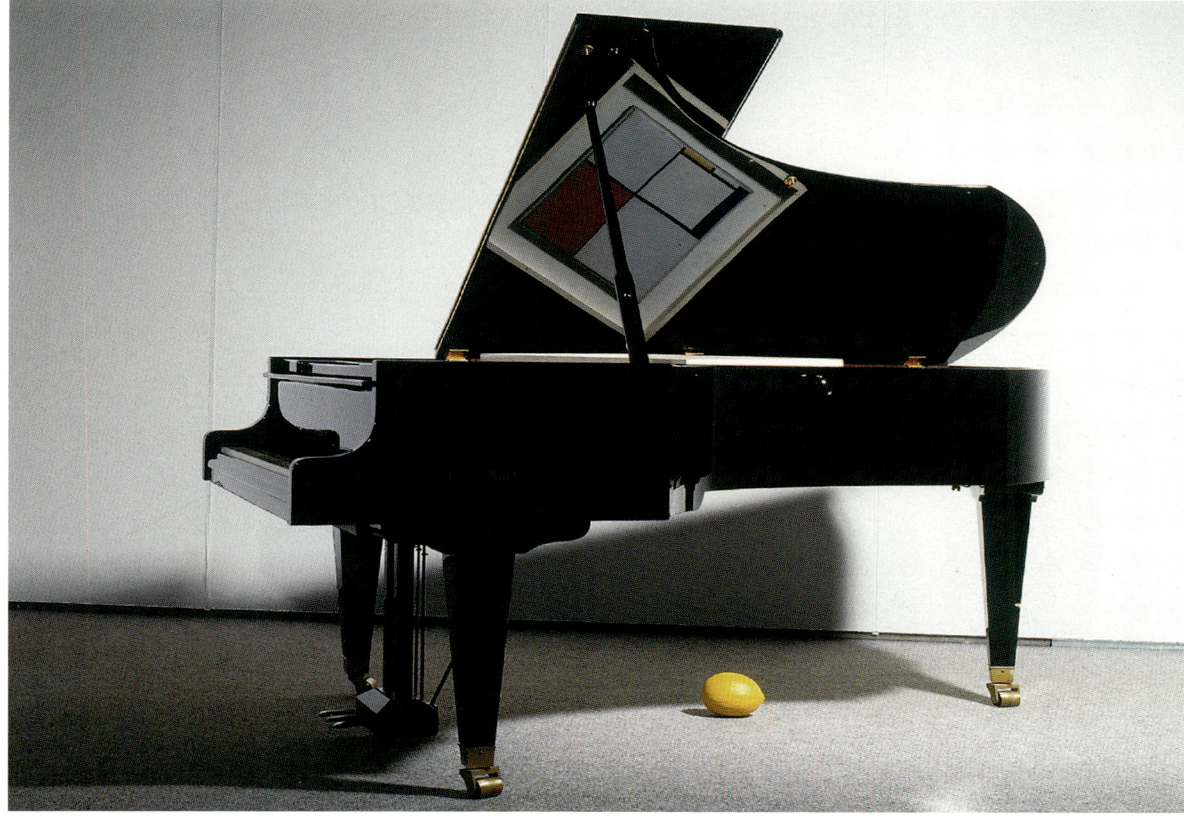

Triptychos Post Historicus
Wilhelm-Hack-Museum, Ludwigshafen, 1985

I: *Composition with Red, Yellow and Blue*, Piet Mondrian, 1928
II: Piano played by Siegbert Panzer; III: Melon
Collection: Wilhelm-Hack-Museum, Ludwigshafen

One-man exhibition at the Tate Gallery, London, 1985

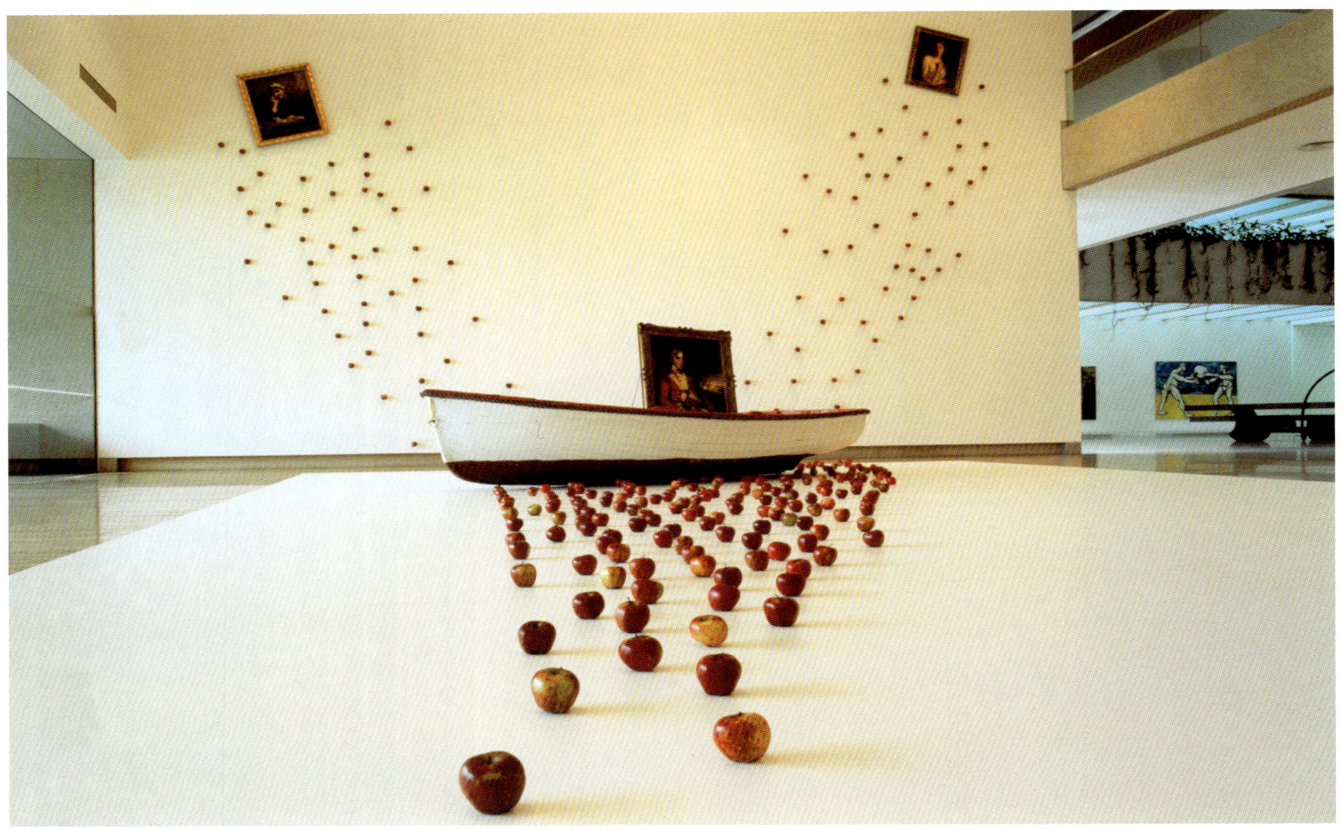

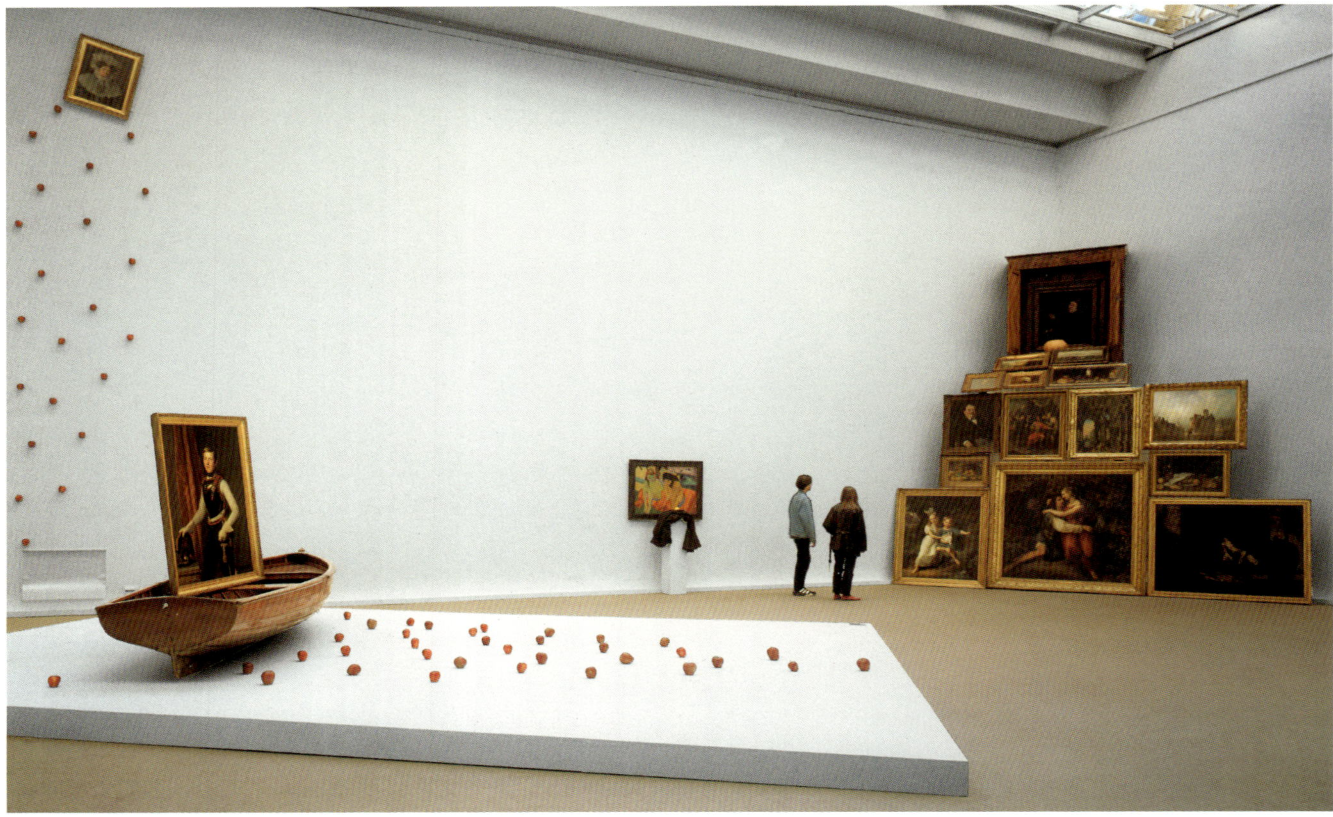

Triptychos Post Historicus or Far from the Harbor, near the Stars
One-man exhibition at the Queensland Art Gallery, Brisbane, Australia, 1989

One-man exhibition at the Kunsthalle, Düsseldorf, 1996

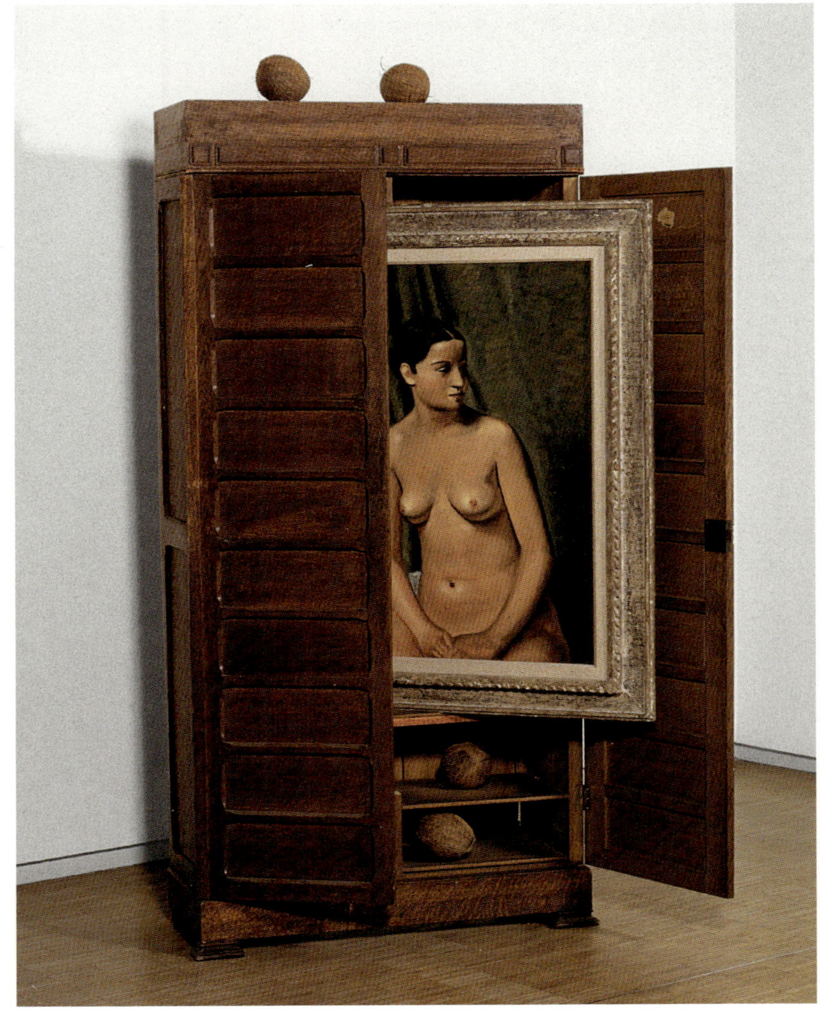

Triptychos Post Historicus or Mother of Romulus and Remus
Musée National d'Art Moderne, Centre Georges Pompidou, Paris, 1989

I: *Nude*, Andre Derain, 1923
II: Wardrobe used by Francois Delschneider; III: Coconuts
Collection: Musée National d'Art Moderne, Centre Georges Pompidou, Paris

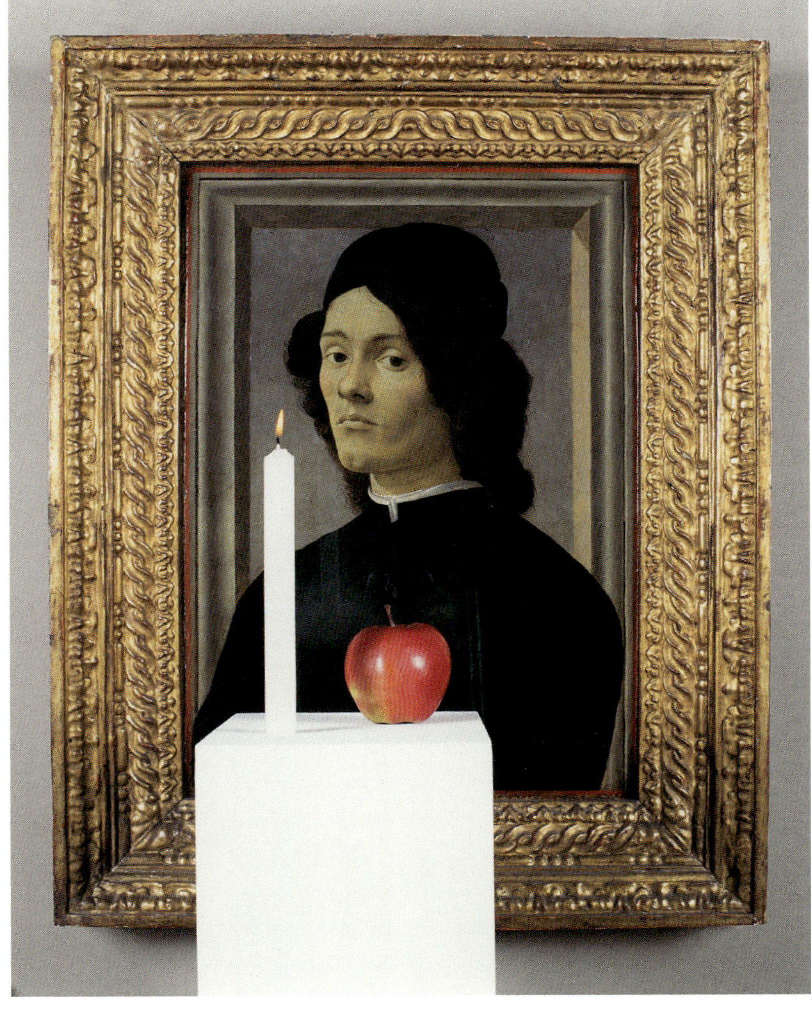

Triptychos Post Historicus
Musée du Louvre, Paris, 1996

I: *Portrait of a Young Man*, Sandro Botticelli, ca. 1470–1475
II: Candle lit by Braco Dimitrijević; III: Apple
Color photograph, 177x132
Collection: Patrick Asseman, London

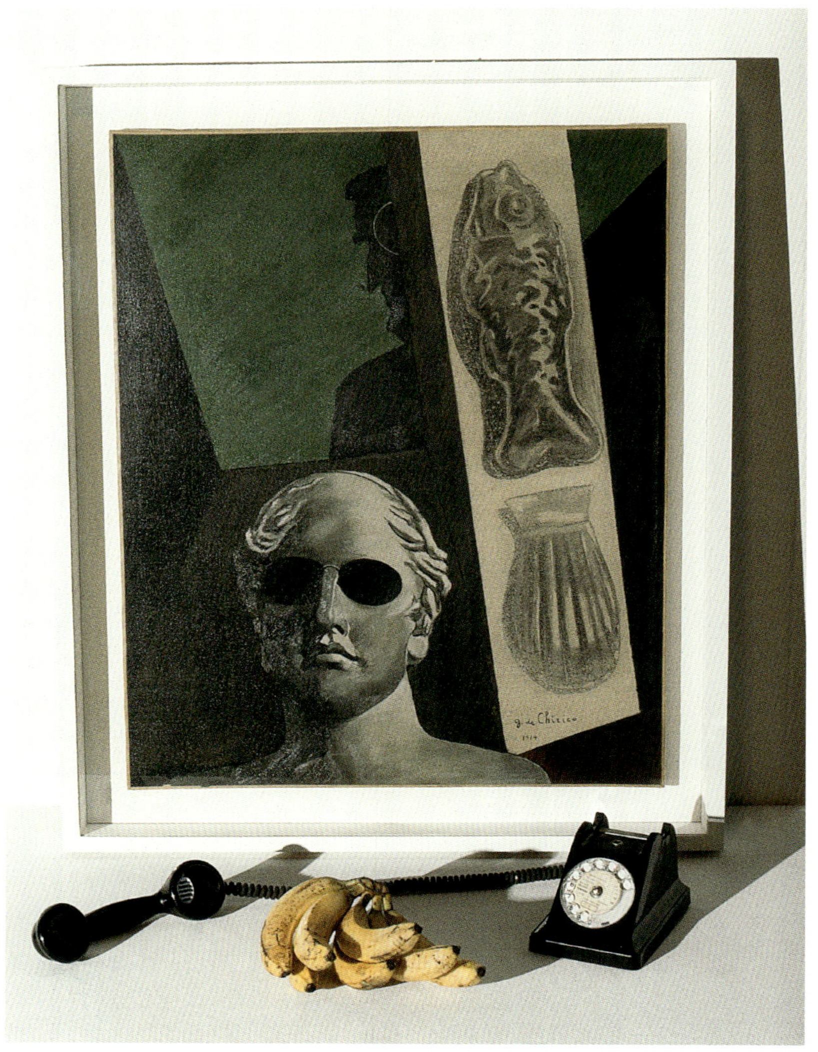

Triptychos Post Historicus or The Late Years Bananas on the Line Again
Musée National d'Art Moderne, Centre Georges Pompidou, Paris, 1981

I: *Premonitory Portrait of Apollinaire*, Giorgio de Chirico, 1914
II: Jean-Hubert Martin's telephone; III: Bananas

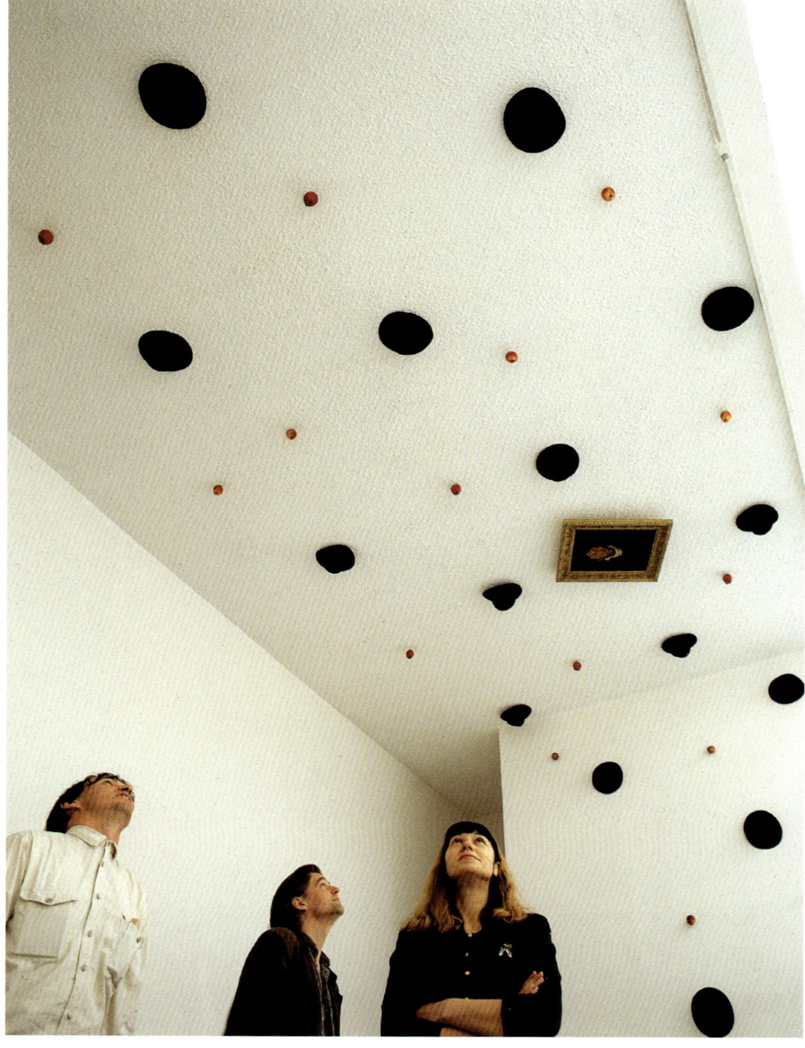

Installation at the Museum Fridericianum,
Documenta IX, Kassel, 1992

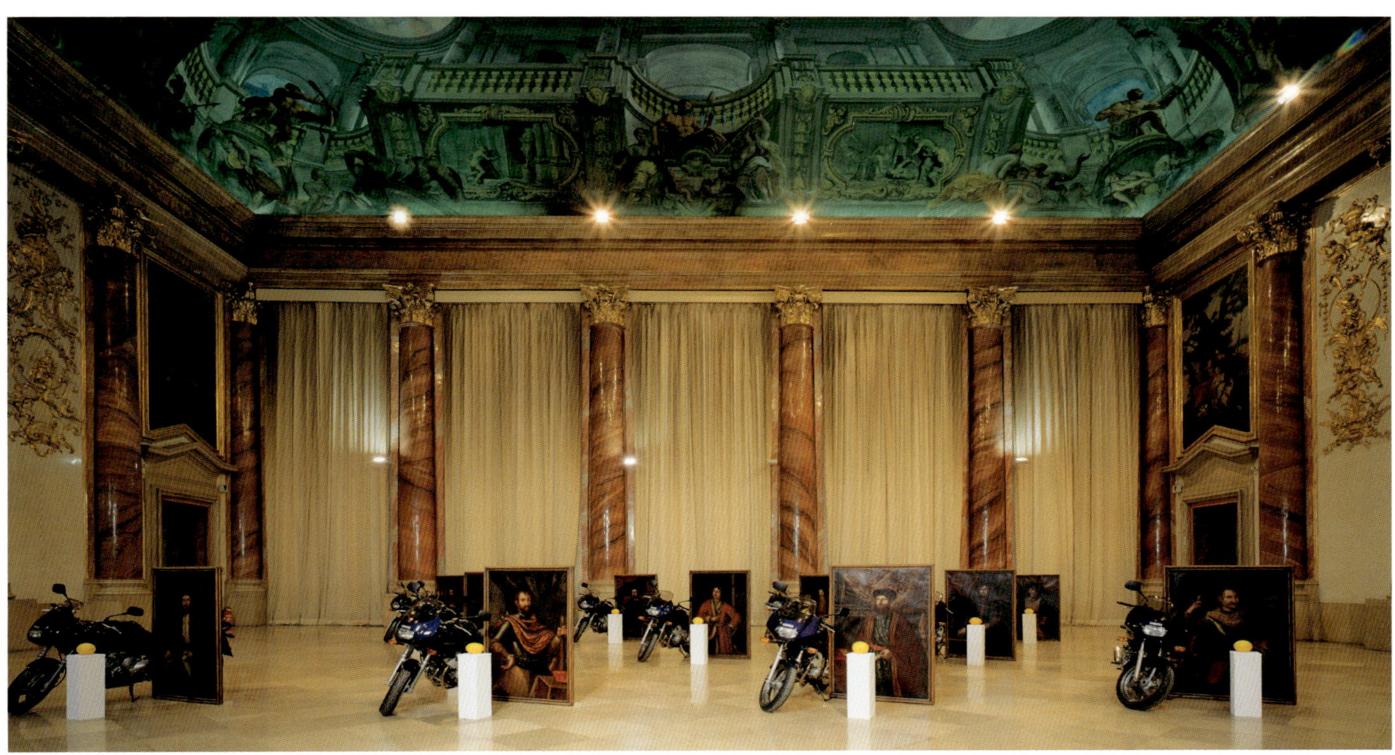

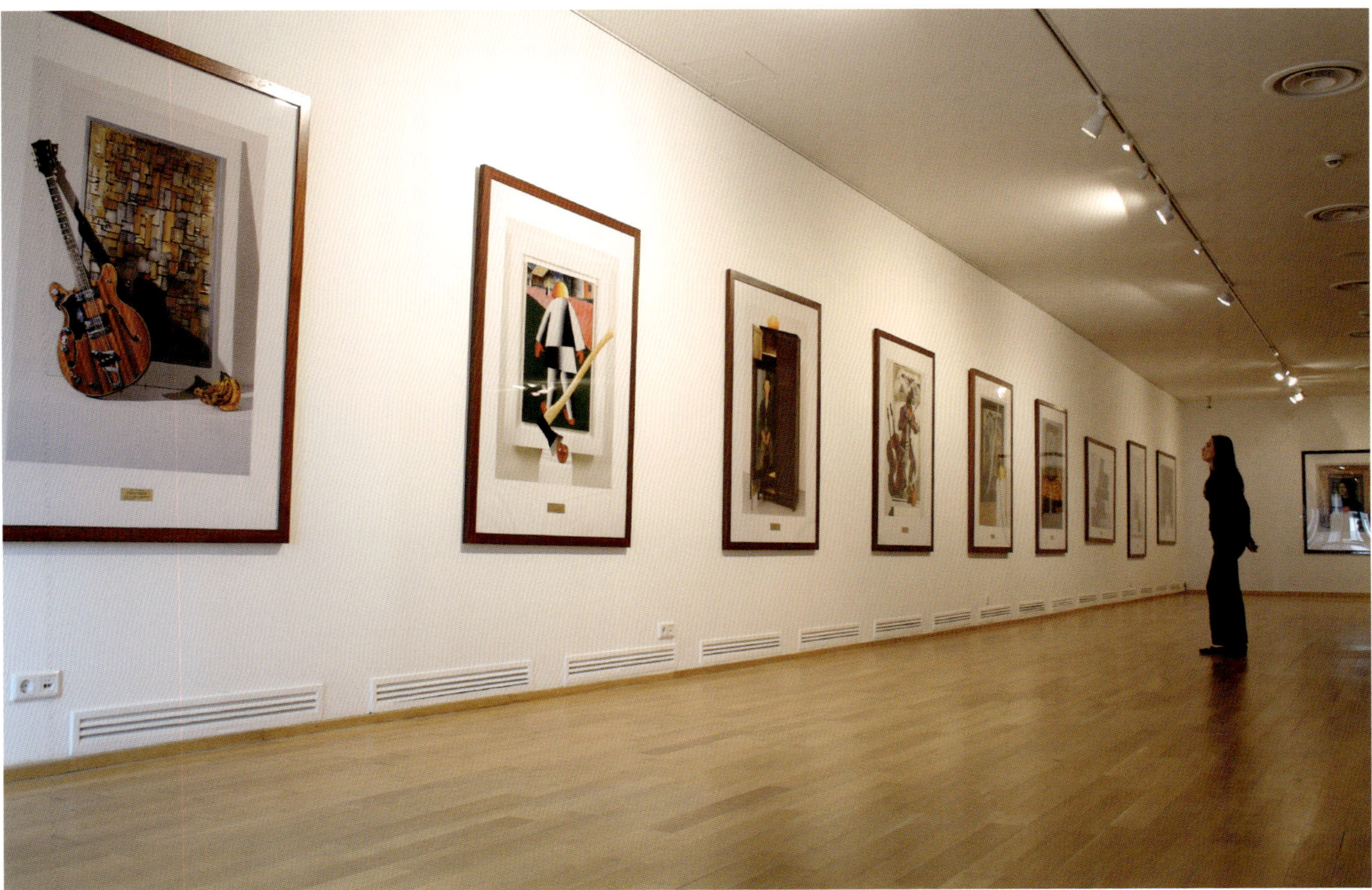

Triptychos Post Historicus or At the Start of the Milky Way
Museum Moderner Kunst, Palais Liechtenstein, Vienna, 1994

I: *Portraits of the Tarzia Family*, Venetian Masters of the 15th–17th century
II: Yamaha motorbikes; III: Melons

View of photographic *Triptychos Post Historicus*
MNAC, Bucharest, 2008

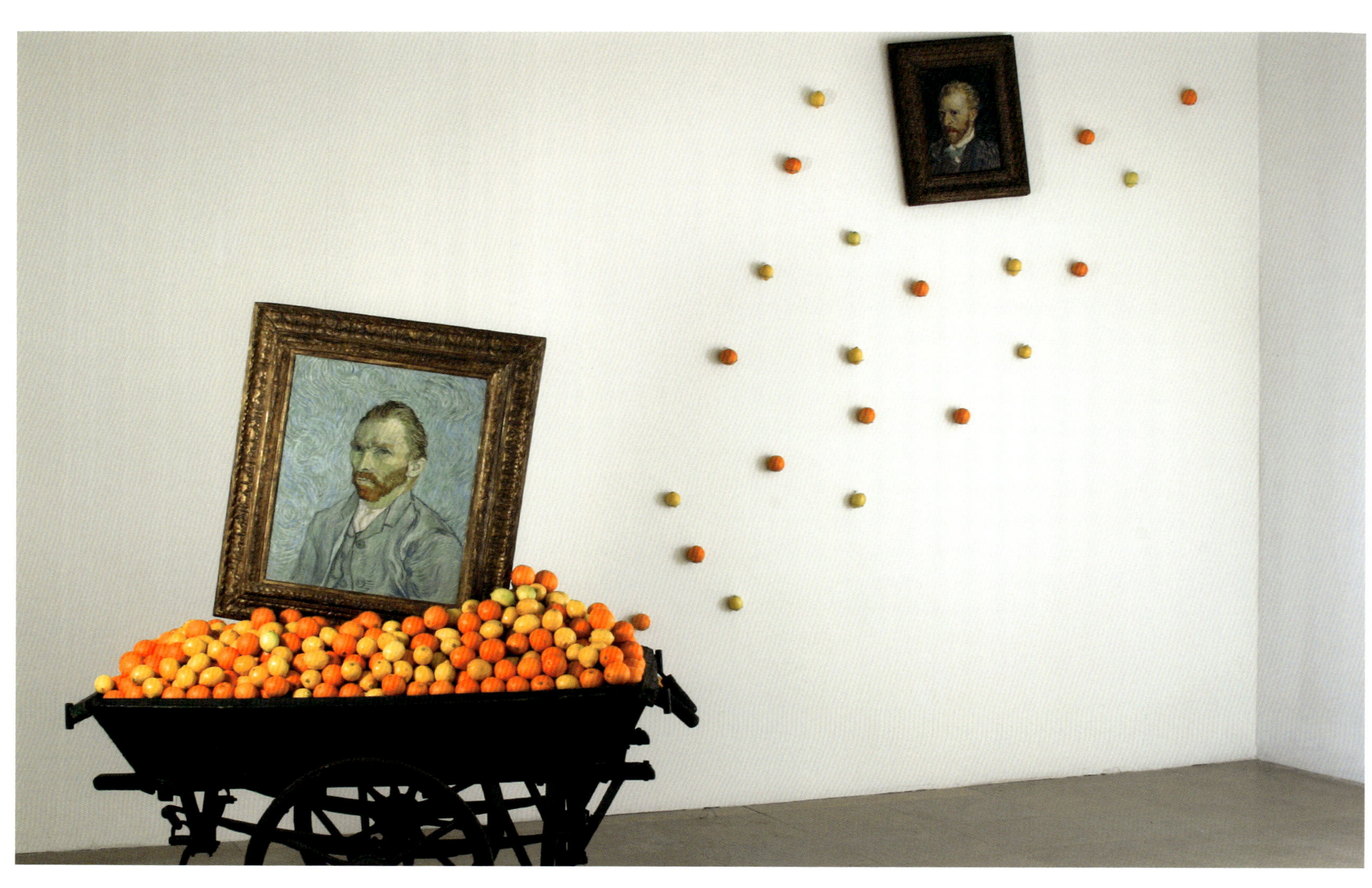

Triptychos Post Historicus or Van Gogh Goes to Paradise
Musée d'Orsay, Paris, 2005

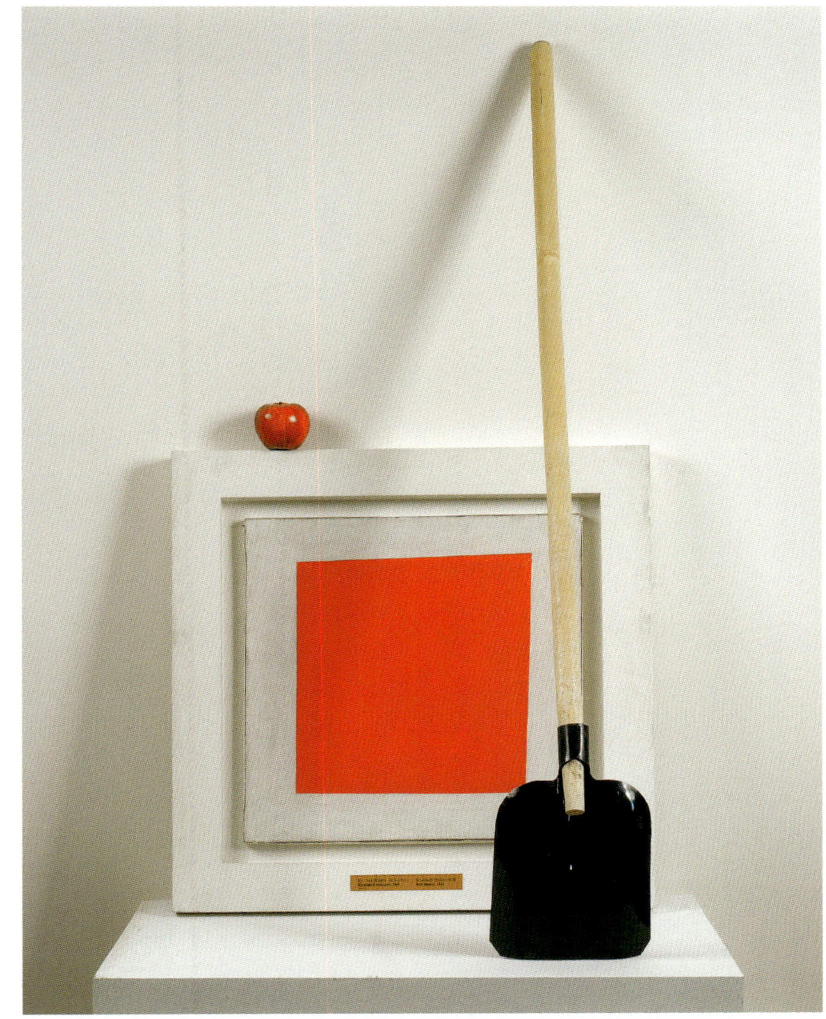

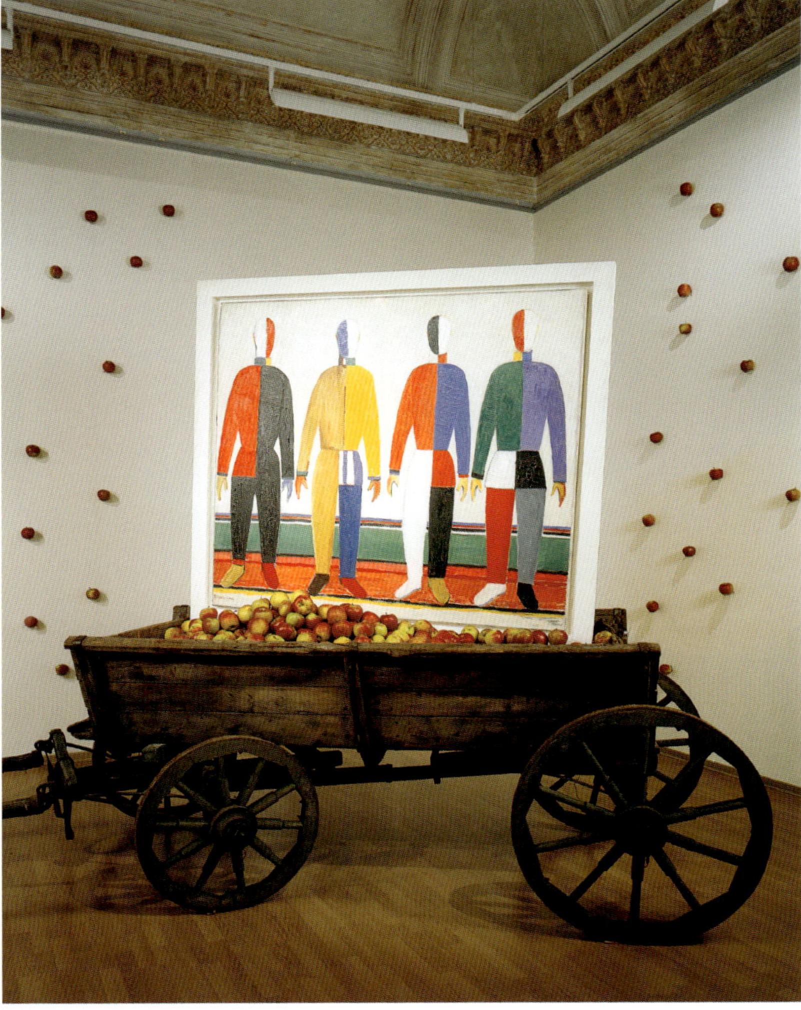

Triptychos Post Historicus
The State Russian Museum, St. Petersburg, 2005

I: *Red Square*, Kasimir Malevich, 1915
II: Shovel used by Mihail Vilich; III: Apple
Color photograph, 160x118
Collection: Caroline and Viet Ha Thuc, London

Triptychos Post Historicus or Mayday 1905
The State Russian Museum, St. Petersburg, 2005

I: *Sportsmen*, Kasimir Malevich, 1931
II: Wagon found by Vasily Senin; III: Apples

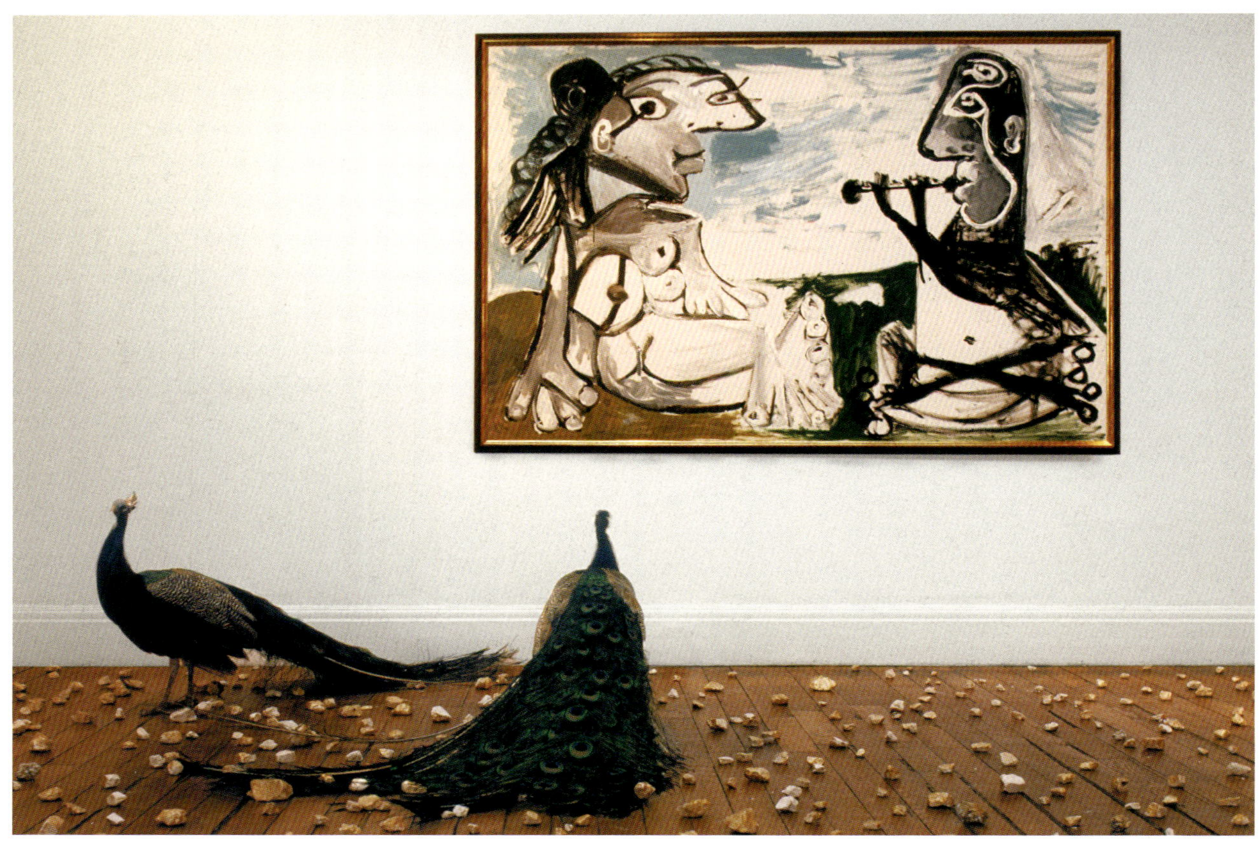

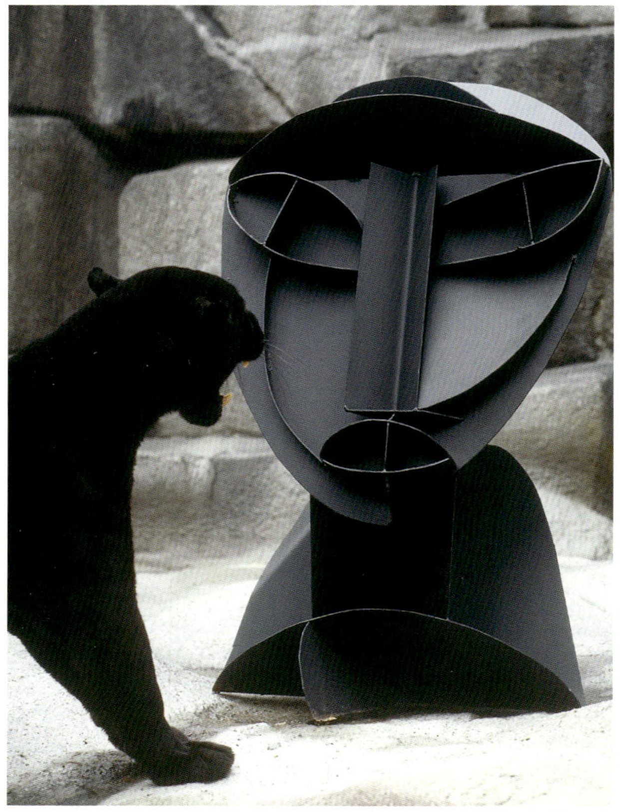

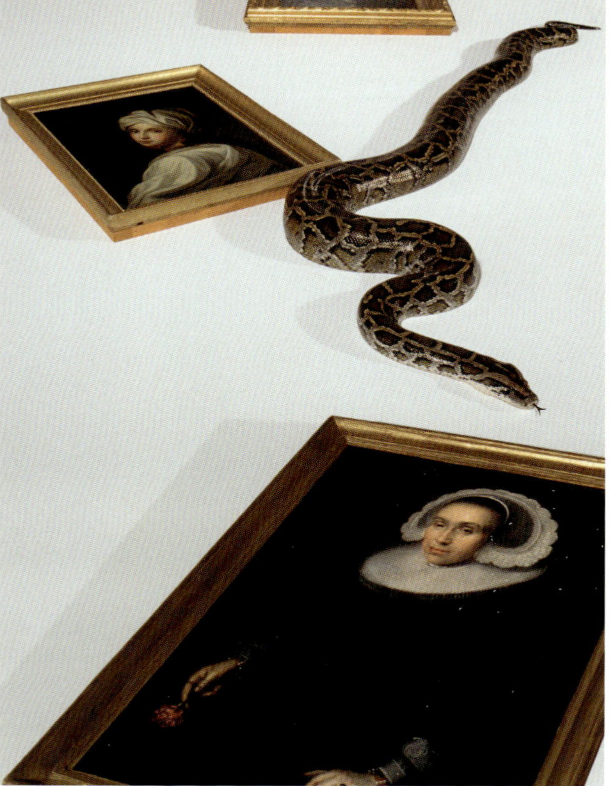

Dust of Louvre and Mist of Amazon, 1981
Waddington Galleries, London

Cas d'evolution, 1998
Ménagerie du Jardin des Plantes, Paris

Against Historic Sense of Gravity, 1995
Hessisches Landesmuseum, Darmstadt

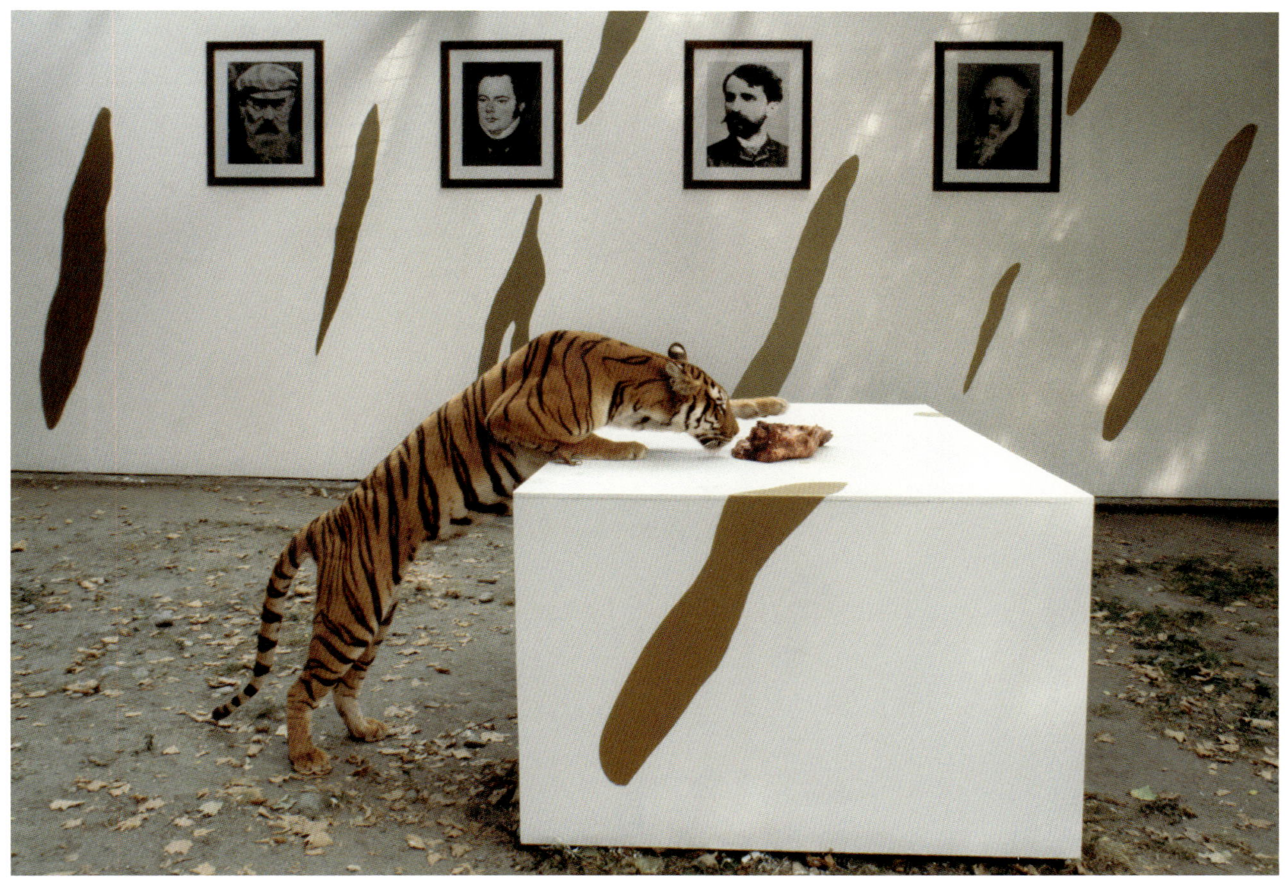

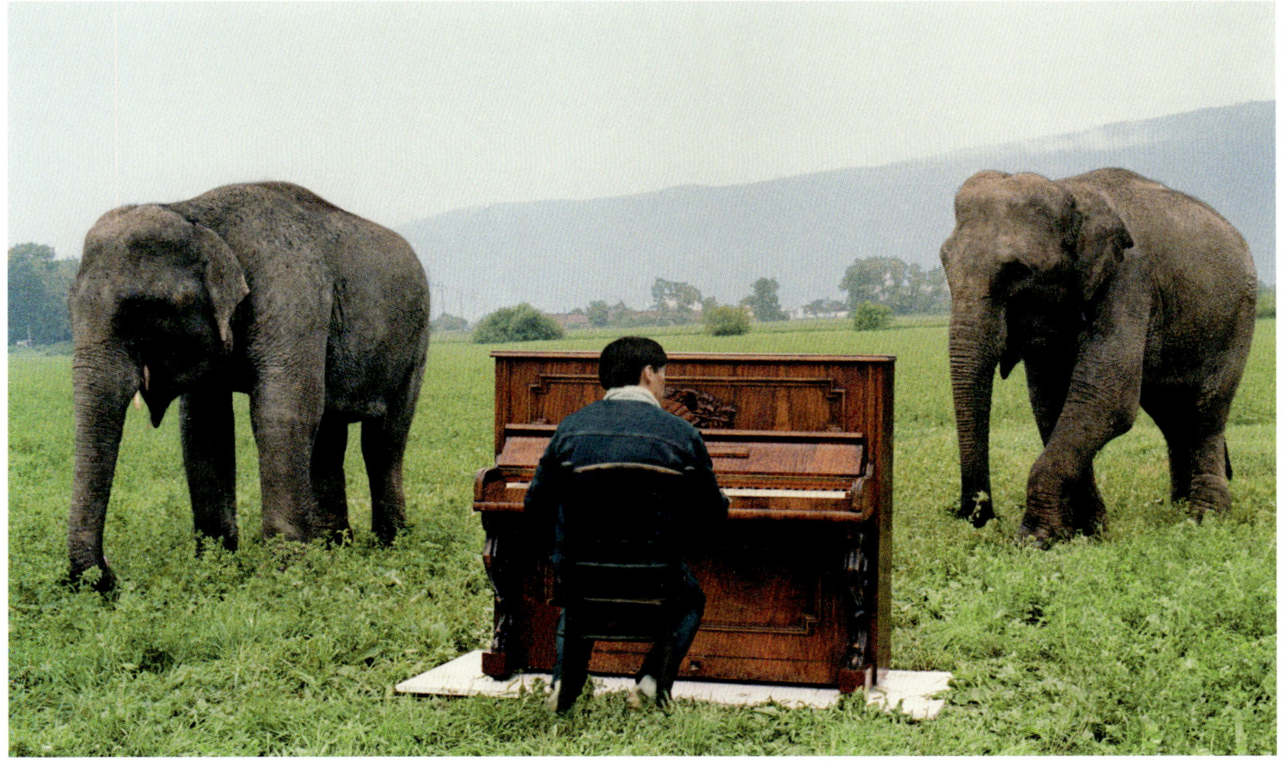

The Last Congress, 1989
Turin Zoo

When Elephants Were Rehearsing Nordic Disciplines in my Home Town, 1983
Color photograph, 170x130 cm
Private Collection, Switzerland

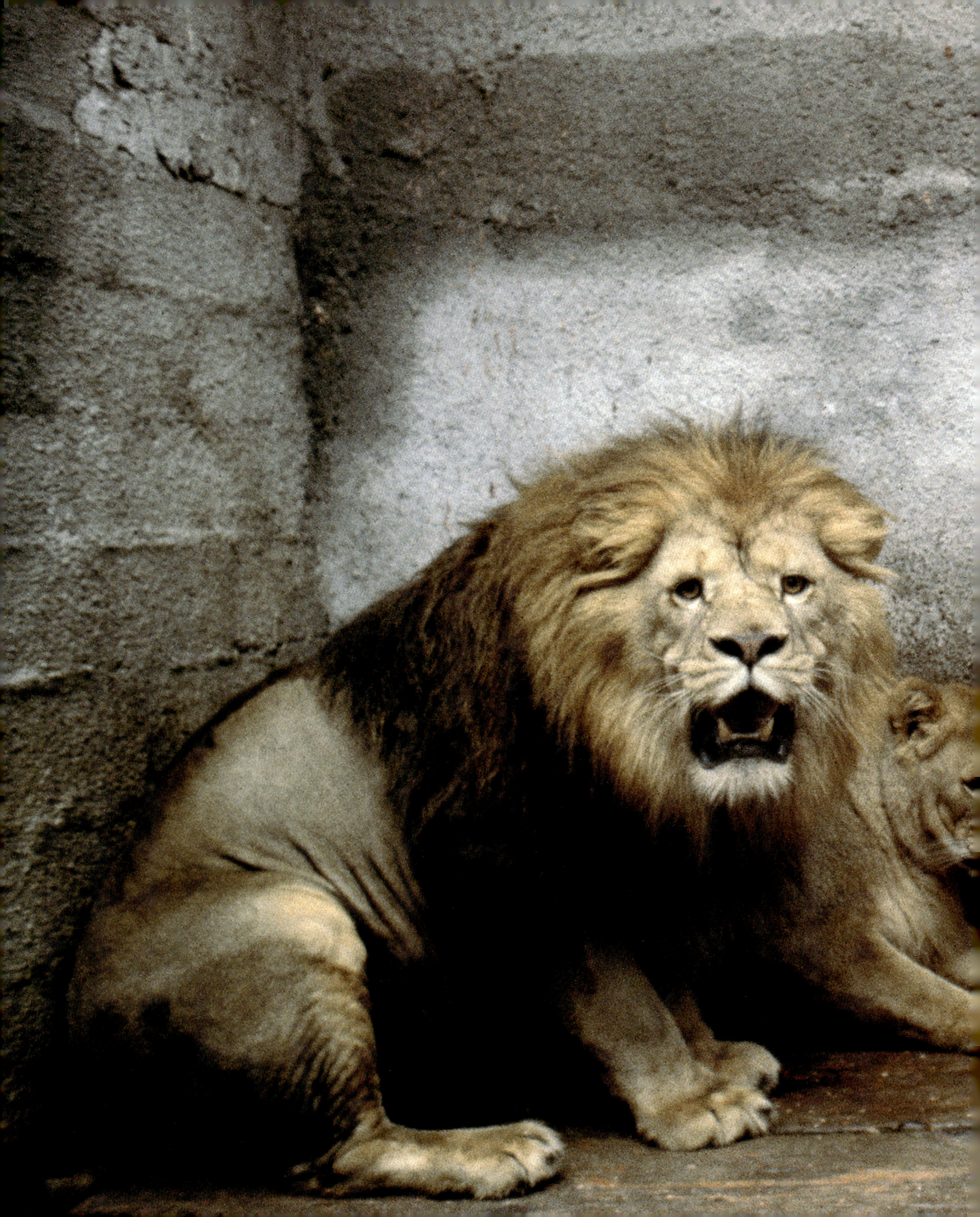

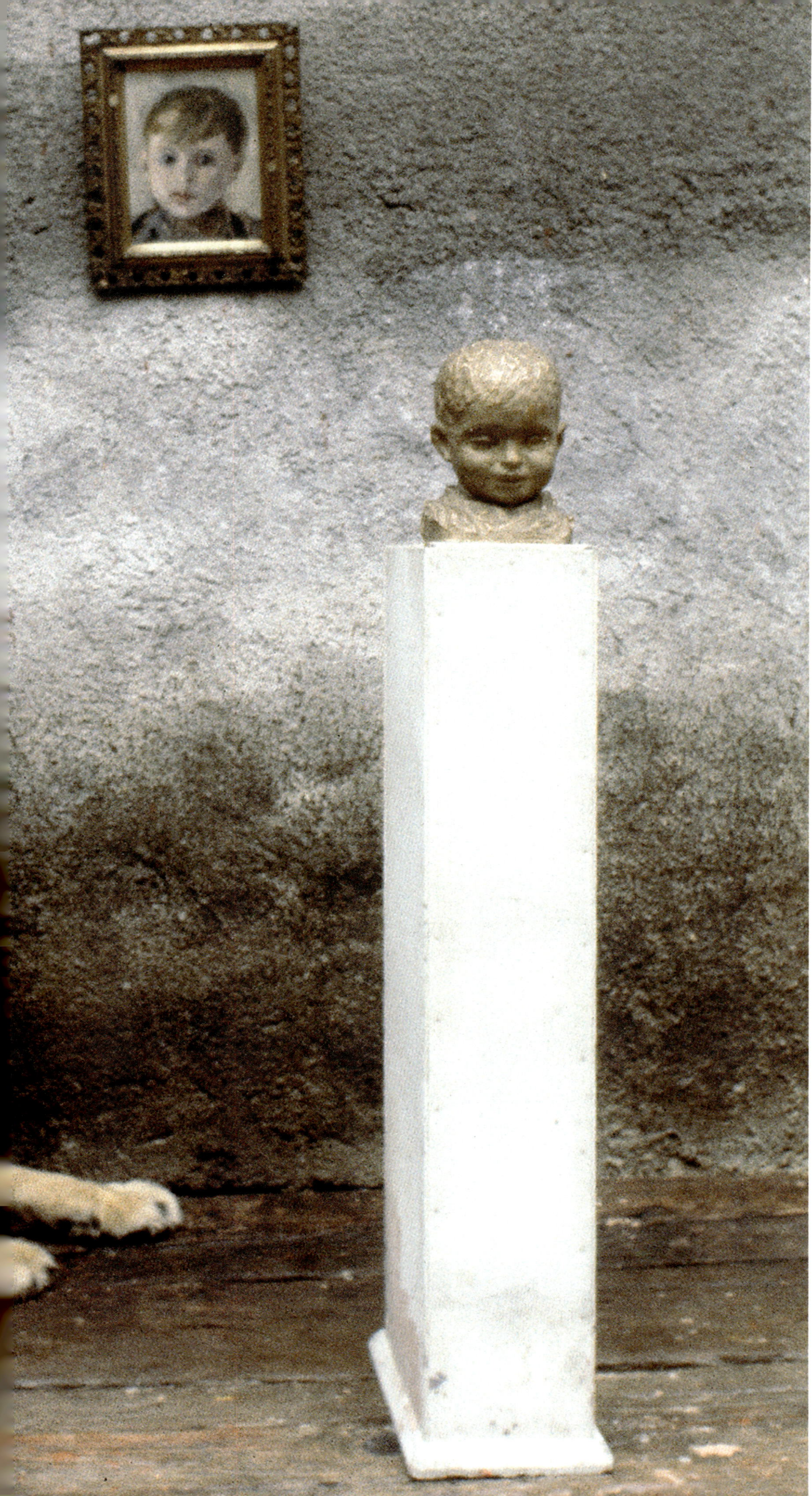

Memories of Childhood, 1983
Color photograph, 125x165 cm
Collection: Kunstmuseum Bern

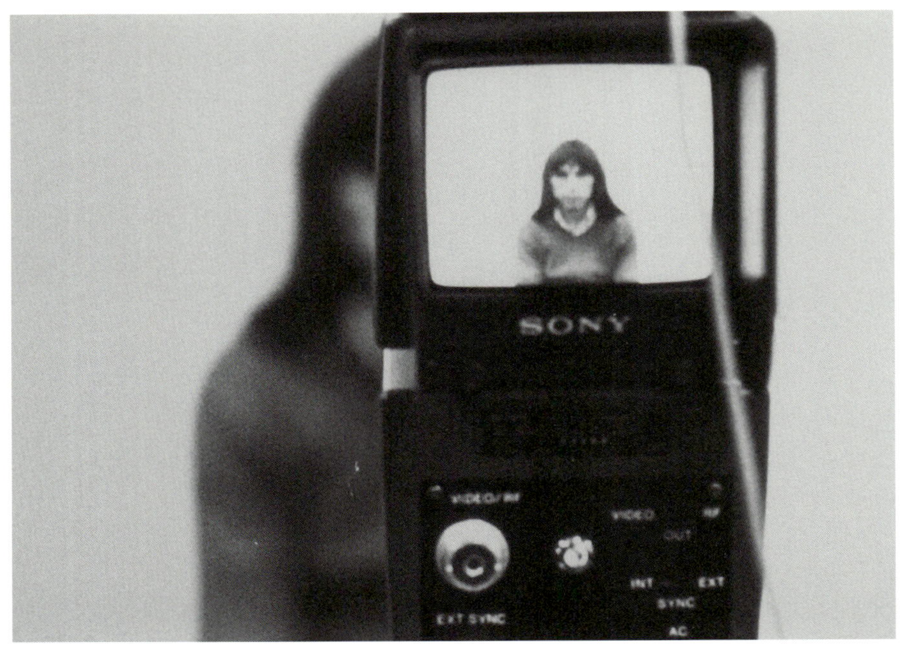

Filming *Metabolysm as a Body Work,* 1971St. Martin's School of Art, London

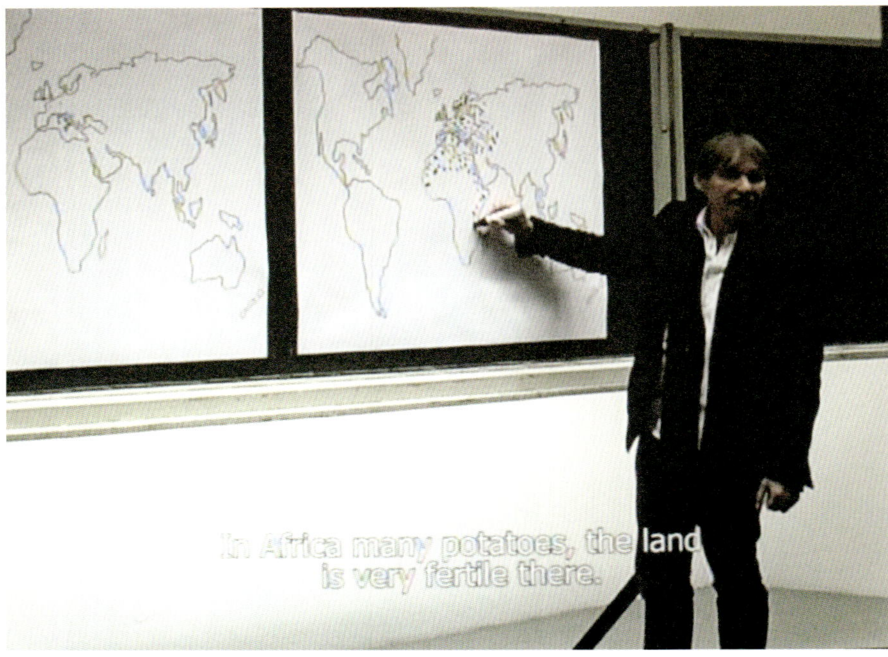

Geography of Arts, 1975- 2006

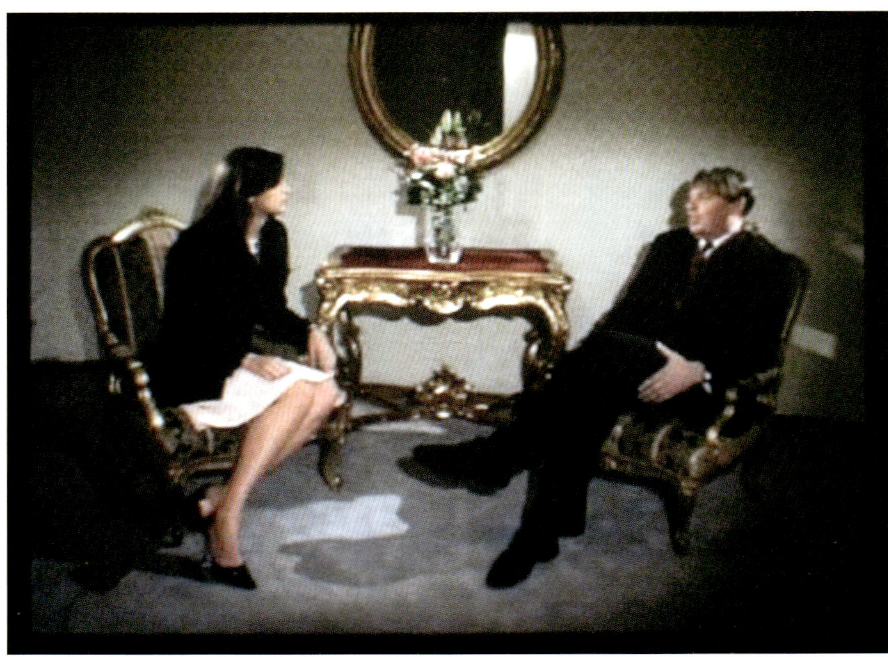

Interview/ Interview, 1974 – 2004

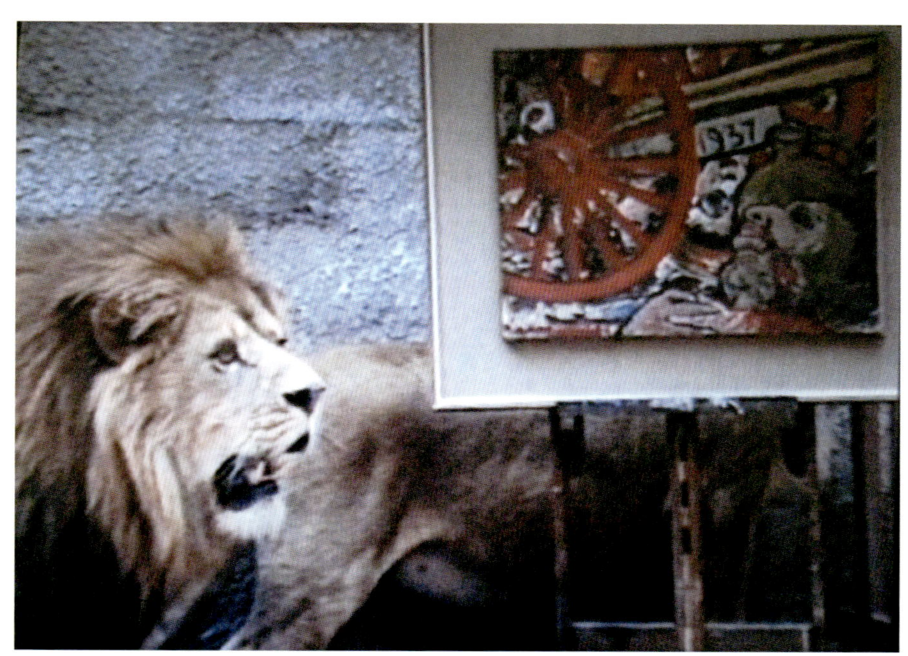

Four Culturescapes, 1983

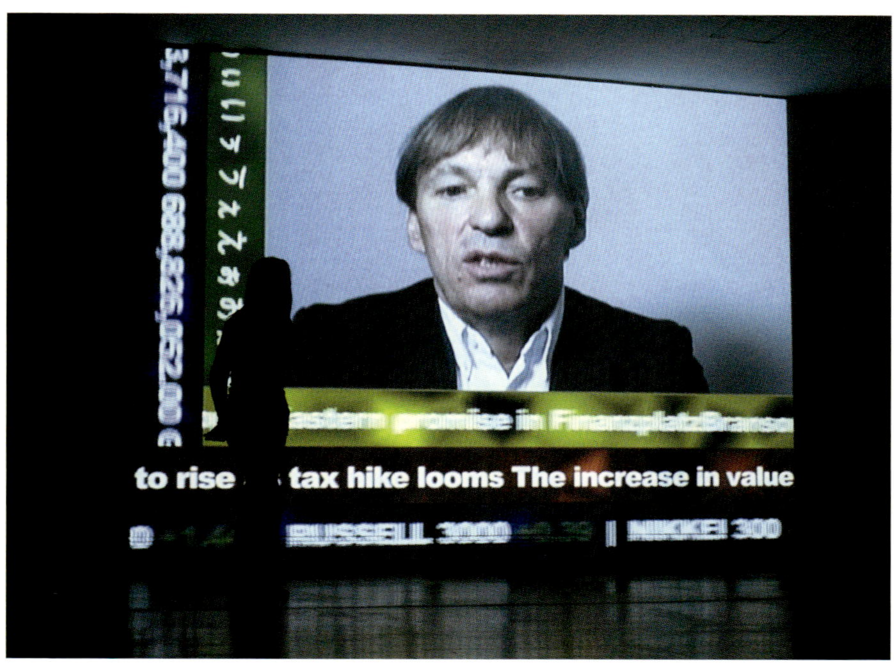

The Resurrection of Alchemists, 2006,
Collection: Tate Modern, London

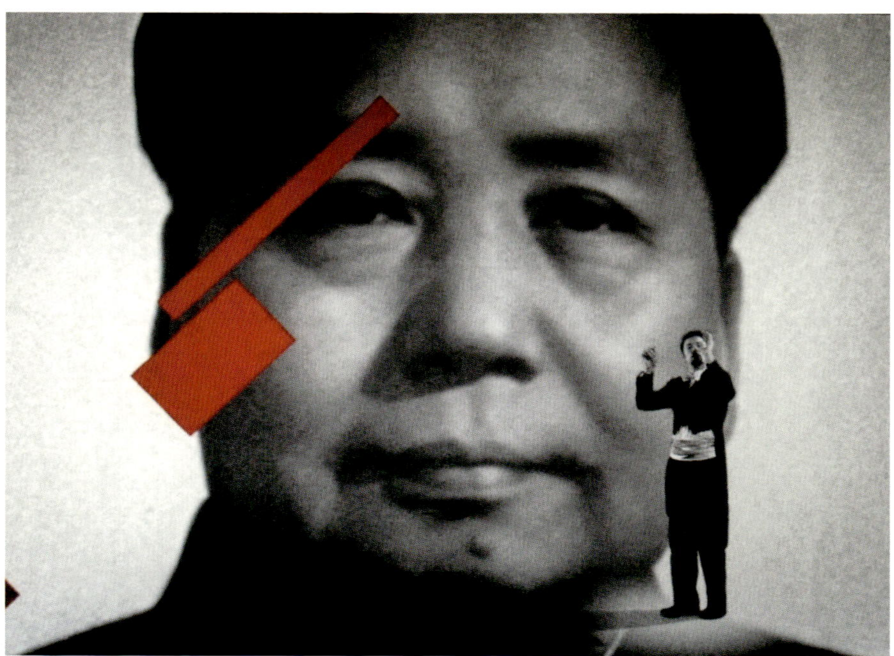

The Century Behind me – One Second of Post Historic Time, 2009

Photo Album

Vojo and Jelena,
Braco Dimitrijević's parents

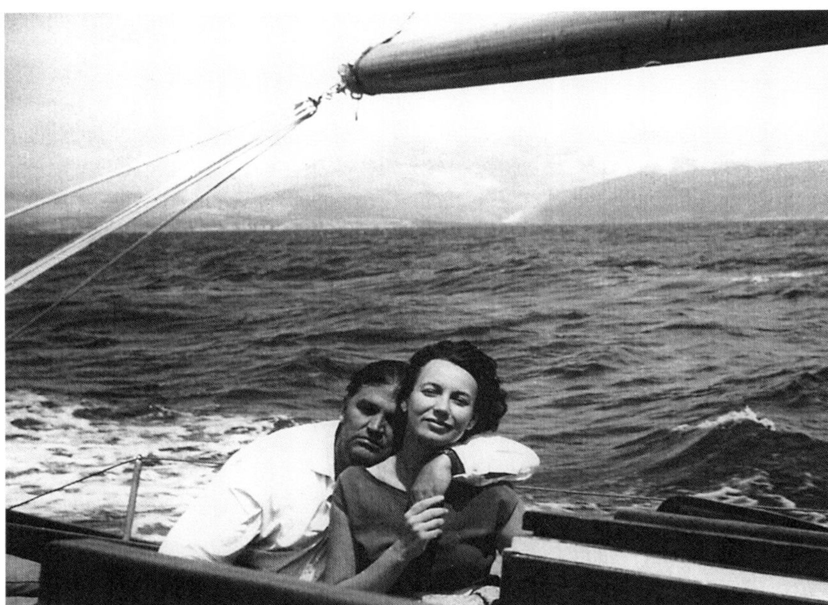

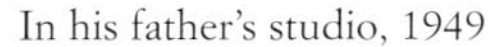

In his father's studio, 1949

Monument made by Vojo Dimitrijević in 1949 to commemorate the event which started World War I in Sarajevo

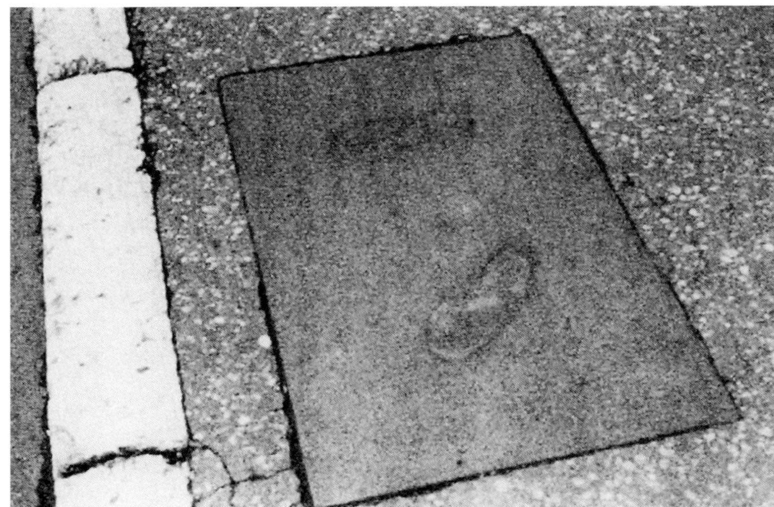

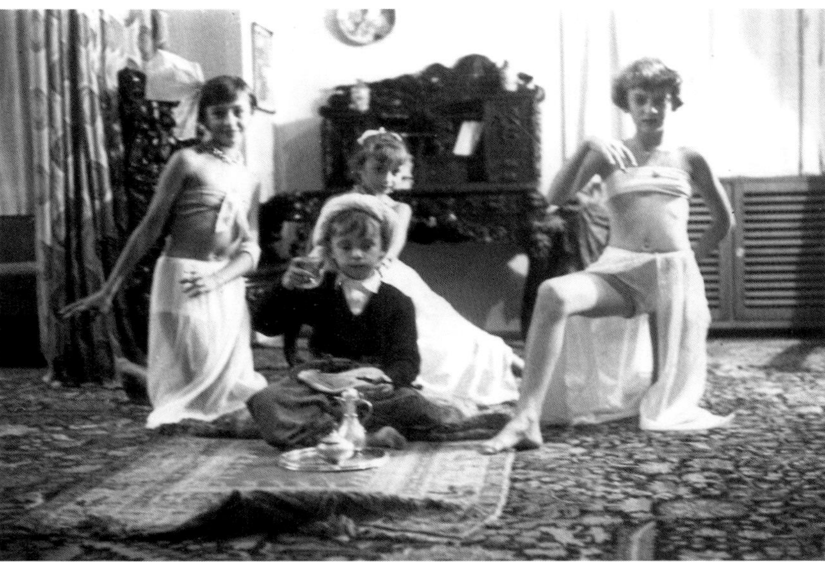

Braco Dimitrijević with his sister and cousins at his parents' home

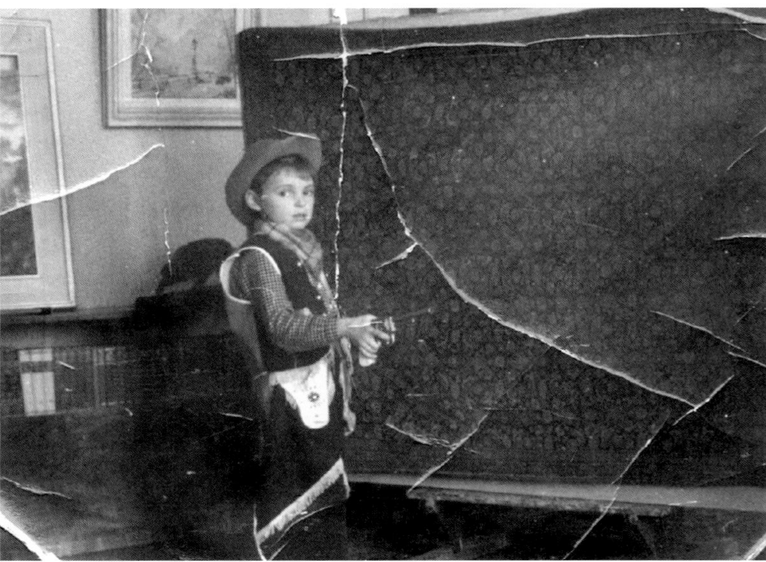

Braco Dimitrijević, 1955

The newspaper *Oslobodjenje*, 1954

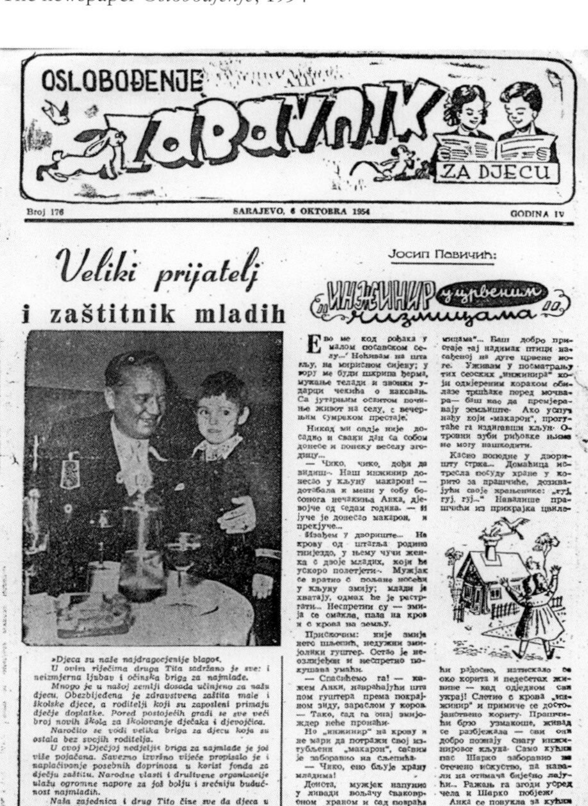

OSLOBOĐENJE ZABAVNIK ZA DJECU

Broj 176 SARAJEVO, 6 OKTOBRA 1954 GODINA IV

Veliki prijatelj i zaštitnik mladih

»Djeca su naše najdragocjenije blago«.

U ovim riječima druga Tita sadržano je sve: i neizmjerna ljubav i očinska briga za najmlađe.

Mnogo je u našoj zemlji dosada učinjeno za našu djecu. Obezbijeđena je zdravstvena zaštita male i školske djece, a roditelji koji su zaposleni primaju dječje doplatke. Pored postojećih gradi se sve veći broj novih škola za školovanje dječaka i djevojčica.

Naročito se vodi velika briga za djecu koja su ostala bez svojih roditelja.

U ovoj »Dječjoj nedjelji« briga za najmlađe je još više pojačana. Savezno izvršno vijeće propisalo je i naplaćivanje posebnih doprinosa u korist fonda za dječju zaštitu. Narodne vlasti i društvene organizacije ulažu ogromne napore za još bolju i srećniju budućnost najmlađih.

Naša zajednica i drug Tito čine sve da djeca u socijalističkoj Jugoslaviji imaju što ljepše, što srećnije i što bezbrižnije djetinjstvo.

Na slici: Mali Slobodan Dimitrijević u zagrljaju druga Tita.

Јосип Павичић:

„Инжињир у црвеним чизмицама"

Ево ме код рођака у малом босанском селу...' Ноћивам на штагљу, на мирисном сијену; у зору ме буди шкрипа ђерма, мукање телади и звонки ударци чекића о наковањ. Са јутарњим освитом почиње живот на селу, с вечерњим сумраком престаје.

...мицама"... Баш добро пристаје тај надимак птици насађеној на дуге црвене ноге. Уживам у посматрању тих сеоских „инжињира" који одмјереним кораком обилазе трштаке поред мочвара— баш као да премјеравају земљиште. Ако успију нађу који „макарон", прогутаће га издигавши кљун. Отровни зуби риђовке њима не могу нашкодити.

(Наставак на 4 страни)

Braco Dimitrijević with President Tito, 1954

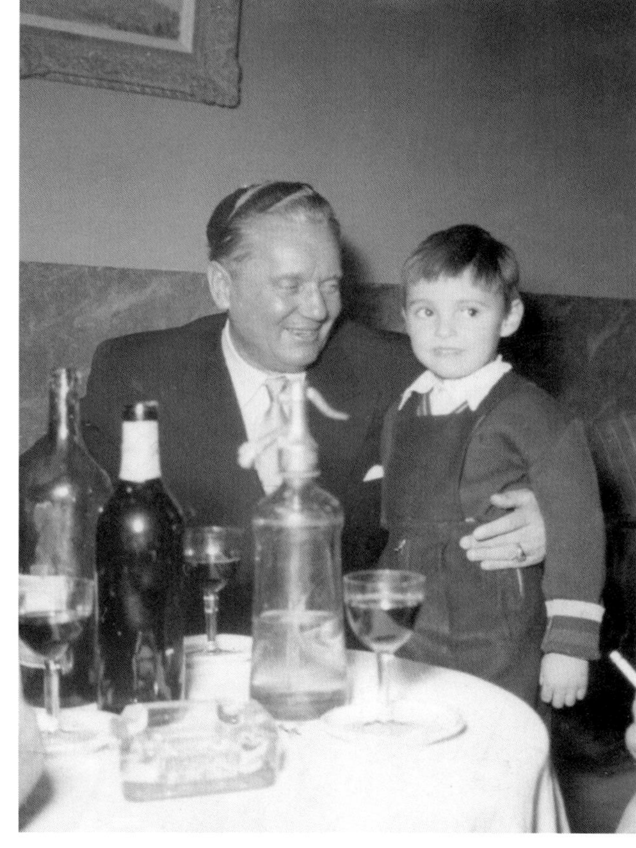

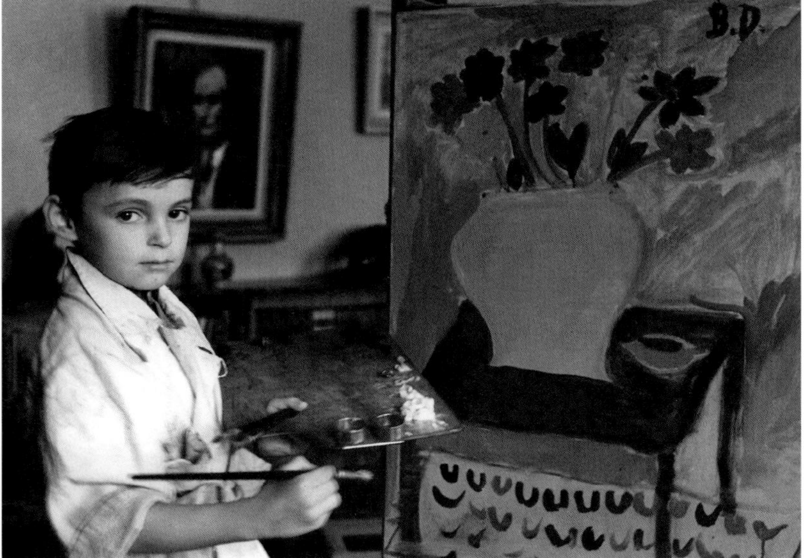

In the studio, 1954

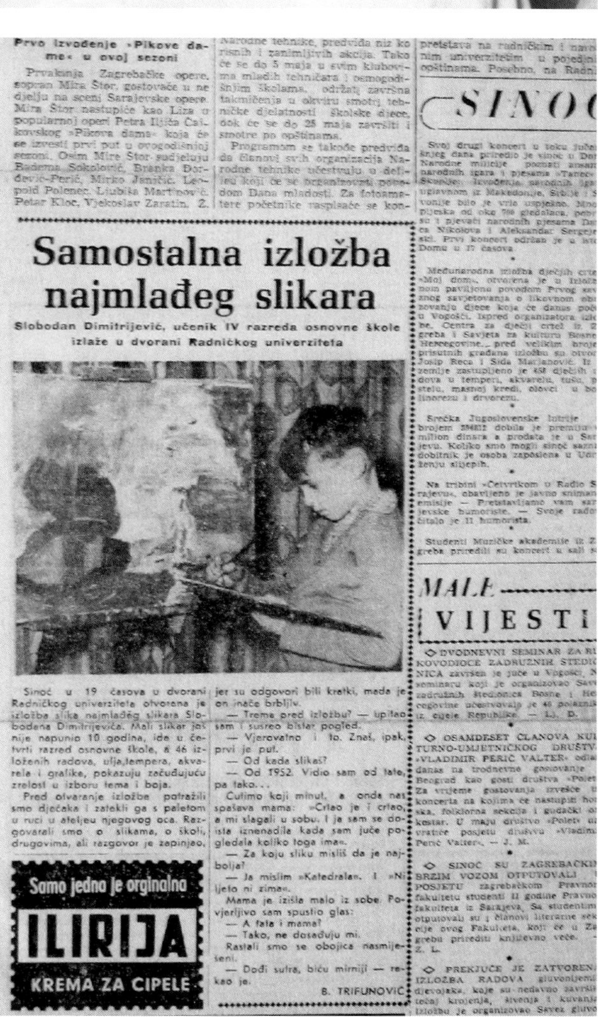

Samostalna izložba najmlađeg slikara

Slobodan Dimitrijević, učenik IV razreda osnovne škole izlaže u dvorani Radničkog univerziteta

Sinoć u 19 časova u dvorani Radničkog univerziteta otvorena je izložba slika najmlađeg slikara Slobodana Dimitrijevića. Mali slikar još nije napunio 10 godina, ide u četvrti razred osnovne škole, a 46 izloženih radova, ulja, tempera, akvarela i grafike, pokazuju začuđujuću zrelost u izboru tema i boja.

Pred otvaranje izložbe potražili smo dječaka i zatekli ga s paletom u ruci u ateljeu njegovog oca. Razgovarali smo o slikama, o školi, drugovima, ali razgovor je zapinjao, jer su odgovori bili kratki, mada je on inače brbljiv.

— Treme pred izložbu? — upitao sam i susreo bistar pogled.

— Vjerovatno i to. Znaš, ipak, prvi je put.

— Od kada slikaš?

— Od 1952. Vidio sam od tate, pa tako...

Ćutimo koji minut, a onda nas spašava mama: »Crtao je i crtao, a mi slagali u sobu. I ja sam se dosta iznenadila kada sam juče pogledala koliko toga ima«.

— Za koju sliku misliš da je najbolja?

— Ja mislim »Katedrala«. I »Ni ljeto ni zima«.

Mama je izišla malo iz sobe. Povjerljivo sam spustio glas:

— A tata i mama?

— Tako, ne dosađuju mi.

Rastali smo se obojica nasmiješeni.

— Dođi sutra, biću mirniji — rekao je.

B. TRIFUNOVIĆ

Samo jedna je orginalna ILIRIJA KREMA ZA CIPELE

Article about Braco Dimitrijević's first exhibition, *Oslobodjenje*, April 6, 1958

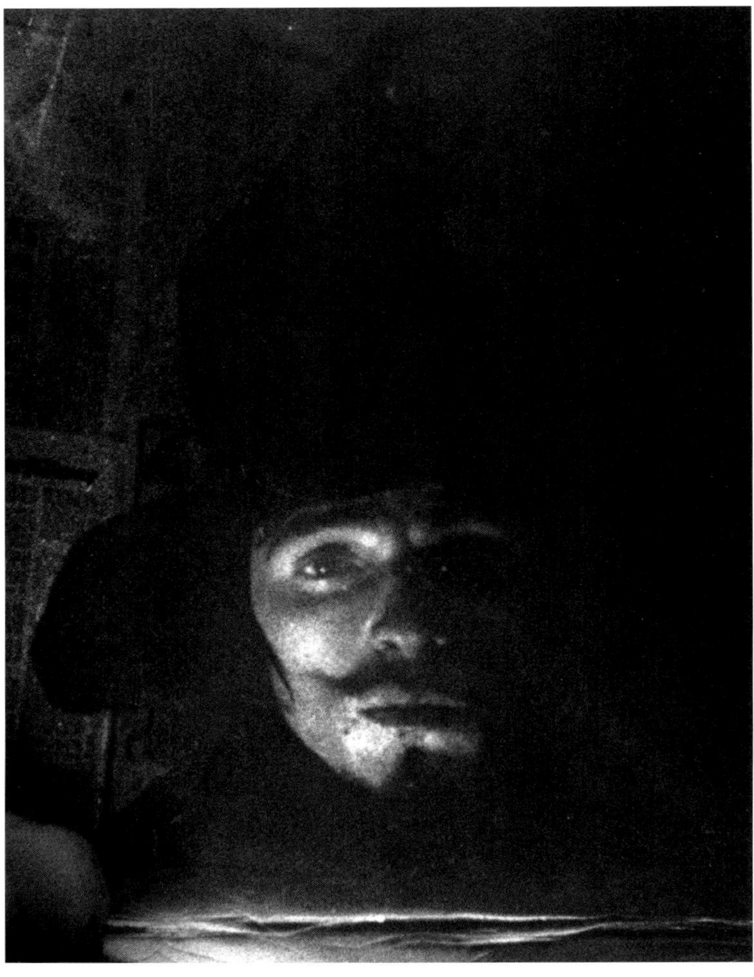

Self-portrait after Rembrandt, 1968

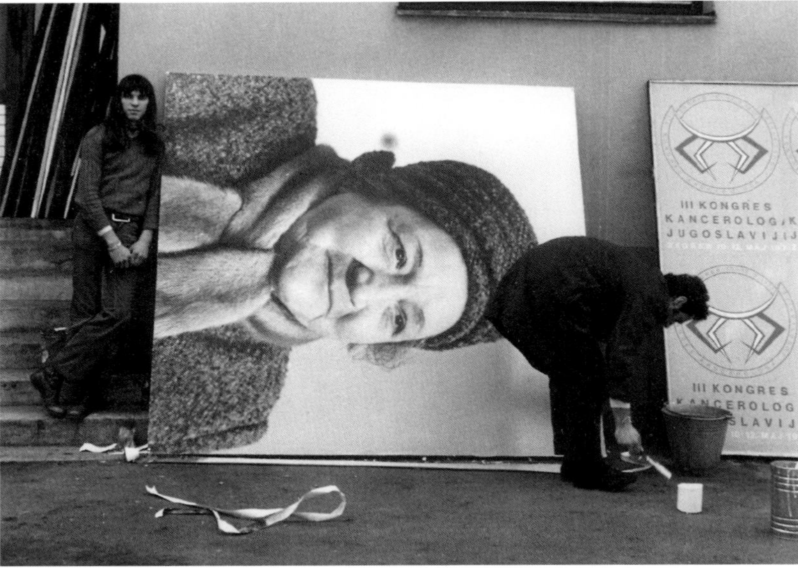

Zagreb, spring 1971

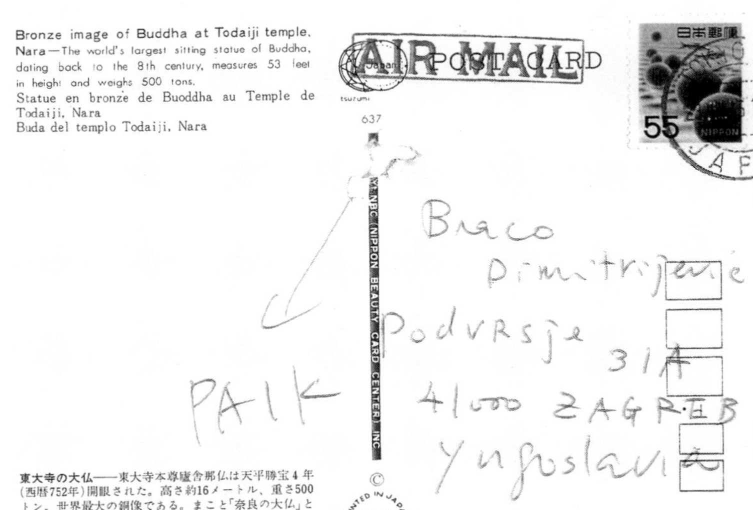

Bronze image of Buddha at Todaiji temple.
Nara—The world's largest sitting statue of Buddha, dating back to the 8th century, measures 53 feet in height and weighs 500 tons.
Statue en bronze de Buoddha au Temple de Todaiji, Nara
Buda del templo Todaiji, Nara

東大寺の大仏——東大寺本尊廬舎那仏は天平勝宝4年(西暦752年)開眼された。高さ約16メートル、重さ500トン。世界最大の銅像である。まこと「奈良の大仏」というにふさわしい。

AIR MAIL
POSTCARD

PAIK

Braco
Dimitrijević
Podvrsje 31A
41000 ZAGREB
Yugoslavia

(C) NBC (NIPPON BEAUTY CARD CENTER) INC
PRINTED IN JAPAN

Postcard piece by Nam June Paik, 1974

S LeWitt
117 Hester St
NYC 10002

N. & B. DIMITRIJEVIC
PANTOVČAK 104 C
ZAGREB YUGOSLAVIA

Letter from Sol LeWitt, 1970

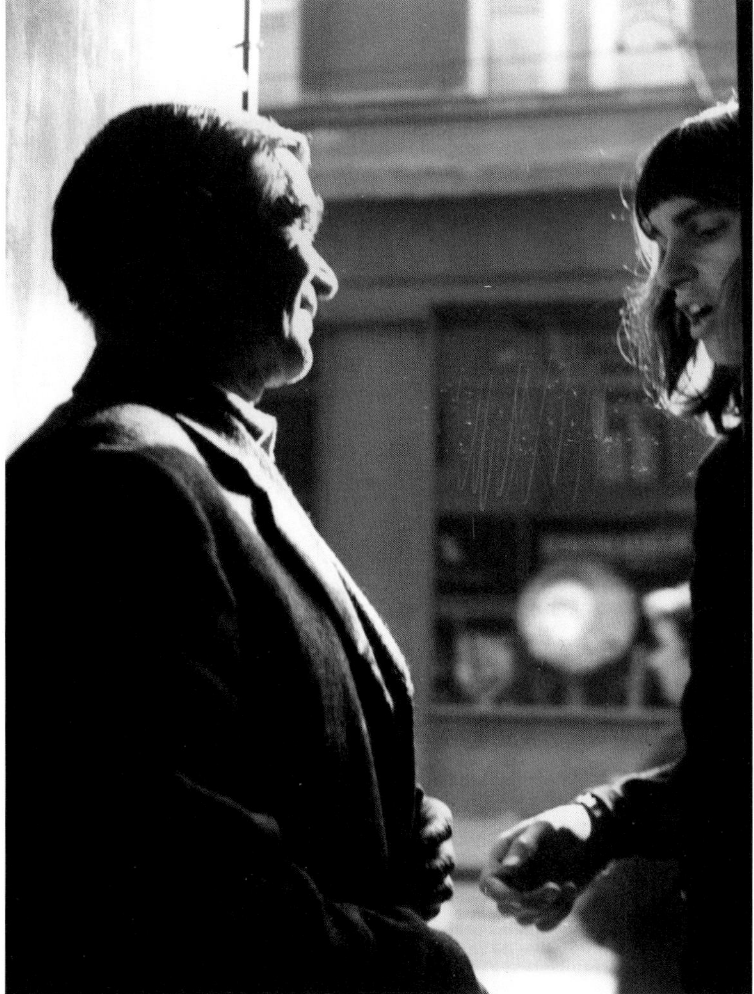

Tihomir Simić in conversation with
Braco Dimitrijević, Zagreb, 1969

Exhibition *At the Moment* with Hido Biscevic, Haustor Frankopanska 2a, 1971

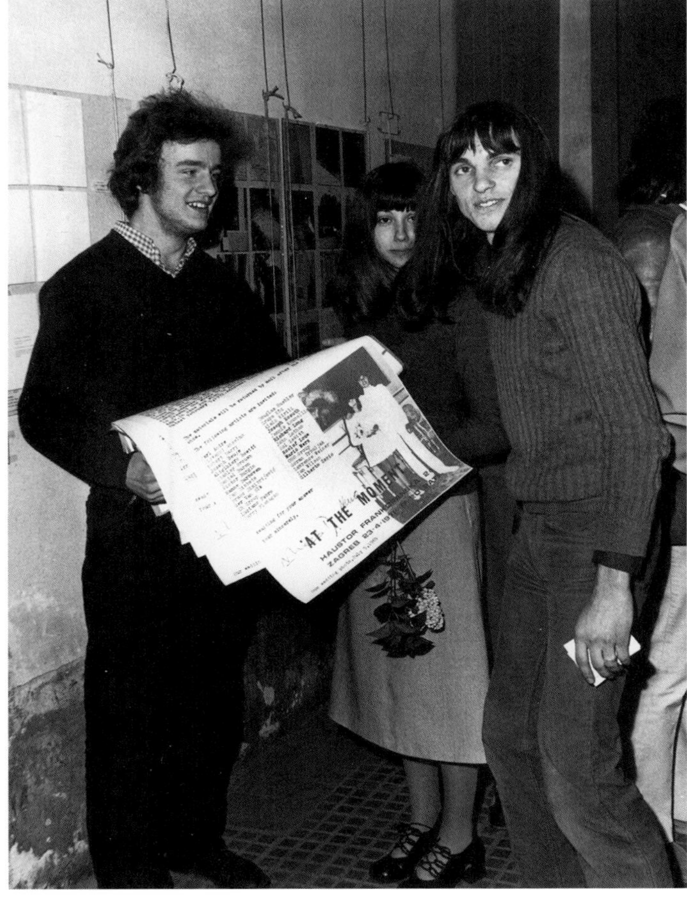

Braco Dimitrijević and Jannis Kounellis in Kounellis' studio, Rome, 1971

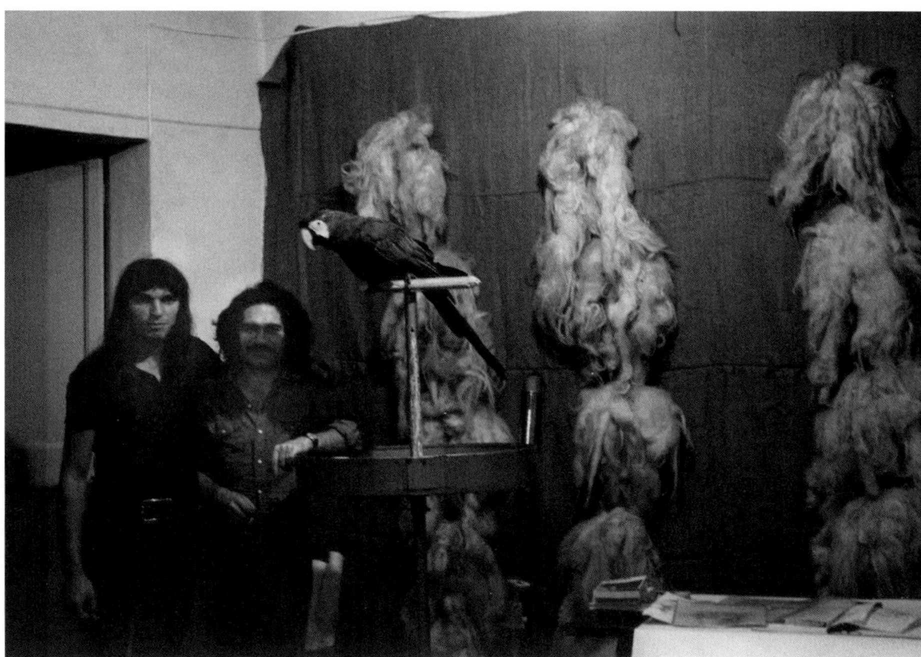

Braco Dimitrijević with his first drip paintings in the style of Jackson Pollock, Dubrovnik, 1972

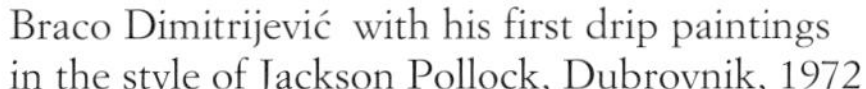

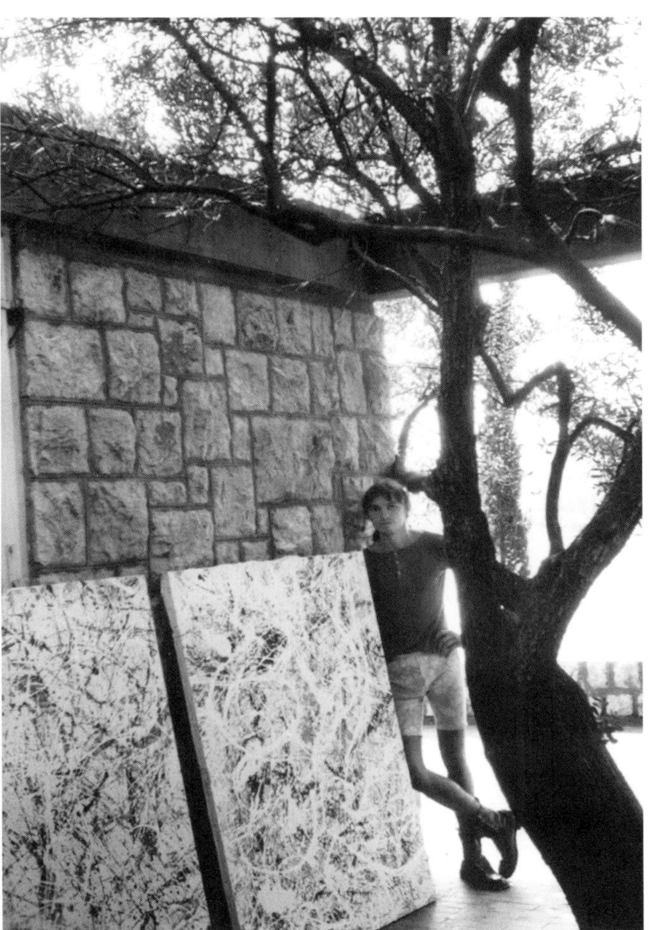

Braco & Nena Dimitrijević
Pantovčak 104 c
Zagreb
Y u g o s l a v i a

Dear Mr.________________

The group show "AT THE MOMENT" is the first international show of conceptual art which will present our audience the works of several artists which they created in last two years.
The show will be open in March or April depending upon the printing of the cataloge-poster, and will take place in the hall of an apartment house in the center of the city, Zagreb Frankopanska 2a, which will together with the gallery audience allow as well the visit of the casual passers-by. In such specificconditions we have the possibilites to present the works by means of film, slides, photographs, texts and tape. In case you wish to participate please send the works at the latest February 5,1971. Address: Nena & Braco Dimitrijević
Pantovčak 104 c
41000 Zagreb
Y u g o s l a v i a

The materials will be returned by mail after the closing of the show.

The following artists are invited:

Carl Andre
Giovanni Anselmo
Robert Barry
Joseph Beuys
Aligihiero Boetti
Stanley Brouwn
Daniel Buren
Victor Burgin
Hanne Darboven
Jan Dibbets
Braco Dimitrijević
Ger Van Elk
ER Group
Luciano Fabro
Barry Flanagan
Douglas Huebler
Grupa Kôd
Alain Kirili
Joseph Kosuth
Jannis Kounellis
Richard Long
John Latham
Sol LeWitt
Roelof Louw
Mario Merz
OHO Group
Goran Trbuljak
Lawrence Weiner
Ian Wilson
Gilberto Zorio

Awaiting for your answer

Your sincerely,

Nena

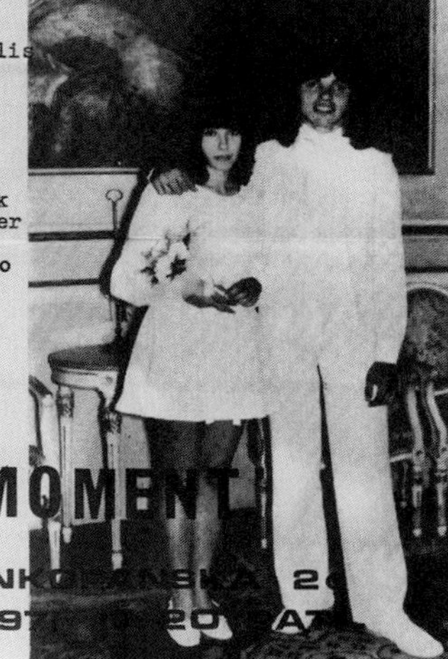

AT THE MOMENT

HAUSTOR FRANKOPANSKA 2a

ZAGREB 23·4·1971

Our wedding photo, July 5,1969

Poster for the exhibition *At the Moment*, 1971

7th Paris Biennale, Braco Dimitrijević, Catherine Millet, Alfred Pacquement, Michael Baldwin, 1971

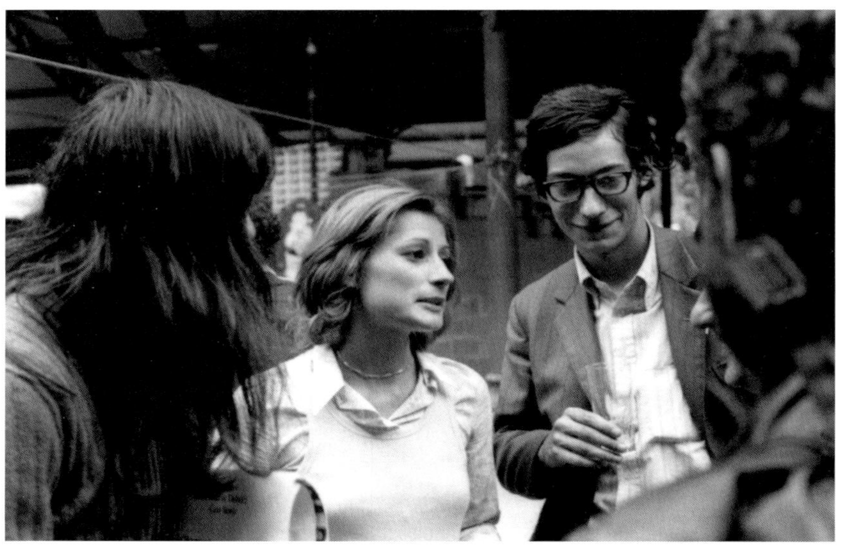

Braco Dimitrijević and Barry Flanagan at the opening of Dimitrijević's show at the Situation Gallery, London, 1972

The police and fire brigade removing a *Casual Passer-by* photograph from Boulevard St. Germain, Paris, 1971

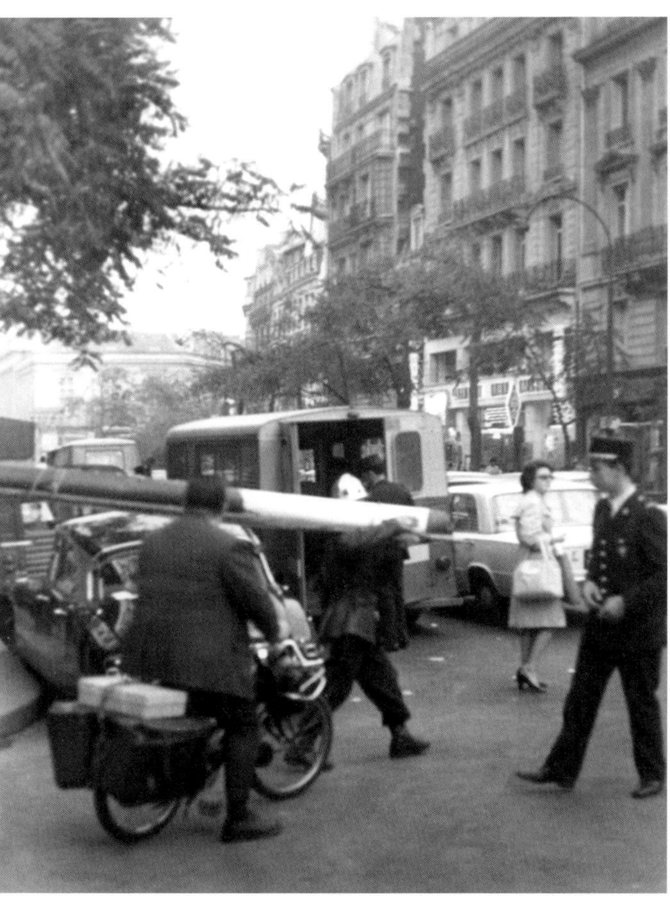

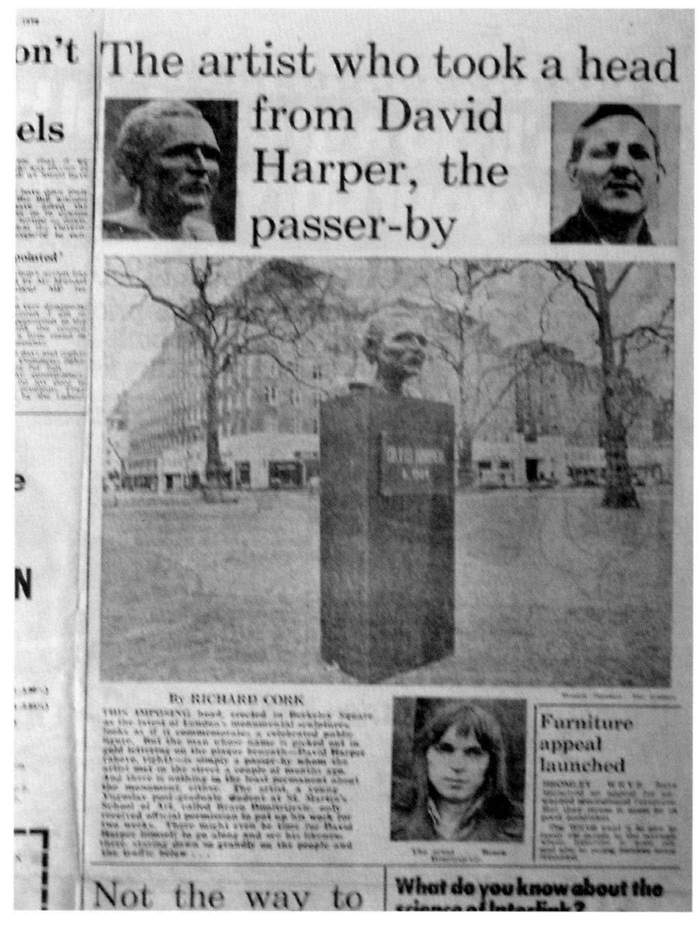

The artist who took a head from David Harper, the passer-by

By RICHARD CORK

Furniture appeal launched

Not the way to

What do you know about the

Newspaper reviews on Braco Dimitrijević's first London exhibition, 1972

Photographs of the artist in motion, 1973

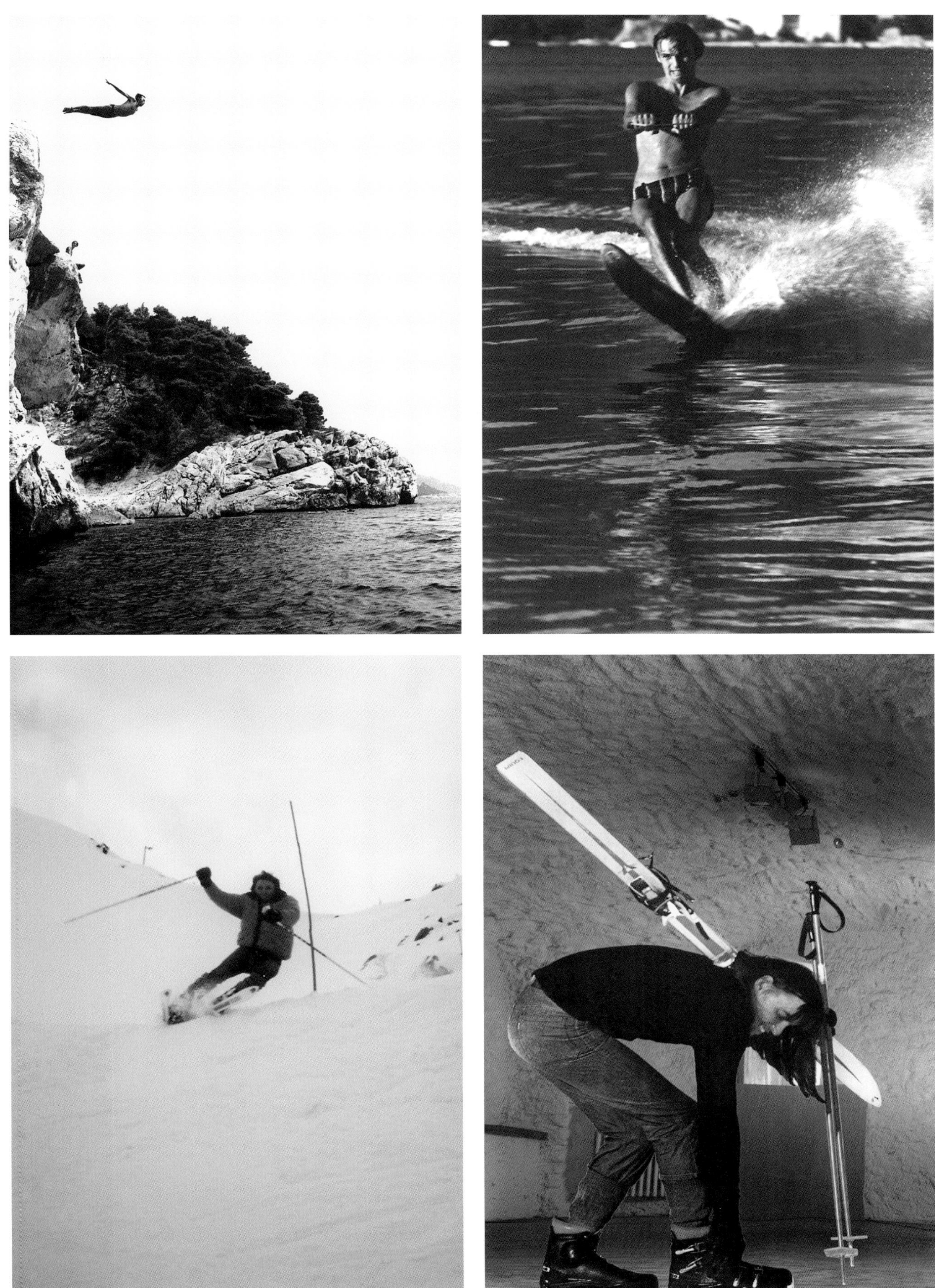

Chamonix, 1968

Braco Dimitrijevic's portrait on a mirror by Michelangelo Pistoletto, 1976

Richard Serra and Braco Dimitrijević at Documenta VI, Kassel, 1977

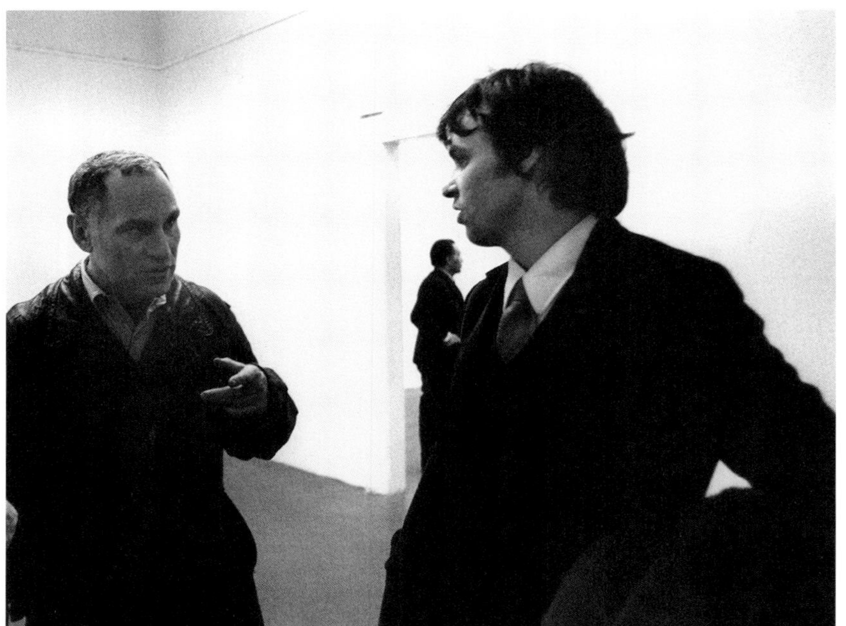

Postcard from Gordon Matta-Clark, 1977

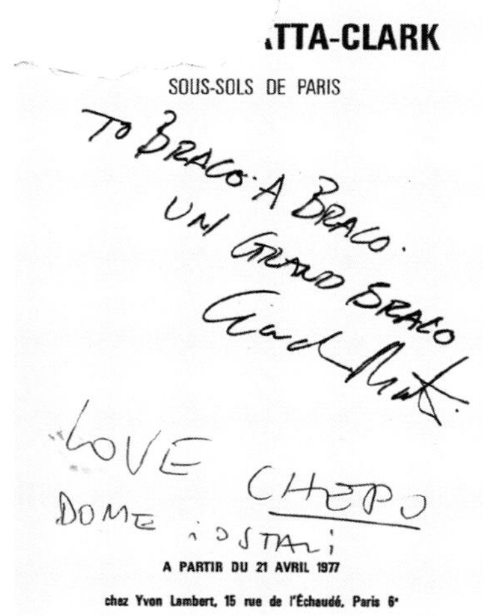

Braco Dimitrijević with Jan Hoet installing *Triptychos Post Historicus* in Ghent, 1978

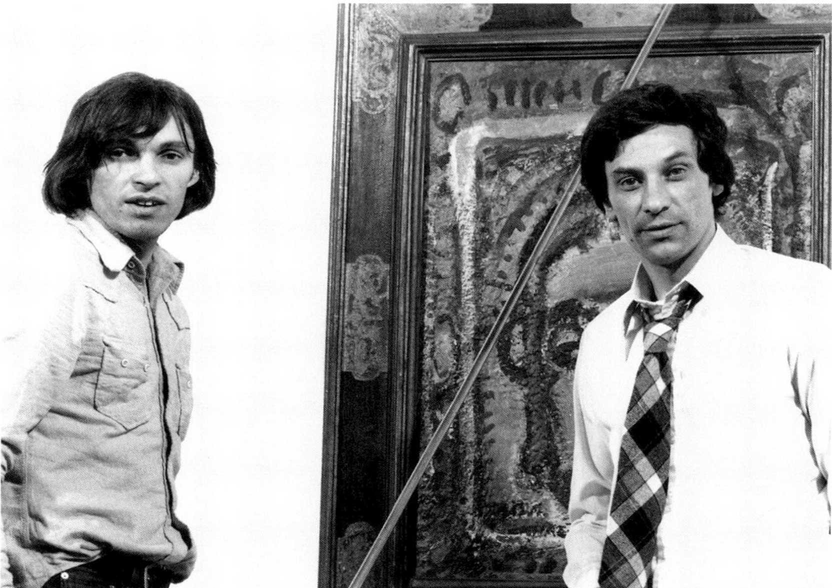

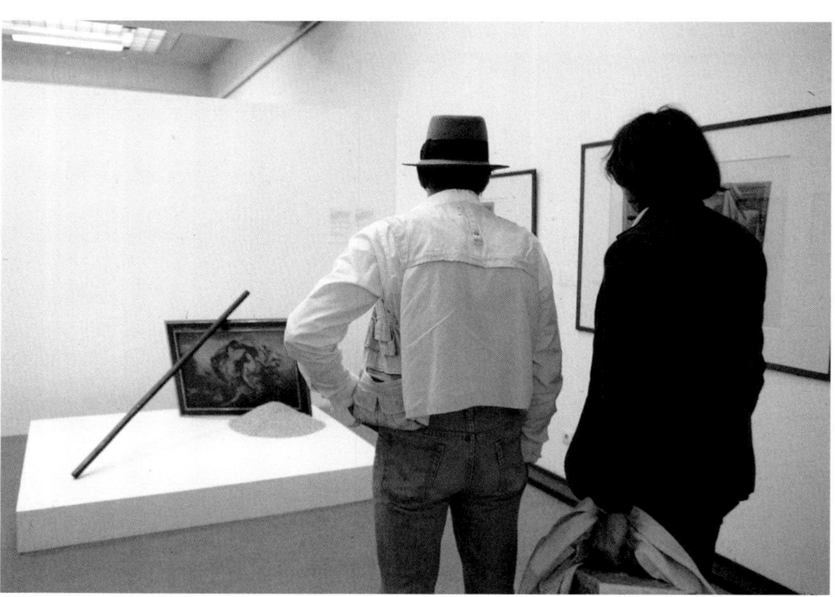

With Joseph Beuys in front of a *Triptychos Post Historicus* at the Kunsthalle, Düsseldorf, 1978

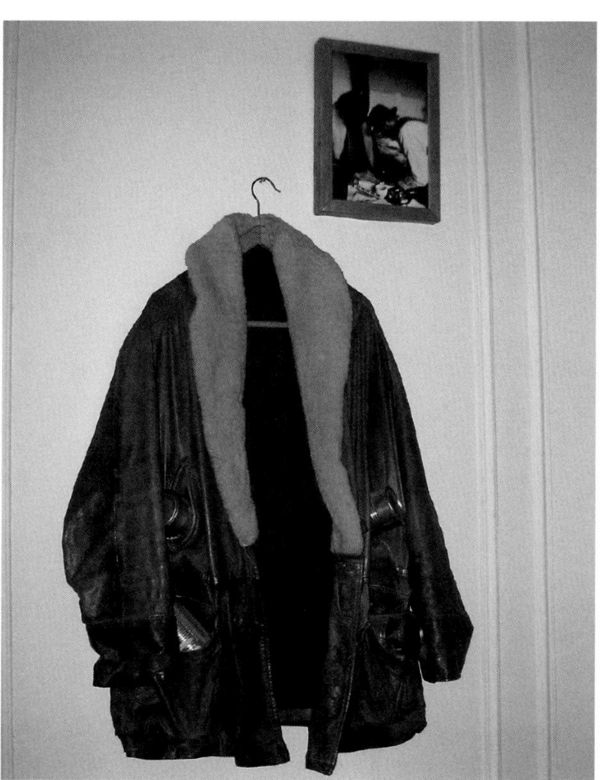

Braco Dimitrijević's portrait by Joseph Beuys, 1984

Braco Dimitrijević, Lucinda Childs, Joan Jonas, Berlin, 1976

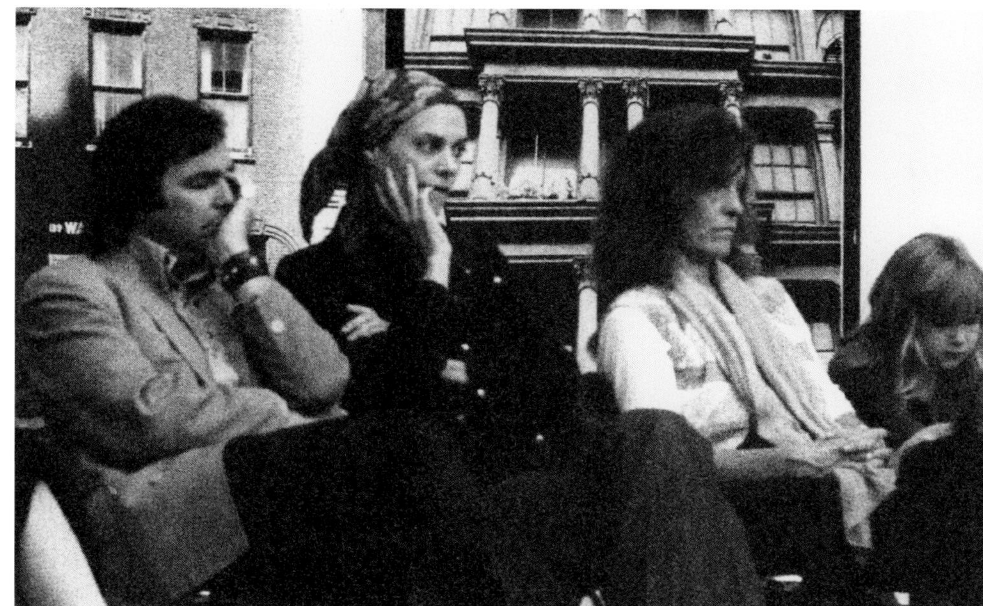

Douglas Hueblerand Braco Dimitrijević

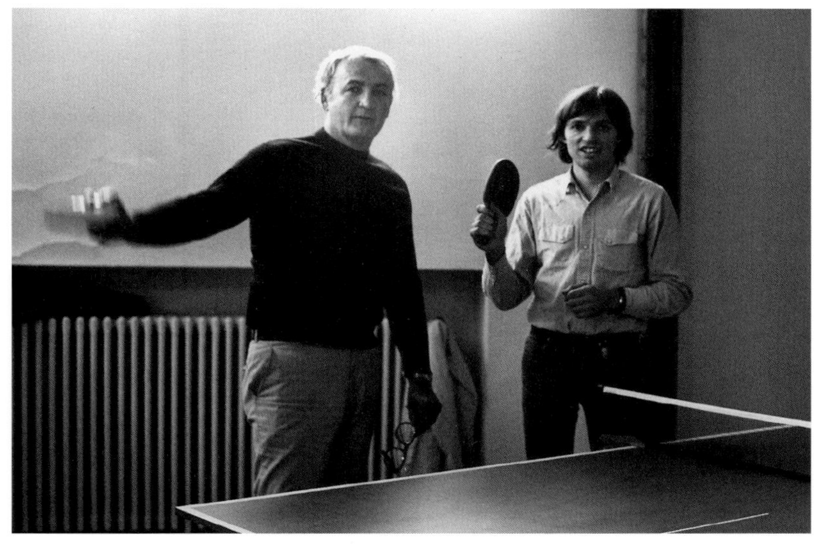

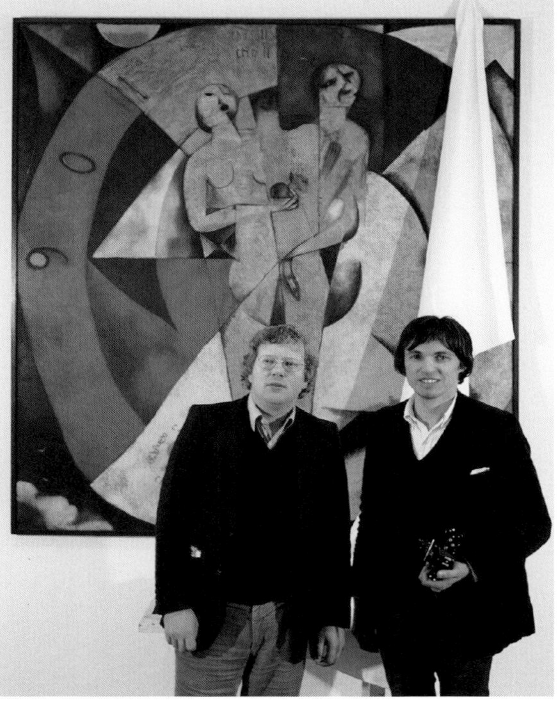

With Rudi Fuchs working on a one-man exhibition at Stedelijk van Abbemuseum, Eindhoven, 1979

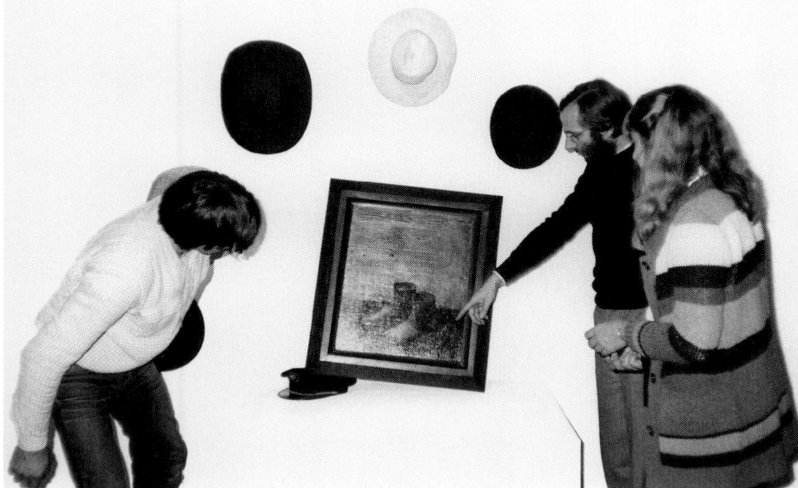

With Jean-Hubert Martin and Nena Dimitrijević working on *Triptychos Post Historicus* installations at the Musée National d'Art Moderne, Centre Georges Pompidou, Paris, 1981

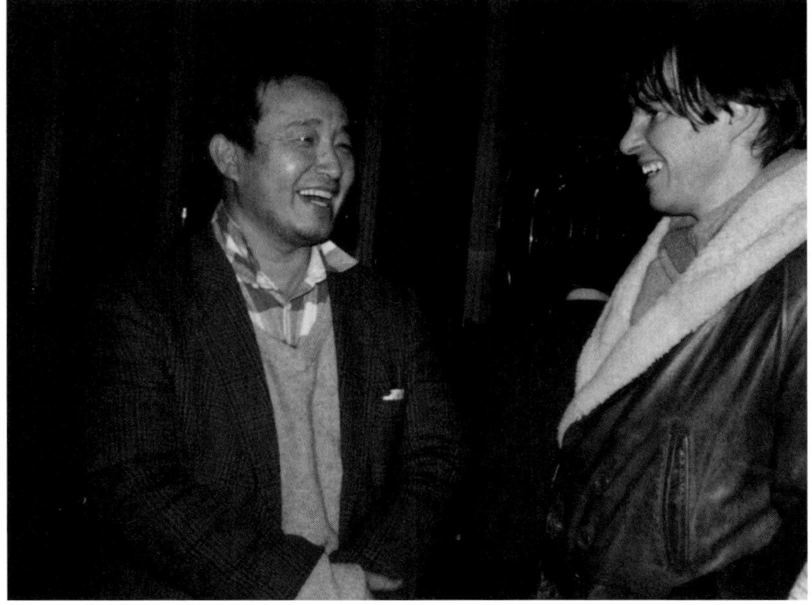

Nam June Paik and Braco Dimitrijević, Cologne, 1983

Claude Lévi-Strauss and Braco Dimitrijević,
Collège de France, Paris, 1982

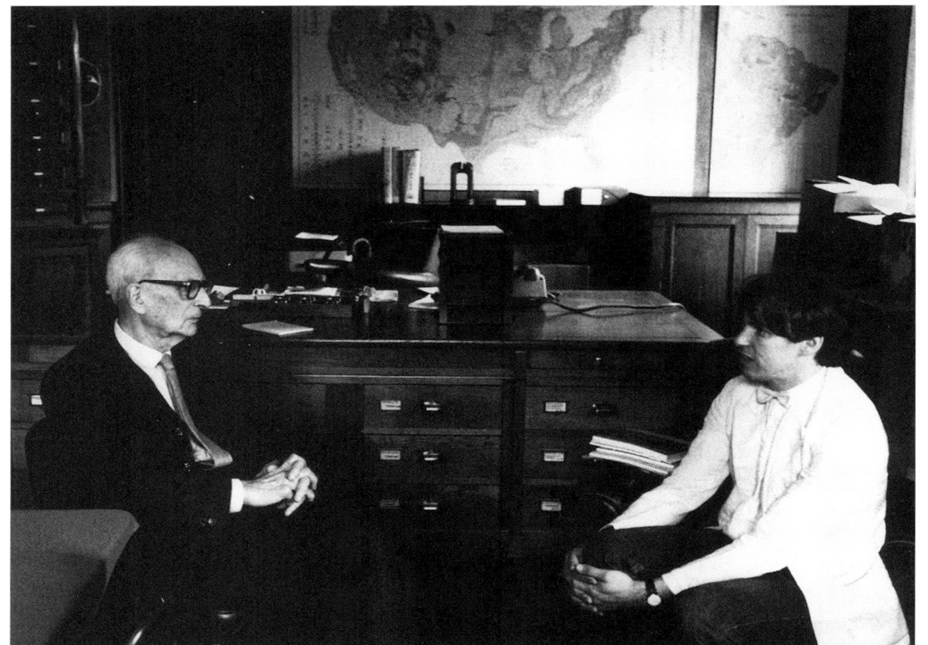

Braco Dimitrijević and Meret Oppenheim,
Parc Lulin, Geneva, 1985

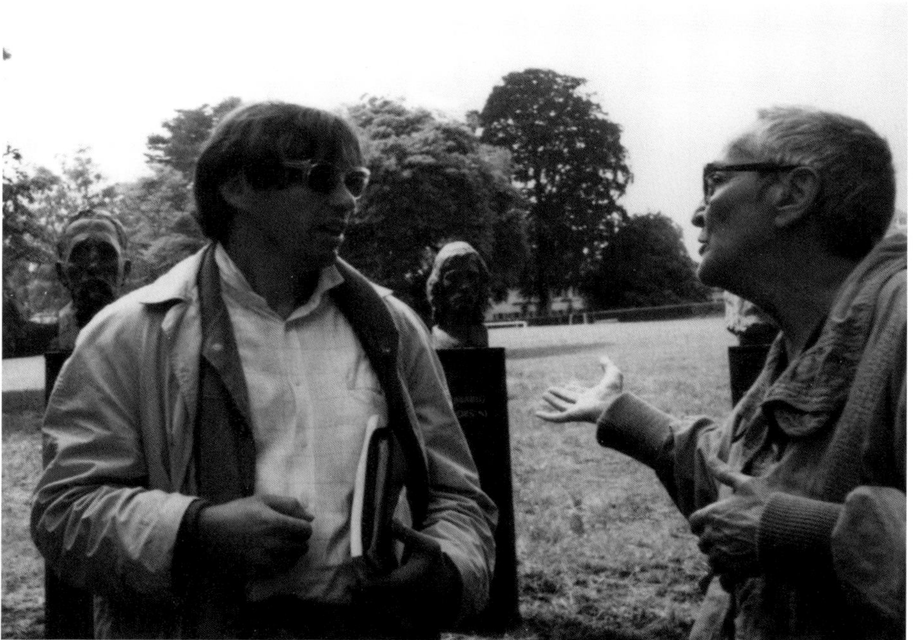

Braco Dimitrijević and John Nixon
near Melbourne, Australia, 1986

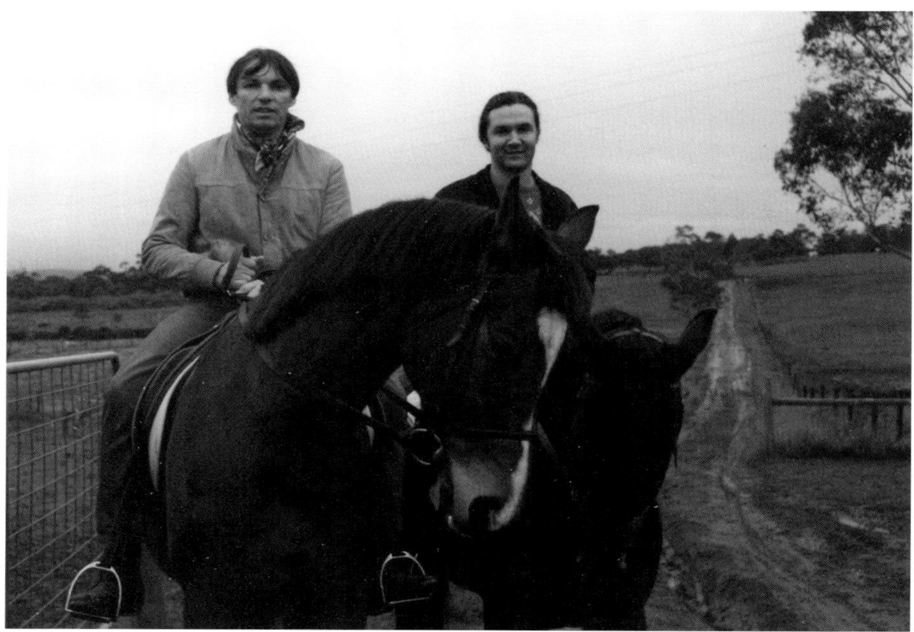

Nena and Braco Dimitrijević,
July 10, 1986, London

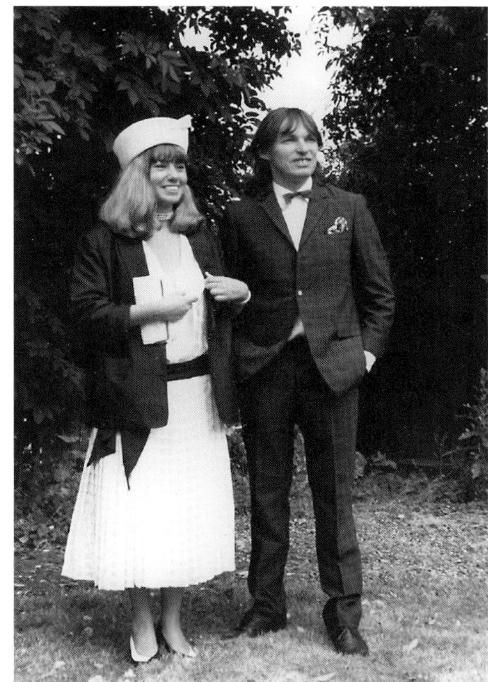

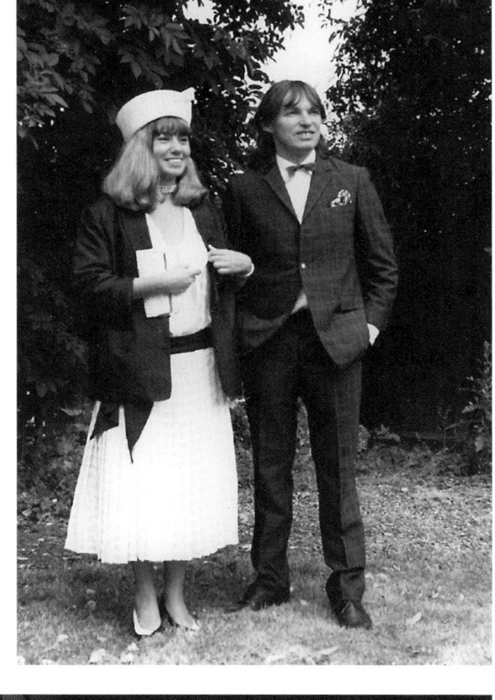

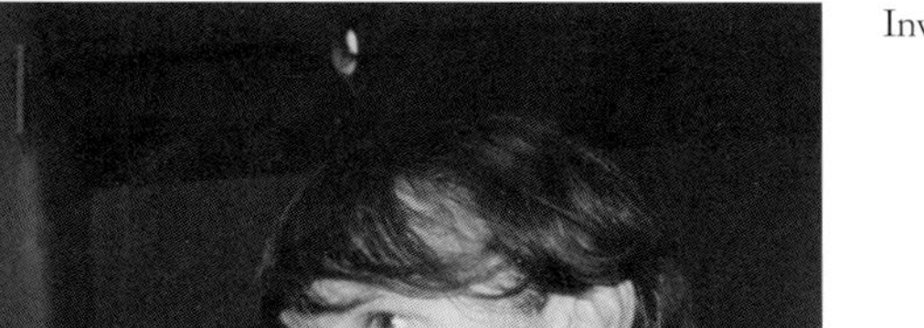

EIIR

The Lord Chamberlain is
commanded by Her Majesty to invite

Mr. and Mrs. Braco Dimitrijevic

to a Garden Party at Buckingham Palace
on Thursday, 10th July, 1986 from 4 to 6 p.m.

Morning Dress, Uniform or Lounge Suit

Invitation to Buckingham Palace, 1986

Malcolm McLaren and Braco Dimitrijević,
Sydney, 1986

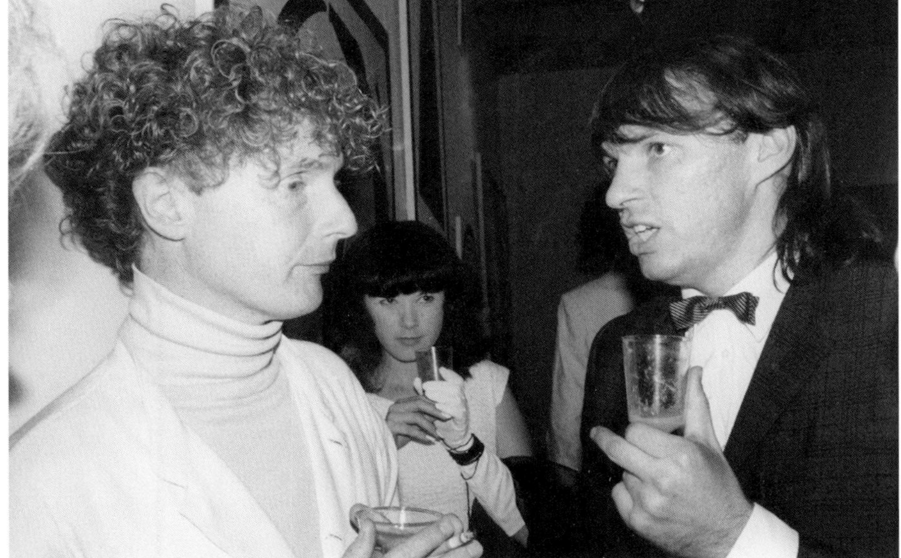

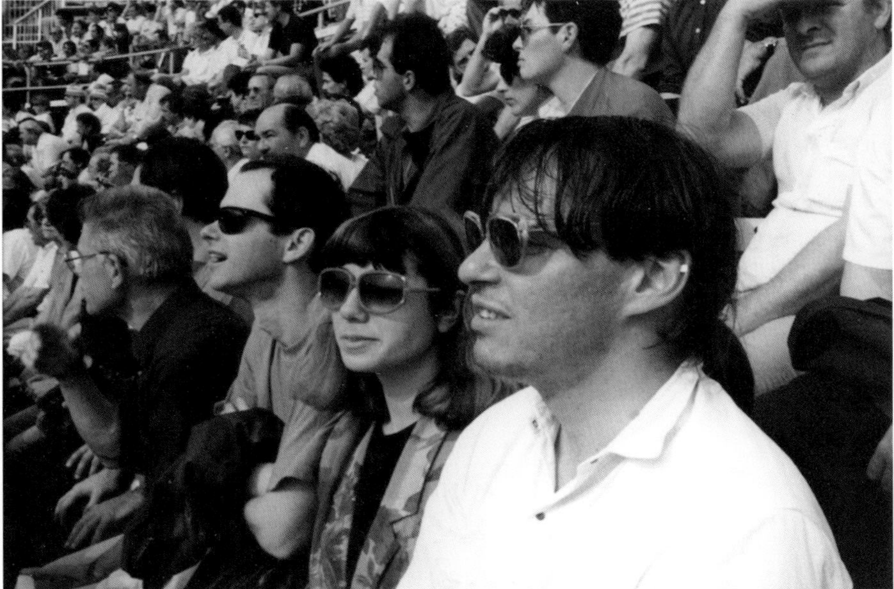

Eric Fabre, Nena and Braco Dimitrijević,
Feria de Nîmes, 1987

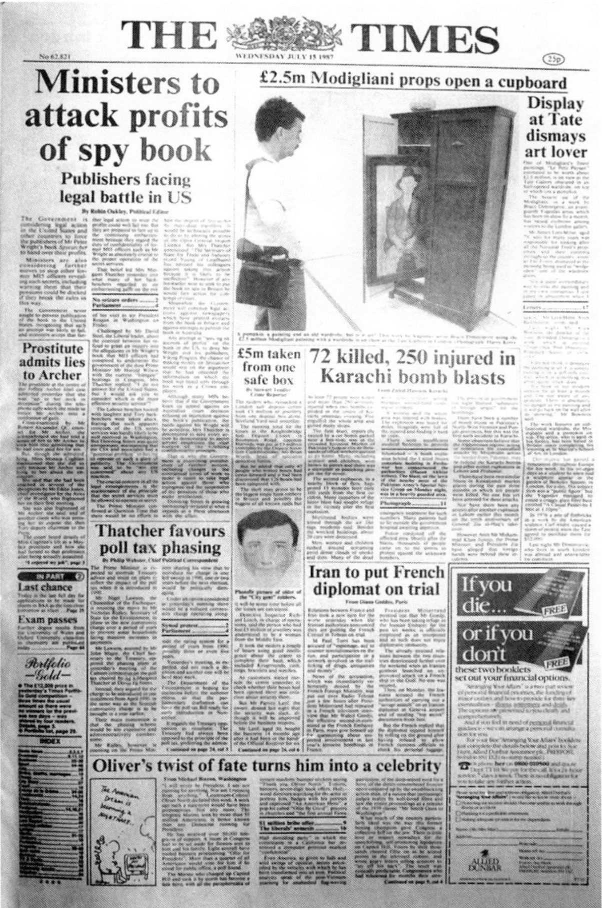

THE TIMES

Ministers to attack profits of spy book

Publishers facing legal battle in US

£2.5m Modigliani props open a cupboard

Display at Tate dismays art lover

Prostitute admits lies to Archer

£5m taken from one safe box

72 killed, 250 injured in Karachi bomb blasts

Thatcher favours poll tax phasing

Iran to put French diplomat on trial

Oliver's twist of fate turns him into a celebrity

If you die... or if you don't

Front page of the *Times* with
Triptychos Post Historicus, July 15, 1987

Mario Merz and Braco Dimitrijević, Parc Lulin, Geneva, 1985

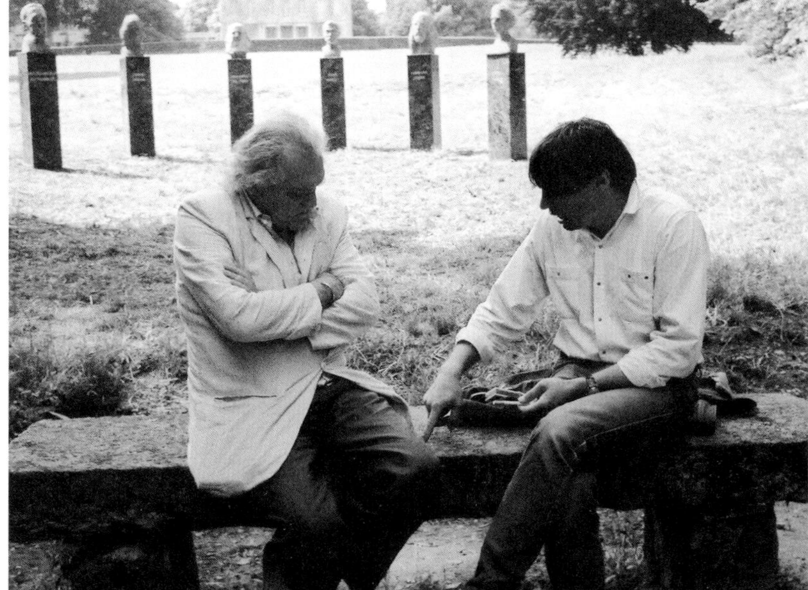

In front of Braco Dimitrijević's work: John Armleder, Braco Dimitrijević, Emmet Williams, Nena Dimitrijević, Rene Block, Ursula Block, and Allan Kaprow, Hamburg, 1985

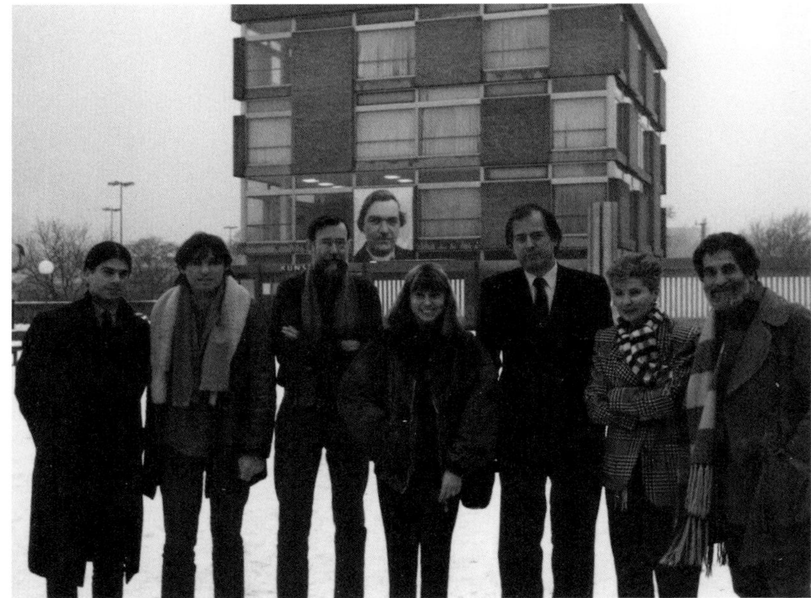

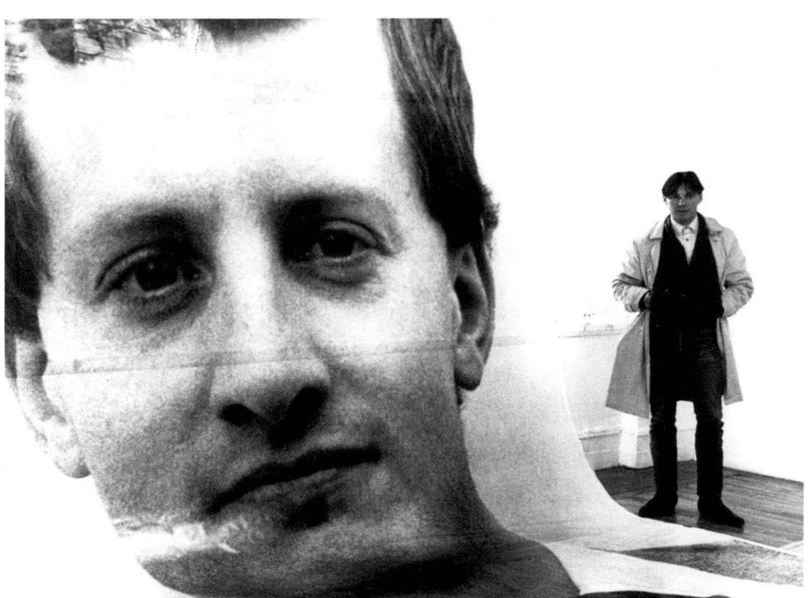

At the Nicole Klagsbrun Gallery on Broadway, New York, 1988

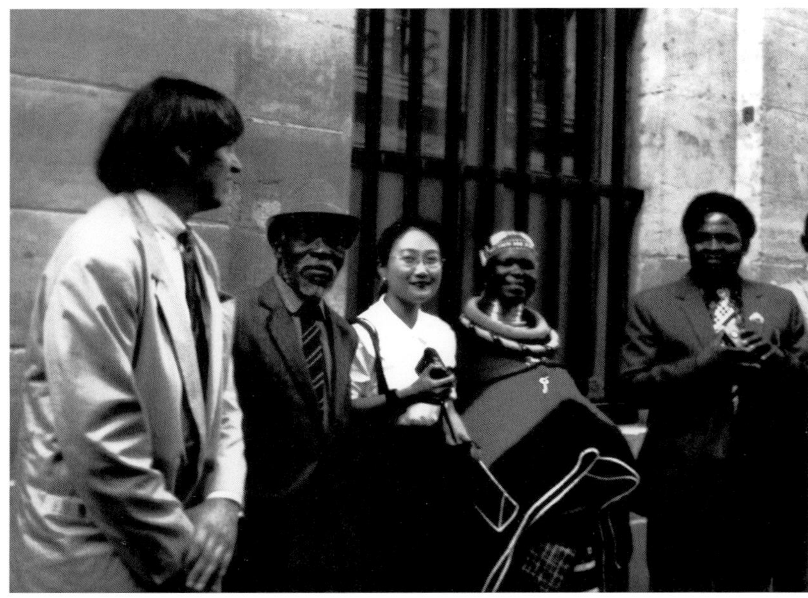

Magiciens de la terre exhibition, Braco Dimitrijevic, Frederic Bruly Bouabre, Ester Mahlangu, Cyprien Tokoudagba, and André Magnin, Paris, 1989

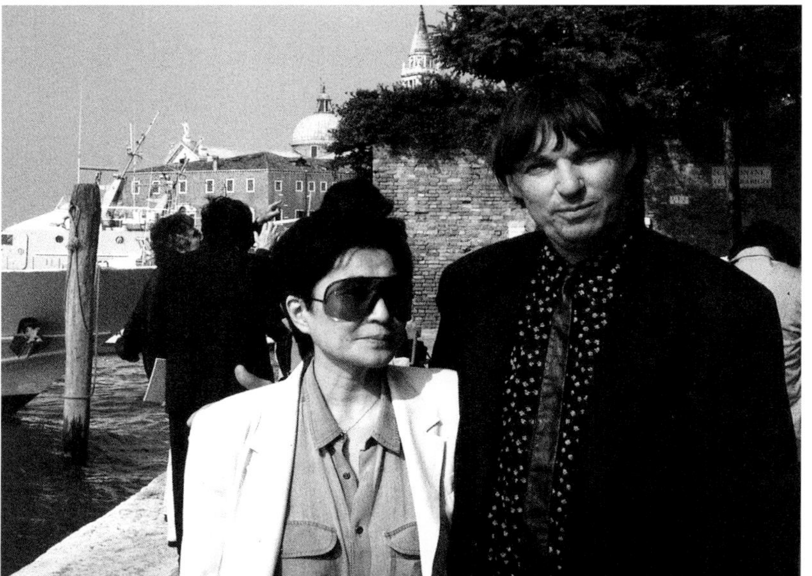

Yoko Ono and Braco Dimitrijević, Venice, 1990

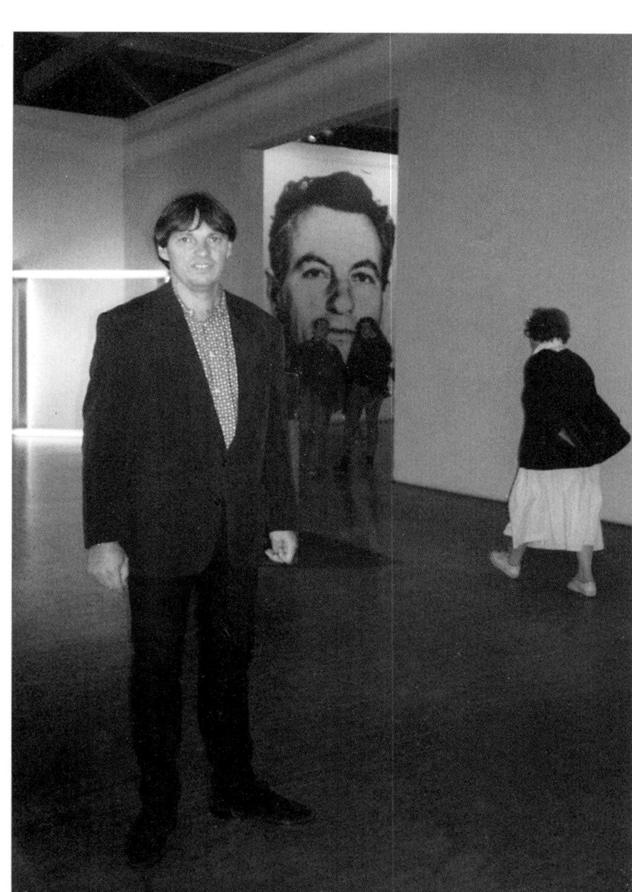

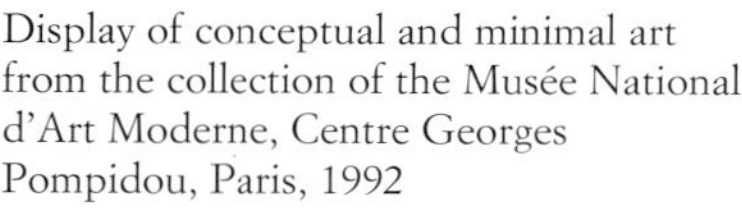

Display of conceptual and minimal art from the collection of the Musée National d'Art Moderne, Centre Georges Pompidou, Paris, 1992

Roman Polanski and Braco Dimitrijević, Palais Royal, Paris, 1992

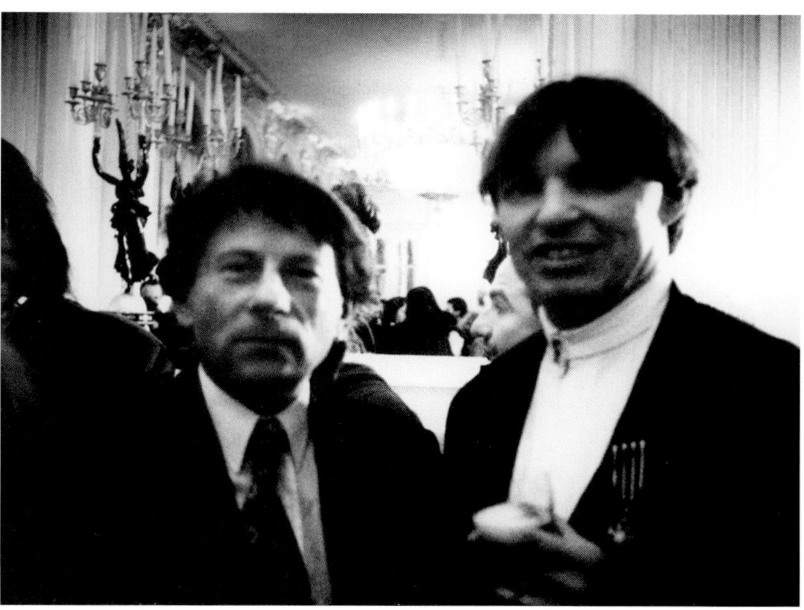

Being made a Chevalier des Arts et des Lettres by Jack Lang, French Minister of Culture, Palais Royal, Paris, 1992

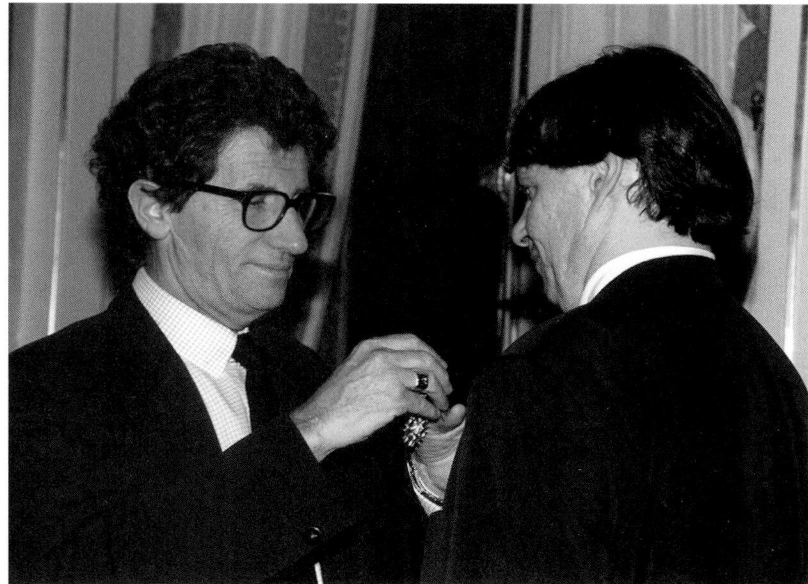

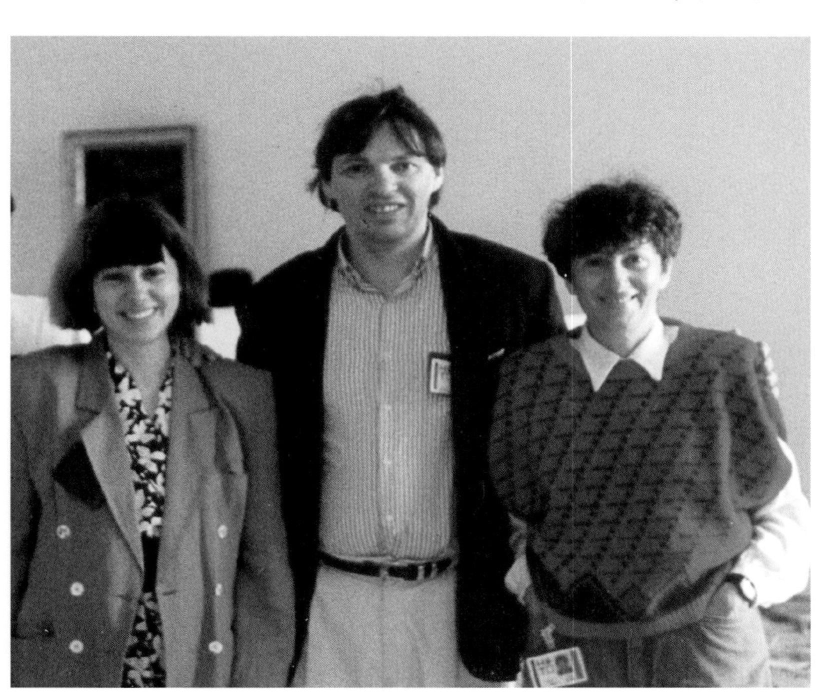

Nena and Braco Dimitrijević, Suzanne Landau, Israel Museum, Jerusalem, 1990

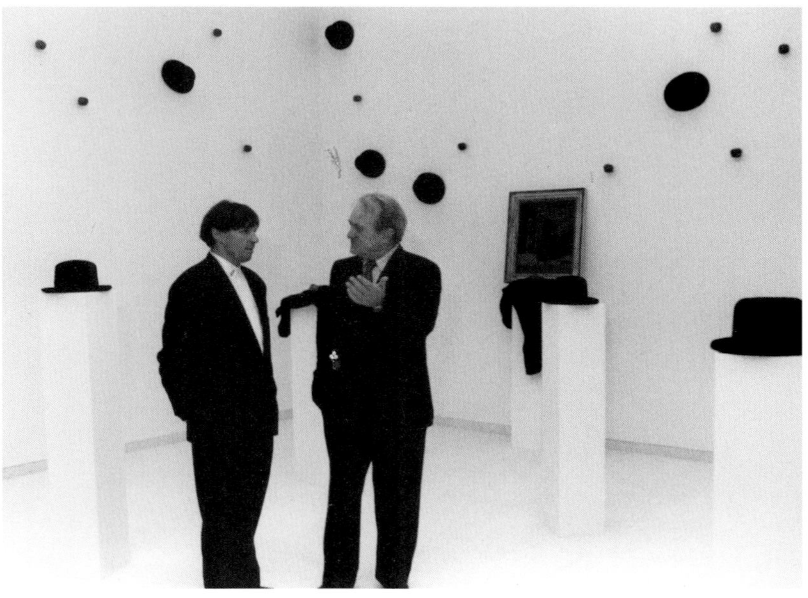

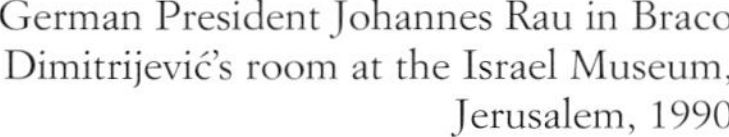

German President Johannes Rau in Braco Dimitrijević's room at the Israel Museum, Jerusalem, 1990

Richard Hamilton and Braco Dimitrijević, Cadaques, 1991

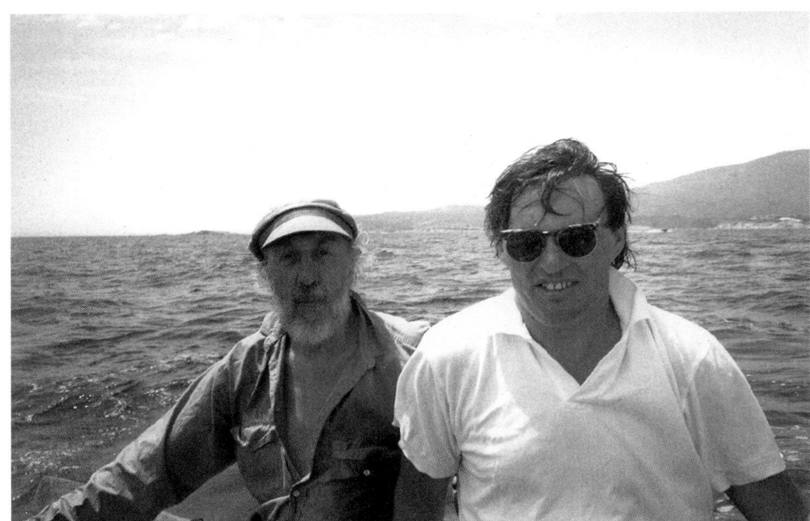

Marie Starkmann, Braco Dimitrijević, and Emma, Praslin Island, Indian Ocean, 1992

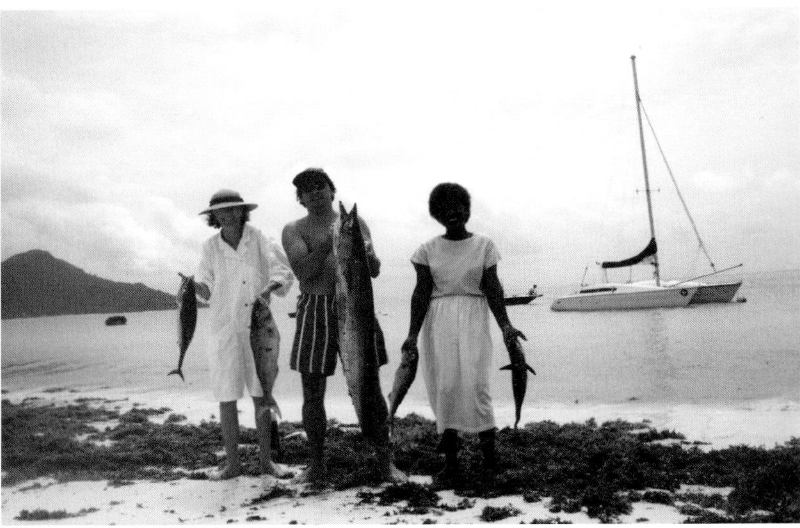

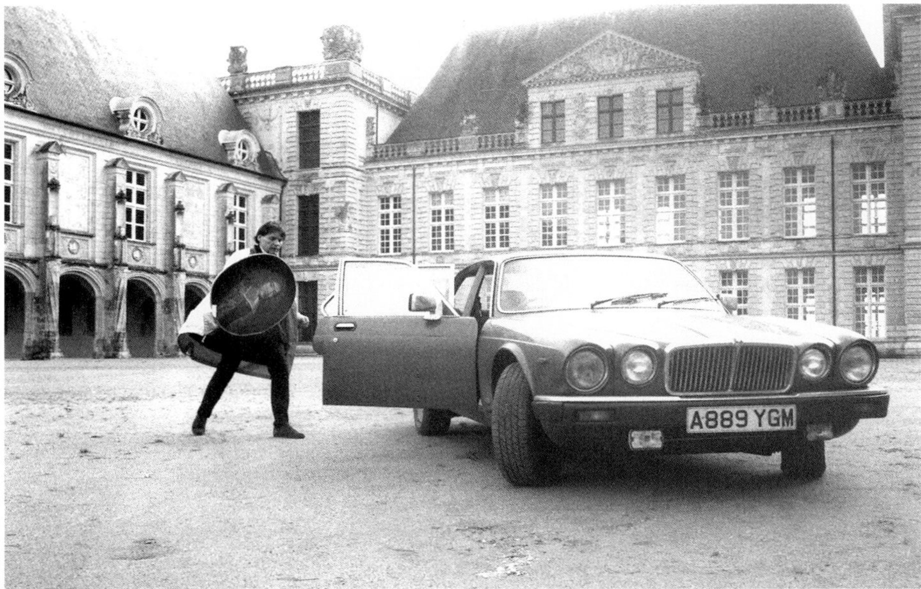

Chateau d'Oiron, France, 1993

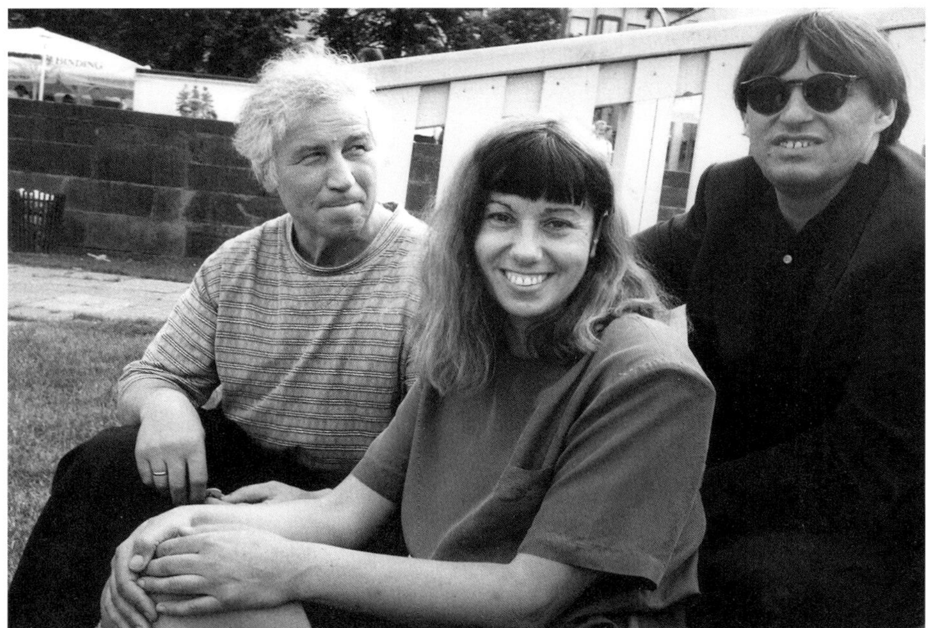

Ilya Kabakov, Nena and Braco Dimitrijević, Documenta IX, Kassel, 1992

Praslin Island, Indian Ocean, 1992

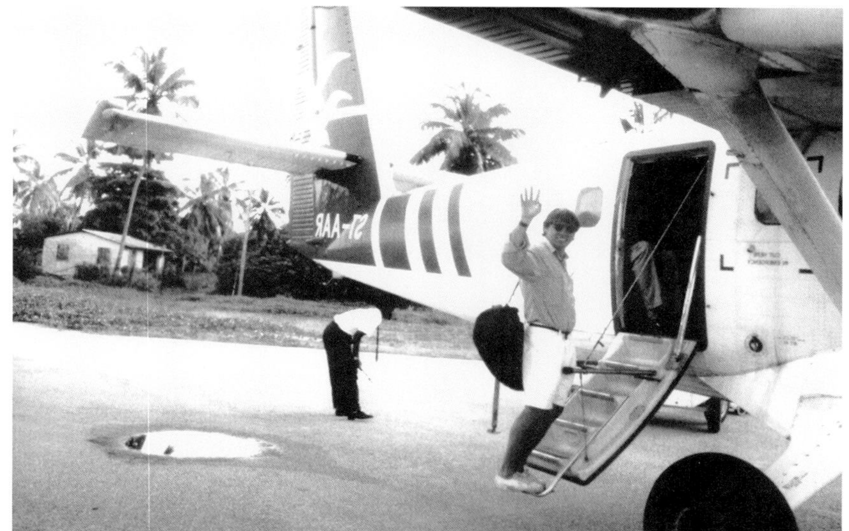

Nena Dimitrijević, Christian Boltanski, Braco Dimitrijević, Nam June Paik, Jannis Kounellis, and Lóránd Hegyi, Venice Biennale, 1993

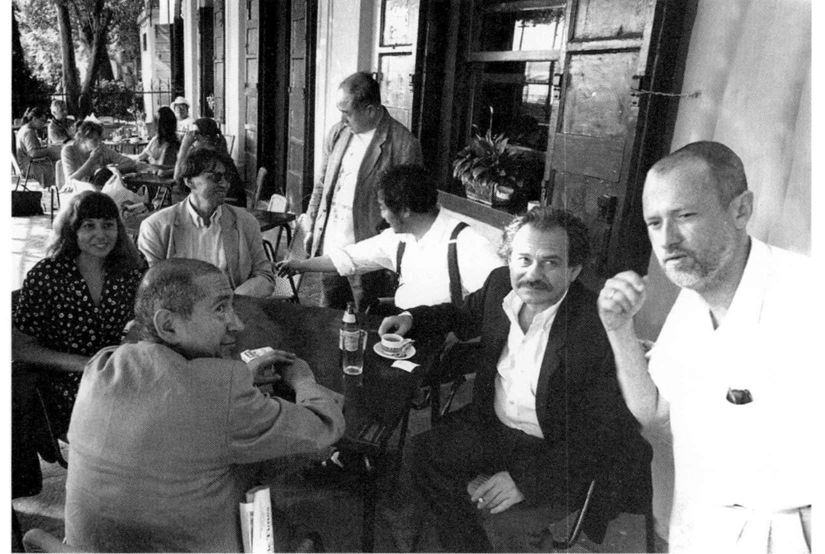

With Bruce Ferguson in Rio Grande, New Mexico, 1995

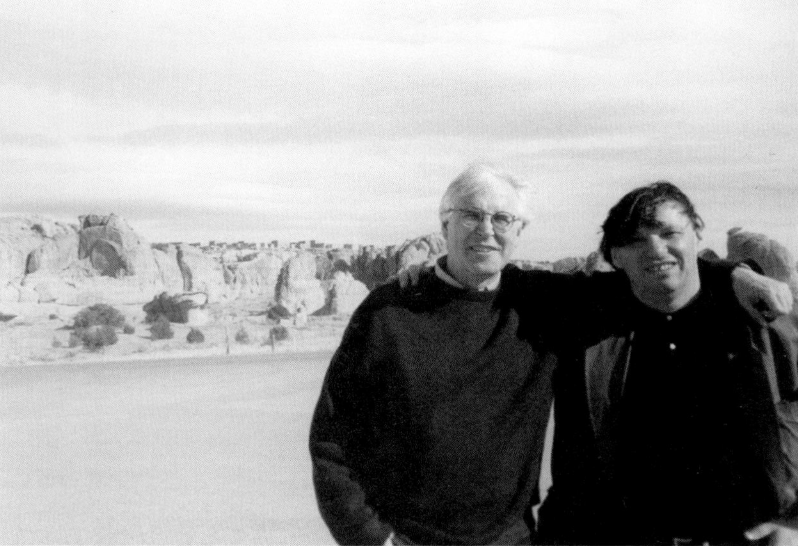

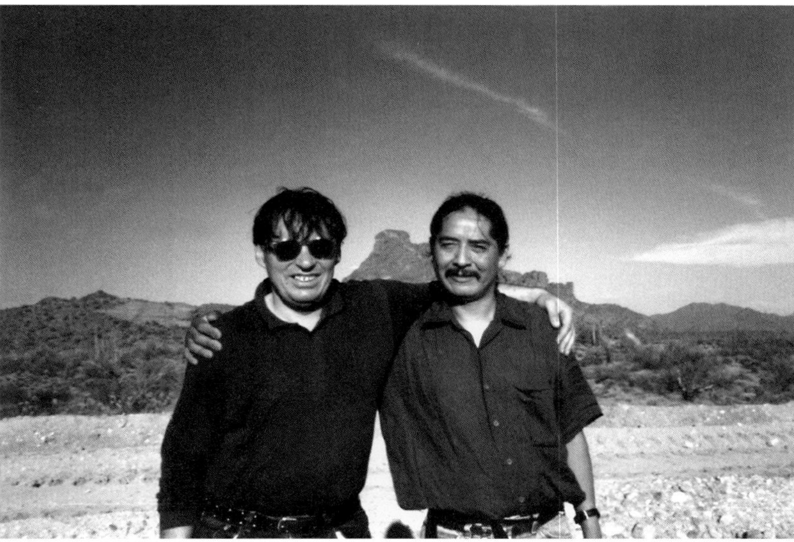

Braco Dimitrijević and Joe Ben Jr., east of Phoenix, Arizona, 1995

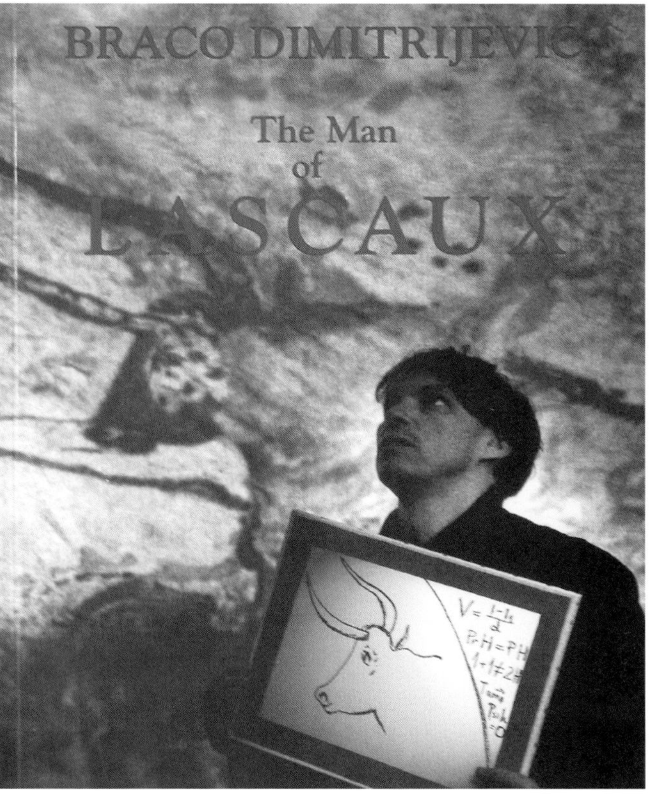

Exhibition in Lascaux, 1993

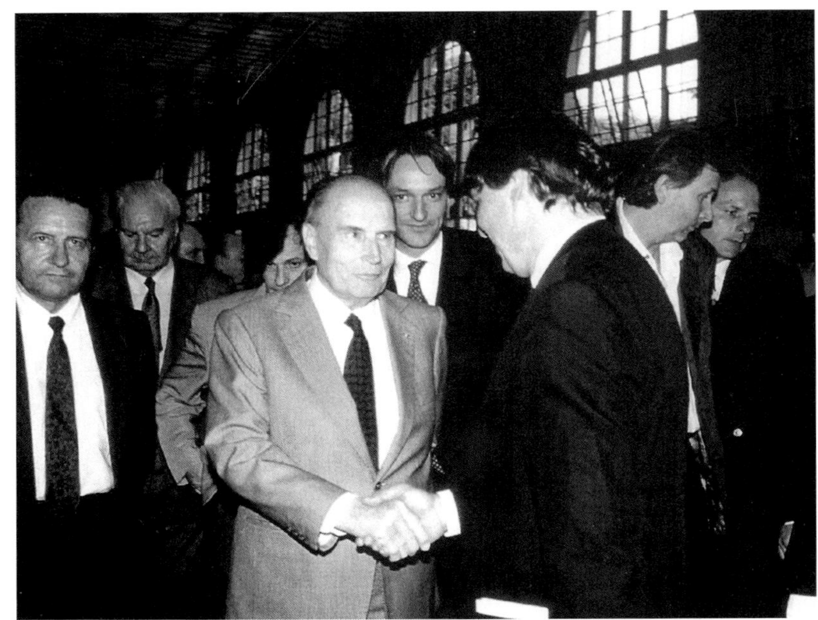

Braco Dimitrijević with President François Mitterrand, Paris, 1995

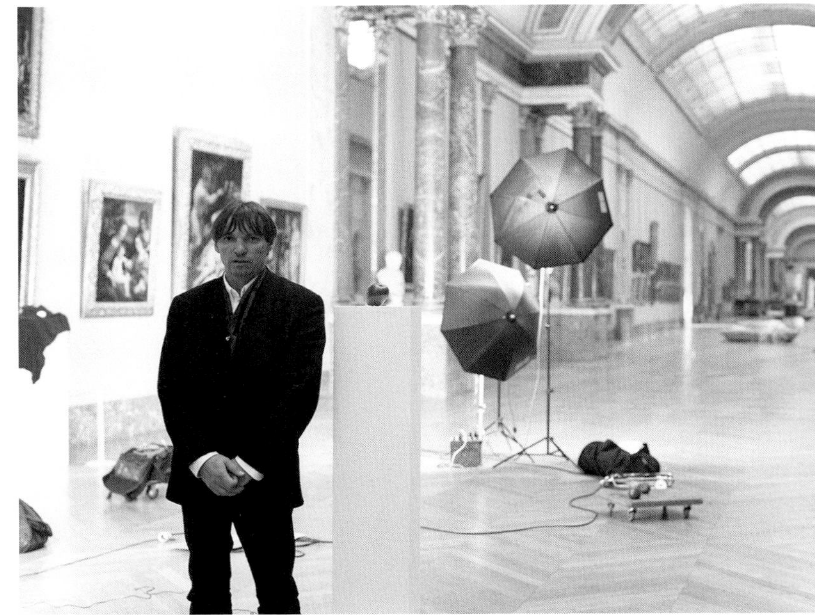

Musée du Louvre, 1996

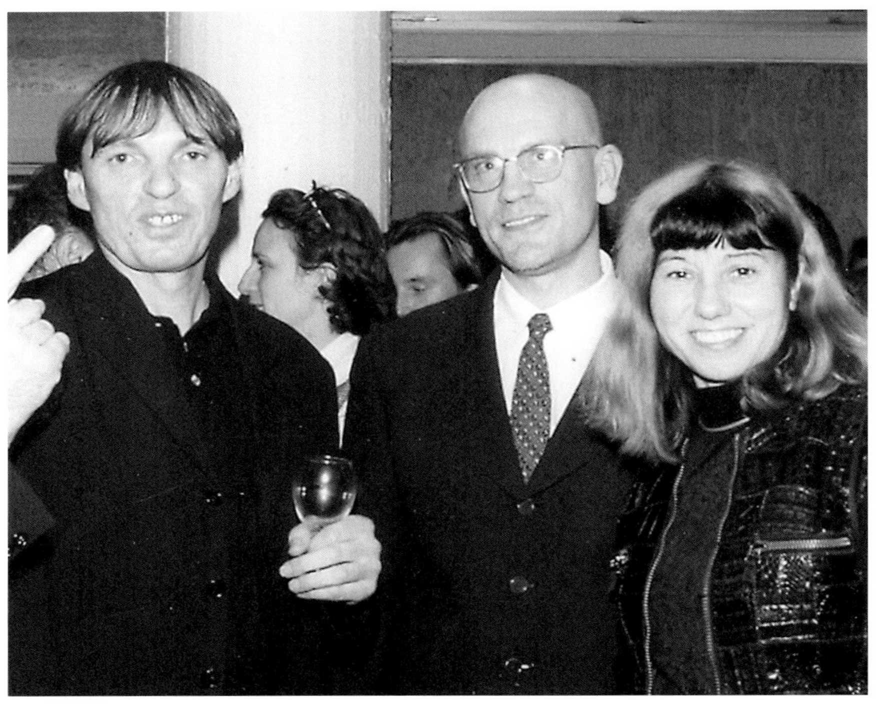

Braco Dimitrijević, John Malkovich, and Nena, Paris, 1997

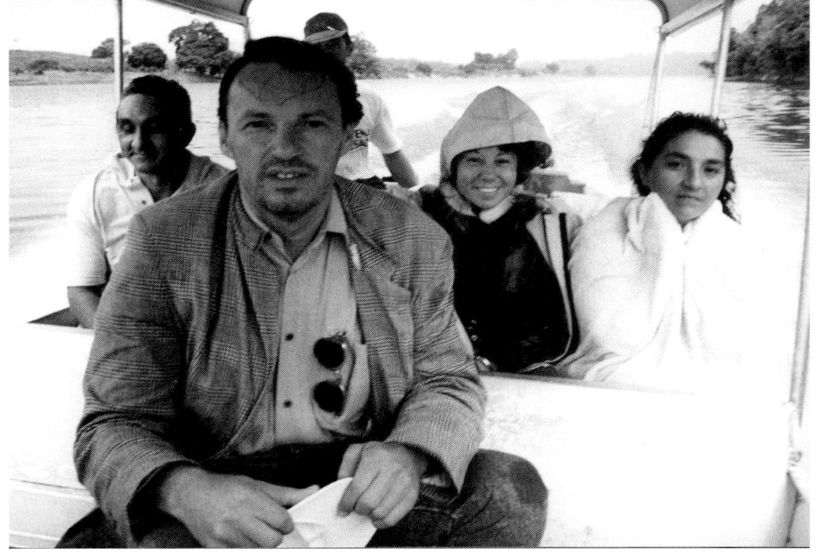

North-western Amazonia, Brazil, 1996

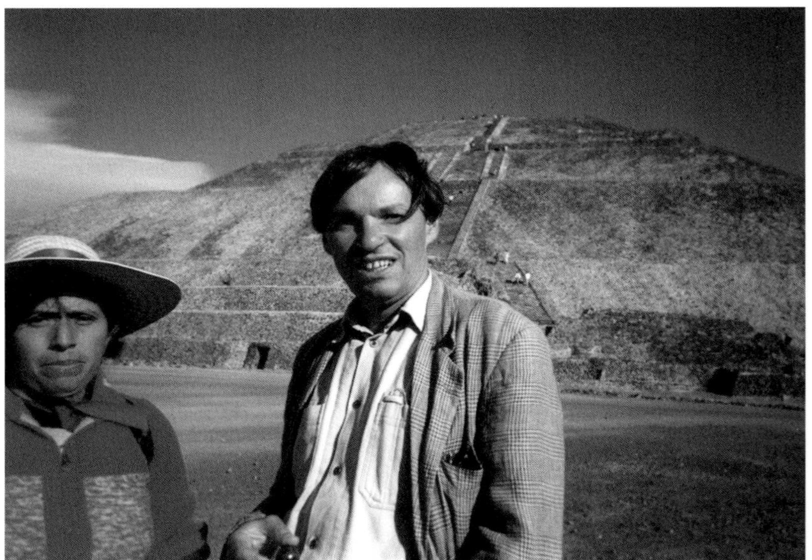

Braco Dimitrijević with Itchu, Teotihuacan, Mexico, 1997

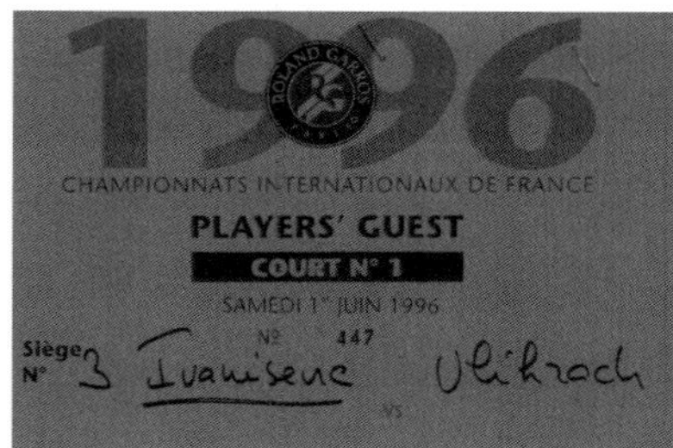

Invitation to Roland Garros, 1996

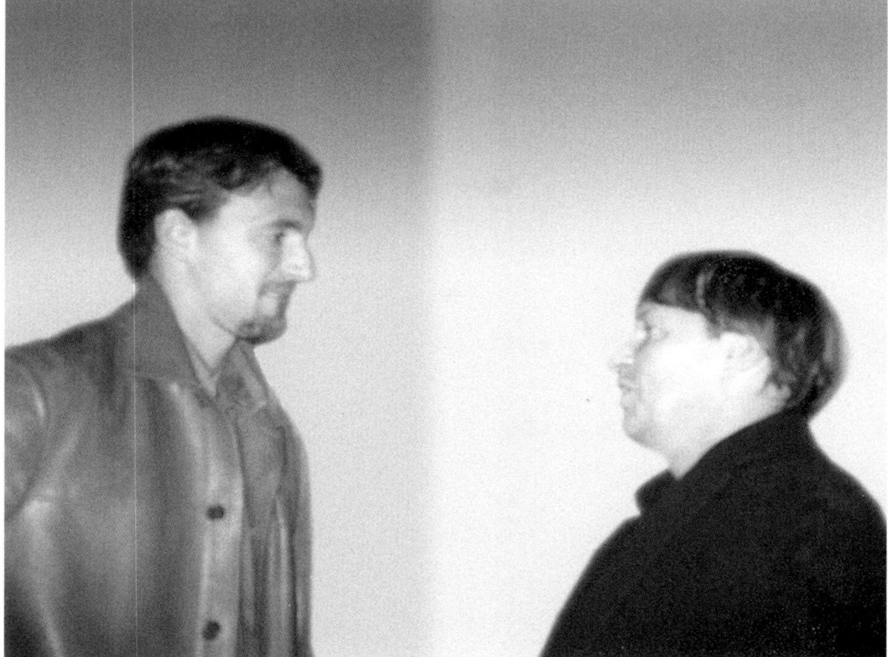

Goran Ivanisević, Braco Dimitrijević,
Paris, 2001

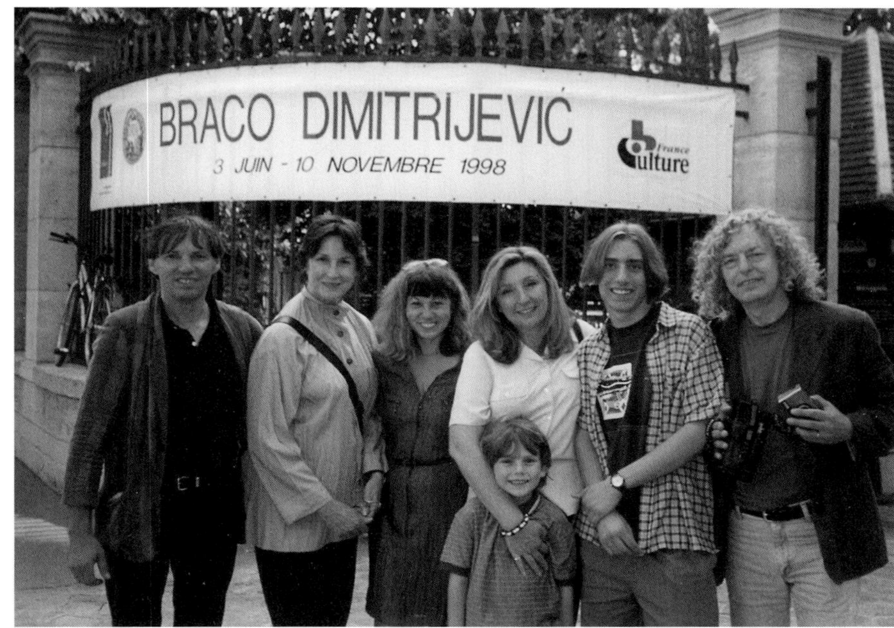

Braco Dimitrijević, Virginia Dwan, Nena Dimitrijević, Candice and Anton Perich with sons during Braco Dimitrijević's exhibition at the Paris zoo, 1998

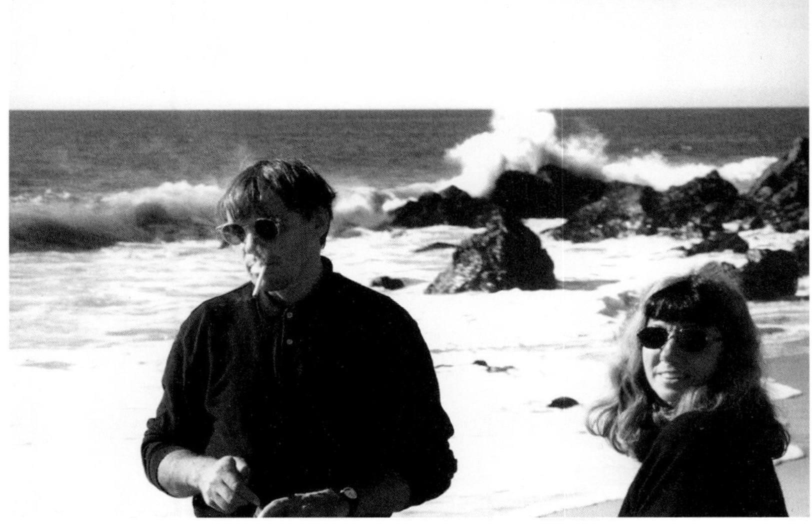

With Nena, Malibu Beach, California, 1996

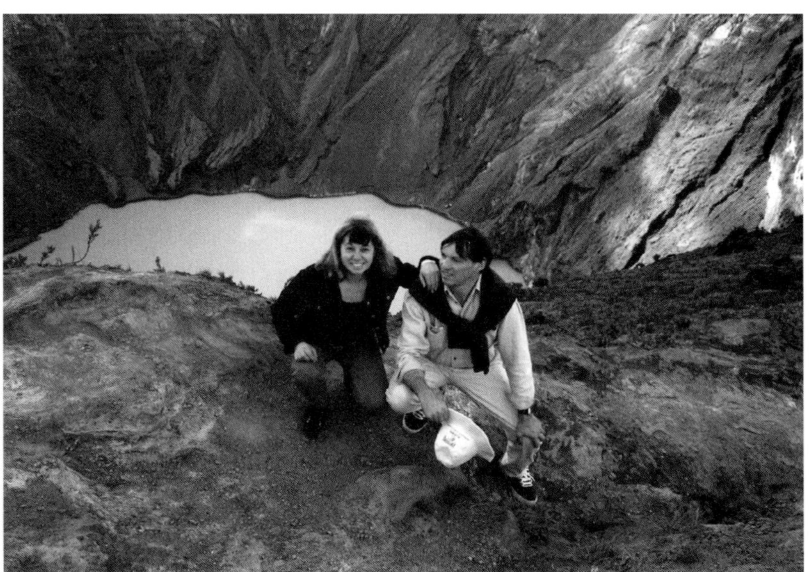

With Nena at the Irasu volcano,
Costa Rica, 1998

Christian Boltanski, Ingrid Blanco Diaz, and Braco Dimitrijević during the Bienal de La Habana, 1997

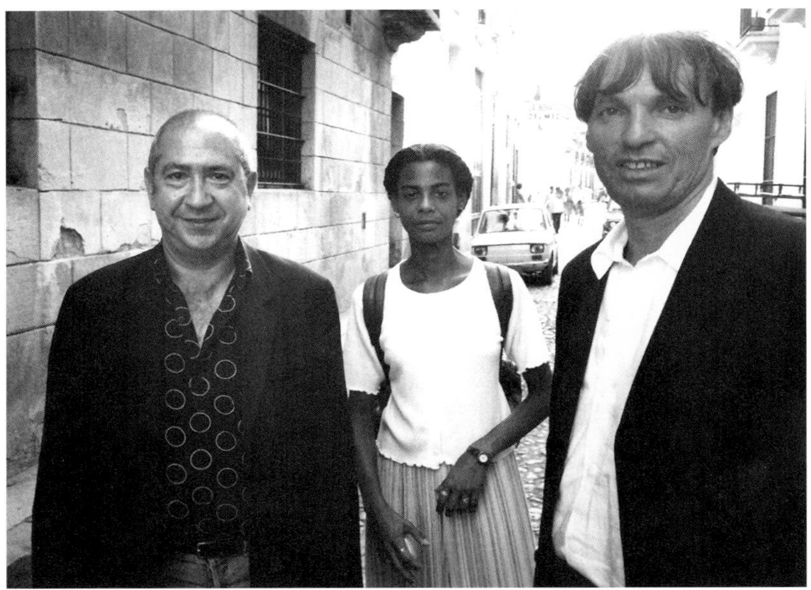

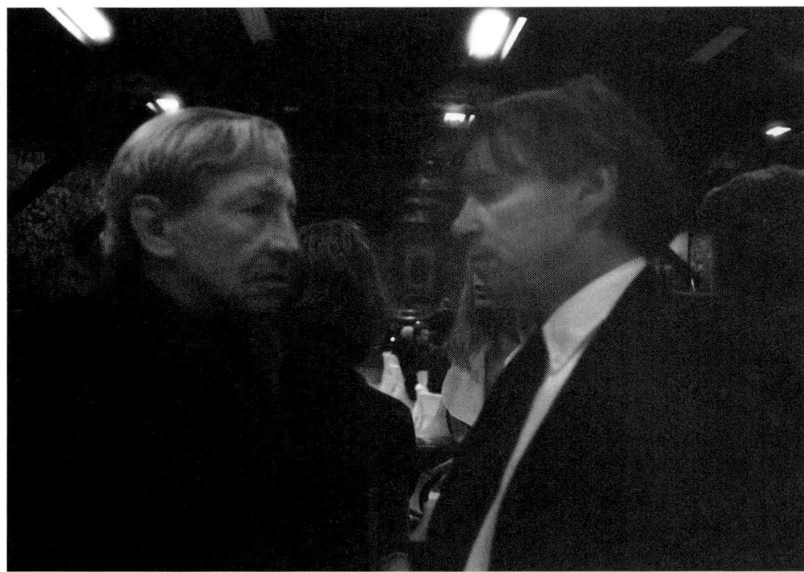

With Robert Rauschenberg, 1998

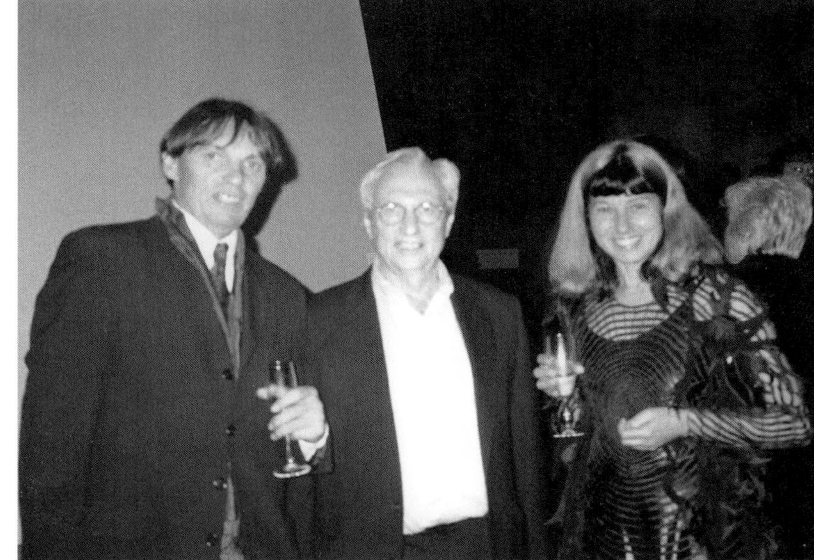

Braco and Nena Dimitrijević with Frank O. Gehry at the opening of the Guggenheim Museum, Bilbao, 1998

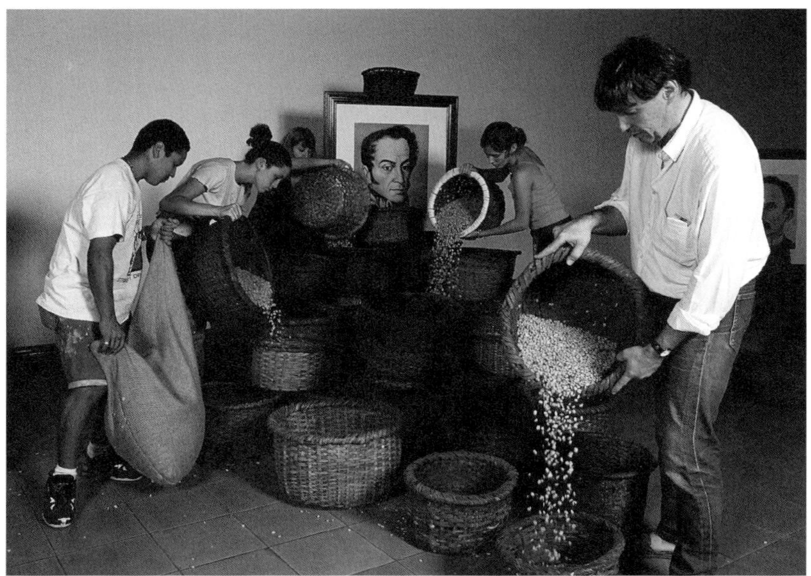

Preparing the exhibition at the Museo de Arte y Diseno Contemporaneo, San Jose, Costa Rica, 1998

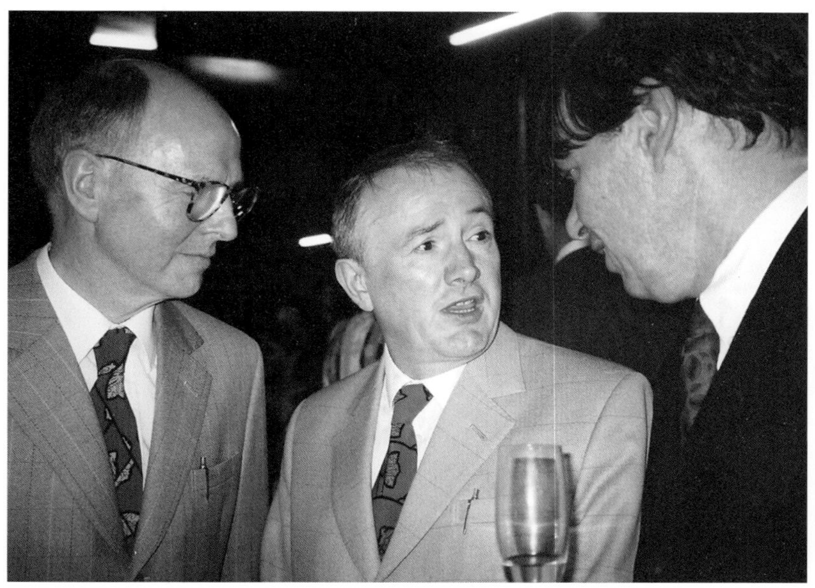

Gilbert and George, Braco Dimitrijević at the *Zeitweneden* exhibition, Bonn, 2000

Queen Sophia of Spain with Braco Dimitrijević at the First Bienal de Valencia, 2001

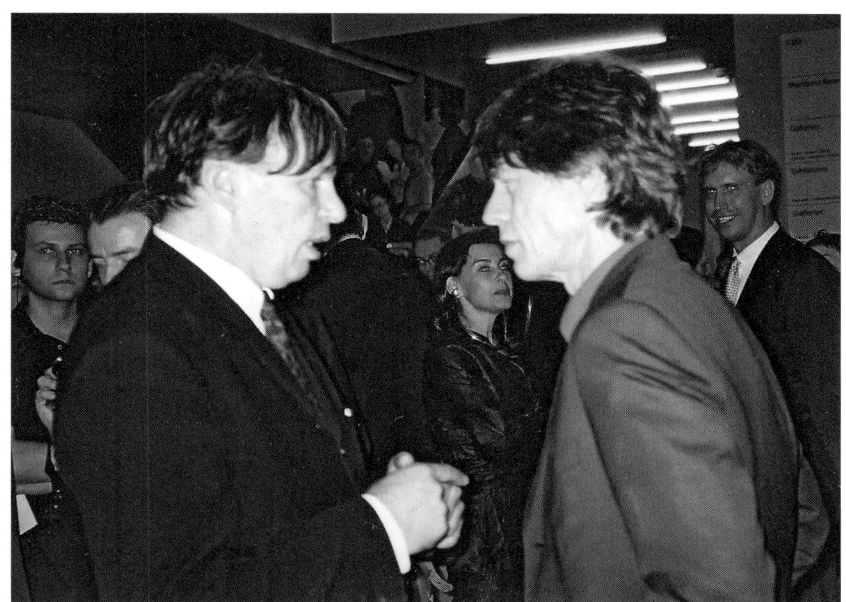

Braco Dimitrijević and Mick Jagger at the opening party for Tate Modern, London, 2001

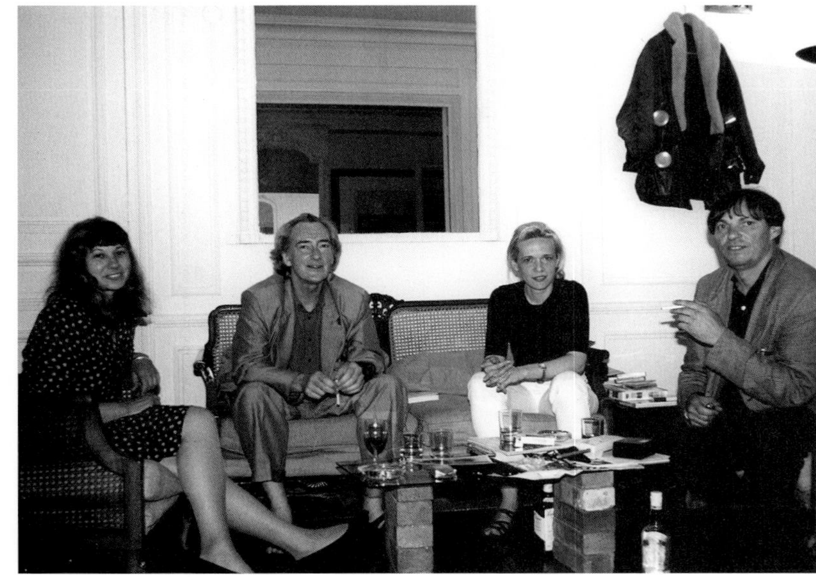

Nena Dimitrijević, Barry Flanagan, Katarina Predic, and Braco Dimitrijević, Paris, 1998

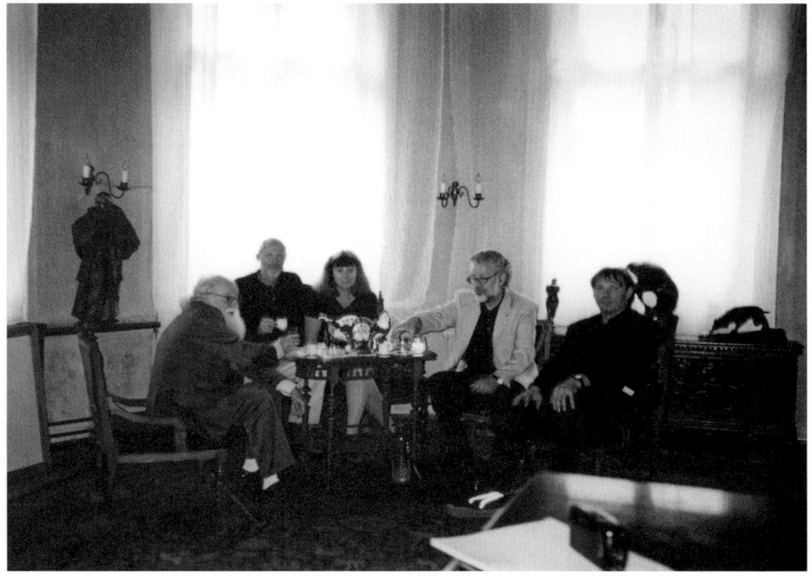

Pierre Restani, Lóránd Hegyi, Nena Dimitrijević, and Bruno Corà in the Dimitrijević family apartment, Sarajevo, 2000

Bozo Biskupic, Nena and Braco Dimitrijević, Zagreb, 2002

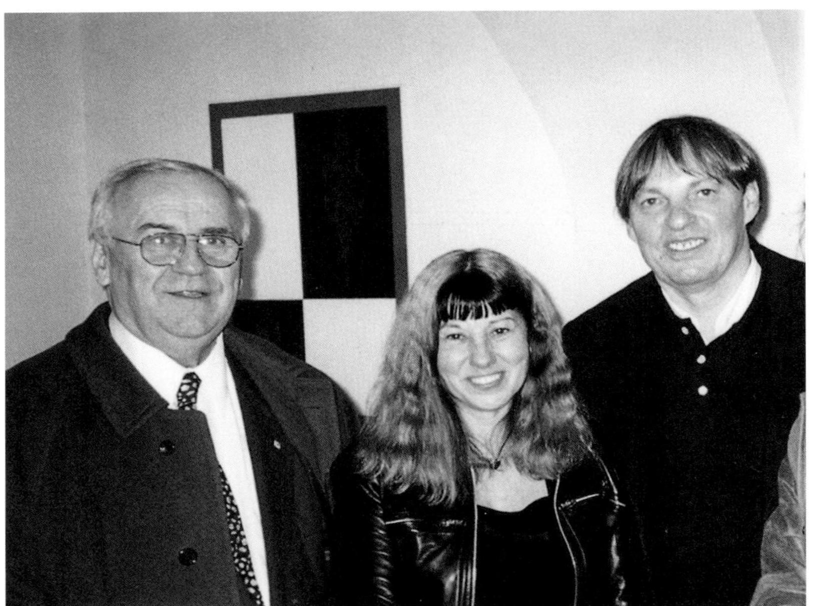

Zaha Hadid, Braco Dimitrijević, Massimilliano Fuksas, Hans Hollein, Architecture Biennale, Venice, 2000

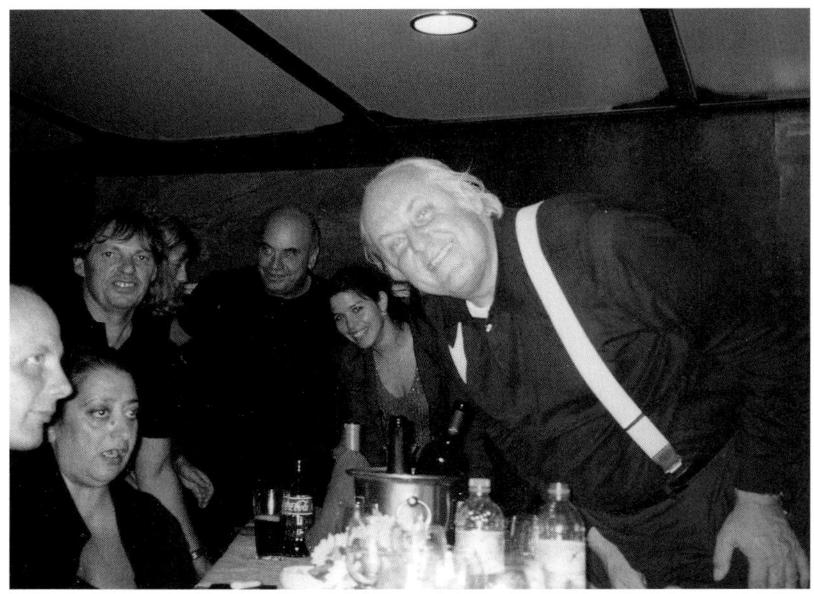

Braco Dimitrijević, Bob Wilson, Paris, 2001

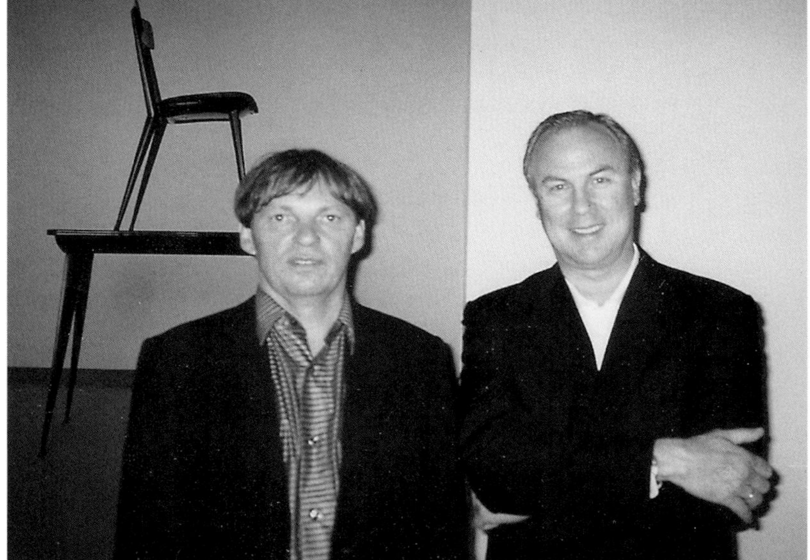

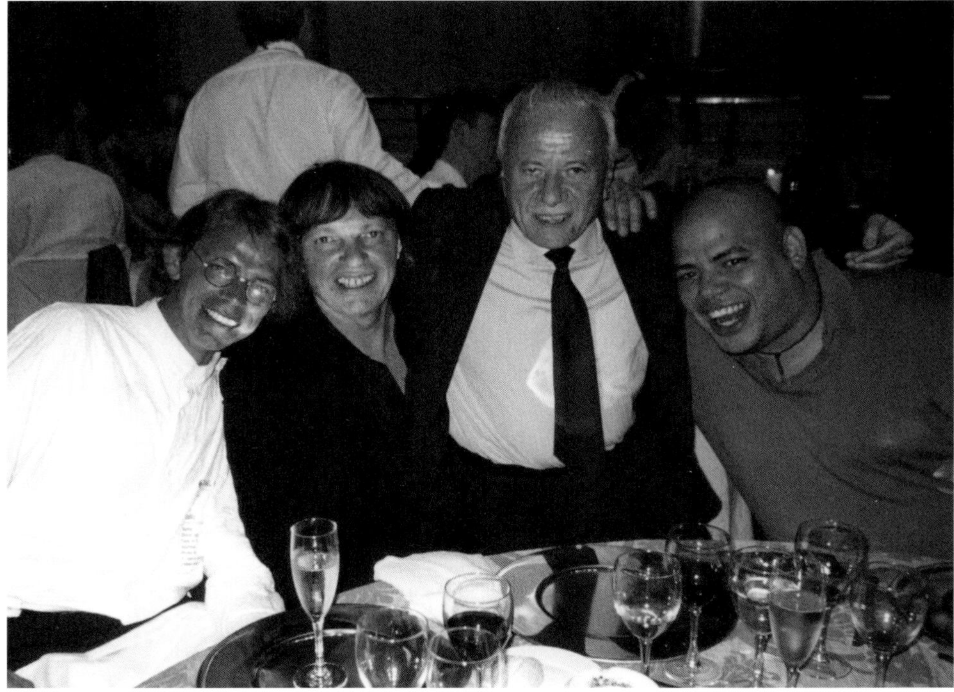

Africa, Braco Dimitrijević, Achille Bonito Oliva, and Kcho, Bienal de Valencia, 2001

Nena and Braco Dimitrijević, Jimmie Durham, Maria Teresa Alves, and Zelimir Koscevic, Zagreb, 2003

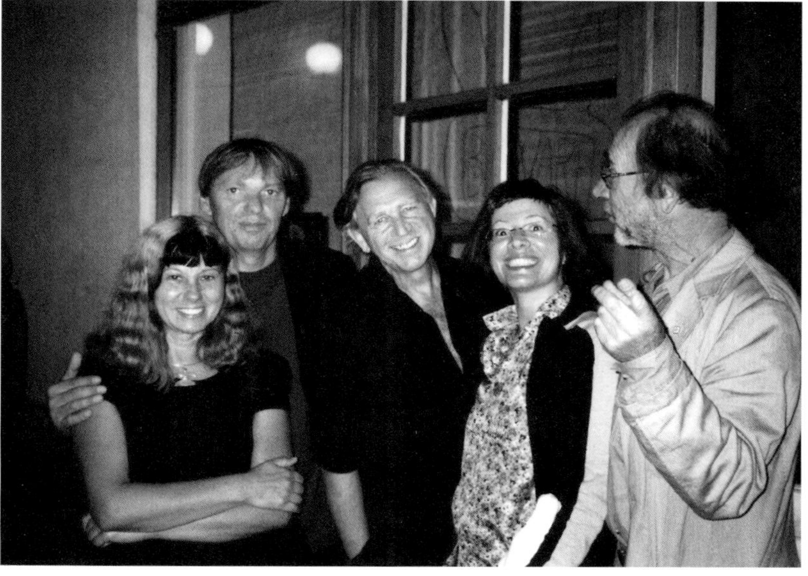

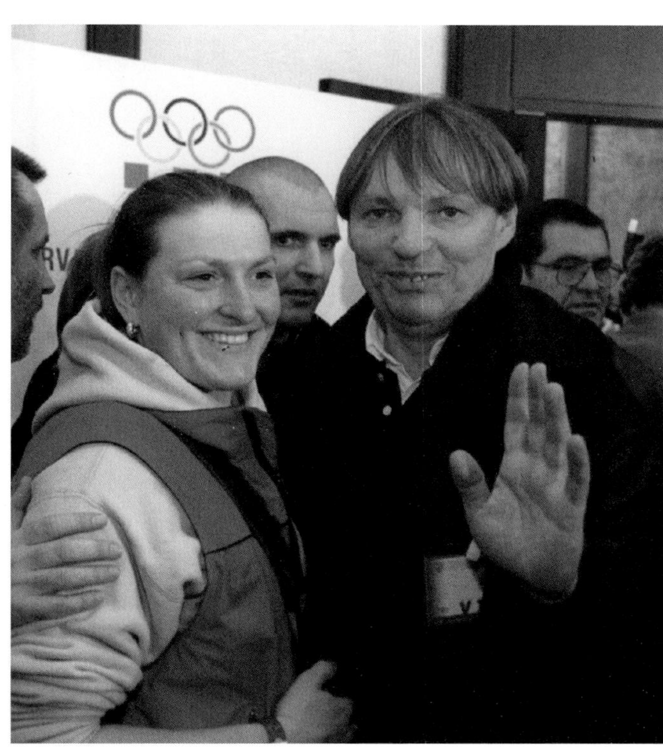

Janica Kostelić, after winning three Olympic gold medals at Salt Lake City, with Braco Dimitrijević, 2002

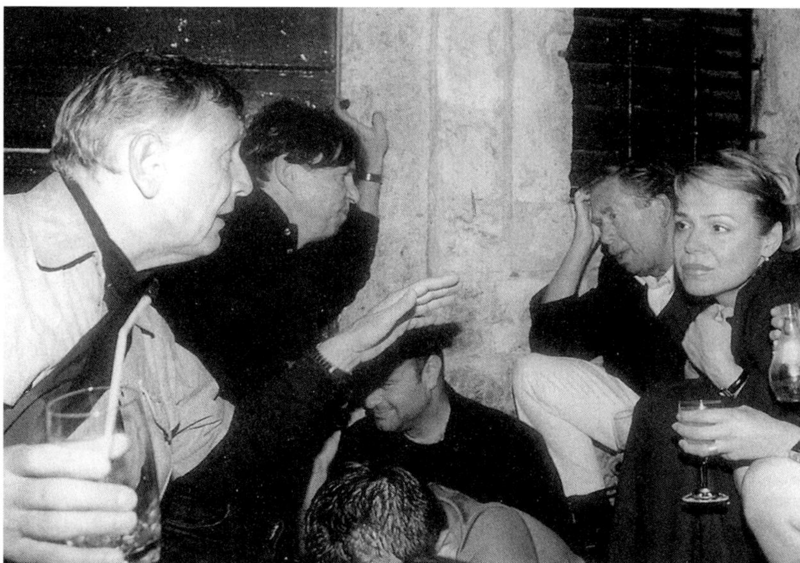

Vaclav Havel, Braco Dimitrijević, Jiri Menzel, and Mrs. Havel, Dubrovnik, 2001

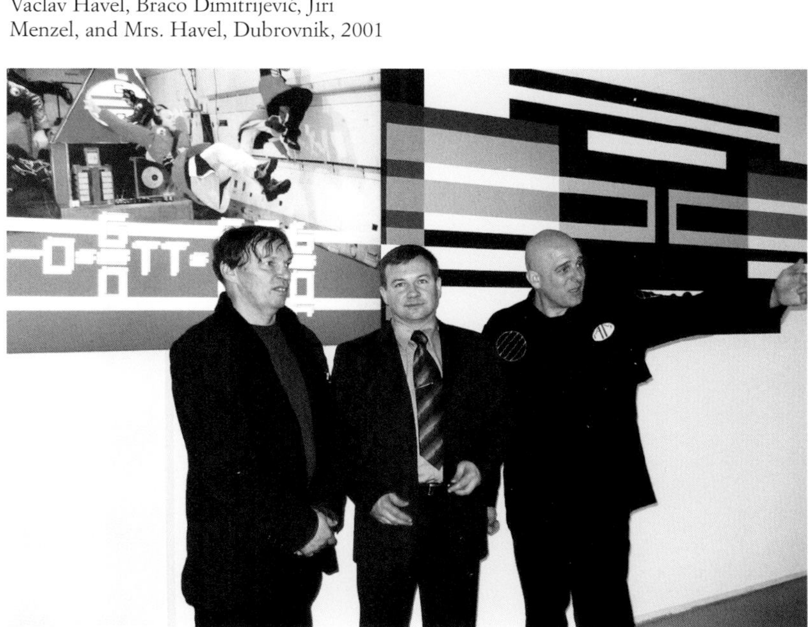

Braco Dimitrijević, Cosmonaut Yuri Lonchakov, Dragan Zivadinov, Zagreb, 2004

Teresa Gleadowe, Nena, Nicholas Serota, and Braco Dimitrijević, Hotel Excelsior, Dubrovnik, 2002

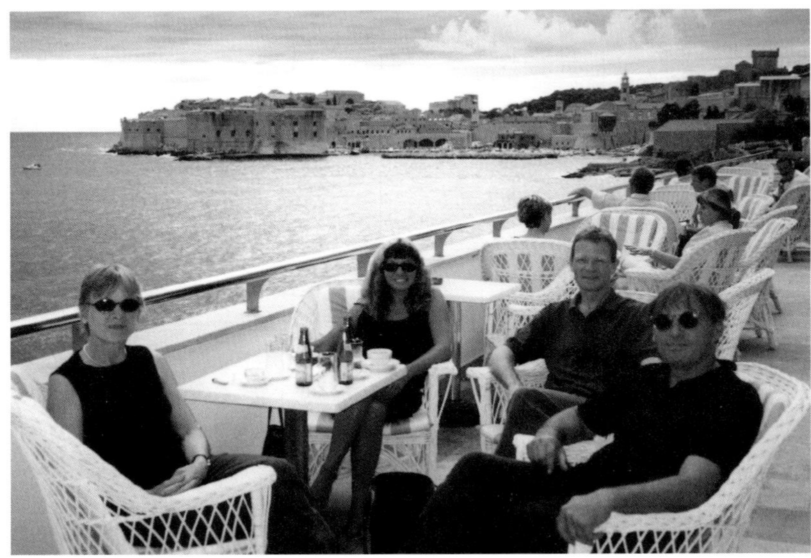

Jannis Kounellis, Michelle Coudray, Enver Hadziomerspahic, Nena and Braco at Braco Dimitrijević's retrospective, Museum of Modern Art, Dubrovnik, 2004

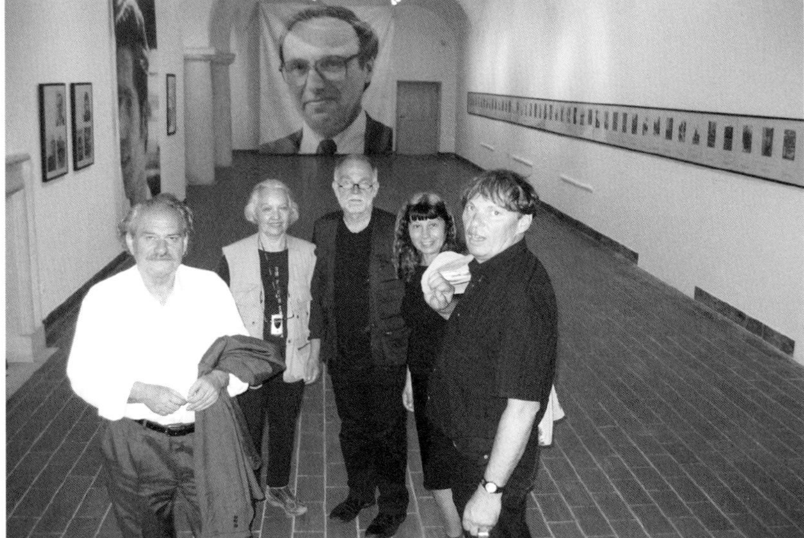

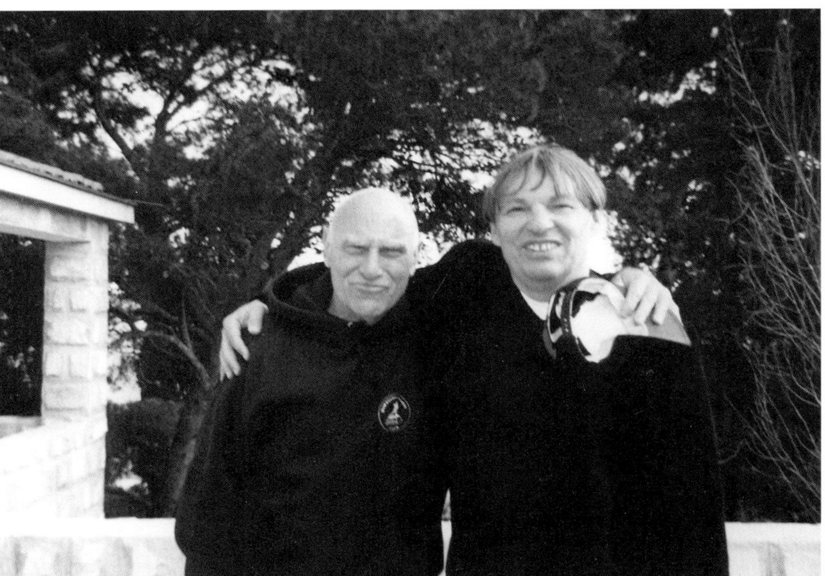

Richard Serra and Braco Dimitrijević, Dubrovnik, 2003

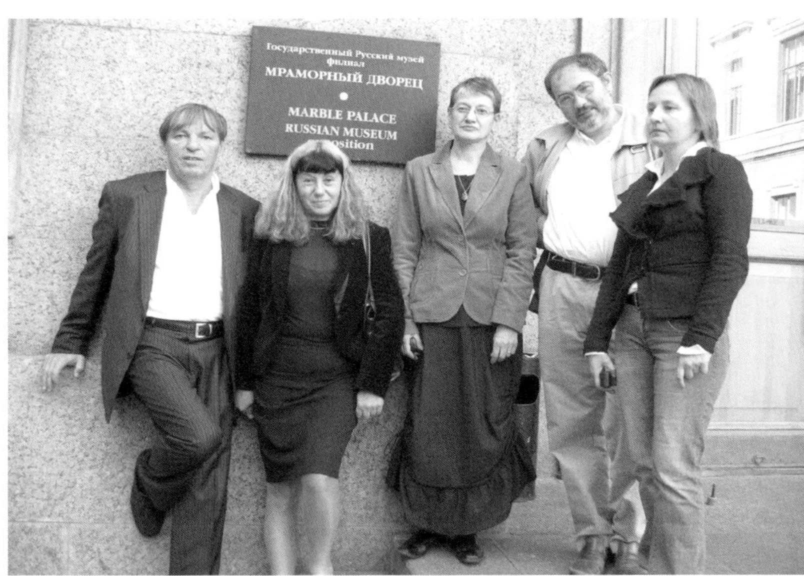

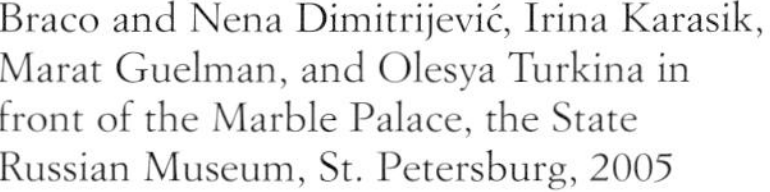

Braco and Nena Dimitrijević, Irina Karasik, Marat Guelman, and Olesya Turkina in front of the Marble Palace, the State Russian Museum, St. Petersburg, 2005

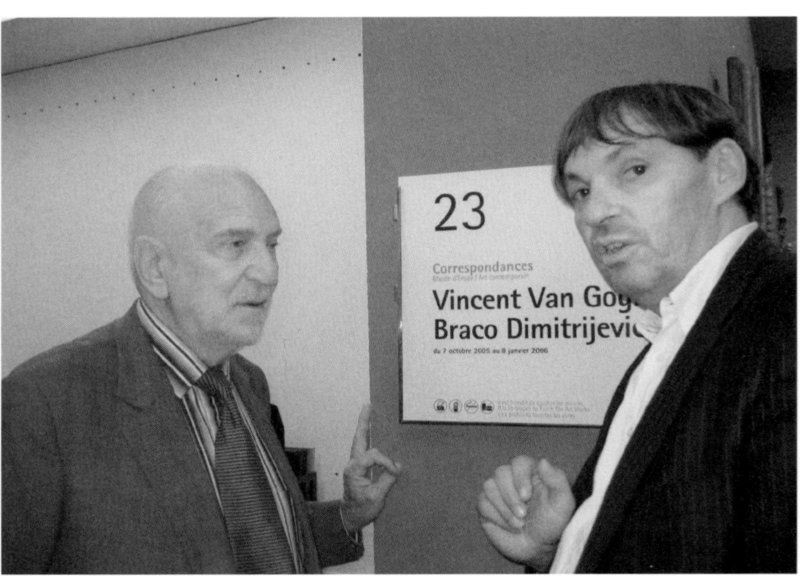

Anthony Caro and Braco Dimitrijević, Musée d'Orsay, Paris, 2005

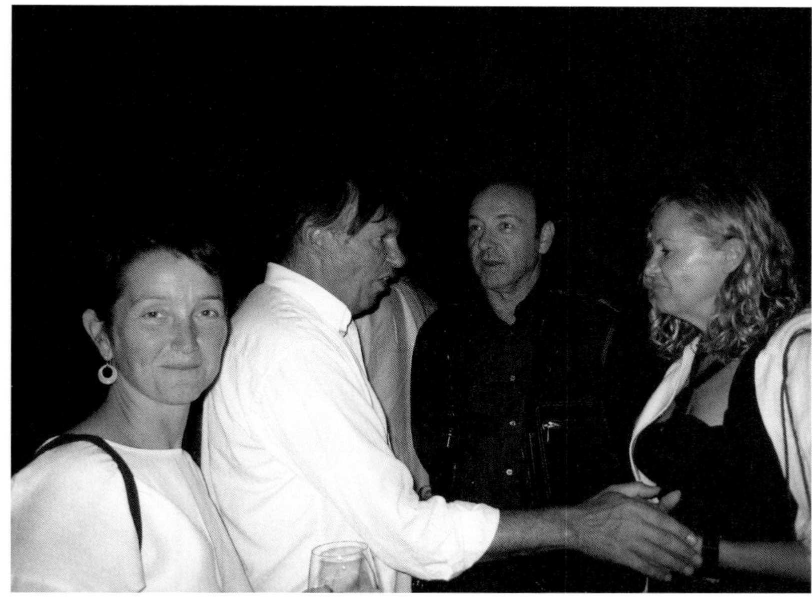

Frances Morris, Braco Dimitrijević, Kevin Spacey and Renate Strok, Dubrovnik, 2007

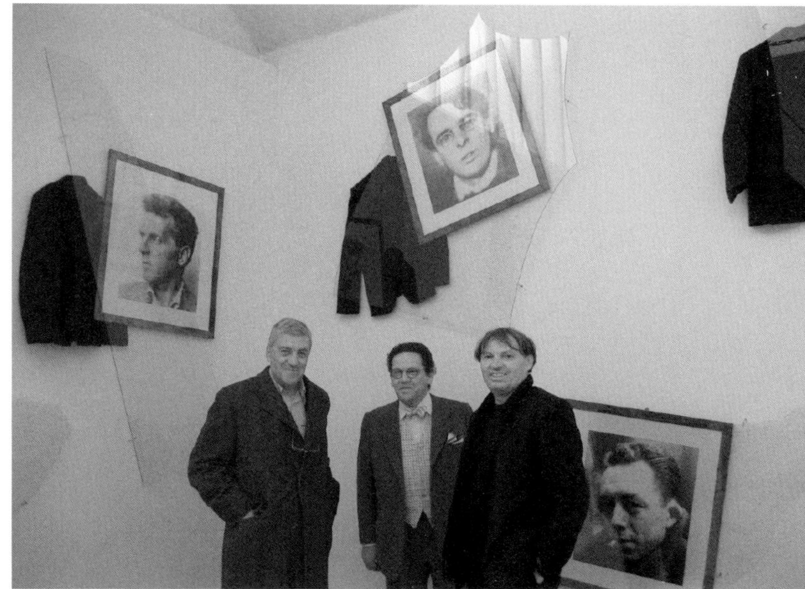

Nino Cerruti, Philippe Daverio, and Braco Dimitrijević, Fondazione Pria, Biella, 2005

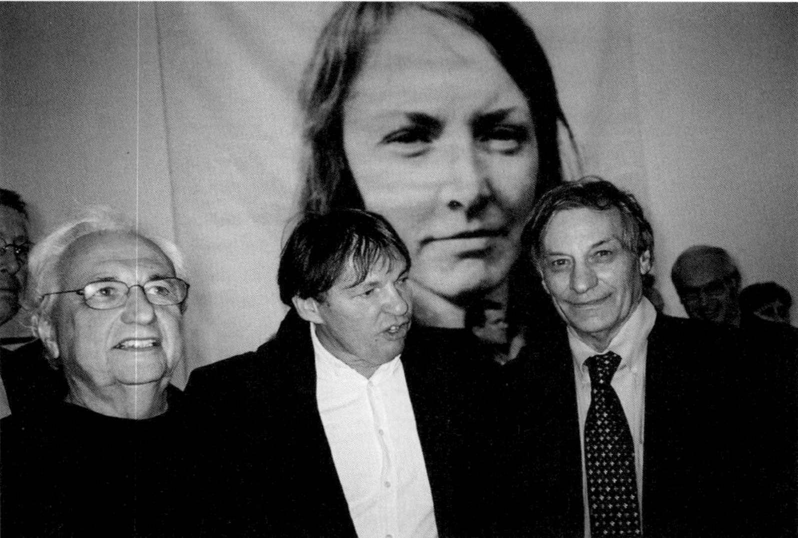

Frank O. Gehry, Braco Dimitrijević , and Jan Hoet at the opening of MARTA, Herford, 2005

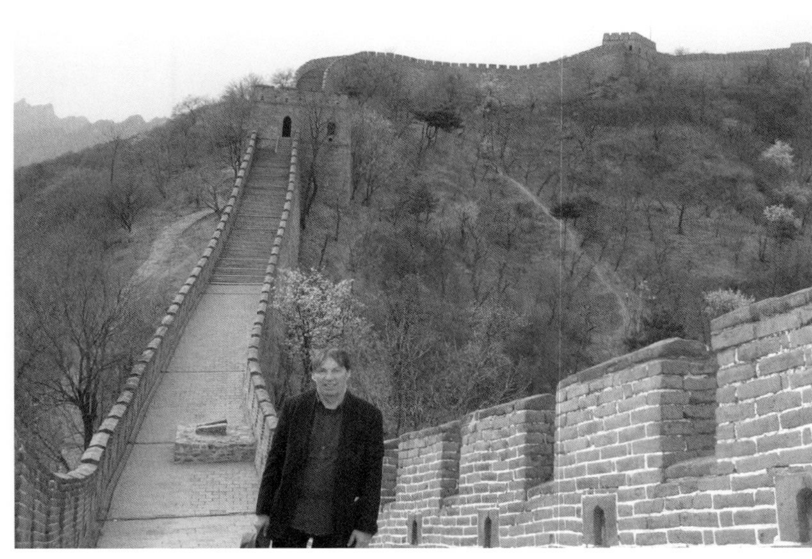

On the Great Wall, North China, 2006

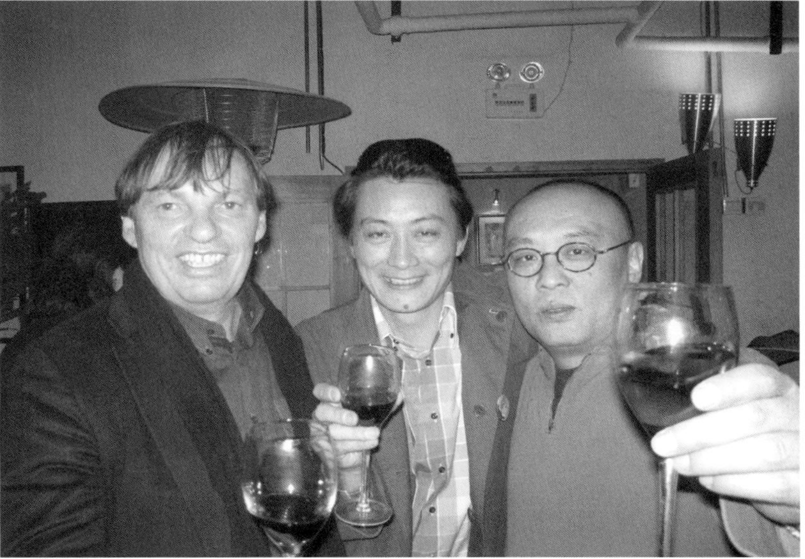

Braco Dimitrijević, Xin-Dong Cheng, Zhang Xiaogang, Peking 2006

Richard Hamilton and Braco Dimitrijević at the opening of "Duchamp – Man Ray – Picabia", Tate Modern London, 2008

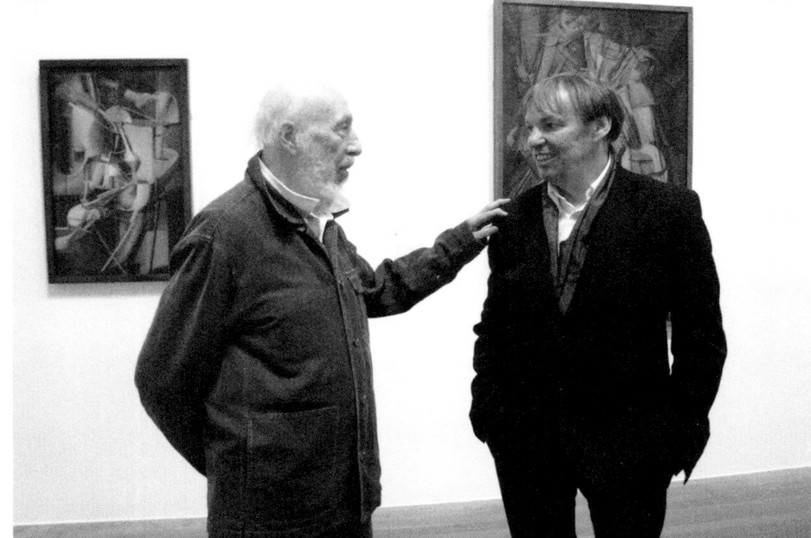

Braco Dimitrijević, Jan Fabre, HM Queen Paola of Belgium, Paris 2008

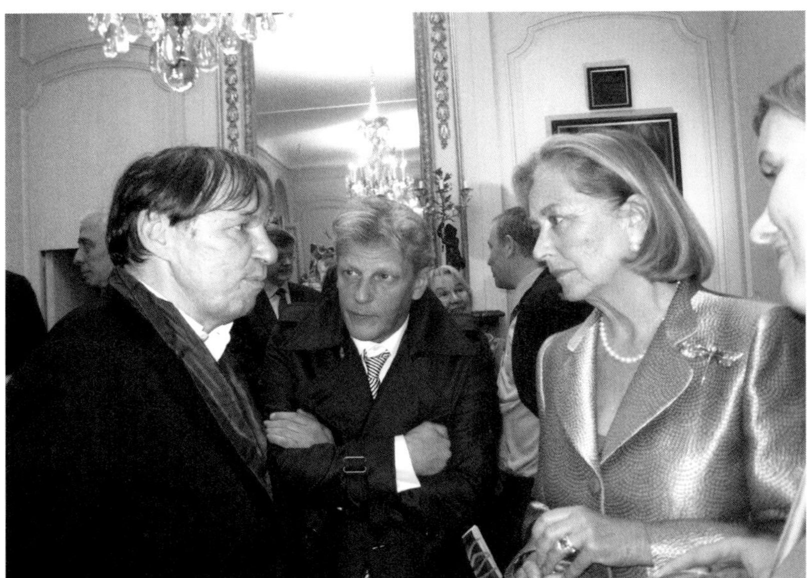

Osvaldo Romberg, Braco Dimitrijević and students at Philadelphia Academy of Fine Arts, 2007

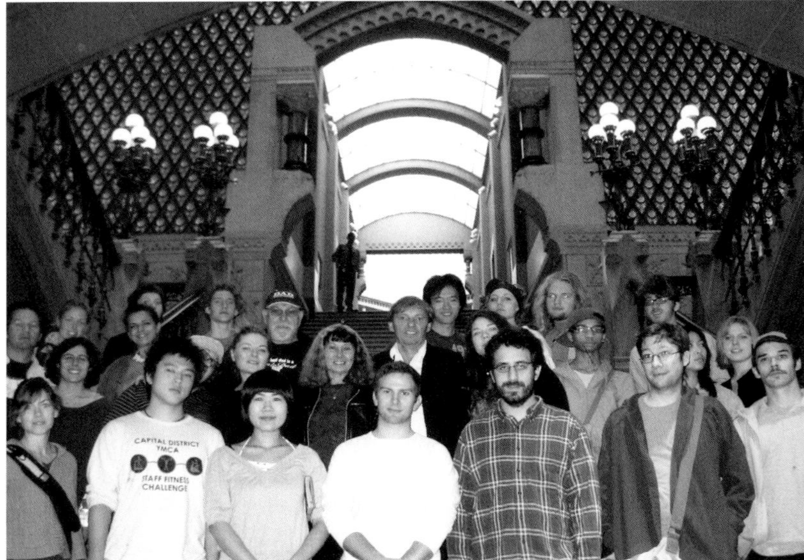

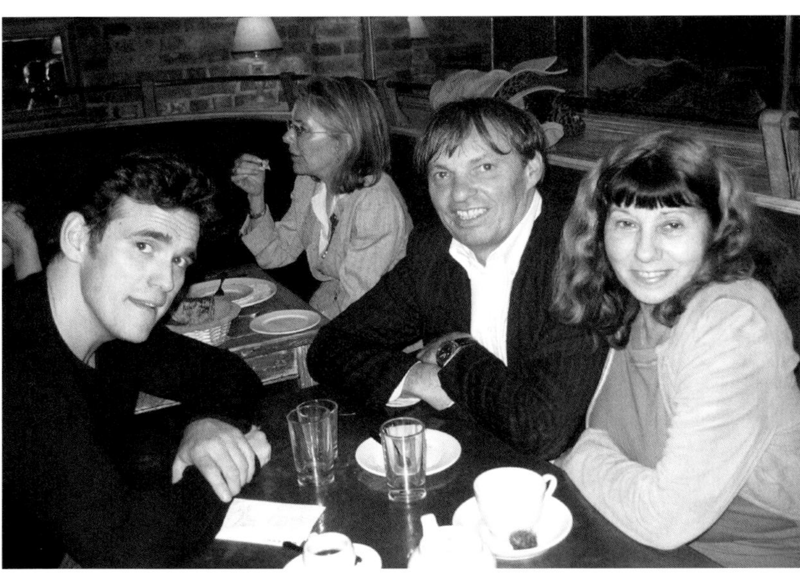

Matt Dillon, Braco Dimitrijević, Nena Dimitrijević, New York, 2007

Braco and Nena Dimitrijević, Aaron Levy, Laura Heffernan, Philadelphia 2007

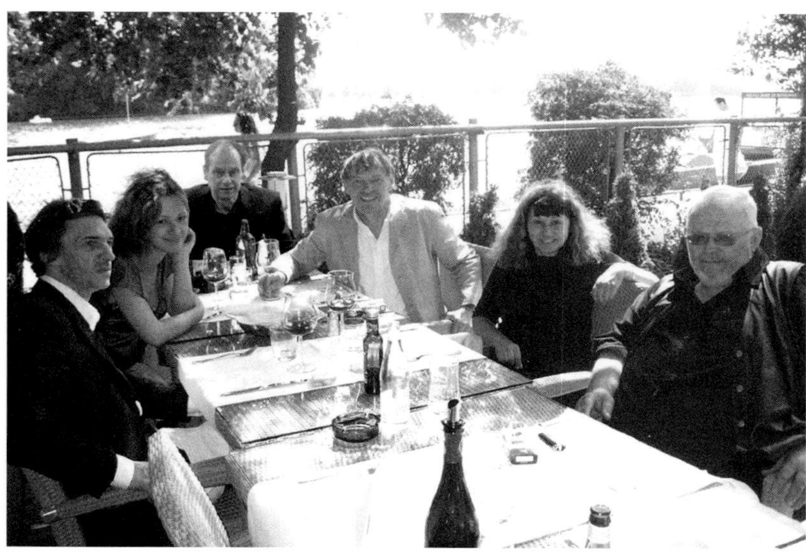

Nicolas Bourriaud, Sinziana Ravini,
Eric Fabre, Braco and Nena Dimitrijević,
Mihai Oroveanu, Bucharest 2008

Danilo Eccher, Erika Hoffmann,
Braco Dimitrijević, Barry
Flanagan, Opening of the
Retrospective at the Museum
Ludwig Budapest, 2008

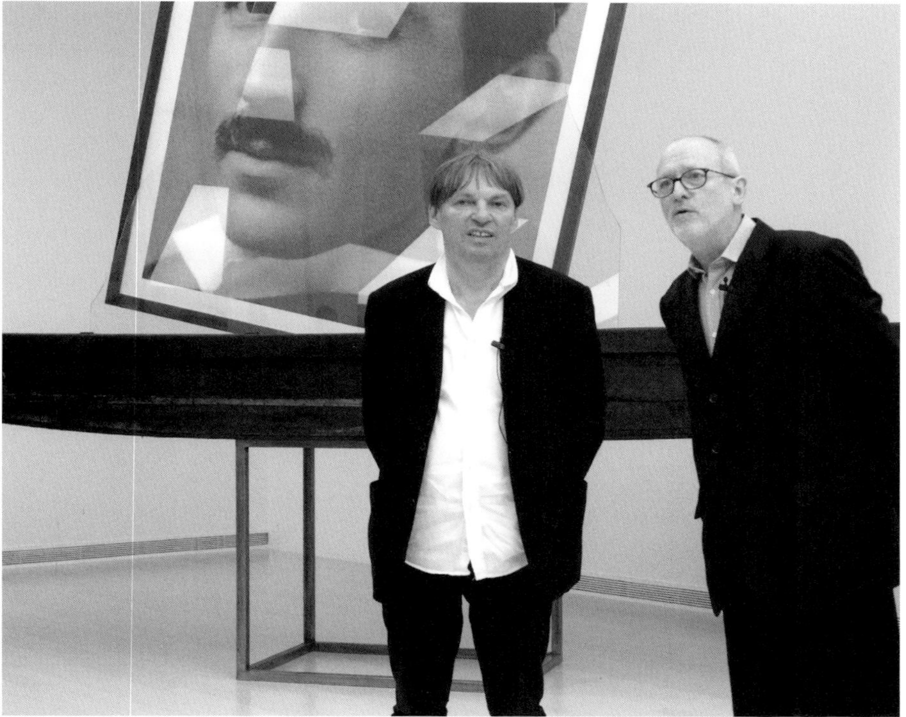

Braco Dimitrijević, Lorand Hegyi,
Museum Ludwig Budapest, 2008

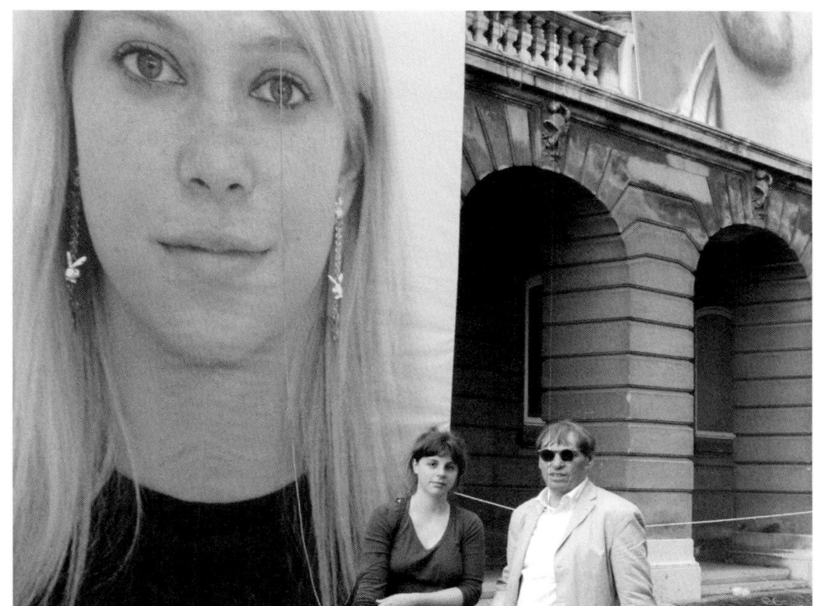

Ronna Kopezcky, Braco Dimitrijević,
Buda Castle, Budapest, 2008

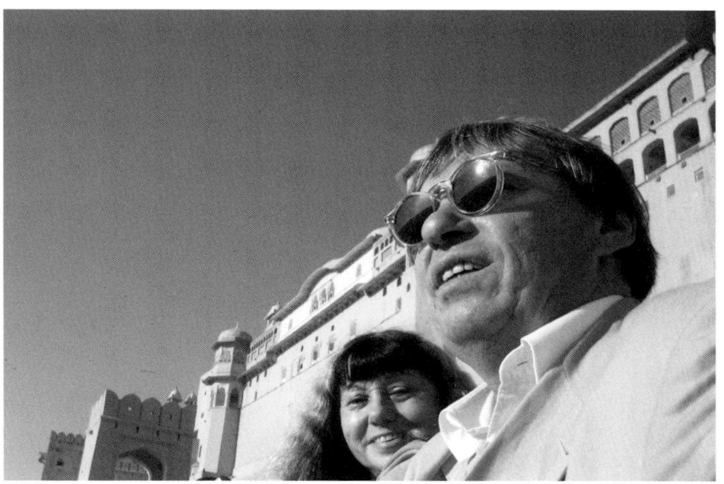

Jaipur, Rajasthan, India 2008

Appendix / Appendices

Biography / Biographie

BRACO DIMITRIJEVIĆ was born in Sarajevo in 1948. He had his first solo show in 1958 at the age of ten. From 1968 to 1971 he studied at the Academy of Fine Arts in Zagreb (MA). Between 1971 and 1973 he did post-graduate work at St Martin's School of Art in London. 1971 - 1972 British Council grant. 1976 - 1977 DAAD fellowship in Berlin. In 1978 received Prix Jean Dominique Ingres from Académie de Muséologie Evocatoire. 1978 received the Major Award from the Arts Council of Great Britain. 1992 received Knighthood for Arts - Chevalier des Arts et des Lettres in Paris. 2005, ABO d'Oro, Rome

BRACO DIMITRIJEVIĆ est né à Sarajevo en 1948. Sa première exposition personnelle a eu lieu en 1958, alors qu'il avait dix ans. Il a étudié à l'Académie des Beaux-Arts de Zagreb de 1968 à 1971. Il a ensuite passé son post-diplome à la St Martin's School of Art de Londres. 1971 - 1972 Bourse du British Council. 1976 - 1977 DAAD résidence à Berlin. En 1978 il a reçu le Prix Jean Dominique Ingres de l'Académie de Muséologie Evocatoire. En 1978 il a reçu le Grand Prix du Arts Council du Royaume-Uni. En 1992 il a été décoré de l'ordre des Chevaliers des Arts et des Lettres à Paris. En 2005, il reçut l'ABO d'Oro à Rome

Selected Solo Exhibitions / Expositions monographiques - Sélection

1969
Galerija SC, Zagreb

1971
Lucio Amelio, Naples

1972
Situation Gallery, London
Galerie Konrad Fischer, Düsseldorf

1973
Muzej Suvremene Umjetnosti, Zagreb

1974
Galleria Gian Enzo Sperone, Turin

1975
Sperone Gallery, New York
Robert Self Gallery, London
Stadtisches Museum Monchengladbach
Palais des Beaux-Arts, Brussels

1976
Galerie Rene Block, Berlin
Galleria Gian Enzo Sperone, Turin

1978
MTL Gallery, Brussels
Centre d'Art Contemporain, Geneva

1979
Institute of Contemporary Arts, London
Stedelijk van Abbemuseum, Eindhoven
Badischer Kunstverein, Karlsruhe

1981
Waddington Galleries, London

1984
Kunsthalle Bern, Bern
Museum Ludwig, Cologne

1985
Tate Gallery, London

1986
Hilman Holland Fine Arts, Atlanta, Georgia

1987
Wilhelm-Hack-Museum, Ludwigshafen
Galerie de Paris, Paris

1988
Outdoor Retrospective 1968–1988, Interim Art in collaboration with
Serpentine Gallery and Hayward Gallery, London
Nicole Klagsbrun, New York

1989
Galerie de Paris, Paris
Galerie Albert Baronian, Brussels
Queensland Art Gallery, Brisbane

1990
Pat Hearn Gallery, New York

1991
Fundacion San German, Puerto Rico
Galerie de Paris, Paris
Winnipeg Art Gallery, Canada

1992
Galerie Albert Baronian, Brussels

1994
Galerie de France, Paris
Museum Moderner Kunst Stiftung Ludwig, Vienna
The Israel Museum, Jerusalem

1995
Hessisches Landesmuseum Darmstadt

1996
Kunsthalle Düsseldorf, Düsseldorf

1998–1999
Galerie Michael Janssen, Cologne

2000
Museo Nacional de Colombia, Bogota
Porin Taidemuseo, Finland

2001
Museum of Contemporary Art and Museum Mimara, Zagreb
Ikon Gallery Birmingham, Birmingham

2003
Medievalmodern, London
Pièce Unique, Paris

2004
Galeria Pino Casagrande, Rome
Museum of Modern Art, Dubrovnik

2005
Fondazione Mudima, Milan
The State Russian Museum, St. Petersburg
Guelman Gallery, Moscow
Musée d'Orsay, Paris
Xin-Dong Cheng Space for Contemporary Art, Beijing
Imperial College of China - Temple of Confucius, Beijing
Galerija Zona, Zagreb

2006–2007
Galleria Il Ponte Contemporanea, Rome

Galleria Pino Casagrande, Rome
Slought Foundation, Philadelphia
1st Floor Gallery, Antwerp
Galerie Heike Curtze, Berlin

2008
National Museum of Contemporary Art, Bucharest
Galerie Heike Curtze, Vienna
Museum Ludwig, Budapest

2009
Musée d'Art Moderne, Saint-Etienne
Ca' Pesaro, 53rd Biennale di Venezia

Selected Group Exhibitions / Expositions de groupe - Sélection

1971
Biennale de Paris
At the Moment, Haustor Frankopanska 2a, Zagreb

1972
Documenta V, Kassel

1973
Contemporanea, Rome

1974
Projekt 74, Walraf Richartz Museum and Kunsthalle, Cologne

1976
Venice Biennale

1977
Documenta VI, Kassel

1978
Biennale of Sydney

1980
Kunst in Europa nach '68, Museum van Hedendaagse Kunst, Ghent
British Art 1940–1980, Hayward Gallery, London

1982
Venice Biennale
Aspects of British Art Today, Metropolitan Museum, Tokyo

1983
New Art, Tate Gallery, London

1985
Promenades, Centre d'Art Contemporain, Geneva

1986
Biennale of Sydney
Terrae Motus, Fondazione Lucio Amelio, Naples

1989
Magiciens de la Terre, Musée National d'Art Moderne, Centre Georges Pompidou, Paris
Prospect 89, Frankfurter Kunstverein and Kunsthalle, Frankfurt

1990
Casino Fantasma, P.S.1 Contemporary Art Center, New York
Venice Biennale
Rhetorical Image, New Museum of Contemporary Art, New York
Life-Size, The Israel Museum, Jerusalem

1992
Documenta IX, Kassel
Manifeste, Musée National d'Art Moderne, Centre Georges Pompidou, Paris

1993
Venice Biennale

1994
Europa-Europa, Bundeskunsthalle, Bonn

1995
SITE Santa Fe, New Mexico
Kwangju Biennial, Korea
Unser Jahrhundert, Museum Ludwig, Cologne

1996
Bienal de São Paulo

1997
Bienal de la Habana
Made in France 1947-1997, Musée National d'Art Moderne, Centre Georges Pompidou, Paris

1998
Hommages. Hommes illustres , héros et hommes du commun, Espace culturel François Mitterrand, Périgueux, France

1999
Global Conceptualism, Queens Museum, New York
Les Champs de la sculpture 2000, Champs-Élysées, Paris

2000
Zeitwenden: Ruckblick und Ausblick, Kunstmuseum, Bonn
L'Autre moitié de l'Europe, Galerie Nationale du Jeu de Paume, Paris
D'après l'antique, Musée du Louvre, Paris

2001
Valencia Biennial

2002
Cetinje Biennale, Montenegro

2003
Blut und Honig, Sammlung Essl, Vienna
In den Schluchten des Balkan, Kunsthalle Friedericianum, Kassel

2004
Passage d'Europe, Musée d'Art Moderne, Saint-Étienne
An Other Epistemology, Slought Foundation, Philadelphia
Open Systems: Rethinking Art c. 1970, Tate Modern London
My Private Heroes, MARTA Herford, Herford
Big Bang, Musée National d'Art Moderne, Centre Georges Pompidou Paris

2006
Conflicts, Slought Foundation, Philadelphia
Force de l'Art, Grand Palais, Paris
Belgrader Oktober Salon, Belgrade
Crossing Frontiers Grenzganger, Kunstforum Ostdeutsche Galerie Regensburg
Fremd bin Ich eingezogen, Kunsthalle Fridericianum, Kassel

2006–2007
Busy Going Crazy, The Parlestein Collection, La Maison Rouge, Paris

2007
Intramoenia Extrart, Castelli di Puglia, Italy

2008
Interiors, Oredaria, Rome
Octobar Salon, Belgrade
Who killed the painting?, Neueus Museum, Nürnberg
Poznan Biennale, Poland

2009
Venice Biennale
Moscow Biennale

Bibliography / Bibliographie

Monographs - Catalogues of Solo Exhibition and Artist's Books / Monographies - Catalogues d'expositions monographiques et Livres d'artistes

1969
Galerija SC, Zagreb. Text by Braco Dimitrijević

1973
Museum of Contemporary Art Zagreb. Texts by Caroline Tisdall and Braco Dimitrijević

1974
Interview-Interview, Galerija SC and SKC, Zagreb/Belgrade

1975
Stadtisches Museum Monchengladbach. Text by Johannes Cladders

1976
Tale of an Artist and a Castle, Kabinett fur aktuelle Kunst, Bremerhaven and DAAD Berlin
Tractatus Post Historicus, Edition Dacic, Tubingen

1978
Self-Portraits after Rembrandt and Miguel Perez, Centre d'Art Contemporain and Ecart Publications, Geneva

1979
An Obelisk beyond History - Ein Obelisk jenseits von Geschichte. Text by Thomas Deecke, DAAD Berlin

1979
Stedelijk van Abbemuseum Eindhoven. Text by Rudi Fuchs
Institute of Contemporary Arts London. Text by Sarah Kent
Arbeiten/Works 1968-1978, Badischer Kunstverein Karlsruhe. Texts by Michael Schwarz and Manfred Schmalriede
Kunsthalle Tubingen. Text by Clara Weyergraf-Serra

1981
Waddington Galleries London. Text by David Brown

1982
Deweer Art Gallery. Text by Jan Hoet

1984
Culturescapes 1976-1984, Museum Ludwig, Cologne/Kunsthalle, Bern. Text by Evelyn Weiss. Interview by Jean-Hubert Martin

1985
Triptychos Post Historicus, Tate Gallery London. Text by David Brown

1987
Fur/For Malewitsch, Mondrian, Einstein, Wilhelm-Hack-Museum Ludwigshafen. Texts by Bernhard Holeczek, Richard Gassen, Lida von Mendgen. Interview by Judith Aminoff

1989
Consortium Dijon, La Criée Rennes, DRAG Limousin. Texts by Joel Benzakin and Guy Tortosa
Institute of Modern Art and Queensland Art Gallery, Brisbane. Text by Sue Cramer

1990
Life of Braco Dimitrijević, Ronny van der Velde Gallery, Antwerp. Text by Jonathan Watkins

1991
Dimension Dimitrijević: Rooms and Thoughts, Municipal Art Gallery, Piran. Interview by Frank Perrin and Olivier Zahm

1994
Slow as Light, Fast as Thought, Museum Moderner Kunst Stiftung Ludwig, Vienna. Texts by Lóránd Hegyi, Dan Cameron, Catherine Millet, Adrian Morris
Histoires de Prix Nobel, Braco Dimitrijević, Editions de la Tempete, Paris

1995
Against Historic Sense of Gravity, Hessisches Landesmuseum, Darmstadt. Text by Nena Dimitrijević. Interview by Klaus D. Pohl

1996
Konstellationen, Kunsthalle, Düsseldorf. Text by Jurgen Harten
The Man of Lascaux, Moderna Galerija, Ljubljana. Text by Braco Dimitrijević. Interview by Jean-Hubert Martin

1998
Braco Dimitrijević- Les transmemoriaux, Editions du Regard, Paris. Text by Michel Gauthier

2001
Braco Dimitrijević, Museum of Contemporary Art and Museum Mimara, Zagreb. Texts by Želimir Koščević and Nada Beros

2002
Braco Dimitrijević Triptychos Post Historicus, Ikon Gallery and The Barber Institute of Fine Arts, Birmingham. Texts by Jonathan Watkins, Richard Cork, Richard Verdi

2004
Braco Dimitrijević, Museum of Modern Art, Dubrovnik. Texts by Antun Maracic, Dan Cameron, Nena Dimitrijević, Cornelia Lauf, Adrian Morris. Interview by Klaus D. Pohl
Braco Dimitrijević, Studio d'Arte Contemporanea Pino Casagrande, Rome. Texts by Achille Bonito Oliva, Marco Delogu, Ana Janevski, Stefano Marson

2005
Braco Dimitrijević/Vincent van Gogh, Musée d'Orsay, Paris. Texts by Achille Bonito Oliva, Olivier Gabet. Interview by Michel Gauthier

2006
Braco Dimitrijević - Monograph, Edizioni Charta, Milan. Texts by Dan Cameron, Achille Bonito Oliva, Jean-Hubert Martin, Cornelia Lauf, Nena Dimitrijević, Irina Karasik, Olesya Turkina
Braco Dimitrijević: Truly Global, Xin-Dong Cheng Publishing House, Beijing. Texts by Achille Bonito Oliva, Lynn Gumpert, Nena Dimitrijević

2008
Braco Dimitrijević: Louvre is my studio, street is my museum, National Museum of Contemporary Art, Bucharest and Museum Ludwig, Budapest. Texts by Achille Bonito Oliva, Nicolas Bourriaud, Magda Carneci, Lóránd Hegyi
Braco Dimitrijević: Museum Ludwig Budapest, museum brochure text by Rona Kopeczky

2009
Braco Dimitrijević: Tractatus Post Historicus, 1976. Republished by Slought Foundation and University of Pennsylvania, Philadelphia.

With critical commentary by Nicolas Bourriaud, Dan Cameron, Nena Dimitrijević, Lóránd Hegyi, Zelimir Koscevic, Cornelia Lauf, Aaron Levy, Jeasn-Hubert Martin, Catherine Millet, Achille Bonito Oliva, Klaus D. Pohl, Osvaldo Romberg

Periodicals - Monographic Articles and Essays by the Artist / Revues - Articles monographiques et articles de l'artiste

Braco Dimitrijević, "Casual Passers-by I met," *Avalanche*, no. 5, summer 1972

Braco Dimitrijević, "Towards a New Way of Behaviour," *Studio International*, vol. 187, no. 963, February 1974

Braco Dimitrijević, "My Mind Is between Sociology and Sculpture," *Flash Art* no. 46–47, June 1974

David Quinn, "Braco Dimitrijević: *Triptychos Post Historicus* at the ICA," *Aspects Magazine*, fall 1979

Jean-Hubert Martin, "Entretien avec Braco Dimitrijević," *Arte Factum*, 1984

Duan Sabo, "Braco Dimitrijević," *Flash Art*, no. 123, summer 1985

Judith Aminoff, "Dix années de Post-Histoire: le Tractatus Post Historicus revisité," *Des Arts*, no. 5, winter 1986–1987

Želimir Koščević, "Interview with Braco Dimitrijević," NIKE, no. 28, June 1989

Evelyn Weiss, "On the Works of Braco Dimitrijević," *Magazine C*, no. 23, fall 1989

Olivier Zahm, "Braco Dimitrijević: La beauté sera contemporaine," *Art Press*, no. 144, February 1990

Mona Thomas, "Braco Dimitrijević," *Beaux Arts*, no. 77, March 1990

Lynn Gumpert, "Braco Dimitrijević-Accidental History," *Art in America*, no. 6, June 1991

Braco Dimitrijević, "Three Museum Exhibitions," *Blocnotes*, no. 1, 1993

Braco Dimitrijević, "Histoires de Prix Nobel – Nobel Prize Stories," *Art Press*, no. 193, July–August 1994

Jean-Hubert Martin, "Braco Dimitrijević: Louvre Is My Studio, Street Is My Museum," *Flash Art*, vol. XXIX, no. 186, January–February 1996

Doris von Drathen, "Braco Dimitrijević: Leonardo und die Mitstgabel," *Kunstforum International*, vol. 135, October 1996–January 1997, pp. 296–311.

Catherine Millet, "Braco Dimitrijević: les animaux devant les tableaux Nature Meets Culture," *Art Press*, no. 238, September 1998

Braco Dimitrijević, *Komersant*, St. Petersburg, September 2005

Braco Dimitrijević, *Afisha Magazine*, no. 17, St. Petersburg, October 2005

Catharina Manchanda, *Staging History*, History of Photography, Spring 2007

Braco Dimitrijević, "Louvre is my Studio, Street is my Museum," Naoko Kaltschmidt Springerin, Band XIV, Heft 3, Wien, Summer 2008

Catherine Millet, "Interview with Braco Dimitrijević," *Art Press*, Paris, May 2009

Braco Dimitrijević features in the following recent Books and Publications / Braco Dimitrijević est mentionné dans les articles, livres, et récentes publications suivants

La Collection, Musée National d'Art Moderne, Centre Georges Pompidou, Paris, 1997

Catherine Millet, *L'Art Contemporain,* Paris, 1998

Lóránd Hegyi, *50 Jahre Kunst aus Mitteleuropa 1949 -1999,* Museum Moderner Kunst Stiftung Ludwig, Vienna, 1999

Gian Enzo Sperone - 35 Years of Exhibitions in Europe and America, Hopeful Monster, Turin, 1999

Global Conceptualism: Points of Origin, 1950s–1980s, Queens Museum of Art, New York, 1999

Achille Bonito Oliva, *A bordo dell'arte,* Skira, Milan, 2000

Conceptual Art, Phaidon, London, 2002

Primary Documents, The Museum of Modern Art, New York, 2002

Giulio Carlo Argan and Achille Bonito Oliva, *L'Arte Moderna, L'Arte oltre il Duemila*, Sansoni, Florence, 2003

Richard Cork, *Everything Seemed Possible. Art in the 1970s,* Yale University Press, New Haven, 2003

Catherine Millet, *L'Art contemporain – Histoire et geographie*, Flammarion, Paris, 2006

Thomas Heyden, *Who killed the painting?*, Neues Museum, Nürnberg, 2008–2009

Brandon Taylor, *Art Today*, Laurence King Publishing Ltd., London, 2005

Donna de Salvo (ed.), *Open Systems: Rethinking Art c. 70*, Tate Modern, London, 2005

David Rosenberg, *The Perlstein Collection*, Ludion, Ghent, 2006

Sandy Nairne, *Portrait Now*, National Portrait Gallery, London, 2006

Lóránd Hegyi, *Fragillita del narativo*, Skira, Milan, 2007

Photographies – La Collection Neuflize Vie, Flamarion, Paris 2007

Rene Block and Maruis Babias (eds.), *The Balkan Trilogy*, Kunsthalle Fridericianum and Verlag Silke Schreiber, Munich, 2007

Achille Bonito Oliva, *Artisti Solitari - Uno sguardo dal ponte sul terzo millenio,* Silvana Editoriale, Milan, 2008

Nadia Candet, *Collections particulières,* Flamarion, Paris, 2008

Kenneth Hayes, *Milk and Melancholy*, Prefix Institute of Contemporary Art, Toronto, 2009

Videography / Vidéographie

1971
Metabolysm As A Body Work, 2 min

1974–2004
Interview/ Interview, 10 min 7 sec

1975–2006
Geography of Art, 12 min 40 sec

1979
Teaching An Egg To Fly, 4 min

1983
Four Culturescapes, 8 min 25 sec

1988
Meeting With The Avant-Gardes,
2 min

2006
The Resurrection Of Alchemists,
2 min

2008
About Two Professions, 2 min 40 sec
Censored, 5 min 27 sec
Democracy, 6 min
Divine Strokes, 3 min 40 sec

2009
The Century Behind Me – One Second Of Post Historic Time, 4 min
The Picture Show, 2 min

Selected Filmography / Filmographie

1957
Braco Dimitrijević – Little Painter, 20 min, 35 mm
Directed by Siba Krvavac
Filmske Novosti, Sarajevo

1971
At The Moment, 15 Min, 16 mm
Directed by Vladimir Petek, Zagreb

1973
Braco Dimitrijević At Museum Of Contemporary Art, 20 min, 16 mm
Directed by Vladimir Petek, Zagreb

1988
Great Expectations, 111 min
Directed by Alfonso Cuaron
Written by Charles Dickens, Michael Glazer, and Braco *Dimitrijević*
Twentieth-Century Fox Film Corporation
Distributed by Twentieth-Century Fox

2006
Tesla – Despite History, 43 min
Directed, written, and narrated by Braco Dimitrijević
Motion R Pictures

2008
Braco Dimitrijević: Louvre Is My Studio, Street Is My Museum,
82 min
Narrated by Philip Talbot
Directed by Gordana Brzovic
Music by Malcolm Mclaren
Motion R Pictures

Works in Public Collections / Oeuvres dans les collections publiques

Tate Gallery, London
Museum of Modern Art, New York
Musée National d'Art Moderne, Centre Georges Pompidou, Paris
Fonds National d'Art Contemporain, Paris
Arts Council of Great Britain
Contemporary Art Society, London
Stedelijk van Abbemuseum, Eindhoven
Scottish National Gallery of Modern Art, Edinburgh
Museum Ludwig, Cologne
MAMCO, Geneva
Stadtiches Museum Abteiberg, Monchengladcbah
SMAK, Ghent
Kunstmuseum, Bern
Israel Museum, Jerusalem
Hessisches Landesmuseum, Darmstadt
Kunsthalle, Bern
Museum of Contemporary Art, Zagreb
Neues Museum, Nürnberg
Cincinnati Museum of Art, Ohio
City of Cologne
Centre d'Art Contemporain, Geneva
Museum of Contemporary Art, Belgrade
City of Geilo, Norway
Museum and Garden Charlottenburg, Berlin
Musée Saint-Denis, Reims
Moderna Museet Beijer Collection, Stockholm
Kunstinstitut, Ghent
Wilhelm-Hack-Museum, Ludwigshaven
Dutch Art Line, Holland
Museum van Hedendaagse Kunst Antwerpen, Antwerp
Fonds Regional d'Art Contemporain du Pays de la Loire
Fonds Regional d'Art Contemporain, Limousin
Fonds Regional d'Art Contemporain Lorraine
Chateau d'Oiron, France
Museum Moderner Kunst (MUMOK), Vienna
State Russian Museum, St. Petersburg
Sammlung Essl, Vienna
City of Ussel, France
City of Saint-Claude
Museum of Fine Arts, Santa Fe, New Mexico
Terrae Motus, Naples
Museo d'Arte Contemporanea, Trevi
Ludwig Museum, Budapest
Moderna Gelerija (Museum of Modern Art), Ljubljana
MMSU, Rijeka
Museum of Modern Art, Dubrovnik
Museum of Modern Art, Sarajevo
Museum of Modern Art, Zagreb
Wadsworth Athenaeum, Hartford, Connecticut
Ars Aevi Museum of Contemporary Art Sarajevo
Musée de la Musique, Paris
Sammlung Hoffmann, Berlin
Museo di Teritorio Biellese, Biella, Italy
Leeds City Galleries, Leeds
Museum of History, Sarajevo
Certosa di San Lorenzo, Padula, Italy
National Museum of Contemporary Art, Bucharest
Vehbi Koc Vakfi, Istanbul
Macura Museum, Belgrade
Neue Galerie, Graz
Xin Dong Cheng Space for Contemporary Art, Beijing

Concept
Braco Dimitrijević

Graphic Coordination / Coordination graphique
Gabriele Nason

Editorial Coordination / Coordination Éditoriale
Filomena Moscatelli

Editing / Relectures
Emily Ligniti

Translation / Traduction
Peter Barta
Josephine Fabre
John Lee
Aaron Levy
Leila & Jean Yves Lopez
Rubina Renan Kopytto
Charles Penwarden

Copywriting and Press Office
Silvia Palombi Arte&Mostre, Milano

Web Design and Online Promotion
Barbara Bonacina

Cover / Couverture
Balkan Walzer, *2004*
(Joseph Strauss)

Back Cover / Quatrième de couverture
Casual Passer-by I met, *Les Champs-Élysées, Paris, 1999–2000*

ISBN 978-88-8158-748-3

Photo Credits / Crédits photographiques
Archives CNAC, Roland Aeillig, Meho Aksamija, Nick Barlow, Dirk Bleicker, Hans Biezen, Braco Dimitrijevic Archive, Prudence Coming Assoc. Hilda Decke, Thierry Domage, Sharon Freundlich, Egon Von Furstemberg, Ray Fulton, Simone Gansheimer, Yves Gevaert, Avi Ganor, Vincent Godeau, Johny H., David Harris, Rony Hierman, Eva Inkeri, Mimmo Jodice, Belinda Lawley, Antoine Lesieur, Lorand Le Cat, Tchepo S. Kaleb, Franz Kuen, Milomir Kovacevic, Pier Luigi Macor, Enes Midzic, Elio Montanari, Tim Morris, Paolo Mussat Sartor, Monika Nikolic, Paolo Pellion di Persano, Dirk Pauwels, Sergey Petrov, Rheinisches Bildarchiv, Joseph Rosta, Michel Saltz, Bruno Scotti, Lothar Schnepf, Heini Schnebeeli, Robert Self, Goran Tacevski, Tate Photography, Goran Trbuljak, Fedor Vucemilovic, Hans-Dieter Weber, Klaus Widler

Special thanks to / Remerciements particuliers à
Mr. Pino Casagrande, Rome, and to a donor in New York who prefers to remain anonymous

Edizioni Charta srl
Milano
via della Moscova, 27 - 20121
Tel. +39-026598098/026598200
Fax +39-026598577
e-mail: edcharta@tin.it

Charta Books Ltd.
New York City
Tribeca Office
Tel. +1-313-406-8468
e-mail:
international@chartaartbooks.it
www.chartaartbooks.it

Printed in Italy

Braco Dimitrijevic
Louvre is my studio,
street is my museum

Exposition au Musée d'Art Moderne de Saint-Etienne Métropole

15 May – 16 August, 2009
15 mai – 16 août 2009

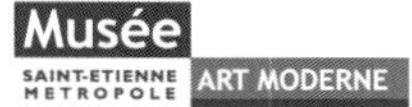

Curator / Commissaire
Lóránd Hegyi

Coordination
Pauline Faure
Sonia Reynaud-Thien

Setting-up / Montage - Installation
Pascal Essertel
Nasser Abdechakour,
Nicolas A. A. Brun, Christian Brun,
Jean-François Heurtier, Jérôme Laisy,
Yves Monmart, Nicolas Tourier,
Gérard Vigneron

Communication
Alicia Treppoz-Vielle

Musée d'art moderne de Saint-Etienne Métropole

Head Director / Directeur Général
Lóránd Hegyi

Communication and Fundraising / Communication et mécénat
Alicia Treppoz-Vielle

Directorial assistants / Assistantes de direction
Blandine Gwizdala, Sandrine Peyre

Exhibitions-Conservation Department / Pôle Conservation – Expositions
Jeanne Brun, Curator / conservateur
Martine Dancer, Curator / conservateur
Exhibitions-Conservation Department / Service Collection – Exposition
Pauline Faure
Marc Bœuf, Cécile Bourgin, Corinne Cazorla, Pascale De Fressanges, Evelyne Granger, Céline Le Bacon, Sonia Reynaud-Thien
Library : Christian Gay / Bibliothèque
Sophie Lepine, Sébastien Terrat
Photographs / Photographie
Yves Bresson

Public Department / Service des Publics
Lorraine Roux, Naïma Jouberton-Lafond
Jessica Mamoum, Nicole Pascal, Dominique Viou, Aude Monasse
Médiateurs / Tour Guides : Delphine Alleaume, Pierre Arnaud, Mélodie Blanchot, Jean-Marc Cerino, Franck Chalendard, Eliane Chavagneux, Patrick Condouret, Bianca Falsetti, Anne Favier, Anne-Laure Gerbelot-Fraisse, Dominique Marel, Alexis Meilland, Marie Mestre, Emma Ré, Philippe Roux
Front desk / Accueil: Nathalie Pauze, Nathalie Darne, Elodie Pignot

Accountance and administrative services / Administration – Comptabilité
Joëlle Verdier, Dominique Jay
Front desk / Standard : Annie Joubert
Boutique : Nelly Imbert, Valérie Lescot
Damien Crabol, Alexandre Segura, Sébastien Terrat

Technical and Security Department / Pôle Technique – Sécurité
Technical staff / Equipe technique:
Pascal Essertel
Nasser Abdechakour, Christian Brun, Gilles Cheminal, Gérald Lima, Yves Monmart, Gérard Vigneron
Security staff / Equipe sécurité
Pascal Devun
Jacques Alu, Laure Bacher, Gilles Bacher, Loïc Cherrier, Patrice Cote, Mohamed Ibrahimi, Christophe Monmarché, Alexis Pain, Gaël Palay, Pierre-Henri Perez

Acknowledgements / Remerciements
Maurice Vincent, Président de Saint-Etienne Métropole
Françoise Gourbeyre, Vice-Présidente de Saint-Etienne Métropole, Chargée de la Culture et des équipements culturels
Alain Lombard, Directeur Régional des Affaires Culturelles Rhône-Alpes

Saint-Etienne Métropole, son service presse et son service communication

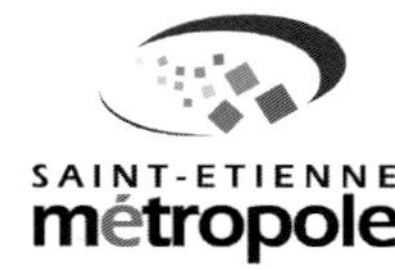

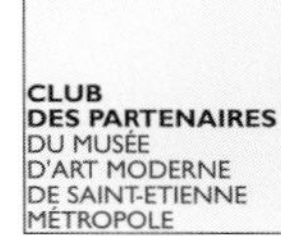

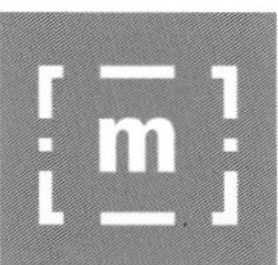

To find out more about Charta, and to learn about our most recent publications, visit

www.chartaartbooks.it

Printed in May 2009
by Tipografia Rumor, Vicenza
for Edizioni Charta